What They Said
in 1976

What They Said
In 1976

The Yearbook of Spoken Opinion

•

Compiled and Edited by

ALAN F. PATER

and

JASON R. PATER

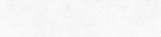

MONITOR BOOK COMPANY, INC.

COPYRIGHT © 1977 BY MONITOR BOOK COMPANY, INC.

EIGHTH ANNUAL EDITION

Printed in the United States of America

Library of Congress catalogue card number 74-111080

ISBN number: 0-9600252-9-4

WHAT THEY SAID is published annually by Monitor Book Company, Inc., Beverly Hills, California. The title, "WHAT THEY SAID," is a trademark owned exclusively by Monitor Book Company, Inc., and has been duly registered with the United States Patent Office. Any unauthorized use is prohibited.

To

The Newsmakers of the World . . .

May they never be at a loss for words

Preface to the First Edition (1969)

WORDS can be powerful or subtle, humorous or maddening. They can be vigorous or feeble, lucid or obscure, inspiring or despairing, wise or foolish, hopeful or pessimistic . . . they can be fearful or confident, timid or articulate, persuasive or perverse, honest or deceitful. As tools at a speaker's command, words can be used to reason, argue, discuss, cajole, plead, debate, declaim, threaten, infuriate, or appease; they can harangue, flourish, recite, preach, discourse, stab to the quick, or gently sermonize.

When casually spoken by a stage or film star, words can go beyond the press-agentry and make-up facade and reveal the inner man or woman. When purposefully uttered in the considered phrasing of a head of state, words can determine the destiny of millions of people, resolve peace or war, or chart the course of a nation on whose direction the fate of the entire world may depend.

Until now, the *copia verborum* of well-known and renowned public figures—the doctors and diplomats, the governors and generals, the potentates and presidents, the entertainers and educators, the bishops and baseball players, the jurists and journalists, the authors and attorneys, the congressmen and chairmen-of-the-board—whether enunciated in speeches, lectures, interviews, radio and television addresses, news conferences, forums, symposiums, town meetings, committee hearings, random remarks to the press, or delivered on the floors of the United States Senate and House of Representatives or in the parliaments and palaces of the world —have been dutifully reported in the media, then filed away and, for the most part, forgotten.

The editors of *WHAT THEY SAID* believe that consigning such a wealth of thoughts, ideas, doctrines, opinions and philosophies to interment in the morgues and archives of the Fourth Estate is lamentable and unnecessary. Yet the media, in all their forms, are constantly engulfing us in a profusion of endless and increasingly voluminous news reports. One is easily disposed to disregard or forget the stimulating discussion of critical issues embodied in so many of the utterances of those who make the news and, in their respective fields, shape the events throughout the world. The conclusion is therefore a natural and compelling one: the educator, the public official, the business executive, the statesman, the philosopher—everyone who has a stake in the complex, often confusing trends of our times—should have material of this kind readily available.

These, then, are the circumstances under which *WHAT THEY SAID* was conceived. It is the culmination of a year of listening to the people in the public eye; a year of scrutinizing, monitoring, reviewing, judging, deciding—a year during which the editors resurrected from almost certain oblivion those quintessential elements of the year's *spoken* opinion which, in their judgment, demanded preservation in book form.

WHAT THEY SAID is a pioneer in its field. Its *raison d'etre* is the firm conviction that presenting, each year, the highlights of vital and interesting views from the lips of prominent people on virtually every aspect of contemporary civilization fulfills the need to give the *spoken* word the permanence and lasting value of the *written* word. For, if it is true that a picture is worth 10,000 words, it is equally true that a verbal conclusion, an apt quote or a candid comment by a person of fame or influence can have more significance and can provide more understanding than an entire page of summary in a standard work of reference.

The editors of *WHAT THEY SAID* did not, however, design their book for researchers and scholars alone. One of the failings of the conventional reference work is that it is blandly written and referred to primarily for facts and figures, lacking inherent "interest value." *WHAT THEY SAID,* on the other hand, was planned for sheer enjoyment and pleasure, for searching glimpses into the lives and thoughts of the world's celebrities, as well as for serious study, intellectual reflection and the philosophical contemplation of our multifaceted life and mores. Furthermore, those pressed for time, yet anxious to know what the newsmakers have been saying, will welcome the short excerpts which will make for quick, intermittent reading—and rereading. And, of course, the topical classifications, the speakers' index, the subject index, the place and date information—documented and authenticated and easily located—will supply a rich fund of hitherto not readily obtainable reference and statistical material.

Finally, the reader will find that the editors have eschewed trite comments and cliches, tedious and boring. The selected quotations, each standing on its own, are pertinent, significant, stimulating—above all, relevant to today's world, expressed in the speakers' own words. And they will, the editors feel, be even more relevant tomorrow. They will be re-examined and reflected upon in the future by men and women eager to learn from the past. The prophecies, the promises, the "golden dreams," the boastings and rantings, the bluster, the bravado, the pleadings and representations of those whose voices echo in these pages (and in those to come) should provide a rare and unique history lesson. The positions held by these luminaries, in their respective callings, are such that what they say today may profoundly affect the future as well as the present, and so will be of lasting importance and meaning.

ALAN F. PATER
Beverly Hills, California   JASON R. PATER

Table of Contents

TWO events make the year 1976 immediately identifiable: It was the year of the Bicentennial of the United States and also a Presidential election year, made even more significant by being the first Presidential election since the Watergate debacle.

The Bicentennial and the election contributed much to this volume of *WHAT THEY SAID*— the former bringing forth a myriad of philosophical musings about the current state and future bodings for America, and the latter accounting for statements on almost all national and international affairs by the various candidates and nominees.

A change of Administrations always brings with it the departure of a number of recognizable personalities, many of whom have regularly appeared in these pages over the years. Gerald Ford, Henry Kissinger, William Simon and others have previously filled a number of pages in *WHAT THEY SAID* all by themselves. We hope and believe that the record of their utterances contained in the volumes covering the years when they served in Washington form an indelible history of their contributions, positive and negative, to the world scene.

The editors of *WHAT THEY SAID* look forward to monitoring and recording the prophecies, the promises, the "golden dreams," the bluster and bravado and the thoughts, ideas and doctrines of the new Administration, as well as the other influential voices that will inevitably be raised around the world.

The Editors of *WHAT THEY SAID* welcome comments and suggestions in an effort to improve the series. Ideas deemed appropriate and practical will always be considered for use in future editions.

With no intention of being a complete news summary of 1976, following are some of the happenings reflected in many of this year's quotations . . .

American Scene:

The American Revolution Bicentennial was celebrated throughout the year across the country and in some areas around the world.

Civil Rights:

The school busing controversy continued unabated, and Presidential candidate Jimmy Carter made his now-famous "ethnic purity" remark, which he quickly corrected.

Commerce:

The argument over government regulation of business grew as signs pointed to possible deregulation experiments. In light of last year's revelation of corporate bribes, business ethics became a popular topic in 1976. There was pressure for the break-up of the oil companies.

WHAT THEY SAID IN 1976

Crime:

Capital punishment, the methods of the FBI and gun control remained frequent subjects of discussion.

Education:

There was growing concern about education standards and the increase in illiterate graduates.

Foreign Affairs:

International arms sales, detente, Congressional vs. Executive authority in foreign policy, supervision of the CIA and the future positions of President-elect Carter were major topics.

Government:

Trust in government was a major campaign thrust of Jimmy Carter's. With a new Administration, new focus was placed on the role of the Vice President.

Labor / Economy:

Inflation, recession and unemployment remained key areas of discussion. Tax reform and public-service jobs were also under consideration.

National Defense:

The debate comparing U.S. and Soviet capabilities continued. There was some talk of labor unions for military personnel.

Politics:

The Presidential election was the big news in 1976. Some of the highlights: Jimmy Carter's rapid ascent to his party's nomination, his controversial *Playboy* magazine interview, and his defeat of President Ford in a close election; Ford's narrow nomination victory over Ronald Reagan (who broke tradition by naming in advance his Vice-Presidential running mate), and Ford's implying, during the newly revived Presidential debates, that Eastern Europe is not under Soviet domination.

Transportation:

The British-French *Concorde* SST began service to Washington's Dulles Airport on a trial basis.

Urban Affairs:

The fiscal crises of New York and other cities remained the Number One urban problem.

Africa:

The Soviet-and-Cuban-backed forces in the Angolan civil war were victorious. Rhodesia agreed to black majority rule in two years, but the plan was rejected by some black African leaders who pressed for quicker conversion and who vowed to continue the struggle militarily.

Americas:

U.S. control of the Panama Canal became an issue in the U.S. Presidential election. In Canada, Quebec province elected a party advocating separation from the rest of the country. Cuban forces in Angola raised anew the subject of continued Cuban foreign intervention.

Asia:

China's Mao Tse-tung died. India's "emergency" and the resultant loss of freedoms continued. United Vietnam pressed for U.S. aid and UN membership. The debate went on regarding the presence of U.S. forces in South Korea.

Europe:

The increasing political strength of the Italian Communist Party sparked debate on its professed independence from Moscow and its effect on NATO. Britain's economic crisis continued. In Sweden, the Social Democrats were voted out of office after 44 years.

Middle East:

Israel's daring raid on Uganda's Entebbe Airport to free hijacked hostages was the year's most dramatic news event.

Journalism:

In a highly publicized affair, broadcast news correspondent Daniel Schorr steadfastly refused to reveal the source of classified government documents he leaked to the press.

Television/ Radio:

The debate over violence in TV programming and the resultant "family hour" concept continued in 1976.

Sports:

The big sports event of the year was the Montreal summer Olympic Games, made more newsworthy because of Canada's refusal to allow Taiwan to participate if it called itself the Republic of China. As a consequence, the Taiwanese withdrew from the Games. Elsewhere in sports, the baseball reserve-system abolition and resultant free-agent status of players were beginning to take effect. Also in baseball, Commissioner Bowie Kuhn negated a proposed sale of three Oakland (Calif.) players to other teams for over $3.5-million. In football, the college draft system was ruled illegal in its present form.

Editorial Treatment

ORGANIZATION OF MATERIAL

Special attention has been given to the arrangement of the book—from the major divisions down to the individual categories and speakers—the objective being a logical progression of related material as follows:

(A) The categories are arranged alphabetically within each of three major sections—

Part One: "National Affairs"
Part Two: "International Affairs"
Part Three: "General"

In this manner, the reader can quickly locate quotations pertaining to particular fields of interest (see also *Indexing*). It should be noted that some quotations contain a number of thoughts or ideas—sometimes on different subjects—while some are vague as to exact subject matter and thus do not fit clearly into a specific topic classification. In such cases, the judgment of the Editors has determined the most appropriate category.

(B) Within each category, the speakers are in alphabetical order by surname, following alphabetization practices used in the speaker's country of origin.

(C) Where there are two or more quotations by one speaker within the same category, they appear chronologically by date spoken or date of source.

SPEAKER IDENTIFICATION

(A) The occupation, profession, rank, position or title of the speaker is given as it was *at the time the statement was made* (except when the speaker's relevant identification is in the past, in which case he is shown as "former"). Thus, due to possible changes in status during the year, a speaker may be shown with different identifications in various portions of the book, or even within the same category.

(B) In the case of speakers who hold more than one position or occupation simultaneously (or who held relevant positions in the past), the judgment of the Editors has determined the most appropriate identification to use with a specific quotation.

(C) Nationality of speakers is normally not given unless this information is of interest or relative to the quotation(s).

THE QUOTATIONS

The quoted material selected for inclusion in this book is shown as it appeared in the source, except as follows:

(A) *Ellipses* have been inserted wherever the Editors have deleted extraneous words or overly long passages within the quoted material used. In no way has the meaning or intention of any quotation been altered. *Ellipses* are also used where they appeared in the source.

(B) *Punctuation and spelling* have been altered by the Editors where they were obviously incorrect in the source, or to make the quotations more intelligible, or to conform to the general style used throughout this book. Again, meaning or intention of the quotations has not been changed.

(C) *Brackets* ([ ]) indicate material inserted by the Editors or by the source to either correct obvious errors or to explain and/or clarify what the speaker is saying.

(D) *Italics* have sometimes been added by the Editors where emphasis is clearly desirable.

Except for the above instances, the quoted material used has been printed verbatim, as reported by the source (even if the speaker made factual errors or was awkward in his choice of words).

Special care has been exercised to make certain that each quotation stands on its own merits and is not taken "out of context." The Editors, however, cannot be responsible for errors made by the original newspaper, periodical or other source, i.e., incorrect reporting, mis-quotations or errors in interpretation.

DOCUMENTATION AND SOURCES

Documentation (circumstance, place, date) of each quotation is provided as fully as could be obtained, and the sources are furnished for all quotations. In some instances no documentation details were available; in those cases only the source is given. Following are the sequence and style used for this information:

Circumstance of quotation, place, date/Name of source, date: section (if applicable), page number.

Example: *Before the Senate, Washington, Dec. 4/The Washington Post, 12:6:(A)13.*

The above example indicates that the quotation was delivered before the Senate in Washington on December 4. It was taken for *WHAT THEY SAID* from *The Washington Post,* issue of December 4, section A, page 13. (When a newspaper publishes more than one edition on the same date, it should be noted that page numbers may vary from edition to edition).

(A) When the source is a television or radio broadcast, the name of the network or local station is indicated, along with the date of the broadcast (obviously, page and/or section information does not apply).

(B) One asterisk (*) before the (/) in the documentation indicates that the quoted material was written rather than spoken. Although the basic policy of *WHAT THEY SAID* is to use only *spoken* statements, there are occasions when written statements are considered by the Editors to be important enough to be included. These occasions are rare and usually involve Presidential messages, Presidential statements released to the press and other such documents attributed to a person in high government office.

(C) Two asterisks (**) after the (/) indicate the speaker supplied the quotation to *WHAT THEY SAID* directly.

INDEXING

(A) The *Index to Speakers* is keyed to the page number. (For alphabetization practices, see *Organization of Material,* paragraph B).

(B) The *Index to Subjects* is keyed to both the page number and the quotation number on the page (thus, 210:3 indicates quotation number 3 on page 210); the quotation number appears at upper right-hand corner of each quotation.

(C) To locate quotations on a particular subject, regardless of speaker, turn to the appropriate category (see *Table of Contents)* or use the detailed *Index to Subjects.*

(D) To locate all quotations by a particular speaker, regardless of subject, use the *Index to Speakers.*

(E) To locate quotations by a particular speaker on a particular subject, turn to the appropriate category and then to that person's quotations within that category.

(F) The reader will find that the basic categorization format of *WHAT THEY SAID* is itself a useful subject index, inasmuch as related quotations are grouped together by their respective categories. All aspects of journalism, for example, are relevant to each other; thus, the section *Journalism* embraces all phases of the news media. Similarly, quotations pertaining to the U.S. Presidency, Congress, revenue-sharing, etc., are together in the section *Government.*

MISCELLANEOUS

(A) Except where otherwise indicated or obviously to the contrary, all universities, colleges, organizations and business firms mentioned in this book are located in the United States; similarly, references made to "national," "Federal," "this country," "the nation," etc., refer to the United States.

(B) In most cases, organizations whose titles end with "of the United States" are Federal government agencies.

SELECTION OF CATEGORIES

The selected categories reflect, in the Editors' opinion, the most widely discussed public-interest subjects, those which readily fall into the over-all sphere of "current events." They represent topics continuously covered by the mass media because of their inherent relevance to the changing world scene. Most of the categories are permanent; they appear in each annual edition of *WHAT THEY SAID.* However, because of the transient character of some subjects, there may be categories which appear one year and may not be repeated.

SELECTION OF SPEAKERS

The following persons are *always* considered eligible for inclusion in *WHAT THEY SAID:* top-level officials of all branches of national, state and major local governments (both U.S. and foreign), including all United States Senators and Representatives; top-echelon military officers; college and university presidents, chancellors and professors; chairmen and presidents of major corporations; heads of national public-oriented organizations and associations; national and internationally known diplomats; recognized celebrities from the entertainment and literary

WHAT THEY SAID IN 1976

spheres and the arts generally; sports figures of national stature; commentators on the world scene who are recognized as such and who command the attention of the mass media.

The determination of what and who are "major" and "recognized" must, necessarily, be made by the Editors of *WHAT THEY SAID* based on objective personal judgment.

Also, some persons, while not recognized as prominent in a particular professional area, have nevertheless attracted an unusual amount of attention in connection with a specific issue or event. These people, too, are considered for inclusion, depending upon the circumstances involved.

SELECTION OF QUOTATIONS

The quotations selected for inclusion in *WHAT THEY SAID* obviously represent a decided minority of the seemingly endless volume of quoted material appearing in the media each year. The process of selection is scrupulously objective insofar as the partisan views of the Editors are concerned (see *About Fairness,* below). However, it is clear that the Editors must decide which quotations *per se* are suitable for inclusion, and in doing so look for comments that are aptly stated, offer insight into the subject being discussed, or into the speaker, and provide—for today as well as for future reference—a thought which readers will find useful for understanding the issues and the personalities that make up a year on this planet.

ABOUT FAIRNESS

The Editors of *WHAT THEY SAID* understand the necessity of being impartial when compiling a book of this kind. As a result, there has been no bias in the selection of the quotations, the choice of speakers or the manner of editing. Relevance of the statements and the status of the speakers are the exclusive criteria for inclusion, without any regard whatsoever to the personal beliefs and views of the Editors. Furthermore, every effort has been made to include a multiplicity of opinions and ideas from a wide cross-section of speakers on each topic. Nevertheless, should there appear to be, on some controversial issues, a majority of material favoring one point of view over another, it is simply the result of there having been more of those views expressed during the year, reported by the media and objectively considered suitable by the Editors of *WHAT THEY SAID* (see *Selection of Quotations,* above). Also, since persons in politics and government account for a large percentage of the speakers in *WHAT THEY SAID,* there may exist a heavier weight of opinion favoring the political philosophy of those in office at the time, whether in the United States Congress, the Administration, or in foreign capitals. This is natural and to be expected and should not be construed as a reflection of agreement or disagreement with that philosophy on the part of the Editors of *WHAT THEY SAID.*

Abbreviations

The following are abbreviations used by the speakers in this volume. Rather than defining them each time they appear in the quotations, this list will facilitate reading and avoid unnecessary repetition.

ABA: American Bar Association/American Basketball Association
ABC: American Broadcasting Company
BBC: British Broadcasting Corporation
B&O: Baltimore & Ohio Railroad
CAB: Civil Aeronautics Board
CBS: Columbia Broadcasting System (CBS, Inc.)
CCC: Civilian Conservation Corps
CIA: Central Intelligence Agency
DH: designated hitter
EEC: European Economic Community (Common Market)
EPA: Environmental Protection Agency
ERA: Equal Rights Amendment
ESP: extra-sensory perception
FBI: Federal Bureau of Investigation
FCC: Federal Communications Commission
FDA: Food and Drug Administration
FEA: Federal Energy Administration
FHA: Federal Housing Administration
FHWA: Federal Highway Administration
FRG: Federal Republic of Germany (West Germany)
FTC: Federal Trade Commission
GDR: German Democratic Republic (East Germany)
GNP: gross national product
GOP: Grand Old Party (Republican Party)
GSA: General Services Administration
HEW: Department of Health, Education and Welfare
HMO: health maintenance organization
ICBM: intercontinental ballistic missile
IOC: International Olympic Committee
IRA: Irish Republican Army
ITT: International Telephone & Telegraph Corporation
LAMDA: London Academy of Music and Dramatic Art
LSD: Lysergic acid diethylamide (hallucinogenic drug)
MIRV: multiple independently targeted re-entry vehicle
MIT: Massachusetts Institute of Technology

MPLA:	Popular Movement for the Liberation of Angola
NAACP:	National Association for the Advancement of Colored People
NASA:	National Aeronautics and Space Administration
NATO:	National Atlantic Treaty Organization
NBA:	National Basketball Association
NBC:	National Broadcasting Company
NFL:	National Football League
NHL:	National Hockey League
NOW:	National Organization for Women
NRA:	National Rifle Association
OAU:	Organization of African Unity
OMB:	Office of Management and Budget
OPEC:	Organization of Petroleum Exporting Countries
OSHA:	Occupational Safety and Health Administration
PBS:	Public Broadcasting Service
PLO:	Palestine Liberation Organization
PRC:	People's Republic of China
RADA:	Royal Academy of Dramatic Art
SAGE:	semi-automatic ground environment (defense system)
SALT:	strategic arms limitation talks
SEC:	Securities and Exchange Commission
SSA:	Social Security Administration
SST:	supersonic transport
TUC:	Trade Unions Council
TV:	television
UN:	United Nations
U.S.:	United States
U.S.A.:	United States of America
U.S.S.R.:	Union of Soviet Socialist Republics
WCT:	World Championship Tennis
WIN:	whip inflation now

Party affiliation of United States Senators, Congressmen and Governors—

C:	Conservative-Republican
D:	Democratic
R:	Republican

The Quote of the Year

"*Nineteen seventy-six appears to have been gloom. We see lasting discord, even wars in the world, little reconciliation, little progress and too many people failing. And with all of this there is the frightening lack of respect for each other's life and well-being, of all life on earth, that is visible again and again in dozens of terrifying shapes. However, all of this is no cause for surprise in a world inhabited by four billion egoists, all of them inclined to fancy themselves to be the focus point of the world.*"

JULIANA
Queen of the Netherlands

Christmas broadcast to the nation, December 25.

PART ONE

National Affairs

The State of the Union Address

Delivered by Gerald R. Ford, President of the United States, to a joint session of Congress, in the House of Representatives, Washington, January 19, 1976.

Mr. Speaker, Mr. Vice President, members of the 94th Congress and distinguished guests:

As we begin our Bicentennial, America is still one of the youngest nations in recorded history. Long before our forefathers came to these shores, men and women had been struggling on this planet to forge a better life for themselves and their families.

In man's long upward march from savagery and slavery—throughout the nearly 2,000 years of the Christian calendar, the nearly 6,000 years of Jewish reckoning—there have been many deep, terrifying valleys, but also many bright and towering peaks.

One peak stands highest in the ranges of human history. One example shines forth of a people uniting to produce abundance and to share the good life fairly and in freedom. One union holds out the promise of justice and opportunity for every citizen.

That union is the United States of America.

Pride in America

We have not remade paradise on earth. We know perfection will not be found here. But think for a minute how far we have come in 200 years.

We came from many roots and have many branches. Yet all Americans across the eight generations that separate us from the stirring deeds of 1776, those who know no other homeland and those who just found refuge on our shores, say in unison:

I am proud of America and proud to be an American. Life will be better here for my children than for me.

I believe this not because I am told to believe it, but because life has been better for me than it was for my father and my mother.

I *know* it will be better for my children because my hands, my brains, my voice and my vote can help make it happen.

And it has happened here in America.

It happened to you and to me.

Mistakes Made

Government exists to create and preserve conditions in which people can translate their ideals into practical reality. In the best of times, much is lost in translation. But we try.

Sometimes we have tried and failed.

Always we have had the best of intentions. But in the recent past we sometimes forgot the sound principles that had guided us through most of our history. We wanted to accomplish great things and solve age-old problems. And we became over-confident of our own abilities. We tried to be a policeman abroad and as an indulgent parent here at home. We thought that we could transform the country through massive national programs.

—But often the programs did not work; too often, they only made things worse.

—In our rush to accomplish great deeds quickly, we trampled on sound principles of restraint, and endangered the rights of individuals.

—We unbalanced our economic system by the huge and unprecedented growth of Federal expenditures and borrowing. And we were not totally honest with ourselves about how much these programs would cost and how we would pay for them.

—Finally, we shifted our emphasis from defense to domestic problems while our adversaries continued a massive buildup of arms.

GERALD R. FORD

Correcting the Mistakes

The time has now come for a fundamentally different approach for a new realism that is true to the great principles upon which this nation was founded.

We must introduce a new balance to our economy—a balance that favors not only sound, active government but also a much more vigorous, healthier economy that can create new jobs and hold down prices.

We must introduce a new balance in the relationship between the individual and the Government—a balance that favors greater individual freedom and self-reliance.

We must strike a new balance in our system of federalism—a balance that favors greater responsibility and freedom for the leaders of our state and local governments.

We must introduce a new balance between spending on domestic programs and spending on defense—a balance that insures we fully meet our obligations to the needy while also protecting our security in a world that is still hostile to freedom.

And in all that we do, we must be more honest with the American people—promising them no more than we can deliver, and delivering all that we promise.

The genius of America has been its incredible ability to improve the lives of its citizens through a unique combination of governmental and free citizen activity.

History and experience tell us that moral progress comes not in comfortable and complacent times, but out of trial and confusion. Tom Paine aroused the troubled Americans of 1776 to stand up to the times that try men's souls because the harder the conflict the more glorious the triumph.

The Year 1975

Just a year ago, I reported that the state of the union was not good.

Tonight I report that the state of our union is better—in many ways a lot better—but still not good enough.

To paraphrase Tom Paine, 1975 was not a year for summer soldiers and sunshine patriots. It was a year of fears and alarms and of dire forecasts—most of which never happened and won't happen.

As you recall, the year 1975 opened with rancor and bitterness. Political misdeeds of the past had neither been forgotten nor forgiven.

The longest, most divisive war in our history was winding toward an unhappy conclusion. Many feared that the end of that foreign war of men and machines meant the beginning of a domestic war of recrimination and reprisal.

Friends and adversaries abroad were asking whether America had lost its nerve.

Finally, our economy was ravaged by inflation—inflation that was plunging us into the worst recession in four decades.

At the same time, Americans became increasingly alienated from all big institutions. They were steadily losing confidence not just in big government, but in big business, big labor and big education, among others.

Ours was a troubled land.

And so, 1975 was a year of hard decisions, difficult compromises, and a new realism that taught us something important about America.

It brought back a needed measure of common sense, steadfastness and self-discipline. Americans did not panic or demand instant or useless cures. In all sectors people met their difficult problems with restraint and responsibility worthy of their great heritage.

Add up the separate pieces of progress in 1975, subtract the setbacks, and the sum total shows that we are not only headed in the new direction I proposed 12 months ago, but that it turned out to be the right direction.

It is the right direction because it follows the truly revolutionary American concept of 1776 which holds that in a free society the making of public policy and successful problem-solving involves much more than government. It involves a full partnership among all branches and levels of government, private institutions and individual citizens.

Common sense tells me to stick to that steady course.

The Economy

Take the state of our economy.

Last January, most things were rapidly getting worse.

This January, most things are slowly but surely getting better.

The worst recession since World War II turned around in April. The best cost of living news of the past year is that double digit inflation of 12 percent or higher was cut almost in half. The worst—unemployment remains too high.

Today, nearly 1.7 million more Americans are working than at the bottom of the recession. At year's end people were again being hired much faster than they were being laid off.

Yet let us be honest: Many Americans have not yet felt these changes in their daily lives. They still see prices going up too fast, and they still know the fear of unemployment.

And we are a growing nation. We need more and more jobs every year. Today's economy has produced over 85 million jobs for Americans, but we need a lot more jobs, especially for the young.

My first objective is to have sound economic growth without inflation.

We all know from recent experience what runaway inflation does to ruin every other worthy purpose. We are slowing it; we must stop it cold.

For many Americans the way to a healthy non-inflationary economy has become increasingly apparent: the Government must stop spending so much and borrowing so much of our money; more money must remain in private hands where it will do the most good. To hold down the cost of living, we must hold down the cost of government.

Federal Spending

In the past decade, the Federal budget has been growing at an average rate of over 10 per cent every year. The budget I am submitting Wednesday cuts this rate of growth in half. I have kept my promise to submit a bud-

get for the next fiscal year of $395 billion. In fact, it is $394.2 billion.

By holding down the growth in Federal spending, we can afford additional tax cuts and return to the people who pay taxes more decision-making power over their own lives.

Last month I signed legislation to extend the 1975 tax reductions for the first six months of this year. I now propose that, effective July, 1, 1976, we give our taxpayers a tax cut of approximately $10 billion more than Congress agreed to in December.

My broader tax reduction would mean that, for a family of four making $15,000 a year, there will be $227 more in take-home pay annually. Hard-working Americans caught in the middle can really use that kind of extra cash.

My recommendations for a firm restraint on the growth of Federal spending and for greater tax reduction are simple and straightforward. For every dollar saved in cutting the growth in the Federal budget we can have an added dollar of Federal tax reduction.

We can achieve a balanced budget by 1979 if we have the courage and wisdom to continue to reduce the growth of Federal spending.

Jobs

One test of a healthy economy is a job for every American who wants to work.

Government—our kind of government—cannot create that many jobs. But the Federal Government *can* create conditions and incentives for private business and industry to make more and more jobs.

Five out of six jobs in this country are in private business and industry. Common sense tells us this is the place to look for more jobs and to find them faster.

I mean real, rewarding, permanent jobs.

To achieve this, we must offer the American people greater incentives to invest in the future. My tax proposals are a major step in that direction.

To supplement these proposals, I ask that Congress enact changes in Federal tax laws that will speed up plant expansion and the

5

purchase of new equipment. My recommendation will concentrate this job-creation tax incentive in areas where the unemployment rate now runs over 7 percent. Legislation to get this started must be approved at the earliest possible date.

Housing

Within the strict budget total I will recommend for the coming year, I will ask for additional housing assistance for 500,000 families. These programs will expand housing opportunities, spur construction and help to house moderate and low income families.

We had a disappointing year in the housing industry in 1975, but it is improving. With lower interest rates and available mortgage money, we can have a healthy recovery in 1976.

Government Regulation

A necessary condition to a healthy economy is freedom from the petty tyranny of massive Government regulation. We are wasting literally millions of working hours, costing billions of consumers' dollars, because of bureaucratic red tape. The American farmer, who not only feeds 215 million Americans but also millions worldwide, has shown how much more he can produce without the shackles of Government control.

Now, we need reforms in other key areas in our economy—the airlines, trucking, railroads and financial institutions. I have concrete plans in each of these areas, not to help this or that industry, but to foster competition and to bring prices down for the consumer.

This Administration will strictly enforce the Federal antitrust laws for the same purpose.

Energy

Taking a longer look at America's future, there can be neither sustained growth nor more jobs unless we continue to have an assured supply of energy to run our economy.

Domestic production of oil and gas is still declining. Our dependence on foreign oil at high prices is still too great, draining jobs and dollars away from our own economy at the rate of $125 per year for every American.

Last month I signed a compromise national energy bill which enacts a part of my comprehensive energy independence program. This legislation was late in coming—not the complete answer to energy independence, but still a start in the right direction.

I again urge the Congress to move ahead immediately on the remainder of my energy proposals to make America invulnerable to the foreign oil cartel. My proposals would:

- Reduce domestic natural gas shortages.
- Allow production from national petroleum reserves.
- Stimulate effective conservation, including revitalization of our railroads and the expansion of our urban transportation systems.
- Develop more and cleaner energy from our vast coal resources.
- Expedite clean and safe nuclear power production.
- Create a new national energy independence authority to stimulate vital energy investment.
- And accelerate development of technology to capture energy from the sun and the earth for this and future generations.

Tax Breaks

Also for the sake of future generations, we must preserve the family farm and family-owned small businesses. Both strengthen America and give stability to our economy.

I will propose estate tax changes so that family businesses and family farms can be handed down from generation to generation without having to be sold to pay taxes.

I propose tax changes to encourage people to invest in America's future, and their own, through a plan that gives moderate income families income tax benefits if they make long-term investments in common stock in American companies.

The Federal Government must and will respond to clearcut national needs—for this and future generations.

Health Care

Hospital and medical services in America are among the world's best, but the cost of a serious and extended illness can quickly wipe out a family's lifetime savings. Increasing health costs are of deep concern to all and a powerful force pushing up the cost of living.

The burden of a catastrophic illness can be borne by very few in our society. We must eliminate this fear from every family.

I propose catastrophic health insurance for everybody covered by Medicare. To finance this added protection, fees for short-term care will go up somewhat, but nobody after reaching age 65 will have to pay more than $500 a year for covered hospital or nursing home care, nor more than $250 for one year's doctors' bills.

We cannot realistically afford federally dictated national health insurance providing full coverage for all 215 million Americans. The experience of other countries raises questions about the quality as well as the cost of such plans. But I do envision the day when we may use the private health insurance system to offer more middle income families high quality health services at prices they can afford and shield them also from catastrophic illnesses.

Using the resources now available, I propose improving the Medicare and other Federal health programs to help those who really need more protection: older people and the poor. To help states and local governments give better health care to the poor, I propose that we combine 16 existing Federal programs, including Medicaid, into a single $10 billion Federal grant.

Funds would be divided among the states under a new formula which provides a larger share of Federal money to those states that have a larger share of low income families.

I will take further steps to improve the quality of medical and hospital care for those who have served in our armed forces.

Social Security

Now let me speak about Social Security.

Our Federal Social Security system for people who have worked hard and contributed to it all their lives is a vital part of our economic system. Its value is no longer debatable. In my budget for fiscal year 1977 I am recommending that the full cost of living increase in Social Security benefits be paid during the coming year.

But I am concerned about the integrity of our Social Security trust fund that enables people—those retired and those still working who will retire—to count on this source of retirement income. Younger workers watch their deduction rise and wonder if they will be adequately protected in the future.

We must meet this challenge head-on.

Simple arithmetic warns all of us that the Social Security trust fund is headed for trouble. Unless we act soon to make sure the fund takes in as much as it pays out, there will be no security for old or young.

I must therefore recommend a three-tenths of 1 percent increase in both employer and employee Social Security taxes effective Jan. 1, 1977. This will cost each covered employee less than one extra dollar a week and will insure the integrity of the trust fund.

Unemployment

As we build our economy, we have a continuing responsibility to provide a temporary cushion to the unemployed. At my request, the Congress enacted two extensions and expansions in unemployment insurance which helped those who were jobless during 1975. These programs will continue in 1976.

In my fiscal 1977 budget, I am also requesting funds to continue proven job training and employment opportunity programs for millions of other Americans.

Welfare

Compassion and a sense of community—two of America's greatest strengths throughout our history—tell us we must take care of

7

our neighbors who cannot take care of themselves. The host of Federal programs in this field reflect our generosity as a people.

But everyone realizes that when it comes to welfare, government at all levels is not doing the job well. Too many of our welfare programs are inequitable and invite abuse. Worse, we are wasting badly needed resources without reaching many of the truly needy.

Complex welfare programs cannot be reformed overnight. Surely we cannot simply dump welfare into the laps of the 50 states, their local taxpayers or private charities, and just walk away from it. Nor is it the right time for massive and sweeping changes while we are still recovering from a recession.

Nevertheless, there are still plenty of improvements we can make. I will ask Congress for Presidential authority to tighten up rules for eligibility and benefits.

Last year I twice sought long-overdue reform of the scandal-riddled food stamp program. This year I say again: Let's give food stamps to those most in need. Let's not give any to those who don't need them.

Crime

Protecting the life and property of the citizen at home is the responsibility of all public officials but is primarily the job of local and state law enforcement authorities.

Americans have always found the very thought of a Federal police force repugnant and so do I. But there are proper ways in which we can help to insure domestic tranquillity as the Constitution charges us.

My recommendations on how to control violent crime were submitted to the Congress last June, with strong emphasis on protecting the innocent victims of crime.

To keep a convicted criminal from committing more crimes we must put him in prison so he cannot harm more law-abiding citizens. To be effective, this punishment must be swift and certain.

Too often, criminals are not sent to prison after conviction but are allowed to return to the streets.

Some judges are reluctant to send convict-ed criminals to prison because of inadequate prison facilities. To alleviate this problem at the Federal level, my new budget proposes the construction of four new Federal facilities.

To speed Federal justice, I propose an increase this year in U.S. attorneys prosecuting Federal crimes and reinforcement of the number of U.S. marshals.

Additional Federal judges are needed, as recommended by me and the Judicial Conference.

Handguns

Another major threat to every American's person and property is the criminal carrying a handgun. The way to cut down on the criminal use of guns is not to take guns away from the law-abiding citizen but to impose mandatory sentences for crimes in which a gun is used, make it harder to obtain cheap guns for criminal purposes, and concentrate gun control enforcement in high crime areas.

My budget recommends 500 additional Federal agents in the 11 largest metropolitan high crime areas to help local authorities stop criminals from selling and using handguns.

Drugs

The sale of hard drugs is on the increase again. I have directed all agencies of the Federal Government to step up enforcement efforts against those who deal in drugs. In 1975, Federal agents seized substantially more heroin coming into our country than in 1974.

I recommended months ago that the Congress enact mandatory fixed sentences for persons convicted of Federal crimes involving the sale of hard drugs. Hard drugs degrade the spirit as they destroy the body of their users.

State/Local Crime Responsibility

It is unrealistic and misleading to hold out the hope that the Federal Government can move into every neighborhood and clean up crime. Under the Constitution, the greatest responsibility for curbing crime lies with state and local authorities. They are the frontline fighters in the war against crime.

There are definite ways in which the Federal Government can help them. I will propose in the new budget that the Congress authorize almost $7 billion over the next five years to assist state and local governments to protect the safety and property of all citizens.

As President, I pledge the strict enforcement of Federal laws and—by example, support and leadership—to help state and local authorities enforce their laws. Together we must protect the victim of crime and insure domestic tranquillity.

Revenue-Sharing

Last year I strongly recommended a five-year extension of the existing revenue-sharing legislation which thus far has provided $19 billion to help state and local units of government solve problems at home. This program has been effective with decision making transferred from the Federal Government to locally elected officials. Congress must act this year, or state and local units of government will have to drop programs or raise local taxes.

Including my health care reforms, I propose to consolidate some 59 separate Federal programs and provide flexible Federal dollar grants to help states, cities and local agencies in such important areas as education, child nutrition and social services. This flexible system will do the job better and do it closer to home.

Foreign Affairs

The protection of the lives and property of Americans from foreign enemies is one of my primary responsibilities as President.

In a world of instant communications and intercontinental missiles, in a world economy that is global and interdependent, our relations with other nations become more, not less, important to the lives of Americans.

America has had a unique role in the world since the day of our independence 200 years ago. And ever since the end of World War II,

we have borne—successfully—a heavy responsibility for insuring a stable world order and hope for human progress.

Today, the state of our foreign policy is sound and strong.

—We are at peace—and I will do all in my power to keep it that way.

—Our military forces are capable and ready; our military power is without equal. And I intend to keep it that way.

Our principal alliances, with the industrial democracies of the Atlantic Community and Japan, have never been more solid.

—A further agreement to limit the strategic arms race may be achieved.

—We have an improving relationship with China, the world's most populous nation.

—The key elements for peace among the nations of the Middle East now exist.

—Our traditional friendships in Latin America, Africa, and Asia continue.

—We have taken the role of leadership in launching a serious and hopeful dialogue between the industrial world and the developing world.

—We have achieved significant reform of the international monetary system.

Downgrading of America

We should be proud of what the United States has accomplished.

The American people have heard too much about how terrible our mistakes, how evil our deeds, and how misguided our purposes. The American people know better.

The truth is we are the world's greatest democracy. We remain the symbol of man's aspirations for liberty and well-being. We are the embodiment of hope for progress.

I say it is time we quit downgrading ourselves as a nation. Of course, it is our responsibility to learn the right lessons from past mistakes. It is our duty to see that they never happen again. But our greater duty is to look to the future. The world's troubles will not go away.

Foreign Affairs Authority of President

The American people want strong and ef-

GERALD R. FORD

fective international and defense policies.

In our constitutional system, these policies should reflect consultation and accomodation between the President and Congress. But in the final analysis, as the framers of our Constitution knew from hard experience, the foreign relations of the United States can be conducted effectively only if there is strong central direction that allows flexibility of action. That responsibility clearly rests with the President.

I pledge to the American people policies which seek a secure, just, and peaceful world. I pledge to the Congress to work *with* you to that end.

We must not face a future in which we can no longer help our friends, such as in Angola—even in limited and carefully controlled ways. We must not lose all capacity to respond short of military intervention. Some hasty actions of the Congress during the past year—most recently in respect to Angola—were in my view very short-sighted. Unfortunately, they are still very much on the minds of our allies and our adversaries.

Defense

A strong defense posture gives weight to our values and our views in international negotiations; it assures the vigor of our alliances; and it sustains our efforts to promote settlements of international conflicts. Only from a position of strength can we negotiate a balanced agreement to limit the growth of nuclear arms. Only a balanced agreement will serve our interest and minimize the threat of nuclear confrontation.

Rise in Defense Budget

The defense budget I will submit to Congress for fiscal 1977 will show an essential increase over last year. It provides for a real growth in purchasing power over last year's defense budget, which includes the costs of our all-volunteer force.

We are continuing to make economies to enhance the efficiency of our military forces. But the budget I will submit represents the

necessity of American strength for the real world in which we live.

Summation

As conflict and rivalries persist in the world, our United States intelligence capabilities must be the best in the world.

The crippling of our foreign intelligence services increases the danger of American involvement in direct armed conflict. Our adversaries are encouraged to attempt new adventures, while our own ability to monitor events—and to influence events short of military action—is undermined.

Without effective intelligence capability, the United States stands blindfolded and hobbled.

In the near future, I will take actions to reform and strengthen our intelligence community. I ask for your *positive* cooperation. It is time to go beyond sensationalism and insure an effective, responsible and responsive intelligence capability.

Tonight I have spoken of our problems at home and abroad. I have recommended policies that will meet the challenge of our third century.

I have no doubt that our union will endure—better, stronger, and with more individual freedom.

We can see forward only dimly—one year, five years, a generation perhaps. Like our forefathers, we know that if we meet the challenges of our own time with a common sense of purpose and conviction—if we remain true to our Constitution and our ideals—then we can know that the future will be better than the past.

I see America today crossing a threshold, not just because it is our Bicentennial, but because we have been tested in adversity. We have taken a new look at what we want to be and what we want our nation to become.

I see America resurgent, certain once again that life will be better for our children than it is for us, seeking strength that cannot be counted in megatons and riches, that cannot be eroded by inflation.

I see these United States of America moving forward, as before, toward a more prefect

10

union where the Government serves and the people rule.

We will not make this happen simply by making speeches, good or bad, yours or mine, but by hard work and hard decisions made with courage and common sense.

I have heard many inspiring Presidential speeches, but the words I remember best were spoken by Dwight D. Eisenhower.

"America is not good because it is great," the President said. "America is great because it is good."

President Eisenhower was raised in a poor

but religious home in the heart of America. His simple words echoed President Lincoln's eloquent testament that "right makes might." And Lincoln in turn evoked the silent image of George Washington kneeling in prayer at Valley Forge.

So all these magic memories, which link eight generations of Americans, are summed up in the inscription just above me.

How many times have we seen it?—"In God We Trust."

Let us engrave it now in each of our hearts as we begin our Bicentennial.

The American Scene

Carl Albert
United States Representative
D—Oklahoma
1

[Upon his retirement]: I leave this nation's capital with confidence in the future of America, its representative form of government and the two-party system. I leave with boundless faith in America's future. The United States is the brightest jewel in the treasure house of history.

Before the House, Washington, Oct. 1/
Los Angeles Herald-Examiner, 10-2:(A)2.

William S. Banowsky
President, Pepperdine University
2

My prescription for the new American vision includes the following: a humble admission of our limitations, along with an awareness that we must always live in an imperfect world; the facility not to take ourselves too seriously and to cultivate a sense of humor; a constant, unrelenting effort to limit and control the power and cost of government at all levels; a strong national defense, second to none, in recognition of the real world in which we live which includes the congenital evil within human nature; a deeper appreciation of the unique greatness of our political system and a rededication to its preservation; a greater and deeper participation by citizens in all levels of government; a clearer understanding that freedom is indivisible, including economic freedom, and that without the preservation of the private, competitive economy none of our dreams will come true. Finally, there is something else. We must restore the spiritual vision which, at its moments of finest expression, was at the heart of the American dream.

Before Philadelphia Society,
Los Angeles, Jan. 31/Vital Speeches, 3-15:344.

3
If America is a sick and corrupt society, it is only by comparison to the standards that we set for ourselves, not by comparison to reality as it exists now, or even has existed anywhere in the world.

U.S. News & World Report, 5-31:30.

Max Beloff
Principal, University College,
Buckingham, England;
Former professor of government and public administration, Oxford University, England
4

. . . on the whole, the United States is in a much healthier condition than the rest of the free world. I feel much more optimistic every time I cross the Atlantic. At the moment, it's true, Americans are passing through a period of self-examination and self-criticism. It's a sort of trauma which I hope will end very quickly, because most of it is totally unnecessary. Apart from a few narrow circles in New York and Washington, I find there is still a great sense in the United States that this is a country of opportunity with an enormous capacity for achievement. I sometimes think if only you would close down *The New York Times* and *The Washington Post,* for a year or two, America would be fine.

Interview, London/
U.S. News & World Report, 3-8:54.

Shirley Temple Black
Chief of Protocol of the United States;
Former U.S. Ambassador to Ghana
5

We've [the U.S.] been in the laundry business for the last several years. No country has washed more dirty laundry in public than we have. I think that time is over now, but we've got to start giving ourselves a pep talk, be like [boxer] Muhammad Ali who says,

"I'm the greatest!" We *are* the greatest. We shouldn't hold our heads down; we should recognize that we're the greatest. Other countries know we are, and they ask: "Why do you keep beating yourselves when you're the greatest country in the world?"

Interview/
U.S. News & World Report, 11-8:42.

David Brinkley
News commentator,
National Broadcasting Company
1

I don't see any easy solutions to America's problems . . . The cities are falling apart, the school systems are failing, transportation systems have already fallen apart. I don't know how a country can survive with all that happening. Congress has been an ineffectual instrument. I don't believe it is representing the American people. Washington generally does not represent the American people. The more leadership we need, the less we seem to get.

Interview, Washington/
The Christian Science Monitor, 8-18:22.

Edmund G. Brown, Jr.
Governor of California (D)
2

The country is rich, but not as rich as we've been led to believe. The choice to do one thing may preclude another. We are now forced to make difficult choices: freeways, child care, schools, income assistance, pensions, health programs, prisons, environmental protection all must compete with one another and be subject to the careful scrutiny of the common purpose we all serve.

Before the Legislature, Sacramento/
San Francisco Examiner & Chronicle, 1-11:(A)8.

3

Right now, no country has done so well at attacking itself as the United States of America. The problems are how do we put it back together and how do we inspire people with confidence and pride in country and family and the things that normally hold people together. Today, it's very easy to find out what's

wrong—the pessimistic side. Mere criticism won't build this unity.

Interview/ Playboy, April:186.

Jimmy Carter
1976 Democratic Presidential nominee
4

I believe in patriotism. I believe that people should love our country and be proud of our country and be willing to fight to defend our country. [But patriotism] is out of fashion or is an object of scorn and jokes. I do not seek a blind or uncritical patriotism. Obviously a government's policies must be deserving of public support. But in recent years, disagreement with our country's policies too often became rejection of our nation itself. There is a great need for the next President to do everything in his power, by word and deed, to restore national pride and patriotism in our country—and, if I am elected, that is what I intend to do.

Before American Legion, Seattle, Aug. 24/
The Washington Post, 8-25:(A)4.

Leonard F. Chapman, Jr.
Commissioner, United States Immigration and Naturalization Service
5

[On such things as bilingual education, lack of "Americanism" training and emphasis on ethnic pride for immigrant children]: America is becoming less and less of a melting pot of many nationalities and is becoming more of a mosaic—a quilted pattern of races and nationalities clinging firmly to their own backgrounds, thinking less of the interests of the United States and more of the interests of the nation they left behind.

U.S. News & World Report, 4-5:26.

John Cheever
Author
6

The future *doesn't* look dismal. I detest the extravagant uses of "decay" and "decline" as applied to this country. I don't see any rampant decline, and I travel a lot around the country. We have the oldest parliamentary government in the world, and a parliamentary government is exploratory and ad-

(JOHN CHEEVER)

venturous. We are a nation of immigrants, which accounts for the unprecedented diversity, richness and vitality of our blood. The Yale magazine wrote me and asked if I thought things were going to get worse in the country, and I wrote back that if people continue to go around asking questions like that, things are *bound* to get worse. There is still a newness in this country, a freshness. We are still experimenting. This is a haunted nation—haunted by a dream of excellence.
Interview/Newsweek, 7-4:36.

Leo Cherne
Executive director,
Research Institute of America
1

Of course there is a crisis of belief in our government, but it is not simply that. We are in the midst of a crisis of all authority, of all our institutions. Those who study the public opinion of the American people agree that our regard for all our institutions—medicine, education, religion, military, Executive Branch, the Supreme Court, Congress, business, organized labor—our confidence in each of them is at the lowest point since we have measured such attitudes . . . . I suggest that when any of us who are leaders in any walk of life think we can repair our own misfortune by identifying the great distress of someone else's trouble, we may be deluding ourselves. While there is still time, I urge we end this orgy of reciprocal abuse and escalating disbelief. We are living in the most complex and dangerous time in the entire history of mankind. We must, I think, very soon put aside our denigrations and concentrate once again on the affirmative tasks of protecting liberty, individual and national. Until then we suffer the consequences of each other's misbehavior.
Before House Select Committee on Intelligence, Washington/
The Christian Science Monitor, 1-28:27.

William Sloane Coffin
Chaplain, Yale University
2

Many of us were sitting around in 1975 in despair, as if in our pride we Americans invented evil. We didn't invent evil. We're only discovering it. Thank God! At last we're ready to join the human race and admit we are not the most virtuous nation. It is our pretensions of innocence, not our sins, that do us in.
The Christian Science Monitor, 1-23:16.

John B. Connally, Jr.
Former Secretary of the Treasury of the United States;
Former Governor of Texas (D, now R)
3

We [in the U.S.] don't understand how affluent and abundant we really are. We use more energy for air-conditioning alone in the United States than 800 million mainland Chinese for all purposes. That's the kind of perspective we need in this country.
The New York Times, 4-27:19.

Alistair Cooke
Journalist, Historian
4

This country, particularly, justifies the pendulum theory of history because we swing from one extreme to another more than most and because the country was founded on an idea, was invented to produce general domestic tranquillity and happiness for everybody. Americans are always grouching that it hasn't done that. Well, I don't think it's possible in human terms, but still it's a very gutty ambition, and I think Americans are always measuring themselves against an ideal life.
Interview, New York/
The Dallas Times Herald, 7-4:(B)3.

Edward M. Davis
Chief of Police of Los Angeles
5

I'm a first-generation American except for one of my grandparents. I sat and listened to my family saying why they chose this country. I think of everything it means to us, of what it meant to our parents and what we mean to oppressed people all over the world. We have a great history and a responsibility to future generations as custodians of liberty. You can't just smell the roses, baby. You have to get out there and do everything you can to

preserve our way of life.
*Upon receiving Freedom's Foundation's
Honor Medal Award, Los Angeles, Feb. 20/
Los Angeles Herald-Examiner, 2-24:(B)1.*

Ronald V. Dellums
*United States Representative,
D—California*
1

This is the Bicentennial year. Is the Congress of the United States fighting valiantly to make sure that democracy is real? No. The Bicentennial has become a sham, a justification for selling red, white and blue everything; but we do not face the reality that democracy must be real for people in this country... The wonderful, beautiful thing about freedom is we cannot compromise it. We cannot make it half freedom or three-quarters freedom. Once we start walking down that road to freedom, we have to continue until everybody is free. So do not give me that line about compromising. The reality is that until we deal with all 25 million hungry people in this country and the one-third in America who are illiterate, we have not done the job. We are still in the process of developing and expanding freedom. We do not have it in this country as yet. What the Bicentennial ought to be about is not our standing on our laurels of the past 200 years but making sure that, in the last quarter of the 20th century, democracy means more than these few monuments we have around Washington, D.C.
*Before the House, Washington, April/
Los Angeles Times, 5-25:(2)5.*

James Dickey
Author, Poet
2

When the Bicentennial first began to roll, I hadn't much faith or interest in it. It just seemed to me like a big Kiwanis Club promotion, or something like that, nation-wide. But I'm coming around to a different view now. I've lived in Europe on several occasions, and Europe is heavy with history. You can't turn a corner in Rome or Paris without seeing where something notable—sometimes

pretty horrible—happened. I think the chief effect of the Bicentennial on this country is to give us a pride and a sense of our history. Ours is only a couple of hundred years old or so, but it is something to be very proud of.
Interview/ U.S. News & World Report, 3-15:55.

3

The South is the future. It is the political pivot of the country now. It's very gratifying to see Jimmy Carter become President, to see the South finally win out after all these years. [The South offers] a better way of life than anywhere else, and it's something people are grasping for. Look at all the magazine articles about it everywhere. It's something people want. Everybody wants to be a Southerner now. Certainly it can make a man feel chauvinistic.
The Dallas Times Herald, 11-19:(A)2.

Paul R. Ehrlich
Professor of biology, Stanford University
4

I think the main thing that's wrong with our society is we've allowed people to think that in this day and age it is sufficient to vote a couple of times a year, at most, in order to be a good citizen. And I think if that's all we do, we're going to continue to get exactly what we deserve. I think that all of us have to start doing what I call tithing to our society—spending at least 10 per cent of our time trying to help run it. That doesn't necessarily mean being a politician, but it may. Getting involved in local government, getting involved in action organizations of certain sorts, informing yourself about issues, and so on.
*Lecture to College of Physicians,
Philadelphia/ The National Observer, 3-6:11.*

Elizabeth II
Queen of England
5

I speak to you as the direct descendent of King George III. He was the last crowned sovereign to rule in this country, and it is therefore with a particular personal interest that I view those events which took place 200 years ago. It seems to me that Independence Day, the Fourth of July, should be celebrated

WHAT THEY SAID IN 1976

(ELIZABETH II)

as much in Britain as in America. Not in rejoicing in the separation of the American colonies from the British crown but in sincere gratitude to the Founding Fathers of the great Republic for having taught Britain a very valuable lesson. We lost the American colonies because we lacked that statesmanship "to know the right time, and the manner of yielding what is impossible to keep." But the lesson was well learned. In the next century and a half we kept more closely to the principles of Magna Carta, which have been the common heritage of both our countries. We learned to respect the right of others to govern themselves in their own ways. This was the outcome of experience learned the hard way in 1776. Without that great act in the cause of liberty, performed in Independence Hall 200 years ago, we could never have transformed an empire into a commonwealth. Ultimately, peace brought a renewal of friendship which has continued and grown over the years and has played a vital part in world affairs. Together, we have fought in two world wars in the defense of our common heritage of freedom. Together, we have striven to keep the peace so dearly won. Together, as friends and allies, we can face the uncertainties of the future, and this is something for which we in Britain can also celebrate the Fourth of July. This morning I saw the famous Liberty Bell. It came here over 200 years ago when Philadelphia, after London, was the largest English-speaking city in the world. It was cast to commemorate the Pennsylvania Charter of Privileges, but is better known for its association with the Declaration of Independence. Today, to mark the 200th anniversary of that declaration, it gives me the greatest pleasure, on behalf of the British people, to present a new bell to the people of the United States of America. It comes from the same foundry as the Liberty Bell; but written on the site of this Bicentennial Bell are the words: "Let Freedom Ring." It is a message in which both our people can join and which I hope will be heard around the world for centuries to come.

Philadelphia, July 6/The New York Times, 7-7:1.

Lord Elwyn-Jones
Lord Chancellor of the United Kingdom

1

[On the U.S.]: Your recovery from the tribulations of recent years has especially impressed us. Both at home and abroad, you have been beset by circumstances and adversities which appeared to shatter your confidence and to threaten the principles on which depends the smooth running of a great democracy—circumstances which might have broken a less resilient people. But now, it is evident to all your friends that your strength is untouched and your resolution firm. Above all, your Constitution has proved its soundness and its vitality.

At ceremony loaning the Magna Carta to the U.S.
for the Bicentennial, Washington, June 3/
The New York Times, 6-4:(A)10.

Gerald R. Ford
President of the United States

2

Other nations have risen to great heights only to weaken in their resolve. We must not repeat their error. A nation born of faith and carried forward by action requires from each of us a commitment to advance individual liberty and to maintain our guard against those who threaten our freedom ... In the two centuries that have passed since 1776, millions upon millions of Americans have worked and taken up arms, when necessary, to make [the American] dream a reality. We can be proud of what they have accomplished. Today, we are the world's oldest republic. We are at peace. Our nation and our way of life endure. And we are free.

Memorial Day address,
Arlington (Va.) National Cemetery, May 31/
The New York Times, 6-1:40.

3

[Addressing new U.S. citizens]: Remember that none of us are more than caretakers of this great country. Remember that the more freedom you give to others, the more you will have for yourself. Remember that without law, there can be no liberty. And remember, as well, the rich treasures you brought with you from whence you came, and let us share your pride in that. This is the way we keep our independence as exciting as the day it was declared, and the United States of America even more beautiful than Joseph's coat.

At Monticello, Charlottesville, Va., July 5/
Los Angeles Herald-Examiner, 7-5:(A)2.

Valery Giscard d'Estaing
President of France

1

You [the U.S.] are now emerging from the most serious economic upheaval the world has known since the great Depression of 1929. Ultimately the foundations of American power . . . were not shaken. You are starting your third century of existence as a nation, with all the means necessary not only to preserve your way of life, but also to shape the destiny of the world.

At luncheon, New Orleans, May 21/
Los Angeles Herald-Examiner, 5-22:(A)2.

Eric F. Goldman
Professor of American history,
Princeton University

2

The word that best describes the [American] mood today is malaise. Americans in the past have had several assumptions as a people that gave us great confidence in the present and the future, and many of these assumptions have been exploded in just the past few years. I suggest that the 1973-75 period was a major watershed in American life.

Interview/The New York Times, 7-5:18.

Robert A. Goldwin
Special Consultant for Education to
President of the United States
Gerald R. Ford

3

Americans are moral judgers, and severe judgers at that. More, we judge no one as severely as ourselves. This may not always have been the mass phenomenon that it is today, but elements of it have always been present. That does not mean that we always, or even regularly, do the right or good thing. It means that when we do not, or when we do the wrong or evil thing, for whatever reasons of necessity, or convenience, or advantage, or whim, or passion, or ignorance, there are

almost always, and almost always promptly, voices raised in self-criticism and self-condemnation. And those morally condemning voices have listeners.

At St. John's College, Annapolis, Md., Feb. 20/
Vital Speeches, 6-1:485.

Alex Haley
Author

4

[Americans today] are in many ways manifesting a condition of rootlessness. You see it in our children and in our old people. We need to start taking charge . . . asking the oldest people to tell us about our families . . . collecting old trunks and boxes in the attics. And we should hold family reunions—everyone walks away from those things feeling a little taller.

San Francisco Examiner & Chronicle,
10-31:(This World)2.

Helen Hayes
Actress

5

What I'm proudest of in America is Americans. I know the American people from having trouped around the country for 50 years, and there are no better people anywhere. The essence of an American is courage and kindness. I know it doesn't sound right to say that when you look at the headlines in the papers. But those, unfortunately, are the splashy events. There's not much written about the majority of Americans, who are secret doers of good—the secret good, good people. They don't make any noise, and they don't make any fuss, and they are very serious about their country and their politics. I know so many like that, and I consider them the typical Americans.

Interview/U.S. News & World Report, 9-13:61.

Alexander Heard
Chancellor, Vanderbilt University

6

The combination of resources now available in the South, including human resources and climate and water, promise the South a level of material prosperity that it has not en-

(ALEXANDER HEARD)

joyed in relation to the rest of the nation for 150 years. I believe that the evolution of black persons to full and equal status will be more rapid and harmonious in the South than elsewhere. The third century of American independence will be distinguished by a massive emergence of the South from the shackles of its inheritance into a major locus of the nation's economic, social and cultural strength.

Time, 9-27:99.

Robert L. Heilbroner
Professor of economics and chairman of the economics department, graduate faculty, New School for Social Research, New York

America will have to accommodate itself to a world that is very different from the past. Within a few years, we're going to wake up to the fact that we're no longer the richest country per capita. We'll be third or fourth. And America will have to struggle to reconcile its individualism with the need for controls, for economic discipline. There's a mood of foreboding in [this country], partly the result of the fact that we are facing problems we never thought we'd face: new international tensions, the spread of the atomic bomb, depletion of resources. Partly it is the worry that capitalism won't work. So there is a sense of stock-taking and sobriety—and a good thing, too, I may add. It's not good for a country to feel it's so blessed by Providence that it's always just naturally on top or naturally a success.

Interview/
U.S. News & World Report, 3-8:56.

Bob Hope
Entertainer

This is a nation with a proud heritage. It is not yet a perfect nation. Anyone who says it is without fault has either flunked political science or Logic 1. There are problems out there, and I don't mean just political prob-

lems. There are diseases out there that have to be cured. There are social ills that need a treatment. There are problems in almost every field of endeavor. That's why we're bringing in the new team—the class of '76. We know there is much work to be done. We already have enough people who are willing to sit back and tell us that we have problems. Besides, you don't really need a college education to do that. We need the people who are going to recognize reality, see the work that has to be done, roll up their sleeves, and say to themselves, "Well, even if I can't make it perfect, I'm gonna make it a little better." That's the new spirit of '76.

At St. Ambrose College commencement,
Davenport, Ia./
The National Observer, 6-12:13.

Hubert H. Humphrey
United States Senator, D—Minnesota

America is a young country with its future before it. The American people are builders. They are restless. They are energetic. They are idealists who want to put their ideals to the test. America looks to new leaders who can make our country both dynamic and just, who have a sense of compassion, but also a dedication to individual initiative—leaders who can inspire and are inspired by our history, but who sense that our greatness is in the future. America's best days—America's great days—have only just begun.

At Democratic National Convention, New York,
July 13/ The New York Times, 7-15:26.

Robert M. Hutchins
President, Center for the Study of Democratic Institutions

I think there is something here [in the U.S.] that doesn't exist anywhere else. This may be just because I was brought up as a lawyer, but I think the Constitution of the United States is just what Gladstone thought of it—the most wonderful work ever struck off at a given time by the brain and purpose of man. There is a Constitution that works fairly

well!; there is a form of government that we don't really understand but it seems to be working fairly well; and there are the history and the spirit of the people."
Television interview/ Center Report, February:23.

Barbara Jordan
United States Representative, D—Texas
1

. . . the basic fundamental institutions of the country are durable. People still repeat those words, "liberty" and "equality" and "justice," with feeling, and somehow point them up as examples of what democracy can do and what masses of people can do when working together. I don't know if you heard the speech by the Prime Minister of Ireland—he came and spoke to us and said that people abroad think a lot more of you [the U.S.] than you think of yourselves. And there was applause, because we were so glad to hear that—that people elsewhere still view us as a pretty good country. I think we think less of ourselves than we deserve.
Interview/ Newsweek, 7-4:70.

2

A nation is formed by the willingness of each of us to share in the responsibility for upholding the common good. A government is invigorated when each of us is willing to participate in the shaping of its future. In this election year, when we must define the common good and begin again to shape our common future, let each person do his or her part. If one citizen is unwilling to participate, we all suffer. For the American idea, though shared by all, is realized in each one of us.
At Democratic National Convention, New York, July 12/ The New York Times, 7-15:26.

Herman Kahn
Director, Hudson Institute
3

About half the country—about 60 per cent —is "squares." That's the first good thing about America. Squares make good taxpayers. They make great soldiers and great citizens. They believe in religion. They know

that people die; they know that people get sick. They know you can't defend frontiers just by being nice. They are realistic. They know you've got to earn a living and it's tough to earn a living—earning a living involves some serious compromise in the real world . . . It's a square country, a Roman country. When the Romans lost their qualities, theirs wasn't a good country any more. The Romans epitomize the total square values: a respect, first of all, for tradition; a respect for the institutions of the country; a respect for older people. It's this kind of respect that makes society operate. I think this basic squareness [in America] will last to the end of the century. That's a very good thing—what makes this country work. You go to Houston, that's America, and you'll be shocked: confident people—they haven't heard about the depression. Go anywhere in the Middle West, South, Southwest—no depression or recession. Things are booming. People are working hard. They expect to make money. They think the place is great. The mood of pessimism is basically that of the Northeast United States—it may go as far south as Atlanta—plus some of the West Coast.
Interview/ Newsweek, 7-4:29

Joseph Kingsbury-Smith
National editor, the Hearst Newspapers
4

Despite all you may hear about disillusionment with America and anti-Americanism abroad, I can assure you from my talks with people in almost every country in Europe, the Middle East and Asia, that if our immigration barriers were removed, millions of foreigners would come rushing to America to share our American way of life.
Before delegates from Senate Youth Program, Washington/
Los Angeles Herald-Examiner, 2-7:(A)5.

Henry A. Kissinger
Secretary of State of the United States
5

Americans have always made history

(HENRY A. KISSINGER)

rather than let history chart our course. We, the present generation of Americans, will do no less. So let this year mark the end of our divisions. Let us usher in an era of national reconciliation and rededication by all Americans to their common destiny. Let us have a clear vision of what is before us—glory and danger alike.

Before Boston World Affairs Council, March 11/
Time, 3-22:6.

1

I came to the United States from Nazi Germany. So I had an experience of America that most Americans take for granted. For me, just to be able to walk across a street without being pursued by a bunch of thugs was a great experience. And not having ever experienced a free society until my fifteenth year, I could appreciate what America means to oppressed people around the world. It's been a very important influence on my life. Because, while I have seen many of the failings of America, and while I don't excuse them, I also have to say there's no other country in the world that I know where it would be possible for a foreigner who had worked four years in a shaving brush factory, and had gone to night school to get into military intelligence, to become a professor at a leading university; to become Secretary of State, without anybody ever saying, "Who are *you* to tell us what to believe?" And therefore I have never been able to join those who wanted to tear up the whole society in order to cure particular ills.

Interview/Newsweek, 7-4:20.

Alan J. Lerner
Playwright, Lyricist

2

This country isn't like any other. We're the only country that's founded, based, on an idea. We didn't go through thousands of years of change, and evolve. Somebody said, "We're gonna make up a country," and they made up the United States of America . . . I have this fantasy that when God created the world He said, "I love colors"—so he made Europe white and Africa black, the Orient yellow, North America brown, South America red, and so on. Then an angel came over and said, "What are you gonna do, Lord—they don't mix." And God said, "I'll invent the United States of America, dump them all there and let them work it out."

Interview, Washington/
The Washington Post, 2-29:(F)3.

David E. Lilienthal
Chairman, Development and Resources
Corporation; Former Chairman,
Atomic Energy Commission of the
United States

3

In the future that I envisage for our country over the next 10 to 20 years, the individual private citizen will have an increased function and importance. Far from becoming of less and less consequence in the decisions that most intimately affect his life, I predict that the individual will become more important than ever. This will be a confirmation of a basic tenet of American life: freedom of the individual to have a part in the shaping of his life. What I see ahead is something more than increased citizen participation in governmental decisions. The most heartening promise of American life is the increased stature of the private individual and his non-governmental organizations in matters close to his daily life . . . I suggest that it is [the] very complexity of our lives, this massive and growing interdependence, that has given and will increasingly give the individual new and increased importance in shaping his life.

Address sponsored by American Institute of
Planners and American Society of Planning
Officials, Washington/
The National Observer, 4-10:13.

Archibald MacLeish
Poet; Former Assistant Secretary of State
of the United States

4

The whole point of the Bicentennial, the thing that has the Russkies and Chinese scared to death of the American, is that it was not a class revolution, but a revolution of all men.

News conference, Washington, March 29/
The Washington Post, 3-30:(B)1.

Mike Mansfield
United States Senator, D—Montana
1

. . . as far as my country is concerned, I'm always optimistic. I become depressed once in a while, did during the war in Southeast Asia. But that's a feeling I can't afford to harbor too long. The country is still young, got lots of room. Hopefully, the purgatory which we've gone through in Watergate and Vietnam, Southeast Asia, will make us better people, a better nation.

Interview, Washington/
The Christian Science Monitor, 6-10:16.

James A. Michener
Author
2

[On the Bicentennial celebration, amid inflation, unemployment and the aftermath of Watergate]: In the middle of all this they ask us to hold a barn dance. It's like a couple trying to celebrate an anniversary after the worst year they ever had.

Before Colorado Legislature, Denver/
The New York Times, 2-19:42.

3

We're [the U.S.] in a better relative position, I think, today than most of the other democracies. Our dollar is stronger. Our productive capacity is unimpaired. We do not have the savage class strife that some of the other countries have. We have a position of strength from which we can build, I think. We have demonstrated that we are a bastion of freedom. We have survived Watergate. We are alarmed by the abuses of the FBI and the CIA and the threat to civil democracy that they pose. I have thought for many years that this nation is good until the year 2050. I am sure we're going to be here. I am sure we're going to be functioning one way or another. Detroit may not be here. A bomb might hit New York. But there will be a society here, and it will be governed, I believe, largely upon the principles that now govern us, because there's no alternative. We must keep this. We must keep it going.

At National Press Club, Washington/
U.S. News & World Report, 7-5: Special Section.

Walter F. Mondale
United States Senator, D—Minnesota;
1976 Democratic Vice-Presidential nominee
4

[Common Cause chairman] John Gardner once said that there are three kinds of persons. [There are] the uncritical lovers who love society in all its rigidities so much they resist any change. Then there are the unloving critics; they hate society so much they become expert in the art of demolition. He said what we need are loving critics, people who care enough, study enough, try enough to reform and make it work. I would like to think I am a loving critic.

Interview/Newsweek, 7-26:26.

Arturo Morales-Carrion
President, University of Puerto Rico
5

Whether one likes it or not, the United States in its bigness and might stands for Western Civilization. It represents, at this watershed of history, its achievements and failings, its strengths and weaknesses. As such, it lives in a glass house more than any other country in the world. It is carefully watched at every twist and turn, as no other country is watched. What is said or done here not only affects Pittsburgh or Kalamazoo, it also influences the thinking and attitudes of far-away lands. By the same token, events in remote places eventually send their ripples to affect American life.

At Temple University, May 27/
Vital Speeches, 8-15:657.

Richard B. Morris
President, American Historical Association;
Professor emeritus of history,
Columbia University
6

I think the notion of America as an asylum for liberty is still a very strong one. Just witness the fact that we were able, in a very short time, to relocate 100,000 Vietnamese—quite a remarkable story. I don't think there's any parallel to that. We are still an asylum for liberty and for opportunity. To the average individual immigrant, the dream of asylum

(RICHARD B. MORRIS)

may be somewhat flawed, but to millions of uprooted and displaced persons of our own generation, the United States is still the last best hope of man.

Interview/U.S. News & World Report,
7-5:Special Section.

Bill Moyers
Television commentator, Public Broadcasting Service; Former Press Secretary to the President of the United States (Lyndon B. Johnson)

1

If the Founding Fathers believed in anything, they believed in ingenuity. The Revolution, the Civil War, the conquering of the West, the world wars were different challenges, but they could all be solved by American ingenuity. Anything was possible. Now we are living in the specter of limits. That's a new word we are learning—limits. It's never been part of the American vocabulary. What has happened? What is so wrong with our democratic system that it can't deal with the problems of the cities, crime, terrorism, higher and higher costs? A recent study showed that the only people in this country who are really satisfied with themselves are the garbagemen. They see a problem, and they cart it away. That's what society wants done with its problems. Most Americans are looking for just one small victory. They are pleading, "Won't somebody do *something*?"

Interview, People, 1-26:69.

Daniel P. Moynihan
Professor of government, Harvard University; Former United States Ambassador/Permanent Representative to the United Nations

2

Anyone who says the condition of man is not better just doesn't know much about the condition of man. But if I were choosing another time to live, I suppose it would be roughly what the French called the "Belle Epoch," around the turn of the century. It was

[a] time when the country [the U.S.] was in its . . . well, an *extraordinary* time, you know. Things were coming to fruition. The age of William James and Henry James. An age of—not to deny its turmoils—but an age of rather extraordinary, surprisingly *high* level of public discourse. It culminated, you know, in the elevation of Woodrow Wilson. Read Wilson's speeches, if you would like to know what you have missed. Read Teddy Roosevelt's. Read about the acquisition of the Philippines. You know, it was a society that was not exhausted, a society with most of its energies left unexpended. Just beginning—a society just beginning to sense its powers. Good time, good time.

Interview, New York/
Los Angeles Times, 4-22:(1)1.

Steven Muller
President, Johns Hopkins University

3

Among the world's people we, as a still-emerging single people, are indeed young. And we are showing classic symptoms of late adolescence. In a telling phrase from our vernacular, we are having trouble "getting it together" . . . Metaphorically, having lost our diverse childhood manners, we have not yet evolved good adult American manners of our own. We indulge in adolescent excesses. We are spoiled by providence and as a nation suffer teen-age delusions of material splendor without a wiser adult judgment of values. We are typically adolescent over-consumers, lacking adult discipline, and we have a national crush on the entertainment industry. Most awkward of all, we have outgrown the clothing of our government and [at] the moment nothing in our Federal wardrobe fits: Our local underwear is badly frayed and bindingly too small; our state shirts and blouses are worn out and patched; and our national outerwear is too new and scratchy and at least a size too small . . . I deeply love the adolescent United States of my vision—this gawky, rowdy, boorish, overweight, self-indulgent, promising teen-ager. Life with a teen-ager is unbearable without love, sometimes nearly unbearable even with it. Love does not prevent criticism, but it can forgive the Bay of Pigs, Watergate, commercial television, the Department of Health, Education and Welfare, and other adolescent horrors. They are not tolerable, but, with love, endurable. With love also comes trust. Of course, I have fears for the America of my vision. A spoiled adolescent can become a rotten adult. A careless and wildly undisciplined one may not even survive. But there is so much promise here. I deem the American heart good, the ideals sound, the energy prodigious, the talent infinite, the prospects auspicious. Thus—with love and trust, and with fear and criticism as well—I have great confidence in the nation's future.

On Johns Hopkins University centennial/
Los Angeles Times, 3-16:(2)5.

Thomas A. Murphy
Chairman, General Motors Corporation

1

One of the problems that we run into today is that people think because the economy is turning up, everything is going to be easy. It's going to be automatic that I'm going to get a job or that people are going to buy more automobiles. Well, nothing is automatic. I remember one day in 1950 when I was living in Stuyvesant Town in New York, and there was a salesman for U.S. Rubber—I used to run into him in the elevator and we'd ride over to the subway together. We were in a real boom situation, and I remember this guy saying, "God, I don't understand this about times being good. I'm having to work my heart out for the business I'm getting." And I wondered what he was expecting—that he didn't have to get out of the office? That people were going to deluge him with orders? He had to get out there and hustle it. The *only* thing that concerns me about this country is that people sometimes have the delusion that somehow the good Lord raised His arms and said, "There it is—America, the land of opportunity," and gave us something more than He gave everybody else. He didn't. I think the system has done that for us. A lot of people sweated and strained for a long time to make America what it is today, and we can improve on it— if we work at it.

Interview/Newsweek, 7-4:16.

Ralph Nader
Lawyer; Consumer advocate

2

The problem with this country is that the immediate sensory perceptions of people are pretty comfortable. And where they're not comfortable, what I call the "anesthesia" is operating. People are irritated by pollution, but they have air-conditioning. People are irritated at unemployment, but they have unemployment compensation. There are a whole host of these "anesthesias" that let people tolerate structural abuses. I'll tell you what the *real* problem is: We ask people to think, instead of asking them to believe. And history has always gone to those who ask people to believe.

The New York Times Magazine, 1-18:52.

John Osborne
British playwright

3

[After a visit to the U.S.]: It is utterly ludicrous over there. There are failures everywhere trying to make out they are successes. There is no conversation, not even gossip. The Americans don't even talk about what they have seen and done. [They] are so idiotic that it almost makes you hope that if there is a war the Russians will win.

The Washington Post, 5-21:(B)2.

Ronald Reagan
Candidate for the 1976 Republican Presidential nomination; Former Governor of California (R)

4

I don't believe that people I've met in almost every state of the Union are ready to consign this—the last island of freedom—to the dustbin of history. Call it mysticism if you will, but I believe God had a divine purpose in placing this land between the two great oceans to be found by those who had a special love of freedom and the courage to leave the countries of their birth. We're Americans and we have a rendezvous with destiny.

National television address, Los Angeles, March 31/The New York Times, 4-1:22.

Ronald Reagan
Former candidate for the 1976
Republican Presidential nomination;
Former Governor of California (R)
1

[On what he would write about in a letter to be placed in a time capsule to be opened in 100 years]: . . . they'll be the domestic problems . . .; the challenges confronting us; the erosion of freedom that has taken place . . . in this country; the invasion of private rights; the controls and restrictions on the vitality of the great free economy that we enjoy. These are our challenges that we must meet. And then again there is that challenge . . . that we live in a world in which the great powers have poised and aimed at each other horrible missiles of destruction, nuclear weapons that can in a matter of minutes arrive in each other's country and destroy virtually the civilized world we live in. And suddenly it dawned on me: those who would read this letter a hundred years from now will *know* whether those missiles were fired. They will know whether we met our challenge. Whether they had the freedom that we have known up until now will depend on what we do here. Will they look back with appreciation and say, thank God for those people in 1976 who headed off that loss of freedom; who kept us now a hundred years later free; who kept our world from nuclear destruction? And if we fail, they probably won't get to read the letter at all because it spoke of individual freedom and they won't be allowed to talk of that or read of it.

At Republican National Convention,
Kansas City, Aug. 19/
The New York Times, 8-21:15.

Nelson A. Rockefeller
Vice President of the United States
2

Like every generation, we face today what seem like insurmountable problems. But the lesson of our extraordinary past is simply this: that every such challenge is an opportunity; that it has been the creative response to such challenges over these 200 years that has brought America its greatness.

At Bicentennial ceremony,
Washington Monument, Washington, July 4/
The New York Times, 7-5:18.

Dean Rusk
Professor of international law,
University of Georgia;
Former Secretary of State of
the United States
3

Our confidence has fallen to an all-time low, not just in politics, but in our institutions, as a result of Watergate. We are in a mood in which we've forgotten that, while self-criticism can be the lifeblood of democracy, self-flagellation can be its destruction.

Before Dallas Assembly, Feb. 6/
The Dallas Times Herald, 2-7:(B)22.

Arthur M. Schlesinger, Jr.
Historian; Professor of humanities,
City University of New York
4

For some reason, self-doubt appears to thrive in our Bicentennial year—perhaps because such anniversaries impel us to recognize how far we have fallen short of the men and hopes of 1776 . . . Let us not succumb too easily to this gloom.

San Francisco Examiner & Chronicle,
4-11:(This World)2.

James R. Schlesinger
Chairman, Washington Study Group on
National Policy Alternatives;
Former Secretary of Defense of the
United States
5

What we need to do is to get back on the track on a consensus. The democratic system requires a consensus. Where there is none, it is much more susceptible to centrifugal forces. Where there is a consensus, our system can pull itself together much more effectively than the other systems. When the American people see there is a problem to be solved, they will respond. The great historical achievement of the United States has been that when the times required unity, we have achieved it.

Interview, Washington/
Los Angeles Times, 3-11:(2)7.

William W. Scranton
United States Ambassador/
Permanent Representative to the
United Nations
1

We are a people who have come through the most rapid and radical change in the world's history. In just a few brief years, we have seen assassinations and riots, unpopular wars and sordid scandals, economic setbacks and moral confusion. We are the first people in history to live with what Alvin Toffler calls "Future Shock," but we have not collapsed under that strain. We are more skeptical than we once were, but we are not cynical. We are more cautious than we were, but we are not fearful. We are more realistic than was once the case, but we are not pessimistic. I believe we are coming of age as a people. The price has been high. Adulthood is hard. We've had to give up some illusions, and that has often been a painful experience. But, above all else, we are maturing in this critical period, and we are becoming a stronger and more-resourceful people, especially as individuals.
At University of Utah commencement/
The National Observer, 8-7:11.

John R. Silber
President, Boston University
2

On the 200th anniversary of the birth of our Republic, we face dangers at home and abroad. We may feel oppressed by the magnitude of our problems, but let us take pride in the fact that . . . men and women the world over still look to America as the last best hope for freedom in the world. Despite our weaknesses, we are very strong. Despite our uncertainty, we are capable of great resolve. Whatever our faults, and they are significant, we have also our virtues, and the former do not eclipse the latter.
Before municipal authorities of Boston, July 4/
Vital Speeches, 9-1:677.

Alexander I. Solzhenitsyn
Exiled Soviet author
3

. . . I believe profoundly in the soundness,

the healthiness of the roots, of the great-spirited, powerful American nation—with the insistent honesty of its youth, and its alert moral sense. With my own eyes I have seen the American country, and precisely because of that I have expressed all this today with steadfast hope.
Upon receiving Freedoms Foundation's Friend-
ship Award, at Hoover Institution,
Stanford University/
Los Angeles Times, 6-13:(1)3.

Jay Sourwine
Chief counsel,
Senate Internal Security Subcommittee
4

There is still a world Communist conspiracy. It is aimed at the domination of the world. We [the U.S.] are the Number 1 target. It has become maybe a fetish in this country to say, "I'm not anti-Communist." Maybe the American people have been brainwashed into believing there's something unwholesome about being anti-Communist. Subversion in the armed forces, government, the schools, from the pulpit, continues. We have a generation, perhaps two, raised in this country to believe that nothing is inherently right or inherently wrong. We've got people adrift.
Interview/The Washington Post, 2-28:(A)2.

Leonard Sussman
Executive director, Freedom House
5

The Founding Fathers did not use the term "moral," but it permeated the structure they established. They never forgot the role of morality in framing the concepts of this government. We have the Constitution; but, before the Constitution is enforced, you expect individual enforcement of the requirements of society, and we have gotten away from that. We have galloped off to stress the material gains that free choice makes possible, and in that drive have underplayed the very rules of the moral structure that make the gains possible.
The Christian Science Monitor, 4-12:16.

A. J. P. Taylor
British historian

No, I've never been to the United States. Why should I go? I like old buildings; there are none of any great age in the United States. I like agreeable, sophisticated food, and I was told by Maurice Bowra, the warden of Wadham College, now dead, that when he went to the United States he never had a decent meal. So if I can't see any lovely buildings and if I can't get any decent food, what should I go for?

Interview, London/
The New York Times, 6-16:2.

Michael Tilson Thomas
Music director,
Buffalo Philharmonic Orchestra

Being born an American has made me more a citizen of the world than I would have been in any other country. This because of the diversity of life I've soaked up from my friends of so many different backgrounds. We're arriving at a point in America where all of us can revel in our own personal histories while at the same time fuse into a stronger new identity.

Interview/U.S. News & World Report, 12-27:65.

Laurens Van der Post
South African author

I think the United States has a true passion for finding the right answers. I think that the way in which it exposed itself through Watergate . . . to the outside world is not a sign of weakness but of immense spiritual strength. I think that the United States really wants a spiritual answer and therefore that ultimately this rediscovery of the classical spirit of the West depends on the rediscovery by the United States of itself and of its power, and rediscovery of its courage and its wish to use that power, this gigantic power, not like a giant but in the interest of the world and humanity.

Interview, London/
The Christian Science Monitor, 7-27:15.

Malcolm Wallop
United States Senator-elect, R—Wyoming

If we all have to be grouped and cared for under some Federal program, then the energy of this country will disappear. Self-reliance, individual mobility and the chance to take risks and fail are all important—and they are disappearing under the liberal attitude we see around us now.

Interview/The Washington Post, 12-12:(F)3.

John W. Warner
Administrator, American Revolution Bicentennial Administration

When I first started making the circuit around the country, I'd be asked: "Here we are in the middle of Watergate, in the aftermath of Vietnam, in the middle of a recession—how in hell can we celebrate anything?" Well, I think the balance has swung. The American spirit hit bottom and it's on the way back up again. I've seen it in hundreds of towns with people saying, "Hey, maybe my voice does count and there are things I can accomplish with my neighbors." I'm of the opinion that there will be residual effects from this in the years ahead. Things are going to get accomplished that don't have a Bicentennial label because these millions of people, literally millions, have come together in all these little communities to accomplish something together. There's a restoration of confidence in all this.

Interview, Washington/
Los Angeles Times, 3-24:(1-A)3.

Shirley Williams
Secretary of State for Prices and Consumer Protection and Paymaster General of the United Kingdom

What impresses me about the U.S. is the sense that almost anything is possible. People are willing to change their attitude, change their place of living and work, far more readily than they are in Europe, and that's very attractive. Secondly, although there's a very marked financial hierarchy, it isn't related to class, birth, accent and education, which is so infuriating. It drives one up the bloody wall. It's not just England, but other European countries, places like Sweden. What distresses me is the extraordinary failure to mobilize the massive resources of the U.S. to deal with poverty. In relations between the Federal, state and city governments they've gone about it in an extraordinarily inefficient and profligate way.

Interview, London/
The New York Times, 9-2:8.

Walter B. Wriston
Chairman, Citicorp
(Citibank, New York) [1]

The emphasis in the last few years on all the negative factors has warped our perspective. It's about time that we restore the optimism that is an essential ingredient of democracy. Unless you believe tomorrow is better than today, you can't have a democracy. You'll have a dictatorship, because the dictator will tell you that that's true, and that never works. Whether this experiment [American democracy] will work for the next 200 years depends on your children and mine. If they're brought up to believe that personal liberty isn't important, or that opportunity is dead, it's not going to work. But if they have the same faith in the democratic experiment that my generation grew up with, it's going to work fine. It's going to be different, but it's going to work.

Interview/Newsweek, 7-4:67.

Daniel Yankelovich
Public-opinion analyst [2]

[Americans] fear that in the pursuit of their organizational goals, the politicians and the businessmen and the unions and the professionals have lost sight of any larger obligation to the public and are indifferent, or worse, to anything that does not benefit immediately and directly—themselves or their institutions.
San Francisco Examiner & Chronicle, 9-26:(This World)2.

Civil Rights

James Baldwin
Author

1

I worked for the Army on the railway in New Jersey. A lot of what happened to me in those years has to do with having had a sense of being utterly helpless, no matter what you did. I learned what it means to be black in America—it means something terrifying. Every generation has to face it, because the spirit of the country doesn't change from generation to generation. Only the details change. I experienced what it means to be despised by your countrymen.

Interview, Paris/Book Digest, December:19.

Terrel H. Bell
Commissioner of Education
of the United States

2

Busing [of schoolchildren for racial balance] has been a mixed bag. Many parents have become embittered and upset. Some of them have taken their children out of public schools and put them in private schools. It has caused a lot of strife, hard feelings and ill will, but there have been some successful desegregations where busing has gone smoothly. I would point to Denver as a good example of that, where racial isolation has been greatly reduced. In other cases, however, busing has gone to the extreme, where the intent was to attain total racial balance regardless of the extent of busing or how much disruption was caused in home, family and neighborhood. On the other hand, we ought not be tolerating a racially isolated society. We should be doing those things, within limits, to encourage integration of schools. But I think education has been forced to mediate problems caused by others, those who set up housing patterns and zoning ordinances.

Interview, Washington/
The National Observer, 8-14:4.

Julian Bond
Georgia State Senator (D)

3

Political scientists don't usually think of courts as the most democratic institutions in a society, but to blacks for a generation the courts have been the essence of our democracy, the main symbol of the fact—or our belief—that we were finally becoming a part of this nation. Today that sense is going fast. The lawyers tell us the Federal courts are inventing new doctrines to justify why they don't even have to hear our cases. I am not an expert on these details, but I read that the Supreme Court has decided that a black defendant isn't entitled to ask his jurors whether they will be prejudiced against him because of his color. I read that the Voting Rights Act doesn't prevent small Southern towns from discriminating against us as long as they are careful not to make things worse than they were in 1965. I read that if ... the judge and prosecutor in Cairo deliberately bring false charges and set unreasonable bonds to shut blacks up—the Federal courts are not interested in any of these. They are closed. In 1965, when I was first elected to the Georgia House, the other members refused to let me be seated because I had said some things about the Vietnam war ... The Supreme Court held that the Georgia Legislature had no business excluding me—and disenfranchising the voters in my district—for exercising my right of free speech. That was only 11 years ago ... I have a real feeling that if the case came up today, we would be told the Federal courts are not in the business of running state legislatures and that we should take our complaints somewhere else. Well, for many people and many issues, there is nowhere else.

Before Senate Subcommittee on
Constitutional Rights, Washington/
The Washington Post, 5-23:(C)6.

Edward W. Brooke
United States Senator, R—Massachusetts 1

For a long time, blacks have rallied to the Democratic Party. Before that, they all rallied to the Republican Party. But we cannot afford the luxury of supporting just one political party.

U.S. News & World Report, 1-26;44.

James L. Buckley
United States Senator, C—New York 2

I've always felt that the best way we could continue the civil-rights movement was to encourage upward movement of minorities in the economic arena. It was the way for minorities to achieve, gain self-respect, satisfaction and bring about mutual respect.

Interview, New York, Dec. 20/
The New York Times, 12-21;37.

Jimmy Carter
Candidate for the
1976 Democratic Presidential nomination;
Former Governor of Georgia (D) 3

[On criticism of his recent use of the term "ethnic purity"]: I should have said, "ethnic character," "ethnic heritage." I see nothing wrong with a heterogeneous type American population. If you have a lower-status neighborhood that is black primarily or Latin American primarily or Polish primarily or of Germanic descent primarily, I see nothing wrong with that. People have a tendency—and it is an unshakable tendency—to want to share common social clubs, common churches, common restaurants. I would not use the forces of the Federal government to break up the ethnic character of such neighborhoods.

At City Club, Cleveland, April 9/
The New York Times, 4-10;10.

4

When I ran for Governor [of Georgia] in 1966 and 1970, I told people that conserva-tism did not mean racism. But if I had gone in and said, "All of you are wrong. You shouldn't have done what you did. I'm better than you are" . . . I wouldn't have been elected. I wouldn't have gotten more than 10 per cent of the votes. The point I'm making is that the South, including Georgia, has moved forward [racially] because it hasn't been put into the position of having to renounce itself. You've got to give people credit for the progress they make and the changes in their attitudes.

Interview/The New York Times, 6-18:(A)23.

Jimmy Carter
1976 Democratic Presidential nominee 5

[On racial progress in the South]: It was a very difficult thing for us in the South to change the pattern of a century or more, but we have done it successfully. [The success of my primary campaign in the South and elsewhere] is a symbol that racial lines have been broken down in the South and also that the sectional prejudice that has held us back so long on the national political scene has also been destroyed. The changes were not made solely by the Supreme Court and by Congress. The changes were made by literally hundreds, even thousands, of school-board members, city councilmen, county officials and others who did accept complete and total integration in the South.

Campaigning, Biloxi, Miss., Sept. 17/
San Francisco Examiner & Chronicle, 9-19:(A)17.

6

I'm strongly opposed to forced busing [of schoolchildren for racial balance]. The only kids that ever get bused are poor children. Rich parents either move or put their kids in private schools. My own preference is a plan whereby any child who wants to be bused can be bused at public expense—but that busing must not contribute to resegregation; you wouldn't be able to be bused away from a school just because it's integrated. Second, black leadership must be adequately represented in the administration of the school

(JIMMY CARTER)

system all the way from the school board down to the classroom, so that black parents feel that it is their school system as well as white folks'. Third, no child should ever be bused against his or her wish.

Interview, Plains, Ga./
The Reader's Digest, October:102.

1

[On whether he will quit his church in Plains, Ga., because it does not allow blacks to attend services]: I can't resign from the human race because there's discrimination. I can't resign as an American because there's still discrimination, and I don't intend to resign from my own church because there's discrimination. I think my best approach is to stay with the church and to change the attitudes which I abhor. Now, if it was a country club, I would have quit. In fact, I have no memberships in country clubs or any private clubs that discriminate because of race. But this is not my church. It is God's church. And I can't quit my lifetime worship habit, commitment, because of a remnant of discrimination which has been alleviated a great deal in the last 10 years. I hope it will be eliminated completely in the next few weeks. I won't speak for the church membership. But I'll do all I can within the church to eliminate that last vestige of racial discrimination . . . I'll do all I can as an American citizen, and as someone who is going to be President of the country, to eliminate the last vestige of racial discrimination in this country to the best of my ability.

News conference, Sacramento, Calif., Nov. 1/
Los Angeles Times, 11-2:(1)3.

W. Montague Cobb
President, National Association for the Advancement of Colored People

2

I really am not interested in the racial aspect of my office. What is more important is that everyone recognize the NAACP as an organization that has made some of the most significant contributions to the American creed of equal justice under law and opportunity for all.

The Christian Science Monitor, 1-30:4.

James S. Coleman
Professor of sociology,
University of Chicago

3

[On the busing of schoolchildren for racial balance]: There is probably no single action that has had as strong and immediate effect in removing whites from already substantially black central cities than the policies of racial balance in the schools . . . An action necessary to bring about equal protection under the law for blacks and whites has the overall effect of defeating social integration among blacks and whites.

Before Massachusetts Legislature, Boston,
March 30/The New York Times, 3-31:50.

James Farmer
Founder, Congress of Racial Equality

4

What we succeeded in doing in the '60s was in dealing with the Constitutional issue of rights—what the 13th, 14th and 15th Amendments mean. We've won that battle. Now we are dealing with issues that transcend Constitutional rights . . . You might call it human rights. We're dealing with real equality, how to close the gaps—gaps in educational achievement, in income, in health, in general well-being.

San Francisco Examiner & Chronicle,
11-21:(This World)2.

Gerald R. Ford
President of the United States

5

I think the individual ought to have a right to send his daughter or his son to a [segregated] private school if he's willing to pay whatever the cost might be . . . I would hope they wouldn't, but individuals have a right where they're willing to make the choice themselves, and there are no taxpayer funds involved. [But] if they get Federal aid, that's a totally different question and I certainly would not, under those circumstances, go along with segregated schools.

TV-radio interview/"Face the Nation,"
Columbia Broadcasting System, 6-6.

S. I. Hayakawa

There is no good reason why we cannot wipe out the vestiges of discrimination in America, achieve quality education for our children and at the same time minimize the massive busing of our children [for racial balance in schools]. Let me re-emphasize that my vision of the future means equal opportunity and equal rights for all of our citizens. The principle of racial equality is indelibly written into our Constitution and into our hearts, and in all that we do we must honor it.

Before U.S. Jaycees, Indianapolis, June 22/
The Washington Post, 6-23:(A)5.

Louise Day Hicks

"Black is beautiful" was a motto of genius which uplifted us far above its first intention. Once Americans had thought about it and perceived its truth, we began to realize that so are brown, white, red and yellow beautiful. When I was young, a Sunday-school teacher told us that the beauty of Joseph's coat was its many colors. I believe Americans are beautiful—individually, in communities, and freely joined together by dedication to the United States of America.

Before newly naturalized citizens,
Monticello, Charlottesville, Va., July 5/
The Washington Post, 7-6:(A)3.

Redd Foxx
Actor, Comedian

Young people need to know [about the accomplishments of black Americans], so their parents can't poison their minds that niggers are lazy and shiftless and never did nothing, and blah blah, and are good for picking cotton. Black kids need it, but white kids need it too; they need it more, because they're the

ones that are going to have to bring down this prejudice. The white kids need it so they can say, "Mom, you're wrong. You know who invented the blood plasma that saved Uncle Willie in World War II? A black man."

Interview, Culver City, Calif./
The New York Times, 6-20:(2)34.

John Hope Franklin
Professor of history,
University of Chicago

Since the first American Revolution has proved inadequate in promoting and achieving a condition of equality for all persons who live under the government it created, and since the first American Revolution has encouraged evasive legalism and downright opposition to the enjoyment of equality for all persons in this country, we need a new American Revolution to achieve the equality that the first one failed to achieve. One need not linger over the matter of assessing blame. The post mortem clearly indicates a failure of will, of sincerity and of integrity. And it is the failure of the first American Revolution that suggests what the nature of the second should be. We need no Lexington and Concord, no Saratoga and Yorktown, to chart the course of victory. We do not even need France or some other foreign power to bail us out, as the Patriots needed. We need no call to arms, no violence, no bloodshed. We need a new declaration, a declaration in favor of the rights of all men. And this time we need to mean what we say. We need a new commitment to a more perfect union, one in which some are not more equal than others. We need a new adherence to the principles of equality, an adherence so unequivocal that it will not permit sly evasion or "clever" side-steppings of the obligation to recognize a man on the basis of merit and not on the basis of race. In a word, we need a new American Revolution that will create a new ideology of comradeship in the great enterprise of building a society in which every man and woman can face tomorrow unencumbered by the burdens of the past or the prejudices of the present. This

WHAT THEY SAID IN 1976

(JOHN HOPE FRANKLIN)

calls for a revolution in the heart and soul of every American. This calls for an unswerving commitment of the will to achieve equality. That is what the first American Revolution did not have. That is what the First and Second Reconstruction did not have. That is what the New American Revolution must have.

Before American Psychiatric Association/
The National Observer, 7-31:7.

Charles V. Hamilton
Professor of government,
Columbia University
1

It is unreasonable to expect people to continue providing their loyal support without some significant return. Those black leaders jockeying for jobs in the new [President-elect Jimmy Carter] Administration should be as mindful of this as any others. The masses of black voters have not engaged in years of struggle simply to receive a few patronage jobs and honorific titles for a handful of their leaders.

San Francisco Examiner & Chronicle,
12-12:(This World)2.

Richard G. Hatcher
Mayor of Gary, Indiana
2

. . . we [blacks] had Cleveland [the Mayor's seat] once. Now we don't. We lost it because of the failure to do what is necessary to retain power. And, too, whites no longer feel civil rights is a major problem. They don't have to elect black Mayors to keep the cities from burning. So we lose a Cleveland because we failed to watch over what we had won. It is one thing to gain power. But it is another to retain power. And one of our goals in 1976 must be the mastery of the art of staying in office once we have won.

U.S. News & World Report, 1-26:44.

3

Our [black's] primary priority is becoming

delegates to both the national [political] conventions or helping elect other blacks as delegates. The new arena of the '70s is politics, and we have to be in the middle of that arena —participating, making decisions, calling the shots.

U.S. News & World Report, 1-26:43.

S. I. Hayakawa
1976 California Republican
U.S. Senatorial nominee
4

It is true that as a nation we have far to go to achieve full racial justice. But in the world context, we are seen as the nation that has gone farther than any other in offering equality of political rights and economic opportunities to all races, including the blacks.

Campaign address,
San Francisco State University, Oct. 4/
Los Angeles Herald-Examiner, 10-5:(A)11.

Louise Day Hicks
President, Boston City Council
5

[Criticizing the busing of schoolchildren for racial balance and the U.S. Supreme Court's refusal to review court-ordered school desegregation]: No people anywhere at any time can be expected to live with the injustice that has been heaped time and time again on the good parents of Boston. They have been had and they will respond. The Supreme Court may have spoken, but the people shall rule, and God help those who have let them down.

Boston, June 14/ The New York Times, 6-15:23.

Herbert Hill
National Labor director,
National Association for the
Advancement of Colored People
6

Rates of unemployment among black youths have reached disaster levels. If they continue, and unfortunately there is every reason to believe they will, it is necessary to conclude that virtually an entire generation of ghetto youths will never enter the labor force . . . This development is the single most volatile factor in potential large-scale urban unrest and holds explosive implications for the future stability of American society.

Los Angeles Times, 4-5:(1)5.

Carl Holman
President,
National Urban Coalition   *1*

The politicians [in this national election year] have evaded and skirted the [civil-rights] issues and nobody is putting them on the spot. They are being shielded by their supporters and by their aides. Too many of them are afraid of quotas and busing. They say they believe in affirmative action, but not in quotas. They believe in fair housing, but not in knocking down covenants. They believe in integration, but not in "forced integration." That burns me. How can you have any law if the power of force is not behind it? We're getting a message, but I'm worried because [we] blacks are not rearing up on our hind legs.

Interview/ The New York Times, 2-8:(1)40.

Benjamin L. Hooks
Executive director-designate,
National Association for the
Advancement of Colored People   *2*

If you take the top 500 corporate entities in this country, the top 500 businesses, I doubt if you could name five black people who are members of the boards of directors of those institutions by virtue of their own line corporate responsibility. They may be on there as outside directors, and I don't deprecate that, but when you have got the majority of business in this country that have no black people, very few women in any position of responsibility, when you look at the banks—when you look at all of the institutions—look at broadcasting, look at public broadcasting, read the top salaries, you hardly see a black name. When you look at all the things that happen in this country, we come to recognize that black folk can drink from the same water fountain, can use the same restrooms, can buy

a hotdog at a stand, but the major task that remains before us is the elimination of racism in this country . . . In other words, I am saying that racism in all of its sensitive implications is still a part of American life, and we plan to fight that.

TV-radio interview, Washington/
"Meet the Press,"
National Broadcasting Company, 11-14.

3

[On the revelation that Griffin Bell, President-elect Jimmy Carter's choice for Attorney General, belongs to private clubs that discriminate racially, and Bell's subsequent decision to resign from those clubs]: You have hundreds of thousands, perhaps millions, of white people who deliberately choose to belong to clubs that either by law or custom will not allow blacks, Jews or women . . . That's racism, pure and simple. To the extent that Mr. Bell resigned, that's great. The problem is, how long will we go on and people . . . only resign when the spotlight gets on them? It seems to me the time has come for men of good-will to drop membership in those clubs. The racism is so widespread, I don't know how many other members of the Cabinet don't belong. It may be Mr. Carter would have a hard time in this country finding the kind of people he wanted who don't belong.

TV-radio interview/"Issues and Answers,"
American Broadcasting Company, 12-26.

Jesse L. Jackson
Civil-rights leader; President,
Operation PUSH
(People United to Save Humanity)   *4*

[Although blacks have been and are victims of racism,] to dwell on it in a negative kind of way is to reinforce in the victims a sense of their own victimization and lead them not to action but only to feeling sorry for themselves. Racism is the enemy, no doubt about it. But it takes strong soldiers to fight a strong enemy, and you don't produce strong soldiers by crying about what the enemy has done to you.

Interview/ The Washington Post, 3-8:(A)19.

(JESSE L. JACKSON)

[Supporting the busing of schoolchildren for racial balance]: More than 60 per cent of the children in America are bused to school every day, less than 3 per cent for racial reasons. The rich are bused to private schools, the handicapped are bused to special schools, the rural consolidated are bused, so many, as a matter of fact, until children have to drive the buses. To be sure, there are areas where logistics will alter a given matter, but right now we are fundamentally, in Boston [for example], not dealing with logistics. In Boston [where many parents object to racial busing] we are dealing with the principle that we have one nation and one tax system and one military system; will we have one school system? Given the fact that there are variations in principle, there must be one proposition, even though logistics may vary.

TV-radio interview, Washington/
"Meet the Press,"
National Broadcasting Company, 5-30.

Vernon E. Jordan, Jr.
Executive director,
National Urban League

2

Not only is participation [in politics] important for blacks, but we must participate in both political parties. I want blacks involved so that at such times as necessary the black presence can be felt—whoever is in power.

U.S. News & World Report, 1-26:44.

3

Traditionally, blacks have been rewarded for playing it safe and penalized for risk-taking. Pervasive discrimination and brutality have channeled us into habits and economic attitudes that mitigate against business success in today's world. The Post Office and teaching drained off many of those individuals who, were they white, would today be affluent businessmen . . . Every ethnic group has turned to businessmen and women for its core leadership group. Every ethnic group has prospered through development of business

enterprises that create capital, goods and jobs for its members. Black people cannot afford the luxury of foregoing such development, of losing such leadership.

Before National Business League, Boston/
The Wall Street Journal, 2-27:6.

4

Our nation has much to be ashamed of in its treatment of black people and other minorities, and affirmative action is a necessary step toward redressing past and present wrongs. Continued opposition to affirmative action, and the persistent, willful distortion of the issues is indicative of the flagging of support for civil rights. In a few brief years our nation has moved from "We Shall Overcome" to "We Don't Care."

Before Los Angeles American Jewish
Committee/The National Observer, 6-19:14.

5

. . . nobody in their right mind, looking at race relations in America today and comparing it to even 25 years ago, can argue that there has not been unprecedented progress. There has been—no question about that. Unbelievable . . . But it's also very clear that there is still one standard, one set of rules for blacks in this country, and another for whites. If we've done all the other things we've done, we could have solved this problem. But we haven't, and what is basically lacking is the will to do it. I think the politicians sense that the vast majority of white Americans have just gotten weary of the problem and think that when what happened in the '60s happened, they had really done their duty. The '60s were *easy*. In the 1960s, we were trying to define the right of black people to check into the downtown motels in the South, and we've done that. But in 1976, we've got another, far more difficult, problem—providing that same black person with the wherewithal to check *out*. That goes to economic security, income maintenance, economic empowerment—the real basic issues of equal opportunity. And now, at the 200th birthday of this country, the vast majority of white Americans have reached the point of moral exhaustion. They didn't have much gas in the tank in the first place, and what little they had they used up so hurriedly.

Interview/Newsweek, 7-4:35.

Herman Kahn
Director, Hudson Institute

1

... I don't believe it's possible in a democracy to bus children long distances to bad schools—forced busing [for racial balance]. You know that people who are trying to do that are doing something crazy, particularly if the reason for the busing has nothing to do with previous illegal actions.

Interview, Croton-on-Hudson, N.Y./
The Dallas Times Herald, 2-22:(B)3.

Edward H. Levi
Attorney General of the United States

2

The legislation which we are discussing in the [Justice] Department ... does have in it a provision that busing [of schoolchildren for racial balance] can, under certain circumstances, be ordered for a three-year period, that it can then be continued for two additional years ... Then, if the orders of the court over that period of five years have been carried out in good faith, the assumption is that busing will not any longer be required unless there are exceptional circumstances .... [In some areas, busing] works well; in others, it does not. But there is a question as to whether it is supposed to be a permanent remedy or a transitional remedy. And I do think that legal scholars are coming more and more to think that it is to be regarded as transitional.

News conference, June 16/
U.S. News & World Report, 6-28:19.

David Mathews
Secretary of Health, Education and Welfare of the United States

3

... some people want to know what I think about ending segregation. I have been com-

mitted to equal opportunity in education all of my professional life, and I don't intend to change. There is a moral imperative that I find compelling which says that no one should be excluded from the benefits of our society by reasons of his or her race. Sometimes people are asking: What do I think about the court orders for busing [of schoolchildren for racial balance] that have been issued? My position is that, whether I agree with a court order or not, it is my responsibility as a public official to act in concert with that order ... There has been evidence that [busing] is not as effective a means as was thought at one time ... there are other means that have been effective, but none is a panacea.

Interview, Washington/
U.S. News & World Report, 4-12:43.

Margaret Mead
Anthropologist

4

The North always made the South into a scapegoat, not realizing that in the South blacks and whites considered each other human. In the North, each group treated the other as if the other was not human ... In the North, we want to make people live on the other side of town so we don't see them. In dealing with this problem it is so much easier for Southerners reared to treat blacks as human beings, because there has been contact between the two groups. In the North, what we have worked for is to prevent contact. In the South, they worked to preserve caste distinction.

Interview, New York/
Los Angeles Times, 7-19:(2)7.

Clarence M. Mitchell, Jr.
Director, Washington, D.C., bureau, National Association for the Advancement of Colored People

5

[Criticizing those who are against the busing of schoolchildren for racial balance]: If they think they've seen some action in Belfast and Beirut and other places, just let somebody try to change the Constitution of the United

WHAT THEY SAID IN 1976

(CLARENCE M. MITCHELL, JR.)

States in a way that will derogate the rights blacks and other minorities have fought and died for. These other outbreaks will look like a picnic . . . What is going on now is a fight against the Constitution of the United States and its laws and its courts. Anybody who talks about "forced busing" knows he is appealing to the basest passions of this nation.

News conference, Washington, Aug. 24/
Los Angeles Times, 8-25:(1)1.

Charles Morgan, Jr.
Director, Washington office,
American Civil Liberties Union
1

[On how to assign white and black children to particular schools]: . . . to achieve equity we can use something called the alphabet—A through Z. I would decide who goes where by assigning children equally—in alphabetical order. I would use the alphabet in this wonderful little community that we've got here of rich white folks, and in the terrible little community over there of poor black folks. Once those rich white folks' kids get in that black folks' school, guess what's going to happen? The windows are going to get fixed, the police are going to be in the neighborhood, the school is suddenly going to be a quality school, and the money is going to come from the board of education. That's what the answer to integration is. White folks aren't going to put their money into anything their children don't go to, and black folks wouldn't if they had the money.

Panel discussion conducted by American
Enterprise Institute for Public Policy Research/
The National Observer, 7-31:7.

Joshua Nkomo
Leader, Zimbabwe (Rhodesian)
African People's Union
2

It's a pity that cattle are more sensible than human beings. Black and white graze peacefully together in the same pen. What makes creatures who have reason attach such importance to color? I don't.

Interview/ The Christian Science Monitor, 11-4:10.

Basil Paterson
Vice chairman,
Democratic National Committee
3

There is a natural progression of more blacks in each succeeding [Federal] Administration that I expect to continue under [President-elect Jimmy] Carter. There were more blacks under President Nixon than under President Johnson; President Ford had more than Nixon; and Carter will have more than Ford. Blacks won't be looking to get all the jobs, but they are looking for full recognition of the realities of politics. On our part, we recognize he has a duty to appoint the best people he can find. On his part, he has to recognize the people who put him where he is. There can be a meeting of the minds. There is a plethora of black talent out there that would be a benefit to any Administration.

The New York Times, 11-7:(1)39.

Ronald Reagan
Candidate for the 1976 Republican
Presidential nomination;
Former Governor of California (R)
4

[On whether the Federal government should intervene to desegregate private schools]: No. While I believe in an open society, some place along the line I think we've gotten out of balance on our recognition of the rights of people to be wrong, if we may think them wrong. People have a right to disagree, and I may look in disfavor myself on some people who would discriminate against anyone . . . for whatever reason, whether religion or race or anything else. But I have to respect their right to be wrong. And this is to me some of the greatness of this country.

At Huntsville (Alabama) Press Club, April 29/
Los Angeles Times, 4-30:(1)30.

5

Certainly no one of us would challenge government's right and responsibility to eliminate discrimination in hiring or education. But in its zeal to accomplish this worthy purpose, government orders what is in effect a quota system both in hiring and in education. They don't call it a quota system; it is an "affirmative action" program with "goals and timetables" for the hiring of particular groups. If you happen to belong to an ethnic group not recognized by the Federal government as entitled to special treatment, you are a victim of reverse discrimination. Goals and timetables are in reality a bureaucratic order for a quota system. For example, if your ancestry or national origin is Czechoslovakian, Polish, Italian, or if you are of a Jewish faith, you may find yourself the victim of discrimination contrary to the civil-rights law.

National television address, July 6/
Los Angeles Times, 7-7:(1)21.

Bayard Rustin
President, A. Philip Randolph Institute
1

If you went into Harlem tomorrow and turned all the blacks into whites, what would you have? Would there be more jobs, more hospital beds? There would not. Would there be more capability of sending kids to college because those people turned white overnight? There would not . . . The danger is that we are moving toward a nation divided between those who have it and those who cannot make it. That cuts across black-white lines. In other words, the future advancement of blacks and other poor in this country has very little to do with the color of their skin. Ten years ago there was indeed widespread discrimination against blacks in work. Now there is still some, but discrimination is not the main enemy where work is concerned. The problem now has to do with the nature of production. We are no longer a society prepared to buy the muscle power of the poor. For every black who cannot get a job because of his race, there are 10 blacks who cannot get a job because this society is not buying muscle power as it did when the immigrants were arriving from Europe.

Interview, New York/
Los Angeles Times, 8-11:(2)5.

Herman E. Talmadge
United States Senator, D—Georgia
2

Busing [of schoolchildren for racial balance] has caused more damage to public education in this country than anything. The Supreme Court intended its laws to prevent classification of students by color. We have now come full cycle, and in the interest of some so-called mythical balance we are doing just that—classifying students by color.

At Senate Youth Program, Washington/
Los Angeles Herald-Examiner, 2-4:(A)5.

C. Delores Tucker
Secretary of State of Pennsylvania
3

For the first time in 20 years, no Democratic [Presidential] candidate has felt it necessary to publish a civil-rights plank. No Democratic candidate still in the field is actively demanding slates with full minority representation . . . The party famed for its positive programs for people has begun to echo the traditional negativism of the Republicans by insisting that it is still for affirmative action—it's just against quotas; it's still for fair housing—but not in their neighborhoods; it's still for integration—but not "forced integration" . . . The party we [blacks] embraced because it remembered all Americans is beginning to forget 25 million of them.

At national issues conference of black Democrats,
Charlotte, N.C., April 30/ The Washington Post,
5-1:(A)12.

Morris K. Udall
United States Representative, D—Arizona;
Candidate for the 1976 Democratic
Presidential nomination
4

[Presidential candidate] Jimmy Carter is a good man and I expect us to have our arms around each other at the end [of the Party's convention] in New York City. But he can't have it both ways. He says he's for voluntary busing [of schoolchildren for racial balance], which means he's turning his back on 25 million Americans. You'll get voluntary busing in south Boston when they celebrate Yom

(MORRIS K. UDALL)

Kippur in Palestine Liberation Organization headquarters.

Boston, Feb. 29/
Los Angeles Herald-Examiner, 3-1:(A)5.

George C. Wallace
Governor of Alabama (D); Candidate for the
1976 Democratic Presidential nomination
1

[On recent public demonstrations against the busing of schoolchildren for racial balance]: Busing is a symptom of the discontent of the average citizen of our country, with the country telling him what to do with his child and his money and every aspect and phase of his life.

TV-radio interview/"Face the Nation,"
Columbia Broadcasting System, 1-11.
2

I supported the system we had of [segregated] schools back in '62 and '63 and I never apologized for it. I'm not who said, "Oh, I was for it, in a way, but it wasn't in my heart." No, I was raised that way . . . and since we lost the legal battles, let's go forward . . . but don't be dishonest about it. Don't tell people, "Oh, well, I had to say that but I didn't mean it." I wasn't raised that way.

Winston-Salem, N.C./
The New York Times, 3-28:(4)15.

Kevin H. White
Mayor of Boston
3

As desirable as racial integration may be, busing [of schoolchildren for racial balance] is not the best vehicle for it. It breaks up the cohesiveness of the neighborhoods, and it compromises parental prerogative to send their children to a nearby neighborhood school.

U.S. News & World Report, 3-15:18.

Roy Wilkins
Executive director, National Association for
the Advancement of Colored People
4

[On the busing of schoolchildren for racial

balance]: Too many blacks remember that busing was all right as long as it was used to segregate. It only became reprehensible when it was used to desegregate. Happily, the courts have paid no attention to the political agitation against busing. When they find a city with a segregated school system, they order it broken up. And busing is the only method for doing that in some cities. The neighborhood school is too often a segregated school. And nearly every white school is better off than the black schools because black schools have been treated with discrimination . . . What's been lost sight of in this whole busing controversy is that the Supreme Court ruled that segregated schools are inherently unequal. As a concomitant of this fact, this country must grow up to the place where it has all the elements of the population in it. Boston is an example of the fact that thousands of white people who went to "lily-white" schools never got to know any black people until they got out into real life. And black children who go to black schools never get to know white people. Black people are never going to accept a return to the old rule of "separate but equal." They know that separate education is not equal education.

Interview/ U.S. News & World Report, 2-2:75.

John Wilks
Director of black political affairs,
Republican National Committee
5

Of course we are interested in blacks becoming Republicans, but the recent history of black Americans has been that they aren't voting. When they do, it is as Democrats. Blacks should demand that both political parties be accountable to them. They should not be taken for granted.

U.S. News & World Report, 1-26:44.

Harold Wilson
Former Prime Minister
of the United Kingdom
6

In Britain a West Indian or Bengali, in the

United States a Puerto Rican, cannot afford to shrug his shoulders when the [terrorist] attack is anti-Semitic. It is not open to any gentile, Jew, black, white, yellow or brown to pass by on the other side, reassuring himself that it is not his quarrel.

At Hadassah banquet, Washington, Aug. 17/
The New York Times, 8-18:43.

James Q. Wilson
Professor of government,
Harvard University

[On U.S. government actions on civil rights]: I don't know of any democratic government . . . which could have behaved more reasonably with respect to the challenge of civil rights. Indeed, we have a civil-rights problem in this country precisely because we, almost alone among nations that have a multiracial society, have tried seriously to do something about it, and this has produced tension and conflict. Most societies wouldn't have the problem because they wouldn't attempt to deal with the situation.

Interview/
U.S. News & World Report, 7-21:18.

Commerce · Industry · Finance

Fred T. Allen
Chairman and president,
Pitney Bowes, Inc.
1

Polls indicate that the credibility of American business has gone down considerably in recent years, especially since political contributions and [questionable] international payments have been revealed. American business is very, very necessary for the growth of the United States. But when people read about these things, they lose faith in a strong part of the whole free-enterprise system . . . The free-enterprise system isn't going to go down the drain, but certainly it's being weakened. What may result are further regulations to prohibit what shouldn't have happened in the first place . . . The revelations have done a lot of good. I think it's necessary for American business people not to hide this thing but to talk out against it and say that we don't condone it. The chief executive should set the tone of how he wants his business run.
Interview/ U.S. News & World Report, 4-12:36.

Malcolm Baldridge, Jr.
Chairman,
Scovill Manufacturing Company
2

Almost all business leaders recognize that increasing corporate involvement in the problems of our society is a necessity, not just an act of good-will. Their difficulty is in developing a partnership with government if the latter has little interest. Whether a combined public-private attack on such problems as structural unemployment ever comes into being is dependent ultimately on the desires of the new [Carter] Administration and Congress. From his statements, I have a feeling Jimmy Carter will take a deep seat in the saddle on this issue, and I hope he does. There will never

be a better time to break with tradition.
Interview/ U.S. News & World Report, 12-20:23.

Walter F. Beran
Partner, Ernst & Ernst
3

There is no escaping the fact that the essence of an individual is his ethics. The more he seeks an ethical path, the more he mirrors the genius of his creator—the potential of his humanity—of one who is fearfully and wonderfully made. On the other hand, the more he treats ethics with scorn or indifference—with a Cain type of rationalization—the more like the jungle animal he becomes . . . To suggest that Americans and American business must submit to less than desirable practices in order to do business in foreign countries, while submitting to ethical conduct at home, is totally inconsistent, absurd and beneath comment. Ethics . . . transcends circumstances. An ethical man is on his good behavior when he is away and not just when he is at home; and so it must be in business and in whatever and wherever humans deal with one another . . .
Before Town Hall, Los Angeles, June 1/
Vital Speeches, 7-15:604.

John C. Biegler
Senior partner,
Price Waterhouse & Company
4

[On government regulation of business]: The regulatory impulse is an old impulse, solidly rooted in the conventional wisdom. We must find a way to deal with the superstition that bad regulation is better than no regulation at all. Whether we like it or not, most Americans, despite the present tide of disenchantment with regulation, feel in their bones that an unregulated economy is a jungle.

At National Conference on Regulatory Reform, Washington/ The Wall Street Journal, 12-30:4.

W. Michael Blumenthal
Chairman, Bendix Corporation

1

[Saying his company follows a code of ethics in its operations]: If we can't do business observing certain absolute standards, we will simply demur from doing business. Instead of growing another $30-million in sales we'll grow a little less, but we'll sleep better for it.

Newsweek, 2-16:58.

2

Business "credibility," whatever that means, is said to be at a low ebb in this country . . . What surprises me is that anyone should think this surprising. Business, after all, and especially the large corporation, continues to provide the essential framework in which we spend our lives—and I need hardly remind you that spending of a life means more than simply making one's way from cradle to grave. The business framework is not merely where we produce and distribute the world's goods and services; it is the terrain on which we meet, interact with each other, work out our ambitions, achieve or fail to achieve our purposes as we see them. So it is only natural that the behavior of corporate leadership should come under intense scrutiny, especially at a time when all the values of our society are being questioned, and that people should look at what we do not only in terms of efficiency and financial results, but also from a moral and an ethical point of view. This, as my children used to say, is where the action is.

At Conference Board seminar, June/ The Washington Post, 12-19:(F)1.

3

Americans want to maintain their high standard of living. They also want the con-

ditions under which they live, which some people call the externalities, to be acceptable and decent. They want safety, humane working conditions, fair play, a high quality of opportunity with an equal chance for all, and a clean environment. These are the things in which business has a responsibility. A good executive must bear all these goals in mind as he leads his company and collaborates with his colleagues in making his contribution toward these things.

Interview, Southfield, Mich./ Nation's Business, November:62.

4

I do not think big is necessarily beautiful. I have noted, however, that an advanced industrial economy such as ours is characterized by bigness—big companies, big government, big labor unions, big newspapers, big universities. Now, apart from whether I think all this bigness is good or bad, I recognize this bigness in the way life now is. I feel that certain tasks require size—large size. A complicated airplane or an advanced computer can only be produced by a big company, not a back-alley shop.

Interview, Southfield, Mich./ Nation's Business, November:62.

W. Michael Blumenthal
Secretary of the Treasury-designate of the United States

5

I see no reason why the growth of our commercial relations must necessarily be restricted in a way which excludes the Communist countries. But trade and technology and the financial relationships that flow from them certainly appear in a political context and I'm a firm believer in the notion of the quid pro quo. Trade with the East simply cannot be looked at only in terms of whether it's good for American business. The overall relationship must also be satisfactory.

Interview/Newsweek, 12-27:16.

WHAT THEY SAID IN 1976

Z. David Bonner
President, Gulf Oil Company-U.S. 1

I have worked in a number of countries around the world in the course of my career. But I have never worked in a country in which the government was less willing to work with the industrial and commercial sectors to achieve national goals than here in the United States. I am not suggesting that the role of government is to acquiesce and serve business; but I do believe it is equally improper for it to constantly throw roadblocks in the way of productive enterprise simply for the sake of control. That sort of attitude is directly responsible for the waste of resources and higher production costs we are experiencing today.

Before Economic Club of Detroit/
The Wall Street Journal, 11-30:20.

Kenneth E. Boulding
Professor of economics,
University of Colorado 2

Business is a workhorse, a mule—and do you ask a mule to be a Pegasus? Business should not be a government or a church. Its main responsibility is to be politically responsible. Businessmen should advocate and support the right kind of public policies. But I'm suspicious of organizations taking over the functions of government.

The Christian Science Monitor, 4-19:17.

Leonid I. Brezhnev
General Secretary,
Communist Party of the Soviet Union 3

[On U.S.-Soviet trade]: We firmly turn away any attempts to link trade with any kind of political conditions and do not permit any interference in our internal affairs. This should be clear once and for all ... We naturally are orienting ourselves more toward partners that do business with us on a normal, equal basis. Discrimination complicates the sale of our products in the U.S.A., increases the imbalance in trade and decreas-

es our interest in the American market.

Before Soviet-American Trade and
Economic Council, Moscow/
Los Angeles Herald-Examiner, 12-1:(A)7.

Alfred Brittain III
Chairman,
Bankers Trust Company, New York 4

I believe it would be wrong for Congress to pass [legislation that restricts or discourages foreign investment in the U.S.]. For 30 years, the United States has been working to reduce trade restrictions around the world ... If the United States substitutes investment restrictions for trade restrictions, we will be signaling our capitulation to shortsighted, politically expedient policies. There is little question in my mind that other nations would then rush to do the same thing, threatening the fragile economic interdependence of nations and jeopardizing U.S. investment abroad. If other governments do retaliate, U.S. companies are in an extremely vulnerable position, with direct investment abroad more than five times as large as foreign direct investment in the United States. Foreign investment, like foreign trade, is not a zero-sum game: A gain for one participant is not necessarily a loss for another. Productive investment, whatever its source, creates jobs, stimulates productivity and strengthens a nation's competitive position. Ultimately it raises the standard of living. Foreign investment in the United States can, in fact, be a positive-sum game in which everyone wins.

Before Columbia Business School Club
of New York, Jan.15/ Vital Speeches, 3-15:337.

Charles L. Brown
Vice chairman, American Telephone
& Telegraph Company 5

... I hope the intensity of the adversary position between business and government will ease under a [President-elect Jimmy] Carter Administration. I'm disturbed and discouraged by the intensity of the conflicts that have flared in recent years. I don't want to be construed as one who blames everything on "the regulators." My business has been under regulation for many, many years, and we understand the need for it. But we and other corporate executives are upset by the investigations, lawsuits and recriminations that have been sparked by the regulatory agencies. It's a condition that is getting worse, and it causes us to divert manpower and energy that ought to go into providing service to our customers.

Interview/ U.S. News & World Report, 12-20:21.

James W. Button
Senior executive vice president,
Sears, Roebuck and Company

1

What was enormously important about many of the early consumer advocates was . . . dedication to careful fact-finding. As best they could, they tempered their zeal with careful research. The new breed of consumer advocates seems to be more frenetic, less interested in careful research, more interested in deciding—of and by themselves—what is best for the consumer. Without a direct constituency, they have the freedom to do this. With this freedom—and the leverage they obtain from the media—they have been partly responsible for the rapid growth of [government] regulations.

At National Conference on Care Labeling,
Washington/ The National Observer, 9-18:13.

Earl L. Butz
Secretary of Agriculture
of the United States

2

Even in the highly literate nation of our own, we have seen repeated attacks on the incentive system for farmers. We have had such campaigns as the beef boycott, eat-one-less-hamburger-per-week, or meatless Tuesdays. It has only been two years since political pressures forced us into a system of Federally imposed price ceilings on meats and other food products . . . Now we must ask, have we learned our lesson from taking those negative acts? Have we learned that if the

United States is indeed to use its great food-productive capacity, then the individual farmer must be free to produce and market his crops as he sees fit? We must *not* dampen the incentives that have made our farmers the producers that they are. We must *not* signal to them in the language of price—the language they understand best—that we want *less,* not more. We must *not* periodically signal to our farmers that they have only limited access to markets beyond their shores. We must *not* periodically throw government controls at them that dampen their plans for investment, their dreams of expansion, their hopes for success.

Before Economic Club of Chicago/
The National Observer, 1-10:11.

3

. . . America is far and away the largest supplier of food to the world today. And as we look down the road 15 or 20 years, the Number 1 problem we face on this globe is how to feed 75 to 80 per cent more people with about the same land resources we have now. There is no new Western Hemisphere to discover, no more virgin prairies to plow. Increasingly, other nations are becoming dependent on the United States for a continuing supply of basic foodstuffs. That's what I mean by American agripower.

Interview, Washington/
U.S. News & World Report, 2-16:26.

4

The other day somebody asked me: "Isn't it evil to be selling grain to those Communist Russians?" My reply was: "Far better we exchange bushels with them than bullets."

Interview, Washington/
U.S. News & World Report, 2-16:26.

Jimmy Carter
Candidate for the 1976 Democratic
Presidential nomination;
Former Governor of Georgia (D)

5

I want to be sure that, as President, the American flag is returned to the seas again.

(JIMMY CARTER)

I believe that American [merchant] ships, built in American yards, designed by American engineers, built by American craftsmen, and manned by American seamen, trained principally as they are now in the industry-operated schools and on the ships themselves, can once again be the envy of the maritime world. I believe that once again our nation can be a maritime nation, a sea-going nation that can compete for and win a right to haul a major portion of our own foreign cargo.

At Maritime Management-Labor Salute, Washington, June 30/ The Washington Post, 10-11:(A)3.

Jimmy Carter
1976 Democratic Presidential nominee 1

The business community is naturally inclined to adhere to rigid standards of morality, ethics and legality—if they know that other component parts will also be required to comply. And that maintenance of high standards is a major responsibility of the President. If the President looks the other way, if the Cabinet members condone illegality, by private action or public statements, then it puts the business community in a status of almost being forced into illegal acts to be competitive with one another.

Interview/ San Francisco Examiner & Chronicle, 9-19:(C)8.

2

Over 50 per cent of the members that have been appointed to all regulatory agencies in our country have come from the industries that are being regulated. And my concept of the regulatory agencies is to be responsible primarily to the consumers who are served by the industries being regulated. There's too much of a sweetheart arrangement now between the industries being regulated and the regulatory agencies themselves.

Interview, Washington/ TV Guide, 10-9:(A)4.

Frank T. Cary
Chairman, International Business Machines Corporation 3

When some businesses turn out shoddy products or engage in misleading advertising or ignore customer complaints, the public gets sour on business as a whole. When some executives have to admit that they bribed foreign officials or illegally channeled corporate funds into political campaigns, the public believes this is standard business conduct. And when we read in the papers about corporate kickbacks and secret Swiss bank accounts, all business suffers. Some businessmen have tried to excuse themselves by saying that everybody does it. Well, everybody *doesn't* do it . . . The time has come for those of us in business to put our house in order . . . to restore the faith of Americans in the basic competence and purpose of business. And this requires a lot more than public-relations efforts.

Newsweek, 2-16:59.

A. W. Clausen
President, Bankamerica Corporation 4

As of this moment, the public is rightly skeptical of our [the business world's] practices and our preachings . . . Integrity is not some impractical notion dreamed up by naive do-gooders. Our integrity is the foundation for, the very basis of, our ability to do business. If the market economy ever goes under, our favorite villains—socialist economies and government regulators—won't be to blame. We will. If we're not concerned, then we're just not sensitive to the reality of the problem or today's world.

Newsweek, 2-16:59.

5

Barring unpredictable holocaust, I believe some future mutation of today's international companies will be the catalytic force in spreading throughout the world the splendid American proposition that "all men are created equal." No other institution, public or private, has the motivation, the resources and the power to tackle global inequities as effectively as multinational corporations.

At seminar, University of Southern California, June 28/ Los Angeles Herald-Examiner, 6-29:(A)15.

Philip E. Coldwell
Member, Federal Reserve Board

1

[Saying recent publicity about recession-related loan losses should not keep banks from taking risks]: Banking is a risk industry. Unless bankers take risks, they cannot support their communities nor the industries and businesses making up those communities. But if risk-taking is to be eliminated in the banking industry, banks will no longer serve the nation, and the nation's economic recovery would be less than assured.

At conference sponsored by Dallas Chamber of Commerce and Dallas Council on World Affairs, Feb. 24/ The Dallas Times Herald, 2-25:(D)14.

Calvin J. Collier
Chairman,
Federal Trade Commission

2

While it is true that the information which advertising provides is essential to the operation of the free market—and therefore to the welfare of all consumers—it needs to be said that this is true only as long as that information is neither deceptive nor misleading . . . For the same reasons that consumers are forced to limit their search efforts, the time and effort a consumer will expend verifying advertising claims is limited. Knowing this, there is an almost irresistible incentive to advertise falsely, particularly in those cases where advertising weighs heavily in the decision to purchase and where the deception cannot be easily discovered . . . The temptation to tell a white lie—or even a blatant one—is increased even more when competitors generally tell the truth and consumers believe they do. In these cases, the government has a strong reason to step in because

it is best situated to prohibit the deceivers from taking a free ride on the good-will of their honest competitors. This, in a nutshell, is the classic role of the FTC. Since its inception over 60 years ago, the Commission has worked to enhance the reliability of marketing claims and prevent the debasement of the value of advertising. Indeed, I think it is safe to predict that if the FTC were abolished tomorrow, the advertising community would be lobbying for its reincarnation the following day, for, without its influence, bad advertising would be just that much more likely to drive out the good.

*Before Peoria (Ill.) Advertising and Selling Club, Sept. 13/ ***

John B. Connally, Jr.
Former Secretary of the Treasury
of the United States;
Former Governor of Texas (D, now R)

3

American business today is rated [by the public] as low as lawyers. And when you reach that low you don't have much further to go—unless you are a member of Congress.

At business seminar, Los Angeles, June 28/ Los Angeles Times, 6-29:(3)9.

Edward W. (Ned) Cook
Chairman, Cook Industries, Inc.

4

The worst thing that's happening in our country today is the overriding obsession for a riskless society. Safety, security—to hell with all that. That's a hell of a way to run a country. They've got that in England, and look at them. I'd just as soon compete. What's wrong with my losing money? Is that bad? That's my privilege, to make money and lose money. If I lose money, tough luck; if I make money, that's great. The assumption of risk is what made this country. It's what everybody's trying to get away from. You should take your raps without being a cry-baby. What's wrong with firms going broke? If New York's going to belly up, let it go. I think if I made a bad decision and Cook Industries went broke . . . tough.

Interview, Memphis/ The Washington Post, 1-4:(A)14.

WHAT THEY SAID IN 1976

John D. deButts
Chairman, American Telephone &
Telegraph Company 1

I'd . . . like to see capital gains on stock-market investments treated like the investment in a home. If you sell your house and buy another within 18 months or build one within two years, you don't pay a capital gain on the sum you put into a new house. It's deferred. Why shouldn't the same principle be applied to capital gains in stock, except over a shorter time—maybe 60 or 90 days? If you were to sell a stock and reinvest the money in another stock in that period, you'd push the capital gain off into the future. The reason I propose this is that the individual investor is about the only one these days who pays a capital-gains tax. Many institutions don't pay any, and they're in and out of the market all the time. It seems to me we should equalize this situation—not forgive capital gains to the individual but postpone them to make the equity market more attractive.

Interview, Washington/
U.S. News & World Report, 7-5:89.

Francis J. Dunleavy
President, International Telephone &
Telegraph Corporation 2

Like so many in American life, businessmen have made their share of mistakes, and often the decisions they made were not popular with those who feared change. But as we celebrate our [U.S.] Bicentennial, it is worth remembering that 200 years ago the American Revolution itself started as a businessmen's revolution. That is, after all, what the Boston Tea Party and the Stamp Act protests were all about. And it is also worth remembering that *one* hundred years ago it was the businessman who began translating the "heroic age of invention" into a better life for Americans, and the world. In our own day, it has been the businessman, with his practical development of medical technology, the computer, the jet, the Xerox machine, new sources of energy, anti-pollution devices, and much else, who has continued to enhance the quality of life not only for the select and the wealthy but for all of us. This is what the American Revolution, with its dedication to free enterprise, promised. And it would be tragic if America were to allow progress to be blunted.

Before Bonneville Knife and Fork Club,
Salt Lake City, Utah, Jan. 21/
Vital Speeches, 3-15:341.

Lewis A. Engman
Former Chairman,
Federal Trade Commission 3

There are some substantial restraints on our economy, which are put in place because of over-regulation, both governmental and private, and all of these areas need to be re-examined to see whether or not a free-market system cannot open things up. I am not saying all regulation ought to be abolished. There is some regulation where the benefits do justify the cost of that regulation; it is most clear in areas affecting health and safety . . . But there is not a need, in my judgment, for regulations which say that some individual who wants to risk his own money and his own time and to open up a one- or two-truck operation hauling some kind of product between Detroit and Toledo has to get the approval of some bureaucracy in Washington before he undertakes that effort. It is in this kind of area where we could do without an awful lot of that regulation.

The Washington Post, 1-11:(H)7.

Gerald R. Ford
President of the United States 4

A necessary condition to a healthy economy is freedom from the petty tyranny of massive government regulation. We are wasting literally millions of working hours costing billions of consumers' dollars because of bureaucratic red tape. The American farmer, who not only feeds 215 million Americans but also millions world-wide, has shown how much more he can produce without the shackles of government control. Now we need reforms in other key areas of our economy—the airlines, trucking, railroads and financial institutions. I have concrete plans in each of these areas, not to help this or that industry, but to foster competition and to bring prices down for the consumer.

State of the Union address, Washington, Jan. 19/
The New York Times, 1-20:18.

1

I oppose any policy that would once again have the farmer producing for government storage, and a government check, on the government's terms. My policy is to let the government govern, and let the farmer farm, and let the people benefit.

At forum sponsored by the Farm Bureau,
Rockford, Ill., March 11/
Los Angeles Times, 3-12(1)5.

2

[On his formation of a task force to determine how to stop U.S. corporate bribes to foreign countries]: The purpose of this task force is not to punish American corporations but to ensure that the U.S. has a clear policy and that we have an effective, active program to implement that policy. To the extent that the questionable payments abroad have arisen from corrupt practices on the part of American corporations, the United States bears a clear responsibility to the entire international community to bring them to a halt. Corrupt business practices strike at the very heart of our own moral code and our faith in free enterprise. Businesses in this country run the risk of ever-greater governmental regulation [when] they illegally take advantage of consumers, investors and taxpayers.

Washington, March 31/
The Washington Post, 4-1:(A)2.

Henry Ford II
Chairman, Ford Motor Company

3

We, in business, have often regarded any governmental effort to modify our products and processes as a death threat to free enterprise. Legislators and governmental officials, on the other hand, have often regarded businessmen as sinners who must be forced to mend their ways by stringent rules and dire penalties. The moralistic approach to problems has been fostered by self-appointed consumer advocates who have built their own careers and influence by foisting on the public a distorted image of business and businessmen, and picturing themselves as righteous crusaders for the public interest. The truth of the matter, of course, is that the costs of government regulation fall ultimately on the same people who are benefited by regulation. The problem is not to abolish sin at any cost, but to find the best balance between benefits to people as citizens and costs to people as consumers.

Oct. 8/ The Washington Post, 10-13:(A)20.

M. L. Frankel
President,
Joint Council on Economic Education

4

There is a strong correlation between people's attitudes toward big business and the amount of correct economic information they have. The higher they score on a test of basic economics, the more favorably they look at business organizations as a group . . . The solution to misunderstanding lies in the formal educational structure—a lifetime program of economic education. Exhortation, speeches, articles, a film, film strip, envelope stuffers have in and of themselves little value.

U.S. News & World Report, 9-13:44.

E. J. (Jake) Garn
United States Senator, R—Utah

5

I know of no other industry that is more regulated than the banking industry. In no other industry can examiners descend unannounced on Friday afternoon and stay for six months, and in no other industry is this protection as necessary to protect depositors' money. Banks have played a major part aggressively boosting the economy by working with businesses to provide capital and allow-

WHAT THEY SAID IN 1976

E. J. (JAKE) GARN

ing people to build homes. A lot of people wouldn't be in business today if it weren't for classified loans and a banking system structured like ours is.

At Senate Banking Committee hearing,
*Washington, Feb. 5/***

1

Many of the problems facing small businesses can be attributed to the U.S. government and its regulating and taxing policies. The infant mortality rate for new business is too high; about five of every 10 fail in the first two years. Of course, not all of it can be blamed on government, but much of it can be traced directly to over-regulation and unfair taxation. I see one of my major tasks in the Senate as convincing my colleagues, and others, that small business is the backbone of our economy; that nearly 95 per cent of the business in this country is small business, and that the other five-plus per cent used to be.

*Washington, March 23/***

Julian Goodman
Chairman,
National Broadcasting Company

2

Responsible reporters don't make news where none exists. The fact is that some critics of business are documenting their grievances, organizing their protest and presenting their case to the public persistently and thoroughly. The business community has not done nearly so much to present its case. In the face of criticism, businessmen too often are silent, defensive, segmented and far too inaccessible to journalists.

Before International Franchise Association,
Palm Springs, Calif., Feb. 10/
Daily Variety, 2-11:10.

C. Howard Hardesty
Vice Chairman,
Continental Oil Company

3

I am becoming convinced that the credi-

bility gap between the oil industry and the public is now so great that the industry cannot do the job of convincing leaders of public opinion and the public as to the true nature of our energy dilemma and what our energy priorities should be. The public will not now accept the facts from us ... We must openly report our reserves, our profits and all the statistics that are essential to intelligent analysis and planning. In addition, we must rid ourselves of and openly condemn bribery and corruption in the business community

At conference sponsored by
Dallas Chamber of Commerce and Dallas Council
on World Affairs, Feb. 24/
The Dallas Times Herald, 2-25:(D)14.

John D. Harper
Former chairman,
Aluminum Company of America
(ALCOA)

4

[On widespread criticism of business]: The goose doesn't worry much about its reputation. It is too busy creating wealth and benefits and providing jobs. In other words, laying golden eggs. But then some dissatisfied person comes along and fires a shot at the goose ... Soon another critic takes a few shots ... [and] finally a crowd has gathered and everyone is blasting away. The goose knows it is getting weaker ... but it still isn't worried. The goose believes it has only to hang up there and one day the crowd will realize where the golden eggs are coming from, come to its senses and cease fire. Meantime, the goose struggles to stay aloft. By now, as all of us are surely aware, the crowd shooting at the golden goose we know as business shows no signs of dispersing. Instead, it has grown huge and even more hostile toward the goose. Perhaps it is time to ask: Why is no one rushing to the defense of this endangered species?

Newsweek, 2-16:58.

Michael J. Harrington
United States Representative,
D—Massachusetts

5

... the long-range fundamental interests of

the major corporations and of the people of the United States are in conflict. The corporations preside over a revolutionary technology, but their criterion of how to use it is profitability. Increasingly, the Adam Smith assumption that profitability yields maximum social allocation is not true. You see this most dramatically in the case of the oil companies, but this kind of conflict between private corporate profit and public good exists throughout the economy.

Interview, New York/
Los Angeles Times, 7-6:(2)5.

Gary W. Hart
United States Senator,
D—Colorado 1

[On why he believes the big oil companies should be broken up]: Because, in my judgment, there is not genuine free enterprise and competition in the oil industry. There are 15 to 20 major, vertically integrated petroleum companies in this country that control anywhere from 75 to 80 per cent of the market ... a product so central to the economy of this country and the world should not be controlled by just a handful of people—as I think it is now. [Reorganization and divestiture of these companies] would permit the government to get out of the price-control and price-regulation business. It's a farce and a myth to talk about decontrol of prices when, in fact, they are susceptible to manipulation, both internationally by OPEC and domestically by a handful of producing companies. It's ridiculous to talk about returning petroleum prices to the "free market" when no such market exists.

Interview/U.S. News & World Report, 2-9:25.

Harold J. Haynes
Chairman,
Standard Oil Company of California 2

[On calls for breaking up the big oil companies]: Those who advocate what they call "divestiture" give only one reason: They claim it would increase competition. They ignore the fact that the petroleum industry, by any accepted measurement, is one of the most competitive and least concentrated businesses in America. I have yet to hear just how their plan would benefit the motorist, the homeowner, our employees, our stockholders, or the economy and security of America . . . There are more than 40,000 oil and gas companies in the United States. Ten thousand are engaged in exploration and production, but the largest accounts for less than eight per cent of the crude-oil output in this country. There are a total of 131 companies that operate 270 refineries, but the largest refiner has less than nine per cent of the total U.S. refining capacity. There are approximately 200,000 service stations in the United States, but the largest share of the gasoline market held by a single company is only 8.2 per cent. The top eight firms in our industry control about 57 per cent of the business. Compare that with the concentration in other industries. To give a few examples: The top eight firms in steel have 65 per cent; copper, 98 per cent; motor vehicles, 98 per cent; aircraft, 87 per cent.

Interview/U.S. News & World Report, 2-9:25.

Roderick M. Hills
Chairman,
Securities and Exchange Commission 3

[Saying self-policing by companies will preclude the need for new laws banning illegal foreign payments and bribes]: Disclosure alone will not restore the lost confidence of the public in business, but the discipline of disclosure will be a powerful tool for ridding that distrust. I don't see any need for greater laws governing foreign activities. We don't have the power to ban bribery as such. And there will always be "grease" payments. But stockholders will be in a position to decide if they want the kind of management that does this kind of thing . . . I've spoken to the chief executive officers of the companies that have confessed, and without exception they are delighted to have the pressure on them removed and to have been relieved of the burden of operating this way. They can now tell these

(RODERICK M. HILLS)

countries that the U.S. government forbids them from doing these things.

Before businessmen, Dallas, Feb. 26/
The Dallas Times Herald, 2-27:(E)7.

Walter E. Hoadley
Executive vice president and chief economist, Bank of America 1

. . . business is operating in a climate of greater uncertainty and change than at any time in history. Old ideas and theories are disappearing. In business planning, it's enough just to try to get a handle on economic developments. The businessman has to be aware of political, social and technological realties that affect management. He has to understand how people react as consumers, jobholders, voters—not merely as statistical dots on a chart.

Interview/Nation's Business, February:24.

Robert T. Howard
President,
National Broadcasting Company Television 2

[On TV coverage of business affairs]: I won't claim perfection for every TV news story, but I would suggest to you that, to a great degree, business' problems with the media are self-created. [On key business issues, industry leaders often hold back while] leaders like Ralph Nader for the consumerists, or Barry Commoner for the environmentalists, have no qualms about meeting the·press and facing public opinion. And when they do, they usually have a good command of the facts and come on strong.

Before Rotary Club, Los Angeles, March 19/
Daily Variety, 3-22:2.

Hubert H. Humphrey
United States Senator,
D—Minnesota 3

We may not be far from a new era of general trust-busting, like the one that swept America in the early 1900s. Frankly, that's what's needed in this country more than anything else to protect the consumer.

At Consumer Federation of America's
Consumer Assembly, Washington, Jan. 22/
The New York Times, 1-23:38.

Edward G. Jordan
Chairman, Conrail 4

I think that you organize companies best with very shallow rather than very deep organizations. The concepts of span of control, which are often articulated in textbooks, are no more than that—a textbook idea of what you do. One of the real problems in American industry, in large organizations such as the railroads, is that you get such incredible depth in management that the nature of a real problem, and the man dealing with it, never gets to the decision-maker. Instead, it gets diffused and interpreted by layers of management.

Interview, Philadelphia/
The New York Times, 3-28:(3)7.

Edward J. Kane
Professor of banking and
monetary economics, Ohio State University 5

Historically, the bankers have tried to portray themselves as leaders and tribal priests, and the banks have been built on the model of temples. I don't see any reason to believe bankers are any worse or any better than anyone else. But because they operate with a special product—money—there's more temptation.

The Washington Post, 2-15:(A)4.

E. Douglas Kenna
President,
National Association of Manufacturers 6

While most government regulation was originally aimed at preventing business abuses, all too often it now prevents business from operating efficiently and has thus become a public abuse in itself. Federal regulatory agencies now exercise direct control over industries like railroads and air and truck transportation that account for 10 per cent of everything made and sold. And *all* businesses have come under more and more control in such areas as environmental protection, consumer satisfaction, job safety and hiring practices. The economic burden of over-regulation amounts to tens of billions of dollars each year—costs that are directly borne by American taxpayers and American consumers in everything they buy. Then, compounding the injury, the same legislators who advocate more and more costly regulation turn around and advocate price controls. The central question both labor and management must ask is whether the benefits of excessive regulation are really worth the costs. How much is *too* much? Where does the public finally reach the point of no return from government's intrusions into the operation of business and the workings of the marketplace?

Before Economic Club of Detroit, April 5/
Vital Speeches, 5-1:427.

Edward M. Kennedy
United States Senator,
D—Massachusetts 1

The linchpin of [President Ford's] program of [business] deregulation [by government] is reliance upon competition and vigorous antitrust enforcement. I am concerned as to whether the definitions of stringent antitrust enforcement means one thing to me and another to the President. I believe that relaxation of government regulation must be accompanied by more-vigorous antitrust enforcement . . . But if the Administration is going to back down and oppose or even waffle on legislation that would better enable both the government and private citizens to police competition and seek to redress antitrust-law violations, this will reduce the prospects for enactment of regulatory reform proposals.

Before the Senate, Washington/
The Washington Post, 4-6:(D)11.

John E. Kircher
Deputy chairman,
Continental Oil Company 2

[Arguing against divestiture in the oil industry]: Petroleum has been and is an intensely competitive industry, with more competitors, lower concentration ratios and greater ease of entry than many other industries. Smaller companies have entered the business, and independent marketers have thrived, increasing their market share, so that today it is in excess of 35 per cent. As an indication of the magnitude of the divestiture effort, consider that the 20 largest petroleum companies have total assets in excess of $146-billion. They employ 800,000 people. The total debt secured by integrated oil companies exceeds $100-billion. They have an estimated 15 million direct and indirect stockholders . . . The dismemberment of a group of companies that supply six per cent of the world's people— just we Americans—with 33 per cent of the world's energy, at a lower cost than anywhere else, certainly does not augur well for America's future. Can there be any doubt that energy and the issue of divestiture will have a dominant impact on our national interest? In the final analysis, while the nation's energy ills are real, I believe they can be solved—with sufficient doses of time-tested American ingenuity, combined with large quantities of capital. However, by every yardstick, divestiture will certainly delay, and perhaps prevent, this "cure."

Before Cleveland Technical Societies Council,
March 25/Vital Speeches, 5-15:478.

Mitchell P. Kobelinski
Administrator,
Small Business Administration
of the United States 3

I think that it's still true in a general way that small business is more innovative than big business. You're drawing on a much broader pool of people in the small-business sector, and the inventor—the ingenious man working on new ideas as they relate to his own profit and well-being—is motivated in a more

WHAT THEY SAID IN 1976

(MITCHELL P. KOBELINSKI)

direct way. I firmly believe that in one respect it's easier for a person to strike out on his own today and pursue a new idea, because our economy is bigger than it's ever been before and should afford more opportunities. Consumers are demanding more, so there's more of a chance to provide goods and services because people have the buying power. That's why you have more people in small business trying to think of better ways to make a buck.

Interview, Washington/
U.S. News & World Report, 8-30:40.

William E. LaMothe
President, Kellogg Company
1

Since the days of Henry Ford, we've learned that mass production lowers the price per item. When production lags and overhead stays the same, the price per item must rise to cover that overhead. Even today, with the cost of materials, labor and energy going up year after year, we have quite a job trying to keep the price of a box of cereal in some relation to what's left in the average pay envelope. If the FTC forces us to give up the economies of big-scale production, distribution and marketing, the price of all of those products has to go up. And that's certainly what would happen if they broke up the cereal industry. I don't really believe that will happen. American common sense is too well-developed to allow the take-over of an industry by the government under the name of "fostering free enterprise." But if we have to, we'll fight all the way to the Supreme Court to keep that from happening to the cereal industry. With companies like Kellogg's, General Mills, General Foods, Quaker Oats, Ralston, Nabisco and Pet in a single industry, there's got to be competition, and there is, every single morning all over America. Don't let anyone force on you the notion that just because there are only a few companies in an industry that they're not competitive. That is another myth that should be kicked out into the open.

Before International Platform Association,
Washington, June 28/Vital Speeches, 9-1:699.

Edwin H. Land
Chairman, Polaroid Corporation
2

The only thing that keeps us alive is our brilliance. The only thing protecting our brilliance is our patents.

At Polaroid annual stockholder meeting/
Newsweek, 5-10:86.

Louis F. Laun
Acting Administrator,
Small Business Administration
of the United States
3

Unfortunately, what many of us either refuse or fail to recognize is the truly awesome power of the *individual* consumer. Speaking from experience, I can tell you that a few letters of complaint on a product or service deficiency sent to a corporation will cause more tremors and action than many times that number dumped into the machinery of government bureaucracy. If you don't believe me, try writing to the president of the company next time you feel you have been treated less than properly. There are many obvious reasons for this reaction, but perhaps the most important one is that businesses look upon such complaints as very real threats to their competitive position. They depend on word of mouth, and, in a free-enterprise system, they have no way to compel you to buy their product. We also know that once a consumer's confidence in a product or service is lost, it is almost impossible to retrieve it without superhuman effort. Examples of this fundamental fact are legend.

At White House Conference on
Consumer Representation, Chicago/
The Wall Street Journal, 1-26:10.

Mary Wells Lawrence
Chairman,
Wells, Rich, Greene, advertising
4

The advertising business is like going to school all the time. You are presented with a very wide variety of problems. You have to learn about all kinds of things—theatre, travel—that are very broad in scope, that keeps it amusing and challenging. You are constantly discovering something.

Interview, Chicago/
The Dallas Times Herald, 12-10:(E)5.

Warren W. Lebeck
President,
Chicago Board of Trade 1

We should not have and do not have any quarrel with the concept of government as an umpire. It is a wholly appropriate role that we can and do accept. But in an era where government seems increasingly to assume an adversary role to the nation's industry, its business and its institutions, then government is no longer the "umpire." It becomes the "other team." This we should not, and cannot, and will not accept. Much too much is at stake.

At National Futures Industry Conference,
Tarpon Springs, Fla./
The Wall Street Journal, 5-21:8.

David F. Linowes
Chairman, Federal Privacy
Protection Study Commission 2

The universality of credit cards means that information about specific people can be selected and made available merely by punching a few keys in a computer. First, the credit bureaus track down credit-worthiness before cards are issued. Then information continues all along the line—what people buy, where they travel, where they stay, the magazines they subscribe to and the reservations they make. All of these things get into computer data banks where a profile of an individual can be designed. The resulting picture can show whether an individual is liberal or conservative, his affluence and habits.

U.S. News & World Report, 2-23:43.

Robert W. Long
Assistant Secretary for Conservation,
Research and Education, Department of
Agriculture of the United States 3

Near the top of the list of grave concerns harbored by farmers is the control over their business held by people who do not understand today's agriculture . . . Non-farm decision-makers, hard as they may try, often have real difficulty in understanding the characteristics of modern farmers and farms. Rather than to think in terms of what has really made the American farmer the envy of the world—voluntary action, hard work, inventiveness, managing his own business, assisted by research, education, credit and technical assistance—they tend to try to motivate him through the use of laws, regulations and compulsion . . . Little wonder agriculture is getting some public decisions that are difficult to live with . . . Family farmers, operating in a free-enterprise climate, for profit, have eagerly and voluntarily used the results of agricultural research, both public and private, brought to them by county extension agents and land-grant university specialists. They have been assisted by Soil Conservation Service professionals and the agribusiness community. Couple these forces with ample supplies of credit and you have the ingredients that created the greatest revolution of all times—the American food production revolution. Note that I have stressed *voluntary* action. Laws, rules, regulations and compulsion had little to do with the progress farmers have made.

Before American Seed Trade Association,
Los Angeles/ The National Observer, 7-31:7.

Ian MacGregor
Chairman, AMAX, Inc.
(American Metal Climax) 4

I am quite prepared to talk about any subject that anyone brings up. For one thing, it helps me to educate myself. For another, if someone asks me something, I have to lay my viewpoint in front of them. If I'm taciturn, I don't help anybody. I think one problem facing businessmen is a lack of articulateness. They may be good at this or that, but they are still regarded as inarticulate. For myself, I delight in throwing out information about our company. This is part of my job: to project knowledge about our company into the

WHAT THEY SAID IN 1976

(IAN MacGREGOR)

minds of people—what the company is doing, why, and what it hopes to do. If that is garrulous, then I'm garrulous. I will talk to anyone who will listen.

Interview/Nation's Business, January:36.

Donald S. MacNaughton
Chairman,
Prudential Insurance Company
of America
1

Probably nothing haunts business-news-media relationships more than the common-place evidence that so many writers, reporters and commentators often don't understand the meaning, uses and benefits of profits. Opinion polls show [that] the vast public mis-understanding of profit and profit margins has grown with the years, probably at least to some degree on the basis of news media coverage . . . For their part, the press and broadcast organizations have learned to be skeptical about the motives of all special interests, including business—maybe even especially business. They look for special pleading when business establishments defend them-selves or seek out public attention, and, un-fortunately, they are too often justified in do-ing so. And the men and women of the news media are often frustrated when digging for business news. They find many business ex-ecutives excessively secretive and often inac-cessible or prone to double-talk. The journal-ists tell us, too, that business arouses their hackles because so many companies press hard for space or air time when they have good news, but remain underground when fortunes are receding. And what an image the businessman usually projects—to both the news media and the public. A hallmark of American business is its willingness to keep up with the times—to innovate. Yet, before the press, radio or television, the businessman comes on like the original Neanderthal man, mouthing cliches that went out with the Stone Age.

At annual meeting of American Life Insurance Association and Institute of Life Insurance/ The New York Times, 3-7:(3)14.

Carl H. Madden
Professor of business,
American University
2

In my opinion, whether we like it or not, the world is moving away from the doctrine that business should limit its activities to clas-sic profit-making. The definition of "profit" itself is changing. The meaning of "cost" is changing. The pursuit of revenue is being regulated. For a corporation, "costs" even now include social objectives: equality of op-portunity, management of natural resources, development of human resources, attainment of a just and stable society.

Interview/U.S. News & World Report, 12-27:84.

Mike Mansfield
United States Senator, D—Montana
3

I think the government is too much into the regulatory field. I hope there will be a re-versal of the present trend. Part of this over-regulation is caused by all the pressure con-stantly being applied on Washington for more government action. What we need is more of a partnership between government and business, a recognition of the fact that the private enterprise system needs that kind of joint participation.

Interview, Washington/ Nation's Business, November:36.

Stanley Marcus
Chairman, Neiman-Marcus stores
4

One of the first declarations of business philosophy I heard from my father, soon after I came to work at Neiman-Marcus in 1926, was, "There is never a good sale for Neiman-Marcus unless it's a good buy for the custo-mer." This was his way of practicing the Golden Rule, and now the same policy pre-vails.

Interview, Dallas/ The Dallas Times Herald, 12-12:(D)11.

Robert P. Mayo
President,
Federal Reserve Bank of Chicago
1

It has become virtually as popular to call for less government regulation [of business] as it is to extol apple pie and motherhood. Everywhere one turns, whether within government or business, talk focuses on the high cost of government regulation . . . I think it is true that in many areas the costs of regulation exceed the benefits, and the economy as a whole would gain from less regulatory oversight. However, what I see behind much of the talk in favor of deregulation amounts to saying: "Let's get rid of the regulations on that industry because I will benefit, but don't deregulate my industry; we're too fragile." "Deregulate natural-gas prices, but don't let the price go up." "Deregulate water-carriers but not trucking." "We're for free trade generally, but our industry needs import quotas." . . . deregulation will remain only a slogan—while the trend toward more regulation will continue—until the business community is willing to accept some of the readjustments needed to operate in a more competitive environment.
Before The Conference Board, Chicago, April 1/
Vital Speeches, 5-1:435,436.

Jerry McAfee
Chairman, Gulf Oil Corporation
2

[On illegal political contributions made by his company, of which he is the new chairman]: I think it is obvious by now that all of us at Gulf regret very deeply that these acts have occurred. It should be also obvious that we have taken every reasonable step possible to put this matter behind us and to regain the public's respect for our labors . . . as difficult as these last few months have been for Gulf, I think it has made us a stronger company, a company with a new sense of determination and purpose and a company which can once again be evaluated on its strength[s] and accomplishments.
Before financial analysts, Boston/
The Dallas Times Herald, 3-23:(D)8.

John F. Mee
Professor,
Graduate School of Business,
Indiana University
3

If all you know about managing people is what you knew ten years ago, you're out of date. Past managerial approaches were based on management as a system of authority. Authority often depended on ownership of the firm. Employees depended on the owner-manager for wages and jobs, and thus employees were more willing to be housebroken and placed into organizational harnesses. Present managerial approaches tend to be based on management as a resource. Younger employees are better-educated and expect the dignity and satisfaction of a management approach that recognizes knowledge, skill, aptitude and expectations. People today expect to work more to achieve objectives and less merely to follow orders or procedures. Management authority today is derived more from personal qualities—possession of knowledge, skills and values—than on ownership of capital or property.
Interview/ Nation's Business, August:23.

J. Irwin Miller
Chairman, Cummins Engine Company
4

[Business] will suffer a new wave of legal restrictions if it does not [morally and ethically] curb itself voluntarily. But at the moment it is reacting to individual incidents and not taking a fresh look. It's generally defensive and not self-critical. If you have a complex interdependent society like ours, it's like people jammed in an elevator. You can't swing your elbows everywhere. We in business must exercise restraint—or it will be imposed. We must do less than the law allows and more than it requires.
The Christian Science Monitor, 4-19:17.

Thomas A. Murphy
Chairman, General Motors Corporation
5

Over the past decade, the principal coun-

WHAT THEY SAID IN 1976

(THOMAS A. MURPHY)

tries of Europe have been investing in plants and capital goods at a rate that is proportionately up to 50 per cent higher than our own. Japan's proportionate investments are almost double ours. We are at the bottom of the list among developed countries in this all-important area . . . Productivity is the single most important instrument we Americans have traditionally used in competing with foreign manufacturers, while paying our workers wages higher than those paid by our overseas competitors. We have lost much of that productive advantage. We dare not lose more.

At publishers seminar/
Los Angeles Herald-Examiner, 1-27:(C)8.

1

Just as political liberty is threatened when men in power violate the spirit of our Constitutional freedoms, so is our free-enterprise system placed in jeopardy when a code of honesty and social responsibility is not honored by business men and women . . . The ethical standards that have come down to us from the world's great religions and through our Judeo-Christian traditions are surprisingly comprehensive in the range of their applications today—and they are even more surprisingly practical. If we remember to be wary of the principle that the end justifies the means, and that the economic benefit of our company is not a supreme good that overrides all other ethical considerations, we will be well on our way to helping restore the good name of our profession. And I suggest that the ethically right decision will ultimately prove to be the economically right decision as well. I don't believe that there has ever been a company that enjoyed a long period of success as a result of unethical or illegal practices.

At University of Michigan/
The Christian Science Monitor, 3-8:11.

2

What is really wrong with over-regulation

[of business] by the government is not that business people don't agree with it, or that we find it burdensome and costly, but that in the long run its principal victim is the consumer. The fall guy is not the businessman; it is the shopper, the person at the end of the line, the one who in the final analysis pays all America's bills. The consumer pays for excessive regulation in higher prices, higher taxes and reduced choices. And apparently he is unaware that he is being had. Every time a government mandates a product standard, it takes away some of the consumer's freedom of choice—and not always with sufficient reason or with compensating benefit. Every regulation poses a threat to economic freedom, and its benefits must always be weighed against its costs, in terms of the average American's liberties as well as his pocketbook.

Before Associated Industries of New York,
Lake Placid, N.Y., Sept. 24/
The Washington Post, 10-12:(A)18.

3

We know that every shoddy product, every neglected service, every reason for complaint is worse than bad business—it invites more regulation by government. Adverse public opinion, the antecedent of government regulation, has been shaped to a great degree by the failures of business to satisfy the customer. Other factors are involved, but much of the public's antipathy toward big business is rooted in the American consumer's own bad experiences in the marketplace. To the extent that it is rooted there, it can be remedied only there . . . we counter the threat of government over-regulation when we do what we must and should to satisfy our customers, when we get back to what competition in business is all about—when we do business as business should be done, openly and honestly, with the customer's needs uppermost in mind.

Before Associated Industries of New York,
Lake Placid, N.Y., Sept. 24/
Vital Speeches, 11-1:58.

Bess Myerson
Consumer advocate
1

I think the marketplace is the most important common denominator in America. It touches us every day . . . How we buy and sell to each other, how we get along with each other in the marketplace is a blueprint for the way we act in every facet of our lives.
Interview, Dallas, June 29/
The Dallas Times Herald, 6-29:(A)10.

James J. Needham
Former chairman,
New York Stock Exchange
2

[Criticizing government intrusion in the securities industry]: It is time for the exchanges to get together and keep the government out of it. The SEC is great at giving a sense of direction and great at reacting, perhaps more than it would want to. But it is not great at implementing change. They don't have the time and the people to do that job. And they can't sit down and design specifications for tasks to be done. The Commission probably prefers that the industry keep that role.
Interview/The New York Times, 11-16:61.

Peter Nehemkis
Emeritus lecturer in international business law and international business negotiations, Graduate School of Management, University of California, Los Angeles
3

[Saying government investigators apply a double standard when condemning foreign business bribes paid by U.S. companies]: Why is it legitimate to invite a member of Congress to make a speech before a trade association and pay him $5,000 when everyone knows he has nothing to say? Isn't that a subtle form of corruption? . . . Why do we sanction the idea that entertaining a prospect or a customer is permitted, even tax-deductible? That's another way of gaining favor and exerting influence, but it is sanctioned under our moral standards; whereas if you make a payment to a prospect overseas, say a government department, we look askance . . . Bribery is an institutionalized fact of international business life. It is, to be sure, no more prevalent in other industrialized countries—Italy is an exception—than in the United States. Bribery is, however, pervasive throughout virtually the entire Third World of Latin America, the Middle East, Africa and Asia.
Interview, Los Angeles/
The Washington Post, 6-1:(D)8.

Edward Ney
President,
Young & Rubicam International,
advertising
4

[On government regulation of business]: Without any regulations, we operate in a jungle. With them, we're frequently in a straitjacket. In our view there are too many regulations, poorly administered, which end up putting a half nelson on the free-enterprise system and not generally benefitting the consumer.
Interview/The Wall Street Journal, 7-20:16.

Neal W. O'Connor
Chairman,
American Association of
Advertising Agencies
5

Truth in advertising, and in business, is neither likely nor entirely possible. I know that I have probably just offended you. But to insist that pure truth is the answer to the public's mistrust of business and advertising is naive, simplistic and utterly impractical. Let me explain. The problem is to define the truth, to know what is the truth. When [consumerist] Ralph Nader said that the Corvair was "unsafe at any speed," I think he very likely believed what he was saying. He may even have had some sort of evidence to back up his claim. Ralph Nader, to give him the benefit of suspending doubt, was telling the truth as he saw it. Actually, he was not telling the truth. After years of test-

WHAT THEY SAID IN 1976

(NEAL W. O'CONNOR)

ing, the Federal government announced that the Corvair was no less safe than other cars of similar size. We have a more current case. The makers of food containing Red Dye Number Two said the foods they sold were healthful. Now we are told that Red Dye Number Two is not healthful. The unmistakable conclusion there: All those food companies were lying. Does it matter whether or not they knew they were lying? *Were* they lying? Is it true that Red Dye Number Two in the amounts consumed by the average person is unhealthful? If it is unhealthful in amounts consumed by humans, why are we, all consumers of Red Dye Number Two, not sick? Knowing the truth isn't a problem just for people in business and advertising. It has always been a problem. Remember your college course in philosophy? How one philosopher proved that everything was always in motion and another proved that everything was always at rest? And how about Columbus who disagreed with a known, observable truth? What's the truth about nuclear power plants? The ecologists say they're unsafe, but we say they keep on operating, safely. If we can't agree about the scientific truths, if we can't even agree on the rules for seeking the truth, how are we going to tell the public the absolute truth?

Before American Association of Advertising Agencies, White Sulphur Springs, W. Va., May 15/ Vital Speeches, 7-1:568.

Norma Pace
Business consultant, Senior vice president, American Paper Institute 1

[Saying business capital formation has got to be stimulated]: We have got to stop neglecting this part of our economy. We don't have the slack in capacity in basic industries that we think we have. Until 1969, the stock of plant and equipment in place was rising faster than man-hours used in production. Thus, our productivity was advancing. But we fell off that track in 1969. So many things have happened as a result. Our inability to advance means that everyone's struggle to get an increasing share of the economic pie has become longer and longer, and conflicts in the system among various worker groups have been getting worse and worse. The desire to redistribute income is becoming an impossibility. It cannot change unless we get after the capital-formation problem.

Interview/ The New York Times, 12-3:(D)9.

Alex Park
Chief executive, British Leyland, Ltd. 2

Decisions regarding the planning of new factories, their location, their financing, the types of new models to go on the drawing board, measures to produce more safety and less pollution—all of these are matters of the greatest social and economic importance and should be planned in partnership with government. While I believe very strongly that there has to be an element of free enterprise in our business, and in the freedom of executive decision in its day-to-day affairs, I also believe that government involvement can lead to more efficiency. Generally, stockholders are poorly informed and generally they ask for information only when things go wrong. Sometimes that is too late. Governments make you constantly accountable.

Before Foreign Press Association, London/ The Wall Street Journal, 6-2:12.

Wright Patman
United States Representative, D—Texas 3

[Criticizing a new law permitting statewide branch banking in New York]: What chance does a small bank in Niagara Falls or Montauk have to compete with these giants [from New York City]? The local bankers in these towns who own small banks will shortly be liquidated, as the owners of small corner grocery stores were by the A&P, Safeway, Acme and Kroger . . . About the only small business we have left in this country is the small independent bank. The rest of the economy has gone the way of the roses—three companies make our cars, two our cans, one our computers, and one our copying machines.

Parade, 2-22:23.

Jeno F. Paulucci
Founder, Chun King Corporation

1

There are damn few entrepreneurs who survive today. If any do survive, it's unusual—and even more unusual if they don't sell out as a last resort to a giant, as I did with Chun King—because we all know that the competition for the marketplace and for working capital is fierce as hell. We also know that more business firms go broke due to lack of working capital than any other reason. Now, one must realize that just 500 giant corporations, per the last *Fortune* magazine list, control 83 per cent of products and services of America's gross national product, now exceeding one trillion dollars a year. Therefore, they also control 83 per cent of the working capital in these United States . . . All the other millions upon millions of individuals, partnerships, cooperatives, corporations—whatever—are fighting for the remaining 17 per cent of the market and 17 per cent of the working capital.

At U.S. Small Business Administration seminar, Washington/The Wall Street Journal, 9-27:16.

Ronald Reagan
*Candidate for the
1976 Republican Presidential nomination;
Former Governor of California (R)*

2

My view on dairy subsidies is that we are subsidizing those who could not compete at the expense of those who could possibly bring the price down in the marketplace. You subsidize the inefficient when you put a floor under the market price.

*News conference, Florida, March 8/
Los Angeles Times, 3-9:(1)14.*

Donald T. Regan
*Chairman,
Merrill Lynch, Pierce, Fenner & Smith, Inc.*

3

[On when a small investor should get into the stock market]: As a rule of thumb, an individual should have sufficient savings to meet any emergency—enough to live on for, say, six months. You must have sufficient life insurance and, if you do not own your own home, at least have the mortgage under control. But speculative buying should by no means be ruled out. We shouldn't knock risk. The market and this country were built on risk.

Interview, New York/People, 2-16:50.

Robert W. Reneker
Chairman, Esmark, Inc.

4

The most important ingredient of good management is the kind of people who can attract and develop and grow. If there's a second ingredient, it's attempting to identify for these people the kind of opportunities they can expect. In other words, an orderly process of planning goals and objectives.

*Interview, Chicago/
Nation's Business, February:45.*

Henry S. Reuss
*United States Representative,
D—Wisconsin*

5

Banks are not accountable to the public, mainly because existing regulatory agencies are all entwined with the banks. The banking lobby is very effective, and the public is almost not represented in the legislative process.

Interview/The Washington Post, 2-15:(A)4.

6

The average price of stocks today is just what it was 10 years ago. You tell me what other commodity you can find that sells for what it was 10 years ago. Not lead, copper, gold, wheat, land or homes. Nothing! Common stocks are what I would regard as a bargain, and I think investors who have the good sense to put their pocketbook ahead of their ideology and are willing to buy now will find they can make a profit out of President-elect Jimmy Carter.

*Interview/
Los Angeles Herald-Examiner, 11-8:(A)5.*

WHAT THEY SAID IN 1976

Cedric E. Ritchie
Chairman, Bank of Nova Scotia
1

The lessons of banking which we have learned in the past two years are as old as banking itself . . . We must know to whom we are lending, and what we are lending for. We must know how we are going to be repaid; we must not avoid taking prudent risks, but we must quantify our risks and qualify our exposures. And, above all, we must look to our internal management . . . Most of the serious troubles in the banking world in recent times have been due to pilot error, and for this the blame can be brought back to our doorstep as the senior executive officers.

Panel discussion at
International Monetary Conference
sponsored by American Bankers Association,
San Francisco, June 18/
The New York Times, 6-19:27,31.

David Rockefeller
Chairman,
Chase Manhattan Bank, New York
2

There is growing world concern about the attitude toward protectionism in the United States, particularly with regard to the provisions of the 1974 Trade Act. After Watergate, we are living in a period of renewed Congressional assertiveness, and 1976, as an election year, is a time for traditional flag-waving. Nevertheless, it is a fact that not one of the several worrisome bills introduced in Congress in recent months that might be considered protectionist has been passed into law. Nor has the present [Ford] Administration wavered in its support of free trade. This, too, is an encouraging sign.

"W": a Fairchild publication, 1-9:16.

3

[On revelations of foreign bribes paid by U.S. companies]: It is disappointing . . . that there has been this kind of thing on the scale that has come out. And it is unfortunate . . . the way it has come out. It would sound as though this was something that only U.S. companies and by implication most U.S. companies, do. I don't think either of those things are true. I think this has been a custom in many parts of the world for decades, maybe centuries, and that American companies have only been among many others that have done it.

News conference, Teheran, Iran, March 2/
The Dallas Times Herald, 3-3:(A)2.

Paul A. Samuelson
Professor of economics,
Massachusetts Institute of Technology
4

"Profit" is today a fighting word. Profits are the lifeblood of the economic system, the magic elixir upon which progress and all good things ultimately depend. But one man's lifeblood is another man's cancer.

At business forum, Harvard University/
Time, 8-16:54.

Hans Martin Schleyer
President, Federal Association of
German Employers
5

[Arguing against worker participation in corporate decision-making]: A functioning company demands decisions. But parity on boards leads to factions, and this invariably leads to paralyzing of decision-making, because there is a deadlock. Anyone who likes to keep the legend alive that *mitbestimmung* has proven its value is wrong. It has only proven its value for the unions.

Nation's Business, February:54.

Jane Scully
President, Carlow College, Pittsburgh;
Member board of directors,
Gulf Oil Company
6

[On corporate leadership]: Sometimes it's done in the most arrogant manner: "Management knows best for the corporation or for the nation or they know better than you." They don't see the validity of complaints from the outside. It's ridiculous for them to say "the laws are strangling us." Government and law are the American people. When you assume the law of the land is your enemy, you're in trouble.

Interview, Pittsburgh/
The New York Times, 3-7(3)7.

Irving S. Shapiro
Chairman,
E. I. du Pont de Nemours & Company 1

In the old days, businessmen thought if they made political contributions, that entitled them to something in Washington. They understand now that it doesn't buy anything. If a businessman wants to have an impact, he better get his facts organized, go to Washington to present them and be prepared to take the heat if he's wrong. We are not always right. But, by God, if we pull our facts together and tell our story we'll come out okay because the facts of business are pretty good.

Newsweek, 2-16:59.

2

Our present economy was designed for a number of basic conditions that are now changing. We must redesign our economy to function effectively with much of the world's raw materials under the control of governments of diverse political systems; with traditional energy sources declining; with energy prices soaring; with a lesser rate of economic growth; with stubbornly high unemployment and inflation; with overseas investment increasingly risky and sometimes unwelcome; with widespread consumer suspicions and demands; with government regulation aimed at the achievement of major quality-of-life goals as well as economic fair play. Any one of these new realities would be a major hurdle by itself. Altogether, they add up to the greatest challenge in history to the ingenuity and integrity of business and industrial management.

Before The Conference Board, New York,
Sept. 16/ Vital Speeches, 10-15:16.

William E. Simon
Secretary of the Treasury
of the United States 3

One of the main tenets of U.S. foreign policy which is especially crucial today is our advocacy of reduced trade-and-investment barriers between nations. This country has traditionally been an outspoken and vigorous proponent of a free and open international trading community, and our voice carries a special weight. We know that, with fewer restrictions, international trade could again serve as a powerful engine for international growth and as a means of reducing the pressures of inflation.

At "Pacem in Terris" convocation, Washington,
December ('75)/ Center Report, February:9.

4

We have this great misconception in the United States that every time we want to raise revenues, let's tax corporations. There's a very simple economic fact of life we must recognize, and that is that corporations don't pay taxes. People do. Businesses are people ... in the sense that businesses are owned by people. For us to continue to punish businesses through higher taxes will mean higher unemployment, higher prices for consumers, lower real earnings for workers . . . I don't consider [abolition of corporate taxes] politically possible; but in a perfect world it makes sense, since individuals ultimately pay the tax anyway.

Interview/ The National Observer, 1-17:1.

5

[On why a new international monetary agreement had to be negotiated recently in Jamaica]: . . . the price of the dollar on world markets is without a doubt the single most important price the United States has to live with. It affects everybody and every business. We all saw during the 1960s that our dollar became extremely over-valued in terms of other currencies because of the rigid Bretton Woods system of fixing currency-exchange rates, which prevented the dollar from adjusting. Under that system, others could ad-

(WILLIAM E. SIMON)

just but the United States couldn't. We were locked in . . . It made us non-competitive with other nations. We saw dollars flowing out of our country. We saw imports increase, and that led to massive deficits in our balance of payments. We saw plants built in many countries overseas that would have been built here, thereby costing America tens of thousands of jobs. The Bretton Woods system collapsed because of its rigidity, its inability to respond to the swift changes that have characterized recent years. The final irony is that under that system the U.S. was forced to borrow billions to, in effect, finance our uncompetitive situation. At the end, our borrowings had become so large that our ability to hold the dollar at the old relationship to other currencies was successfully challenged in the foreign-exchange market. We devalued once and then again, and then floated.

Interview/ U.S. News & World Report, 1-26:67.

1

The whole point of free enterprise—of capitalism—is vigorous, honest competition. Every corner cut, every bribe placed, every little cheating move by a businessman in pursuit of quick plunder instead of honest profit is an outright attack on the real free-enterprise system.

U.S. News & World Report, 9-13:44.

2

The Federal Reserve System is the last bastion of discipline in the United States against the politicians. And any move toward politicizing the Fed, I think, is a move toward the destruction of our society. We've seen throughout history that when the politicians get their hands on the money-making machinery and just print money indiscriminately, the result is economic disaster.

*Interview, Washington/
U.S. News & World Report, 12-13:25.*

Joe Sims
*Deputy Assistant Attorney General,
Antitrust Division, Department of Justice of
the United States*
3

Though many businessmen may view antitrust enforcement as simply another form of regulation, it is no more so than the police officer or the referee in a sports event. And the simple fact is that, like the police officer and the referee, antitrust enforcement is essential to a free-market economy. If you don't believe that, look at the record of over 30 criminal price-fixing cases filed in each of the last two years. Price-fixing, and other business collusion, is just as illegal, and socially unacceptable, as other forms of fraud and robbery, and, in its context, perhaps just as common.

*At Board of Directors Conference, Southern
Methodist University School of Business
Administration/ The National Observer, 3-27:11.*

Ian D. Sinclair
Chairman, Canadian Pacific, Ltd.
4

Antitrust is the greatest thing barristers and lawyers ever had happen to them. If it ever comes up here [to Canada], maybe I'll quit and go back to practicing law. U.S. antitrust is carried to ridiculous extremes. They get hepped on disclosure, too. Those kinds of things haven't come here. And I hope they never do.

*Interview, Montreal/
Business Week, 2-23:68.*

J. Stanford Smith
*Chairman,
International Paper Company*
5

In the economic field, business firms and their managers are subject to the plebiscite of the marketplace every day—the plebiscite of customers for goods and services; employees for their skill and conscientious effort; suppliers for their raw materials or components; and investors for their capital. Let any group withhold their favor, or direct it to another company, or another industry, and the business is in trouble. Thus, the marketplace controls whether the company makes sales, has enough employees or the right type, gets goods and services from its suppliers, and raises capital from lenders or share-owners. This is the process that Adam Smith calls "The Invisible Hand." It usually works silently, though swiftly and surely . . . What Adam Smith saw, and we forget at our peril, is that the marketplace is truly a regulatory agency—that it could regulate most economic activities with [great] speed, effectiveness and freedom . . . The market system of regulation works. It has the power to discipline. It takes into account millions of transactions. It responds rapidly to unanticipated events and to secondary effects arising from its own regulatory action. This rapid response is in direct contrast to government regulation which slows change, inhibits new ideas and frequently thwarts the use of invention.

At National Conference on Regulatory Reform, Washington, May 25/ Vital Speeches, 8-15:664.

Edgar B. Speer
Chairman,
United States Steel Corporation 1

Who has paid the price for the poor decisions and judgments of the Interstate Commerce Commission? The Commission members, or the customers and stockholders of America's railroads—and the taxpayers who are paying for Conrail? Who is paying for two decades of price controls, administered by the Federal Power Commission, that has caused the steady reduction in natural-gas reserves and today's shortages of this clean-burning fuel? And who will pay tomorrow, after the Federal Energy Administration inflicts the same heavy-handed treatment on the nation's oil companies? Study after study, by some of the best minds in the country, have shown that whatever the presumed benefits of regulation, they are far outweighed by the ultimate costs, whether those costs are measured in lost freedoms, destroyed investments, higher taxes or higher prices for the consumer.

Before Economic Club of Detroit, March 15/ Vital Speeches, 4-15:409.

George C. Wallace
Governor of Alabama (D); Candidate for the 1976 Democratic Presidential nomination 2

Big business, and especially big oil, ought to understand that there's nothing like the political fury of middle-class America once it gets unleashed. A lot of workers and middle-class people are losing their affluence, and they're not going to give it up easily. If they see this as the result of monopolistic behavior, damned if they won't fight the money folks in this country and make the liberals in Congress look like John Birch Society members.

Interview, Montgomery, Alabama/ Business Week, 2-23:54.

Rawleigh Warner, Jr.
Chairman, Mobil Oil Corporation 3

How would breaking up the oil industry, which I think most reasonable people would consider a national asset of some importance, improve U.S. energy security or otherwise help our country? How would dismantling the U.S. oil industry increase America's supplies of secure domestic oil and natural gas? Put another way, how great a setback would divestiture cause in the urgently needed effort to develop additional reserves of domestic energy? What effect would divestiture have on the American economy, on the energy costs of American industry, on American jobs and on unemployment? How would dismantling large oil companies, with world-wide access to oil supplies and with the ability to move that oil, strengthen our national defense? How would it benefit Americans to have to rely on the large, strong, *foreign* oil companies that Congress would not be able to dismember? If the oil industry is broken up, what industry will be dismembered next? If the strength of the private sector is sapped, will this not lead to an even more powerful central government? It seems to me that if enough people put enough questions of this sort to their elected representatives in Washington, the resulting dialogue can defeat the present efforts to shatter the U.S. economy as

(RAWLEIGH WARNER, JR.)

the first stage in recasting American society in an elitist image.

At Pace University, New York, April 6/
Vital Speeches, 5-1:433.

Murray L. Weidenbaum
Director, Center for the Study of
American Business,
Washington University, St. Louis 1

The massive expansion of government influence in matters which traditionally have been the province of business firms has resulted in what I call a Second Managerial Revolution. In good measure the shift of decision-making from the internal management of American companies to the cadre of government inspectors and regulators has been unintentional and certainly unnoticed, at least by the public at large. Yet the impacts of this shift of basic economic power have been extremely important. They have resulted, in so many ways, in attenuating the basic risk-bearing and entrepreneurial character of business firms. More specifically, the shift of decision-making authority also has been slowing the process of product innovation, reducing productivity and increasing the prices that consumers pay for the goods and services that they purchase. The evidence on this score has been mounting rapidly. In large measure, the over-regulation of business activity appears to reflect a basic lack of understanding of how the market mechanism operates.

Before Government Operations Committee,
Washington, Feb. 6/Vital Speeches, 3-1:312.

2

Unless you're an anarchist, you believe that there's a role for government in setting rules. The question is: What are the legitimate limits? Should the Federal government be concerned about the cleanliness of our environment, about safety in workplaces, about eliminating discrimination, about the safety of products? Those are the principal areas af-fected by what I call the new wave of regulation. In a complicated modern society, there is an important role for government in these areas. But in each of them, Congress has enacted an excess of regulation, and the agencies in charge have promulgated an excess of rules, with the result that the basic objectives of the laws are not achieved in many instances . . . When the Occupational Safety and Health Administration issues regulations on how often a company has to clean spittoons, how big is a hole, when is a roof a floor, and other nonsense like that, it doesn't have enough manpower to deal with truly lethal hazards. And given the tremendous array of regulations, it's very difficult for an inspector from OSHA to focus on the serious hazards.

Interview, Washington/
U.S. News & World Report, 6-14:31.

Frederic W. West, Jr.
President,
Bethlehem Steel Corporation 3

[Journalists are suspicious of business, but] they're equally suspicious of just about everybody in positions of power, influence and wealth; that's why complaints about press bias come from just about every sector of society. My advice to the business community is to stop worrying so much about whether or not members of the press are prejudiced one way or the other. Let's realize that some of the reporting that gets our blood up is probably more muddled than it is malicious.

Before American Newspaper Publishers
Association, New York, May 4/
The New York Times, 5-5:36.

John H. Williams
Chairman, The Williams Companies 4

When I became chief executive officer back in 1950, I felt I had to do everything myself, and I was rather condescending about those I felt were less capable—I tolerated them. But it didn't take me long to find out that I didn't know everything, that there were capable people available, and that you accomplish ever so much more by having talented associates. This multiplies your ability manyfold, though you still may think you personally can do things best . . . You look for people who have the minds, initiative and drive—all of those things that make top people. Then you have to provide them with the tools with which to work, and with an incentive. Money is an incentive, but there also has to be a certain mystique—they must have a pride in the company . . . The job of a chief executive includes creating the atmosphere that these people operate in. I find the chiefs, who then go out and assemble their teams. We have a saying in our company: In order to succeed in any venture, you don't need a team of people, you need the right man to head up the effort and then he'll develop his own team.

Interview, Tulsa, Okla./
Nation's Business, April:55.

William M. Witter
Chairman, Dean Witter & Company   1

On the West Coast, I don't think we have quite as much of an emotional approach to the [securities] business as they do on Wall Street. Back there, either everything's going to a million—or everything's going to hell. I think we have more perspective out here.

Interview, San Francisco/
The New York Times, 10-10:(3)1.

Crime • Law Enforcement

Robert Blakey
Professor of law, Cornell University

1

For all its shortcomings, the FBI is still the best criminal-investigation agency in this country—perhaps the best in the world. I'd hate to see that destroyed because the Bureau, with precious little guidance from Congresses and Presidents, strayed outside of today's rules in a few intelligence investigations . . . People who grew up with the publicity cranked out during the [late Director J. Edgar] Hoover years thought the FBI was a nearly invincible corps of G-men, hunting down kidnapers and bank robbers with their submachine guns. Nowadays, if you believed some news accounts, you'd think agents spent all their time in headphones, snooping on private citizens. Neither of these images has anything to do with the work most agents do from day to day.

U.S. News & World Report, 3-8:23,24.

Edmund G. Brown, Jr.
Governor of California (D)

2

Certainly, we should try to help those who have been incarcerated re-enter society in a productive way, but to think that psychology and group therapy can change a career criminal into a law-abiding citizen is rather naive. Crime for some is a career and is not easily changed. It becomes part of their emotional and conceptual structure. Punishment is a word that many people shrink from today, but it probably provides more fairness than the much-abused rehabilitation. Using that term, we often permit wide-scale discretion and official arbitrariness. In addition, white-collar crime is often not punished at all, because judges are able to identify with the lifestyle of such criminals and believe them to be

rehabilitated by mere conviction without serving any time in jail. In this sense, punishment may be a very progressive idea.

Interview/Playboy, April:185.

3

I believe in some [gun] controls, such as elimination of "Saturday-night specials." But to go beyond that and attempt to confiscate all the guns in this country might require house-to-house searches and a tremendous new government intrusion in our lives. I wonder if the cure would be better than the disease. We kill over 50,000 people a year in cars, yet I don't hear anybody talking about confiscating them . . . Making something a crime doesn't necessarily stop it. It is a crime to smoke marijuana, but people do it. Just criminalizing some activity is often a non-solution.

Interview/Playboy, April:185.

Warren E. Burger
Chief Justice of the United States

4

It is a very serious matter when whole communities become emotionally aroused—as they can—by a constant stream of news accounts of serious crimes. We should not be heard to complain at the loss of public confidence in our legal institutions if people come to think that government is impotent to protect its citizens. One danger is that loss of belief in governmental institutions leads to what is euphemistically called "self help," and too much self help can lead to a disintegration of the social structure. A civilized society should not have "vigilantes."

At National Conference on the Causes of Popular Dissatisfaction with the Administration of Justice, St. Paul, Minn., April 7/ The National Observer, 4-24:17.

Gerald M. Caplan
Director,
National Institute of Law Enforcement
and Criminal Justice   *1*

An uncanny consensus has emerged on crime—an alliance or coalition of enemies. In the 1960s and early '70s, roles got reversed in the way we looked at crime. There were no more cops and robbers. Punishment and deterrence became taboos. Traditional values were scrambled and we looked at the auto thief as a victim of society. Now we're realizing that crime is a way of our life, and we're coming to terms with it.

Interview/ Los Angeles Times, 6-14:(1)20.

Jimmy Carter
Candidate for the 1976 Democratic
Presidential nomination;
Former Governor of Georgia (D)   *2*

[On reducing crime]: We need judicial reform, a much better administered court system, merit selection of judges and prosecutors, briefer trial periods, recodification of the criminal codes. Next, we need to allot crime-prevention funds in areas that can actually prevent crime, and not just to build jailhouses, or to buy helicopters, and so forth. We need to concentrate police officers in high-crime areas. We need to have full backing for police officers from all public officials. We need to have better street lighting. We need to have surer—and perhaps briefer—sentences for those who commit crimes, so that there's a fairly good certainty that if someone is convicted, they'll be punished. We also need to understand the major causes of increases in the crime rate. I think that the major contributing factor has been high unemployment. That's not an excuse for crime, but it's a cause of crime. We've got about a 40-to-45 per cent unemployment rate among our minority young people, and if they could be gainfully employed, their tendency toward crime would be reduced.

Interview/ U.S. News & World Report, 5-24:23.

Jimmy Carter
1976 Democratic Presidential nominee   *3*

We've had an unprecedented increase in the crime rate in the last eight years under a Republican Administration. I don't blame all the crime rate on the Republicans . . . That would not be fair . . . But there's been a great contribution to the crime rate in this country because of Watergate, because of the CIA revelations and because of the disgraceful actions in the FBI.

Campaigning at Brooklyn (N.Y.) College,
Sept. 7/ The Washington Post, 9-8:(A)4.

4

I favor the registration of handguns only, so we can eliminate the ownership of those guns by those who have been convicted of a crime using handguns and those who are mentally incompetent. I don't favor the confiscation of handguns. I don't favor the registration of rifles or shotguns. I happen to be an avid hunter myself and have been all my life. I happen to have both handguns and rifles and shotguns in my possession at home and I think it's a right of American people, I think a Constitutional right, to own guns.

Campaigning, Portland, Ore., Sept. 27/
Los Angeles Times, 9-28:(1)6.

Ramsey Clark
Candidate for the 1976 New York Democratic
U.S. Senatorial nomination;
Former Attorney General of the
United States   *5*

A mere internal reorganization cannot realistically hope to purge the accumulated problems arising from many years of FBI abuse of freedom, lawlessness and contempt for Constitutional government. The problem grew because the FBI set itself above the law. Its solution will only be found in an FBI operating within the rule of law, in an open manner, independently reviewed—as established and monitored by Congress.

Aug. 21/ The New York Times, 8-22:(1)34.

WHAT THEY SAID IN 1976

John B. Connally, Jr.
*Secretary of the Treasury of
the United States;
Former Governor of Texas (D, now R)*

1

[Saying executions of prisoners should be televised]: [Death] is a horrible thing to contemplate. If it was televised, everyone could see the real horror of it. It would be an even more impressive deterrent [to crime]. I know in some of the Arab countries at one time the penalty for thievery is to cut off their hand. And you know there's just no thievery in those countries; you can leave anything out and no one will touch it.

*Radio interview, San Antonio, Tex., Dec. 1/
The Dallas Times Herald, 12-2:(A)1.*

Richard J. Daley
Mayor of Chicago

2

Why in the name of God can't Congress pass a handgun law to prevent guns from falling into the hands of 11- or 12-year-olds? Too many young people have handguns . . . a handgun is not a hunting weapon for animals and birds. It hunts human beings.

*San Francisco Examiner & Chronicle,
10-24:(This World)2.*

Edward M. Davis
Chief of Police of Los Angeles

3

The reality of crime can be changed. There's no question about it. At any point in history there's probably a very, very small percentage of human beings who are vicious and dangerous, who would do other people in. And at different points in history we handle those people differently. That's what gives us our variations in the crime rates.

Interview/Los Angeles Times, 8-10:(4)1.

4

The complexity of law and the protection of individual rights in our society will require that a police officer have infinitely more legal training—approximately nine months,

or a third of a law education. I think there also will have to be infinitely better training in weaponless self-defense. And so the protective martial arts of defenses against karate and that sort of thing will have to be improved. In the year 2000 you probably won't think of turning a policeman loose unless he has the equivalent of a bachelor's degree, but in a highly specialized way—about a year or so of law, almost a year of martial arts, probably about a year of social sciences with heavy emphasis on psychology.

Interview/Los Angeles Times, 8-10:(4)6.

5

Various restraints on the intelligence function today have caused some police administrators to completely abandon this vital activity. Still other administrators have reduced the amount of material kept by their organization to the point that it cannot be classified as intelligence. In many cases, because of disclosure laws, such as the Federal Freedom of Information Act, it is considered too great a risk to share intelligence information with Federal agencies.

*Before Senate Judiciary Subcommittee
on Internal Security, Washington, Sept. 9/
Los Angeles Times, 9-10:(1)3.*

Robert J. diGrazia
Police Commissioner of Boston

6

The degree to which a police chief exercises leadership should be judged by the risks that he—or she, for that matter—takes in seeking improvement in personnel and the delivery of police services and in educating the public and the politicians about what the police can—and cannot—do. The police chief who challenges the hoary assumptions of our calling, who is willing to innovate in the deployment of patrol and investigative resources, who challenges ingrained civil-service practices when they undermine the efficiency of the department, who seeks a department which represents in its racial and ethnic makeup the community it serves, who rewards higher education for officers, who disdains as destructive myth the image of police work as gunslinging melodrama, who encourages officers to have compassion and decency for the poor and deprived— that police chief takes one hell of a lot of risks. His survival is at stake, but he is acting as a leader.

At conference sponsored by Police Foundation, Washington, April 14/ The National Observer, 6-26:11.

1

As police chiefs, most of us have allowed ourselves to be the underlings of American municipal government, somewhat as pet rocks, unable to move, grow, change or in-novate . . . Mere survival, that's the goal of most of us and that's one major thing wrong with police leadership. For the most part, we police chiefs have no vision of ourselves beyond that of being survivors with gold braid. Few of our colleagues are question-ing traditional practices and promoting innovations, demanding increased produc-tivity and upgrading personnel, encouraging serious research and advocating the hiring of women and members of minority groups. There is one other thing few police chiefs are doing: leveling with the public about crime. Most of us are not telling the public that there is relatively little the police can do about crime. We are not letting the public in on our era's dirty little secret: that those who commit the crime which worries citizens most—violent street crime—are, for the most part, the products of poverty, unem-ployment, broken homes, rotten education, drug addiction and alcoholism, and other social and economic ills about which the police can do little, if anything. Rather than speaking up, most of us stand silent and let politicians get away with law-and-order rhetoric that reinforces the mistaken notion that the police—in ever greater numbers and with more gadgetry—can alone control crime. The politicians, of course, end up perpetuating a system by which the rich get

richer, the poor get poorer, and crime con-tinues.

At conference sponsored by Police Foundation, Washington, April 14/ Los Angeles Times, 4-15:(1)6; The Washington Post, 4-15:(A)3.

2

Here in Boston, most people have the feeling that crime is a black-and-white issue, with the bad guys the blacks, and the whites the ones being picked on. The vast majority of the crime we deal with is not black and white. It's black picking on black or His-panic picking on Hispanic or white picking on white—all in a poor area. All police can really do is displace crime—send it out to the suburbs or take very good action against armed robberies only to see an increase in burglaries. That's because of social problems behind crime—environment, education, jobs, the places we force people to live. No one wants to address that. It doesn't make for great political rhetoric.

Interview, Boston/ Los Angeles Times, 6-14:(1)20.

Clinton T. Duffy
Former warden,
San Quentin (Calif.) State Prison
3

[Arguing against capital punishment]: You have to go back to the community, to the family, and find out what made these people rob and rape and kill in the first place. I don't believe one of the executions I wit-nessed ever stopped anyone from committing a crime. Capital punishment just isn't equal justice. It's the poor and the underprivileged who get executed. Besides that, it's wrong to kill, period. It's wrong that they killed, and two wrongs don't make a right. I was warden for 11½ years—longer than anyone else has ever been warden at San Quentin— and I loved every minute of my job, except for the executions.

Los Angeles Times, 8-18:(1)24.

WHAT THEY SAID IN 1976

Michael S. Dukakis
Governor of Massachusetts (D)

1

I don't favor the death penalty, never have and in fact vetoed a capital-punishment bill passed by my own Legislature. But I don't think the movement of the country back toward this kind of thing and other forms of tougher penalties, mandatory sentences, for example . . . reflects anything more than a genuine and a very deep public concern for what is a rising crime rate, more lawlessness particularly in our cities but now even in our suburban and rural areas— as I say, a perfectly understandable reaction to that and frustration at the inability of those of us in government and increasing amounts of resources we are pouring into law enforcement to cope with this problem. I am hopeful we will begin to make some moves in the other direction and begin to see that reflected in reducing murder rates and crime rates. But so far I must say the country and those of us at the state and local level have been unable to do that.

TV-radio interview, Philadelphia/
"Meet the Press,"
National Broadcasting Company, 7-4.

Jiro Enomoto
California State Director of Corrections

2

I don't think that [prisoner rehabilitation] is what we're here for. The expectation of change is a false one, an illusion. Of course, the reality is that there are success stories, but [the rehabilitated convicts] succeeded because they wanted to. The idea that we can change someone who doesn't want to be changed is a bogus expectation.

San Francisco Examiner & Chronicle,
8-22:(This World)2.

W. J. Estelle, Jr.
Director,
Texas Department of Corrections

3

[On the death penalty]: There is a simple common-sense factor involved. I know that capital punishment would deter you from committing murder and I know it would deter me and I'm sure it deters others to whom the penalty applies. If the penalty is applied equally for all, I have no problem with the morality or legality of it. Certainly the attitude of the country, Texas at least, has hardened against the lawlessness we have increasingly experienced in recent years. There's a widespread desire to reinstate the death penalty. The community is acting out of frustration, anger and, in some cases, real fear. It is reacting the only way it knows how.

Los Angeles Times, 8-18:(1)24.

W. Mark Felt
Former Acting Associate Director,
Federal Bureau of Investigation

4

The FBI has a responsibility to learn of violence in advance. And that involves use of informers and hopefully authority for surreptitious entries . . . It requires an aggressive intelligence agency . . . I think over the years the FBI has very carefully balanced the rights of individuals against the right of society . . . I think it's a very serious mistake to believe that any individual can have total privacy . . . We also want him to have total safety, and the two have to be balanced . . . The only way to provide privacy in a society as complex as ours would be to put the person out in a desert somewhere and leave him completely alone.

Interview, Washington/
The Christian Science Monitor, 9-29:26.

Gerald R. Ford
President of the United States

5

[On capital punishment]: Of course, the maximum penalty should not be applied if there is duress or impaired mental capacity or similar extenuating circumstances. But in murders involving substantial danger to the national security, or when the defendant is a cold-blooded killer, the use of capital punishment is fully justified.

Before South Florida chapter, Federal Bar
Association, Miami, Feb. 14/
The Washington Post, 2-15:(A)1.

1

[On the drug-abuse problem]: The suburban housewife, the worker on the assembly line, the white-collar professional—nobody is immune. I pledge to you tonight that I will spare no effort to crush the menace of drug abuse. Frankly, despite all the rhetoric of recent years, I do not believe that we have yet succeeded in making it tough enough for drug traffickers. As far as I am concerned, the people who traffic in hard drugs are nothing less than merchants of death and should be put behind bars for a long, long time.

Law Day address, Dallas, April 9/
The New York Times, 4-10:10.

2

We hear more about the rights of juvenile offenders than about the rights of their victims. Forty-five per cent of all violent crime is now perpetrated by juveniles. If they are big enough to commit vicious crimes against society, they are big enough to be punished by society.

Before National Association of Chiefs of Police,
Miami Beach, Sept. 27/ The Washington Post,
9-28:(A)3.

3

[The record of gun control] does not show that the registration of a gun, a handgun, or the registration of the gun owner has in any way whatsoever decreased the crime rate or the use of that gun in the committing of a crime. The record just doesn't prove that such legislation or action by a local city council is effective. What we have to do— and this is the crux of the matter—is to make it very, very difficult for a person who uses a gun in the commission of a crime to stay out of jail. If we make the use of a gun in the commission of a crime a serious criminal offense, and that person is prosecuted, then, in my opinion, we are going after the person who uses the gun for the wrong reason . . . Those are the people who ought to be in jail. And the only way to do it is to pass strong legis-

lation so that once apprehended, indicted, convicted, they'll be in jail and off the streets and not using guns in the commission of a crime.

Debate with Democratic Presidential nominee
Jimmy Carter, Williamsburg, Va., Oct. 22/
Los Angeles Times, 10-23:(1)25.

Joseph Freitas, Jr.
District Attorney,
San Francisco County, California
4

[On crime in his city]: We are fighting a cavalier attitude toward offenders. We've always been a liberal, progressive city, and that is a worthy goal. But in terms of law enforcement, it doesn't work very well.

Newsweek, 12-20:34.

Charles R. Gain
Chief of Police of San Francisco
5

No police department in a high-crime city can be expected to stop crime; that is, to reduce it. Witness Oakland; Washington, D.C.; Gary, Indiana; or Detroit—wherever it may be. It's the underlying factors that give rise to criminality, [factors] over which the police have no control. Our responsibility, then, given the resources we have, is to do the best we can to bring about the greatest efficiency and effectiveness to impact on the most serious crimes.

Interview/
San Francisco Examiner & Chronicle, 5-2:(A)16.

Charles E. Goodell
Chairman,
Committee for the Study of Incarceration;
Former United States Senator, R—N.Y.
6

[On the U.S. system of criminal punishment—from courts to prisons]: I think it's quite absurd and quite inhumane. But other adjectives might apply—unjust, erratic,

WHAT THEY SAID IN 1976

(CHARLES E. GOODELL)

wasteful, unpragmatic . . . This country has the highest prison-term rate in the world as well as the highest crime rate. Therefore, there doesn't seem to be a correlation between long sentences and crime reduction . . . The deterrent payoff is much greater for increasing the *certainty* of punishment rather than its severity.

Interview/
San Francisco Examiner and Chronicle,
1-25:(This World)22.

Harold H. Greene
Chief Judge, Superior Court of the
District of Columbia
                                                    1

Police are mainly interested in arrests. Prosecutors and defense attorneys want to win their cases. Courts are the arbiters. And corrections officials want to rehabilitate criminals and get them back into the community as soon as possible. One might say they all have two common goals—to cut crime and render justice. But there's a tension between the two that explains why some people have to go free.

U.S. News & World Report, 5-10:40.

Herman Kahn
Director, Hudson Institute
                                                    2

. . . the American public clearly recognized from the mid-'60s on there's an increase in crime. They were told that everybody who talked about law and order was a bigot, but they could see that that was wrong, because there was an increase in crime. I'm not saying the American public doesn't have a good deal of bigotry in it. It does—but that's not why they were worrying about law and order.

Interview, Croton-on-Hudson, N.Y./
The Dallas Times Herald, 2-22:(B)3.

Kenneth Kaunda
President of Zambia
                                                    3

What use are prisons if they are not going

to help prisoners change their attitude to society? What use are they if they do not teach the inmates useful skills that they can use once they have been freed? The primary responsibility of the prison services is to bring the stray sheep back to the fold.

Interview/
The New York Times Magazine, 3-28:63.

Clarence M. Kelley
Director,
Federal Bureau of Investigation
                                                    4

I'm not saying that our nation is in imminent danger of being devastated by terrorists, but I do consider terrorism a very real and growing problem. And I think it's vital that Americans involve themselves in the effort to stem terrorist acts before they reach crisis intensity . . . Make no mistake about it—the terrorist is . . . committed to an extent that is difficult for rational people to comprehend. They are not political activists. They are criminals. And their number seems to be growing.

At news-media meeting sponsored by
American Security Council, Washington, Jan. 13/
The Washington Post, 1-14:(A)4.

                                                    5

For many people in America today, crime is a business, a full-time job, the principal source of income. They make a living by crime. They find in crime a lucrative profit . . . Criminals feel the odds are largely in their favor . . . Our crime statistics plainly tell us that a high percentage of the criminals beat the risk. They are able, for a variety of reasons, to make a profit out of their crimes.

U.S. News & World Report, 2-9:50.

                                                    6

Maybe some of [the late FBI Director J. Edgar Hoover's] programs were wrong—certainly you can't justify some of them—but he was honest and he devoted his entire life to the organization. You have to be careful in a job like this because, after you've been in it 48 years, you begin to think there is not much anybody can tell you. I think Hoover did the best he could. He just stayed around too long. Ten years is plenty in this job.

People, 5-3:25.

1

The men and women of the FBI knew all along that the FBI never was an organization of immortals with infallible judgment; but we are just as certain that neither is the FBI an organization of demons obsessed with grinding up American rights and sweeping them into the gutter. Yet the brilliant spotlight of publicity has been relentlessly focused upon the warts and blemishes of the FBI's past to the exclusion of anything commendable the FBI has accomplished in the past or present—to the exclusion of any progress we have made to insure the FBI operates in the manner the people desire. We have answered all of the questions regarding the FBI's past activities, some of them repeatedly. We are still answering them. We have responded to demands to amend or discontinue techniques considered improper in today's climate of opinion. In that regard, we have, and are, co-operating fully in drawing up guidelines for the FBI's investigations. I have no desire for my grandchildren to grow up in a totalitarian police state. And neither do I want them to grow up in a defenseless and vulnerable society—a society whose principal Federal peace-keeping agency is so discredited that it is impotent against foreign and domestic enemies of democracy. I say it is time for the FBI's critics to concentrate on the FBI present and the FBI future. Yes, there have been errors; but I say it is time to permit the FBI and all peace-keeping agencies to get on with their mission of trying to assure the continuance of orderly, constituted government with peace and tranquility for the American people.

At Westminster College, Fulton, Mo., May 8/
Vital Speeches, 6-15:516.

2

I can't identify anyone [in the FBI] who is

not actually loyal to the FBI. I think that they are all really loyal to the FBI; not all, however, are confident that the administration which I am now bringing into effect is the proper way to lead the organization. Some cling to traditions. Some cling to the idea that you can do anything you want so long as you follow certain ideas that were imbedded in them throughout the many years of the leadership of [late FBI Director J. Edgar] Hoover. Now I'm not critical of Mr. Hoover; I'm merely saying that it was an authoritarian type of administration. Mine is not that. And I might say that I'm confident some feel more comfortable where they have the fatherly type of control, where they have that—again—very authoritarian type of control. And until this is banished from their minds, until they accept that we're in a different era, we're in a different control situation, we're besieged by the aftermath of Watergate—until that is well recognized by them, I may not get 100 per cent support. Insofar as support to the Bureau —yes, I think that's there.

TV-radio interview/"Face the Nation,"
Columbia Broadcasting System, 8-8.

H. Stuart Knight
Director, United States Secret Service

3

[On the Service's job of protecting political figures]: In 1968, following the assassination of [Attorney General] Robert Kennedy, we were suddenly given all the candidates to cover. The Secret Service agents really got put through the wringer. There is a tremendous emotional and psychological strain, apart from the obvious physical strain. There are long hours, no sleep. The agents get keyed up and it takes a lot out of them. Military doctors have compared it to battle fatigue. One thing that generates this response is that there is very little margin for error in our business. Therefore, we demand perfection.

Interview/People, 3-22:59.

Philip Lesly
Public-relations counsel

4

It may be that the increasing visibility and

(PHILIP LESLY)

closeness to each individual of the scourge of crime is near the point where it can be focused to unify the public in defense of the law. There is, after all, a great deal of similarity between the war thrust upon us at Pearl Harbor and the war all innocent citizens are now confronting on the streets. Someone who uses violence against society has declared war on it, and any society that doesn't defend itself in a war and seek to destroy the enemy that attacks it is doomed. The American people, I believe, are beginning to realize that the necessary response calls for an all-out defense against the attacking enemy.

At Federal Bureau of Investigation
National Executive Institute,
Quantico, Va., May 9/
Vital Speeches, 6-15:526.

Edward H. Levi
Attorney General of the United States

1

There still is a strong sentiment among many judges, and others, that you really shouldn't punish criminals—that you should remove the causes of their criminality . . . [But] it's just not true that poverty necessarily causes crime. Sometimes it accompanies crime; sometimes it doesn't. Affluence somehow seems to accompany crime, too, sometimes, and sometimes not. The greatest weakness of our system is that the punishment is not certain. It's not certain because so few criminals are detected, so few are arrested, so few are convicted and so few are sentenced to penitentiaries.

Interview/Los Angeles Times, 6-14:(1)20.

2

A society that can't discuss gun control without the National Rifle Association going crazy, or that can't discuss warrant procedures for electronic surveillance without the counterpart of the NRA—namely, the American Civil Liberties Union—going crazy, is a society which is having difficulty looking at issues in a candid way.

San Francisco Examiner & Chronicle,
8-15:(This World)2.

Deborah Levy
Director, Capital Punishment Project,
American Civil Liberties Union

3

I think most of the support for capital punishment is from people who just have a fear of crime and don't know what to do about it. For these people, capital punishment sort of seems like it might work, like it might be a solution. For the politicians, it's a lot easier to take a handful of blacks and put them to death than it is to take a real look at the criminal-justice system and admit that it doesn't work.

Los Angeles Times, 8-18:(1)24.

Robert Mark
Commissioner, London (England)
Metropolitan Police

4

We [in Britain] suffer in our whole country in one year less deaths by violence than the single city of Detroit suffered in 1974. I tell you this not to suggest that we do things better than you [in the U.S.]. On the contrary, it is simply that our social conditions make our task easier than that of the police elsewhere.

Before National Press Club,
Washington, April 12/
Los Angeles Herald-Examiner, 4-13:(A)9.

5

My own feeling is that the best deterrent to deliberate, and therefore preventable, crime is not so much the severity of punishment as the likelihood of being caught and, if caught, the near certainty of being convicted, if guilty. In other words, the more effective you can make your preventive measures and your criminal justice, the less you need to think in terms of severity of punishment.

Interview, Washington/
U.S. News & World Report, 5-10:41.

6

. . . I'm totally against the death penalty even though for 29 years I supported it. I believe that the purposes of criminal justice should be the protection of society, the rehabilitation of the offender and the compensation of the victim. The objective of the criminal law should be to establish the truth so you can put these constructive and humane purposes into effect. Punishment should not be the primary objective. Britain abolished the death penalty in 1965, and I wouldn't want to go back to it.

Interview, Washington/
U.S. News & World Report, 5-10:42.

Robert Martinson
Associate professor of criminology,
City College of New York;
Director, Center for Knowledge in
Criminal Justice Planning   *1*

After reviewing thousands of studies of [criminal] rehabilitation programs between 1945 and 1967, I have concluded that the system is irrational. It is broken up into a non-system, with many little parts—the judicial, the police, the penal institution—and with no over-all plan ... The basic elements are probation and parole, both designed in the mid-19th century primarily to handle boy-scout offenders, mildly criminal types; but we are now dumping serious criminals onto this system. We now have a set-up operated on the principle that some young fellow with a master's degree in social work can actually treat 75 or more hard-bitten cons over the telephone or during a half-hour interview a month. No wonder people think it's a farce.

Interview/ People, 2-23:21.

Hans W. Mattick
Director, Center for Research in
Criminal Justice,
University of Illinois, Chicago   *2*

These same people who are hardliners on crime ... are also usually fiscal conservatives who are unwilling to pay the costs of a get-tough policy ... I think most of the public would be appalled to learn what it costs to implement a hard line on crime.

U.S. News & World Report, 3-1:67.

   3

The criminal-justice system can be likened to a vacuum cleaner: The police are the mouth and the suction power; the courts are the hose;

and the prisons are the bag. We've increased the size of the mouth and the suction power but not the other things.

U.S. News & World Report, 5-10:40.

Walter F. Mondale
United States Senator, D—Minnesota   *4*

[On FBI and CIA misconduct]: Those bastards down there [in Washington] have got to figure out that there are some rules in this society that they're going to live with, along with everyone else. They're going to tell the truth, they're going to obey the law and they're going to listen to people ... But the idea that you can defend this nation within the Constitution, under the law, and tell the truth is still considered a sort of childish, feminine position.

Interview/ Time, 7-26:22.

Norval Morris
Dean,
University of Chicago Law School   *5*

I know the push by many people now is for longer sentences; but some studies have shown that what's important is the certainty and the swiftness of punishment, not its length. There's a point of diminishing returns in the length of a sentence, after which a person becomes more likely to commit new crime than if he had served a shorter term.

U.S. News & World Report, 3-1:67.

George Moscone
Mayor of San Francisco   *6*

[On urban crime]: Putting more cops into these areas is like putting more troops in Vietnam. I hate to say it, but crime is an overhead you have to pay if you want to live in the city.

Newsweek, 12-20:34.

Thomas O. Murton
Penologist,
University of Minnesota   *7*

Prison hasn't worked because the dicta-

(THOMAS O. MURTON)

torial setting is antithetical to teaching inmates responsibility. You don't send a man to the Sahara Desert to learn to swim.

San Francisco Examiner & Chronicle,
5-9:(This World)2.

Peter J. Pitchess
Sheriff, Los Angeles County, California
1

We in law enforcement have one overriding interest in the death penalty, and that is the protection of society. When we find killers weighing the punishment against the crime and finding the odds to be in their favor, we have erred badly.

Los Angeles Herald-Examiner, 7-3:(A)3.

Lewis F. Powell, Jr.
Associate Justice,
Supreme Court of the
United States
2

[Citing a 50 per cent jump in the homicide rate in a five-year period]: It is perfectly obvious from these figures that we need some way to deter the slaughter of Americans. I use that term because that was the term that was used to describe the Vietnam war. And more Americans have been killed in the streets of this country than were killed on the battlefields of Vietnam.

At Supreme Court hearing on the
Constitutionality of capital punishment,
Washington, March 31/
Los Angeles Times, 4-1:(1)1.

3

It is . . . true that in recent years the [Supreme] Court has decided a number of criminal cases differently from what might have been expected during the decade of the '60s. But it is alarmist to suggest any significant weakening of the basic rights of persons accused of crime. A more traditional, and in my view a sounder, balance is evolving between the rights of accused persons and the right of a civilized society to have a criminal-justice system that is effective as well as fair. No other country in the world, including some with ancient and respected systems of justice, is as protective of the rights of accused persons as the United States under our Bill of Rights.

Before American Bar Association,
Atlanta, Aug. 11/
The New York Times, 8-12:18.

Dan Rather
News commentator,
Columbia Broadcasting System
4

[On the FBI]: Who polices the police? For a long time nobody, but [the late FBI Director] J. Edgar Hoover did. While Hoover created some remarkable cops and investigators, his greatest skill was as a publicist. He convinced the Bureau not to question the notion that father knows best and he convinced the public that the Bureau had no weaknesses. So far, [current Director Clarence] Kelley's greatest service has been to make it more open to outside scrutiny . . . The task of policing the police is too important to be left to one branch of the government or even the law. In the future, the FBI will have to be seen to be believed.

Television broadcast/
"CBS Reports: Inside the FBI,"
Columbia Broadcasting System, 1-26.

Ronald Reagan
Candidate for the
1976 Republican Presidential nomination;
Former Governor of California (R)
5

We must put on a back burner the idea of reforming and rehabilitating criminals and get back on the front burner the idea of prosecuting, punishment and putting them away. The cards have been stacked long enough against the police and the prosecution in favor of the defendant and defense attorneys. This situation requires rectification. The safety of the people—which is supposed to be the supreme law of the land—has been lost sight of as we have erected an elaborate and complex legal structure around the rights of the criminally accused . . . Specifically, we should make it possible for once-convicted criminals, who are rearrested, to be held in jail pending a trial. We should add an additional penitentiary term for any crime committed while an individual is out on pre-trial release, probation or parole . . . We do have a problem with lenient judges, but far worse is the problem that laws, precedents, procedures and rules of prosecution are stacked on behalf of the criminal defendant—and hence against the society he threatens. If legislation is required at the Federal level to unstack the deck against the prosecution, I am in favor of such legislation.

Before California Peace Officers Association, Anaheim, May 26/ Los Angeles Times, 5-27:(1)20.

1

Piously claiming defense of civil liberties and prodded by a variety of bleeding hearts of the society, we have dismantled much of the intelligence operations of law enforcement that we must have if we are to protect society from [terrorism]. It is time for us to remind the people of this country that the most important civil liberty is the right to be secure in their own home and streets, and not to die at the hands of a bomber, a sniper or an arsonist. It is time for law enforcement to tell the American people just what has been done to them and their civil liberties in the name of civil liberty by those who are so intent on protecting us from any over-reaction by law enforcement . . . What is the cause of crime in America? If one should listen to the Congress of the United States, its most vocal voices, you will hear the old refrain, "Poverty is the root cause of crime; eliminate poverty and you will eliminate crime." But time has proven these people wrong—dead wrong in too many cases. If you want to know why crime proliferates in this nation, don't look at the statistics on income and wealth; look at statistics on arrests, prosecutions, convictions and prison population.

Before California Peace Officers Association, Anaheim, May 26/ The New York Times:5-27:24.

2

The [Ford] Administration [gun-control] bill at present is another one of those attempts which I believe would only result in making it difficult if not impossible for the law-abiding to get a gun, but it wouldn't do anything to keep the criminal from getting one. I believe what we did in California makes more sense. We have passed a law that says if a criminal had a gun in his possession when he committed a crime, add 5 to 15 years to his prison sentence. The second law says no judge can turn a gun-carrying criminal, if he is convicted, back on the street on probation. He has to serve a mandatory prison sentence.

Interview/ The Christian Science Monitor, 6-3:17.

Nelson A. Rockefeller
Vice President of the United States   3

There is a growing tendency in our time to excuse immoral conduct because we think we understand the forces that produced it. No society can endure for long by allowing criminals to escape the penalty for their crimes by reference to some vague theory or concept of a collective guilt or personal stress or because it is alleged that everyone does it. Each of us, as an individual American, must return to the concepts of individual responsibility for our own acts upon which this society was founded.

At Bicentennial celebration sponsored by Synagogue Council of America, Newport, R.I./ The Washington Post, 5-24:(A)10.

Louis B. Schwartz
Professor of law,
University of Pennsylvania   4

People are so reluctant to administer the death penalty until every last doubt is eliminated that the procedural law gets encumbered with a lot of technical rules of evidence. You not only get this in the trial, but you get habeas corpus proceedings after the trial. This highly technical procedure is applied not only to capital cases but to other criminal cases as well. So it makes it hard to convict anybody. I believe the death penalty actually

(LOUIS B. SCHWARTZ)

does more harm to security in this country than it does good. Without it, we would be safer from criminals than with it . . . No society has ever been able to make the death-penalty system operate fairly, even by making it mandatory. Look at the British system, which operated for a century with mandatory death penalties. They found juries just wouldn't convict in many cases where the conviction meant execution. And even if the death penalty was imposed, the Home Office eventually decided who would actually be killed by granting or withholding clemency. Taking human nature as it is, I know of no way of administering a death penalty which would be fair. Not every problem has a solution, you know—and I think this is one of those insoluble problems.

Interview/ U.S. News & World Report, 4-19:38.

Milton J. Shapp
Governor of Pennsylvania (D);
Candidate for the 1976
Democratic Presidential nomination
1

I have been opposed to the reinstitution of the capital-punishment laws in this nation. I think the evidence is quite clear that capital punishment has not reduced crime nor has it reduced the tendency of people who create serious crimes. But . . . with the new makeup of the Supreme Court, being more conservative than the previous Supreme Court, the pendulum is shifting back to where it was 10 or 15 years ago. I think this is the nature of the situation in this country. We do shift back and forth on many important issues, and so I think we are going through a period of time where . . . capital punishment will be reinstated. And then I think some time in the not-too-distant future, because it will be proven that it will not be effective in reducing crime and stopping some of the horrendous problems that we have, it will once again be declared un-Constitutional.

TV-radio interview, Philadelphia/
"Meet the Press,"
National Broadcasting Company, 7-4.

Gay Talese
Author
2

Government interference in [controlling pornography] is usually justified on the grounds that obscenity is harmful to the morals of society, harmful to family life, harmful to juveniles. But in fact there is no proof that exposure to pornography leads to anti-social behavior. There is no proof that watching a pornographic movie leads anybody to go out and commit rape . . . I'm saying that the government should not have the right to deal with this "crime" that it cannot define. The Supreme Court has never been able to define what is obscene to the satisfaction of most Americans. If you are going to give the government the power to tell us what is obscene and to restrict our freedom to read books, see films or look at pictures, if you give government that kind of power over the individual, you are not going to maintain a democracy.

At debate on pornography, New York/
The New York Times, 11-21:(2)26.

Richard L. Thornburgh
Assistant Attorney General,
Criminal Division, Department of
Justice of the United States
3

There is abroad in some quarters today a notion that those of us in law enforcement should be obliged continually to justify our existence; indeed, in some cases, to actually apologize for simply doing our job. This attitude must be resisted to the utmost. There is no way for law enforcement to play only defensive ball. A civilized and orderly society depends upon observance of the law. Forceful and aggressive measures must be taken against all of those who would transgress society's rules. There is, of course, a constant necessity for all of us in law enforcement to be first among those to obey the laws—to conduct ourselves "by the book"—and allegations to the contrary should be, and are being, fully and thoroughly developed through our investigative processes. Those who criticize law enforcement and the intelligence-gathering community today remind me of the protagonist in Joseph Heller's best-selling novel, *Something Happened,* who states: "I don't like cops. Except when they are around to protect me." In truth, "protection" is the constant and essential role which these two institutions serve in our American society— "protection" of our citizens in their homes and of our country in the community of nations. One can only hope that during this period of intense scrutiny of law enforcement and the intelligence community, this fact is not lost sight of.

The Washington Post, 1-30:(A)22.

1

At present, sad to say, the benefits which an offender can anticipate from many white-collar crimes may be measured in millions of dollars. We must increase the costs to him of committing such crimes by ensuring his detection, quick prosecution, and punishment more severe than the possible mere loss of his reputation and community standing. It is hard to justify incarcerating the ghetto youth for theft of a car while at the same time putting on probation the corrupt government official or crooked attorney who has abused his position and milked the public for larger sums of money.

Los Angeles Times, 8-8:(1)24.

Morris K. Udall
United States Representative, D—Arizona;
Candidate for the 1976
Democratic Presidential nomination

2

The prison that makes every effort to rehabilitate [criminals] does no better a job than the prison that does nothing ... Prisons exist to punish dangerous criminals and to keep them out of our midst.

Before Uptown Manhattan
Chamber of Commerce, New York, March 22/
Los Angeles Times, 3-23:(1)6.

John K. Van de Kamp
District Attorney,
Los Angeles County, California

3

I believe that victims should be made

whole insofar as possible. Financial restitution should be sought to make them whole in economic crimes. And in violent crimes, we need to make sure that they have access to the state fund which now provides some recompense to victims of violent crime. More than that, our attitude toward victims needs to change. They are not statistics. They are, after all, the persons we are duty-bound to serve, and they deserve to be treated with compassion and understanding; and if we in law enforcement don't do it, no one will.

Interview, Los Angeles/
Los Angeles Herald-Examiner, 2-8:
(California Living)27.

Ernest van den Haag
Adjunct professor of social philosophy,
New York University

4

For certain kinds of crimes [capital punishment] is indispensable. Thus: The Federal prisons now have custody of a man sentenced to life imprisonment who, since he has been in prison, has committed three more murders on three separate occasions—both of prison guards and inmates. There is no further punishment that he can receive. In effect, he has a license to murder. Take another case: When a man is threatened with life imprisonment for a crime he has already committed, what reason has he not to kill the arresting officer in an attempt to escape? His punishment would be the same. In short, there are many cases where the death penalty is the only penalty available that could possibly deter. I'll go a step further. I hold life sacred. Because I hold it sacred, I feel that anyone who takes someone else's life should know that thereby he forsakes his own and does not just suffer an inconvenience about being put into a prison for some time ... As long as the death penalty existed, largely only people in the grip of passion could not be deterred by the threat of the death penalty. Now that there's no such penalty, people who previously were deterred—who are not in the grip of passion —are no longer deterred from committing murder for the sake of gain. Murder is no longer an irrational act, least of all for juven-

(ERNEST van den HAAG)

iles for whom it means at most a few months of inconvenience. Even if you assume the evidence for the deterrent effect of the death penalty is not clear . . . you have two risks. Risk 1: If you impose the death penalty and it doesn't have an additional deterrent effect, you have possibly lost the life of a convicted murderer without adding to deterrence and thereby sparing future victims. Risk 2: If you fail to execute the convicted murderer and execution would have had an additional deterrent effect, you have failed to spare the lives of a number of future victims. Between the two risks, I'd much rather execute the convicted murderer than risk the lives of innocent people who could have been saved.

Interview/ U.S. News & World Report, 4-19:37.

Richard W. Velde
Administrator, Law Enforcement
Assistance Administration of the
United States
1

Society has assigned the corrections system with tasks that are basically incompatible. In elaborating a prison policy, society appears to want to achieve the twin goals of retribution and rehabilitation in dealing with the offender. This is illustrated by the prison environment where a prisoner receives therapeutic counseling to build self-esteem, then is confined in a cell. We have community work-release programs to give an inmate a sense of responsibility, then strip-search him on his return to prison. The public says it is 100 per cent for such rehabilitation programs as halfway houses and drug-abuse centers, but doesn't want one built near his community or

house. In recent years, we also have seen an unprecedented expansion of the rights of prisoners and a concern with their humane treatment. Overlaying this, however, is an apparent desire for stiffer, tougher sentencing. All of this represents society's ambivalent feelings to try to reach the goals of deterrence, rehabilitation and humane treatment.

Before American Correctional Association,
Denver/ The National Observer, 9-11:13.

Daniel Walker
Governor of Illinois
2

Our response to crime must be predictable. Every criminal must know—and, equally important, every potential criminal must know—that if he commits a crime and goes to prison, he will pay a fixed price. Nobody—not a judge, not a parole board—nobody will give him a discount. We don't favor eliminating judges' discretion completely. We just want to put an end to the kind of discretion that makes it possible for one convict to serve four years and another fifteen years for the same crime . . . we desperately need a good criminal-justice system—a system that recognizes that prisons are for punishment, a system that is fast and firm, but, at the same time fair; a system that recognizes professionalism at all levels, and pays accordingly, and, above all, a system that acts as a realistic deterrent to crime. For 200 years, we've tried to remedy crime by preaching, by teaching, by whip and by chain, by cajoling and counseling, by therapy and psycho-surgery. Maybe, just maybe, it's time we tried justice—simple, swift and certain justice.

At Town Hall, Los Angeles, May 24/
Vital Speeches, 9-15:732,733.

Benjamin Alexander
President, Chicago State University
1

[On his being a black college president]:
Some blacks came in when I first took over
and said, "We're sorry that Chicago State now
has a black president." They said that if they
had come in to see the last president [who was
white] and jumped on the table and used a lot
of four-letter words, he would have given
them anything they wanted. I won't. I told
them, "He loved you but I love you more."

Interview/ People, 6-14:84.

Robert F. Alioto
*Superintendent of Schools
of San Francisco*
2

If a student knows how to read, how to
compute and how to write, then he will get an
ego boost that no amount of social boosting
can provide in the classroom. We are conning
our children if we think we can pass them up
grade to grade without giving them the tools
they need to get along in our society. Youngsters who don't learn the basics are doomed
to failure.

U.S. News & World Report, 9-6:50.

John E. Baldwin
*Dean of liberal arts,
University of Oregon*
3

Professors with social consciences felt it
was important to grade very, very generously.
They felt, historically and philosophically,
that the grading system was inherently corrupt, so they gave grades in such a manner
that no one would take grades too seriously.

The New York Times, 3-28:(1)42.

John Bayley
Author, Critic
4

Learning, like life itself, cannot be interesting all the time, and the greatest mistake
made by educational authorities in recent
times is to suppose that it can; that education,
like a TV program, should be a ceaseless
round of entertainment. Any teacher knows
better, and so does the hard-working student
at any age. We should remember, though,
that even while we are being bored by the hard
stuff of some exacting academic discipline,
an addiction is being implanted in us that will
last as long as we do, that will become a permanent part of our consciousness. Rudyard
Kipling observes in his autobiography that he
was bored by Latin poetry for four years, forgot it for 20, and then enjoyed it for the rest
of his life. Educational theorists who think
the young need study only what appeals to
them when they are young are all too apt to
forget the long-term purpose of the exercise.

*At Eliot Honors Assembly,
Washington University, St. Louis/
The National Observer, 1-17:14.*

Terrel H. Bell
*Commissioner of Education
of the United States*
5

Have we become so preoccupied with adult
concerns that we have neglected to give a full
measure of our attention to the children and
their needs? "Absurd," cries the educator.
"Children are what school is all about." I'm
not so sure. Every day I find on my desk
stacks of news items involving teacher strikes,
violence among adults over busing, chronic
complaints from administrators about the

WHAT THEY SAID IN 1976

shortage of money to build and buy new equipment, and so on. I don't find very much on my desk about the children themselves, how they feel about things, what they're learning and how they're getting along . . . Contemporary society has forced new issues on the education establishment.

Before Council of Great City Schools, Cleveland/
The National Observer, 1-24:11.

1

If state government is to treat all citizens fairly, how can it justify varying the quality of education according to the property-tax valuation? One district may have most of the property wealth and another may have more of the poor children. When a state fails to provide a good equalization program, some are arguing, this discriminates against students who have inferior levels of financing behind them. This is a great problem in America. It lies at the heart of educating children in the inner city, where minorities are concentrated. It is the main reason for their discontent, because their property-tax bases are eroding away. It lies at the root of forced busing out to the suburbs, because of the affluence there and the decline of the tax base in the inner city. Too many states are failing to pass good equalization programs.

Interview, Washington/
The National Observer, 8-14:4.

Charles E. Bishop
President,
University of Arkansas

2

Most professors contend that the greatest service that formal education can render students is to cultivate in them the ability to think critically. Teaching them *how* to think is regarded as infinitely more important than teaching them *what* to think. Formal education, therefore, has leaned heavily upon the theory in pedagogical practice. Heavy emphasis upon theory continues to be necessary in teaching how to acquire knowledge, hy-

pothesize about it, assess it and integrate it into our thinking. Yet it is increasingly apparent that students and the public generally desire a better balance between theoretical and empirical analysis. Therefore, more comprehensive descriptive and predictive analyses are necessary in refining and improving theory and public policy.

At University of North Carolina,
Chapel Hill, March 11/
Vital Speeches, 6-1:511.

Edward J. Bloustein
President,
Rutgers University

3

[Our college's] move into bigger-time intercollegiate athletics is a danger. It's a seductive process. [But] is it worth it? It is well worth it. Athletics identifies us as a state university in all respects in everyone's mind. There are many places we can encounter error. The point at which this help to the university and its education becomes a means for its own ends is that danger point. But an athletic program is part of the legitimate cultural outlets of the people of a state, and I think this is a cultural as well as educational institution for the state of New Jersey.

The New York Times, 11-11:55.

Derek C. Bok
President, Harvard University

4

We must acknowledge the limits of formal instruction and search for other contributions that a school can make to reinforce the moral disposition of its students. Over 2,000 years ago, Plato observed that if you would be virtuous, observe the virtuous man. Clearly, the example that teachers and educators provide by their daily conduct will have an effect, for better or worse, on the minds of the students. Institutions can also set an example. The very act of establishing a course on ethical problems is an expression of the importance that a school attaches to moral questions. But no course by itself will engender respect for very long if it occurs in an institution that fails to pay serious attention to the ethical issues that arise in conducting its own affairs. This will not mean that all students must agree with every action the institution takes, or that the institution must seek to impose its values on all who study and work within its walls. It does mean that schools and colleges must make a serious effort to grapple with the moral issues that inevitably confront them, whether in voting the shares of their endowments, carrying out their employment practices, or devising standards of behavior for their students.

Before National Association of
Independent Schools, Boston/
The National Observer, 3-27:11.

1

Undergraduate education—at least at Harvard—is not designed to prepare you for any specific vocation. We hear a lot about the competition for jobs and the pressure to get into graduate school. But you are making a mistake if you come here with the thought of gaining a degree simply as a passport to a job or a ticket of admission to a graduate school. We have a more important mission. What society lacks today is not people who are trained for skilled jobs and professional careers. What society needs are people with a sufficient breadth of knowledge to provide them with judgment, perspective and taste— people with a sensitivity for the problems of others and a strong sense of ethical principles. These are the subtler goals of a liberal-arts education, and it would be tragic if you were to disregard them in favor of a short-sighted effort to use these college years to get a head start on your professional training.

Before Harvard freshman class, Sept. 30/
Parade, 11-21:7.

2

[Defending his school's giving preferential treatment to minority-group students]: For a court to say race is of no relevance at all is unwise. [Test scores and grades] are by no means the only factor [in making admissions de-

cisions]. We're interested in educating students who will make a distinct contribution. And in a country where there are so few minority persons in leading businesses, law firms, hospitals and government agencies, we feel a minority student may make a distinct contribution, especially in a country which suffers from the racial tensions which we've experienced.

TV-radio interview/"Meet the Press,"
National Broadcasting Company, 11-28.

Ernest L. Boyer
Chancellor, State University of New York 3

The idea that it is the publics [public colleges and universities] who are safe and whose future is assured [rather than the private institutions] may have been true at one time, but it is now a myth. The dramatic new development in higher education is the fiscal crisis that has hit the public sector.

The New York Times, 2-29:(1)44.

Urie Bronfenbrenner
Professor of human development and
family studies, Cornell University 4

When teachers start acting like they know how to raise the very young better than their parents, I say—"Look out, America." Nothing can take the place of a caring family, rich or poor. Schools, on the other hand, have shown how thoroughly they can demoralize and confuse children, even in their later years.

U.S. News & World Report, 6-14:41.

James Callaghan
Prime Minister of the United Kingdom 5

There is no virtue in producing socially well-adjusted members of society who are unemployable because they don't have the skills . . . [The aim of education is] to equip children for a lively constructive place in society and also to fit them to do a job of work . . . [What is required is for children] to be basic-

WHAT THEY SAID IN 1976

(JAMES CALLAGHAN)

ally literate, to be basically numerate, to understand how to live and work together, to have respect for others and respect for the individual.

At Ruskin College, Oxford, England, Oct. 18/
The Christian Science Monitor, 10-20:7.

James O. Cansler
Associate dean of student affairs,
University of North Carolina, Chapel Hill 1

Many people who seek higher education do not want to acquire learning in the classical sense. They are here merely for "credentialing," for gaining the right to pass into a particular postgraduate activity. When learning is not the prime motivator, cheating becomes more prevalent because the student has less of a stake in his educational goals.

U.S. News & World Report, 6-14:36.

Jimmy Carter
1976 Democratic Presidential nominee 2

We've had too long in our country . . . a sharp division beteen academic and career education. In our own state [Georgia], before I became Governor, there was a complete separation between the two. At the age of 16 or 17, a person decided: I'm going to be a licensed practical nurse or secretary, or I'm going to be an automobile mechanic or bricklayer—and that was an irrevocable decision, almost, and they went from the academic instruction or civics and English and mathematics, and so forth, into the more practical aspects of life. I try to meld the two together. Also we found that quite often young people didn't have any idea what they wanted to be, so we tried to move the career education introduction down to the fifth-grade level—although those children are much too young to work. We wanted them to start knowing then what sort of lives they could lead and what the responsibility would be for the different careers. We have an inevitable shift already underway toward more practical or vocational education. I want to make sure it's

not completely divorced from learning about one's government and one's life or music, drama, literature.

Interview, Los Angeles, Aug. 23/
Los Angeles Times, 8-24:(1)16.

Paul M. Cubeta
Director, Bread Loaf School of English,
Middlebury (Vt.) College 3

Perhaps . . . our greatest responsibility as . . . American citizens and patriots is to repledge our continuing devotion as American English teachers, real or potential, to perpetuate a legacy of language in an age when the spoken word is suspected as "glib and oily art," manipulative doublespeak; when the written word—badly written, of course—is unread, and when "vibrations" are alleged to be, not inarticulating throbbing, but true communication where every sentence begins with "I feel" and ends with "you know." Teaching has always been an act of faith . . . The student whose life we illuminate, not whose soul we save to be born again, may never be known to us; but he or she may be there any time we enter a class as human model, as artist committed to the social action of teaching.

Opening address of 1976 session of
Bread Loaf School/
The Christian Science Monitor, 8-2:33.

Robert L. Ebel
Professor of educational psychology,
Michigan State University 4

[On criticism that reading-achievement-test scores are biased against poor and minority students]: What do we mean when we speak of bias in an achievement test? Surely not that the test was badly administered, or the scores misinterpreted, or the pupils unaccustomed to test-taking . . . These are not the faults of the test. They cannot be corrected by constructing an unbiased test. If the children [of minority or poverty backgrounds] do not quickly learn to communicate in standard English—to read it, write it, speak and understand it—their future years in school and as adults will surely be difficult and discouraging. The business of not only the student, but of the worker and the citizen, is conducted mainly in standard English. The pupil who scores low on an achievement test because of his unfamiliarity with standard English reveals a serious deficiency in achievement that urgently requires correction. His low score truly signals low achievement. It is not a biased measure of achievement.

At conference sponsored by
National Institute of Education,
Los Angeles Times, 1-14:(1-A)6.

Edward E. Fields
Acting Superintendent of Schools of
Kansas City, Missouri 1

[On teacher tenure]: My concern is that we must recognize teachers are people, subject to the infirmities of all people, and tenure is no guarantee of competence. The tenure system is intended to keep due process, and the fear of losing that due process for all teachers allows many who are incompetent to get by. But an administrator who allows this to happen has done himself, the children and the teacher an injustice.

The National Observer, 7-31:8.

John Hope Franklin
Professor of history,
University of Chicago 2

I have a commitment to scholarship. When I looked over the field, there were damn few [other] blacks committed to scholarship. They'd all been hooked off into some kind of deanship or presidency or something that was the end of them. I said to myself, "Isn't it possible to make it through this life as a scholar— as a scholar only, pure and simple, unadulterated, doing nothing else?" I said I think so. And I haven't been tempted since. And this is all I've ever wanted to do. I'm in a glorious rut.

Interview/ The Washington Post, 4-28:(B)4.

William C. Friday
President, University of North Carolina,
Chapel Hill 3

In recent years I have sensed a decline in the level of commitment to higher education on the part of some of our national leaders. We need to remind ourselves that the kind and quality of educational experience we provide to our young people in our schools, colleges and universities depend, in substantial measure, on our willingness as citizens to see that our educational institutions have the level of resources they need to perform effectively. In my view, the achievement of our national objectives, in the long run, will be determined by the quality and the vitality of the public schools, the colleges and the universities of the nation.

Interview/ U.S. News & World Report, 12-27:53.

George Gallup
Public-opinion analyst 4

The spread of illiteracy in this country is a scandal as serious as the spread of crime. I believe that the decline of students' verbal facility, shown by every national test, can bring about a decline in the whole intellectual level of the nation. This is true because words are the tools of thought. Certainly, abstract thinking can be carried on only by word concepts and not by picture concepts. A generation brought up in front of television sets may be incapable of performing the intellectual feats of earlier and more-literate generations. Some people believe that reading and writing are not so important today as they were in earlier times, but I think this is absolutely false. The knowledge explosion of the last three decades has made it much more important to read with speed and comprehension. Today, no one in the professional world has a way to keep up with new developments in a field except by spending a lot of time reading. And in the modern business world, with its numerous memoranda and reports, the

WHAT THEY SAID IN 1976

person who knows how to express his ideas in a cogent way has a very great advantage over the others.

Before high-school teachers of journalism,
University of Iowa/
The National Observer, 4-10:13.

John Gargin
Professor of political science,
Kent (Ohio) State University   1

Most of our students are from low-to-middle-income families, many Catholics and ethnics, and they are here to get the credentials they believe are central to admission to the Dream. Everyone does the rhetoric bit—Fascist pig this and that—but push them, and they ask you to write recommendations for jobs with banks and insurance companies.

Interview/ The New York Times, 10-17:(1)26.

Thomas E. Gatewood
President,
National Middle School Association   2

[On the emergence of "middle schools," covering grades 5 through 8]: I honestly believe that this is one movement in education that will not graduate to oblivion. It has lasted because it is a grass-roots movement built by the sweat of teachers. Whatever recognition or identity it has received has come because we have all worked as people who like kids this age; because we believe kids this age have gotten the short end of the stick, nationally, all along.

U.S. News & World Report, 2-2:42.

Theodor Geisel (Dr. Seuss)
Author   3

I came up through the Roaring Twenties, when everybody had a hip-flask, went to football games and got drunk in the afternoon. Adults despised us. We were consid-

ered a lost generation of fools. No surprise, then, that we now have going into university kids who can't write a laundry list; "bonehead" English is to facilitate only the most elementary written expression. Reading is fast becoming an old-fashioned kind of thing. Yet, to me, it is the basis of everything. If you can't write it, you don't know it.

Interview, San Diego, Calif./
The Dallas Times Herald, 12-16:(D)1.

Richard C. Gilman
President, Occidental College   4

Being a college president today is much more complicated—complicated is a very weak word—it is much more complex than it was [10 years ago]. There are financial pressures, and the various government regulations as they affect private institutions have increased tenfold and more, not in 10 years but just in the last five years. There is a tremendous array of government regulations that circumscribe what we do or how we do it. I would be less than candid if I did not admit to some concern about the increasing imposition of governmental regulations—the bad word is "bureaucracy." Many of these regulations have been derived out of an altogether different environment. They are derived for an industrial or business application, and a college is not a business in that sense . . . You don't just look at the bottom line. The job of a college president has become so much more involved and so much more complicated because you have to be sensitive to, aware of and in compliance with many different things.

Interview, Los Angeles/
Los Angeles Times, 2-15:(5)1.

5

[On the differences between "education" and "training"]: We are not involved in vocational training. We're involved in something which we'd like to think of as having much broader implications . . . something that is not irrelevant to jobs but is really relevant to the kinds of people that a liberal education is supposed to provide. These are people who somehow here have learned to learn, people who somehow develop a breadth of understanding, a sensitivity to other people, a capacity to think for themselves, the kind of people who are both interested—that is, interested in a lot of different things—and who are interesting because they can communicate something of the variety of their own knowledge and understandings.

Interview, Los Angeles/
Los Angeles Times, 2-15:(5)10.

Robert A. Goldwin
Special Consultant for Education to
President of the United States
Gerald R. Ford   1

I think the big problem in all of education is that we cannot accept human differences. We have to have different kinds of education unless we're going to do the ruthless, repressive thing that makes everybody the same. There's a secret wish that everybody should be "above average." And yet, "elite" is used as a dirty word and, in many places, the idea is that equality has to mean ignoring the differences of academic ability.

Interview/
"W", a Fairchild publication, 1-9:9.

John A. Greenlee
President,
California State University, Los Angeles   2

One thing hasn't changed, and that is the chief reason for a university or college: to pass on knowledge of the past and to make people ready to pass on information in the future.

Interview, Los Angeles/
Los Angeles Times, 2-15:(5)9.

Andrew Hacker
Professor of political science, Queens College,
City University of New York   3

For all our rhetoric to the contrary, we offer no honorable alternative to college. A

deep and formidable chasm rends our supposedly classless society, dividing citizens with college degrees from those lacking that crucial credential. List even our most estimable occupations for the degreeless: nursing, or perhaps police work, sales clerks and factory foremen. At best, these rank as lower-middle-class jobs having limited responsibility and little prospect for advancement. It is instructive that America, the world's archetypal democracy, provides less self-respecting space for those without college than other, less equalitarian, countries. We like to say that any American can go anywhere, even to the White House . . . Yet we add an unspoken qualifier: We mean anyone who has completed college. And college is also necessary for the mantle of successful parent. The ever-so-edged inquiry, "What's Ellen doing now?" can carry ominous overtones. Much better to be able to answer, "She's in her final year at college and will be going to Columbia Law School," than to offer some semi-audible mumble about a macrobiotic commune in Vermont. Successful parents have successful children. While college no longer brings automatic entry or advancement, it still puts you well at the head of the pack. A few years of driving a taxi does no fatal damage to a graduate. One can usually return to suits, skirts and attache cases if ever that inclination arises. Of course we send our offspring to college so they may expand their intellectual opportunities. But we send them for our own sake as well.

At Hobert and
William Smith Colleges commencement/
The National Observer, 7-10:13.

S. I. Hayakawa
1976 California Republican
U.S. Senatorial nominee;
Former president,
San Francisco State University   4

I did two important things [while president of S.F. State], neither of which I suppose I get a hell of a lot of credit for on campus. One is that I lectured widely . . . telling the story of the needs of higher education, trying to get

WHAT THEY SAID IN 1976

people to understand what the problems were ... Another thing I did ... was exploring ways in which the university could be brought closer to the business community. I was looking for sites for a downtown [campus] center ... asking how can the university better serve the needs of industry. We need an awful lot of that kind of thing on campus ... One of the great, great problems of so many of our professors is a total isolation from the town.

Interview/Los Angeles Times, 10-14:(1)25.

R. J. Henle
President, Georgetown University
1

[Saying that although it is good public policy for government to aid private education, there are too many regulations]: I believe that the sheer multiplicity, duplication, internal conflicts, arbitrariness and so forth of Federal regulations, agencies and bureaucrats have become an enslaving burden. Worse still, this machinery is used to impose on universities the personal philosophies and procedural preferences of Federal officials. The very existence of diverse, free, private institutions is endangered.

U.S. News & World Report, 7-5:93.

Terry Herndon
Executive secretary,
National Education Association
2

I cannot speak for all [labor] strikes in the public sector, but there are several things I can say assuredly about teachers' strikes. One, teachers don't want them. Some school boards may welcome them—there were, I'm told, some prominent persons in New York City who hoped that the schools there would stay on strike for a long time, apparently in the conviction that it would balance the city budget. But, believe me, teachers will go on strike only as a last resort, only if they see no reasonable and logical alternative. Further, the strikes generally reflect the morass of broken promises, the massive layoffs, the threat of further reductions, and the general

insecurity that beset the teaching profession last year. These circumstances are forcing more and more teachers to take the last resort. In 1972 there were fewer than 75 teacher strikes and more than 200 last year. And finally, if they see their cause as vital, and if public management persistently refuses to bargain, it makes precious little difference if there is an anti-strike law or not; teachers will strike. The most important lesson from all this is that teachers want to be treated like the citizens and professionals they are. Teachers care about their product: an educated America. They are not custodians, a role that in too many instances over-crowding and often violent classrooms have forced them to play. They want two things, essentially: to teach the best ways they know how and to live with reasonable economic security.

Before Resurgens, Atlanta, Sept. 14/
Vital Speeches, 10-15:12.

Walter E. Hoadley
Executive vice president and chief economist,
Bank of America
3

Our educational system has been less than successful in preparing young people for the realities of life. We tend to keep them in school as a matter of parental pride and prestige, so that they stay in school longer than the youth of most other countries, and their idealism isn't tested with the experience of real life. Too many people come out of high schools and colleges with black-and-white ideas and find—to their utter amazement and dismay— that most of life is played in the gray zone. By the time I was 25, I'd had a little work experience. I didn't have to learn what a boss was. I didn't have to learn that not everybody loves everybody, that you have to take orders, and that you have to discipline yourself.

Interview/U.S. News & World Report, 11-1:87.

Harold L. Hodgkinson
Director, National Institute of Education
of the United States
4

[Reports of the decline in student achievement have] been presented as if the schools are going to hell in a hand basket, [that] they can't do anything right [and that] students aren't learning anything. I think it's just not a fair criticism. That's not to say for a minute that there are not areas [for] improvement in the schools. But certainly if you compare them to almost any other educational system in the Western world and consider the magnitude of the job that they're asked to do and the fact that the American family has gone through some enormous changes, and that we can't rely on parents to prepare students for schools in terms of values and attitudes, the schools have done, I think, an incredibly good job.

The Washington Post, 8-31:(A)6.

1

The educational system must come to grips with the skills needed in American life—not only for work, but for the quality of one's life. The issue is not going back to basics, in the sense of reading, writing and arithmetic. All the data we have so far leads to the conclusion that we need more emphasis on problem-solving . . . students know how to read words much better than they did in the past. What they don't know is how to set up and solve problems.

Interview/
Los Angeles Herald-Examiner, 12-2:(A)6.

David W. Hornbeck
Maryland State Superintendent-
designate of Education
2

[Saying schools need outside help in providing work experience for students]: I believe every youngster ought to be able to acquire a salable skill by the time he or she completes high school if he or she chooses. Even the so-called academic student should have [on-the-job] vocational trade experience during the school years . . . Actual competence results in part from simulated or real experience. That experience cannot be provided by the school alone.

Baltimore, June 14/
The Washington Post, 6-15:(C)6.

Matina S. Horner
President, Radcliffe College
3

As did our forefathers and mothers, I have incredible faith in education. From the very beginning, this nation placed a premium on education as the essential foundation for freedom and equality. It was the base upon which rested the hope of actually realizing the principles and dreams that motivated the American Revolution and shaped the Declaration of Independence. Ignorance and slavery were synonymous. For Horace Mann, education was the great equalizer and balance-wheel of society. For Jefferson, education readily accessible to all young people regardless of their parental background was "the keystone of the arch of government." He had a strong conviction that democracy depended on the integrity of an educational system and its capacity to produce what he called an "aristocracy of talent." Education was viewed as a personally as well as a collectively liberating force. As the nation grew socially and technologically more complex, education became increasingly central as a means for gaining access to most of the valued opportunities in our society and became, in fact, the ultimate *sine qua non* of the fulfillment of many of our national goals as well as personal aspirations. In many ways, then, the participation of men and women and other groups in the educational system, particularly at the higher levels, is a sensitive index of the value and position they have in that society.

Baccalaureate address/
The Christian Science Monitor,
9-16:31.

Mary Evelyn Huey
Acting president,
Texas Woman's University
4

I am deeply in favor of the concept of an all-woman's college. We should continue the pattern of maintaining purity in undergraduate programs. I think it is important in so-

WHAT THEY SAID IN 1976

(MARY ELLEN HUEY)

ciety that there be choices. I am saddened to see the disappearance of all-male schools just as I am disappointed to see the end of all-female schools.

Interview, Denton, Tex./
The Dallas Times Herald, 5-25:(B)6.

Robert M. Hutchins
President, Center for the
Study of Democratic Institutions

1

I think we do reasonably well in getting everybody into school, and keeping them there as long as possible. The question of what happens to them in school is very seldom raised; but if you went around to an American parent and said, "I understand you are sending your child to school, or college, or to the university because of your respect for the mind," he or she would completely deny any such un-American accusation. Parents send their children to school, or college or university in order to have them get ahead in life. We take degrees seriously, but we don't take education seriously.

Television interview/Center Report,
February:21.

2

... if you don't care anything about education, a university presidency is a great job. I'm serious. If you don't want to do anything except keep an institution going, enjoy a dignified position, have access to the press, subsidized housing, automobiles, and a good salary, a university presidency is great. But if you want to do something about education, in the first place, you'll never be chosen; and in the second place, you couldn't do it.

Television interview/Center Report,
February:22.

Jesse L. Jackson
Civil-rights leader;
President, Operation PUSH
(People United to Save Humanity)

3

What urban education needs is not more

money but more parents willing to give their children care, motivation and chastisement—the will to learn. Do that, and these other things will become less of an issue—things like budgets, or such nonsense as black children can't learn from white teachers.

Interview, Washington/
The Washington Post, 1-30:(A)23.

4

When I go in the schools, I see students with hats on, radios blasting and writing on the walls. When I see those things, I know there's no moral authority in those schools. Without moral authority there's no discipline, and where there's no discipline there's no education.

San Francisco Examiner & Chronicle,
5-2:(This World)2.

J. Martin Klotsche
Chancellor emeritus,
University of Wisconsin, Milwaukee

5

... the virtual elimination of illiteracy has not resulted in our discovering a more intelligent way of living. For if a correlation had existed between literacy and intelligence, we should have witnessed in our lifetime a decline in war, national strife, crime, delinquency and general social maladjustment. Yet quite the reverse is the case. For this literate 20th century of ours has also been the bloodiest and most turbulent. Thus, while we are among the most highly educated people in the world, yet we appear incompetent to deal with many of the major problems that are immediately at hand. Technologically we have moved forward at the terrifying speed of a supersonic plane, but in our social behavior we are still moving at the slow pace of the oxcart. Our technical competence is superb but we have neglected other competencies of greater importance. For many of us the times are like "a tale told by an idiot, full of sound and fury, signifying nothing." In this context we can properly ask: For what do we educate? To answer this question we need to re-examine our goals and redefine our objectives. The two great casualties of our time have been *truth* and *conscience*, and unless we can restore these two values to a position of primary importance our educational efforts will have been in vain.

At Northland College commencement, May 30/
Vital Speeches, 9-1:682.

Leon Lessinger
Dean, College of Education,
University of Southern California 1

Human beings are full of emotion, and the teacher who knows how to use it will have dedicated learners. It means sending dominant signals instead of submissive ones with your eyes, body and voice.

Newsweek, 3-8:58.

William N. Lipscomb
Professor of chemistry, Harvard University;
Winner, 1976 Nobel Prize in chemistry 2

Questions from first-year students often startle me. I tell them: "Well, I've never thought about it just that way. Let me try to answer you . . ." That it is important to do research to keep your teaching fresh is recognized generally. But to me it is also important to do teaching to keep my research fresh.

Interview, Cambridge, Mass./
The Christian Science Monitor, 11-19:29.

Norman Lumian
Professor of history, Orange Coast College,
Costa Mesa, Calif. 3

[Criticizing the use of television programs for student credit]: I am very much in favor of face-to-face teaching. Television might augment and supplement a course, and for older people it's a real blessing. But for young minds that can interact, I think it's a complete prostitution of the entire educational system.

Time, 4-26:33.

Michael P. Marcase
Superintendent of Schools of Philadelphia 4

There seems to be a clear mandate from parents that says: "Forget the coddling, and let's concentrate on quality education, respect and decency in the classroom." Today's trend is toward more structure, greater discipline, standards, competency and moral values.

U.S. News & World Report, 9-6:50.

Charles McC. Mathias, Jr.
United States Senator, R—Maryland 5

I cannot help but wonder whether, by continuing and expanding the school lunch program, we aren't witnessing, if not encouraging, the slow demise of yet another American tradition: the brown bag . . . Perhaps we are beholding yet another break in the chain that links child to home. The brown bag, of course, had its imperfections. While some kids carried roast beef sandwiches, others had peanut butter. I have no way of knowing if all of those brown bags contained "nutritionally adequate diets." But I do know that those brown bags and those lunch pails symbolized parental love and responsibility. In our desire to see to it that all children in America are adequately fed, housed, clothed, educated and kept healthy, let us take care that we do not undermine the role of parents in the lives of their children.

Before the Senate, Washington/Time, 8-16:20.

Jean Mayer
President, Tufts University 6

In this tense, ever-more-crowded, ever-more-interdependent world, decision-making is becoming more and more crucial. I do not hesitate to proclaim that the future of the human race will depend on whether our graduates, citizens of the greatest democracy on earth, members of the most highly developed technological society in the world, have the wisdom and the courage to make, and to carry out, the right decisions . . . Our students will have to learn that there are always costs to decisions, financial and human. There are al-

WHAT THEY SAID IN 1976

ways alternative uses for money. There are always ripple effects, good and bad, to any decision. And there are always risks. Some can be estimated. Some can only be guessed. I submit that, in 1976, education for responsible citizenship must have a component which gives our students, primarily undergraduate, and professional as well, the chance to learn how decisions should be taken.

Inaugural address, Tufts University/
The National Observer, 10-16:13.

John F. Mee
Professor, Graduate School of Business,
Indiana University   1

Early in the century, our professors had one foot in the practical business world and one foot in the university. They taught under a mantle of realism. Today, a large number of our professors have had no business experience beyond shopping for their groceries and counting the change. They teach out of books. Many young professors want to deal in high-level business strategy or theory as though it were a social science. To me, the schools of journalism, law, education, engineering and business are professional schools where there has to be some relationship between the instruction and the practical work the student faces on graduation.

Interview/Nation's Business, August:28.

Bill Moyers
Television commentator,
Public Broadcasting Service; Former Press
Secretary to the President of the United States
(Lyndon B. Johnson)   2

Kids have been changed by the tube [TV]. For many of them, television is their first classroom, and the teacher has to make them unlearn a great deal before he or she can teach. Television has made it harder; the authority of the teacher is shaken. I don't know if that's good or bad. But I believe that what made a good teacher in my day still makes a good teacher today—the ability to stir the mind. It's not a matter of imparting

facts; it's setting a person afire with curiosity and enthusiasm.

Parade, 2-22:4.

Daniel P. Moynihan
Professor of government, Harvard University;
Former United States Ambassador/
Permanent Representative to the
United Nations   3

We're turning out people as high-school graduates who can't pass ninth-grade reading tests, and now we say they have a right to go to the university. Well, there are a lot of people who have taken a lot of public benefits in the process of not teaching kids how to read. Including the little bastards who didn't learn how to read. What in the hell is the matter with them? If you can't pass a ninth-grade reading test, you have no right to be in the university, and you ought to say, "Well, I screwed up" . . . It's this softness getting into our culture.

Interview, New York/
Los Angeles Times, 4-22:(1)7.

Iris Murdoch
Author   4

It is traditionally said to be the task of poets to guard the purity of the language; it is also the task of the university. University leaders, in all subjects, should inculcate and defend clear usage of ordinary language, attack sophistry and obfuscating pseudo-scientific jargon and narrowing cliquish mystification, and preserve the liveliness of plain words in the exposition of truth. Every student, whatever else he does, ought to learn to write his own tongue accurately and clearly and with grace. A culture is as strong and as subtle and as profound as its ordinary language.

At Eliot Honors Assembly,
Washington University, St. Louis/
The National Observer, 1-17:14.

Ewald B. Nyquist
New York State
Commissioner of Education   5

The biggest curriculum change in the next

decade will be in citizenship education, morals education, values education or law-related education—whichever you prefer. How to teach all this in the primary grades is the problem, but it's time we realize the schools have done very little to make kids think about moral values.

*News briefing, Albany, N.Y., Sept. 13/
The New York Times, 9-14:36.*

1

Any college president ought to be in a perpetual state of resignation. By this I do not mean mournful acceptance of the universe. I mean that he must be prepared to get out. None of us must ever forget the only reason for our being in our respective offices—that we can make the important decisions that will provide students with an education which will make them richer on the inside than they ire on the outside.

*At installation of Norman Lamm
as president of Yeshiva University,
Nov. 7/
The New York Times, 11-8:37.*

Dallin H. Oaks
President, Brigham Young University

2

Government authorities need to be just as careful about regulating schools, colleges and universities—especially private institutions which provide the vital diversity and competitive alternative to government—as they are about interferences with newspapers, television, radio, or any other delivery mechanism. Government walks on eggs when it makes any kind of regulation controlling newspapers, radio or television. I contend that the government should be at least as sensitive about any rules that affect the internal operations of schools, colleges and universities, because those institutions—along with the family and the church—are the institutions in our society that develop and communicate the values that give force and meaning to all of the communications otherwise protected by the First Amendment.

*Before National Association of College and
University Attorneys, Dallas, June 18/
Vital Speeches, 9-15:727.*

Charles Pappas
*President, Mott Community College,
Flint, Michigan*

3

We're all under pressure to get rid of "frills." But if taxpayers in a community want to take a course, who is to call it a "frill"? Belly dancing is one of our most popular courses, and I suppose some people would consider it a "frill." However, the women who take it enjoy it, find it an art and think it's good physical education.

The New York Times, 3-21:(1)37.

Laurence J. Peter
Author, Educator

4

I keep hearing that teaching is something mystical—either you are a born teacher or not. But I believe there are certain essential things we can try to do through research and some objective observation to develop a competency-based teacher training program. First, a teacher should be able to teach one child before confronted with an entire classroom. When a student-teacher learns the theory of how to mold his teaching technique, according to what he observes about a child, he should, at the same time, have to practice observing a child and show that he can analyze human behavior correctly. As it stands now, a student-teacher can receive his teaching credentials without ever proving he can even distinguish between disturbed and normal behavior. Today's student-teachers take the introduction to educational psychology, school in society, general methods, then they take classroom teaching—completely unrelated to the theory. Somewhere along the line, competency is supposed to descend upon them; but teaching in the classroom is the most complex task in their whole

WHAT THEY SAID IN 1976

(LAURENCE J. PETER)

program, and they've never even dealt with one child.

At lecture sponsored by Reiss-Davis Women's Division, Los Angeles/ Los Angeles Herald-Examiner, 5-28:(B)1.

Walter Peterson
President, Franklin Pierce College
1

Education in America seems to be moving toward the realization of a long-professed idea—that education is a life-long process. In the years ahead, people of all ages will be free to drop in and out of education. Higher education is already feeling the impact of this trend. The traditional students—those between 18 and 22—will be in fewer numbers in the future. The continual decline in the birth rate determines this, but other markets will definitely expand. Adult students, those over 22, comprise the fastest-growing segment in higher education. They currently make up nearly 50 per cent of the total enrollment of nearly 11 million. In 1970, students beyond age 22 constituted 39 per cent of a total enrollment of eight million . . . Automation, shorter work weeks and fewer demanding jobs will increase the leisure time of most Americans, thus making it essential for colleges to re-emphasize the so-called leisure-time activities such as music, art, literature and so forth.

The National Observer, 10-2:15.

Neil Postman
Professor of communications, New York University
2

The one thing schools can do that TV does not is provide feedback, a give-and-take between students and teachers. There is a whole realm of reason and rationality where people sift through ideas before choosing. The schools ought to take on this function; that is, provide a dialectic where teachers and students argue points of view and learn how to analyze and where teachers can find out what students think.

The Christian Science Monitor, 4-15:17.

Ronald Reagan
Candidate for the 1976 Republican Presidential nomination; Former Governor of California (R)
3

[HEW] has injected itself increasingly into the local schools, interfering in their conduct, prodding, harassing, molding them according to bureaucratic ideas of what school should be like in an age of group dynamism. Federal control of education has become a reality. If I am elected President, it would be my intention to issue strict instructions to the Department of HEW and other Federal departments to get off the back of state and local school systems, to leave the setting of policies and the administration of school affairs to local boards of education.

Before Sacramento (Calif.) Press Club, June 2/ The Washington Post, 6-3:(A)16.

4

. . . morality, sound ethical attitudes and behavior, was regarded as a basic component of education until not long ago. However, a new view has come to prevail in the schools—the view that little differentiation should be made between right and wrong, and between good and evil, because such distinctions are irrelevant.

Before Sacramento (Calif.) Press Club, June 2/ The New York Times, 6-3:29.

Paul C. Reinert
Chancellor, Saint Louis University
5

The existence of private, church-related colleges is an absolute requisite for freedom of choice, diversity, balance, an alternative, which are all the more cherished in this Bicentennial year. *Because* the private schools are fewer, *because* we educate only two of every 10 collegians, we are now, more than ever, the crucial counterweight against a monolithic state system. The public generally and the public institutions specifically need us if we educators are to be successful in discharging our common responsibility as guardians of academic integrity and freedom. The president of Johns Hopkins stated it well a short time ago when he noted that in the hysteria of the McCarthy period, state universities could be required to institute loyalty oaths and to strive for intellectual conformity, but the independents were free to protest and to resist—and many of them did. And on this temptation toward intellectual conformity, I always like to quote Kingman Brewster, president of Yale: "You and I know that there is a correlation between the creative and the screwball. So we must suffer the screwball gladly."

*At Inauguration of William Kinnison as
president of Wittenberg University,
Springfield, Ohio/ The National Observer, 3-6:11.*

Terry Sanford
President, Duke University 1

The avalanche of recent government regulations threatens to dominate campus management. At the present rate, it is not difficult to imagine a day when faculties and administrators spend all their time filling out government forms. It is just preposterous. The regulators must be regulated.

U.S. News & World Report, 7-5:93.

David S. Saxon
President, University of California 2

I believe we can ill afford the risk of foreclosing the maximum cultivation of . . . knowledge and understanding simply because it seems not to be required for immediate vocational purposes. America's vision for 200 years has been longer than that. Over-education is an idea whose time must never come.

*San Francisco Examiner & Chronicle,
8-1:(This World)2.*

William E. Simon
*Secretary of the Treasury
of the United States* 3

[On corporate donations to educational institutions]: It is fundamental to America's strength to continue that generosity. I would advise, however . . . to take a close look at the teaching policies of those schools and foundations being considered for corporate gifts. Find out if the subjects of that generosity are really assisting in the fight to maintain our freedoms or if they're working to erode them —and [I] urge that judgments be made accordingly. Otherwise, the largesse of the free-enterprise system will continue to finance its own destruction.

*Before New York chapter,
Public Relations Society of America/
The Dallas Times Herald, 2-27:(B)3.*

4

The erosion of academic independence during the last 20 years has been directly related to increasing Federal financing and controls which have made higher education one of our most regulated industries. Like any other institution experiencing severe financial strains, colleges and universities are losing their independence as policy-making authority is increasingly shifted to absentee government creditors. An American Council on Education study of a cross-section of colleges and universities showed that institutional costs of implementing Federally mandated social programs had, depending on the specific school analyzed, increased 10 to 20 times in the last decade and now equal "the equivalent of 5 per cent to 18 per cent of tuition revenues" . . . Even more serious is the impact of Federal control over the curriculum and faculties of colleges and universities which have historically held the trust of the general public because they believed that the promulgation of learning and the search for truth were their primary objectives. When government regulators force schools to adopt other goals with even higher priorities, in return for financial assistance, then educators will inevitably surrender institutional responsibilities. No matter how desirable these other priorities are, if the government regulation disrupts the primary goal of education—the promulgation of learning and the search for truth—then it is clearly time to reject such controls.

*At Hillsdale (Mich.) College, Nov. 12/
Vital Speeches, 12-15:130.*

WHAT THEY SAID IN 1976

Joseph J. Sisco
President, American University

1

In the 1960s, the United States went through a period of institutional redefinition. In the universities, one of the forms that redefinition took was a challenge to the ownership of the university. Many students asserted their claim on the grounds that they were its primary constituents. Many faculty, taken aback by this, asserted their claims, arguing that they provided the skill and experience without which no university could exist. Trustees and regents invoked their mandated responsibilities. And so the debate went, with the most important consideration—the educational process—often ignored. Every university is, indeed, owned. There are proprietors. You will not find their names in the front or back pages of your catalogue or on class roles. They are not students, alumni, faculty or regents. Rather, they are Plato and Aristotle and Sophocles; Confucius and Buddha; Moses and Jesus and Muhammad; Michelangelo and Shakespeare; Newton and Franklin; Frederick Douglass and Lincoln; Curie and Einstein; Darwin and Wagner; Hemingway and Paderewski; and so many others. These are the proprietors of this and every university. The rest of us hold the university in trust for them and for those whose names have yet to join this timeless throng. May this always be so.

Inaugural address, Oct. 21/
The Washington Post, 10-24:(B)6.

George Smith
President,
National School Board Association

2

Most of [the nation's school-board members] are of a mind that education is not supposed to be involved in politics. But that is a myth. Every time somebody votes for one of them and makes them a school-board member, that's politics. Today, with the fiscal crunch the schools are in, with collective-bargaining bills for teachers being passed, we have to bind ourselves together like the doctors and lawyers and gun-control people.

San Francisco Examiner & Chronicle,
4-18:(This World)2.

John Trimble
Professor of English,
University of Texas, Austin

3

The bulk of American students today are coming up to college educationally stunted. However bright and sophisticated they are in many other respects, in basic English they give the impression of having skipped high school altogether. They are often incapable of distinguishing between a sentence and a fragment. They don't know how to locate the subject of a sentence, the direct object, even the verb, let alone tell whether the verb is active or passive. They haven't a clue as to how to diagram a sentence. They use commas interchangeably with semicolons, and dashes interchangeably with periods. They blithely confess, "I never was much of a speller," as if that excused them from the inconvenience of having to consult a dictionary. Their ear is as untrained as their visual memory. Many of them can't even hear a jarring disagreement between a singular subject and a plural verb . . . They paragraph whenever the mood strikes them. Their ideas circle and collide with each other. They unconsciously wander back and forth between the past and present tense. On and on it goes . . . Now, if language were not our principal tool of thinking, and if it were not also our principal tool of communicating, and if our democratic system were not utterly dependent on the literacy of its citizens, then this state of affairs might merely be viewed as unfortunate. But as it is, it's frightening.

Before University of Texas alumni, Dallas/
The Dallas Times Herald, 2-1:(B)3.

Roach Van Allen
Professor of elementary education,
University of Arizona, Tucson

4

Television is forcing us to look at alternatives to teach. In many cases, television enhances the reading program because television becomes part of a child's total experience. There is a verbal response to TV shows. Whether a child is from an English-speaking home or not, we can't find one anywhere who doesn't instantly recognize the word "MacDonald's," or "Disney," or "Coke." You see, there is no need for TV to diminish the need to read, but quite the opposite.

Los Angeles/
Los Angeles Herald-Examiner, 5-19:(B)3.

Judson C. Ward, Jr.
Vice president,
Emory University
1

We tend to overemphasize the role of the teacher to the neglect of the learner. Too often the teacher is portrayed as a potter seated at the wheel, molding the mind of the student, producing a finished product. The great teacher is better compared to a gardener. He nurtures, cultivates and stimulates a mind **and spirit** to grow according to its own unique **potential.** Great teachers use their talents to arouse students to action. They cajole, taunt, provoke, flatter, inspire or whatever they think will work to send the learner to the library, to his books, to the laboratory, the computer, the field or bedside in order to test hypotheses, clarify issues, satisfy curiosity, or whatnot. Great teachers themselves continue to learn and share the excitement of learning with students. Teachers and students interact as a community of scholars.

At Emory University, Sept. 23/
Vital Speeches, 12-15:158.

George Weber
Director, Council for
Basic Skills, Washington
2

The purpose [of education] should be the intellectual development of the individual. But the purpose actually varies from school to school, and it varies a great deal . . . What a school's purpose is and what its administrators say it is are two different things. Ask a principal what the purpose of his school is and he'll look at you as if you were kind of silly. Then he'd say the purpose is to educate children. Of course, he's dodging the question. Nowadays, he may talk about basic skills. He wouldn't have, 10 years ago . . .

Really, the question is what schools do. Some cancel an afternoon of studies because that's when the football game is being played. Draw your own conclusions about the purposes of those schools. Some inner-city schools are so poor in terms of student achievement that the only function they can perform well is a custodial one. They keep the kids off the street and out of the rain. They may also provide dental examinations. Oh, and lunch. In some schools, breakfast. And that's education . . . There's a great struggle going on with career education. People say too many are going to college. What does a guy who will work in a service station need to study Shakespeare for? Obviously, he doesn't need Shakespeare to pump gas. But if he's to be an educated person, perhaps he does need Shakespeare.

Interview/
Los Angeles Herald-Examiner, 12-2:(A)6.

Clifton R. Wharton, Jr.
President, Michigan State University
3

Occupying as we do positions of tremendous responsibility for the education of Americans, educators must continually reassess our role and how it is played. We should not be in the business of luring students to our campuses simply to fill up the dormitory and classroom space and to keep our faculty occupied. We must not perpetuate outmoded curricula or fail to develop the courses that more accurately represent the needs of the economic system. We must not ignore our responsibilities to counsel students—both at the time of matriculation and throughout their academic years—as to the validity of their expectations and the realities of what they will find when they leave our cloistered halls. At the same time, however, we must not be stampeded into the worst of all dangers—attempts at human engineering. When we reduce the argument over the value of higher education to its basic elements—to the "bottom line," as the business types would say—we may very well find that we really are talking about manipulation of people. Shorn of its sugar coating, most of the debate means

97

WHAT THEY SAID IN 1976

(CLIFTON R. WHARTON, JR.)

deciding who should and who should not attend college, the courses they should study, the majors they should select, and the job slots they should fill after graduation. These are decisions not made by the persons directly involved but by others. It is this danger that we must avoid at all costs.

At Georgetown University commencement/
The National Observer, 7-3:11.

Barbara M. White
President,
Mills College, Oakland, California

1

I think that the basic purpose of a liberal-arts education is to liberate the human being to exercise his or her potential to the fullest. And that means tearing down some of the walls of provincialism with which a person grows up.

Interview, Oakland, Calif./
The Christian Science Monitor, 9-8:26.

The Environment

Daniel Bell
Professor of sociology,
Harvard University
1

Take the problem of pollution. Here is where I would differ from most of the liberals and radicals. I believe very strongly in the price system; I think it's one of the best mechanisms we have for dealing with social costs. But what's happened in the past is that air and water, for example, have been treated as free goods. If something is treated as free, you despoil it. If you put a price on it, you force people to economize. In the largest theoretical sense, it's a failure to use the price system—not the greed of corporations or the stupidities of municipalities, and so forth—which is the ultimate reason for our failure to manage pollution. I think that the price system is a very useful mechanism because it dispenses with bureaucracy and with administration. It forces people to regulate themselves on the base of an impersonal rule.
Interview/ U.S. News & World Report,
7-5:Special Section.

Peter Bommarito
International president,
United Rubber Workers
2

[On chemical health hazards encountered by workers]: In 1968 you couldn't get a quorum of Congressmen to sit and listen and try to put through a bill on occupational safety and health. But our whole struggle is how do you relate technical progress to human progress. It's a struggle of human rights over property rights. There's got to be an answer to alleviate some of the suffering. What's more important—a job or your life? We wanted both, but we had to make a choice, and it was that we'd rather have vital organs than a job.
Interview, Cleveland, April 21/
The New York Times, 4-22:26.

Peter J. Brennan
Chairman, New York State Committee for
Jobs and Energy Independence;
Former Secretary of Labor of
the United States
3

Serving up a black and white choice between environment and growth is phoney. Every thinking person must come to the conclusion that we can and must use our brains and energy to strike a real and effective balance between environmental protection and growth. Without growth, we pollute our economic environment. The pollution of unemployment is as foul as that of raw sewage—it stinks, and it will poison our economy and society. It's an elementary fact of life that to clean up the environment we have got to spend massive amounts of money. Without a healthy economy, there will be neither income to tax nor the capability for people to enjoy the pleasures of a cleaner environment.
Before Pennsylvania Electric Association,
Philadelphia, Sept. 23/
Vital Speeches, 12-1:117.

Edmund G. Brown, Jr.
Governor of California (D);
Candidate for the 1976
Democratic Presidential nomination
4

A President has to project a vision, something I call planetary realism, to combine foreign-policy and ecological programs, to make people understand that we all drink

WHAT THEY SAID IN 1976

(EDMUND G. BROWN, JR.)

water out of the same well and breathe the same air. You won't need to spend as much militarily if you could promote this idea—and there's power in ideas and ideals.

Interview/Newsweek, 5-31:25.

Lester R. Brown
President, Worldwatch Institute

1

There are now four billion of us in the world, a figure we reached, according to the Population Reference Bureau, on March 28, 1976. This landmark occasion was not the cause for celebration, rather it was a matter which troubled people everywhere. The stresses and strains associated with continuing population growth in a world already inhabited by four billion people confront the urban planner on every front. Occasionally we need to remind ourselves that a three per cent annual rate of population growth leads to a nineteen-fold increase in a century. Algeria, with a 3.4 per cent rate of population growth, and with 15 million people today, would find itself with 285 million people, more than the total population of North America, just four generations hence. Similarly, if recent trends continue, Mexico, with 60 million people today, will have more than 1.1 billion people in a century. This would exceed the current population of Russia, India and Bangladesh combined. I cite these numbers not because they are expected to materialize, but merely to emphasize the urgency of reducing birth rates where they remain high.

At United Nations Conference on Human
Settlements, Vancouver, Canada/
The National Observer, 7-3:11.

Hugh L. Carey
Governor of New York (D)

2

It will do little good if we rescue our environment at the expense of our economy. Anyone who doesn't agree with that principle won't be working in this government.

Before waterfront union leaders/
The New York Times, 2-12:1.

Jimmy Carter
Candidate for the 1976 Democratic
Presidential nomination;
Former Governor of Georgia (D)

3

[On off-shore oil drilling]: I favor it. I would hope that the entire Eastern Seaboard, including all states, would take the same attitude that we took in Georgia, North and South Carolina. We formed a three-state agreement. I think each state put up about $100,000. And we did a complete analysis of our off-shore region, working closely with environmental groups, and local and state—and with the oil companies. We identified five sites where we would like to see oil brought ashore and five sites where refineries could very well be built. We used the strictest environmental criteria and we tried to route the oil pipelines which may be there in the future to prevent any damage to our marshlands and beaches and recreation areas, and we sited the future refineries between 15 and 40 miles inland in areas of our states so that it would be a minimum of damage to the environment.

Interview/The New York Times, 3-31:20.

Jacques-Yves Cousteau
Explorer

4

The ocean is sick, very sick. Marine life in the Mediterranean is getting scarcer and scarcer. Whales now number less than seven per cent of what they did at the turn of the century. Coral is dying. The marine environment everywhere is raped and torn up. If the ocean dies, mankind will die soon after.

San Francisco Examiner & Chronicle,
6-13:(This World)2.

Rene Dubos
Professor emeritus of microbiology,
Rockefeller University

5

I happen to be very active in the anti-pollution movement, not because it kills people but because I believe it makes life much less pleasant. I used to, in my early days in this country, come to this part of the country very often and I remember going to Riverside and seeing mountains around me all the time. Now even on the best days I can't see mountains. And I consider that an enormous loss. But it's not right to talk about it in terms of killing people.

Interview, Los Angeles/
Los Angeles Times, 4-15:(4)9.

Glenn S. Dumke
Chancellor, California State University
and College System
                                                    1

Some feel that we in the United States are entering a new era, an era of continued, but slower, economic growth. In this period we shall re-encounter the old economic bogeyman of scarcity in new and different forms. We shall still be an affluent society, but an affluence that must be generated and reshaped in the face of certain changes in our resource base. Population growth, depletion, and hence shortages of certain resources, increased costs of energy, urban crowding, strictures owing to the environment and to pollution are new factors which must be considered. However, our citizens have been conditioned to rapidly rising standards of material well-being, and will continue to demand these. Clearly, we will be faced more and more with hard and realistic choice-making to cope with scarcity. It will require exceptional economic maturity for the electorate to cope with scarcity in the presence of affluence. If, for example, clean air is a scarce good—how much are we as a society willing to give up to get it? Do we understand that it is increasingly costly to get cleaner and cleaner air—that it may be prohibitively costly to get 100 per cent clean air. How much are we willing to alter our life-styles to achieve our goals of clean air?

Before Commonwealth Club,
San Francisco, Aug. 6/
Vital Speeches, 9-15:728.

Jay W. Forrester
Professor of management,
Massachusetts Institute of Technology
                                                    2

Until a few years ago, economic growth in the United States was unhindered by environmental limits. Population increased, but production increased even faster to raise the standard of living. But we are now at that point where shortages are forcing a rapid diversion of equipment and energy away from direct production and into confrontation with an increasingly recalcitrant Mother Nature. Oil wells must be driven deeper. Iron ore comes from farther away. Less-productive land needs more irrigation. Greater pollution means a higher fraction of equipment diverted to filtering and deactivating contamination. The greater the load on environment, the more rapidly does the cost of pressing against the barriers rise.

Interview, Boston/
The Christian Science Monitor, 12-20:8.

Marshall Green
Coordinator of Population Affairs,
Department of State of the
United States
                                                    3

We [the U.S.] have long been the major aid-donor nation, and our assistance has enabled countries to reduce their mortality rates. This is as it should be, but we have thereby helped to promote the so-called population explosion. To be specific, we have been giving 16 times as much foreign aid to mortality-reduction programs, such as food aid, nutrition and health, as we have to fertility-reduction programs, namely, family planning . . . [We must] take into account the various sensitivities and attitudes involved. We must, for example, avoid the language of "birth control" or "population control" in favor of "family planning" and "responsibility in parenthood," with emphasis on promoting basic human rights and the well-being of mother and child as well as the economic benefits to a community and nation.

Before Commonwealth Club, San Francisco/
Los Angeles Herald-Examiner, 11-10:(C)3.

WHAT THEY SAID IN 1976

Robert L. Heilbroner
Professor of economics and chairman of
the economics department, graduate faculty,
New School for Social Research, New York [1]

In the next 10 years, I see no problem; but in the following 10 to 20 years, I think we're going to see a slowing down of growth, and that will set off intense competition over the division of economic pie . . . Two reasons: pollution and depletion of natural resources. In Japan, the pollution problem is already so great that the government is seeking a less-than-maximum growth policy. As for resources, we can't continue to use the essential minerals on which the earth's industrial plant rests at the same rate as we have for the last 20 years.

Interview/
The National Observer, 11-6:3.

John A. Hill
Deputy Administrator,
Federal Energy Administration [2]

What we in FEA are suggesting is that it is time to take a new reading. The targets set in the Clean Air Act amendments of 1970, in the light of what we know today, were overly ambitious. That act was passed at the end of the '60s when this country thought it could do anything. There was no energy crisis, no recognition of resource limitations. We were the Americans who had put men on the moon. We're in a new world now. We are faced with serious energy and economic problems. We also know that the targets of 1970 were based on inadequate health data. So it's time to take stock and insure that our drive for clean air is not aiming at goals over and above what are needed to protect health. We have too many other national problems that have to be balanced with the Clean Air Act.

Interview/ U.S. News & World Report, 7-19:35.

Herman Kahn
Director, Hudson Institute [3]

[Here] is an example of how bad the "experts" are: For a while, I think about two-thirds of the people who seem to have at least the higher educational qualifications have believed that we're running out of food, out of resources, out of energy. None of this seems to be true. Not only not true, but by a very large amount not true. You may have food shortages, or energy shortage[s], or material shortages for a short period, because you made a mistake, or something happened, but we're talking about shortages like for the next 20 years. To us, it's remarkable how what we might call this neo-Malthusian point of view has been spread around the country, mainly by the educated people, by the experts, which shows you why we're skeptical of both education and expertise.

Interview, Croton-on-Hudson, N.Y./
The Dallas Times Herald, 2-22:(B)3.

[4]

At the Hudson Institute, we argue that we haven't approached the limit [to world growth], and won't in the foreseeable future. We see no reason why the world should not be able to support a population of 30 billion people with per capita earnings of $20,000 and with all the energy, raw materials and food they need. There might be some difficulty supplying a few minerals, such as mercury or chromium, but this is negligible. There is, of course, a caveat—the development of these resources could effect ecological changes that we don't anticipate or even know about. Nevertheless, we are saying that you can give people clean air, clean water, food, energy and raw materials. If technological development should continue, it will make the task easier, but the technology that is expected to be available before the end of the 20th century will be sufficient to deal with all the problems of the next 200 years.

Interview/ New York magazine, 8-9:34.

Thomas S. Kleppe
Secretary of the Interior
of the United States [5]

I am very strong in this area of "balance." I think that is the only way we can go. I don't believe in all-out development without any consideration of the environment, nor do I believe that we ought never destroy another tree or never plow up another section of ground or whatever it might be. The balance has to exist. We have these resources. The nation needs them. I believe very strongly that we have an energy crisis and that we need to get at the development of the two most available sources to us, and that is coal and the oil from the outer continental shelf. All of our decisions so far have been along those lines, and I expect we will continue them that way.

TV-radio interview, Washington/
"Meet the Press,"
National Broadcasting Company, 2-29.

Robert W. Long
Assistant Secretary for Conservation, Research and Education, Department of Agriculture of the United States
1

The "wilderness" issue is apparently not well understood by the people of this country. While there is a certain intrinsic appeal to the idea of sealing off from the public certain forest areas, the need for those areas for timber, recreation and other uses is so great that we cannot afford to allow unlimited increases in wilderness acreage. The pressure for establishment of excessive wilderness areas comes mostly from well-meaning people with a special zeal for the wilderness idea. These "preservationist" groups often can't even stand the idea of building a road through huge, inaccessible forest areas so that the public can see their beauty. The idea of using these areas under the multiple-use concept, including managing them as scenic and recreational areas, of course is also vigorously opposed. This whole single-purpose idea, this concept of exclusive designation of vast forest areas to wilderness, to me simply does violence to the national interest, to the common good. It is not a wise public policy. This nation's natural resources are an asset to be enjoyed and used by the people—the point being that they *can* be managed so that they'll serve Americans 100 years from now just as well or better than they are serving them today.

Before American Plywood Association,
Portland, Ore., June 8/
Vital Speeches, 9-1:702.

Michael H. Moskow
Director, Federal Council on Wage and Price Stability
2

At bottom, the big questions about whether environment goals justify their costs cannot and should not be answered by economists or by Federal bureaucrats. They are questions about social values, about people's preferences. They are, in other words, political questions and must be answered in the political arena . . . The public can cope with subjectivity far better than the analyst. People know what their eyes and lungs are worth. They know how much they value parks and open spaces. They neither need nor want someone else to answer these questions for them. If government can tell the public what the price of environmental protection is and assure the public that the same protection could not be provided at a lower price, the public will tell the government when the price is too high. The question, "At what cost?" then, is not a question for me to answer, but a question to put to the fellow who sits next to you on the bus.

Before The Conference Board, New York/
The National Observer, 3-13:13.

Edmund S. Muskie
United States Senator, D—Maine
3

I believe that an economic growth policy which abandons environmental objectives would be a foolish course. The nation must have clean growth. If the price of that clean growth is to restrain the size of particular activities pending the development of new pollution-control technologies or new production procedures, then new technologies and processes can and will be developed in order to take advantage of the economies of scale. Conversely, if environmental objectives are abandoned simply to accommodate the economies of scale, new pollution-control technologies will not be developed, and the result will be environmental chaos. The facts on the record clearly suggest that subtle and often irrevocable changes are being made in man's basic life-support system as the result of un-

WHAT THEY SAID IN 1976

(EDMUND S. MUSKIE)

controlled dispersion of pollutants into the environment. Almost without exception, research into the effects of dispersal of these pollutants has given us more, rather than less, reason to be concerned. To ignore these problems because they are not fully understood is to court catastrophe.

The Washington Post, 4-29:(A)16.

1

[Saying industry must do more to protect air quality]: I've lived long enough to see us win World War II with technology never dreamed of before. I've seen us go to the moon with technology that was once considered nothing but science fiction. I'm much more optimistic than are these industry people that they can do these things if they are required to do so—if they have to meet deadlines. By what God-given right do they conclude for all the rest of us on this planet that they're going to go only as far as their developed technology today permits, and that there's no reason for them to go any further? Our air is finite, and it must be protected. It will be expensive. Our whole standard of living is expensive. So let's not pick this precious thing that is related to life itself and say that to protect it is peripheral and unnecessary.

Interview/U.S. News & World Report, 7-19:36.

Linus Pauling
Chemist

2

The population of the world will have become stable a century from now. I am not able to predict its value. At the present time the doubling period is 35 years. We have just reached 4 billion people, and it is likely that there will be 8 billion people in the world by the year 2010. My estimate of the optimum population for the world is 1 billion. By 2076 we may well be approaching that limit—from above.

Before American Chemical Society/
U.S. News & World Report, 7-5:Special Section.

Marlin Perkins
Zoologist

3

There are many indications of a lessening of wildlife. Man's population is growing so fast that it's destroying natural habitats. This is what has happened in Africa, where they're busy cutting down the trees and the local people are poaching on their own lands, killing off animals for their skins, horns and tusks. Most people have become so urbanized that they cannot understand nature. There's an interweaving of plants and animals necessary to maintain life. Let's remember that man, who is also an animal, is still evolving. I'm afraid he hasn't yet reached the moral level to realize that he shouldn't be destroying nature, polluting water and fouling the air. He hasn't yet realized that if nature is destroyed, man can't live—he's going to go, too.

Interview, New York/Parade.5-2:13.

Russell W. Peterson
Chairman, Federal Council on
Environmental Quality

4

We have lost touch with our roots in the earth. We have forgotten that it is not gold that supports us, but the soil, the water and the air. In the larger, ancient economics of our ecosystem, "cost" means more than dollars; every creature has its function and value, whether economics places a price tag on it or not. We must recognize now, before we have to cope with a biological crisis, that it is not only a narrow spectrum of the life on this planet that supports our life—not just those few living things which we can convert into bacon, eggs and toast. It is, rather, the whole wonderful, diverse bunch: the birds and the bees, the lions and the whales, the weeds and the bugs—all labor to keep us alive. They do their work for a minimum wage; nevertheless, they do exact a wage—and we must, for our own sake, safeguard the ability of the earth to pay it. We must be careful not to destroy our own life-support system by a reckless, unlimited use of our modern Midas touch ... we must try to convince our fellow citizens that we need to strike a wiser balance between man's ability to change the earth, and the importance of preserving some of it as is. We must help the man in the street realize that our gift for converting natural resources into money—if not controlled by a wiser economics than we are using now—poses a threat to human well-being. It is time for us to halt the heedless golding of America. It is time for the greening of America to begin.

At Wildlife in America symposium, Washington, Sept. 29/Vital Speeches, 11-15:77.

John R. Quarles
Deputy Administrator,
Environmental Protection Agency
of the United States. 1

Several years ago it was commonly believed that environmental goals and economic progress were incompatible. A number of industry spokesmen feared that compliance with environmental requirements would result in the loss of millions of jobs and the forced closing of numerous plants. Recent studies conducted by EPA and outside consultants have demonstrated that these fears were greatly exaggerated. According to the most frequent quarterly report on economic dislocation resulting from environmental controls, only 75 plants have been closed during the past five years—January, 1971 through September, 1975—as a result of environmental regulation. These closings—many of which were only partially due to environmental factors—resulted in the loss of only 15,700 jobs—or sixteen thousandths of one per cent of the U.S. labor force. What is more important, these losses have been more than offset by the creation of an entirely new industry—an industry devoted to the production, installation and operation of anti-pollution equipment. A recent study by a firm of Wall Street analysts for the Council on Environmental Quality found that environmental legislation has generated an industry employing over 1.1 million new workers. What this means is that, on balance, environmental controls created 70 times more jobs than they destroyed. The message is quite clear. Environmental protection is not only

good for America; it is also good for our national economy.

Before The Conference Board/
The Washington Post, 2-17:(A)14.

Ronald Reagan
Candidate for the
1976 Republican Presidential nomination;
Former Governor of California (R) 2

I think we have two groups of [environmental] extremists. There are, of course, those people on the one side who would pave the country over in the name of progress. There is an extremist group on the other extreme that wouldn't let you build a house unless it looked like a bird's nest. Now, I think there has to be common sense in-between that recognizes the people are ecology, too.

Interview/
The Christian Science Monitor, 6-3:17.

William D. Ruckelshaus
Former Administrator,
Environmental Protection Agency
of the United States 3

Congress has an almost neurotic fixation for setting deadlines on environmental matters that are unachievable. Then, by promising something we cannot achieve, we become incapable of measuring progress . . . We've got to stop labeling everybody as a good guy and a bad guy. It gets us nowhere . . . Environmentalists think that industry people are in every nook and cranny of the Executive Branch. What they do not realize is that industry leaders are frustrated, too. They feel EPA is inhabited by nothing but wild-eyed environmentalists. This does not provide for an atmosphere of compromise.

U.S. News & World Report, 1-19:53.

Russell E. Train
Administrator,
Environmental Protection Agency
of the United States 4

[On a bill to require pre-testing of new,

WHAT THEY SAID IN 1976

(RUSSELL E. TRAIN)

potentially hazardous chemicals before they can be marketed]: I do not believe that either the public interest or the interests of the [chemical] industry are well served by charges that the legislation could—in the words of one industry spokesman—"cripple" the chemical industry and give the Administrator of EPA "near-dictatorial authority over the introduction of new chemical products." The only real "crippling" that is going on is the kind this legislation would try to prevent—the crippling of who knows how many Americans every year who contract cancer, or some other affliction, after exposure to some hazardous chemical agent. Nor has it been on the "near-dictatorial authority" of the EPA Administrator that so many such agents are introduced into the environment without any effort to find out what their health effects are, much less let the public have a say about whether or not, or in what circumstances, it is willing to be exposed to them.

Before National Press Club, Washington, Feb. 26/
The New York Times, 2-27:52.

1

The oceans continue to serve as an extranational slop basin for pollutants. Oil spills from either accidental or intentional discharges steadily rise. Chemical contaminants are dumped off the shores of industrial nations. Heavy metals such as cadmium, mercury and vanadium from industrial discharges go into the sea. Agricultural chemicals, including toxic pesticides, wash off the land and down the rivers into the ocean. Nations continue to look to the ocean for disposal of radioactive wastes. When deep-sea mining begins, particularly for manganese nodules—and we are on the threshold of that activity—serious pollution problems may result. Increasingly there is a need for regulation and enforcement, and new institutions and authorities will be required. When one reads of the sinking in the Mediterranean of a freighter carrying a lethal cargo of tetraethyl lead and that the adjacent nations continue

to bicker over whose responsibility it is to do anything about the problem—if anyone's—it is not hard to conclude that present arrangements are inadequate.

Before Senate Foreign Relations Committee,
Washington, May 5/
The Washington Post, 6-1:(A)18.

2

I have long believed that, in no small measure, our energy, environmental and economic problems reflect the fact that—in one way or another—we are living beyond our means, and that no small part of our success in dealing with these problems must depend upon our ability to practice economy in the old-fashioned sense of getting the most, rather than the least, out of the energy and other resources we consume. I hope that our energy, our economic and our environmental experience over the past few years has made us sufficiently aware that the abundant resources of this land are not only ours to consume, but ours to conserve—and that they will remain ours to consume only as long as we have the good sense to conserve them.

Before Portland (Ore.) City Club/
The Washington Post, 9-23:(A)18.

Leonard Woodcock
President,
United Automobile Workers of America   *3*

Contrary to what corporate America and the Ford Administration would have the public believe, there is today more than ever before a common cause between [labor-] union members and environmentalists, between workers, poor people, minorities and those seeking to protect our natural resources. It is in times such as these that the corporate tactics of trying to make workers and communities choose between jobs and ending pollution can be most effective. It is frequently a false conflict. If we had a full-employment economy in America today, corporate polluters would have a far more difficult time with environmental blackmail.

At labor-environment conference,
Black Lake, Mich./ The New York Times, 5-9:(1)27.

Bernardo Zuleta
Secretary General,
Law of the Sea Conference   *1*

[On an international treaty governing use of the oceans and seabed]: The treaty has to be concocted like a *paella* to satisfy all tastes.

One prepares the seafood, the meat, the chicken and the rice, but they are just an assortment of separate dishes until they are blended into perfect unity and the result is *paella*—or a treaty for all.

The New York Times, 3-28:(1)13.

ENERGY

Ali A. Alireza
Saudi Arabian Ambassador
to the United States 1

. . . the ultimate economic cost of anything is what alternative supplies or services would cost. By that long-established standard, oil is still one of the very best buys available. Or if I might use another, not-at-all facetious test, how many Americans know that the cost of a barrel of oil is still cheaper than what we are charged for a barrel of Pepsi-Cola or other cola syrup? More specifically, a barrel of cola syrup costs well over a thousand per cent more than a barrel of oil. Yet which is really the more precious and should be conserved? And where are the values and priorities of those in the West who are complaining about oil prices?
Before National Foreign Trade Council/
The Washington Post, 11-24:(A)14.

George R. Baker
Executive vice president,
Continental Illinois Corporation 2

At the heart of our failure to achieve progress in energy independence is the lack of a clear-cut, decisive national policy. Instead of the emergence of a decisive national policy, we are witnessing the delay and fragmentation caused by partisan politics. There is the problem of sometimes conflicting requirements imposed by energy conservation and air-quality considerations. And there is the smothering growth of bureaucracy that accompanies government attempts at regulation. Political differences between Congress and the Administration prevented conclusive action on some strong measures which would have clearly signalled the direction of energy policy. Escalation of price decontrols on do-

mestic crude or the imposition of new fuel taxes are two such measures which might have brought results, but they floundered in political considerations.
Before National Automobile Dealers Association,
Lake Tahoe, Nev., July 14/
Vital Speeches, 9-15:712.

Howard W. Blauvelt
Chairman,
Continental Oil Company 3

When the members of the Organization of Petroleum Exporting Countries . . .decided in 1973 to increase the prices they charged for their oil, it was inevitable that gasoline prices for the American consumer would have to rise sharply . . . today we pay five times as much for OPEC oil as we did three years ago. Since 40 per cent of the oil consumed in the United States is imported, petroleum prices in this country reflect to that extent prices set by OPEC countries, over which we have no control. Even at today's higher prices, gasoline remains something of a bargain. Over the past 25 years, its price has increased only about three per cent a year, on average. Few other products can match that record. In fact, the retail price of gasoline, including taxes, would have to jump to 80 cents a gallon to consume the same share of family income it did back in 1955.
Before Columbia Business School Club,
New York, Feb. 24/Vital Speeches, 4-1:381.

W. Michael Blumenthal
Secretary of the Treasury-designate
of the United States 4

The OPEC countries need us as much as

we need them and we do not need to speak in terms of leverage or confrontation. I don't believe we should ever be afraid to defend our [energy] interests clearly and forcefully, but in an interrelated world no one gains from chaos, dissension and constant waving of a big stick. If we mean what we say and say what we mean—and above all if we develop our own energy policy on a long-term basis and have the American people behind it—we can find constructive ways of getting along with OPEC.

Interview/Newsweek, 12-27:16.

Thornton F. Bradshaw
President, Atlantic Richfield Company   *1*

. . . the U.S. is producing less crude oil but consuming more. The gap between production and demand is widening at a fast clip. The gap is being filled by importing crude oil from the Arab nations at a very high cost. We're at their mercy.

Interview, Los Angeles/
Los Angeles Times, 2-8:(Home)27.

2

It seems more clear to me than ever that the country needs establishment of goals for energy planning on a national scale. And since energy pervades the economy, I think by extension we need some kind of national economic planning as well . . . I agree that there is surely ample reason to be concerned about the concept of national economic planning. Substituting the planning mechanism for the working of the market does inject the political process deeply into the areas that have traditionally been decided by consumer preference. And yet, it seems to me that such arguments ignore the fact that national planning of a not very satisfactory kind is already a reality in this country. The question is, can a much better system of national planning than we now have be developed.

Before American Petroleum Institute,
Los Angeles, April 5/ Los Angeles Times, 4-6:(3)7.

Peter J. Brennan
Chairman, New York State Committee for
Jobs and Energy Independence;
Former Secretary of Labor
of the United States   *3*

Let's get our [energy] priorities back in order . . . it would be tragic to arrive at the brink of the 21st century only to find that we had built no bridges to cross into it. Those "energy" bridges have to be built *now*. We know the hard choices—coal, nuclear and conservation, with possible additions from domestic oil and hopefully some help from other energy sources yet to be developed commercially. We cannot be dazzled by those peddling a "free lunch" with solar power or promising employment by building a vast ribbon of windmills across the nation or advocating reverting to a wood-burning economy. These energy schemers, who are against every real energy alternative put forward, have got to realize that even "pie in the sky" takes energy to bake it!

Before Pennsylvania Electric Association,
Philadelphia, Sept. 23/ Vital Speeches, 12-1:117.

Harrison Scott Brown
Professor of science and government,
California Institute of Technology   *4*

. . . let's examine what I call the energy trap. That's the trap we allowed ourselves to fall into when we became over-dependent on one source of energy: Middle Eastern oil. We can escape from this trap if the American public accepts the fact that we're all going to have to pay more for energy from now on. We can achieve energy independence if we all share the cost of converting our vast reserves of coal into crude oil, plus the cost of adequate pollution controls, and of the development of nuclear energy, including the substantial additional cost required for improved safety. We also should invest in solar energy, initially as an alternative method of heating homes and water. All of this means that our people will have to stop spoiling themselves with cheap energy. Our people are going to be more careful how they use energy once they realize the cost is going up and will stay up.

WHAT THEY SAID IN 1976

(HARRISON SCOTT BROWN)

That, in turn, is going to decrease environmental problems.

Interview, Pasadena, Calif./
Los Angeles Herald-Examiner,
12-26:(California Living)7.

Jimmy Carter
Candidate for the
1976 Democratic Presidential nomination;
Former Governor of Georgia (D) 1

U.S. dependence on nuclear power should be kept to the minimum necessary to meet our needs. We should apply much stronger safety standards as we regulate its use. And we must be honest with our people concerning its problems and dangers . . . all of us must recognize that the widespread use of nuclear power brings many risks. Power reactors may malfunction and cause widespread radiological damage unless stringent safety requirements are met. Radioactive wastes may be a menace to future generations and civilizations, unless they are effectively isolated within the biosphere forever. And terrorists or other criminals may steal plutonium and make weapons to threaten society or its political leaders with nuclear violence unless strict security measures are developed and implemented to prevent nuclear theft. Beyond these dangers there is the fearsome prospect that the spread of nuclear reactors will mean the spread of nuclear weapons to many nations.

At United Nations, New York, May 13/
The New York Times, 5-14:(A)12.

Jimmy Carter
1976 Democratic Presidential nominee 2

. . . mandatory [energy] conservation measures—yes. Encouragement by the President for people to voluntarily conserve—yes. And also the private sector ought to be encouraged to bring forward to the public the benefits from efficiency. One bank in Washington, for instance, gives lower-interest loans for people who adequately insulate their homes or who buy efficient automobiles. And some major manufacturing companies, like Dow Chemical, have through very effective efficiency mechanisms cut down the use of energy by as much as 40 per cent with the same out-product. These kinds of things ought to be done, they ought to be encouraged and supported, and even required by the government—yes.

Debate with President Ford, Philadelphia,
Sept. 24/ The New York Times, 9-25:9.

John B. Connally, Jr.
Former Secretary of the Treasury
of the United States;
Former Governor of Texas (D, now R) 3

[Saying Congress is foot-dragging on energy production]: They're doing it so they can go to their constituencies and promise them cheap gasoline. What they're really saying is that they're delivering the most powerful nation in the world into the hands of small [oil-producing] nations who can shut down this industrial base any time they want to. They're taking a short-range, short-sighted, very selfish political view saying they're going to take care of these bloated oil companies and give people cheap gasoline. And that's cheap demagoguery of the worst kind.

The New York Times, 4-27:19.

Louis F. Davis
Vice chairman,
Atlantic Richfield Company 4

If the nation won't allow the oil companies to get into alternative forms of energy, it would force them to take their cash flow and put it into other lines of business. That wouldn't further the United States energy objectives. Coal, for instance, will require very large sums of money for its development. It's an ideal way for the oil companies to use their financial resources, as oil and gas opportunities in the United States diminish in the next 20 years. Besides, we have the people and the expertise to develop alternative energy resources.

Interview, Los Angeles/
The New York Times, 12-10:(D)5.

Rene Dubos
Professor emeritus of microbiology,
Rockefeller University 1

[On the world-wide search for new sources of energy, even though the world's oil resources will not run out for another 35 years]: We are discussing problems not of today but of the end of the century. And I find that the most extraordinary aspect of formulation of social policies all over the world. For the first time probably in the history of mankind, in all countries affected by Western civilization, we are developing adaptive responses to situations which will occur in their acute form in only two or three decades.

Interview, Los Angeles/
Los Angeles Times, 4-15:(4)9.

Brian Flowers
Rector, Imperial College of Science
and Technology, London; Chairman,
British Royal Commission on
Environmental Pollution 2

Let us not develop a reliance on nuclear power before we can do it in an acceptable manner. That doesn't mean stop. It means, for heaven's sake, stop to think!

News conference, London, Sept. 22/
The New York Times, 9-23:1.

3

It is almost impossible for the world as a whole with its presently available technology to expect the sort of growth at the sort of rates that people talk about who deduce that there will be a huge energy gap by the end of the century. The concept of an energy gap arises from the assumption that energy demand will continue to grow exponentially. If you assume that, you will always have an energy gap. But growth cannot be exponential. It never is. We are coming to the point in our understanding of technological society that the days of ex-

ponential growth are over or are at least approaching being over.

Interview, London/
The New York Times, 10-24:(1)21.

Gerald R. Ford
President of the United States 4

As I look at the [nuclear-plant] safety record, there hasn't been one incident where there has been any safety loss, other than one or two workmen. The public has had no adverse safety impact under any nuclear program ... I think we've got to proceed with the energy aspects of nuclear power. We have about 50 plants now. We hope to get 250 by 1985. I think it's possible, both from the safety point of view and from the financing point of view.

Interview, Illinois/
San Francisco Examiner & Chronicle, 3-14:(A)25.

Henry Ford II
Chairman, Ford Motor Company 5

Nobody knows how much oil is left in the ground. And the chances are that we will never find out because we will never get to the bottom of the barrel. We do know that the proven, recoverable reserve of petroleum is now at an all-time high of almost 660 billion barrels. That's a 34-year inventory at today's rate of consumption. We know that more oil is discovered each year than is used, and more has been discovered in recent years than ever before. And we know that most of the world is still untouched by oil geologists. Ninety per cent of all the oil and gas wells ever drilled in the world have been drilled in the United States. The rest of the land surface of the globe—including even the Middle East—is virtually undrilled. The same is true of the seas and the polar ice caps which cover 80 per cent of the earth's surface. Even in the United States, only a few thousand wells have gone deeper than 15,000 feet, although it is now possible to go twice that deep. The main reason more oil hasn't been found is that,

(HENRY FORD II)

with a 34-year inventory on hand, there has been little incentive to look farther or deeper for still more . . . As the easily recovered supply of petroleum is depleted, the cost of finding and extracting new supplies will go up and up . . . As the cost of petroleum rises, less will be used under boilers and more will be left for passenger cars and other vehicles. As the cost goes still higher, it will eventually become cheaper to manufacture liquid fuel from oil shale, tar sands, coal and perhaps even organic wastes. When that happens, the remaining oil will be left in the ground. In the still longer run, motor vehicles may be powered by electricity or by new fuels made feasible by an abundance of nuclear or solar electric power.

Dearborn, Mich./
The New York Times, 8-1:(3)12.

Clifton C. Garvin, Jr.
Chairman, Exxon Corporation
1

Other energy forms will certainly supplement oil, but none can be expected to totally replace it in this century. Coal is our nation's most abundant fossil fuel, but the development of coal will take time. Today, it cannot be directly substituted for all oil and gas applications. Nuclear power offers tremendous potential, but concerns over safety and environmental factors have limited nuclear-plant construction. Solar power is promising, and it's being used on a small scale; but years of technical work still lie ahead before it can become a major source of energy. Based on Exxon's forecasts, oil and gas will continue to be America's main source of energy for the rest of the 20th century.

Interview/Los Angeles Times, 7-23:(2)4.

2

Our growing dependence on imported oil puts the U.S. in a difficult situation. As we experienced in 1973, foreign governments can reduce or cut off our oil supplies without warning. Just as important is the fact that the free world is consuming oil faster than it is being found. Total free-world petroleum

consumption is now about 17 billion barrels a year. Yet discoveries have been averaging only about 15 to 16 billion barrels a year. We cannot depend indefinitely on growing amounts of foreign oil to make up for our own petroleum-production shortfall. Energy is simply too important to our economy and living standards to rely increasingly on others for our supplies.

Interview/Los Angeles Times, 12-17:(1-A)7.

Kenneth A. Gibson
Mayor of Newark, New Jersey
3

The reason we have cities is because we need them, and we are going to need them all the more as the energy situation grows worse. Even the oil in the Middle East may run out by the end of this century at the present rate of consumption. That is not so far off. Here we go on building highways and big cars— usually one passenger to a car, driving 15 miles one way in the morning and 15 miles the other at night. In an energy shortage it is more efficient for people to live and work in cities. So cities are more needed than ever on that basis. Wait until the real energy crunch comes! The American people haven't realized yet what people in other countries pay for gas and fuel. Wait until it hits! I have just come from a visit to Israel, where gas is $1.50 to $2 a gallon. We thought things were bad a couple of years ago when people had to stand in line for gas [in the U.S.]. I am talking about a crisis when you don't even get in line because there isn't any gas. We don't understand yet what being without energy is like; but, when we do, then cities are going to be very, very attractive because it isn't going to be much fun riding a bicycle 15 miles in the morning and 15 miles out at night, as people can now do in their big cars.

Interview, Washington/
Los Angeles Times, 12-14:(2)7.

Harold J. Haynes
Chairman,
Standard Oil Company of California
4

There's no reasonably economic alternative to oil and gas on the horizon. We really have only two options: Increase our dependence on oil imports or accelerate exploration for our domestic oil potential. As far as I'm concerned, the second option is the only one that makes sense. Today, we're importing about 40 per cent of the oil we consume. Since there is a great deal of oil in the free world, we could readily increase our imports. But this would only make the U.S. more vulnerable to political upheaval abroad. And if we were to have another embargo, the economic effects would be severe indeed. The last embargo [in 1973-74] was, by and large, not much more than an inconvenience. But we weren't 40 per cent dependent then—as we are now—on foreign oil. Some experts estimate that as many as two million Americans would be put out of work if another embargo took place today. Consequently, I'm convinced we should be stepping up leasing of our outer continental shelf for oil exploration, getting out from under needless government controls and regulations, and getting on with the primary job of making the U.S. reasonably self-sufficient in energy.

Interview, San Francisco/
Nation's Business, March:49.

Henry M. Jackson
United States Senator, D—Washington;
Candidate for the 1976
Democratic Presidential nomination 1

[On his ideas in the energy field]: We would move on the large scale to convert coal and oil shale to oil and to develop our geothermal. In the infinite area, I would give the top priority to solar energy and to fusion and hydrogen . . . I'm talking about the creation of new companies. I'm talking about joint ventures on the part of government and industry. I'm talking about guaranteed loans which the White House rejected. When you build a huge plant, when we built Grand Coulee Dam—after all, we start getting income from that. When you build a coal gasification plant, you get revenue back . . . How do you generate enough capital to do what

you need to do in the next 15 years to provide, in effect, investment totalling $2-trillion? That can only be done with the help and cooperation of the Federal government.

Interview, New York/
The New York Times, 3-30:20.

Herman Kahn
Director, Hudson Institute 2

My guess is that in the future there will be 10 large nuclear reservations in the United States. These will be far from the cities, each occupying 10,000 acres—1,000 times larger than today's plants—supplying nuclear energy for the whole country. Fuel processing and recycling will be done on the reservations. It is easier to protect a few areas—and you are not moving nuclear fuel around. [People living near those areas may object, but] you can't run a modern society without hurting some groups; and, by creating reservations, 90 per cent of the opposition to nuclear power will disappear. And there are so many sources of energy—solar, geothermal, fusion, fission—that there is no way we can run out of energy in the next 200 years.

Interview/New York magazine, 8-9:39.

Khalid (ibn Abdel Aziz)
King of Saudi Arabia 3

If the oil-price level concerned us alone, I can assure you we would have opted for a price freeze until the end of 1977. But our commitment and obligations to OPEC may preclude such a freeze. Bare in mind, however, that we will spare no effort to avoid causing the consumer nations any damage. OPEC did indeed freeze oil prices for almost two years, and this was done on Saudi Arabia's initiative. The decision was taken to allow the consuming nations a transition period during which they could adjust their economies and take adequate measures to conserve energy and control inflation. However, this has not been done. On the contrary, oil consumption has increased by four per cent annually and the increase is expected to go up

(KHALID [ibn ABDEL AZIZ])

to five per cent. So where are these measures to save energy?

Interview, Riyadh/
U.S. News & World Report, 11-22:88.

Kim Il Sung
President of North Korea
1

The U.S. imperialists . . . are in a serious fuel crisis. Saying that the United States has fuel resources to last it only 30 years to come, the Americans themselves speak out loudly that they should secure new fuel markets, new fuel bases. U.S. Secretary of State [Henry] Kissinger cannot be regarded as having spoken for nothing when he openly said that if the Arab nations should use the fuel weapon the United States would resort to real weapons. This we can say is a cry of distress given by the imperialists gripped in the vise of a crisis.

Interview/
The Washington Post, 11-12:(A)8.

Thomas S. Kleppe
Secretary of the Interior
of the United States
2

We are now importing between 40 and 45 per cent of our oil, and this could reach 60 per cent in the 1980s. We are threatened with a political and economic bondage not unlike that which touched off the American Revolution some two centuries ago.

At Assumption College commencement, May 15/
The New York Times, 5-16:(1)26.

Floyd W. Lewis
President, Middle South Utilities, Inc.;
Chairman, Edison Electric Institute
3

Our direct involvement with the energy business has led us to the conclusion that we do indeed have an energy problem; that the energy needs of the nation will grow; that the only options available for meeting such energy needs which are presently available are increased use of coal and nuclear fuels;

that our emphasis as a nation should be on increasing the total available energy rather than spending our time on deciding how to divide up a shortage of energy.

Before Middle South Utilities stockholders,
New Orleans, May 21/
Middle South Utilities reprint.

Charles F. Luce
Chairman,
Consolidated Edison Company, New York
4

Energy independence means, in the short run, higher-priced energy. The threat of gasoline prices going up in the summer of a Presidential-election year is more worrisome to some political leaders than the threat of another oil embargo in 1985, even though they surely know that unless our country immediately undertakes real problems to bring about energy independence, by that time our nation will be desperately committed to imported oil to run our economy.

At Consolidated Edison Company annual meeting,
New York/ Los Angeles Herald-Examiner,
5-19:(A)12.

Tom McCall
Former Governor of Oregon (R)
5

The real reckoning on the energy crisis will be ruder than ever. When Alaskan oil starts flowing in 1978, we'll have a glut, and they'll say to me, "Ha, ha, you idiot" [for warning about the energy shortage]. But we'll use it too fast because nobody believes there's a real shortage—and then the roof falls in.

Interview, Portland, May 24/
The New York Times, 5-25:24.

Mike McCormack
United States Representative,
D—Washington
6

The nuclear [energy] industry, just as any other, has some hazardous aspects, and we must assume that at some time in the future there will be some accident causing property damage, injuries, and even deaths. It is crucial, however, to ask how likely these accidents are, and how this risk compares to that associated with our other everyday activities. While it is essential that every conceivable accident be guarded against, and every reasonable precaution taken, there is a point of absurdity beyond which the rational public should not be expected to go in imagining nuclear hazards or hypothesizing extreme nuclear accidents. Recent studies by Dr. Norman Rasmussen of MIT indicates that with 100 plants on the line —as will be the case by 1980—a major nuclear accident would be 10,000 times less likely to happen than a comparable accident with 100 fatalities in a non-nuclear facility. Thus, the hazard to any individual or group will be about the same in 1980—with 100 [nuclear power] plants on the line—as the hazard of being struck by a meteor.

At energy conservation awards dinner of Owens-Corning Fiberglas Corp., New York/ The Wall Street Journal, 1-30:14.

1

Understanding the nature of the energy crisis and what our response to it must be is a matter of supreme importance, for our nation is truly in mortal danger. Our national security and the stability of our economic systems, and even the freedom of our political institutions, may well depend on our ability to develop responsible energy policies and to implement rational programs to carry them into effect. One of the most dangerous aspects of the energy crisis is that a large portion of our fellow citizens still do not understand it. Indeed, a surprising number of Americans deny that an energy crisis even exists; and many who recognize that it is real believe that it has been contrived by evil forces which could, if they wished, simply decide to make the crisis go away.

Before Public Utilities Advertising Association, Big Sky, Montana, June 4/ Middle South Utilities reprint.

A. J. Meyer
Associate director, Center for Middle Eastern Studies, Harvard University; Authority on oil 2

... we Americans are still in a "witch hunt"

stage in energy matters. Our energy companies —utilities and international oil companies— are constant targets of vote-seeking Congressmen, newspapers, academics and conservationists. Yet, ironically, these firms are probably the one hope we have for energy survival during the next 15 years. Whatever their faults, they have supplied the U.S. economy, and the world, with energy efficiently and at bargain prices for half a century. They are huge, they are ubiquitous, and OPEC has eliminated much of the bargain they delivered earlier. A few oil-company executives behave abroad in ham-handed fashion. Yet integrated oil companies do not earn monopoly profits and they still provide the world with energy more effectively and cheaply than government entities *anywhere*. We should not let outraged indignation drive us to acts of self-mutilation.

Before National Association of Petroleum Investment Analysts/ The Christian Science Monitor, 3-9:31.

Ralph Nader
Lawyer; Consumer advocate 3

[Saying a large number of structures are energy-wasters]: Many existing buildings are over-lighted, over-heated, over-cooled, over-ventilated and over-exposed to the outdoors by poor design and inadequate insulation. If they were automobiles, we would call them lemons—and there would be massive recalls.

At conference sponsored by Public Citizen organization, Washington, May 20/ The Washington Post, 5-21:(A)2.

Gerald L. Parsky
Assistant Secretary for International Affairs, Department of the Treasury of the United States 4

In my mind, the answer to the oil-price question is not to challenge OPEC, such as by advocating counter-embargoes, but to seek and promote alternative supplies of petroleum, such as in Mexico. We should also be extending a lifeline to OPEC by developing more

(GERALD L. PARSKY)

trade with those countries. We should be seeking to develop their import potential from us ... We've got to recognize that it's an interdependent world today, and the U.S. should build upon it and lead it. We should be talking about drawing upon common objectives among nations.

Interview, Dallas/
The Dallas Times Herald, 5-20:(E)9.

Carlos Andres Perez
President of Venezuela
1

The increase of petroleum prices is by no means a selfish act of OPEC members for the exclusive benefit of their countries. It represents the irrevocable decision to dignify the terms of trade, to revalue raw materials and other basic products of the Third World.

At Socialist International Congress, Geneva,
Nov. 28/ The New York Times, 11-29:3.

Russell W. Peterson
Executive director, New Directions;
Former Chairman, Federal Council on
Environmental Quality
2

Coal, oil, gas—and terrestrial fuel—is bound to keep rising in cost. Solar [energy] will keep on being free and become more and more attractive. Now, the executive in the board-room figuring return on investment isn't going to get excited about solar energy. But the same fellow thinking about the future of humanity should get pretty excited, because you're talking about avoiding a potentially disastrous confrontation between the have and have-not peoples of the world.

Interview, Washington/
The New York Times, 11-21:(1)40.

Dixy Lee Ray
Former Chairman,
Atomic Energy Commission of the
United States
3

One of the problems nuclear [power] development is faced with is that scientists—too

clever—have made instruments so sensitive they can detect radiation to the millionth part, a measure that in no way can be construed as a health hazard. If our tongues were as sensitive as these radiation detectors, we could easily taste one drop of vermouth in five carloads of gin.

San Francisco Examiner & Chronicle,
5-9:(This World)2.

Ronald Reagan
Candidate for the 1976 Republican
Presidential nomination;
Former Governor of California (R)
4

... we have deteriorated in our ability to provide energy sources for ourselves in the three years since the Arab [oil] embargo. Today we are producing less than we were three years ago, and we're importing more than half of our consumption. I think it is time for us to turn the industry loose and I would suggest we begin by closing out June 30, when its original term is up, the Federal Energy Agency, and that we should repeal the energy legislation that was signed into law last December, and turn the industry loose in the free-market system to produce the energy we need.

Interview/
The Christian Science Monitor, 6-3:17.

W. F. Rockwell, Jr.
Chairman, Rockwell International
5

It's no coincidence that the energy crisis was closely followed by inflation, recession and growing unemployment. There was and will continue to be a relationship between the amount of energy we have and the amount of work that we'll be able to do with that energy. Now, while our economy is definitely on the road to recovery, is the time to take steps to assure that the United States is no longer at the whim of foreign energy suppliers. Now, when we realize that our oil and natural gas reserves are limited, is the time for the United States to develop and utilize the energy available in coal and nuclear energy. The United States has long been the world leader in the areas of advanced technologies. Why then have Japan, the Soviet Union and West Germany exceeded the U.S. growth index of electricity production for the past 10 years? Why has France exceeded the U.S. in electrical growth for the past four years? It's clear that *our* nation must *use* advanced technology if we are to reap its benefits.

*At Rockwell International shareholders meeting, Los Angeles, Feb. 12/***

1

For years the experts in nuclear energy, the experts in the Energy Research and Development Administration and the experts in business have repeatedly proven the safety and reliability of nuclear energy. After years of study, after millions of dollars for research and testing, after years of delay, the proof of the desirability and safety of nuclear energy has been once again secured—despite the negative cries of the anti-nuclear pseudo-experts. In fact, no member of the public has ever been injured or killed by radiation from a publicly licensed nuclear plant, even though there are currently 56 plants operating in the United States, and some of those plants have been operating for almost 20 years. But these operational proofs seem to have little effect on the negative pseudo-experts who continue to raise their voices against nuclear energy.

*At YMCA Good Friday breakfast, Los Angeles, April 16/***

2

... despite the warnings of business and industry, despite the valiant efforts of the engineers and managers of our nation, despite a lot of talk from government at the Federal, state and local levels, and despite the energy conservation resolutions that American consumers may have made during the New Year's Eve parties on December 31, 1973—as we celebrate our nation's independence this year we are in worse shape energy-wise than we ever were during 1973. For while our nation's political independence is something that we all have cause to celebrate, our nation's lack of energy independence is something that we all have

cause to condemn. The facts stand on their own. In 1970 we were using 14.7 million barrels of oil a day. By 1973, our demand grew to 16.7 million barrels of oil a day before the [Arab] embargo. And, despite our good intentions, today our oil demand has grown to 17.7 million barrels a day. But that's only one-half of the problem. Our imports are also on the rise. In 1970 we were importing 3.4 million barrels a day. By 1973, this grew to 6.4 million barrels before the embargo. This year, again, despite our good intentions, we imported 7.7 million barrels a day—roughly 20 per cent more than we did in 1973. About ten weeks ago the latest figures on United States imports showed just how bad the situation has become. For one week in March, for the first time in the history of our nation, we imported more oil than we produced. As it stands today, unless we take positive steps to fill our energy gap, this imbalance between domestic production and foreign imports will increase every year for the rest of the century.

*Before American Institute of Electrical Engineers, St. Louis, May 19/***

A. David Rossin
Chairman, Chicago section, American Nuclear Society

3

[On nuclear power]: No technology is totally risk-free. Nuclear plants are designed so that for any conceivable combination of equipment malfunction and human error the radioactive material will not escape from the containment building. Studies show that the chance of an accident which would release enough radioactivity to cause death of a member of the public is less than one in 10,000 years. We have to compare that with the risks we accept from floods, lightning, earthquakes and man-made risks ... Nuclear power has less impact on the environment than any of the available alternatives. We know it would be irresponsible to continue burning huge quantities of oil and natural gas to make electricity. When one considers the prospects of a society without enough energy, that looks even worse.

Interview, Chicago/ The Dallas Times Herald, 3-4:(A)25.

WHAT THEY SAID IN 1976

John C. Sawhill
President, New York University;
Former Administrator,
Federal Energy Administration

1

What we need to do immediately is to begin building an oil stockpile in this country. One way to avoid vulnerability is to put ourselves in a position that if an embargo, or threat of embargo, is raised we can rely on our own stockpile. This blunts the oil weapon. We have to encourage conservation and provide financing for an alternative transportation system and research and development. To this end, we have got to begin increasing the Federal excise tax on gasoline. Instead of putting this revenue into highways; it should go into the development of mass transit. The American people have to understand that conditions have changed, and we are going to have to change our life-style to accommodate to them. Forty years from now, more or less, the world is going to run out of oil, or at least there won't be enough to provide energy. Whatever is left will be for petrochemicals—drugs, plastics, fertilizer and those sorts of things. So not only do we have the short-range problem of having to reduce dependence but a long-range problem of moving away from an economy which is so oriented to oil as a primary energy source.

Interview, New York/
Los Angeles Times, 12-28:(2)5.

Patricia Schroeder
United States Representative,
D—Colorado

2

[Calling for the abolition of the Federal Energy Administration]: I think it would be a simple enough matter to take the few worthwhile functions the FEA performs and transfer them to the agencies from whence they came. In two years, the FEA has grown from a handful of employees transferred from other agencies into a horde of 3,400, with the highest-paid staff in government. And now President Ford is recommending we triple the budget of this "temporary" agency—from $142-million to $440-million. Ridiculous.

The Dallas Times Herald, 4-28:(A)19.

Irwin M. Seltzer
President, National Economic
Research Associates

3

After a brief flirtation with the superficial charms of a no-growth economy, we seem to have become aware of the more enduring virtues of steady growth and full employment. The simple fact is that there is no environment as degrading as a welfare line, and no solution to the problems of unemployment and poverty without a steadily growing economy. And such economic growth requires energy.

Testimony in behalf of Virginia Electric
Power Company, in a rate-setting case/
The Wall Street Journal, 12-29:8.

William E. Simon
Secretary of the Treasury
of the United States

4

Just look at the cost of energy in the United States versus every other country in the world. It's a calamity today if the price of a gallon of gasoline is going to go up a few pennies. We have gasoline at an average price today of 61 cents in the United States. In every other country in the world, it ranges from $1.50 to $2.50 a gallon. How in the world are we going to conserve energy when we won't make it cost enough in order to be thoughtful in its usage and provide incentive for additional supplies? . . . We must free the shackles from the private sector to produce the coal and oil and natural gas and allow our technology to move forward to provide us with energy self-sufficiency. But, no, our politicians would rather see us continue to pay the OPEC cartel this year $35-billion versus $3-billion in 1970. And each year our dependence and the dollars continue to flow to the OPEC nations instead of to our domestic producers. It's a nightmare to me.

Interview, Washington/
U.S. News & World Report, 12-13:26.

John G. Tower
United States Senator, R—Texas

5

[Calling for the abolition of the Federal

Energy Administration]: This temporary agency has mushroomed into a formidable agent of Federal regulation. It was intended as a one-act play, but now it supports a cast of thousands.

Washington/
The Dallas Times Herald, 4-30:(A)15.

Wernher Von Braun
Vice-president for engineering and development, Fairchild Industries 1

. . . there is no question in my mind that the price of natural gas is being held artificially low because everyone wants natural gas to heat his home. The price is being kept low because that is where the votes are. With so many people dependent on natural gas, no Congressman wants to take the responsibility of driving the price up. As long as the price of that kind of energy is kept artificially low, there is no incentive to go after more exotic and more expensive forms of energy. Let me give you another example. We have a lot of clean coal in the West, but to get it out of the ground involves strip-mining. Strip-mining, of course, is objectionable to environmentalists. How do you convince a Montana rancher that we should tear up his land so that New Yorkers can be kept warm?

Interview/Nation's Business, September:27.

Aubrey J. Wagner
Chairman,
Tennessee Valley Authority 2

The nature of our nation's energy problem is simple to state: We consume more energy each year than the year before. At the same time, we will soon run out of oil and natural gas—the fuels that have been supplying three-fourths of our energy; they comprise less than 10 per cent of our proven energy reserves. It seems obvious to me that any time you are using more and more of something that you have less and less of, you face a problem. And when that resource is something as vital to the national well-being as energy, the problem can quickly become a crisis with the most dire consequences. The potential for disaster is even greater when you rely—as the U.S. currently does—upon foreign sources for about 40 per cent of our vital oil supply. The broad solution to the problem is equally simple: We must stretch and conserve our presently used fuels—gas and oil. We must, near term, convert to other basic energy sources that will meet our needs through proven technology. And that means coal and nuclear. And, for the long term, we must research vigorously for even better energy supply systems. We must, in my view, solve our energy problem quickly or face economic, social and political consequences that will threaten our very survival.

Before Scripps-Howard editors,
Gatlinburg, Tenn., Sept. 21/
Vital Speeches, 11-15:66.

Ahmed Zaki al-Yamani
Minister of Petroleum and Mineral Resources of Saudi Arabia 3

You [in the U.S.] need Arab oil so much for light crude, and you need the Arabs for future demand since they are the only source of supply which can grow. Alaska and the North Sea will take care of some but not all of your demand. Iran has only very narrow limits for the future . . . Gradually you will have to learn how to conserve and preserve. The Arab embargo [several years ago] was so useful as a shock for Americans. It forced you to recognize that oil will not always be available in abundant quantities. Unfortunately, that lesson is . . . being forgotten.

Interview, Al Hada, Saudi Arabia/
The New York Times Magazine, 11-14:138.

Ardeshir Zahedi
Iranian Ambassador to the United States 4

[On Western criticism of high prices of oil exported by OPEC countries]: You [the U.S.] do not have to buy the oil. Neither do the Europeans or the Japanese. If you do not like the price, why do you not use other sources of energy? The answer, of course, is that other sources—such as coal and nuclear power—are going to cost far more than the price of oil. You are a free country. Your people should go out and invest their money in developing

(ARDESHIR ZAHEDI)

these other sources if you believe the price of our oil is too high. None of these other energy sources, we think, is going to cost you less than a comparable price of $12 to $14 a barrel for oil. Once our oil resources are exhausted, how much will you charge us for your shale oil or liquified coal? Will you ask us what we think is a fair price?

Interview, Washington/
U.S. News & World Report, 1-12:51.

Frank G. Zarb
Administrator,
Federal Energy Administration   *1*

[Saying Federally regulated prices for natural gas are too low]: I have come to the conclusion that we have a very serious natural-gas shortage—with less gas being produced than we need for consumption domestically, forcing us to rely on foreign sources—and that the primary reason for declining production is that Federal regulation has made it economically unfeasible for companies to produce reserves.

Los Angeles Herald-Examiner, 2-16:(A)5.

2

I am personally convinced that we stand a disturbingly great chance of being subjected to another embargo [of oil, such as that of 1973-74 imposed by Arab exporting nations]. The Organization of Petroleum Exporting Countries has the oil we need, and they can be expected to make the most of the seller's market they enjoy. As long as we continue to become increasingly dependent on the OPEC nations for our petroleum supplies, we will be increasingly subject to arbitrary OPEC decisions on price and supply. [If another embargo is imposed,] we won't just have long gasoline lines. In some areas, we won't have any lines, because we won't have any gasoline . . . Like a little boy who tends to forget why he was spanked last week, the country seems to have conveniently erased the memory of

the embargo from its consciousness.

At American Power Conference,
Chicago, April 21/
Los Angeles Herald-Examiner, 4-22:(A)7.

3

If we do five major steps, we'll be [oil-] embargo-proof: 1) We have to reduce our rate of energy growth from about 3.5 per cent to around 2.5 per cent a year. 2) We must maximize every opportunity to extract and produce American oil and gas. That means on the outer continental shelf, north slope of Alaska, and in secondary and tertiary recovery of oil fields. 3) We *have got* to double our coal production in the next 10 years for coal to do its part of the job. That means we have to be able to mine it, move it and burn it. 4)We have got to move nuclear power to a point where it represents 26 per cent of electric power. That's compared to the present 9 per cent. And 5) We need the strategic oil-storage system which has already passed Congress and awaits appropriations. If we get those developments moving, we will have our imports down to six million barrels a day by 1985. And with storage reserve equal to three million barrels a day for about a year, we could ride out an embargo for a good period of time and prevent the U.S. from being held hostage by any one region of the world.

Interview, Washington/
The Christian Science Monitor, 6-25:(B)4.

4

Rather than invest in developing new sources of U.S. energy and alternatives to oil and gas, we satisfied our growing energy appetite with cheap foreign fuel. There were those who raised a voice in alarm, and warned of ultimate disaster, but, for political and other reasons, they were not heard. The chrome-plated gunboats that Americans drove . . . were indicative of the choice that was made. The unfortunate energy course pursued by the United States could be called the great American energy orgy.

Before House Energy and Power Subcommittee,
Washington, Dec. 16/
The Dallas Times Herald, 12-17:(A)10.

Carl Albert
United States Representative,
D—Oklahoma
                                    1

In the field of foreign affairs, I have always been one who has tried to support bipartisan foreign policy . . . But I cannot support a bipartisan foreign policy that I don't know anything about and nobody in the Administration will tell me anything about . . . I think it is a part of the business of the Congress, the duty of the Congress, to involve itself in foreign affairs, and for the Administration to take the Congress in as a partner. Otherwise, why would the Constitution have given the Congress, and only the Congress, the authority to raise money, and all these things cost money, or the authority to raise and support armies? I believe that the Democrats will cooperate with the Administration wherever it is in the national interest. We are not going to be against things just because the Administration is for them. We are not out to destroy the Administration just for our own political advantage. But we are not going to let the Administration write our ticket without consulting us and without giving us anything to do with it.

At New Member Caucus, Jan. 16/
The Washington Post, 1-27:(A)18.

                                    2

One thing about foreign aid, military aid or war itself—you either do enough or you're better off not doing anything.

Washington, Jan. 27/
The New York Times, 1-28:1.

Andrei A. Amalrik
Exiled Soviet historian
                                    3

If America and the entire West stopped all credits and aid to the Soviet Union, that country would reach a state of crisis, followed by reforms. As long as the West aids the Soviet Union, there will be no reforms . . . It was a common tactic of many rich and developed countries in the past to keep undeveloped, nomad countries tranquil by paying them tribute. This system continued until the nomads asked: "Why be content with just tribute? Why not take the lot?" That was the end of the empires. American cereals can never replace the force of the soul.

Before Anglo-American Press Association, Paris/
U.S. News & World Report, 10-25:55.

                                    4

The Soviet Union and the United States now remind me of two poker players—one [the U.S.] is putting his cards on the table and the other [the Soviet Union] is playing them close to the vest. And yet, there is nothing wrong with bluffing once in a while.

Interview, New York/
The New York Times, 12-23:8.

William A. Anders
Chairman, Nuclear Regulatory Commission
of the United States
                                    5

[Saying the U.S. should not embargo the export of nuclear materials and technology]: The technology is not all that magical, and we're not a monopoly. The only way to have our way is to be involved, to not opt out, to set the pace, to set the moral tone, if you will . . . There will be a considerably higher probability of nuclear squabbles if nations are forced by a moratorium to develop the capacity on their own. They will have to go back and start from scratch. It won't be all that hard. If they have to develop the whole pyramid, they'll

WHAT THEY SAID IN 1976

(WILLIAM A. ANDERS)

develop weapons. If we let them in at the apex of the pyramid, they won't have all that base and they will have been precluded from going through the phases essential for developing weapons.

Interview/The New York Times, 2-24:9.

Howard H. Baker, Jr.
United States Senator, R—Tennessee 1

It's essential that the political system take account of evolving and developing new concerns and factors in the construction of new foreign policy. The salient single point to remember is that there is nothing sacrosanct about foreign policy or defense policy that sets them apart from the ordinary conflict of partisan political debate.

Panel discussion/Center Report, June:28.

George W. Ball
Former Under Secretary of State of the United States 2

. . . in 1971, when [Secretary of State Henry] Kissinger was preoccupied with China, while at the same time flying back and forth to Paris in a single-handed attempt to negotiate a Vietnamese cease-fire, we drifted with a policy "tilted" toward Pakistan that assured the Soviets a long-desired foothold in the [Indian] subcontinent. While Kissinger was frantically touring the Middle East, carrying the keys of his office with him, critical decisions with regard to the second phase of the SALT talks and the European Security Conference had to be postponed. Because of this practice of one-man diplomacy, America, as Mr. Kissinger has himself admitted, long had nothing resembling a policy toward Latin America or Africa or the less-developed countries. Only when pressures have grown irresistible in one of those areas has Mr. Kissinger felt compelled to get in his airplane, make a grand tour of the region and try to improvise a policy overnight.

Before Democratic Party platform committee, Washington, May 19/ The Washington Post, 5-20:(A)7.

Sirimavo Bandaranaike
Prime Minister of Sri Lanka 3

Recent developments in many parts of the world show that imperialism and colonialism, though in retreat, show a new face and depend upon new weapons which are just as dangerous. The role of mercenaries in Angola and of multinational corporations in subverting lawfully constituted governments, techniques of destabilization . . . the use of systematic bribery and corruption on a massive scale . . . to influence and interfere with the internal affairs of independent nations are some of these new weapons to which we have to find the answers.

At conference of non-aligned nations, Colombo, Sri Lanka, Aug. 16/ Los Angeles Times, 8-17:(1)5.

4

The non-aligned [countries] do not consider any nation or any people as their enemy. Their fight has always been against injustice, intolerance and inequity. Non-alignment is a creative and constructive philosophy, and the world is all the better for it.

At conference of non-aligned nations, Colombo, Sri Lanka, Aug. 16/ The New York Times, 8-17:9.

5

[Foreign] aid, whether it is bilateral or multilateral, is not and cannot be a permanent solution to the world's economic problems. At best, it can only be a temporary palliative, reinforcing the self-reliant efforts of poorer nations for a better future for their own peoples, thereby enhancing their ability to cooperate with other peoples and nations in equality and self-respect.

At United Nations, New York/ The New York Times, 10-17:(1)22.

John Brademas
United States Representative, D—Indiana 6

Neither Congress nor the American people

are going isolationist. But they are unwilling any longer to support an interventionism that sees our national interests equally at stake everywhere. A thoughtful internationalism—rather than an impossible isolationism or a mindless adventurism—ought to be our prescription for the future.

At "Pacem in Terris" convocation,
Washington, December ('75)/
The Center Magazine, March-April:57.

Willy Brandt
Chairman, Social Democratic Party of
West Germany; Former Chancellor
of West Germany 1

In the past few years, it has become more and more evident that the traditional structures of world-wide politics are subject to profound change. East-West relationships are increasingly overwhelmed by growing tensions between North and South. Still, there is no reason to be pessimistic as far as the future of the West is concerned. I am convinced we will be able to revitalize our Western ideals. The long-term future depends to a high degree on the success of the Western countries in presenting themselves as a democratic alternative in solving problems.

Interview, Bonn/The Washington Post, 5-9:(A)18.

Leonid I. Brezhnev
General Secretary,
Communist Party of the Soviet Union 2

Detente does not in the slightest abolish, and cannot abolish or alter, the laws of the class struggle. No one should expect that because of detente Communists will reconcile themselves with capitalistic exploitation or that monopolists become followers of the revolution. We make no secret of the fact that we see detente as the way to create more favorable conditions for peaceful socialist and Communist construction. This only confirms that socialism and peace are indissoluble.

At Soviet Communist Party Congress, Moscow,
Feb. 24/The New York Times, 3-18:14.

Edmund G. Brown, Jr.
Governor of California (D);
Candidate for the 1976 Democratic
Presidential nomination 3

We can have the ideological initiative around the world, based on a foreign policy based on what we believe at home—on the principles of the environment and the economy and equality which we all believe right here. The real question is what's going to happen to the human species. Equality and self-determination and reverence of life that can once again win the respect of mankind ... This idea we can project around the world.

At dinner honoring California Democrats in
Congress, Los Angeles/
Los Angeles Times, 4-26:(1)12.

Zbigniew Brzezinski
Director, Research Institute on
International Change,
Columbia University 4

[Soviet intervention in] Angola is an indication that the sweeping generalizations made by the [Ford] Administration about a "generation of peace" were wrong and misleading. Detente is going to be a mixed relationship, with elements of both conflict and cooperation.

Newsweek, 1-19:24.

5

The East-West relationship must be improved and detente should be a major purpose of American policy, for this relationship bears directly on the problem of human survival. We realize that the ideological as well as political conflict between us and the Soviet Union will go on for a long time, but we should strive to gradually moderate it. To achieve that moderation, both cooperation as well as vigilance will be necessary. Consequently, the maintenance of a strong military deterrent is a necessary precondition for a stable and increasingly comprehensive as well as reciprocal detente—a detente which will remain competitive as well as cooperative.

Before Democratic Party platform committee/
The Christian Science Monitor, 6-11:31.

WHAT THEY SAID IN 1976

Earl L. Butz
Secretary of Agriculture
of the United States

1

I think our record as a humanitarian nation is clear. We have made a commitment, starting with the Marshall Plan in the Truman Administration, that we're not going to permit starvation anyplace in the world to the extent that we can prevent it. And to back up that commitment we have provided 25 billion dollars' worth of food aid in the last 20 years. In the last 10 years, 80 per cent of all the food that moved in the world-relief channels originated in America. But on the other hand, we don't really send it to the enemy. We haven't sent any to Cuba. We are using food to win friends.

Interview, Washington/
U.S. News & World Report, 2-16:27.

Jimmy Carter
Candidate for the 1976 Democratic
Presidential nomination;
Former Governor of Georgia (D)

2

While detente must be more reciprocal, I reject the strident and bellicose voices of those who would have this country [abandon detente and] return to the days of the cold war with the Soviet Union. I believe the American people want to look to the future. They have seen the tragedy of American involvement in Vietnam and drawn appropriate lessons for tomorrow. They seek new vistas, not a repetition of old rhetoric and old mistakes . . . I support the objectives of detente, but I cannot go along with the way it has been handled by Presidents Nixon and Ford. The Secretary of State [Henry Kissinger] has tied its success too closely to his personal reputation. As a result, he is giving up too much and asking too little. He is trumpeting achievements on paper while failing to insist on them in practice.

News conference, Chicago, March 15/
Los Angeles Times, 3-16:(1)6.

3

The people of other nations have learned, in recent years, that they can sometimes neith-er trust what our government says nor predict what it will do. They want to respect us. They like our people. But our people do not seem to be running our government any more. Because we have let our foreign policy be made for us, we have lost something crucial in the way we talk and the way we act toward other peoples of the world. When our President and Secretary of State speak to the world without the understanding or support of the American people, they speak with an obviously hollow voice. In every foreign venture that has failed —whether it was Vietnam, Cambodia, Chile, Pakistan, Angola or in the excesses of the CIA—our government forged ahead without consulting the American people, and did things that were contrary to our basic character.

Before Chicago Council on Foreign Relations,
March 15/The New York Times, 3-16:24.

4

I would continue the effort to be friendly with Russia, trade with Russia, have student exchange, tourist exchange, and consultations. I recognize that we will never have permanent peace, or an end to the threat to South Korea, a solution to the Middle East question, a substantial reduction in atomic weapons—none of those things—without the co-operation of the Soviet Union. I think, though, that we've come out second-best in every negotiation with the Soviet Union. We've been so eager for some sign of agreement that we've yielded. That includes the Helsinki Conference, the Vladivostok Conference—agreement on nuclear-arms limitations—the wheat deal in 1972, even the space flight last year. I would be a much tougher negotiator and make sure that, whenever the Soviet Union gets an advantage, we get an equivalent advantage from them. I also would not neglect our natural allies and friends, as we have in recent years. I would strengthen those ties, consult with them frequently, let our own positions be predictable.

Interview/
U.S. News & World Report, 5-24:19.

1

I am particularly concerned by our nation's role as the world's leading arms salesman. We sold or gave away billions of dollars of arms last year, mostly to developing nations . . . Sometimes we try to justify this unsavory business on the cynical ground that by rationing out the means of violence we can somehow control the world's violence. The fact is that we cannot have it both ways. Can we be both the world's leading champion of peace and the world's leading supplier of the weapons of war?

Before Foreign Policy Association,
New York, June 23/ The National Observer, 7-3:7.

2

Democratic processes may in some countries bring to power parties or leaders whose ideologies are not shared by most Americans. We may not welcome these changes. We will certainly not encourage them. But we must respect the results of democratic elections and the right of countries to make their own free choice if we are to remain faithful to our own basic idea of freedom.

Before Foreign Policy Association, New York,
June 23/ Los Angeles Times, 6-24:(1)12.

3

As far as the evolution of foreign affairs and policies are concerned, I would not want to have a White House staff in effect superior to the Secretary of State. Now, I believe in putting into office the most competent and qualified people as administrators of that [State] Department and letting them perform their functions without interference from me, but responsible always to me. I really prefer to be the spokesman for the nation in the area of foreign affairs and on matters of major policy and let the American people look to me as the one to represent our country in that respect. So I would not form a powerful White House palace guard to be superior to the Cabinet officers in the administration of their departments.

Interview, June 24/
The New York Times, 7-7:12.

4

The singling out of food as a bargaining

weapon is something that I would not do. If we want to put economic pressure on another nation under any circumstances, to use it as a lever by withholding our products, I would not single out food as a singular product. It would be a total withholding of trade.

Interview, June 24/
The New York Times, 7-7:12.

Jimmy Carter
1976 Democratic Presidential nominee

5

There can be no deleterious consequences to keeping the people and Congress informed [on foreign policy]. If national security is involved on some special issue and it is therefore inadvisable to publicize details, at least Congress must be kept advised. After all, our Secretary of State would speak to the world with a hollow voice if he didn't speak for the people. That is one of our troubles now. The people don't even know what [Secretary of State Henry] Kissinger is talking about much of the time. And as foreign nations become aware of this, it weakens our position overseas. They doubt the value of our proclaimed positions . . . I want a Secretary of State like [George C.] Marshall or [Dean] Acheson, a strong spokesman for U.S. policy, a man who could analyze problems and maintain close relations with the President. But it is the President who must be responsible for ultimate decisions. Right now it isn't clear whether Kissinger or [President] Ford makes the final policy decisions. I personally think it's Kissinger, not Ford.

Interview, Plains, Ga./
The New York Times, 8-22:(4)17.

6

I would never again get militarily involved in the internal affairs of another country, unless our own security was directly threatened . . . I don't think that this is an isolationist attitude at all; I don't think that that's what the American people want.

Interview, Plains, Ga., Aug. 22/
The Washington Post, 8-23:(A)9.

125

WHAT THEY SAID IN 1976

(JIMMY CARTER)

1

The American people feel that under [Secretary of State Henry] Kissinger, [President] Ford and [former President Richard] Nixon, our nation has abandoned moral commitments in foreign affairs. We've espoused the purposes of dictators, we've ignored the rights of human beings to be free, and as we abandon each small incremental group, we in effect abandon our commitment to those principles here at home.

*Before members of
Lithuanian-American community, Pittsburgh,
Oct. 2/ The New York Times, 10-3:(1)32.*

2

I think the main problem with [U.S. Secretary of State Henry] Kissinger is that he does not trust the American people. He does not trust the Congress. I even think there is some evidence, in my opinion, he doesn't trust the President [Ford]. He wants to be a unilateral representative of this country in foreign affairs.

The Christian Science Monitor, 10-5:1.

3

We have suffered enough in this country because Presidents and their advisers have felt it necessary to prove their supposed "toughness" by pursuing rash and ultimately tragic policies. It is time for our foreign policy to concern itself with real wisdom rather than imagined toughness. A strong nation, like a strong person, can afford to be gentle and thoughtful and restrained, and can afford to extend a helping hand to others. It is the weak nation, like the weak person, who must behave with bluster and boasting and rashness and other signs of insecurity.

*Before Liberal Party of New York, New York,
Oct. 14/ Los Angeles Times, 10-15:(1)12.*

Jimmy Carter
President-elect of the United States

4

I hope to establish, as best I can, a position where our country is the leader of the world, based not on military might or economic pressure or political persuasion but on the fact that we are right and decent; that we take a position with every nation as best we can according to what is best for the people who live there ... Second, I plan to appoint diplomatic officials who have superb credentials, strictly on the basis of merit, not reward people for political favors—and that's a commitment that I've made on my word of honor; I'm not going to break it. Another thing is to treat developing nations as individuals, not as a bloc. And this would apply not only to the African nations but also to those in Latin America and in Eastern Europe as well. I'd like to try to cement, as much as I can, a good relationship on trade, cultural exchange, student exchange, tourism and foreign aid. Using myself, the members of my Cabinet, maybe Governors on occasion, as special emissaries, and members of my own family, I hope to get what we call "world order" instead of power politics. World order means to me to try to establish peace.

Interview/ Time, 11-15:24.

5

[Saying there will be times when secret foreign-policy matters will not be revealed to Congress]: I am not naive enough to think that everything that I know or everything that is in progress on an international scale [needs to be disclosed] in the early stages of a sensitive analysis process. There will be times when nobody needs to know about a foreign-policy challenge except me and the Secretary of State, or sometimes perhaps just me and the head of a foreign government. I will have to use my own judgment on all things. But my inclination is whenever possible to consult with you ...

*Before Senate Foreign Relations Committee,
Washington, Nov. 23/
The Washington Post, 12-2:(A)1.*

Fidel Castro
Premier of Cuba
1

One cannot stop the processes of change taking place in the world. Nobody can export revolution and impose it by means of war. But neither can anybody hamper the people from carrying out revolutions.

At Soviet Communist Party Congress, Moscow, Feb. 25/ Los Angeles Times, 2-26:(1)10.

Chou Kua-min
Deputy Minister of Foreign Trade of the People's Republic of (Communist) China
2

[The U.S.] endlessly preaches interdependence as the core of maintaining international order and alleges that global prosperity rests on its leadership. To put it bluntly, it means nothing but to maintain the control, plunder and exploitation against developing countries.

At United Nations Conference on Trade and Development, Nairobi, Kenya, May 11/ The New York Times, 5-12:7.

Dick Clark
United States Senator, D—Iowa
3

We must certainly ask whether it is wise policy to react to Soviet actions any place in the world, whether it involves our strategic or economic interests or not. If we follow this policy, it means that we must react even if the Soviets are themselves making a mistake; in short, it means that we are indeed the policemen of the world and that our policy is not an independent one but rather a reacting one, determined by our adversary.

At Senate Foreign Relations Subcommittee on African Affairs hearing, Washington, Jan. 29/ Los Angeles Herald-Examiner, 1-29:(A)2.

Harlan Cleveland
Director, Program in International Affairs, Aspen Institute; Former president, University of Hawaii
4

Republicans and Democrats yearn in par-

allel—in carefully differentiated wording—for a SALT agreement, for mutual and balanced force reduction in Europe, for a Middle East settlement, for majority rule without massacre in southern Africa, for a continuing stalemate in Korea, for positive-sum North-South bargaining, for a comprehensive ocean-law treaty, for a peaceful settlement to the Panama Canal dispute, for an international agreement to frustrate terrorism. But most of the levers of relevant power are not connected to the Oval Office, and the President's command and control of nuclear forces is not terribly helpful—as both Democrats and Republicans discovered in Vietnam. Suasion and consultation and patience and unremitting diplomatic effort are the only available style of leadership in a leaderless world.

Lecture, Aspen, Colo., July 13/ The National Observer, 7-31:18.

William E. Colby
Director, Central Intelligence Agency of the United States
5

We [the CIA] welcome detente. The more freely information flows, the less we have to scramble for it, the better. I was introduced to [Soviet leader Leonid] Brezhnev in 1973. He said, "Oh, so this is the head of the CIA. He must be a dangerous man." I replied, "Mr. General Secretary, the more we know about each other, the safer we all will be." He didn't answer.

Interview, Washington/ Time, 1-19:17.

John B. Connally, Jr.
Former Secretary of the Treasury of the United States; Former Governor of Texas (D, now R)
6

[Saying Congress has stripped the President of foreign-affairs authority]: You cannot run a foreign policy through Congressional committees, and the responsible members of the Congress know it. We [Republicans] ought to be saying just that on every street corner every day from now until the general

WHAT THEY SAID IN 1976

(JOHN B. CONNALLY, JR.)

elections this fall. Because nothing could be more important. If the United States is not the leader of the free world, then it has no leader. No one [else] can assume the mantle of leadership, not even a combination of countries.

To Republican state chairmen,
Floresville, Tex., March/
The New York Times Magazine, 8-8:11.

1

It is my belief that we have entered an extremely dangerous period of history—comparable, in fact, to the decade prior to the Second World War. Perhaps we are so anxious to reject the cold-war mentality of a few years ago that we are blind to the expansionist policies of the Soviet Union. It seems apparent to me . . . that we have indeed moved quietly and almost unnoticed into a new and perilous era—conceivably, in fact, an era of reckoning for Western civilization, and freedom.

At George Washington University Center for
Strategic Studies, April 2/
The Dallas Times Herald, 4-3:(A)7.

2

There has been a flip-flop. The isolationists of the past—businessmen, people in the farm belt and the conservatives—are the internationalists today. The former internationalists —who were mostly on the Eastern Seaboard and included the liberals and so-called intellectuals—are the isolationists.

Interview/U.S. News & World Report, 4-12:21.

3

We're going to have to fashion a whole new foreign policy, it seems to me, not the least of which would be asking the Germans to probably arm and man an additional four or five divisions on their eastern front. After consultation with our friends and allies, particularly the People's Republic of [Communist] China,

we ought to ask the Japanese to engage in a substantial rearmament of their people. They can be a very great stabilizing force in Southeast Asia. So I think we're looking at a whole restructuring, really, of alliances around the world and the utilization of economic strengths perhaps in such a way that they become even more important to us than military might.

Interview/Newsweek, 4-26:23.

Liam Cosgrave
Prime Minister of Ireland

4

We look to America today with affection, with pride and with hope. We are among your many friends abroad who may differ with you from time to time but who still think more of you, and of what you stand for in the world, than, in this time of self-questioning, you may often appear to think of yourselves.

Before joint session of Congress,
Washington, March 17/
The New York Times, 3-18:6.

Anthony Crosland
Foreign Secretary of the United Kingdom

5

We cannot ignore the evidence before our eyes. It has been precisely during those years when the Soviet Union has advocated detente that we have witnessed the steady build-up of the Soviet armed forces. We have to be equal to this challenge . . . We believe detente is indivisible, that it is a commitment to productive relations between governments and peoples. The Soviet view of detente as [Russian leader Leonid] Brezhnev made plain at the recent [Soviet Communist] Party Congress, is, by contrast, narrow and limited. In his words, it is "a way of creating more favorable conditions for the peaceful building of socialism and Communism."

Los Angeles Herald-Examiner, 5-30:(A)4.

Brian Crozier
Director, Institute for the
Study of Conflict, London

6

Many terrorist groups have ideological or

psychological bonds—such as the common rejection of existing society. And there's also a great impatience among young terrorists to change the system of government overnight. This, more than anything else, distinguishes terrorists even from political extremists, who prefer not to resort to violence. To all this you must add a desire for publicity, an innate flamboyance and a complete contempt for human life. Their motivation is always that "we're going to change everything, and it doesn't matter how we do it." By the time they become terrorists, I think they have gone beyond the point where they are open to argument. What goes on in the mind of the extremists is more important than any objective reality. Basically, they want to make people conform to their views—force them into obedience. That's why they tend to terrorize their own side. In many of the revolutionary situations I've studied, the terrorists have killed far more of their supporters than the so-called enemy.

Interview, London/
U.S. News & World Report, 6-28:33.

Suleyman Demirel
Premier of Turkey
1

[On the forthcoming Administration of U.S. President-elect Jimmy Carter]: I'm not worried. The policies of nations shouldn't change with changes in those who administer them. Policies are based on national interests. I think America is a great country and a great people. Yours are a wonderful, nice people. They have kept a true sense of values, of the dignity of man.

Interview/ The New York Times, 11-14:(4)15.

Anatoly F. Dobrynin
Soviet Ambassador
to the United States
2

. . . foreign policy is common knowledge now. More and more things are no longer secret. If you read the papers very carefully, you'll be informed. Maybe you won't know some figures and details, but if you read well

and are clever enough to observe what is going on, you'll know the basics . . . It's knowing how to approach and handle them that is difficult sometimes.

Interview, Washington/
Parade, 3-7:4.

Thomas O. Enders
United States Ambassador to Canada
3

As countries grow closer . . . they often find that they can't lessen dependence in one sector without increasing it in others. For example, if a country invests heavily in resource self-sufficiency, it may become less competitive in manufacturing; if it restricts trade, it may become more dependent on foreign investment. Most of us are pretty ambivalent about this vast movement toward interdependence. We know that growing exchanges are necessary to our prosperity, to the vitality of our arts and sciences. We know that no government—not yours, not mine—has much power over these trends. We can retard a little here, accelerate a little there, but not change the direction. But our need to be ourselves, to exercise sovereignty, to control our own destiny remains as intense and as fundamental as ever.

Before Canadian Club, Ottawa/
The Wall Street Journal, 7-8:14.

Gerald R. Ford
President of the United States
4

. . . I think it would be very unwise for a President—me or anyone else—to abandon detente. I think detente is in the best interest of this country. It is in the best interest of world stability, world peace. We have to recognize there are deep ideological differences between the United States and the Soviet Union. We have to realize they are a superpower militarily and industrially, just as we are. When you have two superpowers that have such great influence, it is in the best interest of those two countries to work together to ease tensions, to avoid confrontation where possible, to improve relations on a world-

(GERALD R. FORD)

wide basis. To abandon this working relationship, and to go back to a cold war, in my opinion, would be very unwise for we in the United States and the world as a whole . . . If the American people will take a good calculated look at the benefits from detente, I think they will support it rather than oppose it; and, politically, I think any candidate who says abandon detente will be the loser in the long run.

Interview, Washington, Jan. 3/
The New York Times, 1-4:(1)21.

1

In our constitutional system, [foreign policy] should reflect consultation and accommodation between the President and Congress. But in the final analysis, as the framers of our Constitution knew from hard experience, the foreign relations of the United States can be conducted effectively only if there is strong central direction that allows flexibility of action. That responsibility clearly rests with the President.

State of the Union address, Washington, Jan. 19/
The New York Times, 1-20:18.

2

I hope the Congress recognizes that every time we fail to act where aggression is obvious, it just invites a greater action somewhere else . . . [The U.S. henceforth will] meet forthrightly the challenge of any nation that has aggressive interest beyond what we think is reasonable and fair. We're going to meet the challenge unless the Congress continues to hinder us.

Before Inland Daily Press Association,
Washington, Feb. 25/
Los Angeles Times, 2-26:(1)4.

3

I don't use the word "detente" any more. I think that we ought to say that the United States will meet with the superpowers—the

Soviet Union, [Communist] China, and others—and seek to relax tensions so that we can continue a policy of peace through strength. If we're strong militarily, which we are, and if we continue that strength, we can negotiate with the Soviet Union, with China and with others in order to maintain that peace. And "detente" is only a word that was coined. I don't think it's applicable any more.

Interview, Washington, March 1/
Los Angeles Times, 3-2:(1)4.

4

No one should mistake our internal debates as a weakening of our intention to protect our interests and to live up to our obligations to our friends. The United States will not only remain secure in its power, but I assure you we shall not hesitate to use that power when it must be used in our national interst.

Before Daughters of the American Revolution,
Washington, April 21/
Los Angeles Times, 4-22:(1)10.

5

Threats are not only risky but rather old-fashioned in today's world. I will not hesitate to use force when it is clearly required to protect American lives and American interests, but I will make no threats I cannot carry out in full comprehension of the cost . . . It isn't a job for babes and it isn't a job for bullies.

Portland, Ore./ The Washington Post, 5-23:(A)8.

6

Today America is at peace and seeks peace for all nations. Not a single American is at war anywhere on the face of this earth tonight. Our ties with Western Europe and Japan, economic as well as military, were never stronger. Our relations with Eastern Europe, the Soviet Union and mainland China are firm, vigilant and forward-looking. Policies I have initiated offer sound progress for the peoples of the Pacific, Africa and Latin America. Israel and Egypt, both trusting the

United States, have taken an historic first step that promises an eventual just settlement for the whole Middle East. The world now respects America's policy of peace through strength. The United States is again the confident leader of the free world.

Accepting the Presidential nomination at Republican National Convention, Kansas City, Aug. 19/ The New York Times, 8-20:(A)10.

1

There are those in this political year who want to withdraw our troops from their positions overseas. The voices of retreat talk about a phased withdrawal. They talk as if our defenses won't be weakened if we only dismantle them one brick at a time. They are very, very wrong. Preparedness preserves peace, weakness invites war.

Before National Guard Association, Washington, Sept. 1/ The New York Times, 9-2:21.

2

The foreign policy of the United States meets the highest standards of morality. What is more moral than peace? And the United States is at peace today. What is more moral in foreign policy than for the Administration to take the lead in the World Food Conference in Rome in 1974 when the United States committed 6 million metric tons of food, over 60 per cent of the food committed for the disadvantaged and under-developed nations of the world? The Ford Administration wants to eradicate hunger and disease in our under-developed countries through the world. What is more moral than for the United States under the Ford Administration to take the lead in southern Africa, in the Middle East? Those are initiatives in foreign policy which are of the highest moral standards, and that is indicative of the foreign policy of this country.

Debate with Democratic Presidential nominee Jimmy Carter, San Francisco, Oct. 7/ The New York Times, 10-8:(A)19.

. . . American Presidents have always known they should never say in advance precisely what course of action this country would take in the event of an international crisis . . . When a potential adversary knows what you will and won't do in advance, your flexibility is limited and his is increased. He can probe with impunity or redirect his efforts at more tempting targets.

Before Pittsburgh Economic Club, Oct. 26/ Los Angeles Herald-Examiner, 10-26:(A)1.

Malcolm Fraser
Prime Minister of Australia
4

[The conflict between the U.S. Congress and the President on foreign policy] materially contributed to Soviet intervention in Angola and their belief that there would not be a reaction from the United States. Some years ago, there were six or eight significant leaders in Congress, and if a President had their support he would be assured of the support of the Congress in certain policies. There now is a risk of the effectiveness of U.S. foreign policy being reduced very severely because of the differences between Congress and the Executive.

Discussion with Chinese Premier Hua Kuo-feng, Peking, June 20/ The Christian Science Monitor, 6-25:22.

Carlos Fuentes
Mexican Ambassador to France; Author
5

A novelist lives with his characters in a world of the imagination, where idealism and conscience and affairs of the heart dominate life. The might-have-been of human encounters and affairs of state can be imagined idealistically. In an imperfect world, a diplomat has to believe in the possibility of change just as a novelist causes his characters to reach for perfectability. If you can live with the imaginary, you can understand the other man's viewpoint and civilization—and these are central ideas of diplomacy today.

Interview, New York/ The New York Times, 10-28:59.

WHAT THEY SAID IN 1976

E. J. (Jake) Garn
United States Senator, R—Utah

1

The defeats we are suffering in the world today, both real and propaganda losses, with no prospects for any real gains to come out of them, are the result of our failure of will. We have adopted a negative attitude toward our place in the world. The fact is that we must regain our understanding of the nature of international relationships. In Communism, we are faced with an enemy which is out to defeat us; getting this fact firmly established in the minds of the people and their leaders is an important part of the struggle. Adequate defense budgets are part of it, but it does us no good to attain and maintain military superiority if we are not prepared to use our strength. Equally important would be an indication from our political leaders that we understand the challenge, that we are ready to meet it, that we are willing to use the economic and moral power at our command to defend free institutions in the world and that we will live up to our commitments.

*Panel discussion, June 22/***

Valery Giscard d'Estaing
President of France

2

. . . the U.S. is in many ways the most important country in the world today, so it is only natural that you will have a tremendous influence on where the world is going. For 200 years, you have had a history of freedom and independence, and yes, you've been a model in this way. But while we in France come to pay our respects to you, to share your Bicentennial, it is not for us to predict what role you will actually play in the future. That answer . . . is something that still remains to be heard. Meanwhile, I assure you of this: We are all listening.

Interview, Paris/ Parade, 5-16:8.

3

The economic structure of the world in the 1970s and 1990s will be rather different than that of the 1960s because the situation of a certain number of developing countries has profoundly changed and will not go back to what it was. That is true for the oil-producing countries, and for others like Brazil and Mexico. I think there will be a new world economic order, and I want it to be something organized and not simply an empirical situation and more or less turbulent; whereas American policy seems to be more based on the idea that the old situation can be made to work with some rearrangements.

Interview, Washington/
The Washington Post, 5-16:(A)16.

4

Detente is an open and sincere approach. It requires perseverance. It means we must keep our eyes open. It must be based on reciprocity. But opting for detente is the opposite of relaxing our moral defenses. It does not signify, in the slightest degree, that we are renouncing our system of values, or our desire to spread our convictions and preserve our way of life.

Before joint session of Congress,
Washington, May 18/
The Christian Science Monitor, 5-19:2.

Barry M. Goldwater
United States Senator, R—Arizona

5

[Saying foreign-embassy parties for Senators and Congressmen are like "bribes" to obtain favored treatment for the host embassy]: I'm tired of Congressmen picking on business, when this town [Washington] is filled with identical favor-seekers going out night after night. Maybe they should realize that taking favors from embassies is no different than a Colonel or General accepting a weekend trip from Rockwell or Lockheed. Both are trying to influence us to do what the hosts would like us to do.

Washington/
"W": a Fairchild publication, 4-16:6.

6

When people attack [Secretary of State

Henry] Kissinger I say, "All right, stop. Name me a Secretary of State you have liked in your whole life," and they can never think of one. And I can't, either. It is a tough job, and I think he is doing a good job. It is sort of one-man diplomacy. We haven't had this since the days of [John Foster] Dulles. But I will back Kissinger. As long as we don't go to war, and as long as we don't put this country in a position of possibly having to go to war, I think the Secretary of State can be said to be doing a good job.

TV-radio interview, Washington/"Meet the Press,"
National Broadcasting Company, 5-2.

1

The United States has no alternative, I believe, than to develop the capacity to go it alone. We must create a capability whereby we can handle the Soviets unaided by any ally. I don't say we shouldn't seek allies. But there is no potential ally we can seek that would be a bonus.

Before Dallas Council on World Affairs
women's group, Oct. 21/
The Dallas Times Herald, 10-22:(A)21.

Daniel O. Graham
Lieutenant General,
United States Army (Ret.);
Research professor, Center for
Advanced International Studies,
University of Miami
2

American negotiators often seem overly enamoured of "reaching an agreement." That becomes a goal in itself. For the Soviets, "a spirit of detente" is an ephemeral matter, of value largely to inhibit our defense effort. They are looking for agreements that advance their perceived strategic goals. Verification of treaty compliance is also a serious problem. Any successful SALT agreement obviously requires knowledge of what the other side is doing. Unfortunately, the Soviets consistently attempt to deny us information ... In the pre-detente era, Soviet military adven-

ventures such as the Berlin blockade, the grab for South Korea, the aggression against South Vietnam, the attempt to place missiles in Cuba, all failed. During the detente era, we have seen no fewer Communist military adventures—just more successful ones. Consider the conquests of South Vietnam, Cambodia, Laos and Angola; consider the strong positions in Syria, Iraq, India, Somaliland, Mozambique, Guinea. I am convinced that the detente policies that we have pursued led *toward* nuclear war, not *away* from it. The Soviets have consistently shown constraint when faced with superior military power; they have shown less constraint as they perceive us allowing them a military advantage.

Interview/The Reader's Digest, September:81,82.

Samuel L. Gravely, Jr.
Rear Admiral, United States Navy;
Commandant, 11th Naval District
3

Detente does not mean friendship, trust, affection or assured peace. Detente means, simply, a relaxation of tensions—and strength is a prerequisite to acceptable agreements whereby tensions can be relaxed.

Before civic groups, San Diego, Calif., March 10/
Los Angeles Herald-Examiner, 3-11:(A)3.

Alexander M. Haig, Jr.
General, United States Army;
Supreme Allied Commander/Europe
4

[Detente] cannot be, and never has been, a substitute for strength and unity, but rather the fruit of that endeavor. To the degree that it loses that backdrop of strength, it loses its utility for our purposes.

Interview, Casteau, Belgium/
U.S. News & World Report, 3-1:38.

Fred R. Harris
Candidate for the 1976
Democratic Presidential nomination;
Former United States Senator,
D—Oklahoma
5

There is a foreign-policy elite in America. It started with the economically powerful and

WHAT THEY SAID IN 1976

(FRED R. HARRIS)

then reached into the universities, and foundations for the Rostows, the Rusks and the Kissingers, and into business circles for the Dillons, the Wilsons, the Packards and the McNamaras. It has created a virtual monopoly on official and shadow-government foreign-policy thought. The members of this small and powerful group are not consciously evil in intent, but they have devised and administered an American foreign policy which in recent years has caused our influence and reputation in the world to dwindle almost to nothingness. Confused efforts today to develop what is called a "post-Vietnam" foreign policy result from the fact that too many of the leaders of the foreign-policy elite do not see the connection between what America is at home and what it should be abroad. And many do not hold a strong enough commitment to economic and political democracy within our own country. America must be a country here at home which is open and democratic and one which stands for a widespread diffusion of economic and political power. Those are exactly the same principles, too, which must characterize and guide our policies and actions throughout the world.

The Washington Post, 3-4:(A)18.

Mark O. Hatfield
United States Senator, R—Oregon
1

Our greatness is being severely tested. But now, as never before, greatness may be found in restraint—in refraining from becoming involved in situations where our power cannot be used effectively and with justice to ourselves and our traditions.

Before the Senate, Washington, March 29/
The New York Times, 3-29:12.

S. I. Hayakawa
1976 California Republican
U.S. Senatorial nominee
2

[On a question about what the U.S. should do under certain circumstances in explosive

areas of the world]: These are purely rhetorical issues, for goodness sake, and they're rhetorical issues that arise out of reporters trying to corner [politicians] into making a statement. You never say in advance that you'll not use troops. That's giving the show away. You may never intend to use them, but you don't disclose this as a policy. You have to keep some cards up your sleeve. I'm not going to ad-lib foreign policy on a microphone.

News conference, Sacramento, June 22/
Los Angeles Times, 6-23:(1)3.

3

I would hope to encourage insurrection in Hungary, or Poland, or Latvia, or Lithuania, or Estonia, or Tibet for that matter—those poor, crushed nations that have been under Communist tyranny all these years. Nobody seems to give a damn about them any more ... We must not write them off and say, "Too bad, too bad. We'll say a prayer for you."

News conference, Los Angeles, Oct. 27/
Los Angeles Times, 10-28:(1)3.

Martin R. Hoffmann
Secretary of the Army
of the United States
4

There's a tension between disclosure [of information to the public] on the one hand, which is essentially necessary in our society, and the need for secrecy, which has been written about since de Tocqueville, who wrote [in the last century] that democracy is not good for foreign policy.

Interview, Los Angeles, Jan. 9/
Los Angeles Herald-Examiner, 1-10:(A)4.

Hubert H. Humphrey
United States Senator, D—Minnesota
5

I believe that if a Democrat [President] is elected in November the progress made toward the development of an independent Congressional decision-making process in the foreign-policy field must not be curtailed. Collaboration between a Democratic President and Democratic Congress is important and badly needed. But collaboration does not mean that the Congress must acquiesce in every Presidential decision without first giving it careful analysis and consideration. A Democratic Congress must not abandon its own self-consciousness with the advent of a Democratic Chief Executive. In fact, a Democratic President should welcome a more independent foreign-policy view from the Congress. It gives him more diplomatic latitude when there is fundamental agreement. And when there is not a concurrence of views, it serves as a warning to him to proceed with caution and perhaps modify his program . . . I do not believe that the Congress should ever deprive the Executive Branch of its role as chief initiator, negotiator and day-to-day custodian of the nation's foreign-policy interests. These duties are the basic ingredients of Presidential leadership. But it will no longer suffice for Executive Branch officials to dismiss the Congress as hopelessly divided and self-serving in its private assessment of our motives and behavior. There are serious deficiencies in both branches of government that must be solved in an atmosphere of common trust and understanding. If we are to maintain our leadership role in the world, our foreign-policy decision-making processes must be improved.

Before International Relations subcommittee,
Washington/
The Washington Post, 8-15:(C)6.

Samuel P. Huntington
Professor of government,
Harvard University
1

. . . contrary to the rhetoric of the "New Left" and the "new politics," the record shows that the expansion of American power in the world brought with it more-democratic government and strengthened democracy generally. The most obvious evidence, of course, is to be found in Germany and Japan, where democracy was, in effect, imposed by the American occupation and has taken reasonably well. If one looks at the rise and fall of democratic regimes elsewhere, you find that democracy was most prevalent in East Asia in the 1960s, at the peak of American influence there. In Latin America, democratic regimes were most prevalent during the period of the Alliance for Progress, when the U.S. was playing the most active role there. In the past ten years, there has been a decline in American influence in these regions, and that, I think, has been a factor contributing to the decline of democracy.

Interview/ U.S. News & World Report, 3-8:52.

Robert M. Hutchins
President, Center for the Study of
Democratic Institutions
2

We have to have in the United States, first, a strong commitment to the goal of world law. Second, we have to have a strong commitment to the United Nations; if the United Nations is not in a condition to justify such a commitment, then we have to have a commitment to changing that condition. Next, we have to have a strong commitment to work on transnational problems: health, energy, food, pollution, poverty, the atmosphere, the oceans, the multinational corporations; and we have to have a commitment to work on them in ways that announce our desire to solve the problems rather than to advance our interests. Next, we have to stop throwing our weight around; and we have to stop talking about being the most powerful nation on earth—Vietnam should have taught us something about power and strength . . . We are on the road, I think, to a world society, and the process is long and slow and dangerous. Take whichever figure of speech you like: the rebirth we have to go through or the road we have to build. We have to think of the nurture of human life everywhere, otherwise we return to Matthew Arnold's *Dover Beach,* written 100 years ago. "The world," he said, "which seems to lie before us like a land of dreams, so various, so beautiful, so new, hath neither joy, nor love, nor life, nor certitude, nor peace, nor help for pain, and we are here, as on a darkling plain, swept with confused alarms of struggle and flight where ignorant armies clash by night."

Santa Barbara, Calif./ World Issues, December:30.

WHAT THEY SAID IN 1976

Henry M. Jackson
United States Senator, D—Washington;
Candidate for the 1976
Democratic Presidential nomination

1

If we have a detente, it's a hell of a detente that we've got, because the more they talk about detente, the more we're in deeper and deeper trouble, whether it's in Africa or in the Middle East . . . It's obvious detente has become a cover-up for the gross mismanagement of the foreign policy of the United States.

Campaigning in Florida, Jan. 7/
Los Angeles Times, 1-8:(1)6.

2

South Africa and Rhodesia engage in racism against blacks. Uganda does the same against whites and browns. The Soviet Union commits political protestors to insane asylums, stifles the right of intellectuals to speak their minds and publish their views, and denies its citizens the right to leave. Syria persecutes a Jewish minority. Paraguay abuses the Ache Indians. And India, in whom we had great hope, is the latest nation to suppress liberty and repress human rights. [At the UN] there is a growth in self-serving hypocrisy . . . so that human rights concerns are not dealt with on their merits but are, indeed, exploited and manipulated to serve political ends. In such an atmosphere, Zionism is outrageously equated with racism. In such an atmosphere, repression in the U.S.S.R. or racism in Uganda never even reached the agenda. It's time for a foreign policy in Washington which reflects our deepest beliefs as a people, which embodies the best in our democratic and humanitarian heritage . . . The suppression of whole peoples, the persecution of religious and racial minorities, the imprisonment of individuals for their political views remain major sources of international instability and turmoil today . . . We must be willing to use our human-rights concerns in the bargaining process with other nations. Nations seek our grain, our arms, our technology, our managerial know-how . . . Why should

we not seek greater protection for internationally recognized human rights?

Before World Affairs Council of Philadelphia,
April 19/The Washington Post, 4-20:(A)4.

Jacob K. Javits
United States Senator, R—New York

3

We are in danger now of paying too much for detente. It is time to give notice to the Russians that they cannot continue to exercise, at the expense of the interests of America and the free world, the freedom of action they have used in Angola, Cuba, Vietnam and many other places. I am not for quitting detente. I want to continue it and I would not end it yet. But I believe we are very close to the time when we may have to call the turn on the Russians. They must be told that if detente is to continue, they must stop using it to gain advantage over the free world. They must be made to understand that they cannot continue to endanger the interests of America and endanger world peace by bringing us to the brink of confrontation, while at the same time expecting to get the breaks out of detente in terms of their economic situation with increased trade and reduction of armaments.

Interview, Washington/
Los Angeles Herald-Examiner, 2-8:(A)16.

George F. Kennan
American diplomat

4

If we in the West could get over this fixation we have with the idea that the Russians are dying to drop bombs on us, and think, instead, of what is happening to our planet, and address ourselves, resolutely and rapidly, to preventing the catastrophe that looms before us, we would be doing a great deal better . . . Aren't we . . . being unrealistic in the amount of attention we devote to protecting ourselves from the Russians, who, God knows, are not ten feet tall, who have all sorts of troubles of their own, who can't run an agricultural system that really works, who can't adequately house their population, who are rapidly los-

ing their prestige and leadership in the world Communist movement, and have to reckon with China on their long frontier in the East? Show me first an America which has successfully coped with the problems of crime, drugs, deteriorating education standards, urban decay, pornography and decadence of one sort or another—show me an America that has pulled itself together and is what it ought to be —then I will tell you how we are going to defend ourselves from the Russians . . . Please understand that, for purposes of argument, I am given to overstating a case. But isn't it grotesque to spend so much of our energy on opposing such a Russia in order to save a West which is honeycombed with bewilderment and a profound sense of internal decay?
Interview/ The Washington Post, 10-22:(A)26.

Edward M. Kennedy
United States Senator, D— Massachusetts 1

[On the possibility of the U.S. withholding foreign aid to nations that vote against it in the UN and elsewhere]: It is repugnant to me, and I know to many Americans, to suggest that how a country votes in the UN—such as an African nation facing starvation—will affect American foreign assistance in any form. [That policy runs counter to] the entire thrust of the Congressional foreign-assistance-program mandate last year, and the continuing Congressional support for a development program which is free of political encumbrances.
San Francisco Examiner & Chronicle, 2-29:(A)14.

2

It would be intolerable for us to become arms merchants to the world in order to help our balance of payments or even to provide jobs for workers here in this country. Jobs and the balance of payments are both vitally important. But they must not dictate our arms-sales policy, where we run the risk of starting conflicts that could drag us in, at terrible cost in lives and money. It's simply a false and dangerous economy to try solving domestic problems with an arms-sales policy.
Interview/ U.S. News & World Report, 3-8:44.

Jomo Kenyatta
President of Kenya 3

[Peace and security] can never be attained where islands of prosperity make only token recognition of those surrounding oceans of poverty in which they are perpetuated. If peace is indivisible, prosperity is no less so. For this reason, the developed and industrial nations must appreciate that their momentum may only be secure if what is called the developing world is enabled to earn and to enjoy an equitable share of international prosperity.
At United Nations Conference on Trade and Development, Nairobi, Kenya, May 4/ The New York Times, 5-6:3.

Henry A. Kissinger
Secretary of State of the United States 4

When one great power attempts to obtain special positions of influence based on military interventions, the other power is sooner or later bound to act to offset this advantage in some other place or manner. This will inevitably lead to a chain of action and reaction typical of other historic eras in which great powers maneuvered for advantage, only to find themselves sooner or later embroiled in a major crisis, and often in open conflict.
Before Senate Foreign Relations Subcommittee on African Affairs, Washington, Jan. 29/ Vital Speeches, 3-1:291.

5

It is time we recognize that, increasingly, our difficulties abroad are largely of our own making. An effective foreign policy requires a strong national government which can act with assurance and speak with confidence on behalf of all Americans. But when the Executive is disavowed repeatedly and publicly, other governments wonder who speaks for America and what an American commitment means. Our government is in danger of progressively losing the ability to shape events, and a great nation that does not shape history eventually becomes its victim.
At University of Wyoming, Feb. 4/ The New York Times, 2-5:7.

WHAT THEY SAID IN 1976

(HENRY A. KISSINGER)

1

The United States accepts non-alignment as a legitimate national course. Yet too often nations which choose non-alignment to shield themselves from the pressures of powerful global blocs have tended to form a rigid, ideological, confrontationist bloc of their own.

At state dinner, Lima, Peru/
The Washington Post, 2-26:(A)15.

2

The world watches with amazement—our adversaries with glee and our friends with growing dismay—how America seems bent on eroding its influence and destroying its achievements in world affairs through an orgy of recrimination. They see our policies—in Africa, the Eastern Mediterranean, in Latin America, in East-West relations—undermined by arbitrary Congressional actions that may take decades to undo. They see our intelligence system gravely damaged by unremitting, undiscriminating attack. They see a country virtually incapable of behaving with the discretion that is indispensable for diplomacy . . . They see some critics suddenly pretending that the Soviets are ten feet tall and that America, despite all evidence to the contrary, is becoming a second-rate nation. If one group of critics undermines arms-control negotiations and cuts off the prospect of more constructive ties with the Soviet Union, while another group cuts away at our defense budgets and intelligence services and thwarts American resistance to Soviet adventurism, both combined will . . . end by wrecking the nation's ability to conduct a strong, creative, moderate and prudent foreign policy. The result will be paralysis, no matter who wins [the Presidential election] in November. And if America cannot act, others will, and we and all the free peoples of the world will pay the price.

Before Boston World Affairs Council,
March 11/Newsweek, 3-22:23.

3

It is easy to get into a crisis. It is hard to get through one. And those of us who are in positions of responsibility—and have managed crises—must keep in mind not just what looks good in a headline tomorrow, but how we can sustain our policy over a period of time toward our people and toward our allies. And that alone will impress our adversaries. We will show our strength not by rhetoric, but by steadiness, persistence and conviction in defense of the national interest. And America must never be perceived to rely *only* on strength and bluster. It must always stand for something beyond that if it wants sustained domestic and international support.

Interview, Washington/
U.S. News & World Report, 3-15:28.

4

Our policy toward the Soviet Union for the past several years has attempted to take into account the basic realities of the contemporary period: first, that the Soviet Union confronts us for the first time in our recent national experience with a power of roughly equal strength; second, that the existence of nuclear weapons creates conditions that are unprecedented in history, in that a war under current circumstances could lead to the destruction of all civilized life as we know it; third, that around the world and in this country there is a basic yearning for peace. Therefore, our objective must be twofold: We must prevent the Soviet Union from translating its military strength into political advantage, and for that we have to be strong and determined. And, at the same time, we must move beyond a policy of constant confrontation toward the construction of a more stable relationship between the two superpowers. Our purpose is to avoid, if we can, a situation where a succession of crises slides us into a world conflagration. Our policy should be clearly recognized by our people and by the people of the world for what it is: We are determined to protect our interests—those of our allies and of other free peoples—and we also are prepared to explore every reasonable opportunity for peace.

Interview, Washington/
U.S. News & World Report, 3-15:24.

1

[Saying the U.S. is not the world's policeman]: But if we care anything about our security or the fate of freedom in the world, we cannot permit the Soviet Union or its surrogates to become the world's policeman either. It does no good to preach strategic superiority while practicing regional retreat.

At dinner sponsored by Dallas Council on World Affairs and Southern Methodist University, Dallas, March 22/ The Dallas Times Herald, 3-23:(A)1.

2

Ours is not the record of a tired nation, but of a vibrant people ... We are not weak; we have no intention of letting others determine our future. So let us stop disparaging our strength, either moral or material, because if we do, friends of America grow uncertain, enemies become bold and a world yearning for leadership loses hope. America and its allies possess the greatest economic and military power the world has ever seen. And like those Americans who have gone before, we shall not fail.

Before Downtown Rotary Club, Phoenix, April 16/ Los Angeles Times, 4-17:(1)15.

3

I don't want to tie the conduct of foreign policy to me personally. If a foreign policy is well-designed, then it should be able to be carried out by many people. So, on the whole, I would prefer not to stay [after the end of this year]. On the other hand, I don't want to say today, when I don't know the circumstances that exist today ... the necessities that the President may feel he has, that I won't even listen to him; but on the whole I would prefer to leave.

Television interview, May 15/ The New York Times, 7-10:2.

4

[On superpower rivalry]: We have nothing to fear from competition. If there is a military competition, we have the strength to defend our interests. If there is an economic competition, we won it long ago. If there is an ideological competition, the power of our ideas depends on our will to uphold them.

At International Institute for Strategic Studies, London, June 25/ Los Angeles Times, 6-26:(1)3.

5

For America, cooperation among the free nations is a moral, and not merely a practical, necessity. Americans have never been comfortable with calculations of interest and power alone. America, to be itself, needs a sense of identity and collaboration with other nations who share its values. Our association with Western Europe, Canada and Japan thus goes to the heart of our national purpose ... It is not healthy for the United States to be the only center of initiative and leadership in the democratic world.

At International Institute for Strategic Studies, London, June 25/ The Washington Post, 6-26:(A)9.

6

[A year from now,] the policy that has been called detente will be seen to be reflecting ... the only realistic and, for that matter, moral policy that the West can pursue.

Interview, London, June 25/ The Washington Post, 7-1:(A)17.

7

I have always believed that the ultimate test of whatever an American Secretary of State or President does with respect to any other part of the world is the degree to which he contributes to the unity, vitality and strength of free peoples, especially the people of the North Atlantic area. Security by itself is not enough. We have to ask security for what and for what purpose. We therefore owe it to our peoples as we search for security to make clear we are also seeking peace. And we also owe our people that, as we develop our cohesion, we define the purpose that this cohesion serves in terms of a better world. This

WHAT THEY SAID IN 1976

I consider the permanent task of American foreign policy, and history will have to judge how any one Administration carried it out, and I am positive that any new Administration will address itself to the same objectives.

Interview, Brussels, Dec. 10/
The New York Times, 12-11:8.

John D. Lodge
Former United States Representative,
R—Connecticut

1

Why do some turn away in annoyance when the facts are presented regarding the decline, both relatively and absolutely, of American military power? We don't seem to be tuned in. There are certain subjects on which we just don't or won't listen. We hear about Watergate, the CIA, the FBI, crime, inflation, unemployment, recession and oil. But the gradual erosion of the geo-political posture of the United States is either not believed or not noticed, or perhaps not understood. Some members of the House voted to abolish the House Internal Security Committee, known by the press as the "Anti-Red Panel." Does this mean that there are no more Reds or no more threats from the Communists or subversives in the United States, or is it that we can abolish crime simply by abolishing the fire department? Will the self-styled "liberals" give us their assurances? Professor John Kenneth Galbraith, former Chairman of Americans for Democratic Action, speaks derisively of the "cold-war ideologies." Does he think, then, that Communism is the wave of the future? Is it because he thinks that the cold war has become a hot war? Obviously not. He appears to think that all is hunky dory, that those who talk about the East-West conflict are like Neanderthal men, living in the past; they think that the brave new world is the world of detente, convergence, negotiation rather than confrontation. Yet the hard evidence gives the lie to such an assessment of world forces. This of course is why our military posture is so disturbing to responsible thinkers . . . The day of reckoning for the United States has arrived as we Americans are about to celebrate the 200th anniversary of the Declaration of Independence.

At Eisenhower Memorial Scholarship Foundation
awards ceremony, Indianapolis, April 11/
Vital Speeches, 6-1:493.

Clare Boothe Luce
Former American diplomat
and playwright

2

[On detente]: Since its inception, no U.S. foreign policy has ever been harder to come to grips with, or caused so much semantic confusion. Asked in 1973 by a Senate committee to explain his own interpretation of detente, [Secretary of State Henry] Kissinger replied, "Detente is a process, not a final conclusion." But I think you will agree that the claim made for this process was that—for the price of a concession here and a concession there—it would progressively produce a mutual "relaxation" of political and military tensions with the U.S.S.R. which would lead to a "generation of peace." The process of detente is now in its fourth year. The Soviets and the Cubans are in Angola. The Syrians have moved into Lebanon. The PLO has become a Soviet client. And once again, as the war clouds gather over the Middle East, Israel faces a grave hour of peril. The Soviets, who have steadily continued to enlarge their land, air and naval war machine, have started a build-up of military strength in Eastern Europe. The [Communist] Chinese have entertained [former U.S. President] Nixon in order to get across to the White House that Soviet Russia is still very much in the world-domination business. The North Koreans are itching to go. India has passed into the Soviet orbit and is no longer in the democratic fold. The dominoes are still falling in Southeast Asia. In Europe, Portugal, a NATO member, is not yet safely off the democratic danger list. Cyprus and Turkey have not yet composed their differences, and we are threatened with the loss of our Turkish military and intelligence-collection bases. NATO is in a state of shocking disarray . . . And—the subject of the day—Italy: During detente, the

Communist Party in Italy gained an astounding six per cent more of the vote, and is on the verge of the "historic compromise." Finally, the failure of the process of detente has become so visible that President Ford has ordered the State Department to drop the *word* from our diplomatic vocabulary, and to use the term "peace through strength" instead. The truth of the matter is that once again there is a vacuum in U.S. foreign policy which, if it is not soon filled by a policy addressed to the international realities, will lead, on the Soviet Installment Plan, to the isolation of America.

At Conference on the Political Stability of Italy, Washington, April 2/ Vital Speeches, 6-1:483.

1

What has to be done is for the people of the U.S. to achieve some kind of consensus as to what pieces of real estate are of vital importance—and this has never been easy. I hate to have to remind my friends, which I do very often, that the U.S. stood by while France fell. And as far as the majority of the people here were concerned, England would have fallen too, if the Japanese had not misjudged our capacity to respond and attacked us at Pearl Harbor . . . If we cannot get our ducks in a row and decide what and whom we will or will not defend, and, if having made that decision, we don't have what it takes to defend, obviously we are going to have to surrender at some point along the line and accept a tremendous diminishing of our stature and power. Or, we're going to have to go to war, and the likelihood of it being a nuclear war would be very great.

Interview, Washington/ "W": a Fairchild publication, 4-16:9.

Joseph Luns
Secretary General,
North Atlantic Treaty Organization

2

[On U.S. Secretary of State Henry Kissinger, who will leave office next month]: We in the Alliance have been privileged to work with a man to whom the adjective "great" can be applied with sincerity. I am convinced that you [Kissinger] will stand in history as one of the most effective foreign ministers of our century. You have understood the underlying realities of our time. Your goals have been the goals not only of the free world, but of ordinary men and women everywhere—peace, security and prosperity. And to this task you have brought your extraordinary energy and outstanding brilliance.

At NATO conference, Brussels, Dec.10/ San Francisco Examiner & Chronicle, 12-19:(This World)16.

Ian MacGregor
Chairman, AMAX, Inc.
(American Metal Climax)

3

Some countries have nationalized many [foreign] properties. I am rather saddened by this trend, which is continuing. Some leaders abroad apparently are pandering to current political ideas rather than paying attention to the economic needs of their people. I don't see a single developing country that doesn't need capital invested from abroad to help improve living standards. These countries must have industrial activities. Nationalization isn't the way to get them.

Interview/ Nation's Business, January:36.

Mike Mansfield
United States Senator, D—Montana

4

I don't think a bipartisan foreign policy is necessarily a good thing. Congress needn't agree with everything the President does, or, by the same token, the President with the Congress. Instead of using the old Vandenberg phrase that partisan politics stops at the water's edge, we ought to have more consultation between the President and the leadership and the appropriate members of the appropriate committees of the Congress at the take-off point.

Panel discussion/ Center Report, June:28.

5

You can't be isolationist in this world any

(MIKE MANSFIELD)

more. It's too small, getting smaller. The means of communications are improving all the time, and anything which happens anywhere in the world you usually know about within an hour. [But] we've overstretched ourselves too much since the end of the Second World War . . . [And] we don't seem to want to learn. We get out of someplace only when we're ordered out. That was the case in Cambodia, under Sihanouk, when he told us he didn't want our aid, and we did everything except get down on our knees and beg him, "Please, keep on taking our $25-million a year." We were forced out of Indochina. We were almost forced into Angola. We never anticipate. We react to circumstances, whereas we ought to look ahead and recognize that the world is changing; [that] we have to change with it; that as far as our manpower is concerned, it's limited; as far as our resources are concerned, they are not unlimited; that we are rapidly becoming a "have not" nation in many areas; and that we have to get along with the rest of the world, one way or another, whether we like it or not. It's a question of survival. [But] as far as a "fortress America" concept or looking inward or going inward or being isolationist is concerned, it just can't happen—it's an impossibility.

Interview, Washington/
U.S. News & World Report, 8-16:30.

Eugene J. McCarthy
Former United States Senator,
D—Minnesota
1

The militarization of American foreign policy was bipartisan. The ideology was provided mostly by Republicans, but the military hardware was provided by Democrats.

At "Facem in Terris" convocation, Washington,
December ('75)/ Center Report, February:13.

George S. McGovern
United States Senator, D—South Dakota
2

We need to restructure a foreign policy in light of what our limitations are and to seeing ourselves as a member of the family of na-

tions, not as the policeman of the world.

News conference, Anaheim, Calif., Feb. 3/
Los Angeles Times, 2-4:(1)10.

Marcos G. McGrath
Roman Catholic Archbishop of Panama
3

The American people are so provincial, so self-contained. The country is so large they don't think about the rest of the world—an American champion is automatically the "world champion." The most tragic thing in the world today is that self-containment. There is no more-generous people in the world than Americans, but they have no idea what's going on in the rest of the world.

At conference on global justice, Ossining, N.Y./
The Washington Post, 7-30:(B)14.

Robert S. McNamara
President, International Bank for
Reconstruction and Development
(World Bank)
4

The per capita incomes of the more than one billion human beings in the poorest countries have nearly stagnated over the past decade. In statistical terms they have risen only about $2 a year: from $130 in 1965 to $150 in 1975. But what is beyond the power of any set of statistics to illustrate is the inhuman degradation the vast majority of these individuals are condemned to because of poverty. Malnutrition saps their energy, stunts their bodies and shortens their lives. Illiteracy darkens their minds and forecloses their futures. Simple, preventable diseases maim and kill their children. Squalor and ugliness pollute and poison their surroundings . . . By any objective standard, absolute poverty is an anachronistic tragedy in our century. A tragedy because it is a condition of life beneath the level of human decency; and anachronistic because there are now at hand the economic and technological means to end it . . . For [the developed countries] . . . increasing their help to the poorest countries would not require them to diminish in the slightest their own high standards of living, but only to devote a miniscule percentage of the additional per capita real income they will earn over the decade.

At World Bank annual meeting, Manila, Oct. 4/
The Christian Science Monitor, 10-4:25.

Golda Meir
Former Prime Minister of Israel 1

[On U.S. detente with the Soviet Union]: I don't know why you use a fancy French word like "detente" when there's a good English phrase for it—cold war.

Newsweek, 1-19:20.

Walter F. Mondale
United States Senator, D—Minnesota;
1976 Democratic Vice-Presidential
nominee 2

. . . even now that the [Indochina] war is over, there is still no genuinely new direction in American foreign policy . . . We still do not have a government that recognizes that power alone is not enough, that principle must govern our actions overseas . . . A government that believes in itself and is believed-in abroad has the most important security of all. No international expediency will achieve security if security is not based on principle. When we have a foreign policy operating abroad that is inconsistent with the beliefs of the American people, our adversaries know that it is not credible and that it cannot endure.

Campaigning at University of Notre Dame,
Sept. 10/ The Washington Post, 9-11:(A)3.

3

The increasingly dangerous and urgent problem of the international traffic in conventional arms is a particular responsibility of the United States. Many industrialized countries are in the arms-sales business, but in the last eight years we have become the world's largest arms salesman . . . This profligate policy of selling arms to all comers, no matter how repressive or tyrannical the government has had a terrible impact on our

world position and reputation. America was once proud to call itself the arsenal of democracy. But recent Administrations have tried to turn us into just an arsenal. This record in pushing arms sales is scandalous. It has been a practical failure and a moral failure . . . Now, this does not mean that we underestimate the difficulty and complexity of this problem. Countries want arms. Many need arms. Supplier countries are eager for sales. But our problems are no excuse for indifference. Nor do they justify a cynical disregard for the fact that the arms we sow abroad today we may harvest in war tomorrow. The first step must be greater American self-restraint. Improving our balance of payments is not a reason to sell weapons to another country. I believe there should be a presumption against arms sales which should be overcome only if the sale advances American security, foreign policy or world peace.

Campaign address/ World Issues, December:23.

Daniel P. Moynihan
United States Ambassador/
Permanent Representative to the
United Nations 4

The first fact of detente is that it is not a condition, such as peace or war, but a process that can lead away from or toward either, accordingly as we successfully manage the process—or fail to do so. The process arises from the simultaneous necessity to deal with two nominally incompatible imperatives. The first is the technological imperative, which demands that we cooperate as a partner; the other is the ideological imperative that commands that we compete, as with an adversary.

At "Pacem in Terris" convocation, Washington,
December ('75)/ Center Report, February:9.

5

Vietnam taught us the price of intervention. Angola will teach us the price of non-intervention.

Newsweek, 1-19:22.

WHAT THEY SAID IN 1976

(DANIEL P. MOYNIHAN)

1

You must see detente as a situation in which tensions will increase, or you've missed the point altogether. Detente does mean the relaxation of tensions, but we picked the wrong word for the process. If you come to certain accommodations about nuclear armament, you will almost in a mechanical way move the tensions into ideological conflict . . . If you face the nuclear challenge, as God knows we must, the only way to keep it stable is to be very tough on the other area of encounter. If you get unbalanced in that area, then the nuclear area won't hold either . . . If in fact we are in a condition where we won't stand up to the ideological attacks, then we're not well advised to have detente. If we decide that you can't get Americans to take forward positions out there in the world any more—which is the only way that would sustain a technological standoff—then we will get rid of the standoff.

Interview/Newsweek, 1-19:29.

2

It is most disappointing to me that so many of the new nations which were established as democracies after the Second World War, during the decolonization process, have now changed their systems to state-socialism. Small elites run them, and they aren't sharing societies. They aren't even socialist. The power of the state has been merged with business, and you have the greatest concentration of power that's possible . . . What has happened is that the new nations have opted for state-directed economies. There are at least two reasons. First, this was the ideology most in fashion in the European universities where the leaders of the new nations were educated and also was the ideology of the European political parties which most espoused independence. Second, state socialism —or state capitalism, they come to the same thing—has proved a convenient excuse for concentrating power in the hands of those at the head of the government.

Interview, New York/
Nation's Business, February:21.

3

We have got to make [the case for freedom], and if it causes discomfort to those against whom it is made, so be it . . . We came exactly to be feared [in the UN] for the truths we were telling and none of us needs to be ashamed. To the contrary, they are the honor of the Republic and its glory . . . We [Americans] are the party of revolution in the world —we are the revolutionary party—because we stand for freedom. And in this [Bicentennial] year let us never forget it.

Farewell address to U.S. UN mission, New York, Feb. 26/ Los Angeles Herald-Examiner, 2-27:(A)4.

Daniel P. Moynihan
Professor of government, Harvard University; Former United States Ambassador/ Permanent Representative to the United Nations

4

We [the U.S.] are a liberal democracy, and there aren't many of us left. After World War II, 78 nations were created from the lands that had been possessed by the European colonial powers, and 70 of them began as democratic states with constitutions, a free press and the rest. Of those 70 democratic states, only 11 are left—and seven of them are small *islands.*

The National Observer, 4-17:5.

5

In the summer of 1975, the Soviet leaders knew two things. One was that they had a disastrous crop failure; I mean on an Asian level. And they needed to buy 60 million metric tons of wheat from the United States, or else all sorts of troubles would evolve, including those little troubles that have to do with the stability of regimes. And they had to get this wheat from the United States. The second thing they knew was that they had an opportunity to intervene in Africa [in the civil war in Angola] in a way they had never done before and in a place they had never been before—to some advantage to them, whatever it might be. They should surely have known, would surely have made the calculation, that they could do one or the other. They could get American wheat, or they could get Angola. They could not have gotten both; it would have been impossible to get both. Well, you saw what happened. They obviously judged they could get both and they got both. Now, supposing the situation were reversed. Suppose we had an option to have Russia sell us 60 million tons of wheat that we desperately needed, or we could pick up Lithuania, or something absurd like that. Can you imagine the Russians letting us have the wheat and then allowing us to make a military incursion into some region where we—well, the answer is, they wouldn't let you. You could do one of the other; you couldn't do both.

Interview, New York/
Los Angeles Times, 4-22:(1)6.

Edmund S. Muskie
United States Senator, D—Maine
1

A free people deserve to be informed and to consent to the foreign policy we pursue ... So let us seek a foreign policy we can talk about in public and agree to in advance. Let us defend our real interests and leave no doubt of it. But where our interest is not directly or clearly involved, let our adversaries learn, as we did in Vietnam, the expensive lesson of the limits of their power.

National television address, Jan. 21/
U.S. News & World Report, 2-2:64.

Fred Warner Neal
Professor of international relations and government, Graduate School, Claremont (Calif.) College
2

I am for detente because I am primarily interested in the welfare of the United States and because I am for peace in the world, and I do not think that that can be achieved without the collaboration of the Soviet Union. I am for detente because I am for the defense of Israel, and I do not think that that can be achieved unless there is American-Soviet collaboration. [The] cold-war psychology is still deep, and it is reflected in repeated exaggerations about Soviet strength and Soviet aims

and in the assertion that only the Russians get something out of detente, that we [the U.S.] get nothing from it. I don't think we should say, "Let the Russians prove they are worthy of detente." Let us prove, also, that we are worthy of detente.

At "Pacem in Terris" convocation, Washington,
December ('75)/
The Center Magazine, March-April:19.

Robert E. Osgood
Dean, School of International Studies, Johns Hopkins University
3

[In addition to recognizing the benefits of detente,] it is also important to recognize what detente is not. It is not an accommodation of ideological or political objectives—even if it does include a de-escalation of rhetoric. It is not an accommodation of many conflicting interests in important parts of the world, especially in the less-developed world. It does not mean that the Soviet Union has abandoned the pursuit of dominant influence in areas troubled by national and ethnic conflict and with revolutionary ferment. Nor does detente mean that the Soviet Union has abandoned the pursuit of an advantageous global military balance which it can exploit diplomatically and politically, even with the constraints of stabilizing the nuclear strategic competition.

At "Pacem in Terris" convocation, Washington,
December ('75)/
The Center Magazine, March-April:18.

Don Paarlberg
Director of Agricultural Economics, Department of Agriculture of the United States
4

An idea has developed that the food-exporting countries, particularly those like the United States, have food power in the sense that the petroleum-exporting countries have petroleum power. The idea is that the food-exporting countries should organize themselves and use their food power to counter and indeed to break up the power of the OPEC nations. The idea is that food can be

(DON PAARLBERG)

used as a weapon, to coerce other nations into some desired form of behavior. The use of American agricultural capabilities for such a purpose is not in keeping with the policies of the U.S. government. We see our agricultural capability as a means of increasing exports, earning foreign exchange, building interdependence with other countries in the interest of peace, assisting needy countries to get themselves over difficult circumstances, and facilitating the response of foreign governments to diplomatic initiatives in behalf of peace. These uses are peaceful and purposive. An effort to use food as a weapon is likely to engender adverse public reactions throughout the world. This would be an error on diplomatic as well as moral grounds.

Before Japanese Ministry of
Agriculture and Forestry, Tokyo, June 7/
Vital Speeches, 8-1:628.

Otis G. Pike
United States Representative,
D—New York
1

. . . Secretary [of State Henry] Kissinger yells McCarthyism whenever anybody criticizes him. I happen to think that Secretary Kissinger is undoubtedly a tremendously able diplomat, but I don't think he believes much in democracy. I think he is impatient with the democratic process.

Washington/
San Francisco Examiner & Chronicle, 2-29:(A)12.

Ronald Reagan
Candidate for the
1976 Republican Presidential nomination;
Former Governor of California (R)
2

If you were a Russian official and you heard the American Secretary of State [Henry Kissinger] deliver stern warnings to you for trying to dominate the situation in Angola, but all the time you knew he was packing his bags to come to Moscow to negotiate a new arms-limitation agreement, would you really take his words seriously? And if you were a

Chinese official watching these contradictory moves, wouldn't you wonder just how much confidence you could have in America's words?

At Phillips Exeter Academy, Feb. 10/
The New York Times, 2-11:15.

3

Despite [President] Ford's evident decency, honor and patriotism, he has shown neither the vision nor the leadership necessary to halt and reverse the diplomatic and military decline of the United States . . . I believe in the peace of which Mr. Ford speaks, as much as any man. But in places such as Angola, Cambodia and Vietnam, the peace they have come to know is the peace of the grave. All I can see is what other nations the world over see—collapse of the American will and the retreat of American power . . .

Campaigning, Orlando, Fla./
San Francisco Examiner & Chronicle,
3-14:(This World)7.

4

I don't think [Secretary of State Henry] Kissinger is in any way unpatriotic and I don't think that maybe there's any conspiracy or plot on his part. Dr. Kissinger, though, believes that, like the great civilizations of the past—and he's expressed this—that the United States has had its day and we're in our decline, because the people of this country don't have the will any more to keep us up in Number 1. So, therefore, his attitude is one of bowing and scraping to the Soviet Union, saying "they're going to be Number 1, and, therefore, I must make those concessions that'll have them treat us nicely when they're once in charge."

Campaigning in Houston, April 15/
Los Angeles Times, 4-16:(1)14.

5

Detente, which started out worthily and with a good purpose, has become a one-way street. I think the Soviet Union has become more truculent, more aggressive in the world. And we have been responding with pre-emptive concessions without getting anything in return. I think it is time for us to rebuild our strength and at the same time make detente, if it is to exist, a two-way street by telling the Russians that is the only way we will observe it.

Interview/ The Christian Science Monitor, 6-3:17.

John J. Rhodes
United States Representative, R—Arizona

1

The meaning of detente was a lessening of the tension on the bow string, and that is all it was intended to be. It certainly doesn't introduce a brand new world in which we can all go tripping off into the sunset hand in hand with peace in sight. But it does mean—at least I hope it does—that the Russians and the Americans will spend less on armaments and more on helping people. If it doesn't mean that, then it isn't worth having.

TV-radio interview, Washington/
"Meet the Press,"
National Broadcasting Company, 5-9.

Nelson A. Rockefeller
Vice President of the United States

2

[Actions by Congress interfering with the President's role in international affairs] have already caused serious repercussions abroad and have even worse implications for the future of our foreign policy. There is, frankly, no alternative but to return to the Constitutional arrangement of strong Presidential initiative and leadership in foreign affairs with the cooperation of the Congress. The ship of state cannot be steered by 536 hands grasping for the tiller.

Before International Press Institute,
Philadelphia, May 10/
Los Angeles Times, 5-11:(1)12.

3

Whether we like it or not, a continuing attempt is under way to organize the world into

a new empire in which the Soviet sun never sets. The era of old-world imperialism has gone, and yet we find ourselves faced with a new and far more complex form of imperialism—a mixture of Czarism and Marxism with colonial appendages.

At St. Paul's Church, Frankfurt, West Germany,
May 15/ The Dallas Times Herald, 5-16:(A)9.

Donald H. Rumsfeld
Secretary of Defense
of the United States

4

If one thinks that detente means that the Russians are our friends—that we can trust them, and that they will conduct themselves the way we do in our country, that they believe in freedom and individual, God-given rights of man, that they will not continue to support "just wars of national liberation," or that they will not continue to develop substantial military strength to serve their interests—anyone who thinks that is dead wrong. That is not what Soviet policy or behavior is all about. Detente, most precisely, from our standpoint, is an approach that the United States is using with the Soviet Union to determine if it's possible to relax tensions. Is it sensible to try to lower the level of potential confrontation with the Soviet Union, if it can be done in a way that benefits our national interests and does not adversely affect our security? I believe the answer is "Yes." Does that mean that such policy will solve all the problems of the world? No, it does not. Does it mean that it's going to transform the Soviet Union into a system that is compatible with the beliefs of the United States? No, it does not.

Interview, Washington/
U.S. News & World Report, 3-15:31.

James R. Schlesinger
Former Secretary of Defense
of the United States

5

We should remember that the word detente does not exist in the Russian vocabulary—the Russian phrase is peaceful coexistence, one

WHAT THEY SAID IN 1976

(JAMES R. SCHLESINGER)

which has many meanings, tracing back to Lenin, and implying in its original form a continuation of confrontation between the two social systems. This does not imply that we should not aggressively and vigorously pursue detente, true detente; it does not imply that we should not pursue arms-control measures irrespective of what happens to political detente, because there is no need to go on piling up endlessly expansions of strategic force capabilities that augment the security of neither side.

At "Pacem in Terris" convocation, Washington, December ('75)/ Center Report, February:11.

Richard S. Schweiker
United States Senator, R— Pennsylvania
1

I don't think we can have allies who aren't willing to help themselves. We went through Vietnam and unless basically the people are willing to help themselves, there is no sense defending them. This is one of the reasons I felt and voted opposing the war in Vietnam, because I didn't feel they were really willing to defend themselves. I think the same thing is true of [other] things abroad. If they are willing to help themselves and to help support the effort, fine; but we can't be a crutch for everyone.

TV-radio interview, Washington/
"Meet the Press,"
National Broadcasting Company, 8-1.

William W. Scranton
United States Ambassador/
Permanent Representative to the
United Nations
2

. . . I do not think that there is a basic underlying reason for a confrontation between the United States of America and the Third World. After all, there is no nation on earth that believes more fundamentally in the two basic desires, as I understand them, of the Third World. One is independence or liberty; and certainly that's a basic tenet of the United

States. And the second is an opportunity for economic growth; and, once again, we are constantly exhibited around the world as the outstanding example of a nation that believes in economic growth.

News conference, New York, March 19/
The Wall Street Journal, 4-26:14.

James C. H. Shen
Ambassador to the United States
from the Republic of
(Nationalist) China
3

Especially in international affairs, morality is at a low ebb. The ideas of Machiavelli—that physical force and craft instead of right and moral principles were the essential bases for political actions—have received wider acceptance than ever before. Today the contests between the forces of enslavement and freedom have revealed schemes and methods more unscrupulous and cynical than anything Machiavelli had ever thought possible. The ascendancy of Communism has exposed the weaknesses of democracy and the decline of the forces of freedom. There is an apparent lack of resolution in the international community to defend freedom and the democratic system even on the part of nations that outwardly cherish them. Mindful though I am of the deplorable fact that the forsaking of moral principles in foreign relations is as old as diplomacy itself, I do think that a better world order might have come into being if the criteria of judgment in the conduct of nations toward one another were based on morality instead of expediency.

At George Peabody School for
Teachers commencement, Nashville, Tenn./
The Wall Street Journal, 11-4:16.

Sidney Sober
Deputy Assistant Secretary for
Near Eastern and South Asian Affairs,
Department of State of
the United States
4

The U.S. record on self-determination for

the territories under its jurisdiction is clear for all to see. One territory over which the United States exercised jurisdiction in this century has evolved to independence. Others have come to statehood in our Union. Another enjoys commonwealth status and others also elect their governors and legislatures in free and regular elections in accord with their preference. The United States came to its own independence from colonial status. The United States is not a colonial nation, and it does not intend to become one.

At United Nations, New York, Dec. 2/
The Washington Post, 12-17:(A)20.

Alexander I. Solzhenitsyn
Exiled Soviet author 1

[Criticizing the West's detente with the Soviet Union]: You may call this "detente" if you like, but after [the Soviet intervention in] Angola, I just can't understand how one's tongue can utter this word. Your [British] Defense Minister has said that, after [the East-West peace conference in] Helsinki, the Soviet Union is passing the test. I don't know how many countries have still to be taken; maybe the Soviet tanks have to come to London for your Defense Minister to say at last that the Soviet Union has finally passed the test. Or will it still be sitting for the exam? I think there is no such thing as detente.

Television interview, London/"Panorama,"
British Broadcasting Corporation, 3-1.

Stuart Symington
United States Senator, D—Missouri 2

The whole concept of [foreign] aid has gotten to be like coffee—a habit. The habit was started by worthy causes, such as the Truman Doctrine and the Marshall Plan. Now it continues. Around Congress, it's harder to get $100,000 for a dam in Missouri than it is to get $100 million in aid for a foreign country.

U.S. News & World Report, 11-1:57.

Herman E. Talmadge
United States Senator, D—Georgia 3

Agri-business means agri-power: Our

nation is the breadbasket of the world. It has economic punch. It has political clout all over the world. It is a powerful lever in our foreign relations . . . I do not believe, of course, that we ought to use agriculture as some kind of weapon for retribution or economic sanction. Farm and ranch families of America ought not to be made pawns on some kind of world chess board for diplomats to use in grand political schemes. But we most certainly can use the great strength of our food-and-fiber system as a diplomatic bargaining tool.

At dinner for Wheat Center-U.S.A.,
Hutchinson, Kansas/
The Christian Science Monitor, 1-19:18.

John G. Tower
United States Senator, R—Texas 4

We have the power to defend our own people and develop a climate for self-realization for other freedom-loving peoples in the world . . . The question of morality comes when we use [power]. It is immoral to use power for self-aggrandizement or tyranny. It is also immoral to possess great power and not use it to maintain a climate of liberty in the world.

At North Texas Annual Conference of
United Methodist Church, Dallas, May 31/
The Dallas Times Herald, 6-1:(B)1.

John V. Tunney
United States Senator, D—California 5

Why the United States feels compelled to become the major arms supplier of the world, I don't know. But we are selling about two-thirds of the total number of arms in international commerce. Without the United States, many wars could not be fought.

Re-election campaign address,
University of California, Los Angeles, Oct. 26/
Los Angeles Times, 10-27:(1)27.

Adam Ulam
Director, Russian Research Center,
Harvard University 6

If you are decisive and intelligent, detente

WHAT THEY SAID IN 1976

(ADAM ULAM)

means peaceful cooperation. If you are not strong and intelligent, then detente can also mean appeasement. You might say Munich was a form of detente.

Newsweek, 1-19:24.

John Vorster
Prime Minister of South Africa

1

Above all, the United States must take a firm stand against terrorism, regardless of the origin or reasons for that terrorism. You cannot reject terrorism in one part of the world—such as, for example, in Munich or Lebanon—and condone it in parts of Africa. It is a scourge that thrives and spreads on passivity—not to speak of encouragement. Under no circumstances should the United States give aid to countries which are found to be aiding or encouraging terrorism or violence against any other country.

Interview, Cape Town/
U.S. News & World Report, 6-14:60.

Clifton R. Wharton, Jr.
President, Michigan State University;
Chairman, Board for International Food
and Agricultural Development

2

I cannot urge more strongly that the new [Carter] Administration place high on its foreign-policy agenda the increased support and funding of this nation's world-wide activities in famine prevention. Such a step would represent a dramatic shift in our foreign policy emphasis. It would signal to the poorest of the poor in the developing world that the United States believes freedom from hunger is a more important international goal than the sale of arms.

Before agricultural scientists, Houston, Nov. 29/
The New York Times, 11-30:3.

Frederick R. Wills
Foreign Minister of Guyana

3

When dealing with an intransigent tyrant, the use of the sword has often induced a climate of favorable negotiations.

The Dallas Times Herald, 10-1:(A)3.

Ardeshir Zahedi
Iranian Ambassador
to the United States

4

[On criticism that foreign-embassy parties for Senators and Congressmen are forms of "bribes" to obtain favored treatment for the host embassy]: One can't keep relations between two countries so formal. Knowing each other unofficially makes it easier to promote understanding and world peace. It's not a conflict of interest at all. It's the difference between a free society and a closed—maybe even a Communist—society.

"W": a Fairchild publication, 4-16:7.

Elmo R. Zumwalt, Jr.
Candidate for the 1976 Virginia
Democratic U.S. Senatorial nomination;
Admiral (Ret.) and former Chief of
Operations, United States Navy

5

[On detente]: The Soviets see the United States right now as a great placid bovine chewing its cud in the sun, with two huge udders extending over to them—one labelled "grain" and the other labelled "technology." It stands there letting itself be milked dry, twitching its tail contentedly, too lazy and too placid to notice.

Before Virginia Associated Press Newspapers/
The Washington Post, 2-15:(Potomac)12.

INTELLIGENCE

George Bush
Director, Central Intelligence Agency
of the United States
1

I believe the [CIA] abuses of the past are indeed in the past. I think the American people support the concept of a strong Central Intelligence Agency, and if they don't, they'd better, because we are living in an extremely troubled world.

News conference,
Houston, May 7/
The New York Times, 5-9:(1)26.

Jimmy Carter
Candidate for the
1976 Democratic Presidential nomination;
Former Governor of Georgia (D)
2

I think the proper role of the CIA is the role that was spelled out in the original legislation that set up the CIA as a source of information and intelligence. And I would try to have the CIA perform its functions effectively and efficiently and legally for a change, and I would be responsible to the American people for that performance. I would have no objection to Congressional oversight. I personally would favor a joint Congressional committee rather than independent committees of the two branches of Congress. But I don't see any reason for the CIA, through covert means, to try to overthrow governments.

TV-radio interview, New York/
"Meet the Press,"
National Broadcasting Company, 7-11.

Ray S. Cline
Executive director of studies,
Georgetown Center for Strategic and
International Studies; Former Director of
Intelligence and Research, Department of
State of the United States
3

I freely admit that in the 28 years the CIA has been in operation, some very serious mistakes were made. Some were made in the gray areas where guidelines were not adequate, because this was a new part of government, and so misinterpretations were possible. But the worst indiscretions were made by following direct orders from Presidents of the United States to become involved in internal-security functions which were properly the task of other government agencies . . . My fear and conviction is that this year-long bath of criticism of the intelligence agencies, particularly of the CIA, has nearly destroyed the effectiveness of the agencies in collecting information abroad. It has discredited and demoralized the people in the intelligence system, many of whom have not done anything except read newspapers and foreign-intelligence reports and write scholarly essays and reports to the Congress, to the White House, to the State Department, to the Defense Department. Furthermore, these criticisms have given the impression abroad that the CIA is a criminal institution with which it is unpalatable to deal. I assure you we cannot operate effectively in the international arena if we destroy our own institutions.

At "Pacem in Terris" convocation, Washington,
December ('75)/
The Center Magazine, March-April:30.

WHAT THEY SAID IN 1976

William E. Colby
*Director, Central Intelligence Agency
of the United States*

1

Intelligence now enables us to anticipate as well as to know. Anticipation allows us to arm ourselves, if such be necessary, with the right weapon. We need not face the light and accurate slingshot with an unwieldy broadsword. Anticipation also allows us to deter aggressors, demonstrating by our protective shield the futility of attacking us. Anticipation these days also presents us with an opportunity, beyond anything known in the past, to negotiate. When we have knowledge of a foreign weapons system in the research phase, we can then discuss a mutual agreement to forego its development and deployment. This can save millions of dollars on both sides—which can then be spent on plowshares rather than on swords.

*At "Pacem in Terris" convocation, Washington,
December ('75)/ Center Report, February:12.*

2

I believe the U.S. government needs an ability to conduct large, unattributed, unadmitted [covert] operations. Otherwise, we're in a position of either having to complain with a diplomatic protest and be ignored, or having to threaten to use military force, which nobody wants to do.

Interview, Washington/ Time, 1-19:17.

3

[On criticism of CIA methods and actions]: In truth, our misdeeds were few and far between ... We never assassinated anyone. And our own post-mortems of our performance in various intelligence situations have been selectively exposed [by CIA critics] to give a totally erroneous impression of continued failures of American intelligence. In fact, we have the best intelligence service in the world.

*Before Senate Government
Operations Committee, Washington, Jan. 23/
The Washington Post, 1-24:(A)8.*

4

Traditionally, intelligence is assumed to operate in total secrecy and outside the law. This is impossible under our Constitution and

in our society. As a result, when CIA was established in 1947, a compromise was made under which broad, general statutes were drawn and carefully limited arrangements for Congressional review were adopted. It was then believed necessary to sacrifice oversight for secrecy. Our society has changed, however, and a greater degree of oversight is now considered necessary. U.S. intelligence has already moved out of the atmosphere of total secrecy which previously characterized it. We who are in intelligence are well aware of the need to retain public confidence and Congressional support if we are to continue to make our contribution to the safety of our country. Thus, from the earliest days of the current investigation [of the CIA], I have stressed my hope that they will develop better guidelines for our operations and stronger oversight, to insure that our activities do remain within the Constitution and the laws of our country ... In 1947, we took a small step away from total secrecy by enacting general statutes and constructing careful oversight arrangements in the Congress. Proposals now under consideration would alter these arrangements to assure more detailed oversight. But it is essential that the pendulum not swing so far as to destroy the necessary secrecy of intelligence or destroy intelligence itself in the process.

*Before Senate Government
Operations Committee, Washington, Jan. 23/
U.S. News & World Report, 2-9:19.*

William E. Colby
*Former Director, Central Intelligence
Agency of the United States*

5

People ask me if I regret having gone into the intelligence service, and my prompt answer is "no." I found it a fascinating and challenging life. Over the years, we've brought intelligence into the permanent structure of the government and not merely as a wartime emergency. There are cadres in the CIA today far better trained than I was, a group of really brilliant young men and women ... We need an intelligence service in the government. I don't believe anyone would argue against

that. How it's run is another matter. I leave that to my successor and those who follow.
Interview/ Parade, 2-29:4.

Gerald R. Ford
President of the United States   1

The crippling of our foreign-intelligence services increases the danger of American involvement in direct armed conflict. Our adversaries are encouraged to attempt new adventures, while our own ability to monitor events, and to influence events short of military action, is undermined. Without effective intelligence capability, the United States stands blindfolded and hobbled . . . It is time to go beyond sensationalism and insure an effective, responsible and responsive intelligence capability.
State of the Union address, Washington, Jan. 19/
The New York Times, 1-20:18.

2

I strongly believe in covert operations. I have no hesitancy to say so. I don't know how a President could conduct foreign policy without a degree of covert operations. [As for safeguards,] fairly sizable numbers in the Congress are today given information about covert operations—six committees. That is a lot more than used to get it when I was there. Second, as far as I know, no covert operations that have been undertaken by this Administration have involved any commitment beyond the precise operations authorized by me with my signature. Now, with any Administration that is deceptive, of course, I think the Congress and public ought to be wary. But as far as we are concerned, there is not going to be any commitment that the Congress or a fairly sizable number [of Congressmen or Senators] do not know about.
Interview, Washington/ Time, 1-26:12.

3

For over a year, the nation has engaged in exhaustive investigations into the activity of the CIA and other intelligence units of our government. Facts, heresay and closely held secrets—all have been spread out on the public record. We have learned many lessons from this experience, but we must not become obsessed with the deeds of the past. We must act for the future . . . As Americans, we must not and will not tolerate actions by our government which abridge the rights of our citizens. At the same time, we must maintain a strong and effective intelligence capability in the United States. I will not be a party to the dismantling of the CIA and the other intelligence agencies. To be effective, our foreign policy must be based upon a clear understanding of the international environment. To operate without adequate and timely intelligence information will cripple our security in a world that is still hostile to our freedoms. Nor can we confine our intelligence to the question of whether there will be an imminent military attack. We also need information about the world's economy, about political and social trends, about food supply and population growth, and certainly about terrorism. To protect our security diplomatically, militarily and economically, we must have a comprehensive intelligence capability.
News conference, Washington, Feb. 17/
The New York Times, 2-18:20.

Morton Halperin
Senior consultant, Center for National
Security Studies; Former Deputy
Assistant Secretary of Defense
of the United States   4

It is clear that we need information about potential adversaries and potential dangers in the world. We need some kind of intelligence-gathering capability. But it is vitally important that we take the kind of steps . . . to bring that capability under control. We need legislation by the Congress spelling out precisely what the intelligence agencies can and cannot do, and we need to back that up with effective laws making it a crime for those agencies to violate their charter . . . The gathering and evaluating of evidence can be

(MORTON HALPERIN)

controlled by law. But it is an absolute delusion to think we can bring covert operations under democratic controls and make them conform to our democratic ideals. Covert operations are simply inconsistent with the American constitutional system and with the ideal we stand for in the world. The time has come for the United States to abolish its career service for covert operations and to make such operations illegal.

At "Pacem in Terris" convocation, Washington, December ('75)/ The Center Magazine, March-April:29.

David N. Henderson
United States Representative,
D—North Carolina   *1*

[Criticizing publicity given to revelations of past wrongdoing by U.S. intelligence agencies] I think it provides ammunition for our enemies. I am not condoning any illegal actions of the intelligence organizations or the Federal Bureau of Investigation—nor am I critical of the Senate Intelligence Committee in its investigation or in seeking all the facts that could be obtained. But I blow the whistle on the revelation of everything that they learned. It is not in the best interest of our country, nor is it necessary for us to reveal all that we learn in Congressional investigations, especially in the sensitive area of intelligence-gathering. Many editors have suggested that it's good for the soul of America to reveal all the wrongdoings. I think as a people we subscribe to the premise that "confession is good for the soul." But I'm not sure that that premise extends to international operations or national security.

Interview/ U.S. News & World Report, 1-12:21.

Clarence M. Kelley
Director,
Federal Bureau of Investigation   *2*

The intelligence services of the Soviet Union and Soviet-bloc countries look upon the United States as the primary enemy. One priority of these intelligence services is penetration of the United States intelligence community. They also endeavor to penetrate other departments and agencies of the government where they feel they can develop a willing source or asset who can furnish them information of value. A second priority is the collection of scientific and/or technological information, particularly in those areas where these countries are behind the United States. They take information where they can get it. And their purpose is to glean everything they can through their intelligence officers assigned to diplomatic establishments, or in this country as commercial representatives or exchange participants. They also employ "deep" undercover agents, posing as U.S. citizens—the illegals. This is a most difficult area to detect and counter. It's not like the bank-robber or even organized crime. This is actively funded with the total resources of a hostile government.

Interview, Washington/ U.S. News & World Report, 4-5:34.

Henry A. Kissinger
Secretary of State of the
United States   *3*

...leaks, sensational investigations and the demoralization of our intelligence services—at a time when our adversaries are stepping up their own efforts—are systematically depriving our government of the ability to respond. [Unless the country ends its division,] our only option is to retreat—to become an isolated fortress island in a hostile and turbulent global sea, awaiting the ultimate confrontation, with the only response we will not have denied ourselves—massive retaliation.

At University of Wyoming, Feb. 4/ The New York Times, 2-5:7.

Dale Milford
United States Representative, D—Texas   *4*

[On charges that, over the years, the CIA has tried to carry out assassination plots against foreign leaders]: That simply is not true. There is not a single shred of evidence that there has been attempt to execute any of these plots. They were simply plans lying on the shelf to be used only in case of war, and to be executed only after being ordered by competent authority . . . How does that differ, for example, from what is taking place at Fort Hood, where thousands of men are being trained to kill people, but no one is *ordering* them to kill anybody? How does that differ with Carswell Air Force Base planes, with maps in the cockpit to carry out bombing missions? Nobody is sending those planes to the targets.

Interview/ The Dallas Times Herald, 1-5:(A)14.

Walter F. Mondale
United States Senator, D— Minnesota;
1976 Democratic Vice-Presidential nominee 1

I never joined those who wanted to prohibit covert [CIA] activities. I did say they should be much more limited, put under responsible control and used only in those rare instances where it is essential. And I think that is the proper line to draw. I never attacked the need for the best intelligence apparatus in the world. I never attacked the need for the Federal Bureau of Investigation. I attacked the abuse of power.

Interview/ Newsweek, 7-26:26.

Edmund S. Muskie
United States Senator, D— Maine 2

Much of the world today is watching with amazement as a Congress of the United States examines U.S. intelligence operations overseas. I know many of you must have asked yourselves, as I have, whether it is necessary to hang out the dirty linen—to talk about assassination attempts, to admit that the whole world knows about both us and themselves, that nations spy. Yes, it is necessary. How else is the American public to get hold of its foreign policy again? How else can we guarantee that interventions in other countries are an appropriate expression of deliberate U.S. policy,

and not the making of some faceless bureaucrat? Oh, sure, it is inconvenient to conduct foreign policy in the open, and certainly there will always be a need for intelligence work and for secrecy within the bounds of established policy. But a republic gets its strength from the consent of the governed and from a consensus on shared objectives. It gets only weakness and disappointment from secrecy and surprise.

Broadcast address, Jan. 21/
Vital Speeches, 2-15:261.

Otis G. Pike
United States Representative,
D—New York 3

[On a Congressional committee to oversee the activities of the CIA]: You have to make a distinction between what Congress shall be made aware of and what shall be published. I would make a good oversight committee of Congress aware of everything. I would not make every member of Congress aware of everything. When you have gone that far, you have lost your secrecy. The 535 members are too many people to share secrets with. Obviously, we protect the name of our agent in Moscow, if any. We protect the names of people whose lives would be endangered if revealed. But when you get to people who have conducted illegal acts, I wouldn't protect them even if they are agents . . . One of the things that we have learned is that the CIA has been made out as a symbol of all that was wrong with America. But the CIA did not go off and attempt to assassinate people by itself. The CIA was told to do these things. What we have tried very hard to do is to establish the accountability for who told them. In the final analysis, you get back to the integrity and good faith of the people who are involved in the system.

Interview/ U.S. News & World Report, 1-12:21.

Lowell P. Weicker, Jr.
United States Senator, R— Connecticut 4

[Calling for a new Senate committee to oversee the operations of the intelligence

WHAT THEY SAID IN 1976

(LOWELL P. WEICKER, JR.)

agencies]: Intelligence is too important to our national interests and has been proven too dangerous to our individual freedoms to continue to be watchdogged by four Senate committees whose primary jurisdictions lie elsewhere . . . None of the existing committees is authorized to legislate for the consolidated entity that the intelligence community has become. Their fragmented oversight has, in fact, been none at all. Too much is at stake for Congress not to know. The days of comfortable, clubby relations between agencies and senior Senators must end . . . America's children deserve assurances by law, rather than memory or Executive order, that our national nightmare won't for them be an encore of reality.

At Marymount College, Tarrytown, N.Y./ April 21/ The Washington Post, 5-5:(A)22.

Bella S. Abzug
United States Representative, D—New York;
Candidate for the 1976 New York Democratic
U.S. Senatorial nomination 1

A stag Senate means a stagnation. It's time a woman with considerable legislative and parliamentary experience enters into the legislative body that is one of the most exclusive male clubs in the world.
San Francisco Examiner & Chronicle,
8-1:(This World)2.

Fred T. Allen
Chairman and president,
Pitney Bowes, Inc. 2

Let's concede, for a minute, that a private company might be able to deliver first-class mail to Chicago from New York, faster, cheaper, and make a profit, compared with the existing postal system. But who will deliver mail to the Havasupi Indians at the bottom of the Grand Canyon? Or to the loggers in forest camps in northern Maine? Or to isolated ranches in remote spots in Wyoming? Or to the millions of other Americans who live in sparsely populated areas where regular mail service would be too unprofitable for the private entrepreneurs or too costly for the local citizens? They would probably have to do without. And none of this is to mention other problems associated with privately delivered mail, namely, security problems.
Interview, Stamford, Conn./
The Christian Science Monitor, 12-22:8.

John B. Anderson
United States Representative, R—Illinois 3

[Supporting televising of Congressional proceedings]: Basically, it's included within

the framework of the public's right to know. It is a fact that an overwhelming majority of the American people today receive the bulk of their news through the electronic media—radio or television. And it seems to me that, given the present low estate of the Congress—the fact that there is suspicion and distrust at all levels of government—that perhaps what we need to cure the situation is more-precise information on how Congress really functions. I realize that this argument can be turned around and used against me. There will be those who will say that laws are like sausages—you shouldn't see either one of them made. But I think that we can close the credibility gap between the American people and the Congress. We can increase people's understanding of our whole political process. And frankly, it would have some values for the Congress as well. It might exercise a certain discipline.
Interview/U.S. News & World Report, 6-14:39.

Jerry Apodaca
Governor of New Mexico (D) 4

There is a growing sentiment in this nation and among the people of this state that government has grown beyond reasonable bounds; and that it has grown for its own sake and not in the interest of the citizens who pay for it.
State of the State address, before Legislature,
Santa Fe/The New York Times, 2-8:(3)15.

Benjamin F. Bailar
Postmaster General of the
United States 5

Unless increased public funding enables us in the near term to slacken the pace of [post-

WHAT THEY SAID IN 1976

(BENJAMIN F. BAILAR)

age] rate increases, we may be caught in a vicious cycle of rate increases to compensate for volume decreases brought on in turn by rate increases. The types of problems we have faced are not going to disappear. Inflation, rising costs and decreasing volume are likely to be with us for the foreseeable future.

Before Senate Post Office Committee,
Washington, Jan 27/
The Christian Science Monitor, 4-13:34.

1

If the public elects to continue the postal system in its present form, it will have to pay a steep price. It may find the first-class stamp becoming a luxury item in the next decade and the Postal Service a ponderous and costly left-over from simpler, more affluent times. Obviously, we must prevent this from happening. We must seriously examine the possibility of restructuring both the services provided by the postal system and the schedule of payment for these services. We must, I believe, consider trimming back those services that no longer make economic sense, or label them for what they are and arrange a system of subsidies that covers their cost. And we must identify within each class of mail the actual costs of serving various types of users, and charge accordingly. The keynote of the postal future must be flexibility—flexibility to provide *more* service for those who need more and are willing to pay for more—and we can do that—and flexibility to trim service where it is really not needed in order to save all users unnecessary expense . . . To achieve this will require a fundamental change in attitude by citizens. We must recognize that postal service is a service like any other—a service that we pay for through postage and tax dollars—not a political birthright, deeded to us as a gift by our government.

Before Economic Club of Detroit, March 8/
Vital Speeches, 4-1:358.

Birch Bayh
United States Senator, D—Indiana

2

There is only one role for the Vice President and that is presiding over the Senate. He isn't there very often, and he doesn't contribute very much when he is.

At symposium on the Vice-Presidency,
Fordham University Law School, Dec. 3/
The New York Times, 12-4:30.

Kingman Brewster, Jr.
President, Yale University

3

If society's highest aim is to maximize the ability of each citizen to contribute to the potentialities of others, there is plenty for government to do. But it should be done, insofar as possible, without using government to usurp the responsibility for individual actions or to prejudice the freedom of individual choice.

Baccalaureate address, Yale University, May 16/
The New York Times, 5-17:22.

Edmund G. Brown, Jr.
Governor of California (D)

4

[On government spending]: Sometimes I think a very good reform is not to give people everything they want, because often necessity is the mother of invention. Where things become more difficult, people often become more creative. Just to pump in more money often [encourages] the same bad habits we want to reform.

News conference, Sacramento, Jan. 8/
Los Angeles Herald-Examiner, 1-9:(A)2.

5

I don't see leadership as just passing laws. The fascination with legislation as the big solution to everything is overplayed. A person in a significant position of power can lead by the questions he raises and the example he sets. A lot of political energy comes from a certain vision, a faith that communicates itself to other people—as with [the late civil-rights leader] Martin Luther King and other leaders, whose ideas and the way they presented them had a great influence on government. People who stand for an idea that has energy connected with it—that's power.

Interview/ Playboy, April:73.

1

... I lean toward the view that the level of official corruption is intolerable. What I don't know is, are there any human beings so pure, any government so beyond reproach by the existing standards, that we'll ever be satisfied? I wonder, since these things went on in former times, why they didn't seem to bother anyone then. Where do we finally hit bottom? Where do we finally purify the government?

Interview/ Playboy, April:187.

Edmund G. Brown, Jr.
Governor of California (D);
Candidate for the 1976 Democratic
Presidential nomination
2

I don't think the President runs the country, nor do I think the Governor runs the state. Government is a part of an over-all, complex equation—social, economic and environmental. Within that limited framework, a leader can set a tone, can express a philosophy and can describe a future that is either consistent with what is possible or not.

News conference, San Diego, Calif., April 4/
Los Angeles Times, 4-5:(1)3.

James L. Buckley
United States Senator, C—New York
3

I know after six years [in the Senate] that if you work hard enough and long enough and have faith in the people, you can make a difference, you can chart the way, you can raise the sometime lonely cry that in time, and with work, becomes the accepted wisdom.

News conference, New York, April 26/
The New York Times, 4-27:16.

4

I truly believe men and women can be

trusted to govern themselves well with a minimum of governmental interference from Washington. But our freedoms have been eroded by people convinced that once you drink of the waters of the Potomac you are imbued with a particular wisdom that ordinary mortals don't have.

Campaigning for re-election, Kingston, N.Y./
The National Observer, 10-16:4.

Joseph A. Califano, Jr.
Former Special Assistant to the
President of the United States
for Domestic Affairs
(Lyndon B. Johnson)
5

The Congress opens each day with a prayer and fills out statute books with high-sounding phrases. Its members incessantly preach to us. Yet, from 1955 to 1975, 16 members of the Congress were indicted; to date, 12 have been convicted. In the present Congress, one Representative was indicted last week for illegally taking bribes to pass special immigration laws; another has been convicted of bribery; two have plea-bargained for misdemeanors; and five more are under investigation by the Department of Justice, the Watergate special prosecutor's office of the House Ethics Committee. These are the men who each day legislate our morals and impose legal standards on the individual and institutional conduct of American citizens. Is it any wonder that [Presidential candidate] Ronald Reagan, [consumerist] Ralph Nader, [citizens' rights advocate] John Gardner and [Presidential candidate] Jimmy Carter all agree that something is morally awry in Washington today? Is it any wonder that the increasingly regulated American citizen questions the right of such men to tell him what to do? Since [former Attorney General] John Mitchell's invitation, the people have been watching what we do in Washington, not what we say—and they don't like what they see.

Before Woman's National Democratic Club/
The Dallas Times Herald, 6-27:(B)3.

WHAT THEY SAID IN 1976

(JOSEPH A. CALIFANO, JR.)

1

The departments and agencies of the Federal Executive are a mine field of bureaucratic interests jealous of their jurisdictional turf. Each Federal program has a constituency within the Executive Branch itself, in the committees and subcommittees on Capitol Hill and among the interest groups and individuals who benefit through the nation.

U.S. News & World Report, 8-16:26.

Hugh L. Carey
Governor of New York (D)

2

A Governor can confront a problem of state and fail quite adequately on his own. But no Governor can succeed for the people without the support, understanding and wisdom of the Legislature.

State of the State address, Albany, Jan. 7/
The New York Times, 1-8:36.

3

There is no press release so artfully drawn that can convince the investing public to rely upon New York State's credit-worthiness—if our budget is not in balance. There is no speech, no financial sleight-of-hand so clever or quick to get us to market in the spring for approximately $4-billion—funds relied upon by every citizen and community of this state—if our budget is not in balance. The agencies of this state will default, school districts will be driven from the market, programs creating jobs and providing needed services will be ended or severely diminished—if our budget is not in balance.

State of the State address, Albany, Jan. 7/
The New York Times, 2-8:(3)15.

4

For too long, government has been dealing with difficult problems by creating more government, by putting too much money in new programs, new agencies and new bureaucratic structures before it had an adequate understanding of the problems at hand—massive spending on prison systems which do not rehabilitate, schools which do not educate, care for the elderly which became a moral and criminal scandal, medical-care programs which offer little help or improved mental stability. Massive spending on programs which do not work as they were intended to work, no matter how noble their intentions, offers the public neither social nor economic justice . . . We have learned that government and the people it serves cannot afford to solve all the problems of society. So we enter a new age in which our goals are less government, less spending, fewer government employees, less interference in the lives of our citizens and businessmen and a new spirit of cooperation by all individuals in government. I recognize that it is difficult for men and women, drawn to public service in the hope of improving their communities or the lives of their constituents, to face the restraint brought about by our conditions. Our only hope to meet the future challenge of public service lies in removing the imbalance in our accounts and restoring the integrity of our fiscal condition. To do less, while more comfortable in the short term, will prove to be only an expedient act, and every one . . . of us will pay the price.

State of the State address, Albany, Jan. 7/
The New York Times, 1-8:36.

5

Political parties aside, the people are way ahead of their elected representatives. If hard economic decisions must be made, if new goals must be set, if new understandings must be reached in our society, they are ready for it and will participate.

Before American Newspaper Publishers
Association, New York, May 3/
The New York Times, 5-4:15.

6

The definition of a legislature is a body that deals with unfinished business.

The New York Times, 7-11:(4)4.

Jimmy Carter
Candidate for the 1976
Democratic Presidential nomination;
Former Governor of Georgia (D)

1

The people in this country are intensely patriotic; they love their government so much it almost hurts. They feel that they've been betrayed. They don't understand why something is going on in our nation's government that's a matter of embarrassment and shame. The competence of government is not an accepted characteristic any more. No matter what a person hopes to do, ultimately in life, no matter what their top hope or aspiration might be, generally they feel that Washington is an obstacle to the realization of that hope rather than an asset to be tapped in the future in the consummation of that hope.

Interview, March 16/
The Washington Post, 3-21:(B)1.

2

[On controlling the growth of government bureaucracy]: The steps that need to be taken would fall into three general categories: first of all, the reorganization of the structure of government to make it simple, efficient, economical, purposeful and manageable for a change. The second principle is proper budgeting. We had throughout my own term as Governor a concept instituted called zero-based budgeting. Every program that spends the taxpayers' money has to rejustify itself annually. You have an automatic reassessment of priorities; you have an automatic detection with the possibility of eliminating duplication and overlapping of functions. And you have an automatic screening out of obsolete and obsolescent programs. And the third general principle is long-range planning or, to be expressed more simply, the careful delineation of purposes and goals so that the government knows what it hopes to accomplish at the end of a year, two years, five years or 25 years in every realm of human life which is determined by or affected by government.

Interview/ The New York Times, 4-2:9.

3

I respect the Congress, but the Congress is inherently incapable of leadership. Our Founding Fathers never thought that the Congress would lead this country. There's only one person that can speak with a clear voice to the American people, or inspire the American people to reach for greatness or excellence, or call on them to make a sacrifice, or set a standard of morality, or set out the answers to complicated questions, or correct discrimination and injustice, or provide us with the defense posture that would make us feel secure or a foreign policy that would make us feel proud again. And that's the President.

The Washington Post, 5-2:(C)7.

4

I promise you that if I am fortunate enough to be elected President, I will not preside over an Administration which ignores the lessons of my own personal experience . . . It is time that the Federal government recognized that states and localities retain a special knowledge of local problems and that responsive and flexible local leadership is essential to representative government in this nation.

At National Governors Conference, Hershey, Pa.,
July 6/ Los Angeles Herald-Examiner, 7-6:(A)3.

5

[On his ideas for making the Vice-Presidency more meaningful]: In the first place, I don't believe that I would ever feel threatened by the stature or the competence or intelligence or fame of a Vice President. I think the Presidency itself is such a powerful office that there is no reason to feel threatened. Secondly, in the complexities of a modern technological world with the changes coming so rapidly, a President needs more and more to have someone with official status on whom [he] can rely for ceremonial functions, for dealing with the Congress, for the carrying out of major campaign commitments, for dealing with international matters.

Interview, Plains, Ga./ Newsweek, 7-19:17.

WHAT THEY SAID IN 1976

Jimmy Carter
1976 Democratic Presidential nominee 1

All too often in recent years, laxity and the abandonment of rigid high standards among our leaders has caused our nation to suffer and to grieve . . . During this post-Watergate era our nation has been struggling anew with the question of how to establish and maintain higher standards of morality and justice. So far we have failed. [If elected,] I will never turn my back on official misdeeds. I intend to take a broom to Washington and do everything possible to sweep the house of government clean . . . There is a reservoir of honesty and decency and fairness among our people that can, in a democracy, find expression in our government. [But] if we disappoint them again, we may not get another chance.

Before American Bar Association,
Atlanta, Aug. 11/
The Washington Post, 8-12:(A)5.

2

We should decentralize power, eliminate the trappings of authority and remember that public officials are not bosses but the servants of those who put them in office. When we have a choice between government authority and private responsibility, we should always go with private responsibility . . . If there is a choice between governments, we should assign the authority and the responsibility to the level of government that's closest to the individual citizen.

Campaign address, Warm Springs, Ga., Sept. 6/
Los Angeles Times, 9-7:(1)16.

Jimmy Carter
President-elect of the United States 3

Americans . . . want to be told the truth, even when it is unpleasant. We have always responded well to a challenge. Only when our leaders have lost faith in that basic toughness of spirit and willingness to sacrifice have we been disappointed or embarrassed. But there is something else, something less tan-

gible, that our people want. They want to be proud of our government again. They want to trust their government again. They want to be inspired by their leaders again. They want a new spirit of optimism and trust and confidence. They want a government that is both competent and compassionate. As a citizen, those are the things I've always wanted from my President. As President, those are the goals I will try to meet.

Interview/U.S. News & World Report, 11-15:42.

4

I believe in balanced budgets, and before my term is over I intend for the Federal budget to be balanced. I don't believe in wasting money. I believe in careful long-range planning. I believe in maximum openness of government. When there's a choice to be made between the private sector and government sector, my option would be for the private sector to assume the responsibility. When there's a choice to be made between the Federal, state and local levels of government to perform a function, I would prefer that the function be carried out by the level of government closest to the individual citizen. I believe in the tightest possible control over the government process, a simple and comprehensive management entity where the President, through his representatives, can manage the affairs of the government. I believe in giving Cabinet members maximum authority. I don't intend to run the individual departments out of the White House, especially staff members.

News conference, Plains, Ga., Nov. 15/
The New York Times, 11-16:32.

Frank Church
United States Senator, D—Idaho;
Candidate for the 1976
Democratic Presidential nomination 5

The first priority on our political agenda is the restoration of the Federal government to legitimacy in the eyes of the people. The vast majority of Federal employees are honest, law-abiding citizens, but nobody, no matter how highly placed in the government, has the right to break the law, to open our mail, to photograph our cables . . . to open tax investigations against persons not even suspected of tax delinquency but targeted for political harassment instead.

Announcing his candidacy, Idaho City, Idaho,
March 18/
Los Angeles Herald-Examiner, 3-18:(A)3.

William T. Coleman, Jr.
Secretary of Transportation
of the United States
1

Oh, I'm pretty sure I've made mistakes. I mean, baseball players hit .300 which means they make a mistake two out of three or four times and they get paid $100,000 a year. So I don't know why people expect politicians to be right all the time.

Interview, Washington/
The New York Times, 2-1:(3)9.

Charles W. Colson
Former Special Counsel to the
President of the United States
(Richard M. Nixon)
2

If there is one place in the world where everything is there to separate a man from a relationship with God, it is . . . the White House. Everybody is bowing and scraping, and you [as President] begin to think you are God.

Los Angeles Times, 12-8:(1)2.

John B. Connally, Jr.
Former Secretary of the Treasury
of the United States;
Former Governor of Texas (D, now R)
3

I think [the Presidency] has become a very terrible job. It has become a very demanding job. It is a job that requires a total commitment now, not only for yourself, but a total commitment for your wife, for your children and for all your friends. Time was when the job of President carried with it some aura of respect and dignity, and times were such in

this country and around the world where the pressures were not constant seven days a week, 24 hours a day; but that time is past. Now to be President you have to foresake everything else, and it is a terrible thing to ask. So in that sense I would not like to be President.

TV-radio interview, Washington/
"Meet the Press,"
National Broadcasting Company, 6-13.

4

I've never known a happy Vice President. It's a do-nothing job. It all depends on what the President wants him to do. I've been in and out of Washington since 1939 and I've never known a happy Vice President.

To newsmen, Birmingham, Alabama, July 29/
The Dallas Times Herald, 7-30:(A)1.

Alistair Cooke
Journalist, Historian
5

People always hunger for leadership in a democracy, and they've all been saying in Britain and in this country for the past 30 years, "Where are the leaders?" All of the colorful old men have gone. They've gone because there has been increasing democracy, and leadership in a self-governing country is only really effective when you have a war and you have to suspend a very great deal of democracy. I'm as baffled as everybody else about what type of new leader can operate in an industrial democracy, but I think when we do get some crisis of survival, we somehow have thrown up great leaders. Now, curiously enough, we didn't do it in the 1960s. And it may be due in part to the extension of the freedom of the press, really getting over now into every conceivable kind of keyhole investigation, that we're discovering a lot of these leaders had feet of clay.

Interview, New York/
The Dallas Times Herald, 7-4:(B)3.

Philip M. Crane
United States Representative, R—Illinois
6

[Saying private firms should be allowed to deliver first-class mail]: . . . the Postal Service

WHAT THEY SAID IN 1976

(PHILIP M. CRANE)

is clear evidence that the most outrageous monopolies are those created by government. It is inflicting on Americans deteriorating service at higher and higher cost. There has been a 117 per cent increase in the cost of delivering first-class mail over a six-year period. At the same time, the operating deficit of the Postal Service has increased from $13-million in 1972 to $4.5-billion in the fiscal year that ends in 1977. And now postal officials propose a cutback in deliveries of business mail to once a day in nine of the major cities east of the Mississippi—also a change from doorstep- to curbside-delivery mail, and so forth. There simply are no incentives for improvement in the present arrangement . . . I am convinced that ending the Post Office's monopoly on first-class mail would result in faster and more-efficient delivery of letters. I think it would also provide more—rather than fewer—jobs for letter carriers . . . Defenders of the Post Office monopoly on first-class mail always raise the "cream-skimming" argument. They say that Aunt Tilly up on Pike's Peak or the miners down in the Grand Canyon wouldn't get delivery. I say: If necessary, let's subsidize delivery to Aunt Tilly and the miners, but get some competition into this business in areas where the great bulk of the mail goes.

Interview/ U.S. News & World Report, 9-13:63.

Alan Cranston
United States Senator, D—California 1

The duty of a government employee to keep secret information secret must not be used as a gag rule. We must be extremely careful to protect legitimate secrets without throwing into jail conscientious Federal employees who blow the whistle on waste, corruption and illegal activities.

Panel discussion sponsored by California Newspaper Publishers Association, San Diego, Feb. 20/ Los Angeles Times, 2-21:(1)8.

Thomas E. Cronin
Professor of politics, Brandeis University
2

We want more Presidential leadership, not less. We demand that our Presidents stretch and give us everything they've got. In fact, the country has grown too dependent on Presidents. As a result, the office is driving our Presidents into over-extending themselves. They wind up undertaking more domestic programs and more overseas commitments than they can carry out effectively. I worked as a White House Fellow under [the late President Lyndon] Johnson, and I saw what happened to him. He had humanitarian instincts that were half political and half genuine. He wanted to solve everything that was wrong in the country at once. One week it was education of the poor that was Number 1 priority. The next week it was Model Cities. Then it was the War on Poverty. During the course of a year, dozens of programs became the Number 1 priority. But when you make everything top priority, then you have no priorities . . . We keep hearing: "Only the President can do that. Only the President can provide moral leadership." I think that's wrong—or, if it's true, it is very sad. We have to be more understanding of the Presidency and what it's all about—its frailness, if you will. We must ask a President to give us his best, but we must not ask more of the Presidency than it—or any single institution—can give. Some issues must be diverted elsewhere: to the Cabinet, Congress, appointed officials, states, universities, enlightened business leaders, or wherever else those issues can be solved. The alternative is that we will break the individuals we put in the White House. We will drive some of them to political suicide; we'll wind up assassinating some; and we'll physically exhaust others. Unless we start looking at the Presidency in a sensible and understanding way, I think it will be increasingly likely that no one, for one reason or another, will survive eight years of this cruel and very often "no-win" hardship post.

Interview/ U.S. News & World Report, 9-20:61.

Bob Dole
United States Senator, R—Kansas;
1976 Republican Vice-Presidential nominee[1]

Whenever tyranny reigns in this world, it reigns through the instruments of government. All history tells us that to maximize government is to minimize human freedom, and I believe that the promise of America is not told, nor shall it be fulfilled, through the oppressive constraints of government. The question and the purpose of human liberty are not the rights of government, the dignity of government or the future of government. Rather, they are the rights of the individual, the hopes and dreams of the individual.

Accepting the Vice-Presidential nomination, at Republican National Convention, Kansas City, Aug. 19/The New York Times, 8-21:15.

Michael S. Dukakis
Governor of Massachusetts (D)[2]

I think we have gotten ourselves so involved through the national government in so many, many different programs that we have forgotten that the role of the Federal government, in my view at least, has to be concentrated on some very important problems of compelling national significance. What do I mean by that? Obviously a responsible foreign policy, a guarantee of employment to people who want to work in this country, a comprehensive national health-insurance system, a national energy policy, decent national transportation network. If we had national leadership that would concentrate on those major issues, I think those of us in Governors' offices and legislatures would be perfectly happy to assume responsibility for many, many other public programs that I think we can deal with much better. One of the problems has been that there has been so much Federal involvement in so many of the details of so many programs, without the kind of attention to these major issues of compelling national importance, that we have tended to get all balled up in a large, massive Federal bureaucracy, and we have failed to solve the

problems of unemployment and health care and other things at the national level which clearly have to be the responsibility of the national government.

TV-radio interview, Philadelphia/ "Meet the Press," National Broadcasting Company, 7-4.

John A. Durkin
United States Senator,
D—New Hampshire[3]

[On the Senate]: This is the only asylum that I know of that is run by the inmates. We tie ourselves in knots.

The Dallas Times Herald, 4-11:(F)3.

Sam J. Ervin, Jr.
Former United States Senator,
D—North Carolina[4]

I didn't like this business of [President Ford's] recommending that there should be a law to imprison people . . . punish people for leaking government information. I think if the government doesn't want something to be leaked, it ought to have the responsibility of keeping it safe and secure. It's akin to the idea that the American people ought to be kept ignorant by government and if they find out anything they ought to be punished as criminals . . . Sunlight is the best disinfectant for all things. The more sunlight shed on a thing, the less harmful it's going to be. I think we should have a minimum of secrets in government. Many of them are classified not for reason of national security, but for the security of the politicians that devise them.

At Mountain View College, Dallas, Feb. 18/ The Dallas Times Herald, 2-19:(C)5.

Daniel J. Evans
Governor of Washington (R)[5]

A Governor is a single executive who has to make tough decisions on a regular basis and then ask to be re-elected. A Senator or Con-

WHAT THEY SAID IN 1976

(DANIEL J. EVANS)

gressman has to be a fool to lose a re-election bid. What do the voters know? He writes some nice letters. He sends newsletters. Their only understanding of what he does is what he tells them.

Jackson Hole, Wyo./
The Christian Science Monitor, 9-24:26.

Gerald R. Ford
President of the United States
1

If we fail this year to assure continued movement toward general revenue-sharing, there will be new escalation in the categorical programs of an increasingly centralized government. I am determined to shake up and shape up, with your help, the worthwhile and proven programs we now have rather than permit a proliferation of new and untried programs.

At National Governors Conference, Washington,
Feb. 23/ The Dallas Times Herald, 2-23:(A)1.

2

I will never irresponsibly transfer serious problems from the Federal government to state government without regard for human needs or fiscal realities. I am determined to preserve a constructive partnership with the states on all mutual concerns, through cooperation and not through treatment that is worse than the disease.

At National Governors Conference, Washington,
Feb. 23/ The New York Times, 2-24:27.

3

The government has grown too large, too powerful, too costly, too remote, and yet too deeply involved in the daily lives of the American people . . . We need to stop just scratching the surface, stop dealing in piecemeal approaches, stop merely moving agencies around or renaming them. What we need now is an agenda for action, a timetable for progress toward real reform. We cannot untangle

40 years' work of bureaucratic red tape overnight, but we can at least set the process in motion.

Before small-businessmen, Washington, May 13/
The Washington Post, 5-14:(D)11.

4

Public officials have a special responsibility to set a good example for others to follow—in both their private and public conduct . . . The American people, particularly our young people, cannot be expected to take pride—or even participate—in a system of government that is defiled and dishonored, whether in the White House or in the halls of Congress. Jesus said, "Unto whomsoever much is given, of him shall much be required." Personal integrity is not too much to ask of public servants. In fact, we should accept nothing less.

At Southern Baptist convention, Norfolk, Va.,
June 15/ The Washington Post, 6-16:(A)9.

5

. . . individual liberty in this great country means liberty from oppressive, heavy-handed, bureaucratic government. That is a goal we can achieve. That is a goal we must achieve in our third century. I firmly believe that Americans can do anything if other Americans do not tie us down with red tape, tie us up with pessimism or tie us into a knot of frustration and stagnation.

At Jaycee convention, Indianapolis, June 22/
The New York Times, 6-23:16.

6

The Declaration [of Independence] was not a protest against government, but against the excesses of government. It prescribed the proper role of government, to secure the rights of individuals and to effect their safety and happiness. In modern society, no individual can do this alone, so government is not a necessary evil but a necessary good.

At U.S. Bicentennial observance,
Independence Hall, Philadelphia, July 4/
The Washington Post, 7-5:(A)16.

1

[Upon signing the Government-in-the-Sunshine Act requiring many Federal agencies to open their records and meetings to the public]: In a democracy, the public has a right to know not only what the government decides but why and by what process. The Government-in-the-Sunshine Act is in keeping with America's proud heritage that the government serves and the people rule. This afternoon, I am delighted to sign this legislation and to reaffirm that heritage and let the sunshine in.

Washington, Sept. 13/
The New York Times, 9-14:53.

2

The anti-Washington feeling, in my opinion, ought to be focused on the Congress of the United States. For example, this Congress very shortly will spend a billion dollars a year for its housekeeping, its salaries, its expenses and the like. The next Congress will probably be the first billion-dollar Congress in the history of the United States . . . We, in addition, see that in the last four years the number of employees hired by the Congress has gone up substantially—much more than the gross national product, much more than any other increase throughout our society. Congress is hiring people by the drove and the cost as a result has gone up. And I don't see any improvement in the performance of the Congress under the present leadership. So it seems to me [that] instead of the anti-Washington feeling being aimed at everybody in Washington, it seems to me that the focus should be where the problem is, which is the Congress of the United States, and particularly the [Democratic] majority in the Congress.

Debate with Democratic Presidential nominee
Jimmy Carter, Philadelphia, Sept. 24/
The New York Times, 9-25:9.

3

The veto is a President's Constitutional right, given to him by the drafters of the Con-

stitution because they wanted it as a check against irresponsible Congressional action. The veto forces Congress to take another look at legislation that has been passed. I think this is a responsible tool for a President of the United States, and I have sought to use it responsibly.

Interview, Washington/
The Reader's Digest, October:103.

4

[On gavel-to-gavel television coverage of Congress]: I think it would be a stimulant to improved performance in the House as well as in the Senate. I think Congress has to be prodded to do a better job, and, if they're on television, I'm convinced that the public will demand a better result. I know that it's objected to by many up there [in Congress], and I'm not sure I would have agreed entirely when I was there. But nevertheless, as I get off and look back, I think that if the pressure of the public is on them through televised covering of their day-to-day legislative processes, we'll get a better product. We have to do something.

Interview, Washington/TV Guide, 10-2:(A)5.

5

I feel that during my Presidency the greatest achievement was the healing of the divisiveness, the healing of the differences between the American people. When I became President the people were angry with one another, they were disillusioned with government, there was a lack of faith in the White House and in the whole American form of government. I think the healing of America was probably the greatest achievement . . .

Interview, Washington, Dec. 8/
Los Angeles Times, 12-12:(1)16.

Milton Friedman
Professor of economics,
University of Chicago

6

In the past 40 or 50 years, the fraction of our income going for governmental expenses has risen from 10 per cent to 40 per cent. In

WHAT THEY SAID IN 1976

(MILTON FRIEDMAN)

Britain it is now up to 60 per cent. I think it is a real question whether democratic government may not be destroyed in Britain in the next five years. If we [in the U.S.] get to that stage, we cannot avoid a major political crisis. It will be very difficult, if not impossible, to retain an essentially free and democratic society.

Interview, Chicago/ People, 4-5:52.

John H. Glenn, Jr.
United States Senator, D—Ohio 1

Governments can err, Presidents do make mistakes, but . . . Divine Justice weighs the sins of the cold-blooded and the sins of the warmhearted on a different scale. Better the occasional faults of a government living in the spirit of charity than the consistent omissions of a government frozen in the ice of its own indifferences.

At Democratic National Convention, New York, July 12/ Los Angeles Times, 7-13:(1)21.

Arthur J. Goldberg
Lawyer; Former Associate Justice, Supreme Court of the United States 2

Cabinet meetings as now conducted are largely pro forma and a waste of the President's time as well as that of Cabinet officers. But, if properly selected and reinforced by an institutional process requiring regular and full discussions with a record preserved for history, perhaps the Cabinet would give the President what he sorely needs—candid and unfettered advice and counsel. Presidents are prone to reflect that their task and office is a lonely one. It need not be as lonely as recent Presidents have made the office to be.

San Francisco Examiner & Chronicle, 10-10:(This World)2.

Barry M. Goldwater
United States Senator, R—Arizona 3

[Criticizing privileges enjoyed by Senators

and Congressmen]: In all this groveling about military allowances, I have not read one critical word in the *Congressional Record* about our own side benefits. They range all the way from free shoeshines and haircuts to ascending amounts for travel, greatly increased staff allowances, and political contributions available for special purposes. We have not had the guts to increase our salaries openly, after a frank and open discussion. Instead, we hoist our income by means that in some instances are furtive and underhanded and secret. Witness the pay raise in the first session of the 94th Congress during a time of severe unemployment and inflation. While some called loudly for restraint and austerity, the Congress set a tacky example for the unions and others to follow. We got our raise by cloaking it behind the cost-of-living raise for civil servants.

Washington, Feb. 4/ U.S. News & World Report, 2-16:22.

Charles E. Grassley
United States Representative, R—Iowa 4

[Members of Congress] would merit a substantial cut in pay [if their salaries were awarded] on the basis [of] how effective Congress has been in dealing with the nation's major problems. It is obviously very difficult to determine the productive capacity of an elected official. Whereas one can fairly determine the productive capacity of an individual in private industry by measuring the output of a finished product attributable to him or her, this is not the case with elected officials. For instance, if one were to measure the amount of printed material generated each year by Congress and its individual members, one might determine that Congressmen and Senators are grossly underpaid. But if one were to judge their work on the basis of how effective Congress has been in dealing with the nation's major problems, it is clear that our elected representatives in Washington would merit a substantial cut in pay.

Before Quadrennial Commission on Executive, Legislative and Judicial Salaries, Washington, Nov. 10/ The Washington Post, 11-11:(A)30.

Gary W. Hart
United States Senator, D—Colorado

1

The central problem of big government springs from our attitudes and expectations. The problem of big government is big promises that cannot be backed up by performance. The problem of big government is inflated expectations that generate disillusionment rather than hope and progress. The problem of big government is the myth that it can solve every problem and meet every challenge. The problem of big government, frankly, is the demand placed upon it by every interest group in our society . . . This government was established to *promote* prosperity; no government can *guarantee* prosperity. This government can *encourage* the creation of jobs; it cannot *guarantee* everyone a job of his choice. Government can and must try to minimize inflation; but no government can terminate a world-wide problem by act of law. The Federal government must insure and promote the legal rights of minorities; but, in the long haul, subtle human discrimination will be ended by citizens of understanding and compassion who grow beyond narrow prejudice. This nation must grow beyond the arrogant and ill-considered promises that government could "whip" inflation, immediately win a "war on poverty" or guarantee world peace. Does that mean that we give up on these problems and goals? Absolutely not. I am saying that this country, and particularly the Federal government, must learn to live within limits. The days of the unlimited frontier are over. We are up against the last frontier, and it is ourselves.

Before Western Electronic Manufacturers Association. April 20/Vital Speeches, 6-1:497.

2

You can't get the Federal government off your back until you get your hand out of its pocket.

U.S. News & World Report, 8-16:26.

Philip A. Hart
United States Senator, D—Michigan

3

There's a terrible tendency here [in the Senate] to think that everything we do and say, or omit to do, is of world consequence. But you know full well that you can go across the street and the bus-driver couldn't care less.

The Washington Post, 1-26:(A)17.

Walter W. Heller
Professor of economics,
University of Minnesota; Former Chairman,
Council of Economic Advisers to the
President of the United States
(John F. Kennedy)

4

I don't happen to think government is too big. I think there are a lot of uneconomical programs; I think we ought to be focusing on economy in government. That is one thing I don't find in the White House. The President [Ford] is constantly trying to cut programs, but I don't see where he is improving management, where he is getting more output for less input. That is what I would like to see. But *per se,* if our expenditures were properly programmed, properly directed, I don't feel government is too big, no.

TV-radio interview, Washington/
"Meet the Press,"
National Broadcasting Company, 4-11.

Louis Henkin
Professor of international law
and diplomacy,
Columbia University Law School

5

Congress has a right to know what it needs to know, and the President has an obligation to withhold what the public interest requires that he should withhold. The right to know doesn't necessarily mean the right of 500 to know, and the obligation to withhold doesn't impose a duty to conceal. If Congress is disciplined in exercising its right and the President is responsible in fulfilling his obligation, no insuperable conflict need arise.

At conference sponsored by Academy of Political and Social Science, Philadelphia/
The New York Times, 4-10:31.

Gerald Horton
Georgia State Representative
1

The two things you should never see made are sausages and laws.

Before Georgia Legislature, Atlanta/
The Wall Street Journal, 4-1:16.

Roman L. Hruska
United States Senator, R—Nebraska
2

. . . in government, the more programs and the more regulations we have, then the more we are going to have proscription of conduct in business and personal choice. All these programs impinge on the individual's freedom of choice, and therefore they impinge on liberty, too.

Interview/ U.S. News & World Report, 10-4:25.

Hubert H. Humphrey
United States Senator, D—Minnesota
3

. . . I propose that the modern Presidency should include the establishment of a Federal Council consisting of the 50 Governors and the President. This council should meet regularly on a systematic basis so that the President may outline to the Governors his proposals and initiatives, and receive from the Governors their advice and counsel in the preparation of the Federal budget, the administration of the departments and the implementation of Federal laws.

At University of California, Irvine, Jan. 11/
The New York Times, 1-12:18.

4

Any politician who tells you we need less government is lying. More-efficient government, more-responsive government, yes. But let's not junk everything we've built. That's cheap talk.

At luncheon for retired Federal employees,
Minneapolis/ Time, 1-19:13.

5

I have no apologies for the Federal government doing things. Who's going to take care of the environment, establish the standards—you, me? Now, let me tell you, 90 per cent of all funding is spent by state and local governments. The Federal government may appropriate the programs but they are administered locally—and the business people themselves say we can't load any more on them. I have no apologies for the government being interested in people, in nutrition, in education, in health, in transportation. Who's going to work out a national food policy—the Mayor of New York? Who's going to work out our transportation problems —the B&O Railroad? We've got to have Federal government activity. The only question is not the size of government, but does it work? This government doesn't work today because they don't want it to work. The Republicans make big government an issue because they don't run it. They occupy it—but they don't run it.

The Washington Post, 3-14:(A)12.

William L. Hungate
United States Representative,
D—Missouri
6

I think one of the answers [for restoring public trust in government] is restoration of more parliamentary democracy, more power in the Legislative Branch. If one legislator goes crazy or starts stealing, that can be dealt with; if one executive does, the country may be down the tube before you can act on it . . . I hope to see a restoration of more power and more confidence in the body that should be closest to the people, the House of Representatives. Nobody comes in that's not elected and everybody can be removed in two years. I hope for a restoration in the House.

Interview, Washington/
The Christian Science Monitor, 3-31:26.

Samuel P. Huntington
Professor of government,
Harvard University
7

There is, in my view, a distinction between

an electoral coalition and a governing coalition. To get elected President, you have to put together a coalition consisting of certain voting blocs—regional blocs, ethnic groups. In order to govern the country, you need a quite different coalition, although obviously there is some overlap. Recent Presidents have had real problems trying to form governing coalitions. The difficulty stems partly from the pervasive breakdown of authority, and also because times have changed and there are differences of opinions on policy . . . There is a need for a degree of self-confidence on the part of the President so that he can reach out and involve Congress and the bureaucracy in the process of formulating policy and thus create a governing coalition. That's one requirement, I believe, for a President.

Interview/ U.S. News & World Report,3-8:51.

Henry M. Jackson
United States Senator, D—Washington;
Candidate for the 1976 Democratic
Presidential nomination 1

[On big government]: It's very easy to say that because something is big that it's bad. The issue is not big government versus small government. Big government, if it's inefficient, is bad government; small government if it's inefficient, arbitrary, capricious, is bad.

Interview/ The New York Times, 4-2:9.

2

Washington isn't our enemy—it's our capital. And national policies for full employment and a strong defense and a growing America are going to come from Washington—or they're going to come from nowhere.

At Jefferson-Jackson Day dinner,
Philadelphia, April 20/
The Washington Post, 4-21:(A)6.

Barbara Jordan
United States Representative, D—Texas 3

It is hypocritical for us [public servants]

to exhort the people to fulfill their duty to the Republic if we are derelict in ours. More is required of us than slogans, handshakes and press releases. We must hold ourselves strictly accountable. If we promise, we must deliver. If we propose, we must produce. If we ask for sacrifice, we must be the first to give. If we make mistakes, we must be willing to admit them. We must provide the people with a vision of the future that is attainable. We must strike a balance between the idea that the government can do everything and the belief that the government should do nothing.

At Democratic National Convention, New York,
July 12/ The New York Times, 7-15:26.

Bert Lance
Director-designate,
Federal Office of Management and Budget 4

[On the OMB]: I think I can deal with the problems. I know something about people, and I know something about money. And those are the only two resources we have around Washington or Atlanta or any other place.

Interview/ Newsweek, 12-20:23.

Delbert L. Latta
United States Representative, R—Ohio 5

[On televising Congressional proceedings]: I don't object to gavel-to-gavel, on-the-air coverage. But that isn't what's being proposed. What's being proposed is a plan for some unknown network person to daily censor the activities of the House and to pick out two or three minutes of its proceedings for viewing on the evening news. This would give the American people only that small portion of the day's activities which a network person decided they should see. I'm opposed to that . . . [And with gavel-to-gavel coverage,] you run head-on into the interest question on the part of the viewing public. How many housewives would want to sit every afternoon before a television screen and listen to a debate on very technical pieces of legislation having no particular public appeal?

Interview/ U.S. News & World Report, 6-14:39.

WHAT THEY SAID IN 1976

William Lehman
United States Representative, D—Florida 1

Mr. Speaker, I am today introducing a bill, the "Federal Reports Act Amendment of 1976," to reduce the burden of Federal reporting requirements and the avalanche of Washington-generated paper. In the spirit of the bill, I will say no more.

*Before the House, Washington/
The Wall Street Journal, 5-24:10.*

Patrick J. Lucey
Governor of Wisconsin (D) 2

Retrenchment and re-evaluation are particularly painful for Democrats like myself who have toiled so long on behalf of programs that have fallen short of our expectations. It takes considerable discipline—and some political courage—to cast a cold eye on programs which were developed under the inspirational banner of better housing, education and social services for our people. In Wisconsin, the emphasis now is not on goodies, as in the past, but on austerity.

U.S. News & World Report, 3-15:18.

James T. Lynn
*Director,
Federal Office of Management and Budget* 3

There is one area where Congress is not saving money. Congress itself is the greatest growth industry in America today. The number of Congressional employees has grown 84 per cent in the last 10 years. The cost of Congress has risen to a million dollars a year per member—for salaries, buildings, typewriters and things.

*San Francisco Examiner & Chronicle,
10-3:(This World)2.*

Dumas Malone
*Professor of history,
University of Virginia* 4

Checks and counterchecks were put into our government because of fear of tyranny, but they can lead to conflict between the Executive, Legislative and Judicial Branches of the government. The three Branches can pull in opposite directions, and responsibility is so divided that we don't know whom to blame.

Interview/Nation's Business, July:43.

Mike Mansfield
United States Senator, D—Montana 5

For the time being at least, Congress is resurgent. Congress is now trying to bring about an equality of power between the Executive and Legislative Branches . . . I believe that Congress will retain momentum. There will be a slow and deliberate effort by Congress to re-assert its own power. Of course, we have to be sure the pendulum doesn't swing too far in the other direction. But the President will not continue to accumulate more power at the expense of Congress. There will be no more Vietnams.

Interview/The New York Times, 3-28:(1)44.

6

People can find fault with the Congress as an institution, but they don't seem to find much fault with their Representatives or Senators. They must like their Congressmen, or they wouldn't keep sending them back. It is the institution of Congress that they're taking it out on, as they do sometimes on the White House and the courts. It's a factor in life.

*Interview, Washington/
U.S. News & World Report, 8-16:27.*

7

I've felt that we've had too many new laws for too long, and we tend to think that the answer to a difficulty is to pass another law. What we don't seem to recognize is that when we've passed a law, there's usually a concomitant that goes with it, and that is money. And in that respect we [Congress] have contributed tremendously to the build-up of the national debt. I think we'd be better off passing fewer laws and enforcing the laws which are on the books. It seems to me that the important factor is more oversight, so that where there are discrepancies they can be corrected. Where laws do not pan out as the Congress intended, they should be abolished. But I know of very few laws which have been abolished in my 34 years here. Once a law is on the books it's hard to get it off.

Interview, Washington/
U.S. News & World Report, 8-16:28.

1

There is no longer an inner club dictating the Senate's affairs. No Senators are more equal than others. Assignments are made on the basis of geography and philosophy. Seniority is still a factor, but in a declining sense. There is no such thing now as a super-Senator or a second-rate Senator. They all participate. They don't go through a wallflower period or a silent period. I felt that's the way the Senate should operate. The newest Senator's vote should count as much as any other Senator's. The newest Senator should be seen and heard—when he has something to say.

Interview, Washington/
Los Angeles Times, 9-17:(1)12.

2

Notwithstanding the political turmoil of the last decade—a decade of war, political corruption at the highest levels, and a terrible recession—our democratic system is strong and healthy. I believe that this generation, whose faith in government may have been momentarily shaken, has a strong desire to make self-government work. At every level of government, from Congress to city hall, individuals and public-interest groups are making an impact on the decision-making process as never before. They are proving that an individual can make an impact in our system. Decisions being made by Congress, administrative agencies and the courts reflect the fact that the individual *does* count. Why? Because you, the people collectively, are the government of the United States!

At Carroll College, Helena, Mont., Oct. 29/
Vital Speeches, 12-15:137.

3

I would hope that those in the government would never lose sight of the fact that they are here on a temporary basis, whether they are Presidents or members of the Congress. We are all just transients passing through. The government is really not what is concentrated here in Washington or even in regions that are subject to Washington's whim and will. The government is the people of the United States. If those in government would only realize this: We are here at the sufferance of the people of the United States.

Interview, Washington/
Nation's Business, November:36.

Lawrence P. McDonald
United States Representative, D—Georgia 4

[Congress is] loaded with lawyers lacking life skills. It's loaded with vocabulary and intimidation, loaded with wheeler-dealers. The Capitol is loaded with prostitutes. It's the biggest cathouse in the world . . . I see myself as something of a fireman out of necessity. You become one when your house is burning. That's why I'm in Congress. I left the highest profession [medicine], with the highest ethics in the world. I'm here with the lowest ethics. I miss medicine.

Interview, Washington/People, 7-5:58.

John J. McFall
United States Representative,
D—California 5

In this longest period in our history, now in its eighth year, when the Legislative and Executive Branches have been controlled by different parties, Congress has emerged as the leader and the Administration as the reluctant partner.

The Washington Post, 4-15:(A)2.

Gale W. McGee
United States Senator, D—Wyoming 6

[Saying private firms should not be allow-

(GALE W. McGEE)

ed to deliver general first-class mail]: I don't think they could handle first-class mail at a profit if they had to give the same service required of the Postal Service. What those private firms have done well is to handle bulk mail in concentrated areas—in effect, "skimming the cream." One of the basic concepts of a national postal system that must remain untouched is the equality of service, no matter where you live. Perhaps the private firms could meet that requirement, but the price would be prohibitive. It is a government responsibility to absorb the necessary price differential to treat everybody equally . . . the 13-cent stamp is a bargain when compared to what first-class mail costs in other parts of the world. The General Accounting Office, after a four-year study, found that Americans have the cheapest rate in the world, with the exception of Canada, where it is 10 cents on first-class mail.

Interview/
U.S. News & World Report, 9-13:63,64.

George S. McGovern
United States Senator,
D—South Dakota
1

The problem is not that we [in government] have done too much, but that we are doing too little. Let us refuse to join . . . the rush to under-promise the possibilities of American life. We can afford welfare reform if we stand for tax reform. We can afford to save our cities if we stop the waste of military overkill. We can insure the health of the nation if we properly invest the resources of the nation.

Before Americans for Democratic Action,
Washington, May 22/
The Washington Post, 5-23:(A)7.

Walter F. Mondale
United States Senator, D—Minnesota
2

The polls would suggest a total distrust of politicians and government . . . [which] may have helped create an environment in which people are willing to believe almost anything

[said critical of the government]—and which makes us all the less credible when we, as members of Congress, try to explain what the facts really are.

Interview/
The Christian Science Monitor, 2-24:31.

Walter F. Mondale
United States Senator, D—Minnesota;
1976 Democratic Vice-Presidential nominee
3

Government always tries to put the best face on mistakes . . . I would hope our [Carter-Mondale] government, when we blew a good one, would just stand up and say, "Folks, we really goofed today," and just let it stand for what it is. I mean, every American who buys a pencil usually wants one with an eraser on it . . . we're going to make mistakes.

Interview, July 23/
The Washington Post, 7-24:(A)4.

Richard B. Morris
President, American Historical Association;
Professor emeritus of history,
Columbia University
4

To the extent that the decline of patriotism reflects a decline of confidence in leadership, and even the government and its virtue, I think this is a serious manifestation. But to the extent that it represents a critical view of the facade of virtue by which the government hides a lot of its operations, perhaps it might lead us back into a more realistic view of the proper role of the government. The new style may also help to get us back to a state of society in which the government and its leaders demonstrate more integrity than has been exhibited of late, and our country will operate with a deep sense of moral commitment. After all, that is what patriotism involves: a conviction that the country is on the right course, that it holds a strong moral and ethical position. If we can get the sense of moral purpose back, then patriotism will return.

Interview/
U.S. News & World Report, 7-5:Special Section.

Charles A. Mosher
United States Representative, R—Ohio

1

Mosher's Law states that it's better to retire too soon than too late. I am convinced, from observing the sad examples of others, that it usually is a mistake for anyone in public office to seek re-election after age 70.
The New York Times, 1-15:18.

2

. . . the prime function of the Congress is to. be much more than an arena of competing interests, more than a cacophony of many spokesmen. Its imperative function should be to achieve coherent, effective national policy. That is why the Congress is best described as [a] process, essentially a process intended to achieve understanding and at least majority agreement out of disagreement. And that is largely a conceptual process, requiring long periods of time and varied means to obtain basic information and advice, in the search for understanding . . . long sessions of taking testimony, of probing questions, of intensive study, analysis and synthesis, of discussion and argument, argument, argument; of skillfully writing decisions into legislative form; and also of bargaining, amending, accommodating, compromising . . . moving the bills through cumbersome, tortuous parliamentary procedures and levels to that point of final agreement by both houses, and then the President's signature which makes these decisions an Act, the law.
At Ohio State University summer commencement,
Aug. 27/Vital Speeches, 10-1:741.

3

One of the interesting lines that could be drawn in order to divide Congressmen into sheep and goats is the members who are seekers of new knowledge, new information, better advice, who recognize a desperate need for better understanding of the decisions we're making, and those who come into Congress burdened by habitual ways of looking at things—often doctrinaire, often narrow parochial viewpoints—who don't change much,

who use their staffs largely to reinforce prejudices they brought with them.
Interview/The Washington Post, 12-20:(A)8.

Daniel P. Moynihan
Professor of government,
Harvard University;
Former United States Ambassador/
Permanent Representative to the
United Nations

4

The most exciting thing you encounter in government is competence, because it's so rare.
News conference, Boston, March 1/
The New York Times, 3-2:20.

Edmund S. Muskie
United States Senator, D—Maine

5

A republic gets its strength from the consent of the governed and from a consensus on shared objectives. It gets only weakness and disappointment from [government] secrecy and surprise.
Broadcast address, Washington, Jan. 21/
Los Angeles Times, 1-22:(1)29.

6

Government inefficiency is becoming today's Number 1 villain. Until we bring what programs we now have under control, we simply may not have the resources we need, either in the budget or the public's trust, to pursue new legislative solutions to pressing national problems.
U.S. News & World Report, 5-17:39.

Norman J. Ornstein
Assistant professor of political science,
Catholic University of America

7

Two things have changed in Congress in recent years. It has grown distrustful of Presidents; power has become decentralized. Both developments mean there has to be more consultation and conciliation on the part of the President.
The National Observer, 11-13:2.

Bob Packwood
United States Senator, R—Oregon
1

[Criticizing limits placed on honorariums received by Senators for making speeches, writing articles, etc.]: It is perfectly all right for a member of the Senate to own an apartment house, to spend the weekends fixing toilets, putting on sideboards or whatever . . . It is perfectly all right, legally, to practice law and earn income from that. But it is not all right to go out and make a speech or write an article and be paid in excess of $1,000 to do it!
Los Angeles Times, 4-6:(1)10.

John O. Pastore
United States Senator, D—Rhode Island
2

[Criticizing the Senate's vote to kill a cost-of-living pay raise for Congress while allowing it for judges and other high government officials, saying it is an election-year political ploy]: You know why we're voting against this? Because we haven't got the guts to stand up and say what's in our hearts . . . How far must we go in demeaning ourselves as members of Congress? We say, oh, you'll get a good judge if you pay him more money; but we don't say you'll get a better Senator if you pay him more.
The Washington Post, 9-8:(A)2.

Claude Pepper
United States Representative, D—Florida
3

[President-elect Jimmy] Carter will do all right if he remembers it's his job as President to lead the country and it's Congress' job to legislate. Carter mustn't assume it's his job to run the country all by himself. We're going to assert our proper legislative authority no matter who is President.
Interview/U.S. News & World Report, 11-29:18.

Esther Peterson
Co-chairman, domestic affairs task force, Democratic Advisory Council of Elected Officials; Former Assistant Secretary of Labor of the United States
4

Past Administrations, with notable though limited exceptions, have peopled regulatory agencies with cast-off party functionaries, well-connected lawyers whose prior careers were marked with single-minded devotion to the interests of oil companies and other regulated industries, ideological zealots bent upon the destruction of the very laws they were appointed to uphold, cronies of favored Senators and Congressmen surmounting the selection system by affability and contacts; and perhaps worst of all, "inoffensive" mediocrities—narrow, biased, imperceptive strangers to the public interest as embodied by Congress in the laws.
At Democratic Party platform hearing, Washington, Jan. 31/ The New York Times, 2-1:(1)34.

Otis G. Pike
United States Representative, D—New York
5

I think the greatest peril which our democracy faces at the present time is not the Russian threat in Angola, or anywhere else, but the fact that huge numbers of Americans believe that their government does not tell them the truth. And I can think of nothing more sinister to the survival of our democracy than a populace which believes that its government lies to them.
Interview, Washington/ Los Angeles Herald-Examiner, 1-11:(A)12.

Thomas F. Railsback
United States Representative, R—Illinois
6

Unless the activities of all lobbyists are brought out in the open, the secrecy which protects the unsavory conduct of a few will condemn the reputation of all.
U.S. News & World Report, 2-23:23.

Dixy Lee Ray
Former Chairman, Atomic Energy Commission of the United States
7

By and large, throughout our Federal government, I believe firmly that every agency, every office, every commission, every department should have a built-in self-destruct.

At seminar, Stanford University/
The Wall Street Journal, 3-15:10.

Ronald Reagan
Candidate for the 1976
Republican Presidential nomination;
Former Governor of California (R)

1

I do not believe we can continue down a road in which, as of yesterday, the Federal government had gone $95-billion deeper into debt than it was just one year ago. I do not believe we can continue to present budgets with gigantic deficits, all of which are underestimated, all of which ignore that a number of spending programs up to and including the Post Office have been shoved outside the budget so that the people won't be aware, until the end, of the total amount of the deficit.

Campaign address, Winter Haven, Fla., Feb. 28/
The New York Times, 2-29:(1)42.

2

I don't believe Washington is the answer. I think Washington is the problem. Big government makes small people, and what we need is big people making government smaller.

Time, 5-17:12.

3

The American people have learned who is paying the bill and they have learned that Washington is not solving our problems. They don't believe their voices are heard in the marble halls of Washington. It might be wonderful if the government just closed its doors and slipped away for a vacation. They might be surprised how long it would be before anyone missed them.

Television interview, Cleveland, June 6/
The Washington Post, 6-7:(A)4.

Thomas M. Rees
United States Representative,
D—California

4

I will be leaving Congress in the belief

that it is now a more enlightened and responsive body than when I first arrived in 1966. Then it was an institution caught within the grip of a rigid seniority system and dominated by a cabal of powerful aging committee chairmen . . . A new member was expected to adjust to his small spot in the Congressional solar system and let time slowly, through the deaths and defeats of his seniors, push him toward the hub of power. New voices striving to be heard were hidden and suppressed. Much has changed . . . The undue centralization of power has been broken. Younger members are now free to participate far more freely in the forming of policy in committees dealing with policy . . . While the seniority system still reigns on Capitol Hill, it has been modified. Three chairmen were passed over last year, and this in itself has tended to make chairmen more responsive to the membership . . . On the other hand, I am disturbed at the growing tendency of polarization of rhetoric on the complex domestic and international issues before us.

Before the House, Washington, March 16/
The Washington Post, 3-24:(A)14.

John J. Rhodes
United States Representative,
R—Arizona

5

Congress has become an inert body which is creaky in its functions, arrogant in its disregard for ethics and morals, a pitiful, helpless giant that cannot even act when it wants to act.

At Republican National Convention, Kansas City,
Aug. 17/ The New York Times, 8-18:22.

Nelson A. Rockefeller
Vice President of the United States

6

. . . there are growing and legitimate claims that a dominant central government in Washington is already placing impediments and non-productive restraints upon individual activity, voluntary association and economic enterprise. We must ask: Is there a threat to human liberties because economic freedoms are being restricted, initiative discouraged and individual creativity thwarted? Human liber-

WHAT THEY SAID IN 1976

(NELSON A. ROCKEFELLER)

ties are not possible under the statism that now exists in most of today's world. The risk here in America, however, is not so much that we will take up the worship of the false gods of totalitarian ideologies. It is more that we may drift into statism as a reaction to corruption, and by government's progressively legislating such overwhelming and detailed responsibilities for the ordering of society, that liberty will be surrendered in the process.
Before Congressional Joint Economic Committee, Washington, March 18/ Vital Speeches, 4-15:386.

Dean Rusk
*Professor of international law,
University of Georgia;
Former Secretary of State of the
United States*   *1*

In the old days, when we wanted to find out the mood of Congress on any particular issue, all we had to do was talk to five powerful Congressional leaders. President [Lyndon] Johnson called them "whales." But a lot of people were critical of the "whale system," so they got rid of it. And what we have now is 535 minnows swimming around in a bucket.
*Before Dallas Assembly, Feb. 6/
The Dallas Times Herald, 2-7:(B)22.*

Jeffrey St. John
Political columnist and commentator   *2*

Despite the millions of words written during the Bicentennial honoring this historic moment in human history, we as a nation still do not know that the Declaration [of Independence] was something more than a document justifying open rebellion of British Royal authority in 1776. We have galloped through this Bicentennial year like the headless horseman, oblivious to the fact that the Declaration is a testament of a timeless condition: the tyranny of government. If you doubt it, we have this obscure passage from the Declaration: "He has erected a multitude of new offices, and sent hither swarms of officers to harass our people and eat out their

substance." I am sure that each of us can cite a massive body of evidence to prove how relevant such a statement is today when it comes to the growth of government and the web of tyranny that government daily weaves in an ever-tightening net of rules and regulations.
*Before Conservative Caucus leadership training conference, Culver City, Calif., June 25/
Vital Speeches, 10-1:748.*

Arthur M. Schlesinger, Jr.
*Historian; Professor of humanities,
City University of New York*   *3*

[On the Vice-Presidency]: It is positively damaging for those who hold it. Presidents don't even like to see the Vice President around; Vice Presidents are constant reminders of their own mortality. This causes a severe strain on friendships, and that's why Vice Presidents spend so much time traveling, going off to state funerals, weddings and conferences in Helsinki.
*At symposium on the Vice-Presidency,
Fordham University Law School, Dec. 3/
Los Angeles Times, 12-4:(1)23.*

Daniel Schorr
*News correspondent,
Columbia Broadcasting System*   *4*

Whatever restrictive legislation may be passed, and I think there will be some, I believe that government secrecy will never be the same again. If anything has been learned from Watergate and from the investigations of the CIA, it is the same lesson that the Germans were supposed to have learned from Nuremberg. It is that blind obedience does not provide an exemption from conscience. And that the constitutional process, in which government officials are supposed to trust, can be perverted by officials and even very high officials. And no civil servant can any longer hide behind the statement that he simply accepted high authority... I have to confess to you, as one of those journalists who is sort of part of the "Eastern journalistic elite," that I have long been skeptical about large numbers of Americans at the grass roots.

I was among those who thought that they were too easily manipulated and that there was not very much real wisdom out there. Well, it's my impression now that, whatever may be the conventional wisdom in Washington about the American people, many Americans are not ready to see the secrecy lid clamped on again. At least, not until they have more confidence about what happens underneath that lid.

At American University, April 17/
Parade, 6-6:21.

1

It's the job of government to keep secrets, and it's the job of the press to try to find out what's going on. But once a journalist has a secret, there is no Constitutional power for the government to try to grab it back. Until we get back on an even course in this country and get away from Watergate, we will need a certain amount of whistle-blowing and leaking. If our intelligence agencies, in a great and painful inquest, can cover up anything as they have done in the past, one way to be sure they will not in the future is to have a young man who will leak, and leave the salutary benefits of leaking to society.

Panel discussion sponsored by
Princeton University's "The Daily Princetonian,"
Princeton, N.J., June 5/
The New York Times, 6-6:(1)39.

John R. Silber
President, Boston University
2

Democracy, freed from a counterfeit and ultimately destructive egalitarianism, provides a society in which the wisest, the best and the most dedicated assume positions of leadership, offering foresight, direction and energy on which its future depends. The members of a legislature, of a city council, of a school committee, ought to be chosen by democratic process and no other way; we should be prepared to die in defense of this principle. But the persons elected to these offices ought to be better than average. They ought ideally to be the persons best qualified to hold office. They ought to be better in their intellectual capacity and in their commitment to hard work. This does not mean that they should necessarily be college graduates, middle class, white, or members of any specific group. But since lawmakers really are the servants of the people, it follows that for the people nothing can be too good.

Before municipal authorities of Boston, July 4/
Vital Speeches, 9-1:675.

Paul M. Simon
United States Representative, D—Illinois
3

[On a GSA recommendation that government agencies use private mail firms in some cases instead of the U.S. Postal Service in order to save money]: It's another example of how the Postal Service, with its inefficiency and increasing rates, is pricing itself out of the delivery market. There's something seriously wrong when public agencies have to abandon the public mail service in order to save money.

Los Angeles Times, 5-22:(1)8.

William E. Simon
Secretary of the Treasury
of the United States
4

We just cannot have government growing at the rate that it has been growing and sustain a non-inflationary economy and society ... We're not talking about narrow economic issues; we're talking about fundamental issues of equity and social stability. Today, government at all levels is approximately 40 per cent of the gross national product. And if it continues on the trend, it will be 60 per cent at the turn of this century. And that has profound implications as far as our personal freedoms are concerned. The outstanding fact is that in every country where government domination over the economy has grown to these proportions, there is a diminishing— indeed, a destruction—of personal and political freedoms and a threat to a free society.

Interview, Washington/
U.S. News & World Report, 12-13:24.

WHAT THEY SAID IN 1976

(WILLIAM E. SIMON)

1

[Saying Congress requires too many time-consuming appearances by Cabinet members]: When you're testifying three days a week on the average, sometimes four, then how in the world can one be expected to run a department of 120,000 people? I think when I'm called by every single committee on the Hill just to have a show-and-tell, that's silly.

Los Angeles Times, 12-13:(1)2.

Theodore C. Sorensen
*Former Special Counsel to the
President of the United States
(John F. Kennedy)*
2

The Presidency has nothing like the excessive power people attribute to it . . . [For example,] the President is held responsible for the economy, yet he has no power to slow down expenditures or increase expenditures without the approval of Congress. What we need is not less power in the Presidency, but to hold the power accountable. The President does not have the power to order, to command. We do not have a king, a monarch. There is no need to surround our President with a mystique that would only encourage him to get in trouble.

*At conference on government institutions,
Kenosha, Wis./
The Christian Science Monitor, 5-6:6.*

Floyd D. Spence
*United States Representative,
R—South Carolina*
3

I talked to some high-school students the other day, and some of them were turned off about government. So I told them, "You get imperfect people, you're going to have imperfect government. Now, you find all perfect people, you'll have perfect government."

U.S. News & World Report, 5-24:64.

Jerald F. terHorst
*Political columnist; Former Press Secretary
to President of the United States
Gerald R. Ford*
4

The Vice-Presidency is an extraordinary

job. And don't be put off by all those who tell you it's a big nothing. It's so special that you can't even run for it like you must if you want to be President. Vice-Presidential candidates are hand-picked, right off the vine, like any really good tomato. And you have to be a very special kind of person to get to be [Democratic Presidential nominee] Jimmy Carter's running mate or to get the okay of President Ford. Indeed, the job of being Vice President is so important that our Founding Fathers didn't even give him a whole lot to do. That was so he or she could be free to handle all the really big demands of the job. A Vice President has to be a good sport about everything. He has to bow to the President three times a day while keeping his finger ever so lightly on the Presidential pulse. And he has to have a delicate sense of timing. For example, a Vice President has to know when to speak and when to shut up. He needs to know where the Senate is, because it's his job to preside over it, and because most of the Senators themselves don't know where it's at. A Vice President also has to be ready to throw out the first ball, put on a cowboy suit, go to funerals, save Africa, and figure out how to have his picture taken without a drink in his hand. He may be asked to disappear from sight for days and weeks at a time. And he must know how to deal with the press, because one of his biggest duties is explaining to reporters why the President is such a great guy and what it feels like to be Vice President.

*Radio broadcast, "Spectrum,"
Columbia Broadcasting System/
The National Observer, 9-11:13.*

Morris K. Udall
*United States Representative, D—Arizona;
Candidate for the 1976
Democratic Presidential nomination*
5

[Saying it's fiction that Senators are better qualified for the Presidency than Representatives]: We get the same pay, vote on the same issues and are elected by the same damn people.

People, 3-1:12.

1

In order to be a great President, you've got to be great, and you've got to be President.

People, 3-1:13.

2

. . . there's a general feeling in the country that I think is misunderstood. It's an anti-Washington, anti-government feeling among people. But, if you talk to them, they're not against government; they are against government that's unresponsive and can't process your Social Security claim, government that's crooked or dishonest. You talk to these same people who say they are against government and say do you think we ought to have a national health-insurance system, which means more government, and they'll say "oh yes, I think that's good." Do you think we ought to break up oil companies? "Yes." Well, that isn't going to be done in Tallahassee. It's going to be done in Washington.

Interview/The New York Times, 4-2:9.

Daniel Walker
Governor of Illinois (D)
3

It has always been true that demands for dollars for government spending have far exceeded the dollars available. In the last two years, 27 states increased taxes. In Illinois, we held the line on taxes. It was not easy last year. It will not be easy this year. Four years ago, I pledged no new taxes. I have renewed that pledge in each ensuing year. I renew that pledge now. There will be no tax increase. People do not want more taxes. They will not tolerate more taxes . . . To those who say we should spend money we do not have, to those who demand more, more, more, the answer must be No, No, No.

State of the State address, Springfield/
The New York Times, 2-8:(3)15.

George C. Wallace
Governor of Alabama (D);
Candidate for the 1976
Democratic Presidential nomination
4

The Federal government, in taking over all phases and aspects of people's lives, eventually gets to controlling everything—from their unions to their businesses, to their farms and also their schoolchildren and their pocketbooks. I think that is the main and over-riding issue of 1976.

News conference, Boston, Jan. 10/
The Dallas Times Herald, 1-10:(A)5.

James Q. Wilson
Professor of government,
Harvard University
5

I think Congress has changed. I'm not sure it has changed for the better. At one time, Congress simply disposed of things that the President proposed . . . I think that has changed, beginning with the wave of consumer and environmental legislation in the mid-1960s, almost all of which was conceived of in the Legislative Branch and not in the Executive Branch. Congress began for the first time to sense its own power to initiate and carry through legislation without Executive leadership . . . Congress now, I believe, passes legislation far too quickly. It develops new programs, conceives of new subsidies, supports new forms of regulation really without any careful deliberation, scarcely even offering an opportunity for the effective parties to be heard on the matter. Congress has lost the central leadership that it long had—a strong Speaker, a strong Senate Majority Leader—and has weakened the power of the committee chairmen. The result has been an increased tendency, in my view, for it to ride off in 12 different directions at once.

Interview/U.S. News & World Report, 7-21:18.

Labor • The Economy

A. Robert Abboud
Chairman, First Chicago Corporation
1

With seven per cent of the people without jobs, the country is not functioning up to its potential. It's going to be a very delicate thing to balance getting people back to work and holding inflation in line. I want to tell you: I've learned there is no single, simple answer to doing that, no matter what the politicians say.

Interview, Chicago/
The New York Times, 2-22:(3)5.

I. W. Abel
President,
United Steelworkers of America
2

[Calling for a guaranteed annual wage]: The time has come to give our members steady work and wages every week and every year. Not just steady work and wages 30 or 35 weeks a year. But steady work and wages 52 weeks a year . . . We have reached a stage now in our relationship with basic steel where I think management should be able to take another big cooperative step. I refer to the need of granting their workers uninterrupted, steady work and steady, uninterrupted wages.

At Steelworkers union convention,
Las Vegas, Nev./ The New York Times, 9-3:(B)9.

Gardner Ackley
Former Chairman, Council of Economic
Advisers to the President of the
United States (Lyndon B. Johnson)
3

The most important factor in determining

the rate of inflation is what the rate of inflation has been. In other words, it has tremendous inertia. Once inflation develops for whatever reason, it's going to keep right on rolling along with very little modification for quite a long time no matter what you do.

Newsweek, 1-19:64.

Carl Albert
United States Representative,
D—Oklahoma
4

[Saying President Ford knows little about the economy]: I thought once he was President he would be like Truman. I thought he would become a national figure and no longer just a Missouri mule. I know him better than anybody. I told [former President Richard] Nixon that Ford would be the easiest man in Congress to get by the Judiciary Committee and the House because he is well liked. He is a nice fellow but he has hard-headed ideas about the economy.

Feb. 21/ The Dallas Times Herald, 2-23:(A)2.

David L. Babson
Investment counselor
5

. . . the biggest difficulty today is that few people understand that inflation is basically a political problem, not an economic one. The political pressures for more inflation are more powerful now than ever before, and an investor will ignore them at his peril . . . In my view, the most powerful are these: 1) The steady growth in government spending, which in the past 20 years has climbed two-thirds faster than our private economy has expanded; 2) lopsided tax policies that hold down savings and investment and impede the flow of capital into productive channels; 3) the spreading network of government regulation of private business, which cuts efficiency and productivity; and 4) the upward ratchet effect of pay increases which have led to a widening gap between labor costs and output per man-hour. On top of all this, you have wide misunderstanding on the part of people generally about how our economic system works. That aggravates the other problems and causes Congress and the public to demand more from the economy than it can deliver.

Interview/ Nation's Business, January:55.

Carolyn Shaw Bell
Professor of economics,
Wellesley College 1

[On the definition of capitalism]: To an economist, it means private property and ownership of the means of production. To say it is good or evil does not follow—for property can be used for moral good or for evil.

The Christian Science Monitor, 4-19:16.

Daniel Bell
Professor of sociology, Harvard University 2

This country has extraordinary strengths in its educated labor force. Literally one-fourth of the labor force of this country is today classified as managerial and professional. One fourth! There's no other country in the world that has that many.

Interview/ U.S. News & World Report,
7-5:Special Section.

Henry W. Block
President, H & R Block, tax consultants 3

. . . over a period of many years we have developed a tax system that has worked and is indeed a model for many other countries. It is admittedly complex, but I submit that it is also a delicate mechanism which should not be tampered with lightly. Deductions, credits,

specific treatment of specific problems, all were designed to meet tangible needs and to accomplish certain objectives, economic or social, or both. To shout "simplification" from the hilltops and to say nothing more is, in my judgment, not only, in the words of others, "outrageously discriminating, grossly inequitable and unfair," but also meaningless and, in fact, can be mischievous. It offers nothing positive and it does not begin to cope with the problems. If we do have problems and, if changes are necessary, then certainly we in this country have the abilities, the skills and the wisdom to make changes. But let us not lose sight of the basic principle that the equity which we seek must apply to all taxpayers, that provisions designed for incentives must be retained, or the incentives will be lost, and that the loss of such incentives can have a drastic negative impact, both direct and indirect, on large segments of our people.

Before Executives Club of Chicago, Feb. 6/
Vital Speeches, 3-15:334.

Irving Bluestone
Vice president,
United Automobile Workers of America 4

U.S. management has always paid lip service to the idea that it is the people performing the work who are the most important in the productive process. As a matter of fact, however, the treatment given the workers has belied the rhetoric. Traditionally, management has called upon labor to cooperate in increasing productivity and improving the quality of the product. My view is that the other side of the coin is more appropriate; namely, that management should cooperate with the workers to find ways to enhance the human dignity of labor and to tap the creative resources of each human being in developing a more satisfying worklife, with emphasis on worker participation in the decision-making process.

New York, Oct. 20/ Vital Speeches, 12-1:123.

W. Michael Blumenthal
Chairman, Bendix Corporation 5

The [Humphrey-Hawkins Federal national economic-planning] bill calls for too

183

WHAT THEY SAID IN 1976

much detail and too elaborate a structure. It would result in much too much bureaucracy, and it would hamper the functioning of a free economy in ways that I would regret. However, I do believe some kind of economic planning is necessary for the nation, as it is for individual companies. This national planning should look to estimating options and alternatives and providing a general direction for the economy.

Interview, Southfield, Mich./
Nation's Business, November:62.

W. Michael Blumenthal
Secretary of the Treasury-designate
of the United States 1

I simply do not accept the notion that there has to be a trade-off [between unemployment and inflation] or that relatively full employment can only be achieved at the cost of a high inflation rate. With a cautious, well-framed economic program and a collaborative effort in which we get labor and management to understand what we're trying to do, and enlist their help, we can make progress. Once the pie is bigger, it will be more fun to argue about who gets what.

Interview/Newsweek, 12-27:16.

Thornton F. Bradshaw
President,
Atlantic Richfield Company 2

The question that faces America today is not whether we will have a mixed economy, a blending of public and private initiative, but what kind of mix it should be. I believe that there is a strong future for the market system in the country, but only if we who understand that system best can make the case with logic and force, and only if we are willing to acknowledge that government has a growing role in our economic system that must be shaped rather than fought. I am not asking for more government involvement in business *per se.* What I am suggesting is that the enter-

prise system cannot function properly without the right *kind* of government intervention, at the right time, and in the right degree.

Before American Petroleum Institute,
Los Angeles/
The National Observer, 7-17:11.

Harry Bridges
President, International Longshoremen's
and Warehousemen's Union 3

The basic thing about this lousy capitalistic system is that the workers create the wealth; but those who own it, the rich, keep getting richer and the poor get poorer.

The Dallas Times Herald, 7-18:(A)20.

Edmund G. Brown, Jr.
Governor of California (D);
Candidate for the 1976
Democratic Presidential nomination 4

We're going to have to temper our wastes and excesses and consumption. We're building an economy on obsolescence, and that kind of hubris just can't go on without some kind of resistance from nature.

Newsweek, 4-19:18.

5

We've engineered this economy on automation. We've liberated a lot of human energy; but in some ways we've subjugated it, because now it's loose in the cities with nothing to do. I think we have to find a way to match people with work. There's no doubt in my mind we've got the work out there, and if we can't get people together with the work that society needs, then I am somewhat pessimistic about the future of the institutions we have.

Interview/The Washington Post, 5-15:(A)8.

Edmund G. Brown, Jr.
Governor of California (D) 6

If we're going to have a serious property-tax relief, whether by way of reduction or by way of limitation, then people have to face the unpleasant political choice of making choices. And those choices can involve less health care and less education, less police, less fire, less wages for civil servants, less sewer construction, less roads, or at least a rate of growth in all these things much slower than that which we have. And that's really the choice . . . certainly there's only one way to limit taxes and that's to limit spending . . . If you want certain things, you've got to pay for them. If you don't want to pay for them, fine.

To newsmen, Sacramento, Sept. 29/
Los Angeles Times, 9-30:(1)3.

Arthur F. Burns
Chairman, Federal Reserve Board
1

I don't think people ought to be paid for doing nothing. I think government ought to be compassionate, but a 65-week period [for unemployment compensation] tends to be demoralizing for people, and very costly to the taxpayer. I don't think it's good for the country.

TV-radio interview/"Issues and Answers,"
American Broadcasting Company, 1-18.

2

[The government should act] as employer of last resort, but only at wages that are unattractive, deliberately set that way to provide an incentive for individuals to find jobs themselves [in the private market].

Before Congressional Joint Economic Committee,
Washington, March 19/
The Washington Post, 3-20:(C)8.

3

The main source of inflation is the tendency of modern governments to expand their outlays at a rapid rate in response to incessant demands from the electorate. Govern-

ments nowadays try to solve almost every economic and social ill by spending money. With expenditures increasing faster than revenues, our own government has been persistently paying out a great deal more to the public than it takes in from the public by way of taxes. In the past ten years, including the fiscal year that is just coming to a close, the accumulated deficit under the unified budget comes to something like $220-billion. If you add in the off-budget outlays and the outlays of government-sponsored enterprises, as I think you should, the accumulated deficit comes to about $300-billion. This has been the main cause of our inflation since the mid-'60s.

Interview, Washington/
U.S. News & World Report, 5-17:34.

4

Traditional policies of economic stimulation might well be counter-productive [today]. Fears of inflation would intensify and the seeds of another recession may be sown. I cannot stress too strongly the importance of being cautious in launching new Federal programs with a potentially large budgetary impact. The policies for stimulating employment on which we have relied in the past—such as budget deficits and easy credit—cannot work well in an environment that has become highly sensitive to inflationary fears and expectations.

Before Senate Banking Committee, Washington,
Nov. 11/ The New York Times, 11-12:(D)9.

5

The type of tax cut that appeals to me in the abstract is the kind that [the late President] John Kennedy proposed in 1962, and which finally passed in 1964. It avoided social conflict by not favoring one economic level over another. It also recognized the limits of our economic knowledge as to what kind of tax cut provides the most benefits. To favor low-income groups with the biggest cut would cause the most dynamic and energetic part of our population—largely the middle

(ARTHUR F. BURNS)

class—to think our society no longer holds as much prospect for them as they think it should.

News conference, New York/
The Dallas Times Herald, 11-19:(H)8.

Earl L. Butz
Secretary of Agriculture
of the United States
1

I am more convinced each day I spend in government that the most profoundly limiting factor in sound government is the low level of economic literacy among the electorate.

Before Inland Daily Press Association of Chicago/
The Wall Street Journal, 4-2:8.

Jimmy Carter
Candidate for the
1976 Democratic Presidential nomination;
Former Governor of Georgia (D)
2

While the Federal Reserve Board should maintain its independence from the Executive Branch, it is important that throughout a President's term he have a Chairman of the Federal Reserve whose economic views are compatible with his own . . . To ensure greater compatibility between the President and the Federal Reserve Chairman, I propose that, subject to Senate confirmation, the President be given the power to appoint his own Chairman of the Federal Reserve who would serve a term coterminous with the President's.

Los Angeles Times, 5-6:(2)7.

Jimmy Carter
1976 Democratic Presidential nominee
3

The present tax structure is a disgrace to this country. It's just a welfare program for the rich. As a matter of fact, 25 per cent of the total tax deductions go for only one per cent of the richest people in this country, and over 50 per cent of the tax credits go for the 14

per cent of the richest people in this country . . . The whole philosophy of the Republican Party, including my opponent's [President Ford], has been to pile on taxes for low-income people to take them off on the corporations. As a matter of fact, since the late '60s when [former President] Nixon took office, we've had a reduction in the percentage of taxes paid by corporations from 30 per cent down to about 20 per cent. We've had an increase in taxes paid by individuals, payroll taxes, from 14 per cent up to 20 per cent. And this is what the Republicans have done to us. And this is why tax reform is so important.

Debate with President Ford, Philadelphia,
Sept. 24/ The New York Times, 9-25:8.

4

Anyone who works for a living and who reports all their income for tax purposes will never have their income taxes raised under my Administration. I'm not going to raise taxes. I'm going to cut out loopholes, and that will help all of you, and you can depend on it.

Campaign address, Rochester, N.Y., Oct. 14/
The Washington Post, 10-15:(A)2.

5

The Republicans have always felt that the best way to control inflation was to have a certain portion of American people out of work, to hold down the money we have to spend, to make the demand for goods not so great. So they believe in high taxes for working people, low taxes for corporations, high unemployment and, at the same time, high interest rates. Well, if we turn all those things around, lower the taxes on working people, get our people back to work, get interest rates down, we'll put our people back to work, balance the budget, control inflation, and our country will be better in the future.

Campaigning, Rock Island-Moline, Ill., Oct. 26/
Los Angeles Times, 10-27:(1)7.

Jimmy Carter
President-elect of the United States
1

My own economists believe that you don't reach the inevitable inflationary pressures until you get the unemployment rate down to 5½ per cent or less. At that point, you start making trade-offs between unemployment reduction and inflation . . . the reason for that is if you start using industrial capacity that might be marginal [in efficiency], you start employing people whose efficiency is not as high as those who are in the normal work force. But because we have such a great unused industrial capacity—now almost 30 per cent—and such a greatly unused manpower capacity—about eight million Americans—that gives a great reservoir of improvement before the inflationary pressures inevitably build up. The point that I'd like to make is this: By targeting unemployment programs among constituent groups or in geographical areas where the unemployment rate is very high, not having a uniform effort nationwide, you can delay the impact of inflation on an average basis by concentrating in those high-unemployment areas. And some economists have estimated that you could reduce the unemployment rate at least a half per cent or perhaps even more by targeting unemployment programs before the inflationary pressures build up.

News conference, Plains, Ga., Nov. 15/
The New York Times, 11-16:33.

2

I have no intention of asking the Congress to give me standby wage and price controls and have no intention of imposing wage and price controls in the next four years. If some national emergency should arise, and I think that's a very remote possibility, that would be the only indication I can see for a need for wage and price controls. I believe that the primary threat in these next four years is with continued unemployment, and I believe that with strong leadership, with my appealing to both industry and business on the one hand and labor on the other to show constraints, that an adequate mutual responsibility will

be assumed and unnecessary increases of prices and wages can be avoided. So I don't see any possibility or advisability of my having or asking for wage and price control authority.

News conference, Plains, Ga., Dec. 3/
The New York Times, 12-4:12.

John R. Coleman
President, Haverford College
3

. . . all the good jobs in our society go to college-educated people, and in most cases the education has little bearing on the job. Degrees are being used by personnel people as a lazy person's screening device. It tells you only that the graduate stuck with a program long enough to get a degree. The result is you have a lot of jobs being filled by college-educated people, bored to tears with jobs at which they are ineffectively utilized. There was an experiment done at a post office not too long ago where they persuaded the department to hire a certain number of black employees without putting them through any of the screening tests until after they'd been on the job for a while. Then they got their supervisor's ratings and were tested. They found no correlation at all. Guys doing well on the job, rated high by their superiors, couldn't pass the screening tests.

Interview, New York/
The Christian Science Monitor, 12-23:22.

Helen K. Copley
Chairman, Copley Newspapers
4

Economists are fond of saying that there is no such thing as a free lunch. But when we examine the direction of our economy during the last 40 years we know this conclusion is not widely shared by the American public. It certainly was not taken to heart by the people of England. The simple truth seems to be that economics is indeed a dismal science; it is also one that invites controversy. Its impact on the political system is of never-

(HELEN K. COPLEY)

ending conflict and divisiveness. Nevertheless, our mission is to convince the American people that economics and freedom are inseparable.

Los Angeles Herald-Examiner, 11-25:(B)3.

James H. Evans
President, Union Pacific Corporation
1

Is the imminent bankruptcy of New York City to be laid at the doorstep of Macy's and Gimbels—or is it the fault of rent control, free college tuition, monumental welfare and runaway pension costs? Is black teen-age unemployment a problem because employers refuse to give young people a chance—or is it because minimum-wage laws and legally backed union pay scales have made it simply impossible to afford to hire those on the first rungs of the unemployment ladder? Were the shortages and bottlenecks that struck our economy in seemingly random patterns three years ago a symptom of market failure—or were they the inevitable result of Federal wage and price controls? Do we face an impending capital shortfall because of private enterprise—or because of improper government fiscal planning which encourages consumption and penalizes savings and investment? Can we really blame the private sector for the meteoric rise in governmental expenditures which have caused rampant inflation, strained our capacity to raise capital, and so often misallocated our resources? The more deeply we look, the more signs we find of previous government interventions at the root of our present problems. More unnecessary governmental planning and central control will only make things worse, not better.

Before Tax Foundation, Dallas, April 22/
Vital Speeches, 7-1:572.

Robert H. Finch
Candidate for the 1976 California Republican
U.S. Senatorial nomination;
Former Counsellor to the President
of the United States
(Richard M. Nixon)
2

Public-employee groups throughout the country, and in California in particular, have become powerful de facto political parties. If we cannot separate big government and big labor and hold them responsible, by the year 2000 we will be where Great Britain has gone in the [past] two decades.

Los Angeles, May 3/
Los Angeles Herald-Examiner, 5-3:(A)3.

Murray H. Finley
President, Amalgamated Clothing and
Textile Workers Union
3

I believe in building a better world—not just a better house or more material things for myself—but to better people's lives. And I believe trade unions are necessary to preserve the American way of life. I don't think we can have a free democratic society without a free democratic labor movement.

The New York Times, 6-4:(A)11.

Frank E. Fitzsimmons
President,
International Brotherhood of Teamsters
4

. . . I don't think any public employees involved with the public safety—policemen, firemen, people in the water department—should be allowed to strike. I think compulsory arbitration should come into play when there are disagreements over wages and working conditions.

Interview, Washington/
U.S. News & World Report, 1-26:39.

Arthur S. Flemming
Commissioner,
Federal Administration on Aging
5

Forced retirement is nothing but a lazy person's device for dealing with a difficult personnel situation. You simply let the calendar make your decisions for you that way. [There is] no scientific justification for setting an arbitrary retirement age that *should* be based on individual ability. Compulsory retirement at age 65 is in direct conflict with the Judeo-Christian concept of the dignity and worth of each individual.

At conference on aging sponsored by
Washington Journalism Center, Sept. 14/
The Dallas Times Herald, 9-15:(A)13.

Gerald R. Ford
President of the United States
1

[On his veto of the common-site picketing bill which would have expanded the picketing rights of construction unions]: My reasons for this veto focus primarily on the vigorous controversy surrounding the measure, and the possibility that this bill could lead to greater, not lesser, conflict in the construction industry. I have concluded that neither the building industry nor the nation can take the risk that the bill . . . will lead to loss of jobs and work hours for the construction trades, higher costs for the public and further slowdown in a basic industry.

Washington, Jan. 2/
The Washington Post, 1-3:(A)6.

2

For many Americans the way to a healthy non-inflationary economy has become increasingly apparent: The government must stop spending so much and borrowing so much of our money; more money must remain in private hands where it will do the most good. To hold down the cost of living, we must hold down the cost of government.

State of the Union address, Washington, Jan. 19/
The New York Times, 1-20:18.

3

Our test of a healthy economy is a job for every American who wants to work. Government—our kind of government—cannot create that many jobs. But the Federal government *can* create conditions and incentives for private business and industry to make more and more jobs. Five out of six jobs in this country are in private business and industry. Common sense tells us this is the place to look for more jobs and to find them faster.

I mean real, rewarding, permanent jobs.

State of the Union address, Washington, Jan. 19/
The New York Times, 1-20:18.

4

Two years ago, inflation was 12 per cent. Sales fell off, plants shut down, thousands were being laid off every week. Fear of the future was throttling down our economy and threatening millions of families. Let's look at the record since August, 1974. Inflation has been cut in half. Payrolls are up, profits are up, production is up, purchases are up. Since the recession was turned around, almost four million of our fellow Americans have found new jobs or got their old jobs back. This year more men and women have jobs than ever before in the history of the United States. Confidence has returned. We are in the full surge of a sound recovery to steady prosperity.

Accepting the Presidential nomination,
at Republican National Convention, Kansas City,
Aug. 19/The New York Times, 8-20:(A)10.

Henry Ford II
Chairman, Ford Motor Company
5

Will the United States continue to lag behind the rest of the industrial world in economic growth and productivity improvement? We Americans have always taken pride in the fact that our standard of living was by far the highest in the world. But that is no longer true. Today, we are in fourth place among the industrial nations in per-capita income—behind Switzerland, Sweden and Norway, and not far ahead of West Germany and France. How far must we slide before we recognize that our problem is a national tax system that penalizes savings and discourages investment?

Los Angeles Herald-Examiner, 9-2:(A)8.

William C. Freund
Vice president and chief economist,
New York Stock Exchange
6

[On the U.S.' recent double-digit infla-

WHAT THEY SAID IN 1976

(WILLIAM C. FREUND)

tion]: In a sense, we have gone through the same sort of attitudinal catharsis as the Germans did back in the 1920s, though on a much smaller scale. It has been said that the post-war economic "miracle" of Germany rested in large part on the memories of the awful hyper-inflation of the '20s when money became worthless, when work and saving ceased, and speculation became the only worthwhile activity. The memory of that experience, just as our recent experience with the burdens of double-digit inflation, have seemed to emphasize patience and work.

At "Capital Crisis" Conference of
Chamber of Commerce, San Diego, Calif./
The Wall Street Journal, 3-9:20.

Economics is, in a large measure, a science. I stress this because I believe there is too much of a tendency when somebody disagrees with you to say, "that's only a question of your philosophy." I think that's almost completely wrong. Great differences of opinion between people do not reflect differences in philosophy. Most people have the same values; they all believe in human freedom. They would all like to see individuals have the greatest opportunity to express their values and their abilities. The difference then is a difference of judgment about what institutional arrangements will be most effective about producing that result.

Interview/
San Francisco Examiner & Chronicle,
12-5:(C)9.

Milton Friedman
Professor of economics,
University of Chicago

1

... unemployment has been higher than it need have been because of the efforts of the government to fine-tune the economy; ... the people who are really insensitive to human needs are those people who are willing to rush in with supposed professed cures which have in fact not proved cures. What we have observed, not only in the United States but in every Western world, is that the attempt to use inflation to stimulate the economy may work for a short time, but sooner or later backfires. Rising inflation, which is what will be involved in any attempt to stimulate the economy by increasing government spending or by promoting a more rapid growth of the money supply—rising inflation leads to higher unemployment, not less. The way to get unemployment down, in my opinion, is to establish a favorable framework and climate for economic activity, to reduce the scope of government, and to keep government from sitting in the back seat and hitting the driver of the car over the head every once in a while so that he goes off the road.

TV-radio interview, Washington/
"Meet the Press,"
National Broadcasting Company, 10-24.

3

In the modern world, governments are themselves producers of services sold on the market—from postal services to a wide range of other items. Other prices are regulated by government and require government approval for change—from air fares to taxicab fares to charges for electricity. In these cases, governments cannot avoid being involved in the price-fixing process. In addition, the social and political forces unleashed by volatile inflation rates will lead governments to try to repress inflation in still other areas—by explicit price and wage control, or by pressuring private business or unions "voluntarily" to exercise "restraint," or by speculating in foreign exchange in order to alter the exchange rate. The details will vary from time to time and from country to country, but the general result is the same: reduction in the capacity of the price system to guide economic activity; distortions in relative prices because of the introduction of greater friction, as it were, in all markets; and, very likely, a higher recorded rate of unemployment.

Nobel lecture,
Stockholm, Dec. 13/
The New York Times, 12-14:55.

Frank J. Graziano
President,
Crompton & Knowles Corporation   *1*

As a nation, we suffered from illusions of omnipotence that eventually plunged the country into the 1975 recession from which we are now only starting to emerge. The illusions permeated all segments of our society— business, government and labor. One of our principal illusions was that our economy would magically climb ever onward and upward and that we could endlessly consume without someday paying the bill. Hence, we filled our warehouses with giant inventories for which there was no readily discernible market. We believed that we could compete effectively in a highly competitive world market with aging and obsolete plants. Labor suffered from the illusion that it could obtain astronomical wage increases without setting in motion a disastrous inflationary cycle and that it could obtain these increases without eventually paying for them at the corner grocery store. Our banking system was weakened by the illusion that an ever-improving economy would somehow insure the repayment of loans for marginal ventures that were themselves frequently illusory. Our government— Federal, state and local—suffered from the illusion that our society could prosper on printing-press money and that it could endlessly prime the economic pump without the well someday running dry. Nineteen seventy-five —the necessary year—was in many ways a blessing in disguise, because it shattered many of our illusions and helped us return to the world of reality.

At shareholders meeting/
The Wall Street Journal, 7-14:16.

Alan Greenspan
Chairman,
Council of Economic Advisers
to President of the United States
Gerald R. Ford   *2*

Our employment is largely of two types: The vast proportion consists of relatively short spells of unemployment averaging seven or eight weeks for many millions of individuals

each year. The appropriate remedy for that segment of unemployment is to alleviate the hardships involved with unemployment insurance until these people get back into productive jobs, which they do after a short while. There is also a significant amount of chronic high unemployment—people who have difficulty getting jobs. They are not likely to be much affected by public-service employment because the types of people who get public-service employment are too often those who have skills and could get other jobs. To reduce this chronic unemployment we need to improve our training programs and, for teenagers, to improve the transition from school to work. In short, a good deal of the unemployment problem is not caused by economic factors, and it's very difficult to formulate policies and programs that come to grips with it. We can come up with a lot of fancy-titled programs, and we've had one bill after another in the last decade or more with the objective of resolving these problems, and they haven't done the trick.

Interview, Washington/
U.S. News & World Report, 6-28:30.

                    3

The decision in early 1975 not to pull out all the plugs [in the economy] turns out to have been a very courageous one. There was a tremendous pressure then to pump up the economy. Had the President done so, the level of economic activity wouldn't have been any better than it is now, but you would have put into place a huge amount of liquidity that would have significantly increased the risk of inflation.

Interview, Washington/
The New York Times, 8-22:(3)6.

Robert L. Heilbroner
Professor of economics and chairman of the economics department, graduate facility, New School for Social Research, New York
                    4

Aspirations have changed [over the last 25

WHAT THEY SAID IN 1976

(ROBERT L. HEILBRONER)

years] in such a way as to make people feel less well off. Partly, it has to do with what's happening to their environment, their surroundings, and partly to what's happening to those they measure themselves against ... In the old days, I'm quite sure that people like firemen and policemen would never have thought, "Well, a young guy comes out of Harvard Law School and settles down in Wall Street and doesn't know a damn thing and makes $18,000 to begin with—why shouldn't I make $18,000?" Harvard Law School wasn't in his reference group. I think what's happened over the last 20 years is a consequence of democracy. Working-class groups, lower middle-class groups now take high-income groups—professional groups—as being legitimate reference groups. They want that kind of income.

Interview/ The National Observer, 11-6:3.

Walter W. Heller
Professor of economics, University of Minnesota; Former Chairman, Council of Economic Advisers to the President of the United States (John F. Kennedy)
1

I may shock people, but I'd prefer still more stimulus [to the economy]. Unless the Federal Reserve provides more credit than seems likely, I'd opt for either $10-billion more in job programs, or, as a second choice, $10-billion in additional tax cuts this year. And I definitely want to see Congress provide more stimulus for fiscal 1977 than President Ford is going to provide with a $395-billion budget. Even if Ford proposes additional tax cuts on top of those due to expire in June, it wouldn't be enough to assure us a solid growth rate in 1977. We need more fiscal oomph no matter what the popular fears.

Newsweek, 1-19:63.

. . . [Democratic Presidential nominee Jimmy] Carter has made unequivocally clear that he's against across-the-board wage and price controls. He's not talking about putting

a traffic cop in every mom-and-pop grocery store. What he is saying is, "Let's work out some voluntary guidelines," try through Presidential persuasion and public opinion, after clear identification by the Council on Wage and Price Stability, to try to flag down the speeder. With the aid of that persuasion, and pressure of public opinion, then others will slow down as well. And that seems to me a perfectly consistent program with essentially a free-market economy.

Interview/ The New York Times, 10-24:(3)14.

Walter E. Hoadley
Executive vice president and chief economist, Bank of America
3

. . . there are two powerful forces that will be dominant in the next two years. The first is fear of inflation. And, for most people, the remedy for that is: "Watch government spending, because it's going to hit me in taxes. And don't give me any more fancy promises, because I've seen them result in higher costs and waste in the past." The second factor is a feeling that we're a wasteful nation and that all-out growth isn't what we want. We've got enough congestion and pollution. We're not prepared to accept any lower living standards, but we're going to have to watch our ways a bit, and that means slower growth—which is another way of saying that Americans see unemployment and inflation as two sides of the same problem.

Interview/
U.S. News & World Report, 11-1:86.

Hubert H. Humphrey
United States Senator, D—Minnesota
4

Young people today need something to do, and I don't buy from this [Ford] Administration that all you should do is line up for unemployment compensation and food stamps. [Public jobs] are better than the dole—anything is better than the dole.

At Congressional Joint Economic Committee hearing, Washington, Jan.28/
The Washington Post, 1-29:(F)1.

1

It is estimated that in the last two years we have lost over $400-billion in production by not bringing unemployment levels down to 4 per cent. We've lost some $27-billion in revenues for our local and state governments. We've had as many as 20 million people unemployed in one year, and as many as 75 million Americans whose families have been directly affected by unemployment. This is a colossal waste. I happen to believe we can do a better job. I don't want a planned society. I just want a society in which there is planning—where we look ahead beyond the fiscal year and try to see what the food policy of this country ought to be, what transportation policy ought to be, what energy policy ought to be, and so on. And we need to understand the relationship between transportation, energy, food and all the other things that go into making up commerce today. We don't do any of this now.

At discussion sponsored by American Enterprise Institute/The National Observer, 8-21:7.

Jack Kemp
United States Representative,
R—New York
2

Individuals freely pursuing their own ends have pursued coincidentally many of the ends of society, to the extent that capitalism has created more jobs, more opportunities for people, more housing, more education and more chance for people to rise above their economic circumstances than any other system in the history of mankind.

Before the House, Washington/
The Wall Street Journal, 4-8:18.

E. Douglas Kenna
President,
National Association of Manufacturers
3

Both management and labor know that something has gone wrong lately with our economic machinery. Individual Americans certainly do. They are carrying the privations and burdens of unemployment and inflation

—burdens they do not wish to accept and do not need to accept. People generally may not be as learned about the economy as economists but they have great common sense. They know what works and what doesn't work. Even if most Americans don't know the phrase "new economics," they see what it has wrought in their daily lives. And politicians who continue to preach that gospel will, I am confident, do so at their peril.

Before Economic Club of Detroit,
April 5/Vital Speeches, 5-1:428.

Leon H. Keyserling
Former Chairman, Council of Economic
Advisers to the President of the
United States
(Harry S. Truman)
4

Ten million unemployed is un-American, inhumane and contrary to every known economic law as an acceptable or tolerable alternative to inflation.

News conference, New York, May 7/
The New York Times, 5-8:21.

Lane Kirkland
Secretary-treasurer, American
Federation of Labor-Congress of
Industrial Organizations
5

[On multinational corporations that export American jobs overseas in search of low foreign wages]: It would be just fine with us if all these companies stayed home. The workers of America would welcome their coming back. But it's not realistic to think that's going to happen. The very countries whose representatives are here screaming loudest for restrictions on exploitation by the multinationals are themselves holding out the most elaborate concessions to try to attract them.

At International Labor Organization's
World Employment Conference, Geneva/
The New York Times, 6-18:(D)4.

Henry A. Kissinger
Secretary of State of the
United States
1

There is some irony in the fact that after years of disparaging our [industrial democracies'] economic systems, the socialist countries and the developing countries have turned to us to help them advance more rapidly. Today it is the industrial democracies which primarily have the resources, the managerial genius, the advanced technology and the dedication needed for sustained economic development under any political system.

At ministers meeting of Organization for
Economic Cooperation and Development,
Paris, June 21/ The New York Times, 6-22:10.

Mitchell P. Kobelinski
Administrator,
Small Business Administration of the
United States
2

On the wage issue, I hate to sound like I'm against the minimum wage, because I'm not, but there are certain small businesses that almost cannot exist because of it. These firms could use family members and young, school-age help if it weren't for the minimum wage. If we'd approach this situation rationally, we could say that businesses with x numbers of employees or fewer in this or that sector need not comply with minimum wage. We could then give employment to many of our high-school students who would be willing to work part time and learn how to make a dollar.

Interview, Washington/
U.S. News & World Report, 8-30:40.

Alexei N. Kosygin
Premier of the Soviet Union
3

[On the economic recession in Western countries]: [This crisis] is an organic disease of the capitalistic system aggravated by the protracted militarization of the economy and the growth of military spending, severe inflation, the dislocation of the mone-

tary-financial mechanism and the undermined trust in capitalist currencies, and the energy crisis, which is a crisis of the economic structure. Even bourgeois economists reflect on the vices of the capitalist system as a whole, on its inability to cope with the tasks of present-day development, let alone find an answer to the requirements of social and economic progress which the world has faced in the last quarter of the 20th century. The socialist world gives the answer to the basic questions of social development.

At Soviet Communist Party Congress, Moscow,
March 1/ The New York Times, 3-2:1.

Russell B. Long
United States Senator, D—Louisiana
4

[Calling for the reduction in the very high tax rates on incomes over $100,000]: We think it would create a lot of jobs and new payrolls if a person could keep more of his income . . . A 70 per cent tax rate causes people who are successful, who know how to make a business succeed, to spend 10 times as much time figuring a way to save money against taxes than they do trying to find a way to put people to work.

Interview, May/ The National Observer, 6-19:3.

Ian MacGregor
Chairman, AMAX, Inc.
(American Metal Climax)
5

. . . our labor unions have succeeded beyond their wildest dreams in bringing wages up to levels which in many parts of the world would be regarded as fantastic. Labor Department statistics show that about 75 per cent of all incomes in the U.S. lie between $5,000 and $25,000. Most unionized people now enjoy incomes in the middle or upper part of this range. Clearly, what has happened is that our country has become a country with an enormous middle class. The laboring class has been all but eliminated.

Interview/ Nation's Business, January:36.

Carl H. Madden
Professor of business,
American University

1

I don't see any drastic reduction in hours of work a week. The last thing most of us want is to spend more time at home. We don't really want to be idle. It's an issue of status, of our dignity, of a sense of usefulness, of challenge, of participating, and so on. But I think there is going to be more leisure that is described as work. If my grandfather could see us now and anyone suggested to him that any of us was working, he would laugh us out of the room. Nine out of ten people who ever lived on earth have been consigned to a life of unremitting toil on the land. Much work is now like leisure except in the outworn ideology of organizational executives.
Interview/ U.S. News & World Report, 12-27:85.

David J. McDonald
Former president,
United Steelworkers of America

2

[Criticizing the Steelworkers Union's no-strike agreement calling for collective bargaining or binding arbitration in the basic steel industry]: Samuel Gompers said, "It is a fundamental right of an American working man to sell or withhold his services." The experimental [no-strike] agreement removes that right. It eliminates the basic strength of the union, which is to ask its members to withhold their services. It's like sending up a pinch hitter to the plate without a bat, or asking a man at the blast furnace to make steel without iron ore.
Interview, Palm Springs, Calif./
The New York Times, 9-9:25.

George S. McGovern
United States Senator, D—South Dakota

3

It's simply not fair to have a tax structure where money earned by men and women is taxed at a higher rate than money earned by money. People with big money can invest it and get richer and richer and pay less in proportion of their income for taxes.
News conference, Anaheim, Calif., Feb. 3/
Los Angeles Times, 2-4:(1)10.

George Meany
President, American Federation of
Labor-Congress of
Industrial Organizations

4

I don't believe in organizing people just for the sake of organizing. I believe in organizing people when there's a job to be done and when you can accomplish something in behalf of those people. The percentage of organized workers to the work force in America is, I guess, about as low as any industrial country in the world . . . Despite that, we have had greater success in carrying out the objective of the trade-union movement.
U.S. News & World Report, 10-4:31.

Walter F. Mondale
United States Senator, D—Minnesota;
1976 Democratic
Vice-Presidential nominee

5

The best answer to inflation is production and work. It is not good for anybody, young or old, if they're able-bodied, not to work. This country is built on work. We respect work. Not to work and to want to work when you're able to in my opinion is un-American.
Campaign address, Eau Claire, Wis./
The Washington Post, 9-3:(A)4.

John Moore
Member of British Parliament

6

I don't think it has been understood in many of the debates within corporations how great has been the material success of the free-enterprise system, and how intimately linked are the political freedoms that are associated with it. The comparison with the

(JOHN MOORE)

material deprivation and lack of personal and human freedom that is associated with socialism is obvious. We need no barriers, no mined frontiers to keep our people in. But that freedom is limited. To keep it for ourselves, to win it for others, I would pray and ask that all join in an almost evangelical fight for the cause of free enterprise.

At Edison Electric Institute conference,
San Francisco, June 8/ Vital Speeches, 9-1:693.

Rogers C. B. Morton
Secretary of Commerce
of the United States
1

I think that the American people don't want their economy taken away from them and all responsibility for economic activity placed in the hands of the government. I think there is great fear among the American people that, if we begin to develop this tremendous public service corps, we block out the economy and say that government is responsible for employment and therefore the government must absorb all the unemployed through make-work types of programs . . . you can't have a make-work situation and have this country develop and strengthen its economy and strengthen its society. We are a free country and we have to put up not only with some of the difficulties that freedom presents, but we also are able to enjoy the great privileges of it. I just think if we go to a controlled economy and begin to lose that, we lose a lot of what many generations have fought for.

TV-radio interview, Washington/
"Meet the Press,"
National Broadcasting Company, 1-25.

Daniel P. Moynihan
Professor of government, Harvard University;
Former United States Ambassador/
Permanent Representative to the
United Nations
2

[On the free-enterprise system]: It was once

said that if the Communists took over the Sahara, there would be in time a shortage of sand. And to that I added that if such a thing came about, it would be owing to the construction of swimming pools for the rich in the West. No, my friend, it is generally to be observed that if you don't *sell* soap, you don't have much.

Interview, New York/
Los Angeles Times, 4-22:(1)7.

Thomas A. Murphy
Chairman,
General Motors Corporation
3

[Arguing against government economic planning]: The bulk of the American people have good sense; they won't let society be run by a select few. It worries me that some people say we should have a planned economy when it *is* planned [now], by individuals. Some people in academia refuse to relate their models to the real world. There are problems of business, but businessmen are not a mythical beast roaming the scene in a predatory way.

The Washington Post, 11-7:(M)3.

Edmund S. Muskie
United States Senator, D—Maine
4

Experts in both government and private enterprise tell us that we can, if we choose, significantly reduce the present unemployment during the next fiscal year. Direct employment programs—using Federal dollars to pay for public-service jobs like classroom teaching aids and hospital attendants—would produce the most jobs at the lowest total cost. Federal assistance to local communities for short-term public-works projects and to avoid layoffs in local government services—like police protection and trash collection—also have high job yields for the tax dollars invested. Yet President Ford says he intends to veto even the limited program pending in the Congress now for short-term public-works and financial assistance to local communities which have high jobless rates. This anti-recession bill—which the President seeks to block —would create 300,000 jobs this year. The President says we cannot afford to help Americans find work. I say we cannot, as tax-payers, afford not to.

Broadcast address, Jan. 21/
Vital Speeches, 2-15:260.

Gerald L. Parsky
Assistant Secretary for International Affairs,
Department of the Treasury
of the United States 1

Although our economic situation is usually the main election-year issue, I believe that the state of our economy is not the crucial issue today. Rather, the direction of our economic policy is the real issue. At home, there are prominent people calling for greater government control of price and supply, government allocation of credit, government economic planning, and a major expansion of government spending. Internationally, others are seeking governmental redistribution of wealth, government cartels for basic commodities, and governmental intervention into the operations of multinational corporations. Advocates of such policies are no longer the isolated few; they are growing in numbers, and I submit to you that the economic choices we make will determine whether we will preserve the strength of the United States. We simply cannot afford to move blindly down the path of increased government intervention and control without recognizing that the same path leads us away from the economic freedoms which have made us strong.

At Town Hall, Los Angeles, June 1/
Vital Speeches, 8-1:620.

Ronald Reagan
Candidate for the
1976 Republican Presidential nomination;
Former Governor of California (R) 2

The one basic cause of inflation is government spending more than it takes in. When Washington runs in the red, year after year, it cheapens every dollar you earn; it makes a profit on your cost-of-living wage increases by pushing you into higher tax brackets; it borrows on the capital market to cover its deficits, cutting off business and industry from that capital which is needed to fuel our economy and create jobs; it robs your savings of value, and it denies retired people the stability they need and expect for their fixed incomes. The cure is a balanced budget. The Federal government must set a timetable, a systematic plan, to balance the budget—and it must stick to it.

The New York Times, 5-9:(3)1.

3

I think there's a certain amount of dislocation going to take place or you're not going to lick inflation. I think you ease the burden for those who have to pay the highest price for curing it—the unemployed, for example. What has been true in this country is that some of the price of recession, such as high unemployment, is politically unthinkable. Therefore, the minute that economic adjustment begins, the politicians jump in and say, "Nothing is more important than full employment." Well, no one has more feeling than I have for a person who wants a job and can't get one. But there is no escaping the fact that we've got to look at the long haul . . .

Interview/ U.S. News & World Report, 5-31:22.

William B. Saxbe
United States Ambassador to India 4

Those who advocate state socialism can't point to a place in the world where it has worked. Individual enterprise has to be maintained and encouraged. And if there is a place where state socialism has worked to some extent, it is because some form of individual incentives was permitted.

Before Indo-American Chamber of Commerce,
New Delhi/
The Christian Science Monitor, 11-17:2.

WHAT THEY SAID IN 1976

Helmut Schmidt
Chancellor of West Germany
1

[Supporting government involvement and influence in economies]: There is no alternative to economic discipline. I'm not a Marxist, but you just can't build a political superstructure without an economic infrastructure. Of course, the reverse is also true. The economics won't work if the politics are bad. But political will is meaningless without the economic base.

At Common Market conference, Luxembourg/
The New York Times, 4-3:7.

Jay Schmiedeskamp
Director, Gallup Economic Service
2

To an astonishing degree, the American people see inflation and unemployment as two halves of the same problem. In other words, they believe inflation and recession tend to run together. That's been their experience recently. No Administration has talked more than the Nixon and Ford Administrations about the need for business investment in order to increase productivity and thus fight inflation. At the same time, the policy has been to accept a deep recession and a slow recovery in order to reduce inflation. And yet, there is nothing worse for business investment and productivity than a recession. A great majority of the American people believe it makes no sense to try to cure our economy by making it sick.

Interview/
U.S. News & World Report, 10-11:65.

Ray Schoessling
Secretary-treasurer,
International Brotherhood of Teamsters
3

We [Teamsters] have been probed, we have been examined, we have been checked by every agency with any authority, and we have been found the equal—yes, the superior—of any union in the labor movement in terms of proper administration of the affairs of this international union. We are subject to attack because we are effective.

Las Vegas, Nev./
U.S. News & World Report, 6-28:68.

Charles L. Schultze
Economist; Senior fellow,
Brookings Institution
4

The basic problem with achieving and maintaining full employment is not that we lack the economic tools to generate increased employment. The traditional weapons for stimulating economic activity—easy money, tax cuts and government spending for worthwhile purposes—are perfectly capable of generating an increased demand for public and private goods and services. The real problem is that every time we push the rate of unemployment toward acceptably low levels, we set off a new inflation. And, in turn, both the political and economic consequences of inflation make it impossible to achieve full employment or, once having achieved it, to keep the economy there.

Time, 12-27:10.

Irving S. Shapiro
Chairman,
E. I. du Pont de Nemours & Company
5

I believe any public job programs should be aimed at training people for private industry, that make-work ventures should be avoided. But before any such programs are launched, we should encourage the government to review how many of its tax and regulatory policies hamper accumulation of the investment capital on which new jobs in the private sector depend. We also should encourage the government to dissect the unemployment problem into its various components—which then might suggest different kinds of remedial action. For one thing, the work force is significantly different in composition than it was 20 years ago. There are increased numbers of women, who tend to move in and out of jobs more often than men; and there are increased numbers of teen-agers, many of whom need better education and training before they can become good job candidates. Over 40 per cent of today's unemployed are married women or teen-agers.

Before The Conference Board, New York,
Sept. 16/ Vital Speeches, 10-15:18.

William E. Simon
*Secretary of the Treasury
of the United States*
1

. . . we have the finest [income-tax] system in the world that's based on voluntary compliance. But that voluntary compliance has been falling off in recent years. Why is that? I think it's because such a system can only do its job if it is, and is perceived to be, based on the three principles of equity, simplicity and efficiency. And I think the American people perceive that it is not a fair system, and God knows it's not a simple system. Two out of five people have to use a tax preparer, with all the attendant expense involved, and the other three spend countless man-hours filling out all the incredible forms involved. So people feel that many do not pay their share, that a vast number of people, through various loopholes and subsidies, are not paying their fair share of taxes . . . I've come to the conclusion that if we were to design a tax system today to achieve those three goals, we wouldn't have over 6,000 pages of fine print in Internal Revenue manuals . . . I envision a system that would abolish deductions, tax credits and subsidies and substitute for it a system with a simple progressive income tax for individuals, which would range between 10 or 12 per cent at the low end of the income scale to 35 per cent or thereabouts for people on the upper end of the scale.
Interview/ The National Observer, 1-17:1.

2

. . . when we talk about our free-enterprise economy we are talking about food on the table, goods on the shelves and services at the counter. We are talking about medical break-throughs that have added ten years to ur lives in the past generation. We are talking about labor-saving devices that have freed millions of women for productive careers and the pursuit of self-enlightenment. We are talking about five out of every six jobs in America and wages and benefits that stagger the imagination of the rest of the world. We are talking about a productive base that pays for government support of the elderly, the jobless, the poor, the dependent and the disabled. And we are talking about basic freedoms: to choose a career, to choose what and where we buy, to choose where and how we live, and yes, to swim against the tide, as did Fulton and Ford and Edison—things you could never do living in the gray shadow of conformity under a regimented society.
*Before Colby Institute for Management,
Waterville, Maine, April 2/
Vital Speeches, 5-1:421.*

3

. . . while the payoff to good economics is real, it takes time. This lag, as the economists call it, is a politician's nightmare. Fortunately, I think that more and more people now understand that this is the case—and I sense growing suspicion of the proposed instant solution, the quick fix. In a world of unlimited demands and limited resources, finance ministers not only are inevitably unpopular, but indeed cannot afford to be popular. We are frequently required to be the bearers of bad tidings to our political masters—to reiterate the unpleasant but inescapable fact that resources are scarce while wants are limitless. It is our lot, whatever our country's economic system and whatever its circumstances, to speak out for financial responsibility—to call for prudence in an age of fiscal adventure. Announcement of dramatic new programs is greeted with great fanfare; the management of sustained, stable growth is a bit like watching the grass grow. Yet, in the end, it is sustained, stable growth that does the most good.
*Before board of governors, International
Monetary Fund and World Bank, Manila,
Oct. 5/ Vital Speeches, 11-1:41.*

4

I have always found it easier to discuss the basic common-sense fundamentals of economic sanity with housewives, businessmen and women consumers than with some of the most famous—and occasionally the most pettifogging—of economic theorists.
*Before Women's Crusade for a
Common Sense Economy, Los Angeles, Nov. 23/
Los Angeles Times, 11-25:(4)1.*

Page Smith
Historian
1

Every American should have the right to be creatively unemployed for some portion of his or her life; that is to say, have an opportunity to do "work" of broad social utility that benefits the community and the nation. Indeed, public-service work may be more interesting, more rewarding and more important than "private work."
San Francisco Examiner & Chronicle, 7-11:(This World)2.

Herbert Stein
Professor of economics, University of Virginia; Former Chairman, Council of Economic Advisers to the President of the United States (Richard M. Nixon)
2

There is no more sense in saying that conventional economics is bankrupt because there is poverty and inflation than to saying that conventional medicine has failed because people are still ill and dying. Of course there are problems, but we have a better chance of finding the right answers within the existing economic framework than by yearning for new theories or policies which nobody can describe. The mistake of our generation has been in rejecting the conventional wisdom, not in clinging to it. Thirty or 40 years ago, some old-fashioned economists told us that a commitment to full employment, combined with political management of fiscal and monetary policy, would bring us to our present pass—inflation without full employment. They argued that once we abandoned the old rules of balanced budgets, fixed exchange rates and gold convertibility, the political pressures to pump things up would be unrestrained. Eventually, they said, business and labor would demand more and more in profits and wages to stay ahead of the government's game and you'd wind up stimulating only inflation—not jobs. Well, that's exactly what happened.
Newsweek, 1-19:64.

3

In the Democratic platform, he [Presidential nominee Jimmy Carter] has asked for standby authority to control prices and wages, and I don't see why one would do that if one didn't at least contemplate the possibility that that would be necessary. This is all symptomatic of what I observed in Mr. Carter, that he has no fear of the power of the Federal government or of the Presidency. He sees no limitation to what the Federal government ought to do or what the President ought to do; and whenever any problem is raised, he is prepared to propose a Federal Presidential solution. Now, a lot of these solutions are described as leadership. But what leadership means is that we all are going to be led in the direction in which we don't voluntarily go. That is a form of compulsion. I don't think we should beat around the bush about this. We have seen a lot of other countries go sliding into more compulsory kinds of price and wage controls—even we, though ideologically opposed to it, went into it. And I don't have any doubt that this is the outcome of the course on which Mr. Carter would set us.
Interview/ The New York Times, 10-24:(3)14.

Robert T. Thompson
Lawyer; Authority on public-employee labor disputes
4

Public employees cannot be permitted to disrupt the services of government by strikes or otherwise. By the very nature of their work, they hold a unique responsibility, and they should realize this when they accept the work. The taxpayers have a right to uninterrupted essential services paid for by their tax dollars.
Interview/ Nation's Business, September:69.

Morris K. Udall
United States Representative, D—Arizona; Candidate for the 1976 Democratic Presidential nomination
5

I'd say, by God, while the private sector is to be preferred, the overriding importance to society is to create jobs. If we [government] must create them, then we'll create them. [And if this results in inflation,] so be it—we'll deal with inflation directly.
Philadelphia/ The Washington Post, 4-12:(A)3.

Wesley C. Uhlman
Mayor of Seattle   *1*

[On public-employee strikes]: We could prohibit any strike, which I don't think will happen; or we could totally give in to the demands of public workers—a dire possibility because the chaos of a strike is nothing compared to the chaos of impending bankruptcy. So if the conditions are right, binding arbitration may be a feasible solution.

The Christian Science Monitor, 3-19:15.

W. J. Usery, Jr.
Secretary of Labor of the United States   *2*

[On labor-management mediation]: It's hard to explain, but there's no feeling quite like seeing people who have been mad and aggravated come out of a meeting shaking hands.

Time, 5-31:53.

3

. . . we must do everything we can to create jobs in the private sector. That includes looking at tax incentives and other things to encourage business to expand and hire more workers. Now, during a period of recession, such as the one from which we are emerging, I feel the government has a responsibility to temporarily assist people who are out of work until we move into recovery. Our system relies primarily on unemployment insurance. I think we were wise to extend unemployment benefits temporarily, as we have done three separate times in the recent past. When you get to the question of creating public-service jobs on an emergency basis, I find that I have some concern. Sometimes we may just be substituting jobs—as in the case of a city that has just laid off employees. They may use the public-service money to rehire those laid-off workers without creating any new jobs. Another problem: Public-service jobs are supposed to be temporary, not permanent. Once you've put a worker into one of those "temporary" jobs, how do you move him from there into a more meaningful, permanent, full-time job?

Interview, Washington/
U.S. News & World Report, 5-31:48.

4

I have great respect for economists and all their theories. But I try to live in the real world.

People, 8-30:14.

Friedrich A. von Hayek
Economist   *5*

Nobody can seriously doubt the efficiency of the private-enterprise system and its superiority. But many people resent the fact that it distributes wealth according to market values rather than needs or "merits." That is the inevitable consequence of any system, under which people's services are remunerated according to the value their services have to their fellow citizens, which must be the case if people are to be free to choose the direction of their efforts.

Interview, Salzburg, Austria/
U.S. News & World Report, 3-8:65.

George C. Wallace
Governor of Alabama (D); Candidate for the 1976 Democratic Presidential nomination   *6*

The issue is mainly big government which has brought about almost the extinction of the middle class in this country . . . I feel the salvation of this country is the saving of the middle class—that broad spectrum who carry the great tax load of the super rich on one hand and of those who refuse to work when they can find it on the other.

Before Associated Builders and
Contractors of Texas, Houston, Feb. 10/
The Dallas Times Herald, 2-11:(A)9.

Glenn Watts
President,
Communications Workers of America   *7*

I have a rule of thumb that unions have a break-even point of 75,000 members. To that point, it takes all your income just to keep the organization going. Above that, you have the kind of income to do a better job in organization and in a lot of other programs. If you

(GLENN WATTS)

have less than 100,000 members, it's not realistic to think you'll have much impact on anything.

U.S. News & World Report, 10-4:32.

Leonard Woodcock
President,
United Automobile Workers of America 1

[On whether all labor-management disputes may some day be settled without resort to strikes]: There's only one way, given our system, under which that could be accomplished. And that is if we would agree to arbitrate all our differences or to have binding arbitration imposed on us. Management is just as much opposed to that as we are, and I just cannot see the abandonment of the strike as a weapon of last resort . . . The nature of an arbitrator is always to take the middle path. Look at all the innovative things that have happened in collective bargaining over the years. Practically all of them were strongly opposed by management in the beginning, and often right up to the point of agreement. We never would have made the breakthroughs that have been made had we had to do it through the arbitration system. A strike is a messy thing, but it's part of the price of freedom.

Interview, Washington/
U.S. News & World Report, 3-22:68.

2

. . . this society either has to create a full-employment economy based upon a forty-hour week or it has to begin to seriously reduce the forty-hour week to something less so that we can keep our people gainfully employed. You cannot have a democratic society, in my opinion, and look into the future and see seven per cent-plus unemployment without having crime get out of control, having anti-social forces get out of control; and the only solution will be, finally, an authoritarian society. I feel very deeply about this.

TV-radio interview, Washington/
"Meet the Press,"
National Broadcasting Company, 9-5.

Walter B. Wriston
Chairman, Citicorp
(Citibank, New York) 3

[On the U.S. tax system]: Any law which cannot be understood is undemocratic. No one in the world understands our tax law— not the lawyers and not the [accountants]. There's no cop to read you your rights.

At Southern Methodist University
Business School's management briefing, Dallas,
March 31/ The Dallas Times Herald, 4-1:(A)1.

Jerry Wurf
President, American Federation of
State, County and Municipal Employees 4

We [public employees] used to argue simplistically that taxes and revenues were no concern of ours, that our labor was worthy of its hire and we wanted only to deal in the equities due us. "State aid, Federal aid, those are your problems," we told the bosses. But soon it became clear that we were never going to be able to solve our workers' problems solely by collective bargaining. What we are doing here in Washington is simply trying to help the jurisdictions get the wherewithal to meet their responsibilities to us and to the taxpayers. It's not an effort we really wanted to make; but if we don't do it, it's not going to get done.

Washington/
The New York Times Magazine, 4-11:86.

Law · The Judiciary

Morris Abram
Lawyer   *1*

If the public perceives a wide disparity between [judicial] sentences inflicted upon the
rich and the poor, the cement that holds society together is impaired.
June/ The New York Times, 12-19:(4)8.

F. Lee Bailey
Lawyer   *2*

I would like to see the legal system revised
substantially in this nation. Across-the-board
justice is just not available now. If you are
short of funds, you figure to get screwed.
Interview, San Francisco/
Los Angeles Times, 2-20:(1)26.

William J. Bauer
Judge,
United States Court of Appeals, Chicago   *3*

I have found over the years that one of the
reasons pre-trial gag orders are entered is a
misconception that is indulged in by the
judiciary, indulged in by the prosecution, and
believe it or not, fostered by the media, and
that is the impact of the media on the public
at large. I suggest that one of the things that
you [the press] have fostered, because you
have done such a superb job of reporting, editing and publishing, is to think that you really
influence people. And that four days after
they read the story, they remember the first
thing about it. The fact is, I discovered in trying highly publicized cases—highly publicized, where the issues were brought out
daily before, for months and weeks beforehand, daily headlines, Chicago police scandal
cases, involving 24 defendants in a single case,

things of this nature—that when we came to
interrogating the prospective jurors, and
asked them, do you remember reading anything about this story, 94 per cent, by actual
count, never remembered the story. The other
six per cent remembered vaguely that they
had read something about it, but only about
one half of one per cent remembered what it
was they read, and less than half of them had
made up their mind as a result of what they
had read.
Panel discussion before
American Society of Newspaper Editors/
The Wall Street Journal, 5-5:18.

William M. Beaney
Professor of law,
University of Denver   *4*

The Federal judge today plays a highly
significant role in our society. All kinds of
problems fall into his lap. These days, he even
winds up running schools · or businesses.
We've played political games with the judiciary to an extent that's not justified . . . We
don't have to settle now for someone who's
just passable. To appoint mediocre judges
today is a travesty.
Los Angeles Times, 10-6:(6)2.

Daniel Bell
Professor of sociology,
Harvard University   *5*

We . . . have a willingness, still, on the part
of this country to accept the constitutional
rule of law, which is a very extraordinary historical factor. I don't ignore the fact of corrup-

WHAT THEY SAID IN 1976

(DANIEL BELL)

tion; there's been corruption in every institution. But I know of no country where there's been so long a history and so high agreement to accept a rule of a court as final and binding, and, if one loses, to accept the decision peacefully. I would say that this degree of constitutionalism, years from now, will be looked upon as one of the most unique aspects of the American system.

Interview/
U.S. News & World Report, 7-5:Special Section.

Robert H. Bork
Solicitor General of the
United States

1

[Saying he advocates removal of largely factual disputes from Federal courts]: [But] there's an unthinking reflex . . . a feeling that somehow this would give the little people less-effective justice. There's this kind of silly notion that everyone has his right to a shot at the Supreme Court—even if the Supreme Court never takes his kind of case. I think you'd get better justice under alternative systems.

Interview/Los Angeles Times, 8-30:(1)1.

Warren E. Burger
Chief Justice of the United States

2

. . . the inordinate delay in supplying the much-needed judge power has not deterred the Congress from enacting legislation that brings new litigation into the courts . . . The point is that when the courts have more work, they must have more judges, more supporting personnel, more equipment. It is the lag in providing for these needs that provides a valid cause for public dissatisfaction. And I take it upon myself to continue to make this point because there is no one else in as good a position to do so.

State of the Judiciary message, Philadelphia,
Feb. 15/The New York Times, 2-16:20.

3

[On "diversity" cases, involving lawsuits between residents of different states]: . . . diver-

sity cases have no more place in the Federal courts in the second half of the 20th century, and surely not in the final quarter of this century, than overtime parking tickets or speeding on the highways simply because the street or highway is Federally financed. If we really believe what is the subject of so much rhetoric about returning government to the people and to the states, it would help if we had legislative action to match the rhetoric.

State of the Judiciary message, Philadelphia,
Feb. 15/The New York Times, 2-16:20.

4

With few exceptions, it is no longer economically feasible to employ lawyers and conventional litigation processes for many "minor" or small claims—and what is "minor" is a subjective and variable factor. This means that there are few truly effective remedies for usury, for shoddy merchandise, shoddy services on a TV, a washing machine, a refrigerator, or a poor roofing job on a home. This also means lawyers must re-examine what constitutes practice of law; for, if lawyers refuse minor cases on economic grounds, they ought not insist that only lawyers may deal with such cases.

At National Conference on the Causes of Popular
Dissatisfaction with the Administration of Justice,
St. Paul, Minn., April 7/
The New York Times, 4-8:27.

5

It may be time to consider whether this problem of adequately staffing the courts can be better dealt with in some other way. In Florida, for example, the Governor of the state is authorized by its legislature to create a new judgeship by Executive order based on precise criteria of population, caseloads and other relevant factors prescribed in a statutory formula. Were a similar measure adopted on the Federal level, the need for judgeships would not be caught in the complexities of elections and other irrelevant considerations, when both the Executive and Legislative Branches are preoccupied with matters totally foreign to the needs of the courts.

At National Conference on the Causes of
Popular Dissatisfaction with the Administration
of Justice, St. Paul, Minn., April 7/
The Washington Post, 4-8:(A)20.

1

One of the long-range projects of the entire [legal] profession and all persons interested in the proper administration of justice will be to explore some means to see to it that, every time we approach a national election, all additions of demonstrably needed new Federal judgeships are not embroiled in partisan political conflicts and frozen so that the public suffers while it waits, not months, but years for what everyone agrees should be done. This is a situation that cries for correction.

Before American Bar Association,
Atlanta, Aug. 9/
Los Angeles Times, 8-10:(1)14.

Jimmy Carter
1976 Democratic Presidential nominee   *2*

I do favor a shifting back toward the removal of technicalities which obviously prevent the conviction and punishment of those who are guilty. I believe the Burger [Supreme] Court is moving back in the proper direction. We went too far and it got so that sincere, honest, dedicated, competent law-enforcement officers found it almost impossible to comply with all the technicalities that might be raised in court or on appeal, and obviously guilty people were released unpunished, and society in the process suffered.

Campaigning, Oklahoma, Sept. 13/
The Washington Post, 9-15:(A)4.

3

I believe people should honor civil laws. If there is a conflict between God's law and civil law, we should honor God's law. But we should be willing to accept civil punishment . . . Reinhold Niebuhr, a theologian who has

dealt with this problem at length, says that the framework of law is a balancing of forces in a society; the law itself tends to alleviate tensions brought about by these forces. But the laws on the books are not a measure of this balance nearly as much as the degree to which the laws are enforced. So when a law is anachronistic and is carried over from a previous age, it's just not observed.

Interview/ Playboy, November:69.

Robert Coulson
President,
American Arbitration Association   *4*

In most [legal] cases, both sides have much to gain by accommodating and very much to lose by litigating. But in many situations, the lawyers, following their professional attachment to strict adversary loyalties, find themselves obstructing the way toward mutual compromise.

Before American Bar Association/
Los Angeles Times, 8-30:(1)13.

Archibald Cox
Professor of law,
Harvard University   *5*

One of the penalties of being a lawyer is that you don't remember things, and you don't particularly *want* to remember them. As a lawyer, you have to force-feed your mind for your hour in court with all sorts of material you'll never ever need again, and somehow there's no room for anything else. So you get into the habit of letting everything else slide.

Interview/ Publishers Weekly, 3-1:9.

Edward M. Davis
Chief of Police of Los Angeles   *6*

. . . I think the greatest thing that we're going to learn in changing the justice system is to put it out where the people are, where it can feel the pathos, the pain and suffering, the hopes and expectations, the vibrations of a

(EDWARD M. DAVIS)

community. And so the justice can be personalized to those human beings out there instead of being some abstract academic thing based upon what you believe about Freud and the law and all that.

Interview/ Los Angeles Times, 8-10:(4)6.

Myron Du Bain
Chairman and president, Fireman's Fund American Insurance Companies
                                                                    1

The basic purpose of the [insurance/ reparations] system is to restore a person who has had a loss to the position he was in before the loss occurred, but only at the expense of those who owe him a duty of care and whose fault caused the loss. But somehow over the last decade our legal system has strayed from this touchstone, especially the requirement of fault. Jury awards are often in excess of the amount necessary to restore the injured party to the position before the loss, and there is not enough emphasis placed upon fixing responsibility for the loss with the party most directly responsible. Too often now our courts seem to have become gambling places where people who have suffered a loss go to spin some wheel of fortune, expecting a windfall profit. The few who do win big only serve to inflate the expectations of all ... The need for consumers to have ample recourse to any loss must be put back into balance with what society can afford to pay. That balance can be achieved only through a reform of our entire reparations system. That is where the next American revolution will be staged. This reform must develop a system whereby the injured are compensated fairly, promptly and efficiently for their losses, however much they are found to be, at the same time it removes the elements of windfall profits that invites fraud.

Before Western Association of
Insurance Brokers, San Francisco, Jan. 20/
Vital Speeches, 2-15:277.

Percy Foreman
Lawyer
                                                                    2
... courage in the courtroom is more im-

portant than brains. If I were hiring a lawyer and had to choose between one that was all brains and one that was all guts, I would take the guts.

Interview, Houston/ Los Angeles Times, 5-16:(1)5.

Ralph Gampell
President, State Bar of California
                                                                    3

I would hope the media will note the vast amount of good that lawyers do in the society and not only the peccadillos ... The legal profession plays almost a seminal role in the cementing of the social fabric ... it's overly simplistic to extrapolate ... that because 99 per cent of those jailed in Watergate were lawyers, ergo the remaining thousands of lawyers in the country are all crooks ... A high percentage of politicians are lawyers, but once they move into the political sphere they're operating as politicians. I think it's ridiculous to say that the Nixons, the Haldemans, the Ehrlichmans and the rest were flawed lawyers. They were flawed government servants.

Interview/
San Francisco Examiner & Chronicle, 9-26:(A)15.

Jules B. Gerard
Professor of law,
Washington University, St. Louis
                                                                    4

Judges of all kinds—Federal, state, trial and appellate—are assuming more and more power than anyone ever thought they would have. Judges are sticking their noses in and inventing remedies for problems that 15 or 20 years ago people would have said the courts couldn't do anything about. It's a trend that's becoming an avalanche.

The Christian Science Monitor, 1-12:3.

Arthur J. Goldberg
Lawyer; Former Associate Justice, Supreme Court of the United States
                                                                    5

Our country has sustained far greater injury from judicial timidity in vindicating citizens' fundamental rights than from judicial courage in protecting them.

U.S. News & World Report, 1-19:29.

Erwin Griswold
*Former Solicitor General
of the United States* *1*

Some Supreme Court Justices employ the ruse of saying, "What we are doing is interpreting the Constitution," when what the Court is doing is deciding what is good for the country . . . Judges may be doing good things in the name of activism today, but activism can also be used to order bad things if the principle of intervention is accepted.

U.S. News & World Report, 1-19:29.

Avrum M. Gross
Attorney General of Alaska *2*

The public image of plea-bargaining is terrible. The public sees justice disbursed in terms of deals—that if you get a good lawyer you can get off, not necessarily by winning a trial, but by out-snookering the DA. Sentencing should be determined after a plea is entered and not to get a plea to end a criminal proceeding. It should be a separate function . . . It doesn't do much good for the criminal-justice system to indict someone for assault with a deadly weapon, then find out that you didn't have any evidence on which to prove the charge; so you end up reducing it to an assault-and-battery misdemeanor with an agreed-upon deal for a suspended sentence. That, I don't think, did anything but send all of us through the motions and convince everybody that the whole thing was basically a sham. Now we don't handle that kind of case any more. If we can't prove them, we don't file them. The police are making better cases for our office because they know that for the most part they're going to have to justify their cases in court. Now we can make more cases stick when we file them.

*Anchorage, Alaska/
The Washington Post, 8-20:(A)10.*

Philip B. Kurland
Professor of law, University of Chicago *3*

If the judiciary is to be the primary agency for social reform, shouldn't we be more concerned about the quality of the people we choose for judges? For the most part, judges are narrow-minded lawyers with little background for making social judgments.

U.S. News & World Report, 1-19:29.

Edward H. Levi
Attorney General of the United States *4*

[On a lawsuit by 44 Federal judges seeking an increase in salary]: I hate to say it, but I think it's a silly case. I don't think you can read the Constitution as taking into account the changes in life-style and inflation . . . I wish they did have higher salaries. I know that there are a lot of nice people who don't think [the lawsuit] is silly . . . But I think it's . . . rather strange.

*To reporters at luncheon meeting, Washington,
March 8/ The Washington Post, 3-9:(A)10.*

5

There is tension among the criteria presented for judicial reform. There is doubt about the courts' competence or authority to become a problem-solver for society and a desire that courts confine themselves to their traditional role. At the same time, there is a great reluctance to deny access to the courts, or to deny protection of rights when, as it is said, other institutions have defaulted.

*Before American Bar Association, St. Paul, Minn.,
April 9/ The New York Times, 4-11:(1)30.*

6

The bar must attempt to make clear to the public, with an eloquence that suits the importance and subtlety of the matter, the nature and importance of its special role. This need for eloquence and clarity is generally required of us, particularly in this period, to persuade the society of what we know true: that the law deserves the people's faith and

(EDWARD H. LEVI)

that without this faith the law fails.

At dedication of Texas Law Center, Austin, July 4/
The Dallas Times Herald, 7-5:(A)26.

1

The law has to encourage a kind of reasoning together. That is going to be hard for some people who don't regard the law as a reasoning device. They say use it as a weapon and go as far as you can. The danger is that you lose the case or get something established that you can't live with or, more likely, something so ambiguous that it leads to all kinds of problems.

Interview/ Time, 12-20:72.

Walter F. Mondale
United States Senator, D—Minnesota;
1976 Democratic
Vice-Presidential nominee
2

We can't have a safe America unless everyone agrees to obey the law . . . including those big shots in high public office who also commit crimes. There is nothing more sacred to this country than equality under the law.

At campaign rally, Morton Grove, Ill./
The Washington Post, 9-5:(A)11.

Robert M. Morgenthau
District Attorney,
New York County, New York
3

[Saying he will be giving his assistant prosecutors authority to handle complete cases individually]: Lawyers responsible for a case from the beginning to end are going to do better than a lawyer handling a single piece of a case. Now the prosecutor is like the guy on the assembly line doing one task, but not responsible for the whole car.

New York, April 20/ The New York Times, 4-21:1.

Stanley Mosk
Chief Justice,
Supreme Court of California
4

[On class-action lawsuits]: While it may be true that class actions are not a panacea, they are also not, in the words of some of the

more vehement critics, "legalized blackmail," "potentially dangerous" or a "Frankenstein monster." Unquestionably there have been gross abuses of the class action. But I suggest abuses can be curbed without destroying a useful legal tool . . . If courts are too far committed to the ultimate demise of such proceedings, then appropriate action through Congress and state legislatures may be indicated.

Before environmental lawyers, San Francisco/
The New York Times, 2-8:(1)33.

Philip J. Murphy
Lawyer; Staff director, special committee on
prepaid legal services,
American Bar Association
5

For many middle-income people, using a lawyer is like going to a dentist. They only go when they have to, because the costs of legal services prevents their using lawyers for preventive services.

The New York Times, 1-18:(3)3.

Thomas A. Murphy
Chairman,
General Motors Corporation
6

Unnecessary laws are bad laws, if for no other reason than they substitute legal coercion for freedom of choice.

At Junior Achievement
National Business Leadership Conference,
Dallas, Jan. 30/ The New York Times, 1-31:38.

William H. Rehnquist
Associate Justice, Supreme Court
of the United States
7

[Saying judges today are engulfed in minor and petty details and are becoming dissatisfied with their jobs]: Somewhere there comes a tipping point . . . at which the number of routine and uninteresting tasks in the course of a long day becomes so large a portion of the whole that the number of qualified people willing to take the job diminishes sharply. I suggest we are beginning to approach that point . . . I believe that more and more judges are experiencing growing disappointment with their role in our legal system and in society in general . . . I would estimate that the changes in the professional life of a judge over the period I have been in practice have on net balance been for the worse.

*Before American Bar Association,
Atlanta, Aug. 9/ Los Angeles Times, 8-10:(1)14.*

Charles S. Rhyne
*President, World Peace
Through Law Center*
1

If we are to achieve that more perfect system of justice, it is we lawyers, judges and professors of law who know the current system best who must do the major leadership job of reforms, corrections and innovations. It is we who must recognize that in the United States, the mounting of public opinion for change is the way we get change. It is we who must educate the public on the needs of the justice system and on how to get them. This is a job of leadership that we who have dedicated our lives to the law must perform. If we do not do this leadership job, it will not be done at all.

*Before International Lawyers Club, Geneva/
The National Observer, 10-2:15.*

A. M. Rosenthal
*Managing editor,
"The New York Times"*
2

[Criticizing judges who restrict press coverage of trials, such as by issuing gag orders]: The trend is for judges to try to reach out of the courtroom, control a reporter's typewriter and the newspapers. Obviously this also pertains to television and radio . . . There is a huge body of evidence, the very history of our country, to show that a free press and free reporting of judicial decisions are pillars of all our freedoms. But there is almost no evidence to show that, in effect, the First Amendment and the Sixth Amendment do

collide to the damage of defendants.

*Before Fordham University Law Alumni
Association, New York, Jan. 30./
The New York Times, 1-31:42.*

Justin A. Stanley
*Lawyer; President-elect,
American Bar Association*
3

The cost of rendering legal services today has become so high that in modest matters lawyers cannot afford to undertake the work and prospective clients cannot afford to retain lawyers.

*At Law Day banquet,
Southern Illinois University, April 28/
The New York Times, 5-2:(1)54.*

Potter Stewart
*Associate Justice,
Supreme Court of the United States*
4

[On the exclusionary rule which limits the use of evidence obtained illegally]: The exclusionary rule was designed to protect the Fourth Amendment right to privacy [from unreasonable searches] and has nothing to do with giving a person a fair trial. In fact, isn't it actually unfair to the trial to suppress evidence [obtained by an illegal search], because it impairs the disclosure of truth?

*At Supreme Court hearing, Washington/
The Dallas Times Herald, 2-25:(A)14.*

5
It's true that, for a period in the 1950s and '60s, the [Supreme] Court in many areas was out front. This was really the first time and the only time in the history of our nation when it has been. Mr. Justice [Robert] Jackson wrote a book shortly before he came on the Court—kind of an angry book. And in it he said, as a simple statement of fact, that there's never been a time in the history of our nation when the Supreme Court of the United States did not stand for the conservative forces in American society. That was a historical fact. And that's interesting to remember. The Court was a conservative force. And when it became something *other* than a con-

(POTTER STEWART)

servative force, in the '50s and '60s, that was an unprecedented role for the Supreme Court to be playing. I think those who miss the days of the so-called Warren Court are inclined to think, "Well, golly—the Court was always in the forefront." Actually, it was just a brief moment in American history.

Interview/ Newsweek, 7-4:36.

John A. Sutro
Lawyer; Chairman, standing committee on judicial selection,
American Bar Association

1

In the past we had no difficulty attracting the very best qualified lawyers to the Federal bench, since the salary was somewhat comparable to what one could earn in private practice. Today, however, attorneys are making substantially more than the salary of Federal judges, and won't—or generally can't—accept a Federal appointment unless they have other sources of income.

Los Angeles Times, 2-11:(1)35.

John K. Van de Kamp
District Attorney,
Los Angeles County, California

2

[Saying witnesses and defendants should have more protection in grand-jury proceedings]: Persons ordered to appear before the grand jury have no right to be told what crime, if any, is being investigated or whether they are themselves potential defendants. There are no rules of evidence to restrict the scope of the prosecutor's questions. Unprotected by the presence of either court or counsel, witnesses may face intimidation, harassment and interrogation into virtually any aspect of their lives . . . The Federal agent assigned to the case will typically present the evidence against the accused in a summary fashion, thus eliminating the need for the government to bring any "live witnesses" before the grand jury. In this way, the grand jury is deprived of an opportunity to see and hear [other] witnesses,

or to evaluate their credibility and demeanor.

Before Senate Judiciary subcommittee,
Washington, Sept. 28/
The Dallas Times Herald, 9-29:(A)16.

Lawrence E. Walsh
President,
American Bar Association

3

One idea that ought to be looked at very carefully is to decriminalize many acts that are now prosecuted as crimes. I'm talking about such activities as gambling, prostitution or marijuana smoking. There are also many kinds of business offenses that are presently misdemeanors that might be deterred by administrative or civil proceedings . . . I wouldn't necessarily take these cases out of the courts. I'd shift them from the criminal side to the civil side—or have them dealt with by an administrative or regulatory agency where you have less-elaborate procedures, and cases could move more rapidly than they do in criminal courts. Either way, this would free more judges to handle more-serious crimes because civil cases can be handled more efficiently than criminal.

Interview, Washington/
U.S. News & World Report, 8-2:40.

4

[On the Justice Department's criticism of ABA rules prohibiting lawyers advertising their services and costs]: The claim of the Department of Justice is that the restraint on advertising reduces price competition and so disserves the public and violates the anti-trust laws. In some fields, particularly those providing uniform products, advertising is sometimes useful in holding down prices. But a heavy majority of lawyers commenting on advertising have felt it would not be useful in the practice of law. They are concerned that advertising has in it the danger of deceit and overstatement. There is also concern that the expense of advertising would bear hardest on the new members of the profession, rather than on established law firms, and that all advertising costs would inevitably be passed on to the public.

Interview, Washington/
U.S. News & World Report, 8-2:41.

1

[Saying trial by jury in civil cases may have outlived its usefulness]: I'm in an awkward position. I like juries. I'd hate to see them go. They've been the public's representatives in the administration of justice. But I'm on the verge of being convinced that a 40 per cent delay factor [in court time] is just too big a price to pay in civil cases . . . Our courts are so far behind.

At American Bar
Association annual meeting,
Atlanta, Aug. 6/
Los Angeles Times, 8-7:(1)9.

Andrew Young
United States Representative, D—Georgia 2

My problem with lawyers is they believe in the law . . . as a static concept, for the most part. It's almost as if going to law school brainwashes you out of any real creativity . . . [The law] is designed to protect the power and privilege of those who write the law [and] to ward off any values or vision that threatens it.

Panel discussion at
American Bar Association convention, Atlanta,
Aug. 6/ The New York Times, 8-7:7.

National Defense · The Military

Les Aspin
United States Representative,
D—Wisconsin
1

I don't see how any rational human being, looking at the two superpowers as they exist now—I am not talking about future trends—can say that the Soviets have a strategic advantage. There is absolutely no question that the United States has complete predominance with regard to its nuclear force, solely because of the warheads. Warheads are what count. In 1970, the Soviet Union had 1,800 warheads and we had 4,000—about a two-to-one advantage. Today the Soviet Union has 2,800 warheads and we have 8,500—so now we have almost a three-to-one advantage. We have not just superior, but overwhelming, advantage.

At "Pacem in Terris" convocation, Washington,
December ('75)/
The Center Magazine, March-April:53.

2

Weapons systems have a life of their own, for it seems that whatever strategic doctrine happens to be enunciated by the Secretary of Defense, the armed services have always recognized only one doctrine, the same one that Samuel Gompers had for labor unions: "We want more." It is helpful if a weapons program fits into the prevailing doctrine. But if not, the Pentagon has learned how to fit whatever it wants into the policy and contingencies being enunciated . . . Sometimes we buy weapons simply because we have mastered the technology, and, like the mountain, they are there.

At "Pacem in Terris" convocation, Washington,
December ('75)/
Center Report, February:11.

3

Our biggest problem is trying to figure out the real utility of military power. We make a lot of casual assumptions about the kinds of difficulties which can be solved by military force. For example, we are dependent on foreign sources for raw materials; or we are having trouble with some of the countries along the Mediterranean that have been our allies—and we are told that these troubles justify increasing the size of our Navy, or increasing our air power. But if we stop and think about that for a moment, we begin to realize that military force is just not the appropriate response in such situations. In fact, military force can exacerbate such problems.

Interview, Washington/
The Center Magazine, May-June:31

Alphonzo Bell
United States Representative, R—California;
Candidate for the 1976 California
Republican U.S. Senatorial nomination
4

Quantitative military balance of power in the world is now held by the Soviet Union, and the qualitative balance is rapidly slipping away [from the U.S.]. The pattern of votes cast . . . in Congress during the last five years constitutes an abandonment of the policy of maintaining "rough equivalence" with the Soviet Union in military power.

Los Angeles Herald-Examiner, 4-1:(A)19.

Edmund G. Brown, Jr.
Governor of California (D)
5

I don't think you can be naive about the world. It's a competitive place, and the strong survive and the weak don't. We're still a few generations away from the time when swords will be turned into plowshares. And, until then, we ought to be ready . . . Russia's obviously the strongest military power [the U.S. faces]. We're all becoming more interdependent, but we ought to realize that without substantial military strength, we're obviously jeopardizing our security.

Interview/ Playboy, April:186.

George S. Brown
General, United States Air Force;
Chairman, Joint Chiefs of Staff   1

We believe that U.S. military strength . . . is sufficient today. But we are greatly concerned about adverse military trends and what they portend for the future . . . War does not have a rational beginning, and we must be aware that the Soviet Union is developing forces to win.

Newsweek, 3-1:39.

Yvonne B. Burke
United States Representative,
D—California   2

Blind support for massive military spending must not continue. It must be recognized that the threat to our society from decay within our society is at least equal to the threat from outside. Money from essential social programs must stop being diverted to the military.

Los Angeles Times, 10-14:(1-A)1.

Jimmy Carter
Candidate for the 1976
Democratic Presidential nomination;
Former Governor of Georgia (D)   3

We need to have a simplification of the purposes of the military. I think that a singular purpose of the military ought to be the capability to fight, and with that capability will come the best hope of permanent peace. Now the military duplicates. There's an unbelievable bureaucratic hierarchy that's been established since the Second World War.

We've got an overloaded number of high officials—Admirals, Generals and their immediate subordinates. We've got too many support troops for combat troops. Some management improvements, I think, would restore to a great degree the confidence of our people in the military. It would also let the President and the Congress play a much more legitimate and continuing role in the planning and evolution of new weapons systems, which quite often have been wasteful . . . I think these management-improvement efforts would result in roughly a 5-to-7-billion-dollar decrease in the defense budget. I might add, however, that the Number 1 responsibility of any President is to guarantee the security of our country. I would never permit our nation to be subjected to successful attack, threat of attack or blackmail. And I would keep our defense capabilities adequate to carry out a legitimate foreign policy.

Interview/ U.S. News & World Report, 5-24:19.

4

Exotic weapons which serve no real function do not contribute to the defense of this country. The B-1 bomber is an example of a proposed system which should not be funded and would be wasteful of taxpayers' dollars.

Before Democratic Platform Committee,
June 16/ The Washington Post, 12-3:(A)8.

Jimmy Carter
1976 Democratic Presidential nominee   5

I would try to build about one *Trident* submarine per year. I think we are getting into a dangerous position with respect to the Soviet Union on naval strength. I have a deep belief that our most important element in the entire defense mechanism of our country is nuclear-powered submarines. They are almost completely invulnerable to missile attack and their deterrent value is superb.

Interview, New York/
San Francisco Examiner & Chronicle, 7-25:(A)15.

WHAT THEY SAID IN 1976

(JIMMY CARTER)

1

If we should permit in the future, which I would never do, the Soviet Union to acquire an acknowledged [military] superiority, it might be an encouragement to them to try to overwhelm us with a nuclear strike. We have been discussing the fact that there is a rough equivalency in over-all strategic capability between our country and the Soviet Union. The trend in the future must be maintained to assure that we keep a rough equivalency between ourselves and the Soviet Union in strategic atomic weapons . . . I don't think we're second-best militarily. As you know, we've got some areas wherein we are second-best. The total amount of throw-weight for atomic weapons is one area where the Soviet Union is superior to us. The throw-weight per missile for the Soviet Union is superior to our own. Ground forces, the total number of personnel and total number of tanks is superior with the Soviet Union. Of course, they've got two possible enemies—ourselves and the People's Republic of China. We are superior, I think, in the deployment of strategic weapons at sea. We have much higher accuracy per weapon. We're much further advanced in the MIRV missiles. We also have cruise-missile capabilities that the Soviet Union does not have. We are far superior to them in manned bomber fleets, primarily B-52s. So the over-all statement is that we do have rough equivalency and in some areas we're superior and in some areas they are superior.

News conference, Plains, Ga., July 26/
Los Angeles Times, 7-27:(1)6.

2

Where I come from, most of the men who went off to fight in Vietnam were poor. They didn't know where Canada was; they didn't know where Sweden was; they didn't have the money to hide from the draft in college. Many of them thought it was a bad war, but they went anyway. A lot of them came back with scarred minds or bodies, or with missing limbs. Some didn't come back at all . . . I could never equate what they have done with those who left this country to avoid the draft. But I think it is time for the damage, hatred and divisiveness of the Vietnam war to be over. I do not favor a blanket amnesty, but for those who violated Selective Service laws, I intend to grant a blanket pardon. To me, there is a difference [between pardon and amnesty]. Amnesty means that what you did is right. A pardon means that what you did— right or wrong—is forgiven. So, pardon— yes; amnesty—no. For deserters, each case should be handled on an individual basis in accordance with our nation's system of military justice.

Before American Legion, Seattle, Aug. 24/
The National Observer, 9-4:5.

3

We are a powerful nation but we can be more powerful. We must have a strong defense—tough, muscular, simple, well organized, supported and appreciated by all Americans, with waste and confusion eliminated and with a sharply focused purpose: the ability to fight.

Campaign address, Warm Springs, Ga., Sept. 6/
Los Angeles Times, 9-7:(1)16.

Ramsey Clark
Candidate for the 1976 New York Democratic U.S. Senatorial nomination;
Former Attorney General
of the United States

4

Pentagon over-spending is cheating our city, our state and our nation. What will it benefit us to have the most massive military machine in human history if our society wastes away internally in . . . illness, ignorance, decaying cities, rising crime, loss of liberty? We can no longer afford to indulge in cold-war cliches about America's military might while our cities sink into bankruptcy.

Campaigning, New York, Aug. 28/
The New York Times, 8-29:(1)43.

William P. Clements, Jr.
*Deputy Secretary of Defense
of the United States*
1

We get sniping and snipping at the [defense] budget at a moment when we are running out of time. It takes years to develop some of the new sophisticated items. And we don't have time. The attitude of our armies, now principally volunteer, is superb. The same attitude needs to penetrate to all the people.

Interview/ The Dallas Times Herald, 2-1:(B)2.

2

. . . without any question whatsoever, our Navy is superior to the Russian Navy. So they have more tanks. We have a bigger and better Navy. We have a better Air Force. They have a bigger Army. They have about 2½ times as many people in uniform as we do. But they have, as an example, a common frontier with China on which they have between 500,000 and 600,000 people deployed. You could just go on forever talking about these kinds of comparisons. I don't think they in themselves are important, and I think that's the part that is far, far too simplistic. When you start talking about our production base, our technology—wherein we have probably a 10-year lead overall to the Russians—these things are terribly important . . . the Russians understand this, and it's fortunate that they do.

Interview/ The National Observer, 6-26:1.

Ronald V. Dellums
*United States Representative,
D—California*
3

[Criticizing the military-spending portion of the Federal budget]: What does this budget do? Does it reflect human values? Does it reflect priorities that speak to the millions of human beings in this country who are unemployed, who are desperate, who are victims of racial oppression, of classism, of chauvinism and of sexism? No, it does not. We continue to build monuments to our military madness, spending over $100-billion in this budget for those purposes. Probably it will be

over $150-billion in 1980 and $200-billion in 1985. And why? Because Russia is going to attack the United States? On the scale of 1 to 100, the possibility is somewhere between zero and maybe one. Will we be attacked by the Warsaw Pact? Life is hell for millions of people in this country. They cannot pay their rent. They cannot pay for food. Many of them cannot find jobs. What do we do? We build B-1 bombers that will be obsolete by the time they get into the inventory. We want to build *Trident* submarines that serve no useful purpose. Can we say to the American people that we can be the police officer of the world when any reasonably sophisticated human being understands that our world has changed?

*Before the House, Washington, April/
Los Angeles Times, 5-25:(2)5.*

Bob Dole
*United States Senator, R—Kansas;
1976 Republican Vice-Presidential
nominee*
4

[On U.S. Vietnam-war draft evaders and deserters]: Let there be no confusion as to President Ford's position on this issue. It is unequivocal—and applies equally to draft evaders and deserters: no blanket pardon, no blanket amnesty, no blanket clemency. Today, we have those who would signal weakness and generate strife by declaring that those who served this nation in her armed forces deserve no greater consideration than those who turned their backs and scurried away. President Ford extended the hand of mercy to those who fled America when she needed their service. He offered them a chance to earn clemency by proving their right to resume their place in this nation. The offer was extended to draft dodgers and deserters alike, on a case-by-case basis. Some accepted. Some refused. As far as I know, the effort is finished.

*Before American Legion, Seattle,
Aug. 25/ The National Observer, 9-4:5.*

5

[On those who call for large cuts in defense

(BOB DOLE)

spending]: They tell us we need to reduce our defense budget even further, while increasing spending for even more well-intentioned but ill-conceived domestic programs. There are those who say we spend too much on planes and tanks and warships and troops, and not enough on people. They say we are callous. They say we are indifferent. I say I would rather spend a million dollars, or a billion dollars, to preserve peace, than expend a single human life to pursue war.

Before American Legion, Seattle, Aug. 25/
The Washington Post, 8-26:(A)1.

Robert F. Ellsworth
Assistant Secretary of Defense
of the United States for
International Security Affairs
1

In a very general sense, any statement about America's military power today—in an age of peace which also involves violence, disruption and danger—is at least partially a statement about the role the United States will play in world affairs. This is true not only in the sense that rhetoric unsupported by capability invites failure; it is also true in the sense that other states will mold their own policies and behavior upon their expectations with regard to U.S. actions. Those expectations are based partly on estimates of the capability of America's military forces in being, partly on assessments of the trends between ourselves and the Russians—and partly on estimates of our readiness to act. Today there is some imprecise but uncomfortably large area of doubt with regard to our readiness to act, and with regard to the U.S.-Soviet balance after 1980. There is virtually no doubt whatever about the strength, flexibility, professional competence and weapons sophistication of our military force capabilities in being today, both nuclear and conventional.

Before Rotary Club, Montgomery, Alabama,
Jan. 26/Vital Speeches, 3-1:301.

Frank E. Fitzsimmons
President,
International Brotherhood of Teamsters
2

Despite continued denials by myself and members of the general executive board, reports persist that the Teamsters union is making plans to organize members of the armed forces. I want to put these unfounded reports to rest once and for all. I personally believe that unionization of the armed forces would neither be desirable nor feasible. We view such organizations as very impractical from a trade-union posture. Therefore, it can be written as absolute fact that the Teamsters will not be conducting organizing campaigns to bring members of the armed forces into our union now or in the future.

The Dallas Times Herald, 12-12:(A)13.

Gerald R. Ford
President of the United States
3

A strong defense posture gives weight to our values and our views in international negotiations; it assures the vigor of our alliances; and it sustains our efforts to promote settlements of international conflicts . . . The defense budget I will submit to Congress for fiscal 1977 will show an essential increase over last year . . . We are continuing to make economies to enhance the efficiency of our military forces. But the budget I will submit represents the necessity of American strength for the real world in which we live.

State of the Union address, Washington,
Jan. 19/The New York Times, 1-20:18.

4

Now, I know some questions have been raised about whether we are as strong as the Russians. The allegation is made that they have four million people in the Army, in their military forces, and we have two-million-one. The problems are a little different. The Soviet Union has a 1,000-mile or more border with the People's Republic of [Communist] China and they have at least half of their forces on that border. We, the United States, have friendly relations with the Canadians on the one hand and the Mexicans on the other, so we don't have to have half of our military forces on either the northern or southern border. In addition, the Soviet Union has to face the NATO forces to the west, so they have two borders that they have to man fully, completely, totally. So, just taking numbers without understanding the problem doesn't explain the facts of life. Now, let's take another question that has been raised. The allegation is made that the Soviet Union has more missiles than we. That is true, but what do we have? We have more warheads than they by about four to one. And it is warheads, not missiles, that destroy the target. Our missiles and warheads are more accurate and our launching pads are more survivable, so we are in a better position to survive and we are in a better position because our warheads, what we want, are in greater number. So, I just caution people that before you take a chart that compares numbers, that you understand something broader than just the numbers. You have to compare apples and apples, not apples and oranges, as some people try to do.

San Antonio, Tex., April 9/
The Washington Post, 4-18:(B)6.

1

Our military capability is fully sufficient to deter aggression, keep the peace and to protect our national security. But strength involves more than military might. A nation's real power is measured more completely by considering a combination of its military, agricultural, industrial, technological and moral strength. And in every one of these areas, the Number 1 nation in the world is the United States of America.

Before Texas Grain and Feed Association,
El Paso, April 10/
San Francisco Examiner & Chronicle, 4-11:(A)15.

2

Recent charges that the United States is in a position of military inferiority and that we have accepted Soviet world domination are complete and utter nonsense. To charge

that this Administration—an Administration that has fought for the two biggest defense budgets in history and for the first time in ten years is convincing Congress to spend enough on defense—to charge that we have led our nation into military inferiority is preposterous on its face.

Before Daughters of the American Revolution,
Washington, April 21/
The Washington Post, 4-22:(A)6.

3

There are those in this political year who want to withdraw our troops from their positions overseas. The voices of retreat talk about a phased withdrawal. They talk as if our defenses won't be weakened if we only dismantle them one brick at a time. They are wrong. The world is still a dangerous place ... we cannot retreat from the front lines of freedom if we are to preserve our freedom here at home.

Before National Guard Association, Washington,
Sept. 1/ Los Angeles Herald-Examiner, 9-2:(A)5.

4

[Democratic Presidential nominee Jimmy] Carter in November of 1975 indicated that he wanted to cut the defense budget by $15-billion. A few months later, he said he wanted to cut the defense budget by $8- or $9-billion. And, more recently, he talks about cutting the defense budget by $5- to $7-billion. There is no way you can be strong militarily and have those kinds of reductions in our military appropriation . . . Let me tell you this straight from the shoulder: You don't negotiate with [Soviet leader Leonid] Brezhnev from weakness. And this kind of a defense program that Mr. Carter wants will mean a weaker defense and a poor negotiating position.

Debate with Democratic Presidential nominee
Jimmy Carter, San Francisco, Oct. 7/
The New York Times, 10-8:(A)18.

E. J. (Jake) Garn
United States Senator, R—Utah
1

[On labor unions for the military]: Collective bargaining, arbitration and the right to strike must remain alien to members of the armed forces. The United States Supreme Court has set forth some of the reasons why unions and the armed forces are not compatible. One of the basic distinctions made by the Court is that our civilian and military societies must of necessity be separate. For no matter how much rhetoric we hear, in the final analysis when the armed forces are called upon to defend our country, we must know that the Commander has the unquestioned authority to order his men into battle and the power to enforce his order. Under such circumstances, there is no time or place for union grievances. If the services were allowed to unionize, it would severely hamper, if not destroy, the country's defense capabilities.

Washington, March 9/ **

Barry M. Goldwater
United States Senator, R—Arizona
2

[On members of Congress who criticize various fringe benefits granted to members of the military]: Congressional stone-throwers who attack legal and earned benefits of our soldiers, sailors, and airmen should remember the little-known and often blatant privileges enjoyed by legislators in this glass house on [Capitol] Hill. These hypocrites seek to get their names in print and their faces and voices on TV and radio by sarcastic and demeaning assaults on our servicemen. They assail proper inducements given to members of the armed forces to help in recruiting, to maintain morale and to make the entire career military service more effective and attractive . . . These attacks are hypocritical, for no group in the United States has more fringe benefits, allowances—call them what you will—than members of Congress. Moreover, we voted them for ourselves, often as amendments to other legislation, and without fanfare. There were no press releases, no letters to our districts or states, when we slipped by a new or enlarged benefit . . . Some

of our rock-throwers worry volubly about military commissaries, avoiding the fact that we have heavily subsidized Senate and House restaurants. Some attack post exchanges, conveniently forgetting our own basement stores, which sell at reduced prices . . . Summed up, we take pretty good care of ourselves, and Congressional press releases don't indicate any of us are upset about it. The military should not be above criticism; abuses in the services should be exposed and corrected. But we should apply the same standards to Congress or to any other part of the government.

Before Army & Navy Club, Washington/
The National Observer,2-28:7.

3

It stands to reason that unionizing the uniformed military personnel of this nation would not strengthen but seriously weaken America's preparedness for any eventuality, be it a threat from the Soviet Union or some other aggressor. It would destroy the military chain of command and ruin the discipline so necessary for the proper performance of military missions . . . When you project a military man's right to strike into a combat situation, you come up with a ridiculous situation which cannot be explained away under any circumstances.

Before the Senate, Washington/
U.S. News & World Report, 9-20:84.

Andrew J. Goodpaster
General, United States Army (Ret.);
Former Supreme Allied
Commander/Europe
4

[On the U.S. Military Academy honor code]: What the code does is establish a set of personal principles and ethics of personal behavior and performance of duty, based on honesty and integrity. It is so deeply and strongly inculcated during the period at West Point that it becomes just a mode of life—the way you approach and attack and deal with all your problems and your relationships, individual to individual . . . A review of the West Point code, in my opinion, will simply revalidate it. My expectation would be that a review would show that the code is more valuable than ever. Our country at this particular moment in its history, after the traumas of the last few years, needs more acutely than ever those elements that strengthen principles of ethics and apply higher values to our public life.

Interview, Washington/
Los Angeles Times, 6-9:(2)5.

Otis Graham
Professor of history, University of
California, Santa Barbara 1

National defense is not simply a matter of arms, but also of the natural-resource base and its wise conservation; of the human resources of the nation, not merely armed people but healthy, educated, productive people; of the transportation and communication infrastructure; of scientific and technological talent. In fact, recently we have begun to discover the bottom line in national-security affairs, and it is not the latest nuclear delivery system but the very social cohesion of our 200-year-old country, based on a social compact which has been undercut by the rule of a garrison state which has policed the globe with an arsenal of unspeakable weapons while disorder mounted at home. As a beginning to a remedy, the term "national security" must now be reclaimed from the five-sided [Pentagon] building on the south bank of the Potomac and from the House Armed Services Committee. It must be broadened so that more voices are heard when we formulate policies to insure national strength and survival.

At "Pacem in Terris" convocation,
Washington, December ('75)/
The Center Magazine, March-April:67.

Alexander M. Haig, Jr.
General, United States Army;
Supreme Allied Commander/Europe 2

The greatest danger is giving in to the temptation to cut defense at a time of socio-economic crisis . . . That temptation must be combatted, not just for security reasons, but because if we erode our sense of self-confidence and security . . . we shall never achieve cooperation in broader areas such as energy, monetary matters and trade.

U.S. News & World Report, 3-1:38.

3

To the degree we experience inadequate conventional military capabilities we then find ourselves lowering the so-called nuclear threshold, which raises the risk of our reliance on nuclear weapons to defend our interests.

Interview,
Canadian Broadcasting Corporation,
The New York Times, 3-6:2

F. Edward Hebert
United States Representative,
D—Louisiana 4

There is no "place" and "show" in national defense and security. There is only a winner and a loser. And if America is to survive the cradle of its birth, it must be prepared to win.

Retirement statement/
Los Angeles Times, 3-31:(1)2.

Jesse A. Helms
United States Senator,
D—North Carolina 5

In the field of defense, the United States must never be merely "second to none"; we must be superior to all, or tyranny will win the day, and the totalitarian way of life will be imposed upon us. Other nations can equivocate because they presume they can hide beneath our umbrella. But if we lose our prominence, we have nowhere to hide except in subjection or extinction.

Before Republican Party platform
committee, Aug. 11/
The Washington Post, 8-22:(C)7.

Lewis B. Hershey
General, United States Army (Ret.);
Former Director,
Selective Service System

6

As soon as you let the draft lag, you just

WHAT THEY SAID IN 1976

(LEWIS B. HERSHEY)

simply cut off one of your arms. Twice I've gone through the change from an all-volunteer Army and I know the months it takes. If somebody's eating you up at that time, you may not be still alive by the time you get organized to do something about it.

Interview/ The New York Times, 8-11:7.

Martin R. Hoffmann
*Secretary of the Army
of the United States* 1

For the times we're in, for the condition of the world, and the hope that there will not be a war—I think the volunteer Army is a great success. Many critics who were against the all-volunteer force at the outset will say, "Well, it's a success, and it's the right thing for the times, but it's on the wrong philosophical basis." These critics are usually advocates—as I suppose I am—of a period of required national service. These critics also worry about what happens when a war breaks out, because I don't think anybody thinks the all-volunteer force means that you will never again have to conscript . . . But in terms of the quality of people we're getting, our ability to fill the various skill needs that we have, getting a quality soldier who will retain his motivation and do the traditional job of the Army and be ready to fight—it's been very successful.

The Washington Post, 1-3:(A)3.

2

[On the West Point honor code and revelations of cadet cheating at the Military Academy]: I have no need to come before you and defend the code of honor—it is timeless. This institution, however small, must continue in these troubled times to keep the flame of conscience alive. If West Point does not do it, where else will it be done?

*At Military Academy graduation,
West Point, N.Y., June 2/
The Washington Post, 6-3:(A)8.*

Daniel James, Jr.
*General, United States Air Force;
Commander, North American
Air Defense Command* 3

The greatest form of international suicide would be unilateral disarmament. The other guy has to know we've got it and that we're willing to hit somebody over the head with it if all else fails.

*Before Veterans of Foreign Wars, New York,
Aug. 16/ The New York Times, 8-17:17.*

David C. Jones
*General and Chief of Staff,
United States Air Force* 4

We should bear in mind that in defense as in nature, there are no rewards or punishments, only consequences. The decisions reached in 1976 will have consequences extending far into the future, consequences which ought to be examined, judged and, insofar as possible, controlled. A democracy has a perfect right to select whatever course it wishes—superiority, equivalence or inferiority. In my judgment, superiority, or at least equivalence, are the only rational courses for this nation to follow. American strategic inferiority would pose too many destablilizing political and military risks, and, if history is any guide, would remove *any* incentive for the Soviets to negotiate reciprocal reductions in strategic arms. This year's [defense] budget has arrested the trend of ever-declining resources for national defense. However, the nation cannot regain lost momentum in a single year or with a single budget. If we are to remain committed to maintaining at least strategic equivalence, we must increase the pace at which we modernize our position of unassailable strength.

*At Air Force Association luncheon for him,
Washington, Sept. 21/ Vital Speeches, 11-1:64.*

Henry A. Kissinger
*Secretary of State
of the United States* 5

As we assess SALT, we must face squarely one question: What is the alternative to the agreement we have and seek? If the SALT process falters, we must consider what new or additional strategic programs we would undertake, their likely cost and, above all, their strategic purpose. An accelerated strategic build-up over the next five years could cost as much as an additional $20-billion. Failing a satisfactory agreement, this will surely be the path we must travel. It would be a tragically missed opportunity. For in the process of such a build-up, and the atmosphere it would engender, it would be difficult to return to serious negotiations for some time. Tensions are likely to increase; a new, higher baseline will emerge from which future negotiations would eventually have to begin. And, in the end, neither side will have gained a strategic advantage. At the least, they will have wasted resources. At worst, they will have increased the risks of nuclear war.

At joint luncheon of Commonwealth Club and World Affairs Council of Northern California, San Francisco, Feb. 3/ The New York Times, 2-4:10.

1

I want to make clear that the United States has to be physically strong, and the United States cannot permit any nation to appear to be militarily superior to us. Without adequate military strength in all relevant categories, no diplomacy, however skillful, can help us. For this reason I have strongly supported a strong national defense in all categories, and not just in strategic arms.

Interview, Washington/ U.S. News & World Report, 3-15:27.

2

We need a defense posture that is relevant to our dangers, comprehensible to our friends, credible to our adversaries, and that we are prepared to sustain over the long term.

At dinner sponsored by Dallas Council on World Affairs and Southern Methodist University, March 22/ The Dallas Times Herald, 3-23:(A)1.

3

. . . no responsible leader should encourage the illusion that America can ever again recapture the strategic superiority of the early post-was period. In the '40s we had a nuclear monopoly. In the '50s and early '60s we had overwhelming preponderance. As late as the Cuban missile crisis of 1962 the Soviet Union possessed less than 100 strategic systems while we had thousands. But today, when each side has thousands of launchers and many more warheads, a decisive or politically significant margin of superiority is out of reach. If one side expands or improves its forces, sooner or later the other side will balance the effort.

At dinner sponsored by Dallas Council on World Affairs and Southern Methodist University, March 22/ The Dallas Times Herald, 3-23:(A)11.

4

Democratic societies have always fluctuated in their attitude toward defense— between complacency and alarmist concern. The long lead-times of modern weapons and their complexity make both these aberrations dangerous. We cannot afford alternation between neglect and bursts of frenzy if we are to have a coherent defense program and public support for the necessary exertions . . . To maintain the necessary defense is a question of leadership more than of power. Our security responsibility is both manageable and unending. We must undertake significant additional efforts for the indefinite future. For, as far ahead as we can see, we will live in a twilight area between tranquility and open confrontation.

At International Institute for Strategic Studies, London, June 25/ The New York Times, 6-26:7.

Eugene J. McCarthy
Independent candidate for the Presidency of the United States; Former U.S. Senator, D—Minnesota

5

The "arms race" has not been between the U.S. and Russia; it's been between each Administration and the previous one. If we could stop *that* arms race we would be in pretty good shape. In the Eisenhower campaign they said we were under-defended by Truman, so they raised the ante to 46 billion. Kennedy said we were under-defended by Eisenhower,

WHAT THEY SAID IN 1976

(EUGENE J. McCARTHY)

so they got the budget up to 65 or 70 billion. Johnson said we were under-defended; Nixon said we were under-defended. Gerald Ford said that we were now the strongest we had ever been, and when [Donald] Rumsfeld was sworn in as Defense Secretary he said we were ready to take on everybody. We ought to inaugurate a President sometimes who doesn't . . . declare war on the rest of the world.

Panel discussion/ Center Report, June:29.

1

Three times we've got ourselves all saddled up at enormous expense because "the Russians were coming." They weren't, but we got ready anyway. The first time was in the 1950s, and they were coming by bomber. So we built the Distant Early Warning Line and SAGE, systems that were out of date before they were completed. Then, in 1960, the Russians were coming by missiles, and we discovered the missile gap. There wasn't any gap, but we spent billions preserving a gap of our own between our strength and the Russians'. Now they're coming by submarines, and we've got a submarine man—[Jimmy] Carter—running for President. One of the reasons I'm running is that I think the people should hear from someone who won't say we're under-defended. Of course, I've discoverd a gap—the cavalry gap. The Russian Army has 3,000 horses and our Army has only 29 and never uses them except for military funerals. We should be on our guard. What if it turns out the Russians are coming by horse?

At National Press Club, Washington/ The New York Times, 9-4:19.

J. William Middendorf II
Secretary of the Navy of the United States

2

Our Navy today continues to be an essential part of our national defense. The Soviets realize the importance of a strong Navy too. Fleet Admiral Gorshkov has stated: "The Soviet Navy is the only armed force capable of supporting state interests in peacetime." In the early days and in fact even during World War II, as Pearl Harbor will attest, we had time to rebuild. What about today? [With] today's technology, with missiles capable of traveling 1,000 miles in half an hour, we no longer have the luxury of the long 1-2 year lead time in order to rebuild. A land invasion is no longer a concern; the real threat is obvious and much of it is sea-based. Hence, our only solution is to maintain a strong Navy—always ready. Furthermore, this country of ours has vital overseas interests— interests we must protect. With our reliance on the sea growing by leaps and bounds, and since we have extensive exposed coastlines bounded by two different oceans, in addition to two states and three territories—Puerto Rico, Virgin Islands and Guam—which lie overseas, a primary mission is to protect the U.S. Coasts and mainland areas threatened by sea-based missiles.

Before Rotary Club, Chicago, July 20/ Vital Speeches, 9-15:709.

Walter F. Mondale
United States Senator, D— Minnesota; 1976 Democratic Vice-Presidential nominee

3

[On U.S.-Soviet military balance]: I agree with rough equivalency. You can't be in a position in which the Soviet Union would have a disproportionate lead over our nation, for several reasons. One, it would undermine the deterrent principle. It would shake the confidence of our allies in Western Europe, and elsewhere, and could have political implications. But my hope is that rough equivalency can be achieved more through hard bargaining with the Soviet Union and our mutual realization that that's the best way for both nations, because it reduces the defense budget and increases stability and reduces tensions. Now, of course, it takes two to achieve that, and I'm very realistic, I think, about the difficulties of negotiating with the Soviet Union. But I think we must try.

Interview, Plains, Ga., July 27/ Los Angeles Times, 7-28:(1)6.

Paul H. Nitze
Chairman, advisory council, Johns Hopkins
School of Advanced International Studies;
Former Deputy Secretary of Defense
of the United States 1

The Russians feel that the fulcrum on which all other levers of power and influence depend is the strategic nuclear relationship. Nuclear power isn't something the Russians would wish to use, but it is the fulcrum on which the exploitation of other military, economic and political sources of influence depends. In the strategic nuclear field, the Soviets have made great progress in the last 10 years, while our effort in that field has declined. It would be wise for the United States to reverse that trend—to improve its nuclear arsenal and defenses against attack. It wouldn't be terribly expensive to do so, but there isn't strong support for it today because people don't understand what is happening.
Interview/ U.S. News & World Report, 12-27:51.

Sam Nunn
United States Senator, D—Georgia
2

[On comparisons of the military strength of the U.S. and the Soviet Union]: . . . the debate implies that the comparative military positions of the two superpowers, like the respective automobile fleets of the Hertz and Avis rent-a-car agencies, are subject to precise measurement. On the contrary, military power is not simply the sum total of all the soldiers, tanks, ships, aircraft and missiles in the national inventory. If it were, the United States probably would be permanently relegated to a position of military inferiority vis-a-vis the Soviet Union. But, unlike the Russians, we have never relied on sheer weight of numbers for a decision on the battlefield. The key to our true military capacity has always been the maintenance of technological supremacy over our potential adversaries, a supremacy which traditionally has offset our quantitative inferiority.
The Washington Post, 4-8:(A)18.

Thomas P. O'Neill, Jr.
United States Representative,
D—Massachusetts
3

[Saying many former Congressional critics of the Pentagon are now backing a stronger defense posture]: There's an over-all feeling that the world is a tinder box. We all know that we are not as strong as we used to be. The Navy is obsolete. We've neglected conventional weaponry. The feeling in Congress is that our equipment is worn out, and we better get it ready.
Time, 4-12:12.

William Proxmire
United States Senator, D—Wisconsin
4

The most serious military problem facing the nation is the decline in the United States force levels. Dwindling numbers of military vehicles, aircraft and vessels can be directly attributed to unit price increases which have resulted in less than one-for-one replacement of older, obsolete equipment. Continuation of this policy will result in a U.S. force structure containing a very small number of highly sophisticated weapons. Although on paper this small force may show an improved effectiveness, the capital-intensive nature of general-purpose warfare makes this policy extremely dangerous. The U.S. appears to be engaging in its own form of unilateral disarmament. Insistence on ever-more-sophisticated weapons irreversibly leads to lower force levels. The only conclusion that can be drawn is that the Defense Department is engaged in a replacement policy detrimental to our national well-being.
*Before the Seante, Washington, March 29/***

5

The age of the manned strategic penetrating bomber is over. Flying missions into the heart of the U.S.S.R. with gravity bombs is virtually a suicide flight. But just as the Navy could not give up its battleships, the Air Force refuses to recognize the end of the World War

WHAT THEY SAID IN 1976

II bomber mission. If the Air Force had a ground-force mission, we would still be breeding cavalry horses.

*Before the Senate, Washington, May 19/***

Ronald Reagan
Candidate for the 1976 Republican Presidential nomination; Former Governor of California (R) 1

My critcism of our defense posture is not based on a crystal ball. I have cited Defense Department statistics; statements by the current Secretary of Defense and his immediate predecessor; our arms-control chief; the Pentagon's research chief; former SALT negotiators; our NATO commander—among others. [President] Ford's protestations that he has an "impeccable record of standing for a strong Defense Department and a fully capable, fully trained, fully equipped and ready military force" missed the point. No one is questioning his patriotism, only the record. Since the mid-1960s we've frittered away a clear military superiority over the Soviet Union. The trend has continued under Mr. Ford's and [Secretary of State Henry] Kissinger's leadership and I have yet to see it change. The American people must be told the facts so they can demand a change. That is what I am working to do.

News conference, Dallas/
The New York Times, 4-6:24.

2

How does [President Ford] refute the figures? The figures reveal that we're outnumbered in ships in the Navy by the Soviet Union 2 to 1; we're outmanned in the Army 2 to 1; their artillery outnumbers us 3 to 1; their tanks outnumber us 4 to 1; their missiles are bigger, more powerful, more numerous, and now they're years ahead of where we thought they were in adding multiple warheads to each missile . . . If Mr. Ford wants to take me up on that, I'm prepared and have wanted a legitimate debate on the issues. But he's also

going to have to answer some people like his own Secretary of Defense.

News conference, Georgia, April 21/
The Washington Post, 4-22:(A)6.

3

Defense spending is something I don't believe is very much subject to argument or opinion. I think you have to spend. That is dictated by necessity. You have to spend what is necessary to ensure that no other nation acquires the strength to challenge you and violate the peace.

Interview/The Christian Science Monitor, 6-3:17.

Thomas C. Reed
Secretary of the Air Force of the United States 4

[On "overkill"]: It's the only way to maintain stability. They, the Soviets, are not likely to attack, as long as they know the United States has the capability of responding in a controlled and responsible way. But if they knew our weapons were outdated, that would be another story. What counts is the ability to retaliate.

Interview, New York/
The Christian Science Monitor, 4-21:30.

5

Why should the U.S. have a strategic deterrent? The answer is because the Soviets have embarked on a steady, determined program of building up their military capability. Ten years from now, unless we take prompt action, we're going to be faced with a very serious military-strategic imbalance. Given that we are to have a strategic deterrent, what should it be? The concept of the "triad" has proved to be most useful and satisfactory. The "triad" means the strategic forces have three legs: submarine-launched missiles, surface-based missiles, and manned aircraft—which together have posed an unsolvable targeting challenge to the Soviets. Ten years from now the bomber leg is going to be facing a very difficult defense. By then we will need a better manned, penetrating bomber for the core targets.

Interview/ U.S. News & World Report, 4-26:63.

1

It would be irresponsible not to initiate B-1 [bomber] production [in view of the] expansion [of Soviet strategic forces]. There is every indication that the Soviets are driving for strategic superiority by the early 1980s. The B-1 is the strategic initiative that can redress that imbalance by the early '80s.

News conference, Washington, Dec. 2/
The New York Times, 12-3:(A)18.

Bernard W. Rogers
Commanding General, United States
Army Forces Command
2

. . . defense preparedness is unpopular with those persons who wish to see more and more of the national budget spent on social services. They tend to forget, as Sir John Slessor reminds us, that "the most important social service a government can do for its people is to keep them alive and free." In conjunction with our allies, America must ensure that a world-wide equilibrium of force is maintained. The burden of maintaining such a world balance is substantial, but it is a burden which must be borne. In contributing its part to such a balance, America's defense must meet three requirements: (1) Its strategic forces must be adequate to deter attack and maintain the nuclear balance in a credible fashion . . . (2) Its forces for regional and local defense, along with those of its Allies, must clearly be able to resist threats and pressures. It is in this area especially that some of us are concerned by the downtrend in real —or constant—defense expenditures. (3) Within America we must have the national will to exercise necessary power when appropriate and to unite behind the proposition that aggression unresisted is aggression encouraged.

At Army Staff College, Camberley, England,
May 11/ Vital Speeches, 8-15:650.

Donald H. Rumsfeld
Secretary of Defense of the
United States
3

There is no doubt in my mind but that the debate will shift, either this year or next year, to serious considerations of ways to maintain rough equivalence to Soviet military power. The debate up in the Congress cannot be, "Can we cut $5-billion out of defense or $8-billion?" It must be, "Is this budget sufficient?" Because the American people, I believe, somewhere, down deep in their bones, recognize the importance of stability . . . I am not given to over-statement. It is not that the Soviets are ten feet tall; but where they used to be five-foot-three, they have become five-foot-nine-and-a-half; and they are growing, and we are not.

Interview, Washington/
San Francisco Examiner & Chronicle, 3-7:(A)12.

4

Weakness can be as provocative as belligerence.

Interview, Washington/
San Francisco Examiner & Chronicle, 3-7:(A)12.

5

While Soviet military power has continued to expand at an impressive rate in the past decade or two, we [the U.S.] have experienced repeated reductions in our defense budget. The facts of our position relative to the Soviet Union drive one to the conclusion that continued shifting of the balance of power—shifting in the direction it has been for the past 10 or 20 years—would be unacceptable from the standpoint of peace in the world.

March 10/
Los Angeles Herald-Examiner, 3-11:(A)4.

6

The need to modernize our fleet is clear. The task is made all the more urgent by the expansion of Soviet maritime capability over the past 10 or 15 years. Recent world-wide Soviet naval exercises; expanding patterns

WHAT THEY SAID IN 1976

of deployment in the Mediterranean, the Atlantic, the Pacific and the Indian Oceans; launching of the *Kiev*, the first Soviet aircraft carrier . . . all are indications of increasing Soviet capabilities and interest in projecting power far from their shores.

San Francisco Examiner & Chronicle, 10-3: (This World)2.

James R. Schlesinger
Chairman, Washington Study Group on National Policy Alternatives; Former Secretary of Defense of the United States 1

Our Navy has shrunk and continues to shrink. The reason is twofold. For one thing, more than 30 years have passed since World War II. Ships are being retired at a fairly rapid rate of 25 a year. In addition, one of the ways we conserved on funds during the Vietnam war was to dramatically hold back ship-construction money. The Navy was the service that primarily suffered in investment as a result of Vietnam.

Interview, Washington/ Los Angeles Times, 3-11:(2)7.

Bryan M. Shotts
Commander, 15th (U.S.) Air Force 2

For those of us in the military, there is a need to stop apologizing for the cost of national defense. We need not appear as beggars before Congress and the American people. We can hold our heads high because we know our military profession is honorable, and vital to the survival of our nation. We have other tasks, too, we who wear the military uniform. We must show the American people that we've pared every excess dollar from our defense budget, that what we ask for is what we honestly believe is the minimum for our nation's security. We must try to make our American people listen to the words of Somerset Maugham who wrote . . . "If any nation values anything more than freedom, it

will lose its freedom; and the irony of it is that if it is comfort or money that it values more, it will lose that too." Yes, although we may all long for the day when the prophecy of Micah comes to pass, it seems certain that its time is not yet come. Let us then put our plowshares and pruninghooks to use for the good of our people, but let us not yet cast our swords and spears into the foundry . . . Our freedom is still defended by the sword, and it is a double-edged sword. One edge represents the rights and privileges of free men, and the other the *responsibilities* of free men. Unless both edges are untarnished and finely honed, the blade is flawed.

At Air Force Association regional meeting, Merced, Calif., May 21/ Vital Speeches, 7-15:581.

John C. Stennis
United States Senator, D—Mississippi 3

[Advocating a return to the military draft]: The services have all tried and I've backed them [in the all-volunteer system]. But this volunteer-forces concept is a bothersome matter. Bothersome matter. We're now having to spend 58 to 60 per cent of the military dollar on personnel, and that doesn't leave too much out of that dollar to buy all of the expensive weapons . . . I think, with these conditions I've been talking about, we're going to have to have a Selective Service bill put back on the books in the course of some few years where we'll be assured [of enough talent, dedication and manpower].

News conference, Jackson, Miss., Dec. 28/ The Washington Post, 12-30:(A)6.

Samuel S. Stratton
United States Representative, D—New York 4

Almost every item [in the 1976 Federal budget] has been increased with the single exception of the defense budget, which was cut by $8-billion . . . We cannot continue to reduce year after year after year while the Soviets keep on going up year after year after year; or else, suddenly one day we will wake up and wonder why we no longer have any credible deterrent power.

Before the House, Washington/
Nation's Business, March:33.

John G. Tower
United States Senator, R—Texas
1

[Arguing against unions in the military]: Imagine an army in which enlisted soldiers refuse to carry out orders from superior officers until they have been cleared by a shop steward or agreed to in a union meeting. Imagine an army unprepared to perform its mission because the union blocked unpleasant working conditions such as night marches, weekend duty and rugged physical-fitness training.

Parade, 4-11:19.

Frederick C. Turner
Vice Admiral, United States Navy;
Commander, Sixth Fleet
2

There is one significant difference between us and Russia in that we, as a maritime nation, vitally need the sea. Our society, our way of life, depends on the sea. Therefore, we need a navy to insure our use of the sea. The Soviet Union, on the other hand, is a land power. It does not need the sea as we do. I think the Soviet perception is that the West, and particularly the United States, is so dependent upon the sea that if they could deny us the use of the sea, they would be able to deprive us of the basic materials we need to propel our industry, and cut us off from our allies.

Interview, aboard U.S.S. "Little Rock"
in Mediterranean/
Los Angeles Herald-Examiner, 6-13:(A)4.

Morris K. Udall
United States Representative, D—Arizona;
Candidate for the 1976 Democratic
Presidential nomination
3

[On reports of the Soviet Union's increasing military strength]: . . . you can lay out 20

different criteria by which the U.S. and Soviets are compared, and on 10 or 12 we will be ahead and on seven or eight they will be ahead. What the Pentagon wants to do, this whole idea from the '50s and '60s that we have to be ahead in everything, well—national security, in my judgment, is balanced, is an adequate, lean, tough national defense system both conventional and nuclear, but it is also a strong economy and it is also a country that has justice for its citizens and has its head on straight, is helping its old people and its young people and education system. That is part of national security too . . . If the Russians want to spend themselves into bankruptcy on some of these goldplated systems that don't make them any safer, that don't make us any safer, let them go ahead.

TV-radio interview, Washington/
"Meet the Press,"
National Broadcasting Company, 4-4.

4

. . . I don't recognize the claim of the Defense Department to a certain proportion of the GNP. I think the function of the Defense Department is to defend and that when you've got enough, you've got enough, whether it's two per cent or eight per cent.

Interview/The Washington Post, 4-25:(C)1.

John Vorster
Prime Minister of South Africa
5

I am genuinely afraid that the United States and other nations with which it is allied may be staring themselves blind against the threat of an A-bomb war when, in reality, the Russians are preparing for a conventional war. They are, according to reports, outstripping the free world in the manufacture of every conceivable weapon of conventional war: warships, tanks, guns, bombers and fighters—everything.

Interview, Cape Town/
U.S. News & World Report, 6-14:59.

WHAT THEY SAID IN 1976

William C. Westmoreland
General (Ret.) and former Chief of Staff,
United States Army; Former Superintendent,
U.S. Military Academy, West Point

1

[Criticizing the enrollment of women at West Point]: The purpose of West Point is to train combat officers, and women are not physically able to lead in combat. Maybe you could find one woman in 10,000 who could lead in combat, but she would be a freak and we're not running the military academy for freaks . . . The pendulum has gone too far. They're asking women to do impossible things. I don't believe women can carry a pack, live in a foxhole, or go a week without taking a bath.

News conference, Middletown, Ohio/
The Christian Science Monitor, 6-7:26.

Louis H. Wilson
General and Commandant,
United States Marine Corps

2

If we expect diplomatic efforts to be effective, we must maintain a capability to defend these interests whenever and wherever necessary. Yet we cannot maintain pre-positioned forces in every potential overseas crisis area . . . This is the principal reason why the United States has a continuing need for its fleet Marine forces—instantly ready and highly mobile—to provide the nation's only major capability of forcible entry. The need for this capability in crisis management is fundamental.

Before House Armed Services Committee,
Washington, Feb. 2/
The Washington Post, 2-3:(A)5.

3

I've just authorized doubling the number of women Marines over the next three years to about 6,000 and a 50 per cent increase in women officers. They're doing a fine job in all fields. . . . We're getting all high-school graduates. We don't require that, but we have so many women who want to enlist that we take only high-school graduates. Twenty per cent of the women officers have master's degrees, and I

believe that 15 per cent of the enlisted women have had some college . . . The law now says women can't go into combat. The American people are not ready for it, nor am I. But I have authorized a woman to be an explosives ordnance disposal officer; she'll defuse bombs. And of the top four Marines at the engineers' school at Camp Lejeune, three were women. I fully expect a woman to take my place one day.

Interview/People, 9-13:63.

Elmo R. Zumwalt, Jr.
Admiral, United States Navy (Ret.);
Former Chief of Naval Operations

4

During my four years as Chief of Naval Operations, I believe that the probability of a U.S. victory in a war with the Soviet Union went from 55 per cent to about 35 per cent, because of major reductions in our naval capability vis-a-vis the Soviet Union. This should not be surprising to any of us who look at history. We lost hundreds of thousands of lives in World War I because we were not prepared and the enemy felt he could get away with a strike. Prior to World War II, we talked ourselves into the same posture and encouraged the strikes. Prior to the Korean war, we turned our posture into a very poor one in conventional-force terms, and [the late Soviet leader Josef] Stalin thought he could get away with the North Korean invasion of South Korea. Now we are in another period when the American people . . . are encouraged to put themselves into a posture that hazards war. I do not believe that the odds are very high that war will come. I believe, rather, that careful and rational leadership will continue to accommodate to Soviet demands as we began to do during the Yom Kippur war [in the Middle East in 1973] when, in response to a Soviet ultimatum, we ordered Israel to release the Egyptian Third Army. The victory the Soviet Union won in that war—the opening of the Suez Canal and the quadrupling of the oil prices which followed the oil embargo, both of which they urged the Arabs to do—is the kind of victory we can expect to see the Soviet Union win under their ever-increasing military superiority in the years ahead.

At "Pacem in Terris" convocation,
Washington, December ('75)/
The Center Magazine, March-April:52.

1

[For each expensive, nuclear-powered warship, the Navy, instead, could] build five much smaller frigates that are too small to carry a nuclear reactor—and it's quite obvious that that's the way to go. When the United States Navy loses the war—if we have to fight one in the next five years—it will be for two reasons, in my judgment. One is that the Soviets will have outspent us for ten years by 50 per cent in the ship-construction field. And the other is that we will have spent our money wrong by about 50 per cent in the last ten years.

At foreign and military policy symposium,
Mt. Vernon College, Washington/
The Christian Science Monitor, 4-12:10.

Politics

Howard H. Baker, Jr.
United States Senator, R—Tennessee   1

. . . the American political scene is unique, special and different, I believe, from the political situation in any other part of the world. The two-party system . . . tends to attenuate the grosser aspects of confrontation between the candidates. The fact that both [parties] accommodate a wide spectrum of ideas . . . tends to provide, in effect, the primary system that weeds out . . . institutional confrontations and narrows the range of controversy . . . Unlike the Conservative and Labor confrontation in England . . . much of that is out of the way by the time you finish the selection process . . . So you no longer have the big cataclysmic upheavals in the campaign that we once had here, and which frequently still occur in other areas of the world. You do have campaigns that turn on specific issues . . . but this turns out to be a continuing public dialogue in the U.S. and not a great wrestling match.

News conference, United Nations, New York/
The Washington Post, 11-10:(A)14.

Birch Bayh
United States Senator, D—Indiana;
Candidate for the 1976 Democratic
Presidential nomination   2

One of the real problems we have had in the last seven or eight years is the politics of division. We have had [President] Jerry Ford running against New York City; we have had [former President] Richard Nixon and [former Vice President] Spiro Agnew running against "radiclibs" and "pusillanimous pussyfooters" and "nattering nabobs of negativism." We have really had the politics of polarization, the politics of hatred and division; it's

been very divisive, very costly to this country. I want to conduct a campaign, and I want to see whoever is President run a government that really pulls us together, that weaves together the common threads that exist in most all of our hearts.

TV-radio interview, Des Moines, Iowa/
"Meet the Press,"
National Broadcasting Company, 1-11.

Richard Bolling
United States Representative,
D—Missouri   3

[On the recent sex scandals involving members of Congress]: Hell, the behavior of Congressmen hasn't changed. We've still got the same number of alcoholics, the same number of guys who chase women, the same number who bully women, as we did 25 years ago. That's no different. Perhaps 25 years ago they were a little smoother about it and didn't let it get out of hand the way it has, but what you're talking about is a small minority. What has changed, though, is the coverage. I don't know if the coverage we've been seeing lately does more good or bad, but I would suggest that the press do some careful thinking when it's messing with a guy's life.

Los Angeles Times, 7-29:(1)12.

Julian Bond
Georgia State Senator (D)   4

[On 1976 Democratic Presidential nominee, Jimmy Carter]: I think he wants to do good. He wants to be President so he can do good. Now, what his good is, I don't know, but I think that's his motivation. He has the kind of self-righteousness of the absolutely convinced person—which is a frightening phenomenon to find in people. But what bothers me most about the Carter candidacy and his eventual Presidency is that I have no way of predicting what he is going to do. You can't really take many cues from his campaign because—although he has been more specific than he lets people think he is—even his specifics tend to be general. It bothers me to think that a year from now an occasion will come up when some response is called for from him as President and I have no way of knowing what it would be.

Interview/ Newsweek, 7-19:26.

Edmund G. Brown, Jr.
Governor of California (D);
Candidate for the 1976 Democratic
Presidential nomination
1

[On politics and campaigning]: There seems to be a premise that a good candidate can produce the Holy Grail. All you can really do is say your piece, which isn't all that different from anybody else's. But I can't come up with a better substitute [to campaigning]. It's a testing process that brings out what people are like.

Interview/ Time, 5-31:10.

James L. Buckley
United States Senator, C—New York
2

[The] underlying principles [of conservatism]: The primacy of liberty in the political life of America; confidence in private initiatives; hostility to any concentration of power; distrust of government planning and regulation; a commitment to the traditional fiscal virtues; a belief in our system of free enterprise; a subordination of government to the individual; and a rejection of government as an instrument of social manipulation.

Interview/ U.S. News & World Report, 10-4:25.

3

[On his re-election defeat in the just-concluded election]: I continue to believe that until and unless the Republican Party identifies itself with a set of broad propositions that are clearly distinguishable from those associated with the Democrats, the Republican Party will lose ground because it offers nobody a reason to join it. In New York, even though the real issues were not the ones that

were focused on, I nevertheless got 46 per cent of the vote. Given the lopsided party registrations [in favor of the Democrats] in this state, I think that says something. In other words, I think that the Republican Party has a natural constituency, but, by failing to define its positions with that constituency in mind, it is not enlisting them.

Interview, New York/
U.S. News & World Report, 11-15:110.

Yvonne B. Burke
United States Representative,
D—California
4

If a Democratic Convention or a Republican Convention is ever deadlocked and there is a woman with the right background and popularity, she will get the [Presidential] nomination. The American people are willing to accept a woman President. It's just a matter of getting the right candidate. We recognize that most Presidential candidates are either Senators or Governors, and there is only one woman Governor and no women Senators. Until we change that pattern, we're at a disadvantage. It's a disgrace that we haven't had a woman on the national ticket for President or Vice President, but I think that time is coming—just as it did in Israel for Golda Meir and like it may happen in Britain. If those systems can recognize a woman leader, the United States can, too.

Interview/ U.S. News & World Report, 4-26:50.

Walter D. Burnham
Professor of political science,
Massachusetts Institute of Technology
5

The average Republican comes across as an old-fashioned kind of guy who clips coupons and is well enough off so that he does not want to share anything with anyone else and wants to hold down the public sector so that the private sector can rip people off.

Time, 8-23:11.

Hugh L. Carey
Governor of New York (D)
6

[Criticizing recent Republican Administrations in Washington]: Who broke and entered

(HUGH L. CAREY)

in the night? Who opened the mails? Who tapped the phones? Who kept lists of enemies? Who preached patriotic virtue while mocking the dictates of the law and the commands of the Constitution? Our problem is not that the enemy of the people is government; our problem is that the Republicans rule as if the enemy of government were the people.

At Democratic National Convention, New York, July 21/The New York Times, 7-13:27.

Jimmy Carter
Candidate for the 1976
Democratic Presidential nomination;
Former Governor of Georgia (D) 1

I don't believe the nation appreciates personal animosities and attacks among candidates hoping to be President of the American people. One of the things that concerns the people of our country is the bickering, squabbling, hatred and animosity and blame handed back and forth in our great nation's capital in Washington. This is not good for our country. I want to be the next President of this country. I expect to be the next President. That does not mean that I have to take my political success from personal hatred [and] attacks on the character or identity of my opponents.

Campaign address, Boston, Feb. 27/
The Washington Post, 2-28:(A)6.

2

I have been accused of being an outsider. I plead guilty. Unfortunately, the vast majority of Americans are also outsiders. We are not going to get changes by simply shifting around the same groups of insiders, the same tired old rhetoric, the same unkept promises and the same divisive appeals to one party, one faction, one section of the country, one race or religion or one interest group. The insiders have had their chances and they have not delivered. Their time has run out.

Time, 3-8:16.

3

A lot of people have been deeply concerned —particularly the news media—about my ability to get support from farmers and from city dwellers, from young and old, from conservatives and from liberals. I've never had to modify my positions because I've been able, through my close personal relationships with the people of our nation, to understand and express common ideals. I come from probably one of the most conservative areas of the nation, in deep, rural, southwest Georgia. It used to be the conservatism identified with racism, with withdrawal from the fast-changing technological world, with callousness about one's fellow human beings. That's no longer the case. Conservatism means, in its best sense, a pride in individuals, strengthening local government, careful planning, not wasting money, tough management, a good delivery of services. And the liberals of this country who have always wanted, above all else, human rights, civil rights, the elevation of suffering, now understand very clearly that those hopes can be realized best through a well-structured government and openness and an ability to work in harmony with other people. So I never have been able to detect the incompatibility that formerly had been a matter of concern and which has at times, I admit, divided our party.

At five-state caucus,
Democratic National Convention,
New York, July 14/Los Angeles Times, 7-15:(1)16.

Jimmy Carter
1976 Democratic Presidential nominee 4

[On his selection of Senator Walter Mondale as his Vice-Presidential running mate]: Had he come from a metropolitan area and had he been a Catholic, that would probably have been an asset. But, you know, I can't balance the ticket geographically, and between me and the Congress, and between an aggressive campaigner and a more dormant campaigner, and in a religious way. I just can't balance a ticket all that kind of ways. And I finally just eliminated that process and I came to the conclusion . . . that if I took a person that I felt would be the best President or Vice President regardless of race or location or background or religion, that I was making the right political decision.

New York, July 15/Los Angeles Times, 7-16:(1)1.

1

[On the Democratic Party]: Ours is the party of the man who . . . inspired and restored this nation in its darkest hours—Franklin D. Roosevelt. Ours is the party of a fighting Democrat who showed us that a common man could be an uncommon leader—Harry S. Truman. Ours is the party of a brave young President who called the young at heart, regardless of age—John F. Kennedy. And ours is also the party of a great-hearted Texan who took the office in a tragic hour and who went on to do more than any other President in this century to advance the cause of human rights —Lyndon Johnson. Our party was built out of the sweatshops of the old Lower East Side [of New York], the dark mills of New Hampshire, the blazing hearths of Illinois, the coal mines of Pennsylvania, the hardscrabble farms of the southern coastal plains, and the unlimited frontiers of America. Ours is the party that welcomed generations of immigrants—the Jews, the Irish, the Italians, the Poles and all the others—enlisted them in its ranks and fought the political battles that helped bring them into the American mainstream. And they have shaped the character of our party. That is our heritage. Our party has not been perfect. We have made mistakes, and we have paid for them. But ours is a tradition of leadership and compassion and progress.

Accepting the Democratic Presidential nomination at Democratic National Convention, New York, July 15/ U.S. News & World Report, 7-26:77.

2

I believe that we understand the need for a change now that we've experienced almost eight years of the Nixon-Ford Administration, an Administration of vetoes and not vision, an Administration of scandals and not stability and pride, an Administration of rhetoric and not reason, an Administration of WIN buttons and empty promises instead of progress and prosperity . . . In the last few months, we've seen an almost unbelievable spectacle in Washington. The President of the United States [Ford] deeply concerned about an ex-movie actor [rival Republican Presidential candidate Ronald Reagan], traveling

all over the nation to get a handful of delegates here, a handful of delegates there— which is okay—but neglecting the basic responsibility of leadership in governing the greatest nation on earth and 215 million Americans. The lack of leadership is the greatest single handicap the Republican Party will face this year.

At rally, Manchester, N.H., Aug. 3/ Los Angeles Times, 8-4:(1)7.

3

I have to admit that in the heat of the campaign . . . I've made some mistakes. And I think this is part of just being a human being. I have to say that my campaign has been an open one and the *Playboy* [magazine] interview has been of very great concern to me. I don't know how to deal with it exactly. I agreed to give the interview to *Playboy*. Other people have done it and are notable . . . But they weren't running for President. And in retrospect, from hindsight, I would not have given that interview had I to do it over again.

At debate with President Ford, Williamsburg, Va.; Oct. 22/ Los Angeles Times, 10-23:(1)23.

Jimmy Carter
President-elect of the United States

4

The Republican Party continues to reflect the political views of millions of Americans. I expect to include Republicans in my Administration. I will seek the advice of Republican leaders in Congress, in the business world and elsewhere, and I hope that a great many Republicans will support my goals and programs. I recognize and respect the role of the GOP as the "loyal opposition" in both foreign and domestic matters.

Interview/ U.S. News & World Report, 11-15:42.

Frank Church
United States Senator, D—Idaho; Candidate for the 1976 Democratic Presidential nomination

5

We have produced in this country perhaps history's most irrational method of electing a President, particularly of nominating a President, and it gets worse with each passing year

(FRANK CHURCH)

because of a number of primaries, each with different laws and requirements.

Campaigning in Rhode Island/
Los Angeles Times, 4-8:(1)14.

Ramsey Clark
Candidate for the 1976 New York Democratic
U.S. Senatorial nomination;
Former Attorney General
of the United States   1

I don't know that [Democratic Presidential nominee Jimmy] Carter really wants to make a difference in the way this country operates. You see, making a difference is what it is all about. Lyndon Johnson was consumed with a desire to make a difference—that desire was tearing him apart. It was the same with John Kennedy. Carter talks in terms of empathy, but rarely in terms of action. I don't know what he wants to do as President.

Interview, New York/
The Dallas Times Herald, 7-11:(A)23.

John B. Connally, Jr.
Former Secretary of the
Treasury of the United States; Former
Governor of Texas (D, now R)   2

We just can't talk about being Republicans and get elected. We represent just 21 per cent of the people, and, unless we appeal to those who call themselves independents and Democrats, we're not going to get elected to anything. It's not enough for you to sit in smoke-filled rooms and plan a little strategy. It's hard work that wins elections.

To Republican state chairmen,
Floresville, Tex., March/
The New York Times Magazine, 8-8:10.

3

[Democratic Presidential candidate] Jimmy Carter's gotten where he is by running on Republican issues. He's against big government, against budget deficits, against bureaucracy, against everything Washington and the Democrats symbolize. He's running away with the Republican issues. At some point he's going to have to change his image or renounce his party.

June 27/The New York Times, 6-28:19.

4

[Saying that the Democratic Party, which now controls Congress, should not also be given the Presidency]: [The Democrats say] that they should be given final, absolute and total dominion over all the power in this system by control of the Executive Branch of the Federal government. I believe that is an argument which thoughtful Americans must view with grave alarm. For I say to you it is time—it is long past time—that we must awaken to the reality that our system is in danger of losing the very balances which assure its success and our personal freedom. Not in the lifetime of any present here—not in the lifetime of the Republic itself—have we been so near as we are now to subjugation of the system under the rule of a single party . . . Is this the party which the people want to hold all power over them without a President in the White House willing and able to exercise restraint over that party's willful excesses?

At Republican National Convention, Kansas City/
The Dallas Times Herald, 8-30:(B)2.

5

[Comparing President Ford and Democratic Presidential nominee Jimmy Carter]: President Ford believes in less Federal government, less Federal intervention, less Federal spending, less Federal interference in the business and the lives of the American people. And Governor Carter believes in more Federal government, more deficits, more spending, more programs, more control at the Federal level. And that's the simple difference between these two men. In President Ford we have a leader. We know how he will act. We know how he will react. His opponent we do not know. We don't really know what he would do, or how he would act, or how he would react.

Campaign rally, Houston, Oct. 30/
The New York Times, 10-31:(1)34.

James E. Connor
Secretary to the Cabinet and Staff Secretary
to President of the United States
Gerald R. Ford
1

[On President Ford, who recently was defeated in his bid for re-election]: My hunch is that the man will be treated awfully kindly by history. Measure his accomplishments against August, 1974, [when he took over the Presidency from the resigned Richard Nixon,] when the world seemed bleak and frightening, when every day brought a new surprise, when today didn't look much like yesterday and tomorrow promised to be radically different. The anchors weren't there. The most obvious was the Presidency of the United States. It had damn near been destroyed [before Ford took office].
The New York Times, 11-14:(4)5.

Archibald Cox
Professor of law, Harvard University;
Former special government prosecutor
for Watergate
2

Someone once told me you're supposed to always vote for the best man. Well, in my lifetime, anyway, all the best men have happened to be Democrats.
News conference, Boston, Jan. 24/
The Dallas Times Herald, 1-25:(A)6.

Carl T. Curtis
United States Senator, R—Nebraska
3

I do not favor a law that would compel public disclosure [of Federal officials' personal finances]. It is in no way a proper qualification for holding office . . . It would serve no good purpose whatever. Someone may be of very modest means. They might have quite a few debts. Forced disclosure would subject them to ridicule and the charge that they were a failure. On the other hand, disclosure by people of considerable wealth would invite opposition and stir up prejudice against them. It would keep many well-qualified, public-spirited people from serving in public office . . . There is no justification for applying a property qualification to holding office. Such a rule would satisfy the curiosity of some people. It might make good copy for a lot of stories. But there's no way you could translate it into good, honest government. Bribery and cheating and similar conduct are always hidden, and somebody that would resort to criminal acts wouldn't hesitate to file a deceptive financial statement.
Interview/
U.S. News & World Report, 1-5:45.

John W. Dean III
Former Counsel to the President
of the United States
(Richard M. Nixon)
4

[On his revelations of the Watergate cover-up and of an off-color remark by former Agriculture Secretary Earl Butz]: I don't want to be known as the all-time snitch. I'm sitting on several interviews now because there's the same kind of stuff in them, and I don't want to make any more news. [Former President Richard] Nixon once told me, "The snitch is the pariah of society," and he's right. People claim they want the truth, but they have more respect for the perjurer. You learn from kindergarten, "Don't be a tattletale," and that's where the whole dilemma begins.
Interview, Los Angeles/
"W": a Fairchild publication, 11-12:16.

5

The country is better off, in a sense, because Watergate happened. Because someday there would have been another Watergate that would have been worse than the one we had. I think people have a better understanding of their government because of it. It was a tremendous educational process, and it's still going on. Books like mine [about Watergate] are showing people more about the internal workings of their government. I hope [President-elect] Jimmy Carter reads it.
Interview, Dallas/
The Dallas Times Herald, 11-28:(F)6.

E. L. Doctorow
Author
6

On the face of it, there seems to be a greater degree of sophistication in American politics

235

WHAT THEY SAID IN 1976

(E. L. DOCTOROW)

than there was 30 or 40 years ago. We all know that politicians are divorced and married again and we elect them. We know they get drunk and get into trouble and we elect them. We grant them their adulteries and mental problems and give them the right to be always expedient in their ideas and programs because, like us, they have their careers to think of. But if a politician speaks too well, we think of him as a writer and we don't elect him.

Before Authors Guild/
The New York Times, 4-11:(4)17.

Bob Dole
United States Senator, R—Kansas;
1976 Republican Vice-Presidential
nominee   1

[On Democratic Presidential nominee Jimmy Carter]: He can say what he wants in *Playboy* [magazine]; that only affects Jimmy Carter. He can look at all the pictures he wants to; that only affects Jimmy Carter. He can tell Norman Mailer anything he wants, which will not be reprinted in *The New York Times* because of its vulgarity. And he can say what he wants—or his son can say what he wants—about [evangelist] Billy Graham, a great North Carolinian, because that only affects the Carters and the Carter family. He can call former President [Lyndon] Johnson a liar and a cheater and a distorter of facts. And don't you kind of wonder sometimes about someone who can always judge somebody else? Whether it's your neighbor or whether it's your friend or whether it may be somebody in business or in the bank or whatever? Don't you kind of wonder at those people who make snap judgments, then rush to the phone to apologize? I just say as long as he makes those judgments, [and they] affect Mr. Carter, his family and his business, that's his business. But I doubt a man's judgment when he does those things. I don't want him making decisions that affect me—more importantly, the rest of America.

Campaigning, Wilmington, N.C., Oct. 6/
The New York Times, 10-7:36.

Bob Dole
United States Senator, R—Kansas   2

We [Republicans] do not have to wait four years to make our comeback. We can begin now. Indeed, if we don't begin now, if we sit idly by in the complacent belief that [Democratic President-elect Jimmy] Carter will make a botch of things, give us a new lease on life, we may not have a comeback. We have off-year elections coming up; we have Congressional elections in 1978. And we have to look to the electing of dog catchers, sheriffs and aldermen just as we do to state legislators, Mayors and Governors. Our minority status isn't legislated; we don't have to remain a minority party. On the other hand, neither is our existence legislated.

Before Republican Governors,
Washington, Nov. 30/
Los Angeles Herald-Examiner, 11-30:(A)3.

3

We [Republicans] seem to appeal rather exclusively to white Americans, to most of the better-educated people in our society and to higher-income groups. And, as long as we are seen in exclusionary terms, we are going to fall behind in registration . . . I do think we have to learn to present what we stand for in a way that doesn't make us appear to be an elitist group. We need to look for answers and not sit back taking stiff-necked pride in our refusal to explore new avenues of approach to the affections of the American people. We simply cannot afford to keep winning moral victories and sustaining political defeat.

At Hillsborough County Republican dinner,
Tampa, Fla., Dec. 14/
Rocky Mountain News, 12-15:54.

Mike Douglas
Television talk-show host   4

The hardest people to interview are politicians. They don't have the words "yes" or "no" in their vocabularies. They qualify everything.

Interview, Philadelphia/
San Francisco Examiner & Chronicle, 11-28:
(Datebook)31.

Henry Fairlie
Former chief editorial writer,
"The London Times"   *1*

Something unique in American Presidential elections is the upstart as candidate. There is no political arena in America for a Presidential candidate to gain the experience he needs to qualify for the office. Presidential elections are contests between upstarts, except, of course, when one of the candidates is an incumbent. A candidate is a *tabula rasa.* He writes his own political character during the process of a campaign and in response to what he feels the people want. One of the things voters respond to positively in their political candidates is the attitude of the candidates themselves toward politics and government. The American people liked the fact that [the late President] Franklin Roosevelt smiled a lot, that he kept his chin tilted, that he enjoyed the office and running for the offie, that he enjoyed his country and the age in which he lived. That is an important part of a candidate's political appeal. It is also an important way by which voters can judge whether a candidate will have the political character needed for the office. When you get the other kind of person, although he may be a very fine and honorable person, one senses there is something wrong.

Discussion at Center for the Study of
Democratic Institutions, Santa Barbara, Calif./
The Center Magazine, Sept.-Oct.:74.

Frank E. Fitzsimmons
President,
International Brotherhood of Teamsters   *2*

Generally speaking, where politics is concerned, I don't let myself be governed by an individual's personal ambitions; I try to look at what is best for the country. In that respect I've been criticized for discouraging any of our Teamsters members from running for public office. I don't think a person with a labor background can take a political job and serve the community well. An individual who serves labor and goes into public office certainly owes some responsibility to the organization he came from. If he's elected and there's a question to be decided for the good of the community, he can be criticized if he goes against the desires of his labor organization, and he can be criticized by the community for going along with what his group wants. So it's best for him to stay out of politics.

Interview, Washington/
U.S. News & World Report, 1-26:38.

Gerald R. Ford
President of the United States   *3*

. . . I am the first to admit that I am no great orator or no person that got where I have gotten by any William Jennings Bryan technique. But I am not sure that the American people want that. I think they are more interested in honesty, trustworthiness and a feeling of security. So maybe out in the hustings it will pay off to make those kinds of flamboyant speeches, but the American people for a long time have been made grandiose promises, and there have been an awful lot of disappointments. We aren't going to do that.

Interview, Washington/ Time, 1-26:12.
4

[On why he is vetoing a bill that would remove the Hatch Act's ban on partisan political activity by Federal government workers]: The public expects the government service will be provided in a neutral, nonpartisan fashion. This bill would produce the opposite result . . . If this bill were to become law, I believe pressures could be brought to bear on Federal employees in extremely subtle ways beyond the reach of any anti-coercion statute so that they would inevitably feel compelled to engage in partisan political activity. This would be bad for the employee, bad for the government and bad for the public.

Washington, April 12/
The Washington Post, 4-13:(A)1.

5

I believe that a man who is campaigning for the highest office in the land must be will-

WHAT THEY SAID IN 1976

(GERALD R. FORD)

ing to talk seriously about his policies and the consequences of his policies. When it comes to the life-and-death decisions of our national security, the decisions made must be the right ones. There are no retakes in the Oval Office. Glibness is not good enough; superficiality is not good enough. Every serious candidate for the Presidency must be equal to the burdens and responsibilities of the Presidency.

Campaign address, Tyler, Tex., April 28/
Los Angeles Herald-Examiner, 4-28:(A)2.

1

I have been called an unelected President, an accidental President. We may even hear that again from the other [Democratic] party, despite the fact that its elected representatives in Congress certified my fitness for our highest office. They voted for me 387 to 35 in the House of Representatives and 92 to 3 in the Senate. Having become Vice President and President, without expecting or seeking either, I have a special feeling toward these high offices. To me, the Presidency and the Vice Presidency were not prizes to be won, but a duty to be done. So tonight, it is not the power and glamor of the Presidency that leads me to ask another four years. It is something every hard-working American will understand—the challenge of a job well begun, but far from being finished.

Accepting the Presidential nomination, at
Republican National Convention, Kansas City,
Aug. 19/ The New York Times, 8-20:(A)10.

2

A Republican President has been a good safeguard against the excesses of Democratic Congresses over the last several years. If you don't have a safety valve against their spending, against their legislative program—which inevitably means more government—this government could be in very serious circumstances. Let's take this specific example: If there had been a Democratic President in the White House for the last two years—a Demo-

cratic President who would not have vetoed 55 proposals coming out of a Democratic Congress, as I did—the American people would have been saddled with a minimum of $13-billion more in Federal spending. The fact that the Ford Administration has been here protecting the American people and their tax money has been a very, very important safeguard against the excesses of the Democratic Congress.

Interview/ U.S. News & World Report, 9-13:30.

3

If the Democrats make the mistake of trying to relate this Administration to Watergate, I think the American people will see through that synthetic issue . . . The record is very clear that I had nothing to do with Watergate, and this Administration has had nothing to do with Watergate. It has been the most open, candid and straightforward Administration in recent years—certainly in the memory of most people. So any charge of that kind is totally and completely inaccurate, and I think the American people would see through it.

Interview/ U.S. News & World Report, 9-13:26.

4

[Criticizing Democratic Presidential nominee Jimmy Carter]: It is not enough for anyone to say "trust me." Trust must be earned. Trust is not having to guess what a candidate means. Trust is leveling with the people *before* the election about what you're going to do *after* the election. Trust is not being all things to all people, but being the same thing to all people. Trust is not cleverly shading words so that each separate audience can hear what it wants to hear, but saying plainly and simply what you mean—and meaning what you say.

Campaign address, University of Michigan,
Sept. 15/ The Washington Post, 9-16:(A)1.

5

[On his 1974 pre-indictment pardon of former President Richard Nixon for any possible Watergate crimes]: . . . the reason the pardon was given was that, when I took office this country was in a very, very divided condition. There was hatred, there was divisiveness—people had lost faith in their government in many, many respects. Mr. Nixon resigned, and I became President. It seemed to me that if I was to adequately and effectively handle the problem of high inflation, a growing recession, the involvement of the United States still in Vietnam, that I had to give 100 per cent of my time to those two major problems. Mr. Nixon resigned. That is disgrace. The first President out of 38 that ever resigned from public office under pressure. So when you look at the penalty that he paid, and when you analyze the requirements that I had to spend all of my time working on the economy, which was in trouble, that I inherited, working on our problems in Southeast Asia which were still plaguing us, it seemed to me that Mr. Nixon had been penalized enough by his resignation in disgrace, and the need and necessity for me to concentrate on the problems of the country fully justified the action that I took.

Debate with Democratic Presidential nominee
Jimmy Carter, Philadelphia, Sept. 24/
The New York Times, 9-25:8.

1

[On Democratic Presidential nominee Jimmy Carter]: Mr. Carter does have a strange way of changing his accent as he moves about this great country. In California, he tries to sound like [farm labor leader] Cesar Chavez. In Chicago, he sounds like Mayor Daley. In New York, he sounds like [consumerist] Ralph Nader. In Washington, D.C., he sounds like [AFL-CIO president] George Meany. Then Mr. Carter comes to the farm belt—he becomes a little old peanut farmer. The President has to take the same position wherever he goes. That is the kind of President I have been and will continue to be for the next four years.

Election campaign address, Iowa State University,
Oct. 15/ Los Angeles Times, 10-16:22.

2

The history of human politics is a history of demagogues. I don't think it's special to democracy. Faith in democracy has to rest essentially on something Lincoln said—that you can't fool all the people *all* the time. Our democracy makes mistakes. But what I find reassuring, at least about America, is that by and large the figures who get chosen President are figures around the center. Loudmouths don't make it, in the end. Even [former President] Richard Nixon was not a demagogue.

Interview/ U.S. News & World Report, 3-8:60.

Milton Friedman
Professor of economics,
University of Chicago

3

Everybody has some good elements in them and everyone has weak elements. [Former President Richard] Nixon had the capacity to be one of the greatest Presidents of this country if only he had been a little less interested in political expediency. I think it's one of the tragic cases in which he did not give more weight to principle and less weight to political expediency.

San Francisco Examiner & Chronicle, 12-12:
(This World)2.

Betty Glad
Professor of political science,
University of Illinois, Urbana-Champaign

4

[On President-elect Jimmy Carter]: In a sense, what we've had from him is the presentation of a kind of perfection that is not humanly possible. He talks in the abstract about learning humility and compassion, but at the same time his self-presentation has been of one who doesn't really have doubts or fears, even when he should be doubtful or fearful. He is, by his own statements, a very ambitious person who doesn't intend to lose. This indicates that power is very important to him, and to fall short is in some way shameful.

Interview/ U.S. News & World Report, 11-22:29.

John H. Glenn, Jr.
United States Senator, D—Ohio
1

[On the Democratic Party]: Of course, we must correct any excesses and inefficiencies, and on a high-priority basis, but this party is a great party because of its compassion, and we must wear that compassion like a medal. We are the best hope, the best hope for those searching for jobs, for senior citizens trying to make a go of it on eroded income, for the sick unable to afford good medical care, for the handicapped and the underprivileged. Our compassion, our willingness to help, we must never lose.

At Democratic National Convention, New York, July 12/Los Angeles Times, 7-13:(1)21.

Barry M. Goldwater
United States Senator, R—Arizona
2

[On who he thinks will be the 1976 Democratic Presidential nominee]: Hubert Humphrey. I've got money on it. A Humphrey-Udall ticket would be very attractive because Hubert does not come through as a screaming liberal. He *is*, of course, but he can be conservative in the morning and liberal in the afternoon, and he admits it.

Interview, Washington/People, 3-22:10.

3

We [Republicans] are people who believe in limited government, unlimited individual opportunity and maximum personal freedom. And we know that what we are is less important than what we believe in. In that one perception, especially, we are different from our opponents. Freedom was never mentioned even once at the Democratic Convention. We must take ourselves less seriously. We must take more seriously the things in which we believe. In short, this is where we battle for the freedom of the individual—our Party stands for freedom and strength. It is what we believe in and it is what America wants. Make no mistake about it—we are the last, best hope on earth for sound, Constitutional government, and we must fight to realize that hope before it is too late.

At Republican National Convention, Kansas City, Aug. 16/The New York Times, 8-17:20.

Bryce N. Harlow
Former Counsellor to the President of the United States (Richard M. Nixon)
4

The public image of the man [President Ford] is exact. It is quite exact. He's guileless, you know. He truly is. And he can't help it. He's what he is. You see the same fellow in the White House privately that you see outside the White House. The President remarkably easily accepts criticism. He welcomes it, as a matter of fact. It doesn't bother him at all to be criticized—not only face to face, but also in a group . . . This is extraordinary with Presidents. Truly extraordinary. I have seen people criticize Presidents and then never be invited back because it was regarded as *lese majesty*, and impudent. But it's quite easy to do that even now with Gerald Ford, even though he's been President for two years.

Interview/Newsweek, 10-18:44.

S. I. Hayakawa
Candidate for the 1976 California Republican U.S. Senatorial nomination
5

Politics is the biggest forum for public communication, just as courtship is the best forum for private communication.

Interview/ Los Angeles Herald-Examiner, 2-10:(A)5.

S. I. Hayakawa
1976 California Republican U.S. Senatorial nominee
6

Republicans are people who, if you were drowning 50 feet from shore, would throw you a 25-foot rope and tell you to swim the other 25 feet because it would be good for your character. Democrats would throw you a 100-foot rope and then walk away looking for other good deeds to do.

Time, 6-14:8.

7

There is not one image of me the public has —there are many. Some who have read my newspaper column and my textbooks know me best—thoughtful, compassionate, sensi-

tive. A lot of extreme conservatives think I'm
an extreme conservative because I tried [when
president of San Francisco State University]
to preserve the college against attack. I'm a
political Rorschach test. People see whatever
they want in me.

The New York Times, 9-24:(A)21.

Jesse A. Helms
United States Senator,
R—North Carolina
1

There are some who view politics as the
art of compromise. I view it as a challenge
to provide principled leadership. A political
party unable to set forth a forthright course
of action to inspire the nation to rise to
greatness is a political party that will wither
and blow away. There are some who may be
content with a political party as a coalition
of competing interests, interests that may even
be contradictory, divergent and clashing. But
there are millions of Americans yearning for
a political party composed of citizens willing
to subordinate their personal and selfish interests for the common good and for the
political health of the nation.

Before Republican Party platform committee,
Aug. 11/The Washington Post, 8-22:(C)7.

Linwood Holton
Former Governor of Virginia (R)
2

A Senator can get more TV time in a week
than we [Governors] can in a year. So if a
Governor wants to get ahead in national
politics, he pretty much has to get elected
to the Senate.

The Christian Science Monitor, 1-20:12.

Hubert H. Humphrey
United States Senator, D—Minnesota
3

I don't think he [former President Rich-

ard Nixon] was mentally unbalanced—that's
been overdone—but his whole life attitude
has been one of suspicion and conspiracy
from day one. That's the way he started in
politics. He never passed a constructive piece
of legislation. He was always investigating
someone. He never thought about the joy in
America, the happiness in the streets. It's
like I always say: If a man hates long enough
he'll destroy himself. This fellow was so suspicious of everybody that when he got to be
President it consumed him.

Interview, Waverly, Minn./People, 2-9:10.

4

If you went through the campaigns of
every Congressman and Senator in the past
you'd find illegal [campaign] contributions.
There's just no way you could prevent them.
We didn't solicit them. But big companies
go out of their way to hire clever people to
launder money. They don't come to you and
say, "Here's a corporate campaign gift."

Interview, Waverly, Minn./People, 2-9:11.

5

[On pressure put on him by Democratic
Party leaders to run for the Presidential
nomination]: Everytime that something happens, there's a whole new group that comes
down to you and says, "Now, you've got to
do something, Hubert." After New Hampshire, you know, it was "Stop Jimmy Carter." After Massachusetts, "Hurry up, we've
got to stop Scoop Jackson." And I keep
telling them the Democrats better quit stopping and start starting. You know, we've been
stopping each other around here for the last
eight years. We stopped in '68; we stopped
in '72. And Democrats better learn that what
this country wants is somebody who can get
up and go, not somebody that can stop.
We've got a stop artist right now in the government [President Ford] where we've had
vetoes and go-slows and no-noes and all of

(HUBERT H. HUMPHREY)

that I think the country wants leadership and I believe Democrats have to prove that they are capable of governing. And they've got to get on the stick and start uniting around a candidate . . .

Television interview/"Today Show,"
National Broadcasting Company, 3-10.

1

[On why he is not actively seeking the 1976 Democratic Presidential nomination]: Look at my beautiful home in Minnesota! Look at the job I've got. I'm a respected United States Senator. And that's not bad. I've been Vice President of the United States. I came within a hair of being President. The Prime Ministers call me on this telephone as often as the head of a trade union in Minnesota does. They know me. I can go to the Soviet Union; I can go to Germany, France, China. So why should I scramble? If it happens, it happens. And if it doesn't, the country will get along.

Interview, Washington/
The New York Times Magazine, 4-4:16.

2

After eight years of [Republican] phases, freezes and failure—of start-ups and slowdowns, of high prices and fewer jobs, we are still being asked for "just a little more time and patience." Go slow, not now, no, no, veto—this is the Republican theme. This is their policy. Well, we've had enough of this defeatism. For eight years these modern Tories have deceived the people, destroyed confidence in our government and caused widespread suffering. These inventors of "WIN" buttons have given our country its highest level of inflation in three decades. These self-proclaimed champions of the work ethic have given us more unemployment than at any time since the Great Depression. These advocates of balanced budgets have given us the largest Federal budget deficits ever in our history. These true believers in the rugged individualism of free enterprise have been ready to bail out giant corpora-

tions, yet they would deny school lunches to needy children. These self-appointed experts on law and order have presided over alarming increases in crime. Worse, crime has reached into the highest offices in the land.

At Democratic National Convention, New York,
July 13/Los Angeles Times, 7-14:(1)16.

3

We [Democrats] will win [in the forthcoming election], not because we have some magic cure for our ills, not because of political gimmicks or opportunism. We will win because the people know we care. They know we dare to try. We are in the tradition of America—a tradition of pioneering, of adventure, of optimism, confidence and faith; a tradition of caring and sharing. That is the story of America. This Democratic Party has always believed that no challenge is too great for the American nation.

At Democratic National Convention, New York,
July 13/The New York Times, 7-15:26.

4

Liberalism means freedom. It means freedom for the individual from the forces of oppression, discrimination and prejudice and the freedom to enjoy the widest possible opportunity—to become the best that we can be. In government, it means the commitment to make our institutions as responsible as possible in creating and maintaining those freedoms.

Interview/
U.S. News & World Report, 10-4:25.

Eugene Ionesco
French playwright

5

. . . French politicians are politicians but they are not like American politicians. They have had literature to humanize them. [The late French Presidents Charles] de Gaulle, [Georges] Pompidou were literary men; [current President Valery] Giscard has written books. They have a humanistic sense of culture in them that is very strong. Whereas the Russian and the American politicians are ignorant or brutes.

Interview, Washington/
The Washington Post, 11-24:(B)3.

Henry M. Jackson
United States Senator, D—Washington;
Candidate for the 1976 Democratic
Presidential nomination 1

Our political currency—the meanings of liberalism and conservatism—have been debased. I look at a problem and try to solve it, and I don't worry about liberal or conservative labels.

Interview, Massachusetts/
The Christian Science Monitor, 3-10:12.

Jerome H. Jaffe
Professor of psychiatry,
Columbia University; Former Director,
White House Special Action Office for
Drug Abuse Prevention 2

[On his opinion of the Nixon Administration after serving in the Executive Office, 1971-1973]: The Administration admired people who could be cold and dispassionate in making personnel decisions. To make concessions to people's feelings, to recognize that a particular objective was not worth destroying people in the process of its attainment, was not something that elicited any admiration. Such concern was viewed as a fatal flaw.

Interview/ The New York Times, 1-12:12.

Barbara Jordan
United States Representative, D—Texas 3

What is it . . . about the Democratic Party that makes it the instrument that people use when they search for ways to shape their future? Well, I believe the answer to that question lies in our concept of governing. Our concept of governing is derived from our view of people. It is a concept deeply rooted in a set of beliefs firmly etched in the national conscience, of all of us. Now what are these beliefs? First, we believe in equality for all and privileges for none. This is a belief that each American, regardless of background, has equal standing in the public forum, all of us. Because we believe this idea so firmly, we are an inclusive rather than an exclusive party. Let everybody come. I think it no accident that most of those emigrating to America in the 19th century identified with the Democratic Party. We are a heterogeneous party made up of Americans of diverse backgrounds. We believe that the people are the source of all governmental power; that the authority of the people is to be extended, not restricted. This can be accomplished only by providing each citizen with every opportunity to participate in the management of the government. They must have that. We believe that the government which represents the authority of all the people—not just one interest group, but all the people—has an obligation to actively underscore, actively seek to remove those obstacles which would block individual achievement . . . obstacles emanating from race, sex, economic condition. The government must seek to remove them. We are a party of innovation. We do not reject our traditions, but we are willing to adapt to changing circumstances, when change we must. We are willing to suffer the discomfort of change in order to achieve a better future. We have a positive vision of the future founded on the belief that the gap between the promise and reality of America can one day be finally closed. We believe that. This, my friends, is the bedrock of our concept of governing. This is a part of the reason why Americans have turned to the Democratic Party. These are the foundations upon which a national community can be built.

At Democratic National Convention, New York,
July 12/ Vital Speeches, 8-15:645.

4

The people who vote [in the Presidential election] on November 2 are going to make a choice between competing personalities, devoid of issues. If you watched the debates

WHAT THEY SAID IN 1976

(BARBARA JORDAN)

Thursday night [between Presidential nominees Gerald Ford and Jimmy Carter] . . . if you read any of the assessments of the debates, you do not hear people talk about the issues discussed. [The talk you hear is] about style, class, oomph, machismo. You don't hear them talk about issues . . . We're going to make a choice that is going to affect the future of America on November 2, and it's going to be a choice between competing personalities.

At Democratic fund-raising luncheon,
Denver, Sept. 24/
The Dallas Times Herald, 9-25:(A)11.

Robert W. Kastenmeier
United States Representative,
D—Wisconsin
                                                    1

[On whether public officials should be forced to make public declarations of their personal finances]: Definitely—so that the people of this country can decide whether a Federal official's interests may conflict with his judgment. We've already acknowledged the necessity. The House of Representatives has had a partial-disclosure system for some six years now. But it is inadequate. We are in a time, this post-Watergate period, where government has to improve itself. The Congress particularly, and government generally, look bad in the public eye. There is very little public confidence in us. One way that we can help restore it is by making disclosures of this sort, letting the light of day in.

Interview/
U.S. News & World Report, 1-5:45.

Edward M. Kennedy
United States Senator,
D—Massachusetts
                                                    2

People keep asking me what I think of [Presidential candidate Jimmy] Carter. I still don't have any real feel for the dimensions of the man, no sense of the human being. People ask if I agree with his positions on the issues. I have to say "what positions?" When he sends a statement to the [Demo-

cratic Party] Platform Committee saying he is not going to take up the substance of the issues, how is one going to know? That's obviously his strategy.

Time, 5-31:18.

Louis W. Koenig
Professor of government,
New York University
                                                    3

Many argue our [political] parties are dwindling because it's the age of television, which seems to favor personality over issues. In that sense, the Presidency, of course, shines—it's very much a "personality type" of institution. This tends, then, to weaken the party as an institution which has other functions than serving the Presidency and other Branches of the government. You can say, too, the expansion of the primary system has hurt the parties. Frequently it appears that the favorites of the party regulars are defeated in the primaries and the outsider tends to win.

Interview/
U.S. News & World Report, 11-8:24.

Marvin Kranz
Senior historian, Library of Congress
                                                    4

[On the recent sex scandals involving members of Congress]: If you want to talk about sex scandals in Washington, you can go all the way back to the Founding Fathers. It's hardly a new phenomonon. Remember, a person doesn't get to be a politician by not loving himself. He has to preen. It shouldn't be thought of as unusual that dalliance is sometimes involved. These are ambitious people with pretty great drives. Why shouldn't they have strong sex drives as well?

Los Angeles Times, 7-29:(1)1.

Everett C. Ladd, Jr.
Professor of political science,
University of Connecticut, Storrs
                                                    5

The Republican Party has become a permanent minority party because it has not made the transition to the post-industrial society . . . The idea-generating community in this country sees the Republican Party as a basket case.

Before American Political Science Association, Chicago/ The Washington Post, 9-5:(A)21.

Alfred M. Landon
Former Governor of Kansas (R)　　1

The art of winning—of winning an election—must precede the art of governing.

At Republican National Convention, Kansas City/ The New York Times, 8-18:1.

Clare Boothe Luce
Former American diplomat and playwright　　2

Now, you take the Democratic and Republican Parties. They hold conventions and what do they do? They go shopping from one city to another asking, "How much money will you pay me to bring the convention here?" Is that a bribe? How is that any different than some of the things they're complaining about business doing?

Interview, Washington/ "W": a Fairchild publication, 4-16:9.

Lester G. Maddox
Former Governor of Georgia (D)　　3

[On 1976 Democratic Presidential nominee, Jimmy Carter]: From a temperamental standpoint, from a standpoint of emotions, truth and honesty, he is opposite from the way he appears on radio and television. He's sort of a Dr. Jekyll-and-Mr. Hyde sort of a fellow. He's cold, cunning, cruel, and will destroy anything or anyone who stands in his way . . . He's a typical politician, the type of person I have always detested in campaigning or in public office. As for race, I believe that he is so motivated by his political madness that he doesn't care what happens to any race—and I believe that type of a person is a true racist.

Interview/ Newsweek, 7-19:25.

Eddie Mahe
Executive director, Republican National Committee　　4

I expected we [Republicans] would pick up 30 seats in the House of Representatives [in the national election] on November 2. I was sure—absolutely certain—we would pick up 15. But we were beaten, and beaten so badly. We actually lost seats, and none of us expected that. The thing is, we did the very best we could. By and large, we were so pleased with our candidates. We spent enough money. But we lost. We cannot survive another decade like this. Now we are faced with a terrible problem: redistricting after the 1980 census. If we keep going the way we are now—and I see nothing changing—we will be destroyed as a national party in 1981.

The National Observer, 11-27:1.

Mike Mansfield
United States Senator, D—Montana　　5

[Franklin] Roosevelt was the most effective [President] . . . Truman the most courageous, Eisenhower for his two terms the best because he was a man of his times and presented a father image. Kennedy would have been a great President, in my opinion, but tragedy cut it short. [Lyndon] Johnson, the best President on domestic policy; on foreign policy, the Dominican Republic and Southeast Asia were tragedies. Nixon will be remembered for two things: opening the door to [Communist] China and the Watergate affair. Ford: a more open White House, a candid President, very conservative, consistent in that respect, and really a difficult man for the Democrats to beat [in the forthcoming election], so we can't take him lightly.

Interview, Washington/ The Christian Science Monitor, 6-10:16.

　　6

The two major parties [Democratic and Republican] have become progressively less

WHAT THEY SAID IN 1976

(MIKE MANSFIELD)

well organized. If you'll follow the statistics down through the years, you'll see there are more and more independents all the time—people who shift from one party to the other and try to pick those they consider the best. Neither party has a lock on virtue. Neither party has been scandal-free. I think it's a good trend for voters to elect people not on the basis of party but on the basis of what they think officials can do, and they can check on from time to time. By the way, they are checking on us more and more. That's a good thing.

Interview, Washington/
U.S. News & World Report, 8-16:27.

1

If the Republicans lose [in the national elections] this fall, they'll look moribund, but maybe this time they'll learn some lessons. And, if they do, they might find that they have room in their party for liberals as well as conservatives, as we do in the Democratic Party. No reason why they shouldn't come back. I don't want a one-party system in this country. I think it would be bad, so I wish the Republicans wel. in their comeback—but not too well.

Interview, Washington/
U.S. News & World Report, 8-16:30.

Charles McC. Mathias, Jr.
United States Senator, R—Maryland

2

Today the Republican Party can claim the allegiance of less than 18 per cent of our registered voters. Less than one voter in five wants to own up to being a Republican. If our showing is this poor among registered voters—the people who care enough to participate in the election process—imagine where we must stand with the tens of thousands of Americans who have grown too cynical, too apathetic and too frustrated by the political shadowplay of our times to even register. They are the real warning sign; they are the unknown, a vast threatening amorphous growth on the political scene. It's not that they are turning

to the Democratic Party either. That might even be a healthy sign, for at least then we could say that the inevitable pendulum-swing of our two-party system might turn back our way some day. Rather, it appears that the growing numbers of unaffiliated independents are simply disillusioned with the entire political process. They're disenchanted and disappointed by the way our government operates, or, more precisely, doesn't operate. They see a political system that has failed to live up to its promise and that has failed to live up to its principles. This alienation is not a fad. It's not merely an aberration brought about by the post-Watergate blahs. It's not a temporarily-out-of-order sign. I believe it is rooted in growing mistrust of our political institutions' ability to respond to the needs of the people, and in the fear that government cannot resolve any of our problems either.

The Washington Post, 3-26:(A)26.

3

The conservatives keep agitating for two pure, sharply defined [political] parties. That kind of polarization is wrong. The two parties need a constant dialogue, to watch and challenge and demand things of each other. That's what the American system is all about: to keep power divided, to prevent a small core from either pole suddenly thrusting its decisions on the country.

Interview/ Time, 8-23:17.

4

All my life the Republican Party has been my home and I've been comfortable in it. I've done my best to water its roots, which were planted in the great movement to abolish slavery and to establish human rights for all Americans. I've tried to keep faith with its progressive beginnings. Now, if we are truly to revive our two-party system, the Republicans must rekindle their historic commitment to civil liberties. From that renewed commitment will flow a concern for our cities and the people in them; a concern about jobs and health and crime and the young and the old; a concern about the quality of our life. There are lessons in defeat, just as there are rewards in victory. A resurgent Republican Party, competing in healthy tension with a vigorous, conscientious Democratic Party, interacting with the press and with the courts, is an important safeguard against a future "tyrannous majority" [of which James Madison warned]. Two strong parties are as vital to us as the three strong branches of government. It is by balancing one another and checking one another that they strike the sparks that are the light of democracy.

Before Anti-Defamation League of B'nai B'rith,
Los Angeles, Dec./
Los Angeles Times, 12-17:(2)7.

Tom McCall
Former Governor of Oregon (R)
1

[On political partisanship]: You have one label that begins with "D" and one that begins with "R," and they use them to hack at each other so they can avoid serious work on the problems. I went over to Idaho and kicked off a campaign for Cecil Andrus, the Governor. He's a Democrat, so I'm on the shelf with a lot of Republicans. It's impossible enough to find a decent Governor without throwing him out because he has a label you don't like.

Interview, Portland, May 24/
The New York Times, 5-25:24.

Eugene J. McCarthy
Independent candidate for the Presidency of the United States;
Former U.S. Senator, D—Minnesota
2

[Lamenting the rights and the news coverage afforded the Democratic and Republican Parties compared with independents like himself]: I can anticipate a time when Democrats and Republicans will be the only ones allowed even to vote in Presidential elections, with independents effectively excluded. This is not altogether different from the practice in Communist countries, where the members of the Party pick the candidates, lay out the platform and then allow the rest of the people to approve what they have done.

National broadcast address, Sept. 7/
Los Angeles Times, 9-8:(1)7.

3

Vice-Presidential candidates just clutter up the campaign. We should not ask the country to make two judgments. Every one knows Vice Presidents have no influence on Presidents, once elected. Presidents' wives have much more influence. Perhaps we should have the candidates' wives debate.

To newsmen, Washington, Oct. 8/
The New York Times, 10-10:(1)42.

4

The Republican Party is a lower form of plant life, like moss on a rock. It has very low vitality—green in the summer, slightly gray in the winter—but it never dies. If the Republicans had any decency, they'd just go away.

Interview/
The New York Times Magazine, 10-24:13.

George S. McGovern
United States Senator,
D—South Dakota
5

After eight years of Nixon, Agnew and Ford, after 20 years of Vietnam and 30 years of the arms race, after Watergate and the White House "horrors," what America needs is not expediency and timidity but a renaissance of liberalism. Nothing in recent years provides a proof or even a pretext for losing the liberal faith. Today we face not a failure of liberalism, but a shortfall. The problem is not that we have done too much, but that we are doing too little. It was not the liberals who wasted our resources on a war in Vietnam.

Upon election as President of Americans for
Democratic Action, Washington, May 22/
The New York Times, 5-23:(1)38.

6

[Criticizing President-elect Jimmy Carter's choices for his Cabinet]: Members of the Cabinet, whether in Democratic or Republican Administrations, have been selected, pretty much, from the same group of individuals. I had thought that in view of [the] impact of Watergate, in view of the disillusionment over Vietnam, and in view of the

WHAT THEY SAID IN 1976

(GEORGE S. McGOVERN)

nature of Governor Carter's own bid for the Presidency, that perhaps this time we would see a more definite change in the composition of the Cabinet. But this is the kind of a Cabinet that could have been picked by [current Vice President] Nelson Rockefeller, [the late President] Lyndon Johnson or, for the most part, [former President] Richard Nixon.

> *Radio interview/*
> *The Dallas Times Herald, 12-30:(A)1.*

Abner J.Mikva
United States Representative, D—Illinois

1

I've changed my views about a lot of things in the last 20 years. My definition of liberalism is someone who can look at an old idea and say it doesn't work, and so let's try something else. We forget that some of these liberal ideas are 40 or 50 years old. It's partly our own fault. Those of us who call ourselves liberals have failed to persuade the public that we do have flexibility—that we do understand that you can't be locked into an idea or a program forever.

> *Interview, Chicago/*
> *The National Observer, 11-20:5.*

Walter F. Mondale
United States Senator, D—Minnesota;
1976 Democratic Vice-Presidential nominee

2

I called three great Minnesota [former] candidates for President and asked for their advice [for the forthcoming election campaign]—Harold Stassen, Eugene McCarthy and Hubert Humphrey. Stassen said, "Be humble." McCarthy said, "Work hard." Hubert said, "Keep it short."

> *Before Democratic National Committee,*
> *New York/The Dallas Times Herald, 7-18:(A)7.*

3

I believe that my record is that of a pragmatic, progressive Democrat. I think I am part of the mainstream of American life. I be-

lieve in free enterprise. I believe in competition. I believe in work. I get different labels, but I think my record will reflect that I am not an ideologue.

> *Interview/Newsweek, 7-26:26.*

4

[On the Republican Party and their Presidential candidates, President Gerald Ford and Ronald Reagan]: It doesn't make any difference to them what the status quo is, they will defend it. If there are tax preferences that permit some wealthy people to pay nothing in taxes, that is all right with them. If nine million people can't find work, if people can't get decent housing, that is all right with them. They . . . can destroy this country because their ideological position is resistant to change. That is where they are most vulnerable.

> *Interview/Newsweek, 7-26:27.*

5

[On the past two Republican Administrations, which involved the resignation of President Richard Nixon]: I realize that this is the Democratic Convention and that this is not the place to say complimentary things about Republicans . . . But no other party has done the things the Republican Party has done. They've given us two Presidents and three Vice Presidents with one election.

> *At South Dakota Democratic convention, Pierre,*
> *July 31/The Washington Post, 8-1:(A)12.*

6

[Criticizing President Ford's 1974 pre-indictment pardon of former President Richard Nixon for any possible Watergate crimes]: No act more perpetuated Nixon's own dangerous doctrine that a President is somehow above the law. Few would have objected to a Nixon pardon after a judicial process—if in fact Mr. Nixon was indicted. But the Ford pardon snuffed out that process and made a mockery of the notion that in America there is no sovereign who stands above the law.

> *At University of Missouri Law School,*
> *Kansas City, Oct. 5/*
> *The New York Times, 10-6:22.*

Daniel P. Moynihan
1976 New York Democratic
U.S. Senatorial nominee
1

I always think of [former U.S. President Richard] Nixon as a man who saw more enemies than there were until there were more than he saw. I think of [President] Ford as totally unreached by all the alarums that swarm about him.

Interview, New York/
San Francisco Examiner & Chronicle, 9-19:
(This World)29.

Reg Murphy
Editor and publisher,
"San Francisco Examiner"; Former editor,
"The Atlanta Constitution"
2

[On 1976 Democratic Presidential nominee, and former Governor of Georgia, Jimmy Carter]: . . . he's absolutely ruthless; he will win. He will win this Presidential campaign because he's more determined to win than anybody else. He will do what it takes to win. He will change what views it takes for him to win. He will expand and expound on any topic . . . and he will do it with what a lot of people take to be grace and style and talent . . . If politics is the art of the possible, Jimmy Carter won't get along with anybody in Washington, because he is a mean, hard-eyed sort of fellow who tolerates nobody who opposes him. The [former Georgia] Governor just absolutely does not take challenges from anybody . . . I think his strongest point is determination to achieve and to prevail, and he brings a good mind to politics although his stubbornness would probably be important. My problem is that I just don't understand him as a leader. I don't think he has human warmth in him, and so I just can't imagine anybody being led by him. I can imagine him sounding good to people for a day or two; I can't imagine him sounding very good to them for four years. His attitudes wear very thin very quickly. I also believe that leadership demands more than just the cold-eyed ability to calculate where the votes are and that sort of thing, and I just don't think he has that.

Interview/Newsweek, 7-19:23.

Ron Nessen
Press Secretary to President of the
United States Gerald R. Ford
3

To say that [President Ford] makes . . . decisions for political reasons is just to ignore a whole set of decisions the President has made this year . . . If the President is interested only in votes and only in [Republican Convention] delegates, why does he have the Pentagon draw up a list of bases to be closed? Why does he propose an energy program which is going to raise prices? Why does he propose an increase in Social Security taxes? Why does he hold New York City's feet to the fire, and so forth? Why did he veto a tax cut on Christmas Eve, for goodness sake?

Press briefing, Washington, July 2/
The New York Times, 7-3:19.

Thomas P. O'Neill, Jr.
United States Representative,
D—Massachusetts
4

I like [Gerald Ford] as an individual, but cripes, he's an awful President. He hasn't instilled any confidence in America, that's Number 1. Number 2, he just hasn't put the staff around him that he really should have put. And Number 3, honestly, after looking at our record of override of vetoes. I just don't think he tries that hard. The only thing that I know he's come up with is the swine-flu [inoculation] thing. Don't misunderstand me. Jerry Ford is no dunce by any means. Jerry Ford's a smart fellow. But Jerry Ford doesn't want to learn new tricks. Jerry wants to go along with the past. The past to Jerry is the greatness of America.

Interview/
U.S. News & World Report, 10-18:41.

Shirley N. Pettis
United States Representative,
D—California
5

[On the sex scandal involving Representative Wayne Hays and his secretary]: I think

WHAT THEY SAID IN 1976

(SHIRLEY N. PETTIS)

this is a tragedy which diminishes anyone in politics. As far as Mr. Hays specifically is concerned, the point at issue is whether or not public funds have been misused and I think that is the area of responsibility that we as the members of the House have to resolve. It is our responsibility to be sure that public funds are appropriately spent in the public interest. The American public is apt to feel this is a pattern of conduct applicable to many people in public life, and I would certainly hope that is not true.

Los Angeles Herald-Examiner, 6-23:(B)3.

Milton Rakove
Professor of political science,
University of Illinois 1

Corruption is endemic and almost a normal part of politics. It's a normal part of life. I don't think politicians are more corrupt than the rest of us—than doctors or lawyers or college professors ... The theory of democratic politics is that people are elected to deal with public interests. But once they get into office, they realize that the only way to stay there is by appealing to private interests at the expense of public interests. Now, you have to pay lip service to the public interest. I've written a lot of political speeches and you've got to give them God, Motherhood and Country. So you say: "Here's what I'm going to do for you and it's going to be good for the country." Most people want to be good and they want their politicians to be decent—but their private interests come first.

The Washington Post, 12-26:(A)1,5.

Dixy Lee Ray
Governor-elect of Washington (R) 2

If you are going to run for office and you believe in the two-party system—which I do—you have to choose one or the other. And my answer to why did I choose the Democratic Party is that I spent three years in Washington under a Republican Administration.

San Francisco Examiner & Chronicle, 12-12:
(This World)2.

Robert D. Ray
Governor of Iowa (R) 3

I think we [Republicans] can become a majority party. I don't think it is easy. I think we had things going our way up until Watergate, and I think many, many excellent candidates that were Republicans went down as a result of the American people wanting to purge the Party because of what happened in Washington. I think that is unfortunate, but it is understandable. And so we have a long trail to come back, and it is not going to be easy. We are the first to acknowledge and recognize that, but I think it is possible. I can remember being a state chairman when we had to come back after '64. Maybe the conditions are different, not the same, but nonetheless there were many of the press and others who were saying at that time that we were about to see the demise of the Republican Party. It didn't happen. The Party came back strong, electing a Republican President, not once but twice. And so I think that we can come back ...

TV-radio interview, Philadelphia/
"Meet the Press,"
National Broadcasting Company, 7-4.

Ronald Reagan
Candidate for the 1976
Republican Presidential nomination;
Former Governor of California (R) 4

My own feeling has been that it is an uphill fight against an incumbent. An incumbent [President] has a great many things that he can do. For example, he can make news and be virtually on the network news and on the front page of the papers every day without moving out of the Oval Office. In addition, an incumbent can go into an area and announce that the shipyard is going to stay open. He can go to another area and say that the highway is going to be built. He can stand in front of a group of disabled veterans and tell them he is going to build a new hospital. These are all the things that go with an incumbency that a challenger can't do.

TV-radio interview, Miami/"Meet the Press,"
National Broadcasting Company, 3-7.

1

[On his choice of Senator Richard Schweiker, a liberal, as his Vice-Presidential running mate, when he himself is a conservative]: I have not retreated one iota from positions upon which I campaigned. The Senator has not found it necessary, in doing what he is doing, to compromise principle. What we are really doing for the first time in the history of the Republican Party is trying to bring segments of this party together to win an election instead of winning a convention. It's high time somebody did this.

News conference, Philadelphia, Aug. 6/
The New York Times, 8-7:6.

Ronald Reagan
Former Governor of California (R)
2

[On his losing the Presidential nomination]: The convention turnaround against us was in the [political] machine states. I don't mind saying that whenever the people had a real chance to vote in this campaign we did very well. But none of us ever anticipated the kind of pressure that can be exerted in the organizational states like Pennsylvania, New York and New Jersey. There's no place in America for some of the things we saw happen here . . . Maybe the only answer is regional primaries. The old-fashioned concept of party bossism—with the heirarchy able to lean on delegates—is so much in contrast with the states where the decisions are reached at the grass roots.

Interview, Kansas City, Aug. 19/
The New York Times, 8-20:(A)12.

3

. . . I do think the Republican Party is long overdue for a reassessment of itself, where it stands and where it is heading. It hasn't recognized that, for the past several years, an increasing number of people have drifted away from both parties, calling themselves independents. I think if these people understood what the Republican Party stands for, we could appeal to them. There are also many dissident Democrats who demonstrated in 1972, and again in '76, that they cannot fol-

low the leadership of their party any longer. The real story of this [just-concluded Presidential] election is not in what gave [Jimmy] Carter his squeak-through victory. The real story is: How did he almost lose an election when his party outnumbers ours 2 to 1 or better? The Republican Party, with less than a fifth of the registered voters in this country, got almost 50 per cent of the vote. I think that proves my point that if the Republican Party can decide what it stands for and where it is heading, we can attract the votes to win.

Interview/ U.S. News & World Report, 11-22:21.

Thomas M. Rees
United States Representative,
D—California
4

[On why he has decided not to seek re-election]: Watergate has changed politics completely, and it's almost as if groups like Common Cause and Ralph Nader assume all politicians are guilty until proven innocent. I find that my mail gets nastier, not so much because I'm Rees but because I'm a politician. The whole life is just getting more difficult, more restricted, and it's kind of like being in the trenches.

Interview, Washington/
Los Angeles Times, 2-13:(1)7.

John J. Rhodes
United States Representative, R—Arizona
5

A conservative believes that, fundamentally, the individual is responsible for his own well-being, but that government should do those things for him that he can't do for himself. The liberal's first reaction to a problem is to ask: "How can government solve it?" The conservative first asks: "How can we help the individual solve it, and should we?"

Interview/ U.S. News & World Report, 10-4:25.

6

I am at a loss to understand how anyone can view the results of the last election as evidence that the Republican Party is dying.

WHAT THEY SAID IN 1976

(JOHN J. RHODES)

For behind the raw, depressing win-loss statistics was a truly incredible Party performance. Why is it so many people overlook the fact that the GOP is a minority party outnumbered in registration by better than two to one? Too often people judge our electoral performance as if we have parity with the Democrats, and, of course, we do not. Virtually any Republican running today almost anywhere in the country is an inherent underdog! He or she must campaign twice as hard, twice as effectively as the opposition in order to win. Viewed in this context, the performance of the GOP in the 1976 election was hardly weak. President Ford trailed Jimmy Carter by 33 points in the polls in mid-August, yet by election day he and [Vice-Presidential nominee] Senator [Bob] Dole had rallied to within one percentage point of victory . . . In races for the House of Representatives, ten Republican candidates failed to win election by a mere two percentage points or less; 40 Republicans lost by only five points or less. In all but a few of these cases, the edge in registration belonged to the Democrats, as did the enormous advantages of incumbency. Yet so many of our races were close ones. The point is that, while Republicans have every reason to be disappointed in the final election results, there is absolutely no reason on earth for us to become despondent. We fought a good fight on just about every front, and, given the right spirit and the right planning, have every reason to look forward to substantial gains down the road.

The Washington Post, 12-12:(B)6.

Elliot L. Richardson
Secretary of Commerce
of the United States
                                              1

[On his recent posts as Secretary of Defense, Secretary of Health, Education and Welfare, Attorney General, Ambassador to Britain, and now Secretary of Commerce]: I may be, at this very moment, entering the *Guinness Book of [World] Records* as the most sworn-in of Americans. If I hadn't been moving so fast from place to place, I might well have become the most sworn-*at* of Americans.

At his swearing-in as Commerce Secretary,
Washington, Feb. 2/
The National Observer, 2-14:6.

Donald W. Riegle, Jr.
United States Representative,
D—Michigan
                                              2

You notice that on the Republican side [of the House of Representatives] there are no black members, not many women, very few from ethnic groups, very few from modest economic circumstances. What you see is a group like an Establishment men's service club. On the Democratic side you have the whole country represented. Because of this, the Democratic Party has a tolerance for differences, and that is its real strength. [Because of its limited membership, the Republican Party] fails to understand the problems faced by the rest of the country. It can't dope out answers.

Time, 8-23:12.

Nelson A. Rockefeller
Vice President of the United States
                                              3

[Democratic Presidential nominee Jimmy] Carter has talked love and compassion and the family. These are all things like motherhood, and we believe in them. It is wonderful, and I admire him for talking about love. But when it comes to the issues, it is very hard to tell exactly where he stands. He takes a conservative position, he takes a liberal position; but in each case he always in the small print puts in some clauses which give him an escape hatch, so that when he gets to make the final decision, should he get there, he has got total latitude. I think the American people, when they get right down to it, are going to want to know, where does this man stand?

TV-radio interview, Kansas City/
"Meet the Press,"
National Broadcasting Company, 8-15.

1

. . . I think the two-party system is essential in America. I happen to personally believe both parties should be centrist parties which come up with different concepts for solutions but representing all of the people, not a special interest. That is the strength of our democracy; in fact, it is the future of freedom. If we lose that two-party strength, then I think we are going to lose the basis for preserving freedom and opportunity in America.

TV-radio interview, Kansas City/
"Meet the Press,"
National Broadcasting Company, 8-15.

2

Frankly, this Republican Party of ours has been shrinking—not growing—and it's time to face up to this reality. We know we can have a broad appeal. We've won four of the last seven Presidential elections. But we did it with candidates and campaigns that appealed to the broad spectrum of the American populace—not a narrow few. Every problem America faces is an opportunity. And at no period in history have the opportunities been greater if we but have the vision and the courage to grasp them, to build an America of opportunity for all people to achieve what their capacities, talents and ambitions can produce. If the Republican Party is to be a viable political force, it must seize these opportunities. I hope for a new spirit of unity and vigorous program from this Republican Convention. The Republican Party needs this—and more importantly, the nation needs it.

At Republican National Convention,
Kansas City, Aug. 16/
The New York Times, 8-17:20.

George W. Romney
Former Governor of Michigan (R)

3

[Criticizing the press for blowing verbal mistakes by politicians way out of proportion]: In politics, the media is an anthropologist. An anthropologist resurrects a tooth or jawbone and builds a whole man.

Interview, Bloomfield Hills, Mich./
The Dallas Times Herald, 4-18:(A)27.

Elton H. Rule
President,
American Broadcasting Companies

4

No large corporation or other institution would dream of selecting a president without subjecting his policies and proposals to the most searching examination. Nor would Congress pass an important law without extensive debate. Yet the two major Presidential candidates of this country have debated publicly just once in the television era—in 1960. Those debates between John Kennedy and Richard Nixon may in time be regarded as the greatest single contribution the broadcast medium has made to the democratic process in this country. No one thinks it a coincidence that the greatest percentage of voters went to the polls that year than in any other year in this country.

Before ABC affiliates, Los Angeles/
San Francisco Examiner & Chronicle, 7-11:
(Datebook)27.

William Rusher
Publisher, "National Review"

5

[On his conservative third-party movement]: What we're after is conservative influence on American society. So when the Democrats have nominated the first non-incumbent Southerner of relatively conservative stripe since 1844 [Jimmy Carter], and when President Ford is running around [the Republican Convention in] Kansas City insisting he is just as conservative as [Republican candidate] Ronald Reagan, who is only inches behind him and gaining, I have to say that the glass is not simply half-empty, alas, but half-full—so maybe we can make it a little fuller.

The New York Times, 8-17:23.

Richard M. Scammon
Public-opinion analyst

6

. . . independent [non-party-affiliated] voters are a mishmash: Wallaceites, for example, then the truly Jovian independents who sit up there on Mount Olympus and study the candi-

253

WHAT THEY SAID IN 1976

(RICHARD M. SCAMMON)

dates and make judgments, and many others including what I would call the *Lumpenwahler*, or electoral slob. Studies show that among independents you find fewer people who know their member of Congress, fewer people who intend to vote, fewer people who know anything about the issues. So-called independents include some of our best- informed voters—and some of our worst. There's this terrible tendency in this country to think of the independents as a cohesive force. Inchoate would be a better word to describe them. They include everything—a big garbage pail.
Interview/ U.S. News & World Report, 10-25:29.

1

The Swiss have a lower voter turnout than we [in the U.S.] have, and almost everybody in the Western world regards Switzerland as a stable, well-governed democracy. The idea that high voter turnout necessarily means good government and low turnout means bad government is nonsense. It's something that we've been fed in high-school civics class. We've salivated over this thing like a Pavlovian dog, and it just isn't true. The Soviet Union, Hitler's Germany, Italy under Mussolini—all had very high participation, but not many people would hold them up as examples to be emulated. What it boils down to is that freedom means the freedom not to vote, as well as the right to vote.
Interview/ U.S. News & World Report, 10-25:30.

Richard S. Schweiker
United States Senator,
R—Pennsylvania
2

[On Presidential candidate Ronald Reagan's naming him his Vice-Presidential running mate before Reagan has received the Republican Presidential nomination]: This bold, unprecedented action dramatizes the leadership, the courage and the openness which Governor Reagan will bring to the White House . . . I am proud to be the running

mate of the only Presidential candidate who had the common decency and goodness to refuse to play the old, callous Vice-Presidential guessing game. Governor Reagan's candor in naming his running mate three weeks before the [Republican National] Convention is a bold and refreshing departure from the old politics.
News conference, Washington, July 26/
Los Angeles Herald-Examiner, 7-26:(A)1.

Eric Sevareid
News commentator,
Columbia Broadcasting System
3

I'm often called left-of-center. These labels get fastened on you. I don't know what liberal or conservative means any more. I get attacked by the left wing as a square conservative; I get attacked by Goldwater types as a left-wing extremist. I get it from all sides in just about equal proportions. I suppose I am a liberal in the humanitarian sense. But I am also one of those liberals who grew up in the '30s and who are now very concerned by that liberal approach and how to find new paths, because an awful lot of New Dealism didn't work very well. We have to find new ways for the government to serve people more effectively. You can't just throw money around and expect that to accomplish anything. If this is neo-conservatism, all right. But you have to have the guts to change your mind if what you once believed no longer adds up. So call me a second-look liberal.
Interview/ The Christian Science Monitor, 8-19:27.

Mark Siegel
Executive director,
Democratic National Committee
4

The Republican Party is dying. The old theory that parties go up and down in cycles doesn't apply now. The Republican Party can't bounce back any more. It has the brain wave of a dead person.
The National Observer, 11-27:1.

William E. Simon
*Secretary of the Treasury
of the United States*
1

The trouble with the Republican Party, as Woodrow Wilson once observed, is that it has not had a new idea for 30 years. Well, it has been another 51 years since Wilson made his observation, and I'm afraid it still holds true, at least for a growing number of voters. We need to spell out in plain language what we [Republicans] stand for and what we believe in.

*Before Republican Party platform committee/
Time, 8-23:11.*

Howard K. Smith
*News commentator,
American Broadcasting Company*
2

[On the current Presidential election campaign]: Every election contains portions of fluff and nonsense, but this is the first Presidential one, since Al Smith was beaten for allegedly aiming to put the Pope in the White House, that has been almost entirely fluff. No really sharp issues have developed in either of the two Presidential debates. The headline grabbers have been Jimmy Carter's blooper about ethnic purity and his interview with *Playboy*, and the dirty joke of Gerald Ford's ex-Agriculture Secretary and Ford's own boo-boo about the independence of Eastern Europe. To these earth-shakers there have been allegations that Carter has had mistresses, which he promptly said was nonsense. It's not as though there aren't serious subjects in every day's news. Last week the economic indicators went down and wholesale prices and the number of unemployed household heads went up. *The New York Times* says that New York City's crisis, like that of many other cities, is going to get worse. And it reported that in ten years 36 nations will have enough plutonium to build whole arsenals of atomic bombs. Those are a few of a hundred things that cry out for serious talk and creative plans. Consolations in the campaign are few and scrawny. One is that the next debate will be between the Vice-Presidential candidates.

They may just possibly say something pertinent. The other is that we're doing numerically better off than ancient Rome. They had one Nero fiddling while Rome burned; we've got two.

*ABC News commentary, Oct. 11/
The Washington Post, 10-14:(A)19.*

Mary Louise Smith
*Chairman,
Republican National Committee*
3

As chairman of the Republican Party, I must say in all candor that the sum of the [just-concluded national] election returns points out clearly that our Party must embark on a relentless effort to broaden its base in this nation. We must do a better job of getting our message of personal and economic freedom to the people. We must convey more accurately our concern about people and their well-being. To the extent that we have failed to do this in the past, we are reaping its ill effects.

U.S. News & World Report, 11-15:40.

Adlai E. Stevenson
United States Senator, D—Illinois
4

The liberal really is a conservative who tries to protect the freedom of the individual from encroachment by the state and other forces beyond his control, with a minimum of government activity. People are threatened by big business, big unions and big government. In contrast, that which is defined now as conservatism is defense of the status quo.

Interview/ U.S. News & World Report, 10-4:25.

Robert S. Strauss
*Chairman,
Democratic National Committee*
5

The Democratic Party fully understands now what we couldn't understand in the past—that our internal bickering and internal warfare brought the nation nothing but disaster. The Democratic Party, in myopia, bitterness, pettiness and often downright stu-

(ROBERT S. STRAUSS)

pidity, brought [former President] Richard Nixon and [President] Gerald Ford upon the American people. And that burden we will never be able to shed from our shoulders, for the nation has suffered. [But we Democrats] have fully learned our lessons, and we will not make the same mistakes again.

At Democratic Party platform committee hearing, Washington, May 17/
Los Angeles Herald-Examiner, 5-18:(A)11.

1

[On the condition of the Democratic Party when he took over its stewardship in 1972]: I didn't inherit a party four years ago. It's like someone saying I got a nice watch because someone hands me 24 pieces and calls it a nice watch.

The Wall Street Journal, 7-16:6.

Herman E. Talmadge
United States Senator, D—Georgia

2

[Senator Hubert Humphrey] has probably the best coordination of mind and tongue of any man that I ever saw. He can make an eloquent speech on any side of any issue with or without notice. I don't know that Hubert has strong convictions on any subject. He is always ostensibly for the underdog, and he is strong for every program to give away more assets of the Federal Treasury to all citizens.

Interview/
Los Angeles Times, 2-25:(1)9.

Jerald F. terHorst
Political columnist; Former Press Secretary to President of the United States Gerald R. Ford

3

I don't think [President] Ford is terribly cunning—or devious. He's rather open— open-faced about things. And if he has anything going for him it may be that the good quality is that he is genuinely a person without a devious nature. In politics, of course, I

guess we forgive everything except lack of shrewdness. We like a politician to be shrewd. Ford is not shrewd. And when he tries to be, he comes out ham-handed.

Interview/Newsweek, 10-18:36.

James R. Thompson
Governor-elect of Illinois (R)

4

[On the Republican Party]: To a lot of people, we're the don't-call-us, we'll-call-you party. And the people are sending us a message—political defeats. And I agree with the people who say we're too negative. We shouldn't stand up and holler that every program costs too much money. We should come up with a program of our own that costs less money. We can't worry all the time about ideology. In some parts of the country, people want conservative candidates. Let's have them. In other parts, they want liberal candidates. So let's have them . . . I didn't exclude anyone in my campaign [for Governor]. I went into black wards in Chicago all by myself. No reporters, no nothing. The reaction was outstanding. They'd never seen a candidate for Governor. And they'd never seen a Republican at all.

At Republican Governors Conference, Washington/ The National Observer, 12-11:5.

Morris K. Udall
United States Representative, D—Arizona; Candidate for the 1976 Democratic Presidential nomination

5

[On Alabama Governor George Wallace and former California Governor Ronald Reagan, who are seeking the respective Democratic and Republican Presidential nominations]: They are well-financed, they are well-organized, they are well-publicized, they are clever and they are dangerous. [They] are ruled by ambition—and ambition drives them to pander to deep prejudices, fears and resentments they can uncover or create. They are spearheading an assault on our common sense, our compassion and our confidence in democracy itself.

At Faneuil Hall, Boston, Feb.5/
The Dallas Times Herald, 2-5:(A)11.

1

I frankly concede that I want to be elected [President]; I want to do a lot of things. But I do not have this desperate feeling that I have got to be President. That's the dilemma: Can you be elected without this? . . . I enjoy the contact [of campaigning], talking to people, but I do not want to do that 18 hours a day, 365 days a year. I think one of the key things people ought to look at is not just his [a candidate's] public personality, his smile, but what friends does he have, what outside interests. [Former President Richard] Nixon didn't have any friends, didn't have any outside interests.

Interview, Keene, N.H./
The New York Times, 2-28:18.

2

[On the word "liberal"]: Everywhere I go it's become what I call a worry word. I don't run away from it—I'm a liberal, you know; I haven't changed a speech or program or policy statement or anything else—it's simply a worry word. You stop a fellow in the street and say, "Excuse me, sir, I'm that great liberal Mo Udall and I want to tell you about my great liberal program"; he turns you out before you start. You say, "Just a minute, sir; the country's in trouble, and I'm a progressive, and the country's always made progress when we've got some things to do and here's my program: Humphrey-Hawkins full-employment, tax-reform, break up the corporations, and so on." He says, "Yeah, that sounds good." And it simply became clear to me that it's a worry word that blocks communication, and when you run into one of those situations you change and you joke about it a little bit.

Interview/ The Washington Post, 4-25:(C)1.

Guy Vander Jagt
United States Representative,
R—Michigan
3

This is the most scandal-ridden Congress in this century, and it isn't a case of our saying that every Republican is a saint and every Democrat is a sinner. We are saying the truth of Lord Acton's adage of 1866 which is, "Pow-

er corrupts and absolute power corrupts absolutely." And absolute power by one party, The Democrat Party, over the Congress for 22 consecutive years, has led to an attitude of self-gratification, rather than public service, that breeds the temptation of that type of scandal. That is what needs to be changed, and I think that is what the people are fed up with.

TV-radio interview, Washington/
"Meet the Press,"
National Broadcasting Company, 10-10.

Gore Vidal
Author
4

[On the 1976 Presidential race]: It doesn't make much difference who's elected. The system doesn't work. Our elections are an expensive public charade to celebrate the owners of the country.

Interview/ Time, 3-1:64.

George C. Wallace
Governor of Alabama (D);
Candidate for the 1976
Democratic Presidential nomination
5

I don't want anyone to vote for me because I'm in a wheelchair. But I also don't want anyone to vote against me because of it. I'm just paralyzed in the legs. Some of these other fellows are paralyzed in the head.

Durham, N.C./ Time, 3-29:13.

Harrison A. Williams, Jr.
United States Senator, D—New Jersey
6

If there is one thing [of] which we can be assured, it is that every Presidential candidate, whether he is of the liberal left or the radical right, will indulge in preposterous exaggeration. All of them will make statements, espouse policies and voice exhortations on the hustings which, in the quietness and calm of their own living-rooms, they would laugh at. Unfortunately, for the people of the country, this laughing will only be done after the fact, and not before. I have often felt that in every election each candidate should be required by

WHAT THEY SAID IN 1976

(HARRISON A. WILLIAMS, JR.)

law to cease and desist from campaigning for
one week in every month, and be required also
to spend those seven days reading in detail
every speech he has made in the three weeks
preceding the moratorium. It is entirely possible that the level of campaign oratory would
rise dramatically. It is also possible that the
nation would be spared a lot of impractical,
immature and impossible nostrums for curing
the country's ills . . . I would leave you, therefore, with this plea: when, over the next nine
months, your ears and eyes are assailed by the
millions of words of campaign rhetoric that
are an inescapable adjunct to a Presidential
election, you carry with you at all times a
small bag of salt. At intervals to suit yourselves, take a generous pinch. This seasoning
will help preserve your sanity.

Before New Jersey State Chamber of Commerce/
The Washington Post, 2-19:(A)18.

Harold Wilson
Former Prime Minister of the
United Kingdom
1

The Watergate situation would never have
occurred in this country [Britain]. Even supposing that it had happened, within no time at
all the parliamentary party, whether it be
Labor or Conservative, would have got rid of
its leader. They would have said, "Enough
is enough; we can't go on with this," and it
would have been done just by people talking
to each other in the tearoom or drinking a
rather stronger drink in the Members' smoke-
room or the bars.

Interview, London/ Time, 10-25:40.

Leonard Woodcock
President, United Automobile
Workers of America
2

[Endorsing Jimmy Carter for the Democratic Presidential nomination]: It is time
to end the Civil War and bring this country
together into one nation. There could be no
better symbol of reconciliation than to elect
a President from the genuine South—the new
South—one who listens to the people instead
of the traditional politicians . . . Too many
Americans long had been taught from childhood that certain citizens could not be considered as contenders for the Presidency—no
Catholic, Southerner, Jew, Black, woman
and so on. But in 1960, the Democratic Party,
despite the cries of the naysayers, did nomi-
nate and elect a Catholic President [John
Kennedy]. That taboo is behind us . . . If a
political genius had offered to produce a
candidate who could carry the working class
as well as the crucial black, moderate and
liberal vote in the North and, at the same time,
defeat the strident segregationists of the
South, he would have been a dreamer. And
yet, that is what Jimmy Carter has already
done.

News conference, Detroit, May 7/
Los Angeles Times, 5-8:(1)3.

Frank G. Zarb
Administrator,
Federal Energy Administration
3

[Washington] is a hard, cruel town. One of
the things that strikes me about this town is
its political nature. Back home I had partners
who were Democrats and Republicans, but I
don't remember ever having continuing political discussions with them. Here, politics
dominates everything. My view has always
been that I'm just here temporarily, that I'm
just passing through. I think that's healthier.

The Washington Post, 12-19:(A)6.

Social Welfare

Brock Adams
United States Representative,
D—Washington
1

There is something wrong with a system that permits the sale and construction of expensive condominium[s] and megalithic corporate monuments, but permits whole sections of central cities to slide into slums, and has practically priced the middle-income family out of the housing market.

At National Housing Conference, Washington/
The Washington Post, 3-6:(E)25.

Dewey F. Bartlett
United States Senator, R—Oklahoma
2

[Arguing against unemployment payments to retirees in addition to their pensions]: Unemployment compensation is designed to help a person who loses his job and is facing a rather bleak period of time trying to obtain another job. It's to carry him over, perhaps not to the level of living to which he has become accustomed, but as an emergency subsistence allowance to enable him to make it. To allow persons with a guaranteed income from retirement to receive bonus benefits—intended solely for those who had no job—is a travesty.

The Dallas Times Herald, 3-28:(A)23.

Andrew F. Brimmer
Economist, Harvard Business School;
Former member, Federal Reserve Board
3

In general, over the last five years, income has been redistributed so as to favor whites vs. blacks, the better-off vs. the poor, the newer regions of the country vs. the old, and the suburbs vs. both rural areas and central cities . . . during the last five years—under the combined impact of high inflation rates and slower economic growth—these disadvantaged groups [blacks, the poor and unskilled] have fallen further behind the more fortunate members of society. Moreover, the outlook for a more equal distribution of income over the rest of this decade is far from bright.

Before American Association for the
Advancement of Science, Boston, Feb. 23/
The Dallas Times Herald, 2-24:(A)7.

Edmund G. Brown, Jr.
Governor of California (D)
4

We have a welfare program in California. We have food stamps. We have Medi-Cal. We put hundreds of thousands of people to work through direct and indirect investment. But I would prefer to see stable neighborhoods and communities where people have jobs and a future and are part of the mainstream of society.

Interview/Playboy, April:80.

Yvonne B. Burke
United States Representative,
D—California
5

I think there's a great fallacy among American people generally that Americans are affluent. That happens not to be true. One half of the families in the United States earn less than $13,000 a year. But we're brainwashed. We believe that we're affluent, and, as a result, there has been a polarization and a lack of identification of all American people with the problem of the lower half.

San Francisco Examiner & Chronicle, 5-2:
(This World)2.

259

WHAT THEY SAID IN 1976

Robert N. Butler
Director,
National Institute on Aging
1

Retirement cuts several ways. If you have been an assembly-line worker, done back-breaking work on a farm or worked in a hazardous occupation, you may be delighted to retire. You may even get healthier after retirement. But if you've been in an occupation that you love, you may be hastened into death after retirement. You'll notice that self-employed people often don't retire if they can avoid it. The people who retire, generally speaking, are those working under a compulsory-retirement system. For some of them, the retirement syndrome can be devastating. Actually, retirement had always been functional throughout the world until relatively recently. It was introduced partly through an entitlement system of social welfare by Chancellor von Bismarck in Germany in the 1880s and really became established in the United States during the depression of the 1930s. But now the trend is in the other direction. Sweden is moving its retirement age up to 67. Japan is moving away from 55. The United Kingdom and the Soviet Union also are changing their retirement policies. It's too expensive otherwise, and it's too destructive to people. I have no doubt that the day will come when mandatory retirement will cease.

Interview, Washington/
U.S. News & World Report, 7-12:31.

James B. Cardwell
Commissioner,
Social Security Administration
of the United States
2

We're [the SSA] going to break down. Somebody has to start worrying about it . . . Partly because of the rapid growth and the need to respond on short notice to legislative initiatives, SSA has not always had the opportunity to devise and implement systems and process refinements in a planned, orderly fashion. [As a result,] SSA's processes have become fragmented, and in many ways op-

erationally unwieldy. Our experience shows that our present processes are not always responsive to either the agency's needs or those of the public it is designed to serve.

Before Senate Appropriations subcommittee,
Washington, Feb. 26/
Los Angeles Herald-Examiner, 2-27:(A)1.

Jimmy Carter
Candidate for the 1976 Democratic
Presidential nomination;
Former Governor of Georgia (D)
3

We've got about 12 million people on welfare, permanently. We've got 2 million welfare workers. That's a worker for every six recipients. Good people. But they don't spend their time alleviating affliction or dealing with the aged or helping people get a job that are out of work. They spend their time in offices, bogged down in red tape, shuffling papers, trying to administer about 100 different welfare programs . . . you need to simplify the whole system. Remove from the welfare system those people who can work fulltime. That's about 1.3 million. Put them under the responsibility of the Labor Department, the Education Department; treat them as temporarily unemployed people. The other 90 per cent can't work fulltime; they ought to stay under the welfare system. There ought to be one nation-wide payment to meet the basic necessities of life—varying in amount only to accommodate the cost of living. This varies from one community to another. There ought to be a work-incentive aspect built in, which is absent . . . And cut down the number of programs to no more than one or two. That would eliminate the food-stamp program. Just one basic payment would mean a great deal.

Interview, March 16/
The Washington Post, 3-21:(B)5.

4

We now have developers who want to build homes. We've got construction workers who want to go back to work. We've got families who want to rent or buy homes.

We've got savings-and-loan institutions and others who have money to lend. But last year we only built about a million homes, when the need in this country is 2.5 million and we have a normal construction rate of two million. So something's wrong. And the thing that's wrong is that there's not [a] predictable Federal policy on housing. There are several things that ought to be done. One is to have mortgage guarantees at the Federal and private level. Also, renewed construction for low-cost rent homes. The restoration of the 202 Program, which I thought was very effective in building homes for the elderly. Some interest supplements: I would favor that as a preference to tax credits for the ownership of new homes. And I think that we ought to continue the Section 8 programs which pay part of the rent. At the present time, the last one that I mentioned is the only one that's ongoing. I would orient the housing-and-urban-development funds toward the more-deprived areas, instead of to the suburbs where most of the political influence lies, and assure that the program was predictable. The major hamstring of housing development is the unpredictability of the Federal policies, for that's a four- or five-year proposition for a developer who buys a tract of land to build housing units on it.

Interview/The New York Times, 3-31:20.

1

I think the Federal and state governments ought to share the responsibilities for welfare. The local government shouldn't have to pay any of it. But you would have an enormous additional cost shifted to the Federal government if the welfare system was completely Federalized with no commensurate increase in the quality of services to the people; and, as the welfare costs increase in future years, it might be that the Federal government could pick up the entire increase. But I would not want to merely shift the present welfare responsibility from the states entirely to the Federal government.

Interview/The New York Times, 3-31:20.

Jimmy Carter
1976 Democratic Presidential nominee   *2*

Everything we do, within our churches, our schools and our government, ought to be designed to strengthen the family because, as the family is strengthened, we prevent a weakening of the churches, the schools and the government . . . If we're going to have less government interfering in our lives, what must we strengthen? The family, because the government has to step in when the family fails. Our national government ought to have a strong, understandable, more concerned, deeply committed, close family policy. The present [Ford] Administration doesn't have one, and that's the same thing as having an anti-family policy.

At rally, Manchester, N.H., Aug.3/
Los Angeles Times, 8-4:(1)7.

Robert Coles
Research psychiatrist, Harvard University
Health Services   *3*

In our system, the family is the means by which moral values are inculcated. This built-in authority that we give to families is an integral part of the American social and economic system, and it separates us from much of the rest of the world. That is why some of the radical critics of American society want to undercut the authority of the family and move toward communes, or toward a statist social control of family life. Now, the same thing goes for the family legislation. Are we going to have government social workers with the power to intrude upon family life? In many poor families—who are the most seriously shackled by bureaucratic intrusions—the welfare workers sometimes want to take away the children. They have decided that some families are unsuited to have children. I would be in favor of removing the power of these bureaucrats—get them off the backs of the poor. I certainly wouldn't want to extend their power into the middle class.

Interview, Washington/
U.S. News & World Report, 9-6:61.

WHAT THEY SAID IN 1976

Alex Comfort
Author, Biologist   1

The attitude to aging, an attitude of putting old people out of society as unfit or incapable, is a form of prejudice, and I think it's about to change. Intelligence does not decline with age except in the case of high blood pressure or other illness, and a man who needs a wheelchair needs a wheelchair whether he is 19 or 90.
Interview/The New York Times, 10-1:(C)23.

Daniel J. Evans
Governor of Washington (R)   2

The Federal publications on individual welfare eligibility alone are a yard high and impossible to follow. We don't have a genuine national welfare program. As a consequence, many of the nation's poor who need help don't get it, and many who do get it don't really need it.
At National Governors Conference, Hershey, Pa., July 5/The New York Times, 7-6:15.

Bernard Gifford
Deputy Chancellor, New York City
Public School System   3

New York City has always had a large number of poor children in its school [s]. The difference today is that we now have a large number of *dependent* poor, and that involves a different mindset than just being poor. The difference between poor and dependent poor is the difference between a father who does not make enough to get his income above the poverty level and a situation where the father does not work at all. The dependent poor children come in contact with a welfare system that is dehumanizing, insensitive and denigrating. They come to school profoundly scarred by their out-of-school experiences.
The New York Times, 6-21:34.

Vernon E. Jordan, Jr.
Executive director,
National Urban League   4

FHA mortgage insurance and tax-relief programs have grown to the point where they cost the Treasury more than four times the subsidies for lower-income housing. [These programs] have helped to create a privileged class whose claim on the Federal Treasury is seen as a matter of right. It is politically inconceivable that the government would ever impose a moratorium on such subsidies in the manner that a moratorium on aid to lower-income families was so ruthlessly imposed by the Nixon Administration. This housing welfare program is as sacrosanct as the limited subsidies for low-income housing is vulnerable. Federal mortgage and tax-relief policies encouraged middle-income families to become home-owners and then assisted them to trade up to increasingly more-costly dwellings. Because land and housing values have risen so sharply in recent years, such families have benefited by a windfall rise in their net worth accounting to many billions of dollars . . . The indirect, tax-relief subsidy structure is unfair in that it affects a relatively better-situated economic class, and it is an inflationary factor, distorting market values.
At National Housing Conference, Washington/ The Washington Post, 3-6:(E)25.

5

Cutting across the ideological spectrum and afflicting liberals and conservatives alike, there is a mood I have called "the new minimalism" that preaches less government, less spending, less Federal manpower and less government regulation. Somehow the new minimalists don't include fat Pentagon budgets, or tax expenditures that benefit the well-off, in their calculations. They ignore the fact that less government means less protection for people without resources; less spending means fewer desperately needed social programs and stark hunger for those in poverty; fewer government employees means fewer public services; and less government regulation means abandonment of civil-rights enforcement. Beneath the facade of the new minimalism one can detect an attitude of enmity toward the plight of the poor, the black and the cities in which they live. Beneath the facade of self-styled, hard-nosed, bottom-line-oriented administrators lurks the profound ignorance of the fact that social spending is social investment that pays for itself in the long run. And sometimes in the short run.

Before Los Angeles American Jewish Committee/
The National Observer, 6-19:14.

Kenneth Keniston
Chairman,
Carnegie Council on Children 1

Just try living for a year or so on the poverty-line income, or even the Department of Labor "minimum budget," for a family of four: See what it does not only to the material conditions of your family life, but to your mood, your feeling about yourself, your responsiveness to your children. And watch especially what happens during those crises that inevitably beset most families—parental or child illness, unemployment or job frustration, parental discord. You all know the consequences: Both children and parents suffer. Or try getting good health care when you can't pay for it, try finding decent child care when you can't afford it. And finally, recall that family poverty is a relative concept, related to family need. Ninety-five per cent of American families are "poor" if they have a severely handicapped child who requires special education over a period of years. Only a handful of families have enough savings or insurance to tide them over a year of parental unemployment.

The Washington Post, 2-13:(A)22.

David Mathews
Secretary of Health, Education and Welfare
of the United States 2

I think the present welfare system is problematic not just because of the size of the state bureaucracies, although that certainly is part of the issue, but because of the inconsistencies created by their varying criteria and methods. If we can simplify our programs, then bureaucracies at all levels can do a better job at reduced operating levels. While recognizing the need for national-policy consistency in wel-

fare, we also get indications that there is a correlation between the immediacy of the unit administering a social-service program and its effectiveness. If we are able to use those governmental units close to the people—as are state and local governments—then we have a better chance that the programs will be more effective and more humane.

Interview, Washington/
U.S. News & World Report, 4-12:42.

Daniel P. Moynihan
Professor of government, Harvard University;
Former United States
Ambassador/Permanent Representative
to the United Nations 3

[On whether there are some Americans who are starving]: . . . there are people who have never heard of food stamps and there are people who have never heard of welfare, and there are, no doubt, some of them who are not well-off. But it's a wholly individualized thing, and no citizen who is going off to Queens College has a right to say Americans are starving. It's a lot of crap. They are not starving. What kind of people are we? We do not let people starve in this country.

Interview, New York/
Los Angeles Times, 4-22:(1)7.

Ronald Reagan
Candidate for the 1976
Republican Presidential nomination;
Former Governor of California (R) 4

. . . if someone set out to design a welfare program that wouldn't work, he couldn't do better than food stamps. You probably had that same thought when you were standing in a checkout line with your package of hamburger watching some young fellow ahead of you buy T-bone steak with food stamps.

At campaign fund-raising luncheon,
Fort Walton Beach, Fla./
The Washington Post, 1-28:(A)2.

WHAT THEY SAID IN 1976

Bayard Rustin
President,
A. Philip Randolph Institute

1

I am not jumping on the capitalists; I want that understood. But the Chase Manhattan Bank, or any other bank, cannot put up any money to build housing for poor people. They can't get an adequate return on their money. American charity is no longer able, given the size of the population, to provide hospital care and, therefore, there must be some kind of national hospital and medical insurance for all, in which this class of people do not have to pay. With the price of education being what it is, these people will not be able adequately to educate and train their children. Therefore, it will increasingly become the job of the Federal government to provide free education in schools and universities. The price will be high, but it will be higher in both economic and psychological terms if we do not do it. We are going to have to have an updated Civilian Conservation Corps program of the New Deal days, where we can get these youngsters out of these environments of the ghettos and give them training, with the understanding that a job of some kind will be waiting for them. In the CCC-type of environment it will be possible for them to take on new values and work habits. American capitalism has given the majority of Americans a standard of living undreamed of. Therefore, what the capitalists can do well they should continue to do well. What they cannot provide for this out-class must, therefore, be provided by the government. All I am asking is that government provide steps so people can climb.

Interview, New York/
Los Angeles Times, 8-11:(2)5.

Herbert Stein
Professor of economics, University of Virginia; Former Chairman, Council of Economic Advisers to the President of the United States (Richard M. Nixon)

2

Sixty-five weeks of unemployment compensation is too much. We ought to deal with the problem of people who are really in pover-

ty in a more straightforward way. Unemployment compensation goes in considerable part to people who are not in poverty. We ought to deal directly with the very poor by something like the Nixon Family Assistance Program or the negative income tax, and not create a system which at this time encourages people who are not poor to remain unemployed while they draw their unemployment compensation for 65 weeks.

Interview/
The New York Times Magazine, 10-24:(3)14.

Morris K. Udall
United States Representative, D—Arizona;
Candidate for the 1976
Democratic Presidential nomination

3

[The welfare system] ought to be Federalized: it's a national problem and it's a national obligation . . . there ought to be essentially one national system of benefits with a cost-of-living factor in there. This would not only help the cities but it would tend to keep people in their own regions and homes, near their friends, where opportunities might be better. One of the key causes of urban concentration and urban poverty—city problems—has been the welfare system, which like a magnet drew people off the farms in Appalachia and other areas into the big cities. Largely or in part— or one of the main causes—was the humane level of welfare payments here [in New York], and the outrageous level in states like mine and Alabama and Georgia.

Interview, New York/
The New York Times, 3-29:25.

G. C. Wiegand
Professor emeritus of economics,
Southern Illinois University

4

Nobody objects to helping the truly needy. The strong have always looked after the weak to protect the family and the social order. But there is a fundamental difference between the paternalism of the traditional family, and of a tribal and feudal order on the one hand, and the modern impersonal welfare state on the other. The very word "paternalism," once symbolizing a sense of social responsibility, has acquired meaning. The steadily expanding modern notion of welfare does not imply a willingness of the more fortunate to help the needy, but a so-called "right" of the "poor"—whether truly needy or not—to be supported by society at an ever-rising standard of living—whatever the cost to the community as a whole.

At Columbia University, March 20/
Vital Speeches, 6-15:519.

Transportation

Marvin J. Barloon
Professor emeritus of economics,
Case Western Reserve University
1

Productivity in transportation is of the very essence of all productivity. Efficient movement of freight brings into play the illimitable productivity of regional specialization, provides access to the richest natural resources, however remote, and releases the potentials of mass production by opening the door to continental markets. You may name any great civilization of wealth and culture in history, from Athens to Venice, and from Babylon to Britain, and you will be naming a civilization resting on a base of far-flung commerce and massive movements of freight between specialized and prosperous regions. I know of no exception.

At National Conference on Domestic Shipping,
New Orleans, March 10/.Vital Speeches, 4-15:390.

Birch Bayh
United States Senator, D—Indiana;
Candidate for the 1976
Democratic Presidential nomination
2

[On Transportation Secretary William Coleman's decision to allow the British-French *Concorde* SST to land in the U.S. for a trial period]: I regard this as a very serious mistake. The *Concorde* is wrong economically, wrong environmentally, and wrong in terms of energy. It is a means of transportation available only to a very few rich people. I will push strongly for legislation to overturn the Secretary's decision.

Feb. 4/ The New York Times, 2-5:16.

Bill Benton
General manager,
Ford division, Ford Motor Company
3

Eventually, if government-mandated standards are rammed down the public's throat, forcing more of them into small cars than really want to be . . . yes, if it ever gets that far you will find a rebellion on the part of the American public . . . If a consumer says I need a large car to carry my wife and four or five kids, then he'll also say, by golly, I want to be able to buy that kind of car. That is one of the freedoms in this country of ours. Why should they [the government] dictate to the American car-buying public what size car they buy when they don't dictate what color suit they wear or what size house they buy, or whether they buy a blue bicycle or white bicycle for their kids. The same thing applies in car purchasing. If it gets that far, then the American public will stand up and be heard.

Interview, Dallas/
The Dallas Times Herald, 2-22:(E)5.

Frank Borman
President, Eastern Airlines
4

[On government regulation of airlines]: It's against my nature to seek regulation, but we have to recognize that the airlines are a quasi utility . . . People say we can't stand the competition. Well, that's a superficial answer. You wouldn't consider deregulating the banks, or the utilities. I hope we've gotten past the time of providing simple, black-and-white answers to problems.

Before House subcommittees,
Washington, March/
The New York Times Magazine, 5-9:45.

Alan S. Boyd
Vice chairman,
Illinois Central Gulf Railroad
1

. . . we've got to have a mass-transit system which provides a comparable alternative to the private automobile. It must be an alternative not only in terms of time to get from one place to another, but also in relative comfort. The way mass-transit systems are now, I don't believe that people riding the expressways to and from work are willingly going to get out of their nice, warm automobiles and, instead, stand nose to nose with a bunch of strangers every morning in discomfort. It's going to be costly to change it. But if people are going to change voluntarily, it's got to be done. Energy requirements are going to grow to such a degree that more and more people are going to find they have to go to mass transit. We'd better be sure we've got our existing systems functioning well.
Interview/ U.S. News & World Report, 12-27:56.

Jimmy Carter
Candidate for the 1976
Democratic Presidential nomination;
Former Governor of Georgia (D)
2

In the field of transportation, we have seen a derogation of the quality of our railroads, inadequate attention given to mass transit. We have got too much blocking of streets unnecessarily because of inactivity or weakness on the part of local officials. We are spending enormous amounts of money putting in subways when just off-street parking and one-way streets might solve some of the problems.
TV-radio interview, New York/
"Meet the Press,"
National Broadcasting Company, 7-11.

W. Graham Claytor, Jr.
Chairman, Southern Railway System
3

We [railroads] are a regulated industry. I think we are grossly over-regulated. But we have to be regulated, to an extent. I am not one of those who think you should repeal the Interstate Commerce Act and totally de-

regulate common-carrier transportation. The whole concept of the common carrier is based on regulation. It is certainly regulation that requires you to carry anything that is offered at published rates that are the same for everyone. You eliminate this requirement, and I think you destroy transportation as we know it today . . . The biggest problem we face is to get across to government the thought that, if you want a privately owned and operated transportation system, you have to take drastic action to reduce existing subsidies to competing modes of transportation.
Interview, Washington/
Nation's Business, October:34.

William T. Coleman, Jr.
Secretary of Transportation
of the United States
4

[On his decision to allow the British-French *Concorde* SST to land in the U.S. for a trial period of 16 months]: Those who ask us to pay much more attention to the environment have taught us a valuable lesson. Also, a society might be better off in the long run if we did not always equate progress with doing something faster. Restraint and time for leisure are also high values for a civilized person. But there is so much on both sides of the equation that we do not know and cannot know without observing the *Concorde* in actual commercial operations into the United States, that a firm decision at this time either to admit or to ban the *Concorde* would be irresponsible, a reaction to the flurry of publicity that has preceded its arrival or an attempt to curry favor with one or another constituency. If we would seek the truth about a number of the controversial questions that surround this airplane, we must gain some practical experience.
News conference, Washington, Feb. 4/
The New York Times, 2-5:16.

5

Stated plainly, the present system of airline regulation is fundamentally and inherent-

WHAT THEY SAID IN 1976

(WILLIAM T. COLEMAN, JR.)

ly deficient. The answer is not found in fine-tuning the present statute or in appointing better people. The appropriate answer lies only in allowing the industry to operate in a naturally competitive fashion . . . The airlines have recruited a veritable army of artisans—painters, musicians, film-makers, chefs, beauticians, clothing designers and athletes—to help attract our patronage with various amenities, [when a consumer might instead choose if given the option] a less-costly flight.

Before Senate Commerce Aviation Subcommittee,
Washington, April 7/
The Washington Post, 4-8:(E)11.

J. R. Coupal, Jr.
Deputy Administrator,
Federal Highway Administration
1

I . . . hear on every side around Washington that the automobile is the villain that has caused air pollution, urban congestion, kills and maims people indiscriminately and causes intolerable community disruption. It is also charged that it doesn't pay its own way—and then the critics hurry to say not "economically," but in "social costs." Therefore, say the critics, the solution to all of these problems is to get rid of the automobile. This is a lot of hogwash. We at the FHWA think that the private automobile is one of the most obvious proofs of American technology and productivity, and we are going to work night and day to see to it that no American loses the right to use a car. Sure the automobile has caused problems: urban congestion, pollution and waste of finite resources. But we recognize these problems and we are working to overcome them. The FHWA is developing ways of getting people into the downtown area of cities, and is supporting research and development of new sources of energy and more energy-efficient vehicles. The automobile has provided mankind with the greatest mobility he has ever known and he is not

going to give it up—and he need not give it up. Instead, we are going to solve its problems.

Before Georgia Highway Contractors'
Association, Boca Raton, Fla./
The National Observer, 3-6:11.

Gerald R. Ford
President of the United States
2

[Upon signing a bill to reorganize and reform regulation of the nation's railroads]: An equally important task facing us now is to extend the principles of reform embodied in this legislation to the aviation and motor-carrier industries. In these industries, we must strive to create a regulatory climate which relies on competitive forces, rather than on inflexible and bureaucratic directives of Federal agencies, to determine which firm will provide the desired transportation services and at what price.

Washington, Feb. 5/
The Dallas Times Herald, 2-6:(B)6.

Henry Ford II
Chairman, Ford Motor Company
3

It is important to notice . . . that better fuel economy is not free. To get better fuel economy, the consumer has to give up some combination of [automobile] roominess, comfort, convenience, performance, safety or money. Since the [Arab] oil embargo [of 1973], consumers have shown increased interest in fuel economy, but few of them are interested in fuel economy at any price. The most popular cars today are not the smallest and most fuel-efficient, but the compacts and intermediates. I believe that most people will pay a lot more . . . for the comfortable, convenient and flexible mobility the automobile provides. For the proof of that proposition, we need only look at the rest of the world, where gasoline generally costs two or more times its United States price— and the auto industry is growing faster than it is here.

Dearborn, Mich./
The New York Times, 8-1:(3)12.

Barry M. Goldwater
United States Senator, R—Arizona
1

[On criticism of the British-French *Concorde* SST as posing dangers to the environment]: In all of my experience, I have never known of so much misinformation being put out on any one subject as on the supersonic transport plane. These threats are so ill-founded and unsupported by facts that the Europeans could justly interpret a decision against *Concorde* [being allowed to land at U.S. airports] as being based upon nothing more than economic protectionism meant to isolate our airlines from foreign competition in our own market.

> *At Federal hearing on the "Concorde,"*
> *Washington, Jan. 5/*
> *The New York Times, 1-6:40.*

Gerald Kaufman
Minister of State, Department of Industry of the United Kingdom
2

[On the British-French *Concorde* SST]: Environmental issues such as the possible impact of noise on the community, such as the possibility of significant ozone depletion, if they are recognized as matters of serious concern, must be weighed against other considerations: the benefits of *Concorde* service; the benefits to be gained in the long term from the utilization of new and promising technologies; the value of cooperation among nations; and the importance of equity among friendly peoples.

> *At hearing on whether the "Concorde"*
> *be allowed into the U.S., Washington, Jan. 5/*
> *The Christian Science Monitor, 1-6:9.*

Charles D. Kirkpatrick
Vice president for marketing, Greyhound Bus Lines
3

Amtrak has been a massive money-loser since its inception and I'm very sorry to see the state of California and its taxpayers being misled by slick publicity and by uninformed but well-intentioned public officials . . . Now, let's take a quick look at this year's Los Angeles-to-San Diego operation. By the end of the fiscal year, revenues on that route will total about $1.8-million. Expenses over that same period of time will total a staggering $6.3-million. That's a $4.5-million deficit. That's more money than the James and Dalton gangs ever stole in their collective lives as train robbers. Although Amtrak has not made the "Ten Most Wanted List," by the end of this year Amtrak is going to cost the American taxpayer more than a million dollars a day. To me, that's the greatest American train robbery, and no one, least of all the Federal government, seems to want to put an end to it.

> *News conference, Pasadena, Calif., Dec. 8/*
> *Los Angeles Times, 12-9:(1)30.*

William M. Magruder
Vice president, Piedmont Airlines; Former Director, Office of Supersonic Transport Development, Department of Transportation of the United States
4

When [Congress] canceled the SST program [several years ago], the costs to cancel were estimated to exceed the costs to go ahead and finish the experiment. In the end, the taxpayers paid $1.4-billion for the privilege of fiddling with this thing for ten years, and then quitting. We don't know if our plane would have been better or worse than the [British-French] *Concorde*. We never really got a chance to find out. But if it had been successful, and the theories correct, we would have had an airplane that carried 300 people compared to the *Concorde's* 120, at half the noise and at 1,800 m.p.h. compared to the *Concorde's* 1,450. Opponents of the SST program always said that if our airplane was shot down, the *Concorde* program would go down the next day. But here we are four years later, and the *Concorde* is flying commercial service, and about to fly into New York and Washington.

> *Los Angeles Times, 3-26:(7)4.*

James A. McClure
United States Senator, R—Idaho
5

The single largest use of petroleum supplies in the United States is in the field of

WHAT THEY SAID IN 1976

(JAMES A. McCLURE)

transportation, for gasoline- and diesel-powered motor vehicles. Yet, electric vehicles do not emit any significant pollutants·or noise. In the congested, noisy cities of today, such a vehicle is of unquestionable value . . . I believe the average citizen has no idea what already is and what could be available in the electric-car field. If he knew, he would be significantly more interested in trying one out. Once that demand begins, market forces will take over, and you and I will not be stuck having to make embarrassing explanations to our grandchildren about why we burn such valuable and useful substances as oil and natural gas liquids, in the face of excellent alternatives.

At International Electric Vehicle Symposium,
*Dusseldorf, West Germany/***

John L. McLucas
Administrator,
Federal Aviation Administration
1

We probably have the technical ability to make flight completely automatic from take-off to landing, with the pilot just riding along to monitor the machines. But do we really want to do this? How can we expect a person who never does the job to take over from the machine on the rare occasion when the machine breaks down? And what about the social consequences of driving the pilot to the point where he feels he is just an appendage to a machine? I don't know. But I do know these considerations require serious thought and evaluation.

Before Institute of Electronic and Electrical
Engineers/ The National Observer, 8-14:11.

Gerald C. Meyers
Executive vice president,
American Motors Corporation
2

Don't sell the small car short. [The] more people-efficient car is still the market of the future . . . [Today there is] the new-value automobile consumer, who demands econ-

omy, utility and basic good looks, which are replacing the old values of excess, prestige and grandeur.

Before Adcraft Club, Detroit, Feb. 27/
The New York Times, 2-28:37.

Gaylord Nelson
United States Senator, D—Wisconsin
3

[Criticizing Transportation Secretary William Coleman's decision to permit the British-French *Concorde* SST to land in the U.S. on a trial basis despite warnings that the plane would deplete the atmosphere's ozone layer]: Secretary Coleman appears to require dead bodies piled in the streets before he admits we have an ozone problem. Unfortunately, this situation does not lend itself to black and white solutions. If the Secretary needs bodies before he acts, he will have to use the bodies of the next generation.

Before the Senate, Washington/
The Dallas Times Herald, 2-22:(A)24.

Edward W. Pattison
United States Representative,
D—New York
4

[On government regulation of business, such as of air transportation]: The notion that regulation can be done away with holds up until just the time when you get on that airplane and you find out they've contracted out the piloting to the ABC Cheapo Corporation. They've got a bunch of guys up there with floppy hats and long beards saying, "Man, we'll fly the wings right off this crate." Then everybody says, "Hold on. Regulation's okay in that area."

The New York Times, 4-27:42.

Paul H. Reistrup
President, Amtrak
5

There is no more-efficient means for handling volumes of passengers than . . . a railroad. On Easter weekend, we can handle 1,000 people a train every 30 minutes between

Washington and New York. There's just no other way to do that.

Interview/
The Christian Science Monitor, 9-9:14.

John E. Robson
Chairman, Civil Aeronautics Board
of the United States
1

I think it's important that the Congress—which put this agency [the CAB] into the business, which created the regulatory framework we now operate under—be a participant in changing that mandate. If they agree that regulatory policy ought to go in the direction of more competition, I think it is important that they recognize that the welfare of each individual carrier [airline] can't be the first priority under such a system, and that there are the possibilities of winners and losers in a more competitive environment.

Interview/ The Washington Post, 5-16:(F)8.

2

There is the experience of hundreds of businesses in this country that competition will produce the most efficient system. There is the favorable experience of the intrastate air markets like Texas and California, where the CAB doesn't regulate; and lower fares have had a tremendous stimulative effect on traffic. Also, our experience with commuter airlines and charter operators who are functioning well under less regulation. None of these are perfect laboratories, but they lend support to our view that more competition would lower costs and hold prices down.

Interview/ The National Observer, 7-17:7.

William T. Seawell
Chairman,
Pan American World Airways
3

[Calling for an "assistant secretariat" for aviation in the State Department to help U.S. airlines compete with foreign carriers]: Traditional United States policies of free enterprise and competition appropriate to the United States' domestic environment are not applicable in the international arena where competition is extreme and our competitors operate in an international system of pools and cartels, which support, almost everywhere, airlines that are either government-owned, government-supported or government subsidized.

Before House Aviation subcommittee,
Washington, May 26/
The New York Times, 5-27:60.

Milton J. Shapp
Governor of Pennsylvania (D);
Candidate for the 1976
Democratic Presidential nomination
4

We have the worst railroad system in the world, and yet we are the most industrialized nation. There is no reason for that. For $13-billion we can put 300,000 people to work laying down new track, electrifying the main lines so we can have greater efficiency and use less oil; we can revamp all the classification yards and signaling equipment. Most of these 300,000 jobs are going to be with the steel companies manufacturing electrical equipment, and so the program over a six-year period would stimulate the economy. But it is not spending; it is an investment, and it will be paid back to the Treasury of the United States in two ways: One, through the added taxes that are collected from the working people, and also the savings in welfare and unemployment compensation—it would benefit there. And secondly, you could have a small surcharge on each freight bill for a period of time, just like we have on the interstate highway program, where we have a small gas tax and a tax on accessories, that has more than paid for all interstate highways that have been constructed. If you could put this program into effect, it would pay for itself, just like any other investment, and we would have a modern railroad system.

TV-radio interview, Des Moines, Iowa/
"Meet the Press,"
National Broadcasting Company, 1-11.

Robert F. Six
Chairman, Continental Airlines
1

I feel [the airline industry is] vastly over-regulated, and the cost of over-regulation is high. For example, look at the current government requirements for reducing the noise of airplanes. It so happens that Continental is not affected, because our entire fleet meets the requirements. But if all the carriers that do not meet the requirements are forced to re-equip their planes, it will cost a couple of billion dollars. And the public will not know the difference, because the reduction in noise will not be that great. Since all the planes coming off the lines today meet these requirements, why shouldn't the government allow the airlines to go through a phaseout program? This kind of government over-regulation is hurting the consumer by forcing the airlines to raise fares . . . [But] the government sets the route schedule, and that is good. If the government did not, you would always have some bright entrepreneur coming along and picking out the profitable routes and ignoring the others. There must be a balance. People must be treated equitably.

Interview, Los Angeles/
Nation's Business, September:46.

Alexei Tupolev
Aircraft designer
2

Frankly, there *is* some truth to our critics' arguments [against the SST]. The supersonic requires a more powerful engine, which makes it somewhat noisier than subsonic jets; and there is an effect on the ozone layer, though this also, to some degree, is true of the subsonics. So what do we do about it? In our desire not to harm the environment do we, as some critics suggest, abandon the supersonic? I don't think so. Look, in order to preserve nature, we do not need to stop technological progress. We do not need to give up our machines and go back to being cavemen, or climb trees to pluck bananas; or better yet, in order not to disturb the trees, wait until the bananas fall. No, the way we have to cope with this is to improve our machines. And in

the case of the supersonic, the answer lies in improving the engine design. I am sure we can do it. But, to work out all the so-called "bugs," it will take time and a little patience—hopefully, on the part of our critics, too—because in this field there is simply no way of coming up·with a finished product overnight.

Interview, Domodedovo Airport, U.S.S.R./
Parade, 3-21:26.

Morris K. Udall
United States Representative, D—Arizona;
Candidate for the 1976
Democratic Presidential nomination
3

[On the British-French *Concorde* SST]: It's a turkey, and it should never land here. It's an energy disaster. It's an economic disaster. It's a disaster for people around airports . . . It's interesting to note that we made a decision in '71 about the U.S. SST and there were those who tried very hard to have it built through a large Federal subsidy. That vote was very, very close; and, if the proponents of the SST had had their way, we would probably be landing large numbers of American SSTs right now. I think it's wrong.

Interview, New York/
The New York Times, 3-29:25.

Hays T. Watkins, Jr.
Chairman and president, Chessie System
4

For over a half-century, for roughly as long a period of time as that between the Declaration of Independence and the laying of the First Stone of the B&O, America's railroads operated without Federal regulation. In that time, the strap-iron rails that had first been laid at the door of what is now the B&O Railroad Museum in Baltimore had blossomed into a web of steel, binding together a great nation. And then, as you know, in 1887 there was enacted the Interstate Commerce Act. It established the Interstate Commerce Commission, the first of all the Federal regulatory agencies. Now, government regulation is something we in transportation have learned to live with. It is a fact of life. We do not expect it to end. But what is disturbing to me is the steady *increase* I see taking place in government participation in our business and private lives . . . The railroads must be released from outmoded regulatory shackles if they are to prosper and provide the type of service this nation's shippers have a right to expect. We of the transportation industry have more than burgeoning regulation with which to contend. Actual government *participation* has cast its shadow over the roundhouse door.

Before Traffic Club of Chicago, May 20/
Vital Speeches, 7-1:555,556.

Thornton A. Wilson
Chairman, Boeing Company
1

It has been said the jet transport shrank the world by 40 per cent. Actually, jet travel has enlarged each individual's world by making more places accessible to him. Until recent times most of us relied upon explorers, missionaries, military personnel or news-media representatives to make the unfamiliar portions of our world more familiar. Air travel now provides the means for all of us to participate directly in this process. In effect, what Marco Polo did in 1272 A.D., thousands now do daily. Before the end of this century the number will increase to millions . . . Air transportation is providing significant benefits daily to travelers and non-travelers alike. One only has to sit down to breakfast, order fresh papaya flown in from Hawaii, and pick up the morning newspaper to find out where [U.S. Secretary of State] Henry Kissinger is—to realize the impact of air transportation. The point I'm trying to make is that air travel is not just for Henry Kissinger, but for Henry Smith, Henry Jones—even Henry Ford.

Before Economic Club of Detroit, Sept. 27/
Vital Speeches, 10-15:27,28.

Lester L. Wolff
United States Representative,
D—New York
2

[Criticizing the government's recent approval of the British-French *Concorde* SST to land in the U.S. for a 16-month trial period]: We are united in a common concern—the desire to stop hundreds of thousands of American men, women and children from being used as test subjects to mollify the British and French governments. I hope we can persuade the court that there is little legal, and even less moral, excuse for allowing our citizens to serve as involuntary sounding boards—perhaps "victims" would be better—for *Concorde*.

News conference, Washington, Feb. 11/
Los Angeles Herald-Examiner, 2-12:(A)11.

Urban Affairs

Abraham D. Beame
Mayor of New York
                                    1

We [the City of New York] confront an economic paradox: When we lay off workers, our welfare and social costs increase. When we raise taxes, we drive corporate and individual taxpayers from our borders. When we cut programs and reduce services, we jeopardize the quality of life in our city. If we borrow to pay for current needs, we mortgage our future. If we increase the subway fare, the responsive Consumer Price Index tightens its inflationary grip. If we abandon and defer capital projects, we kill both jobs and hopes. If we fail our museums and cultural institutions, we dim the light that regenerates the spirit and attracts visitors from around the corner and around the world. It's obvious, very obvious, that the city cannot solve its problems alone. In this [national] election year, the stage is set for a great drama—the struggle for the future of our cities. Our cities cannot be the forgotten repository of national social problems.

State of the City address, New York, Jan. 22/
The New York Times, 1-23:39.

Tom Bradley
Mayor of Los Angeles
                                    2

The Mayors of our cities, playing the role of domestic statesmen, are on the front line. We face the legitimate demands for clean sidewalks, for streets where people can walk without fear, for schools, for jobs where men and women can earn decent wages, and for a climate of progress that attracts rather than repels investments. There is something wrong when our vital requests are answered by White House vetoes . . . The Federal government seems to understand inflation *only* when it comes to the defense budget. If the Federal government can keep pace with inflation for the Defense Department, then it can keep pace with inflation for the cities of America. If the Federal government can maintain the U.S. commitment to foreign defense budgets, then it can maintain a national commitment to social progress in our cities. If the Federal government can listen to the pleas of foreign heads of state and to our own Generals and Admirals, then it can listen to the pleas of its Mayors and citizens. We are making a grave error if we continue to allow our cities and towns to suffocate or stagnate while trying to cover all our bets in the international game of economic roulette.

At "Pacem in Terris" convocation,
Washington, December ('75)/
Center Report, February:10.

Erskine Caldwell
Author
                                    3

I don't know that there's been any change in this country [in the past 40 years] other than the movement from the country to the city. The big exodus, that's the difference. In Europe, peasants stayed where they were. Here, they moved to the city. Now they're no better off in the city than they were in the country and probably worse off. Urban living, I think, is an anti-civilized thing. You put people in the slums of the city and lock them up in those high-rises and complexes with no outlet whatsoever for their lives. There are bound to be problems.

Interview, Dunedin, Fla./
The Washington Post, 1-29:(G)15.

274

Jimmy Carter
Candidate for the 1976
Democratic Presidential nomination;
Former Governor of Georgia (D)   1

There needs to be . . . a fair delineation of a national policy on urban problems, so there's some predictability of what they're sharing, what future responsibility—fiscally and otherwise—among the city, among the local, state and Federal levels of government. That relationship—which formerly comprised our system of Federalism—has now been almost completely destroyed. Because of the highly regressive nature of local government income, based primarily on sales taxes and property taxes, they grow very slowly. And I think they are already too heavily overloaded.
Interview/ The New York Times, 3-31:20.

2

The Mayors are very demanding. I don't blame you for it, and I'll accept your demands as President, if I'm elected. But I also intend to be demanding from you. As I struggle to reorganize the Federal government, I'll expect you to struggle to reorganize your own governments, to root out inefficiency and waste, to deal with administrative problems in a courageous and effective way, to try to deal at first hand with the social problems—transportation, pollution, recreation, law enforcement. And to the extent that I'm convinced that you're doing the best you can, I'll be there as a solid partner on which you can always depend . . . For eight years, our cities and their people and their elected officials have too often been viewed by the White House as adversaries and quite often used as political whipping boys. Too often, our highest Federal officials have tried to score political points by pitting the suburbs and the rural areas against the cities . . . I pledge to you an open urban policy based on a new bipartisan coalition—recognizing that the President, Governors and Mayors represent exactly the same urban constituency.
At United States Conference of Mayors,
Milwaukee, June 29/
Los Angeles Times, 6-30:(1)13.

Jimmy Carter
1976 Democratic Presidential nominee   3

. . . this [Ford] Administration has no urban policy. It's impossible for Mayors or Governors to cooperate with the President, because they can't anticipate what's going to happen next. A Mayor of a city like New York, for instance, needs to know 18 months or two years ahead of time what responsibilities the city will have in administration and in financing things like housing, pollution control, crime control, education, welfare and health. This has not been done, unfortunately. I remember the headline in the [New York] *Daily News* that said, "Ford to New York: Drop Dead." I think it's very important that our cities know that they have a partner in the Federal government.
Debate with President Ford, Williamsburg, Va.,
Oct. 22/ Los Angeles Times, 10-23:(1)24.

William T. Coleman, Jr.
Secretary of Transportation of the
United States   4

The city that is not accessible cannot serve its people. The city that lacks mobility is a poor host, a harsh landlord.
U.S. News & World Report, 8-16:48.

Pierre de Vise
Professor of urban sciences,
University of Illinois, Chicago   5

We no longer need very large cities. We developed these behemoths like New York, Chicago and Philadelphia on the basis of late 19th-century transportation and technology. The railroad, for instance, was important not only in the development of the large cities but also in the concentration of industry near the downtown. After supplies got to the railroad terminal, it was literally a matter of using horses and carts to get them to the industries that needed them. This kind of central location is no longer justified for most industries. They're better off in the suburbs because of the need for more land, more floor space, and off-street parking for employees. Also, business organization itself

(PIERRE de VISE)

has changed. Today, the large holding companies that used to operate giant factories in the central city operate out of many small, dispersed plants. I really see little in the cards that will make the city attractive to industry.

Interview/ U.S. News & World Report, 4-5:54.

Gerald R. Ford
President of the United States
1

[Saying revenue-sharing must be renewed this year]: Congress did not share my sense of urgency. It is becoming increasingly apparent that the Congress fails to understand the importance of this program to the people of the cities and counties and states of our nation. Failure to renew this program would weaken the fiscal stability of our cities. You know that expiration of this program, or a reduction in the payments you now receive, would mean cutbacks in essential services, increased public and related private-sector unemployment, or the imposition of more taxes. Maybe this is what some partisans want. But I don't.

At legislative conference of U.S. Conference of Mayors and National League of Cities, Washington, March 15/ The Dallas Times Herald, 3-15:(A)8.

2

If cities in the future are not able to pull themselves up as New York is doing, then, of course, they will have to go into bankruptcy just like a business or an individual does . . . We hope we can avoid it and we will do our utmost to work with cities . . . But until they do something to straighten out their own mess, I don't think the Federal government should move in.

Broadcast interview, Dallas/ The Washington Post, 4-18:(A)11.

3

The Ford Administration does have a very

comprehensive program to help the urban areas. I fought for, and the Congress finally went along with, a general revenue-sharing program whereby cities and states—the cities two-thirds and the states one-third—get over $6-billion a year in cash, through which they can provide many services, whatever they really want. In addition, we in the Federal government make available to cities about $3-billion, 300-million in what we call community development. In addition, as a result of my pressure on the Congress, we got a major mass-transit program over a four-year period, $11.8-billion. We have a good housing program that will result in cutting the down payments by 50 per cent and having mortgage payments lower at the beginning of any mortgage period. We're expanding our homestead housing program. The net result is . . . we will really do a first-class job in helping the communities throughout the country.

Debate with Democratic Presidential nominee Jimmy Carter, Williamsburg, Va., Oct. 22/ Los Angeles Times, 10-23:(1)24.

Kenneth A. Gibson
Mayor of Newark, New Jersey
4

We destroyed the cities of Western Europe in World War II and then rebuilt them. It didn't take so long. But we had the Marshall Plan to bring it about. That is the kind of effort we need now for the rebuilding of our own cities. It would not take so long, once we decided it could be done . . . cities are the vital organs of the country—the heart and lungs. If the heart stops, the body dies. Bear in mind that as long as the cities go on deteriorating it will cost more money to deliver the services and protections they provide. Like an old, run-down car leaking oil, a city government doesn't run efficiently if it is deteriorating. This is a good reason for a repair job.

Interview, Washington/ Los Angeles Times, 12-14:(2)7.

Charles M. Haar
Professor of law, Harvard University;
Former Assistant Secretary, Department of
Housing and Urban Development
of the United States
1

The crisis that many cities face—particularly the older cities of the Northeast and Midwest—goes far beyond the problem of inadequate housing. Jobs and the state of the economy are prime considerations. Personal security is also crucial. There's the issue of mounting municipal debt, which makes it more difficult for cities to maintain services at the quality that citizens and businesses expect. One solution might be a bank for cities, which would enable local governments to obtain funds other than through selling tax-exempt bonds. Patterned after the World Bank, this new institution could restructure the arrangements for financing their activities and services. Local lenders and community organizers should also be encouraged to expand their programs for rehabilitating city neighborhoods. There are also natural demographic forces at work that might signal a revival of the cities, such as the two-career family which often gravitates to the central city, or the increased proportions of singles and aged in the population. But all this depends on rethinking of our national housing programs and on the effort and commitment of the new leadership so sorely needed in this area.
Interview/ U.S. News & World Report, 12-27:58.

Helen Hayes
Actress
2

The saddest thing in America today is the decline of the cities. The American city was, and I trust once again will be, one of man's most exciting creations. There was nothing more exciting and wondrous than the American city when I was growing up. I loved to visit them—many of them—when I was at the peak of my life and touring around. I don't know what will bring them back, but I just pray that we will find in our American in-

genuity a way of getting them into shape and supporting them properly.
Interview/ U.S. News & World Report, 9-13:61.

Carla A. Hills
Secretary of Housing and Urban
Development of the United States
3

Too many Americans have abandoned the cities to their problems. Rather than attack deteriorating neighborhoods, increasing crime, segregated education and jobless minorities with our votes, our tax dollars and with all the creativity and energy that we could muster, we have too often cursed the ineptitude of our cities' leaders from the sanctity of our suburbs. As individuals, we must take ourselves back to the fight to rehabilitate the structures, the government and the schools of the cities. As government officials, we must acknowledge that it took our cities a long time to reach their present state of affairs, and it will take a long time and great ingenuity to turn the trend—but turn it can. Our adversity carries with it the opportunity to restore the urban centers to their key economic, historic and cultural place.
At U.S. conference of Mayors, Milwaukee,
June 30/ The Washington Post, 7-13:(A)18.

Gerald D. Hines
Real-estate and building developer
4

[On his desire for quality and character in the buildings he develops]: You know, the vehicle to improve the American city is the American corporation—that's where the money is. Corporations are today's equivalent of the Medici, or they can be. I think I understand corporate executives because they are basically pragmatists, and what we've tried to do is create a way in which they can make some sort of real contribution to the quality of the city and yet not get sued by their stockholders.
The New York Times Magazine, 11-14:88.

Hubert H. Humphrey
United States Senator, D—Minnesota
5

No person can occupy the power of the Presidency of the United States without being knowledgeable about, and dedicated to, the

WHAT THEY SAID IN 1976

(HUBERT H. HUMPHREY)

well-being of the American cities. That's where we start. To govern America, you have to know how to govern a city; and to have cities that are ungovernable, is to have an America that is ungovernable.

*At National Conference
of Democratic Mayors, New York/
The Dallas Times Herald, 4-2:(A)11.*

Jesse L. Jackson
*Civil-rights leader;
President, Operation PUSH
(People United to Save Humanity)* 1

We blacks have populated the cities; we must now learn to run them. The need is urgent. The ethical collapse, the heroin epidemic, the large numbers of our people who are out of work and on welfare, and the disruptive violence in the schools all indicate that the cities may be destroying us.

*San Francisco Examiner & Chronicle, 6-27:
(This World)2.*

Thomas J. Kutznick
*President, Aetna Life Insurance Company's
Urban Investment and
Development Corporation* 2

The suburban population trend has slowed and the problems of the suburbs are beginning to reflect the problems of the cities. For future development, it is quite possible that cities are the best place for major building projects. The infrastructure is there—transportation, utilities, sewage and so on. The environmental problem is no more complex than elsewhere. The zoning is there. And, most important, the market is there.

The New York Times, 4-11:(3)1.

Moon Landrieu
Mayor of New Orleans 3

Most cities are locked into their corporate limits. They have very little room to grow. Consequently most of the growth takes place in the suburbs. As the most mobile people—the white, Middle American, newly married—go to the suburbs, they leave the city increas-

ingly occupied by the poor, the elderly, the minorities. Because cities can't touch the suburbs, they tax anything that moves inside their borders.

Interview/People, 11-8:81.

Charles McC. Mathias, Jr.
United States Senator, R—Maryland 4

America is an urban nation. Our rural days are far behind us. At last census, close to three-quarters of all Americans live in cities. What better national goal could we set for ourselves than the total revitalization of our cities? How better could we improve the quality of life for all the people of this nation than by transforming our decaying cities into vibrant, wholesome, safe and humane environments where the human spirit can prosper.

*Nashville, Tenn., May 21/
The Washington Post, 5-27:(A)26.*

Morris K. Udall
*United States Representative, D—Arizona;
Candidate for the 1976
Democratic Presidential nomination* 5

I'm prepared to take from 10 per cent to 15 per cent of the defense budget and put it in the city programs. Until we confront that and make that hard decision, you're really not talking about the problems of the city. You're fooling yourself. You can't do both.

*At forum on urban affairs, New York/
Los Angeles Times, 4-4:(1)14.*

6

We have got to save our cities, and we have to do whatever has to be done. New York is just the first. Detroit and Newark and Atlanta and St. Louis are going to be next ... We have had a whole range of Federal programs—everything from taxes to transportation to the highway programs. Nearly every program we have had has discriminated against cities. I want to give them a fair shake in the '70s and '80s, because America is going down if we don't save the cities.

*TV-radio interview, Washington/
"Meet the Press,"
National Broadcasting Company,4-4.*

PART TWO

International Affairs

Alphonzo Bell
United States Representative,
R—California

1

[On the Angolan civil war]: Nobody in his right mind is advocating that we send American troops into Angola. But there is a big area between sending troops and just turning your back on the problem. For example, there is aid that we can send to neighboring countries, such as Zaire and Zambia, which they could use to support the people who are fighting the pro-Russian forces in Angola. It's a matter of our rolling the spitballs and letting somebody else throw them. What's wrong with that? The Soviet Union does it all the time.

Interview/
U.S. News & World Report, 2-23:35.

Leonid I. Brezhnev
General Secretary,
Communist Party of the Soviet Union

2

[On the recent Angolan civil war]: Barely constituted, this progressive state became an object of a foreign intervention—the handiwork of imperialism and the South African racists, the mortal enemies of independent Africa, and also of those who undertook the unseemly role of their henchmen. This was why Angola's struggle for independence was supported by the world's progressive forces, and its success [the victory of the Soviet-backed faction] testified once again that nothing can crush the people's aspirations to freedom.

At Soviet Communist Party Congress, Moscow,
Feb. 24/ The New York Times, 2-25:14.

Gatsha Buthelezi
Political leader of
South Africa's Zulu people

3

[Arguing against self-governing "homelands" for black South Africans]: South Africa is one country. It has one destiny. Those who are attempting to divide the land of our birth are attempting to stem the tide of history. The majority of black people do not want to abandon their birthright. They have toiled for generations to create the wealth of South Africa. They intend to participate in the wealth of the land . . . We cannot wait for [Prime Minister John] Vorster's government to do something about black decision-making at the national level. We must therefore act unilaterally in defining South Africa's policies. It is the policies we blacks define that will be heard and heeded by our brothers in Africa, as well as in many other quarters of the world.

Soweto, South Africa, March 14/
The Christian Science Monitor, 3-15:5.

4

I believe that now the whites can see the writing on the wall, and that surely they can now realize that [South Africa] must move toward [black] majority rule. It is this single principle that is central to any question concerning southern Africa's politics. This is the burning question in Namibia [South-West Africa]. This is the burning question in Zimbabwe [Rhodesia], as much as it has been the burning question in Mozambique and Angola. Before other countries became independent, it was the burning question in every other African state. We blacks are concerned first and foremost with liberation. We want

(GATSHA BUTHELEZI)

to be free from oppression. We want to be free from the stigma of being unworthy of full citizenship or of being worthy of only fourth-class citizenship and unworthy of having a real vote in the country of our birth. We want to be free to be equal to all other men. We want to be free to participate in majority decisions about the future of our country and our common destiny with other South Africans. The white minority has foisted on us political circumstances which make a mockery of our dignity and our responsibility.

Soweto, South Africa/
Los Angeles Times, 5-2:(8)1.

James Callaghan
Foreign Secretary
of the United Kingdom
1

[Rhodesian Prime Minister Ian] Smith is his own man and he will go his own way, but whether to heaven or perdition I am still not quite sure. If Mr. Smith would accept the principle of [black] majority rule, the position of the Europeans in Rhodesia would be much better safeguarded than by anything else that could be done.

Before House of Commons, London, March 2/
The New York Times, 3-3:5.

Burgess Carr
Secretary General,
All-African Council of Churches
2

Africans have not found a way to change governments except through a coup d'etat. It is unique that in 20 years you can't point to a single leader who has been replaced as head of government by the electoral process.

U.S. News & World Report, 11-8:39.

Jimmy Carter
Candidate for the 1976
Democratic U.S. Presidential nomination;
Former Governor of Georgia (D)
3

I personally favor majority rule [in Africa]. I would do everything I could to let, for in-

stance, Great Britain, who still claims dominion over the Rhodesian area, play a major role in outside influence. I see no reason for us to play a pre-eminent role. I would do everything I could to encourage this change toward majority rule with peace, and let our posture be maintained through open expressions of our concern and through . . . legitimate use of economic and political pressure. So, ultimately, majority rule, acquired as early as possible, minimum of conflict or bloodshed, and using our influence through peaceful means and letting other nations who have a more direct relationship play the pre-eminent role.

Before Foreign Policy Association, New York,
June 23/ The New York Times, 6-24:22.

Fidel Castro
Premier of Cuba
4

Cuban military units and arms will remain in Angola to help the Angola republic in case of foreign aggression. They will stay as long as necessary until the Angolan armed forces are organized, equipped and trained; for the time they need us to turn back any invasion; until when they don't need our military assistance.

Radio broadcast, Pinar del Rio, Cuba, July 26/
Los Angeles Herald-Examiner, 7-27:(A)5.

Winston S. Churchill II
Member of British Parliament
5

[On Soviet activism in Africa]: I feel that what is at risk with the challenge they are putting to us is Africa, and that is a very difficult challenge to meet because, if we don't meet it, the Soviets win, and if we meet it in a clumsy way we will allow ourselves to be identified only with the white minority in southern Africa. In that context I don't think liberal and left-wing sentiment on either side of the Atlantic would permit a level of aid to southern Africa equal to what the Soviet Union will put in on the other side. I think we must have to be clear that the path of resistance, if the

West has the will to meet this challenge, must be on a wholly non-racial basis.

Interview, London/
Los Angeles Times, 3-21:(1)9.

Dick Clark
United States Senator, D—Iowa
1

My view is that, when the [U.S.] Senate acted in December [1975] to deny further aid to Angola [in that country's civil war], it would have made no significant difference to the course of the conflict in Angola if we had approved another $9-million—or even 28 million, which Secretary [of State Henry] Kissinger really wanted. By then it was quite impossible for us to offset 6,000 Cuban troops, $200-million in Soviet equipment and 400 Russian advisers with such funds. It would have been like spitting in the ocean. So in mid-December we found ourselves with two alternatives: either get out—or get much, much, much more deeply involved. A decision to get involved effectively would have required not just more money, but troops and advisers. Or it would have required much closer collaboration on our part with South Africa . . . I think that not even the Secretary of State would have felt that the public in this country would support the commitment of American troops and advisers to Angola . . . Our handling of the Angola problem has been wrong since the moment it became apparent that the Soviets were intervening last March or April. We should have made a direct approach to the Russians then, to try by diplomatic means to prevent the situation from getting out of hand.

Interview/ U.S. News & World Report, 2-23:35.

2

[Criticizing apartheid and the way blacks are treated in South Africa]: You might well ask why an American has any right to look critically at your society. Why is it any of our business how you conduct your affairs? It is not up to America, on another hemisphere, to dictate to you. But the nature of your society has to do with whether we are to be close

friends or bitter enemies, or something in between . . . The vast majority of Americans will not relate favorably to the continuation and promotion of such a [discriminatory] system. You must remember we subscribe to the idea of equality of opportunity for all Americans, regardless of race, creed or color. We have not always lived up to our ideals, but they remain our ideals and goals and we are moving toward their fulfillment.

News conference, Johannesburg, Dec.7/
Los Angeles Times, 12-8:(1)4.

Charles C. Diggs, Jr.
United States Representative,
D— Michigan
3

[Critcizing U.S. aid to the pro-West factions in the Angolan civil war]: The error of allowing U.S. policy to converge with that of white-supremacist South Africa was compounded by the covert nature of the operation and further exacerbated by the revelation that the United States had no vital interest in Angola. The tragedy of U.S. Angolan policy is that this fiasco was not inevitable . . . But once again African specialists [in the U.S. State Department] were circumvented by [Secretary of State Henry Kissinger's] imperious attitude and proclivity toward viewing conflicts in terms of exercises in East-West one-upsmanship.

News conference, Addis Ababa, Ethiopia, Jan. 11/
The Dallas Times Herald, 1-12:(A)1.

Colin Eglin
Member of South African Parliament
4

I think it is a pity that we do not have in this house black leaders who could tell us the mood and the attitude of the black people. There will be some blacks who will rally round the white government, but the masses of young people, the educated people, the articulate, the politically aware people perhaps will not. We would like to ascertain the attitude of blacks. It is not easy, but there is no doubt that more and more of them are seeing what is happening to the north of us as a white-man's war. Far too many black people see what is happening in the north and in An-

(COLIN EGLIN)

gola as part of the process of liberation from discrimination within South Africa. I believe many of the black people of South Africa are getting silent satisfaction out of the successes of the MPLA [Soviet-backed faction in the Angolan civil war].

Before Parliament, Cape Town/
The New York Times, 2-21:3.

David Ennals
Minister of State of the
United Kingdom   *1*

[On Rhodesia]: Let us not forget that the people who are now talking of Britain as the protector of last resort have been in rebellion against the Crown for more than a decade. Their claim on Britain's protection is value-less while that rebellion continues . . . Let no one imagine that today's fearful prospects of a bloodbath in Rhodesia are just the result of a revolutionary situation in Angola. They are the direct result of more than 10 years of illegal independence, and the refusal of the white minority to recognize that the interests of white and black alike can only be protected by the sharing of political power, which, in a country where 95 per cent of the people are black, must mean majority rule.

Before Royal Commonwealth Society, London,
Feb. 19/ The New York Times, 2-20:9.

Gerald R. Ford
President of the United States   *2*

The only place that the Communists have made any inroads is when the Soviet Union and Cuba went into Angola. Secretary of State [Henry] Kissinger said to the Congress, "We have a plan that will stop them. If the Congress will approve the money, $28-million, we will be able to take two Angolan groups that form the majority of the population of Angola and they will be able to gain control against the Soviet-Cuban-backed group." But when the Congress turned us

down, wouldn't give us the money, we couldn't support the two factions that could have won. Communism, whether it is Soviet Union or Cuba, wouldn't be in there today. That is unforgivable, but that is the fact.

At Lenoir Rhyne College, March 20/
The Christian Science Monitor, 4-1:12.

                                          3

[On Rhodesian Prime Minister Ian Smith's agreement to black majority rule in his country within two years]: The road is now open for an African solution to an African prob-lem—free of outside intervention, violence and bitterness. We call on other countries to support—not impede—the African search for a peaceful settlement. It is my earnest hope that the several parties will now move swiftly to establish the conditions for [Rhodesian] independence in which all of its peoples can live together in harmony . . . We [the U.S.] can take satisfaction in the role we have played.

Washington, Sept. 24/
Los Angeles Times, 9-25:(1)1.

Barry M. Goldwater
United States Senator, R—Arizona   *4*

[On black rule in Rhodesia]: I have been to Rhodesia quite a few times. I know their peo-ple. I know it is a very tough situation. There are about 17 black tribes. They don't agree amongst themselves. The younger blacks want participation in government, and I can't blame them. Some of the older blacks don't seem to care, but with 300,000 whites living in a country with about four and a half mil-lion blacks, I think the day has to come when the black man has a part in the government that affects his life. It is a hard question be-cause they are very friendly people, friendly to us. They fought on our side in World War II. [Prime Minister] Ian Smith himself was a pilot in World War II. They are good peo-ple. They are people that I think should, on their own hook, without being pushed by anybody, just tell the blacks, "we are going to take you into government."

*TV-radio interview, Washington/
"Meet the Press,"
National Broadcasting Company, 5-2.*

Peter Hill-Norton
*Admiral of the Fleet, British Navy;
Chairman, Military Committee,
North Atlantic Treaty Organization*   *1*

Ten years ago, there was an overwhelming preponderance of friendly or allied naval forces south of the Tropic of Cancer in the Atlantic. The Soviet fleet seldom ventured into blue water and there was no requirement for the Supreme Commander-Atlantic to concern himself with maritime supply routes outside of the NATO area. But the position is now reversed. Units of the Soviet fleet are now deployed in strength in the South Atlantic and the Indian Ocean. Their newly acquired bases on the east and west coasts of Africa provide them with the capability of mounting sea and air attacks on our supply routes, and at any time of their choosing they could effectively disrupt the essential supplies of oil and other raw materials on which not only our fighting capacity but our economy and indeed our lives depend.

*Before NATO defense ministers, Brussels,
June 10/ Los Angeles Times, 6-11:(1)5.*

Henry M. Jackson
*United States Senator, D— Washington;
Candidate for the 1976
Democratic Presidential nomination*   *2*

The bad start that we [the U.S.] made in Africa was to get lined up with South Africa so that white men are killing black men. And again in Namibia or South-West Africa, which is a part of the old League of Nations mandate, there again we are confronted with that kind of problem, and that is not the dilemma we should be confronted with. Rhodesia is the same thing. The last thing we should do is to be aligned with any group trying to preserve a white minority ruling the black majority.

*TV-radio interview, Washington/
"Meet the Press,"
National Broadcasting Company, 3-14.*

Jesse L. Jackson
*American civil-rights leader;
President, Operation PUSH
(People United to Save Humanity)*   *3*

We want intervention in South Africa. [The United States could,] if it has the will, construct a meaningful and effective relationship with those black and white Africans who are willing to accept and live within societies dedicated to equal justice, self-determination and human dignity for all. Now that black South Africans, led by their children, have chosen to confront the government and openly protest various forms of racial minority rule, and have, as a result, been subjected to beatings, imprisonment and murder, we black Americans can no longer stand idle while our government pursues "business as usual" with such a state.

*Washington, Aug. 23/
The New York Times, 8-24:7.*

Kenneth Kaunda
President of Zambia   *4*

[Criticizing Soviet and Cuban involvement in the Angolan civil war]: Africa has fought and driven out the ravenous wolves of colonialism, racism and Fascism from Angola through the front door. But a plundering tiger [the Soviet Union] with its deadly cubs [Cuba] is now coming in through the back door, and the effects of this foreign intervention are now being felt in Zambia.

*Announcing emergency rule in his country,
January/ The Washington Post, 2-5:(A)14.*

5

[On Soviet and Cuban intervention in the Angolan civil war]: The Angolan situation is a very sad one. We see this situation: that governments which are socialist at home are imperialistic abroad, resulting in a political Irish stew in Angola. Zambia has no interest in Angola apart from seeing that there is peace in that country, and we want all foreign forces out of Angola. Cuban and Soviet liberators should leave the task of liberating

WHAT THEY SAID IN 1976

to Africa and Africans.

News conference, Lusaka, Zambia, Feb. 20/
The New York Times, 2-21:4.

1

I do believe that there is a distinctively African way of looking at things, of problem-solving and indeed of thinking. We have our own logic system which makes sense to us, however confusing it might be to the Westerner. The Westerner has a problem-solving mind, while the African has a situation-experiencing mind. The Westerner has an aggressive mentality: When he sees a problem he will not stop until he has solved it. He cannot live with contradictory ideas in his mind, and he is rigorously scientific in rejecting solutions for which there is no basis in logic. He dismisses the supernatural and non-rational as superstition. Africans, being a pre-scientific people, do not recognize any conceptual cleavage between the natural and supernatural. They experience a situation rather than face a problem. They allow both rational and non-rational elements to make an impact on them. I think, too, that the African can hold contradictory ideas in fruitful tension within his mind without any sense of incongruity, and he will act on the basis of the one which seems most appropriate to the particular situation.

Interview/
The New York Times Magazine, 3-28:53.

2

It has been said that the Russians have a right to be in Angola because they helped to fight the Portuguese Fascists. I am the first to agree that they did help, but the question is: Why are they helping? Was it to stay there, or to chase away the Portuguese? It was the duty of the socialist countries, after Angola became independent, to say, "Very good, we have helped you; now you should remain on your own."

Before Zambian Army/
The New York Times Magazine, 3-28:54.

3

We have consistently urged the whites [of Rhodesia] to be reasonable and to accept a peaceful transfer of power to the [black] majority of the people. The Rhodesian whites refused; now they have only themselves to blame. They must now squarely face the bitter consequences on the battlefield. We say to the Rhodesian Front [ruling party] that when majority rule has come through the barrel of the gun, they should blame no one but themselves for the consequences of their own intransigence. It is they who have destroyed the basis of non-racialism in Rhodesia. The die is cast. The end is near. We can see it.

The New York Times Magazine, 3-28:64.

4

[Addressing U.S. Secretary of State Henry Kissinger on his forthcoming talks with South African Prime Minister John Vorster on black-African rights]: I pray very hard that you should succeed. Because, if you don't, I can only use Mr. Vorster's own words: "The alternative will be too ghastly to contemplate" . . . We want peace. But we want peace for every human being in this part of the world. We want peace with honor. We want peace with justice and freedom and independence. Less than that is not peace at all. In the next few days, we will be able to know whether your mission will succeed or not . . . if the mission fails, we will fight. Yes, we will fight until the last man, if necessary.

Lusaka, Zambia, Sept. 16/
The Dallas Times Herald, 9-17:(A)9.

Edward M. Kennedy
United States Senator,
D—Massachusetts

5

There are ways in which we can make a genuine contribution to Africa, both in our interest and that of local countries themselves, while minimizing the risks of superpower competition there. We should begin by recognizing the need for new policies and attitudes based on the realities and the needs of the 1970s, not on the past practices and outmoded beliefs. We should follow the policies set forth by [U.S. Secretary of State Henry] Kissinger toward Rhodesia . . . Namibia and South Africa, in order to speed the gaining of [black] majority rule. This approach has become even more critical as fighting increases in Rhodesia, and as racial violence flares in South Africa . . . We should increase our commitment of resources to economic development of the African continent. In particular, we should help in crisis areas like the Sahel; emphasize the poorest of the poor and efforts to help meet their specific problems; and work primarily through multilateral institutions like the International Development Association and the African Development Fund. We should demonstrate greater respect for, and understanding of, the individuality of each African nation, and [the] full awareness of their own hopes and aspirations. We should keep our direct involvement in African states to a minimum and related to specific needs such as helping with economic development. And we should seek in every possible way to minimize military approaches to involvement, not only by the United States, but also by other nations, including the Soviet Union.

Before the Senate, Washington, Aug. 5/
The Washington Post, 8-12:(A)14.

Henry A. Kissinger
Secretary of State
of the United States   *1*

[The civil war in] Angola represents the first time since the aftermath of World War II that the Soviets have moved militarily at long distances to impose a regime of their choice. It is the first time that the U.S. has failed to respond to Soviet military moves outside their immediate orbit. And it is the first time that Congress has halted the Executive's action while it was in the process of meeting this kind of threat. Thus to claim that Angola is not an important country or that the United States has no important interests there begs the principal question. The objectives which the United States has sought in Angola have not been aimed at defending or acquiring intrinsic interests in that country.

We are not opposing any particular faction. We could develop constructive relations with any Angolan government that derives from the will of the people. We have never been involved militarily in Angola. We are not so involved now. We do not seek to be so involved in the future. Our objective is clear and simple: to help those African countries and those groups within Angola that would resist external aggression by providing them with needed *financial* support. Those who we seek to assist are our friends; they share our hopes for negotiated solutions and for African self-determination . . . But our deeper concern is for global stability. If the United States is seen to emasculate itself in the face of massive, unprecedented Soviet and Cuban intervention, what will be the perception of leaders around the world as they make decisions concerning their future security?

Before Senate Foreign Relations Subcommittee
on African Affairs, Washington, Jan. 29/
Vital Speeches, 3-1:291.

2

The United States position on Rhodesia is clear and unmistakable. As President Ford has said, "The United States is totally dedicated to seeing to it that the [black] majority becomes the ruling power in Rhodesia." We do not recognize the [white] Rhodesian minority regime. The United States voted for, and is committed to, the UN Security Council resolutions of 1966 and 1968 that imposed mandatory economic sanctions against the illegal Rhodesian regime. Earlier this year, we co-sponsored a Security Council resolution, which was passed unanimously, expanding mandatory sanctions. And in March of this year, we joined with others to commend Mozambique for its decisions to enforce these sanctions even at great economic cost to itself. It is the responsibility of all who seek a negotiated solution to make clear to the Rhodesian minority that the world community is united in its insistence on rapid change. It is the responsibility of those in Rhodesia who believe in peace to take the steps necessary to avert a great tragedy.

Addressing the people of Zambia, Lusaka,
April 27/ Vital Speeches, 5-15:456.

WHAT THEY SAID IN 1976

(HENRY A. KISSINGER)

1

No one—including the leaders of black Africa—challenges the right of white South Africans to live in their country. They are not colonialists; historically, they are an African people. But white South Africans must recognize as well that the world will continue to insist that the institutionalized separation of the races must end. The United States appeals to South Africa to heed the warning signals of the past two years. There is still time to bring about a reconciliation of South Africa's peoples for the benefit of all. But there is a limit to that time—a limit of far shorter duration than was generally perceived even a few years ago.

Addressing the people of Zambia, Lusaka,
April 27/ Vital Speeches, 5-15:458.

2

South Africa's internal structure [of apartheid] is incompatible with any concept of human dignity. We are deeply saddened by the recent and continuing clashes in black urban townships, universities and schools . . . No system that leads to periodic upheavals and violence can possibly be just or acceptable—nor can it last.

Philadelphia, Aug. 31/
U.S. News & World Report, 9-13:35.

Kaiser D. Matanzima
Prime Minister of Transkei

3

It has been alleged in certain quarters that our independence [from South Africa] is an essential element of South Africa's policy of apartheid. If this implies that Transkei is in agreement with or actively supports the racial discrimination which has, let us face it, for centuries typified the so-called South African way of life, I must reject it with the contempt it deserves! Certainly we are a party to the break-up of the Republic of South Africa in the form which has satisfied only a minority of its inhabitants.

At ceremony marking Transkei independence,
Umtata, Transkei, Oct. 26/
The New York Times, 10-26:7.

4

[Addressing South African President Nicolaas Diederichs]: For normalization of our relations as neighbors, I hope your government will steadily improve the living conditions of blacks and, as soon as possible, treat them no differently from white alien residents in the Republic . . . therein lies the key to Africa and the world for your country and, incidentally, your best weapon against Communism.

At ceremony marking
Transkei independence,
Umtata, Transkei, Oct. 26/
Los Angeles Herald-Examiner, 11-7:(G)6.

5

[On his country's new independence from South Africa]: I have no doubt there will be people who will immediately point to the economic interdependence of the Republic of South Africa and Transkei as justification for withholding recognition. [But in fact,] all the neighboring states of southern Africa are economically dependent on South Africa.

Umtata, Transkei, Oct. 26/
Los Angeles Times, 10-26:(1)8.

Mobutu Sese Seko
President of Zaire

6

[On war in Rhodesia]: It is inevitable. It is absolutely inevitable. The only people still being dragged down in the world are black people. Black people cannot go to colonize in Britain. They cannot go to the U.S. and colonize Connecticut. As far as Zimbabwe [Rhodesia] is concerned, as far as justice is concerned, Africa cannot stay with its arms crossed. It has got to do something to get rid of [Rhodesian Prime Minister] Ian Smith. I am not saying that all white Rhodesia must go—just the clique that holds power there. I am sure a lot of whites would like to stay in the country, and, if they do, their rights as a minority group will be respected.

Interview, Zaire/ Time, 5-31:30.

1

I am power with a capital "P." Power is me and not the church.

Interview/ The Washington Post, 7-4:(K)1.

Muritala Mohammed
Head of Government of Nigeria
2

We are all aware of the heroic role which the Soviet Union and other socialist countries have played in the struggle of the African peoples for liberation. On the other hand, the United States, which now sheds crocodile tears on Angola, has not only completely ignored the freedom fighters whom successive U.S. Administrations have branded as terrorists, she even openly supported the Fascist Portuguese government. The American Administration continues to support the apartheid regime of South Africa whom they see as the defenders of Western interests.

At Assembly of Heads of State of the Organization
of African Unity, Addis Ababa, Ethiopia/
The New York Times, 1-13:4.

Daniel P. Moynihan
United States Ambassador/
Permanent Representative
to the United Nations
3

[On Soviet involvement in the civil war in Angola]: Why do we talk of Soviet colonization? To bring to the minds of some Africans something they would understandably like to avoid having to even notice, which is the fact that Russian armies, men with blue eyes and European guns, are back on their continent . . . What these Africans don't want to have to acknowledge is something that is inexplicable in their world view: that Communist armies can be in a colonial role in Africa. And yet . . . when white troops land and start shooting up blacks and taking over places, what do you call that? *Anti*-colonialism? As a matter of fact, that's what it will be called.

Interview/ Newsweek, 1-19:29.

Edmund S. Muskie
United States Senator, D—Maine
4

. . . just last month, we discovered that the President [Ford] has involved our nation in a major way in yet another far-off land—in [the civil war in] Angola, where our nation's interests and those of the free world are far from clear. The Senate voted against any further expenditures for Angola. As in Vietnam, we find ourselves deeply committed, without prior notice or consultation with our people, in a country where United States interests could not possibly be served at any price.

National television address, Jan. 21/
U.S. News & World Report, 2-2:64.

Abel Muzorewa
Rhodesian black nationalist leader;
President, African National Council
5

[On Rhodesia after the white minority government is out of office]: In a completely new situation such as this, people are bound to be affected emotionally. Uncertainty always breeds uneasiness. Along with the high euphoria that is bound to greet our independence, I look for a good deal of anxiety and fear. This will be particularly true of those whites who may feel that their whole way of life is doomed. We want to assure the whites that we regard them as fellow human beings who are welcome to stay in the country. But they must be brave enough to face the need for change and to come to terms with the future. There will be big problems of adjustment for the blacks, too. To my mind, nothing will be more important than the building of positive new relationships between the political parties in the delicate early period. The country's peace and stability for years ahead will hinge on the success of that effort.

Interview, Geneva/
U.S. News & World Report, 12-6:35.

Lopo do Nascimento
Prime Minister of Angola
6

The Yankee imperialists say that the Cuban comrades [who helped his new gov-

WHAT THEY SAID IN 1976

(LOPO do NASCIMENTO)

ernment attain power] came to exploit Angola; but Cuba has no concessions in Angola, no oil, no mines, no forests. They are here with clean hands. Who has concessions in our country are the Americans, not the Cubans. The Cubans don't have them and never will. They will return to their land one day, when we decide so, the same way they came—as friends of our people and without dollars in their pockets.

Cabinda, Angola/ The New York Times, 5-16:(1)3.

1

During our armed struggle, we benefited from Soviet help, without which it would have been impossible to obtain victory over Portuguese colonialism . . . We attach an extraordinary importance to our relations with the Soviet Union and we will develop our relations with the socialist countries, at the head of which is the Soviet Union.

Television interview, Luanda/ The New York Times, 5-24:3.

Agostinho Neto
President of Angola

2

Let's get one basic point clear. All throughout the struggle against Portuguese colonialism and all the time we were subject to exploitation, oppression and the worst brutalities, [U.S. Secretary of State Henry] Kissinger had absolutely nothing to say. Even at that time, the Soviet Union was helping us by sending supplies of arms for our liberation struggle, and for this we are very grateful. It is when we have become independent and free, and beginning to build our state, that the United States State Department becomes worried by the fact that we have Soviet arms. Just because the Soviet Union supplies us with weapons, it doesn't mean that we have become a satellite. We've never been one. We've never asked Moscow for advice on how to set up our state. All the major decisions in our

country are taken by our movement, our government and our people. Once again the [U.S.] State Department is operating as international imperialism's chief agent.

Interview/ The New York Times, 1-9:31.

3

We cannot limit ourselves to our own independence. Our people, the first in Africa to fight South African forces, will extend their action to liberate other countries like Namibia, at present occupied by the racists [South Africa], and Rhodesia, which can achieve independence only through armed struggle.

Brazzaville, Congo, Feb. 29/ The Christian Science Monitor, 3-2:2.

Joshua Nkomo
Leader, Zimbabwe (Rhodesian) African People's Union

4

We want independence for the people of Zimbabwe [Rhodesia], that's the important thing. What we are doing is not for a section of the people. It's for all the people of our country. It is the greedy whites who have refused to accept reality. We have no time for greedy people. We want to have independence for the people of Zimbabwe—the people, not black people, not white people, not yellow people, but people. People keep asking me what will the role of the whites be [in a black majority government]. Well, why whites? White what? It is people, the liberation of people, the freedom of people from oppression, that we are talking about.

Interview, Geneva/ The New York Times, 10-28:3.

Julius Nyerere
President of Tanzania

5

[On the movement for black majority rule in places such as South Africa and Rhodesia]: Countries like South Africa would like to confuse the issue. They would like to think we are fighting for the Communists in southern Africa, that we are fighting for the Russians, for the Chinese and the Cubans. We want the United States to be big enough to realize that we are not fighting for a Cuban southern Africa, we are not fighting for Russia, we are not fighting for China. We are fighting for Africa.

News conference, Dar es Salaam, April 26/
The New York Times, 4-27:2.

1

[Saying armed struggle is the only way to achieve majority black rule in Rhodesia]: Mozambique and Angola did not become independent because we talked. They became independent because we acted [with long guerrilla wars by black nationalists]. We are re-dedicating ourselves to what brought about the independence of Angola and Mozambique. We are simply reminding the enemy we shall continue, and no amount of threats is going to make us move back ... and when we say that, we are not talking lightly.

To reporters, Dar es Salaam, Nov. 6/
The Washington Post, 11-7:(A)16.

Harry F. Oppenheimer
Chairman, Anglo-American
Corporation of South Africa

2

. . . those of us who believe that private enterprise is the system best calculated to widen the areas of individual choice, to open new opportunities and raise the standard of life, have to show very clearly that this private-enterprise system is not something which bears the label "for whites only." In South Africa we need, for our security and for our development, a real unity of the country to resist events such as one has seen taking place in Angola. But it is surely intensely illogical to ask a lot of black people to stand together with whites in order to oppose Communist aggression if at the same time, by your laws and your customs, you exclude them from most of the benefits which are conferred by the free-enterprise system. Fortunately, I would say that in South Africa there are many signs of real progress. In industry as a whole over the last five years, wages per head of the black workers, after allowing for inflation, have increased by almost 40 per cent. In the mining industry, if you consider that alone, in which black wages scarcely rose in real terms for a generation, largely due to the fact that the price of gold was pegged to $35 an ounce, wages have risen over the last five years, after allowing for changes in the value of money, by about 165 per cent. One must not exaggerate what has been done, because all this started from a very low level; but nevertheless, even making allowances for that, increases of this magnitude are very massive indeed and to my mind should give cause for thought to those who suppose that the black population can best be helped by cutting South Africa off from the resources needed for economic growth. Nor was this important increase in earnings brought about by pressure from the black workers themselves but was initiated because of the employers' own sense of what was proper in all the circumstances. I would say this must surely be something highly unusual, if not unique, in economic history anywhere in the world.

At Stock Exchange, London, May 18/
Vital Speeches, 9-15:716.

George Palmer
Editor,
"The Financial Mail," Johannesburg

3

The greatest fear I find is that so little has been done to foster an appreciation of the values of private enterprise among [South Africa's] black people. There is a growing concern that as power is transferred to the black population—as it surely will be—it will fall into the hands of people who have little sympathy for private enterprise but lean instead to some form of African socialism.

The New York Times, 11-21:(3)5.

Muammar el-Qaddafi
Chief of State of Libya

4

In the sense that the age of the popular masses has begun all over the world—though

291

WHAT THEY SAID IN 1976

(MUAMMAR el-QADDAFI)

some regimes are resisting it—you can consider me an international revolutionary . . . We are supporting causes we see as just ones . . . because there are still people who need our help to liberate themselves from colonial or neo-colonial or racist regimes . . . If we could get arms and equipment to the liberation forces in southern Africa, we certainly would. If our geographic location was closer to the racist regimes of southern Africa, we would fight them openly . . . We are arming the Palestinian resistance movement. We consider all these causes just and we feel that they are a sacred responsibility for us.

Interview, Tripoli/ Newsweek, 9-20:59.

Yitzhak Rabin
Prime Minister of Israel

1

There is no reason at all why Israel should not have relations with Africa. I must admit we were disappointed and very sorry [when African nations broke diplomatic relations with Israel following the 1973 Arab-Israeli war]. But on our part we are ready and will continue to be ready to enter diplomatic relations. I tend to believe that it will be settled because I believe in the common interest of Israel, on the one hand, and African states, on the other.

Interview/ The New York Times, 11-21:(1)7.

Ronald Reagan
Candidate for the 1976
Republican U.S. Presidential nomination;
Former Governor of California (R)

2

[Criticizing U.S. Secretary of State Henry Kissinger for calling for black majority rule in southern Africa and U.S. participation in sanctions against white-minority governments there]: We seem to be embarking on a policy of dictating to the people of southern Africa and running the risk of increased violence and blooshed in an area already beset by tremendous antagonism and difficulties. It is imperative that we avoid impulsive reactions in a potentially explosive situation.

The peoples of Rhodesia—black and white—have never been our enemies. They fought with us in World War II against Hitler and in the Pacific. If they show a creative attitude that can lead to a peaceful settlement, ourselves and others should avoid rhetoric or actions that could trigger chaos or violence. They have special problems which will require time to solve. We're not going to cure the ills of the world overnight. The great issue of racial justice is as vital here at home [in the U.S.] as it is in Africa, and it would be well to make sure our own house is in order before we fly off to other lands to attempt to dictate policies to them.

At luncheon, San Antonio, Tex., April 30/
The New York Times, 5-1:10.

3

[On what the U.S. should do regarding the Rhodesian racial dispute]: This is one that I think you would have to be completely involved with the Rhodesian government to find out if that [a peace-keeping force] would be necessary. Whether it would be enough to have simply the show of strength, the promise that we would [supply troops], or whether you would have to go in with occupational forces or not, I don't know. But in the interest of peace and avoiding bloodshed, and to achieve democratic majority rule, I think it would be worth this—for us to do it.

At Sacramento (Calif.) Press Club/ Time, 6-14:15.

Holden Roberto
Leader, National Front for the
Liberation of Angola (FNLA)

4

[On why the West is not aiding his cause]: Because the West is sated, prosperous, self-centered, and because our war [against the Soviet-backed MPLA], for so long an obscure, forgotten war, is taking place very far away, even though it is now front-page news. People are like that. We are the same. It's like the story of the old African mother pounding her millet while one of her children is listening to the news on the transistor radio. The child cries out very excitedly, "Mama,

292

an earthquake has just killed 1,000 people in Turkey." "That is sad," says the mother, continuing to pound her millet. "Mama, a plane has crashed in China; 100 people are dead." "Very unfortunate," says the mother, continuing her work. "Mama, the neighbor has just broken her leg." And the old woman is crazed with grief and starts crying . . . And then there is detente, behind which people will continue to live their lives without care. But what detente? The Cubans and the Russians don't give a damn for detente. For the Soviets, Angola is a fundamental question over which they will not enter into any global deal. They control Somalia. They want to dominate southern Africa and the ocean routes. And the West, terrified, lets them swallow everything. Peace, peace, peace for me, and war in other peoples' countries. After all, you [the West] went down on your knees before Hitler, then before Stalin, and now before [Soviet leader Leonid] Brezhnev. You are used to doing that . . . the West will finally wake up when the house across the street is burning, when the neighbor breaks her leg.

Interview, Sao Antonio do Zaire, Angola/
The Washington Post, 2-15:(K)5.

1

. . . no African will ever, ever accept the policy of apartheid. But we must not dream empty dreams. How many resolutions have been adopted at the OAU and the UN, and with what results? Do you believe that we'll settle the question of South Africa once and for all by expelling her from the General Assembly of the UN and by printing stamps glorifying Namibia? That she will be brought down like the walls of Jericho by trumpets blown at her borders? No more playing the fool! We will not deliver our brothers from the yoke of apartheid by means of a "holy crusade," but by means of the ineluctable political revolution of that country. Realism will finally prevail, even in Pretoria. I consider also that, if we build a multiracial Angola, which is free and prosperous, something will relax in South African society.

There are liberal elements in all the families of the white community. They must be helped, and not made prisoners of fear and irrationality.

Interview, Sao Antonio do Zaire, Angola/
The Washington Post, 2-15:(K)5.

Donald H. Rumsfeld
Secretary of Defense
of the United States
2

It is not for the Soviet Union or Cuba or any nation to dictate to African nations. Just as we believe in freedom and self-determination for ourselves, so, too, we believe that no alien power should dictate policy on this continent. The destiny of Africa must lie in African hands.

At luncheon, Nairobi, Kenya, June 16/
The New York Times, 6-17:1.

James R. Schlesinger
Chairman, Washington Study Group on
National Policy Alternatives;
Former Secretary of Defense
of the United States
3

Africa is getting to be a problem, and one must recognize that Soviet ambitions are increasing there, partly because the Soviets think that the fall of large chunks of Africa under their domination will adversely affect Europe and the United States. We are in the political season now [in the U.S.], and everyone talks about momentum in international as well as political affairs; and, particularly since Vietnam, it has been on the side of the Soviets. That momentum has got to be arrested.

Interview, Washington/
Los Angeles Times, 3-11:(2)7.

William W. Scranton
United States Ambassador/
Permanent Representative
to the United Nations
4

[On the Angolan civil war]: Just as the end to South Africa's wrongful intervention

WHAT THEY SAID IN 1976

(WILLIAM W. SCRANTON)

is very welcome, so the continuing Cuban and Soviet intervention is wrong: wrong because it deprived the Angolan people of the ability to exercise self-determination freely, uncoerced by foreign military intervention; wrong because of its massive size—Soviet aid to Angola, in 1975 and early 1976, far exceeded the entire amount of military aid to sub-Saharan Africa from *all* sources in 1974; wrong because it can no longer be related to any of the alleged purposes it pretended to serve; wrong because of its implication for the future, in Africa and elsewhere in the world. What are the implications of the presence of such combat forces in Africa supplied and equipped by a great power? First, the central development in the entire history of modern Africa has been the emergence of African nations from colonial status to independence ... In Angola, the Cuban military presence in large numbers has been and continues to be inconsistent with this history, with the great traditions of modern Africa, and with the firmly stated convictions of Africa's leaders. Second, the radical departure from modern African tradition represented by the massive Cuban movement in Angola must be terminated. The continued presence of Cuban combat forces in Africa risks establishing a pattern of action and competition for foreign sponsorship which can fundamentally undermine what has been achieved in Africa these past 20 years.

At United Nations, New York, March 31/
The Washington Post, 4-6:(A)14.

Ian Smith
Prime Minister of Rhodesia

1

[If the alternative to a settlement with the black nationalists in his country] is simply a continuation of the terrorist war we have known for many years, it doesn't worry us all that much. Of course, if this was to escalate into something completely different, if a new dimension came into the picture such as Russians and Cubans along the lines of Angola, this would create a new problem ...

If we get to this stage, I think it would mean that the free world would have failed us once again as they did in Angola. I think this will be the beginning [of the end] not only for us but for the whole of southern Africa, and I am sure I don't have to tell you what a tragedy this would be for the free world. It would make a tremendous difference to the balance of power between the free world and the Communist world. So we are hoping that the free world wouldn't [fail Rhodesia]. However, if in the end it does, we will go on fighting. What else do you do? It may be a little old-fashioned in the world today, but I believe it is what any man of backbone would do—stand up and fight. We may in the end lose. But I think it's better to lose while you're standing up and fighting than crawling on your knees.

Television interview, March 15/
Los Angeles Times, 3-16:(1)4.

2

I don't believe in black-majority rule ever in Rhodesia—not in a thousand years ... I am opposed to a government in Rhodesia based on color. We must try to get the best Rhodesians, whatever their color.

Newsweek, 4-5:31.

3

We've had terrorist incursions [in Rhodesia] for 12 years now, and these haven't worried us. In the past, when they came by the hundreds, they were killed by the hundreds. If in the future they come by the thousands, they will be killed by the thousands.

Time, 4-12:44.

4

It is clear that both the American and British governments, having been caught on the wrong foot in Angola by the Russian intervention there, are in mortal dread of a recurrence in Rhodesia. They believe, quite wrongly, that if the whites in Rhodesia could be persuaded to surrender, the Russians would then have no excuse to intervene here. Therefore, they are prepared to sacrifice the whites of Rhodesia—and if necessary of the whole of southern Africa—in order to buy time for themselves, in order to avoid being confronted by further Russian aggression in the subcontinent. To this end they are prepared to extend to the terrorists, and the black governments that harbor them, every moral and economic encouragement short of actual weapons of war,which in any case are supplied in ample quantities by the Communists themselves. They could not be more wrong in their assessments. A white surrender in Rhodesia and the dismantling of our highly efficient and effective security forces would lead swiftly and inevitably to a black power struggle within Rhodesia on a scale that would make the Angolan civil war pale into insignificance. Let me say in the strongest terms that we have no intention whatever of surrendering our country as part of a policy of appeasing the Communists. We have no intention of allowing our country to degenerate into the sort of shambles which we see in Mozambique and Angola today.

Salisbury, April 27/
The New York Times, 4-28:17.

1

I am surprised at how many black Rhodesians are more reluctant about black majority rule than they were a few years ago ... It is the white leftist in Europe and America who feels that men with colored skins can do no wrong and those with white ones no right—unless, of course, they call themselves Communists . . . Our best chance of [achieving a fundamental change in the relationship between blacks and whites] would be for the rest of the world to leave us alone. The more they interfere in our country, the more they set us back. I often wonder why world opinion virtually ignored the Cambodian massacres during the last year—the worst slaughter since Hitler's gas ovens—while they busied themselves with our problem.

Interview, Salisbury/Newsweek, 5-24:41.

2

Southern Africa is in the Western camp and is vital for strategic reasons. We supply many of your essential raw materials. Our high-grade chrome, for example, goes into your [the West's] ICBM nose cones. Before the Byrd amendment [permitting the U.S. to buy Rhodesian chrome despite UN sanctions], our chrome was finding its way to the Soviet Union through a number of third parties. Then Moscow was selling it to you at a premium price while you had a ban on Rhodesian imports — a really preposterous situation.

Interview, Salisbury/Newsweek, 5-24:41.

3

It is clear to me that [U.S. Secretary of State Henry] Kissinger intends to pressure white Rhodesians into handing over this country to a black government in the vain hope that this will discourage Communist intervention. If Mr. Kissinger were better informed, he would know about the deep tribal divisions and relentless leadership quarrels among black Rhodesians. He would know that any premature hand-over of power by the whites would swiftly lead to fighting between rival black factions—on a scale even greater than in Angola. That would be the signal for active Communist intervention on the Angolan pattern through neighboring Mozambique, and would inevitably result in the extinction of the civilized, prospering multiracial state of Rhodesia and its replacement by a black Marxist dictatorship. Let me assure you that we have no intention of appeasing Communism by surrendering our country, despite the fact that the American and British governments deny us the arms to defend ourselves.

Interview, Salisbury/
U.S. News & World Report, 5-24:31.

4

I think our approach to the question of majority rule is clear and consistent. Majority rule remains the ultimate goal of our Constitution. This has been Rhodesia's constant position since 1923, when we received the

WHAT THEY SAID IN 1976

(IAN SMITH)

right to govern ourselves—self-government—under our first Constitution. But it must be responsible majority rule, as opposed to irresponsible majority rule. Our aim is the best possible government, irrespective of color, and we believe in the ideal of change being based on orderly evolutionary progress.

Interview, Salisbury/
U.S. News & World Report, 5-24:31.

1

This question of quick [black] majority rule is a facile, superficial argument to our plan. I want to assure you that not only the whites in Rhodesia but the majority of black people in Rhodesia oppose that sort of thing. I think it would be unfortunate if [the U.S.] simply accepted the views of the present British government [which calls for majority rule in two years] because I believe those are far removed from reality . . . We find ourselves in the incredibly stupid position that we are fighting against other members of the free world more than we are fighting our natural enemies, the Communist world. Countries like Britain and the United States are leading the campaign against us in posing sanctions and trying to destroy us economically. So, clearly, we must try to overcome this ridiculous, this stupid, position in which we have got ourselves to see if we cannot get back to normality.

Interview, Salisbury/
The Washington Post, 8-25:(A)16.

2

[Extending the right to vote to all black Rhodesians is] contrary to my thinking. I believe this would be a bad decision for Rhodesia, and I think the majority of black Rhodesians, as well as the majority of white Rhodesians, would agree with what I have said. One-man, one-vote is something that we believe would lead to chaos in Rhodesia. In fact, it would be an invitation to a Communist take-over. We have no objection to

majority rule. We have majority rule in Rhodesia today. It is simply based on a qualification. What we have not got, and we don't think would be right, would be a counting of heads, as I see it, like a counting of sheep. There is nothing to stop a black man obtaining the vote in Rhodesia. He has the same chances as a white man to become a member of Parliament, or even to form a government in our country. The only thing that we have here are certain standards, qualifications.

Television interview/
"Today" show,
National Broadcasting Company, 9-7.

3

[Announcing agreement on a two-year transition to black majority rule in his country]: We live in a world of rapid change, and if we are to survive in such a world we must be prepared to adapt ourselves to change. I believe that it is incumbent on all of us, white and black alike, to act with dignity and restraint in the testing time which lies before us, and to create the right atmosphere to enable those charged with drawing up the new constitution to proceed expeditiously with their important task. Clearly, this agreement doesn't give us the answer which we would have liked. However, it does present us with an opportunity which we have never had before—an offer to Rhodesians to work out amongst themselves, without interference from outside, our future constitution. This is our best choice to keep Rhodesia in the free world and to keep it free from Communist penetration.

Broadcast address to the nation, Salisbury,
Sept. 24/ The Washington Post, 9-25:(A)10.

4

[On his country's unilateral declaration of independence from Britain]: It has given us the eleven best years of our lives. Overnight we created a virile young nation. Our economy is growing and expanding. I have heard economists from all over the world say that our economy over the past ten years has grown at double the pace it would have if there had been no [foreign] economic sanctions imposed against us. Had we not done it, we would have succumbed to what I believe to have been British blackmail. If we had tamely accepted that, it would have shown a distinct lack of backbone and from then on, I am satisfied, the Rhodesian nation would have gone backward. So we have had a wonderful decade in which Rhodesia has grown much stronger and better able to face the kind of problems that we are now facing up to. [As for the blacks,] it has brought them to their senses.

Interview, Geneva/ Time, 11-15:62.

Helen Suzman
Member of South African Parliament   *1*

I wish Americans would understand that white South Africans have a very decided stake in their country. The whites have been there since 1652—they're not Johnnies-come-lately. Unlike the Belgians who left the Belgian Congo or the Portuguese who've recently gone back to Lisbon, the whites in South Africa are there to stay. They have no intention of leaving—and no place else to go . . . Unless whites can be assured that their existence will be protected, it will be very difficult for them to give up the status quo [vis-a-vis the blacks]. We are trying hard to change this and have shown some success. In an either/ or situation, you won't see whites giving up without a tremendous fight.

Interview/ People, 7-19:59.

Pieter van der Byl
*Foreign and Defense Minister
of Rhodesia*   *2*

We are negotiating with a man [Joshua Nkomo, leader of the African National Council] who represents a limited number of people in the country. The reason we are doing it is because the world, thanks to the build-up these people get from the media, believes that the African population . . .that

these people go along with him. They don't, but the rest of the world believes that these African nationalists have this enormous following. We have no option but to go along with it . . . The average African living in the Tribal Trust Lands doesn't know what it's all about and probably thinks that something like self-determination is something on the menu, and he has no idea about this business that's going on.

*Interview, Salisbury, March 5/
The New York Times, 3-6:7.*

3

[Cuban Premier] Fidel Castro has now largely turned his back on South America, where for many years his troops have caused so much death and destruction, and this bloodthirsty dictator now sees his historic role as the revolutionary Communist liberator of Africa. He has been greatly encouraged in this enterprise by his success in Angola, which came about because of the cowardly and treacherous behavior of the American Congress in opposing the efforts of [U.S.] President Ford to sustain the pro-Western movements in Angola, thus causing the Americans and others to abandon their support for the South African peacekeeping efforts. Spurred on by this, he [Castro] will try another adventure somewhere else. In the unlikely event of them [the Cubans] attacking us, let us see them for what they are—certainly not supermen or anything wonderful at all. We will beat the life out of them in the same way we are beating the life out of the terrorists [in Rhodesia] whenever we meet them in battle.

*At parade of Rhodesian Army recruits, May 14/
Los Angeles Times, 5-15:(1)19.*

Laurens Van der Post
South African author

4

Unless change comes from within the human being, it isn't change at all. It's pushing humanity back into a less-advanced stage. That's what bothers me about the whole pattern in Africa. Change is being brought from

WHAT THEY SAID IN 1976

(LAURENS VAN der POST)

without and not coming quietly as a process of growth, when it would really be good and it would really be African.

Interview, London/
The Christian Science Monitor, 7-27:15.

John Vorster
Prime Minister of South Africa
1

South Africa wishes to live in peace with all its neighboring states. It has proved this over and over again in recent years. It is accepted and admitted by all unbiased people that South Africa's immediate neighbors, in this dangerous world in which we live, are among the happiest people in the world. As a result of South Africa's well-known attitude, which it has demonstrated in practice, it is not necessary for them to spend a single cent of their budget on defense. They do not need a defense budget because they know, in spite of all propaganda to the contrary, that they have nothing to fear from South Africa, that South Africa desires nothing that belongs to them, that South Africa does not want any land which is theirs, and that South Africa is at all times willing to meet their wishes.

The Washington Post, 1-12:(A)19.

2

[On whether U.S. Secretary of State Henry Kissinger is trying to compete with the Soviet Union for the "liberation" of southern Africa]: I couldn't agree more, and I would like to add that he is putting the U.S. on a no-win course because, in fact, he is now sitting down to sup with the devil and he should know that his spoon isn't long enough to do that.

Interview/Newsweek, 5-17:53.

3

International Communism is not only a threat to Africa. It is now, and will be for the foreseeable future, a threat to each and every country. The final goal is still world domination. It is for this reason, I believe, that Communist nations put a high priority on extending their control to the southernmost tip of Africa. Possession of this strategic region would give them a tremendous advantage over the free world—particularly in a conventional war . . . Not only would the Communist nations thereby deprive the free world of vital raw materials—and one can easily list a whole page of these—but they would straddle the Cape sea-shipping route. It should be remembered that two-thirds of Europe's oil still passes around the Cape of Good Hope. The number of ships traveling this route annually amounts to 22,000 or more. In other words, one of the most important lifelines of the free world could be cut off at will if the Communists managed to seize control of this region.

Interview, Cape Town/
U.S. News & World Report, 6-14:59.

4

[On the recent black unrest in his country against the white minority government, which some have called a crisis]: If there is a crisis, then all I can say is that in my lifetime I have seen bigger crises. Those people who want to cry wolf! wolf! are doing South Africa an ill service. They are playing right into the hands of the enemy. The enemy want to find us in a crisis, and they want us to admit that we have a guilty conscience. But looking over South Africa's achievements, I say we have no reason to have a guilty conscience about anything. I want to make it clear that nowhere in the world have four million [whites] done so much for the 18 million [blacks] as in this despised South Africa.

Before National Party, Springs, South Africa,
Aug. 27/The New York Times, 8-29:(1)8.

5

There will be no sharing of power [with blacks] . . . This is my answer to those who want political representation for blacks in a white parliament. I will grant political right to everyone in this country, but the black man's political rights, now and in the future, are in his own area and his own parliament.

At National Party rally, Johannesburg, Sept. 8/
The New York Times, 9-9:3.

1

In our part of the world the Communists, in the case of Angola, have made an experiment. They risked quite a lot in making it, but today they know the answer. They know that, on the Angolan pattern, they can subdue or attack any country in any part of Africa, including southern Africa, just as they did with Hungary, that voices will be raised in protest and that perhaps even threats will be made, but nothing else will be done about it. If, therefore, a Communist onslaught should be made against South Africa directly or under camouflage, then South Africa will have to face it alone and certain countries who profess to be anti-Communist will even refuse to sell arms to South Africa to beat off the attack.

Broadcast address to the nation, Dec. 31/
Los Angeles Times, 1-1:('77):(1)22.

Roy Welensky
Former Prime Minister of the
Federation of Rhodesia and Nyasaland
2

We're headed for [black-white] confrontation [in Rhodesia], and most people don't seem to realize how terrible it can be unless some settlement can emerge. We should move on to a mixed government, black and white, a gray government, and then the government should be predominantly black. If you get a change by evolution, then violence can be avoided; but if change comes by revolutionary means, who can tell what will happen? It can be terrible, because the white man will not run. He'll fight. He's known no other country. It's our country, too, you know, as well as [the] Africans'. We've got to work out an evolutionary change.

Interview, Salisbury/
The New York Times, 6-30:3.

Andrew Young
United States Representative,
D—Georgia
3

[On his recent African trip]: I [as a black] felt very much at home in South Africa. It was just like traveling in Mississippi or Louisiana or Georgia when I was a child. The Afrikaners reminded me—it's a terrible thing to say—of the old Southern Baptists; there's this awful familiarity. But that's why I can't give up on South Africa, because I know how far people can come if they have to. And I saw stirrings among the whites in South Africa that reminded me of the early days of our own civil-rights movement in the [U.S.] South.

Before Foreign Policy Association, New York,
Dec. 14/ The New York Times, 12-15:(B)13.

The Americas

Claude T. Bissell
Canadian historian; Former president,
University of Toronto
1

The French Canadian certainly longs for a sense of his own identity and a sense of his own cultural solidarity. But every indication so far is that he would stop short of independence or separation [of Quebec from Canada]. Of course, a lot depends on his definition of what is meant by independence. That really has never been made clear by the separatist group. I think most English Canadians agree that French Canada is a province quite unlike the others and must be given certain concessions. But there are profound doubts as to just how great those concessions should be, and what the limits are as to how far English Canada should and can go.

Interview, Toronto/
U.S. News & World Report, 12-13:51.

Aquilino Boyd
Foreign Minister of Panama
2

[On the controversy in the U.S. about a possible relinquishing of sovereignty over the Panama Canal to Panama]: It seems like an unusual campaign issue. But I understand your election-year politics and I understand how you worship Teddy Roosevelt, the Rough Rider, and how the Daughters of the American Revolution and the Veterans of Foreign Wars would like America to be forever the sole and dominant power on earth. I do believe, though, that the United States is negotiating in good faith. I am hopeful that after your [Presidential] election, perhaps within the next 12 months, we will have a new treaty. I think Panama has been patient and reasonable. Twelve years [of negotiating]

is a long time and, no matter how you put it, a foreign enclave divides my country in two and in these modern times that is an anachronism.

Interview/
Los Angeles Times, 5-21:(1)9.

Forbes Burnham
Prime Minister of Guyana
3

We are making an earnest attempt to institute a non-capitalist system, and there are some circles who don't like it. Maybe they think that if we succeed we will set a bad example to other developing nations ... I think we have been able to nationalize [the economy] without any great upheaval because we don't have a classical bourgeoisie as, for instance, in Jamaica or Chile. What we call middle class here are really small businessmen and shopowners, and some government bureaucrats.

Interview, Georgetown/
The New York Times, 5-25:2.

Jimmy Carter
1976 U.S. Democratic Presidential nominee
4

I would never give up complete control or practical control of the Panama Canal Zone, but I would continue to negotiate with the Panamanians. When the original treaty was signed back in the early 1900s, when Theodore Roosevelt was [U.S.] President, Panama retained sovereignty over the Panama Canal Zone. We retained control as though we had sovereignty. Now I would be willing to go ahead with negotiations. I believe that we could share more fully responsibilities for the Panama Canal Zone with Panama. I would be willing to continue to raise the payment for shipment of goods through the Panama Canal Zone. I might even be willing to reduce to some degree our military emplacements in the Panama Canal Zone. But I would not relinquish practical control of the Panama Canal Zone any time in the foreseeable future.

Debate with President Ford, San Francisco, Oct. 7/ The New York Times, 10-8:(A)19.

Fidel Castro
Premier of Cuba 1

Possibly no other nation has improved itself so much, has learned so much, in so short a time as our [Cuban] people have. And this process continues to grow and no one knows how far it will reach . . . We now have a great people forged in struggle and capable of any feat . . . a people that are invincible.

September/ Los Angeles Times, 12-9:(7)7.

Frank Church
United States Senator, D—Idaho 2

The only plausible explanation for our [U.S.] intervention in Chile [in 1973] is the persistence of the myth that Communism is a single, hydra-headed serpent, and that it remains our duty to cut off each ugly head, wherever and however it may appear . . . Before Chile, we insisted that Communism had never been freely chosen by any people, but forced upon them against their will. The Communists countered that they resorted to revolution because the United States would never permit the establishment of a Communist regime by peaceful means. In Chile, [then-U.S.] President Nixon confirmed the Communist thesis. Like Caesar peering into the colonies from distant Rome, Nixon said the choice of government by the Chileans was unacceptable to the President of the United States. The attitude in the White House seems to be: "If—in the wake of Vietnam—

I can no longer send the Marines, then I will send in the CIA."

At "Pacem in Terris" convocation, Washington, December ('75)/ Center Report, February:13.

Thomas O. Enders
United States Ambassador to Canada 3

[Canadians] feel the United States has played too big a role in their affairs—in the economy, in television and other forms of communication. Canadians want to be less dependent, less focused on the U.S. We encourage them in that. But we want them to do it in a positive way—by building new ties with other countries rather than loosening their ties with us. We are also trying to get this message across: Canada can't simply unilaterally cut back on its relations with the United States and expect there won't be reaction from us.

Interview, Ottawa/ U.S. News & World Report, 6-21:67.

Gonzalo Facio
Foreign Minister of Costa Rica 4

[Saying many Central American countries fear that Cuban forces will back any leftist coup in Latin America]: The rationalization for intervention will be the same as [when Cuba recently intervened] in Angola. The Cuban government does not respect the principles of non-intervention and may use as an excuse for sending troops any provisional government or faction that is fighting.

San Jose, Costa Rica, Feb. 24/ The Washington Post, 2-25:(A)10.

Wilson Ferreira (Aldunate)
Exiled former Uruguayan Senator 5

[Accusing the U.S. of supporting the current dictatorship in Uruguay]: Our countrymen are struggling in all possible ways for the defense of the principles, ideals and way of life that our country took from the Con-

WHAT THEY SAID IN 1976

stitution of the United States. Not one of us could ever understand that the immense weight of the same nation that defined those ideals 200 years ago, and today celebrates them with joy, could continue to be given in support for the enemies of our people.

Before House Subcommittee on International Organizations, Washington/ The Washington Post, 6-21:(A)21.

Daniel J. Flood
United States Representative,
D— Pennsylvania

1

You go from Maine to Puget Sound, and there is no stream of water anywhere, in the whole perimeter, as important to the Western Hemisphere as the Panama Canal, and certainly to the United States . . . If and when, God forbid under any circumstances, the sovereignty of the United States would be surrendered in the Panama Canal, somebody would have to run it. Now, Panama certainly can't run it . . . With the type of leadership you have in Panama, with Cuba where it is— you can stand in the plaza in Havana, and if you have a good right arm you can hit the Canal with a bottle of Bacardi rum—and you know the relationship between Cuba and the Soviet. I'll give you one guess who would operate it. Not Panama. It wouldn't be Uganda. It'd be the Soviet.

Interview/ The New York Times Magazine, 5-16:22.

Gerald R. Ford
President of the United States

2

My Administration will have nothing to do with the Cuba of Fidel Castro. It is a regime of aggression. And I solemnly warn Fidel Castro against any temptation to armed intervention in the Western Hemisphere. Let his regime, or any like-minded government, be assured the United States would take appropriate actions.

At naturalization ceremonies for former Cuban refugees, Miami, Feb. 28/ The Washington Post, 2-29:(A)4.

3

[On Republican Presidential candidate Ronald Reagan's criticism of Ford Administration policy regarding the Panama Canal]: Mr. Reagan wants to discontinue the [U.S.-Panamanian] negotiations and lead to more riots, more bloodshed, antagonize 309 million South Americans and inevitably leading to doubling or tripling our military forces in the Panama. I think that's irresponsible. Our policy is one of negotiations that will seek to maintain [U.S.] operational and defense capabilities in the Panama and will under no circumstances give away anything involving our national security. I don't think that's an issue where we are going to lose. We're on the right side and he [Reagan] is on the wrong side.

News conference, Longview, Tex., April 27/ The Dallas Times Herald, 4-28:(A)10.

4

There are those . . . who seek to distort the facts, to mislead others about our relationship with Puerto Rico. The record is clear and open. We are proud of the relationship that we have developed together and invite the world to examine it. We commend to its critics the same freedom of choice through the free and open election which is enjoyed by the people of Puerto Rico. Those who might be inclined to interfere in our freely determined relations should know that such an act will be considered as intervention in the domestic affairs of Puerto Rico and the United States; it will be an unfriendly act which will be resisted by appropriate means.

San Juan, Puerto Rico, June 26/ The Dallas Times Herald, 6-27:(A)7.

Carlos Fuentes
Mexican Ambassador to France

5

As an Ambassador, I hope to help bring Europe economically closer to Mexico so that we can be less dependent on what happens in the United States. It's an old saying in our country that when the United States catches a cold, Mexico catches pneumonia.

Our heritage is filled with failures. Mexicans have always asked themselves why a people so close to God should be so near the United States.

Interview, New York/
"W": a Fairchild publication, 10-29:9.

Harold S. Geneen
Chairman, International Telephone
& Telegraph Corporation 1

We have recent information tending to show that $350,000 of ITT funds may have been sent to Chile in the year 1970 for the purpose of supporting the democratic, anti-Communist cause there within the framework of their normal democratic process . . . [But] there is no information that even suggests any support of any irregular or violent action, [and] such political contributions would be legal both under Chile and U.S. law. Moreover, it would appear from published reports that authorities of the U.S. government both knew of and encouraged at that time funding of this type, by several corporations, as encouraging the U.S. government's own objectives.

At ITT stockholders meeting, Phoenix, Ariz.,
May 12/ Los Angeles Times, 5-13:(3)13.

Barry M. Goldwater
United States Senator, R—Arizona 2

. . . I am as completely opposed to giving the [Panama] Canal away as anyone. I also know from personal visits to that part of the world, and my personal friendship with people in that part of the world, that unless the United States begins to bend a little bit —now, this could be a gradual little more economic control, a gradual little less military occupation—that we are going to be faced with the problem of guerrilla warfare, whether we like it or not. And the question I ask anyone who comes to me on the subject is: "Are you willing to go to war over the Panama?" I would say 10, 15 years ago the answer would have been yes; but I can tell you that this Congress is not going to allow

the President to use arms to defend our position in Panama.

TV-radio interview, Washington/
"Meet the Press,"
National Broadcasting Company, 5-2.

3

[Cuban Premier] Fidel Castro is a real problem to the whole [Western] Hemisphere, and I frankly think that sooner or later he's got to go. Now, whether he goes by our supporting Cubans who want to go back and create a revolt, or whether it takes the combined activities of the free countries of the Hemisphere, I don't know . . . In my opinion, he has to be stopped.

News conference, Phoenix, Ariz., Dec. 2/
Los Angeles Herald-Examiner, 12-3:(A)4.

Nicolas Gonzalez (Revilla)
Panamanian Ambassador
to the United States 4

[On his country's desire to gain sovereignty over the Panama Canal from the U.S.]: It's a symbol of identity more than anything else. Panamanians feel that the biggest piece of wealth in the nation they have not been able to use for their own benefit, that they have been humiliated by the excessive presence of the United States.

The New York Times Magazine, 5-16:24.

Floyd K. Haskell
United States Senator, D—Colorado 5

[Saying the U.S. should re-establish relations with Cuba]: The more we stay out and the more we deny them access to some of the goods we could supply them, the further we push them into the hands of the Russians, and they don't want to be there. I think we're laying an egg not to recognize it.

The Dallas Times Herald, 12-13:(A)5.

Rafael Hernandez-Colon
Governor of Puerto Rico 6

Terrorist activities in Puerto Rico are

WHAT THEY SAID IN 1976

(RAFAEL HERNANDEZ-COLON)

being sponsored and they are within the mantle of [Cuban Premier Fidel] Castro's Communist objectives in general. In general, it is true as to the pro-Communist Socialist forces working for the independence of Puerto Rico. There is a clear and undeniable link to Castro . . . I don't think that the Cubans can realistically hope to promote a successful revolution in Puerto Rico by any stretch of the imagination. But they can make trouble for us. They can, as they have done in the past, train these people in terrorist activities.
Before National Press Club, Washington, May 19/
The New York Times, 5-20:11.

1

. . . Puerto Rico is debated at the UN as another Vietnam or Angola or Mozambique, by people who do not have the faintest idea of what or where the island is. In Paris it was even stated recently that life in Puerto Rico today is worse than in France under Nazi occupation! . . . The facts are: that throughout the years a very close-knit relationship has developed between Puerto Rico and the United States; that we have maintained our Puerto Rican identity with deep loyalty to our American citizenship; that democracy is as much a way of life in Puerto Rico as it is in the United States; that working through our political system the Puerto Rican people accomplished a dramatic transformation of the island; that current hardships have shown that, though improvable, the system is basically sound; that we have worked out the structural framework of a dynamic relationship with the United States; that the basic framework has the overwhelming support of the Puerto Rican people; and that the processes for solving the problems arising in our ongoing relationship are being worked out . . . Puerto Rico's basic importance is that it is the key citadel of democracy and stability in the Caribbean. Indeed, just as Cuba has become the symbol of militant and expansionist Marxism, the Commonwealth of Puerto Rico is the symbol of liberty, democracy and peaceful development in the Caribbean. It is against this larger background that we must view the role of Puerto Rico today.
Before National Press Club, Washington, May 19/
The Washington Post, 5-21:(A)24.

Henry A. Kissinger
Secretary of State
of the United States

2

The Latin-American nations still seemed to think that the United States, with its great strength and responsibilities, could act unilaterally to resolve all issues, that any compromise was surrender, that Latin America should propose and the United States should respond. Latin America demanded quick results: Each meeting became a deadline by which time the United States had to show "results" or be judged lacking. But as economic difficulties beset us all in a period of world recession, it became obvious that if Latin-American aspirations were expressed to the people of the United States in terms of categorical and propagandistic demands, they could not elicit a sufficiently positive response.
At symposium, Macuto, Venezuela, Feb. 17/
Los Angeles Times, 2-18:(1)4.

3

The United States is prepared to give more systematic consideration to Latin America's quest for regional identity. On the other hand, Latin America must overcome its own apprehensions about our policies . . . We believe the major Latin-American countries need concessional foreign assistance less than they need support for their drive to participate in the international economy on a more equal footing with the industrialized nations.
Carabedella, Venezuela, Feb. 17/
The New York Times, 2-18:6.

4

There has never been any doubt in my mind that Brazil's diplomats speak for a nation of greatness—a people taking their place in the front rank of nations, a country of continental proportions with a heart as massive as its geography, a nation now playing a role in the world commensurate with its great history and its even greater promise.

At dinner in his honor, Brasilia, Brazil, Feb. 19/
The New York Times, 2-20:3.

1

Latin American nations have grown in power and influence and become major forces in their own right on the world scene. This is one of the most striking events of this era.

Caracas, Venezuela/
The Washington Post, 2-26:(A)15.

2

Our policy in the Americas in the years ahead must recognize . . . new realities—of change in Latin America and of the fundamental importance of Latin America to the world interests of the United States. We cannot take the nations of this hemisphere for granted. We should put aside earlier temptations to crusade. We must create a new, healthier relationship. We can accept and, indeed, welcome the emergence of the nations of Latin America into global importance. And we must preserve our special hemispheric ties, without slogans, so that our cooperation as equals in this hemisphere can be a model for cooperation in the world arena.

Before House International Relations Committee,
Washington, March 4/
Vital Speeches, 4-15:387.

3

We cannot tolerate again [after Cuban intervention in Angola] a Cuban military adventure anywhere. This is a major challenge to the United States. If a little country of eight million people in the Caribbean, supported by a major foreign power [the Soviet Union], can establish a right of intervention

and a capability of intervention all over the world—while the United States is incapable of even providing the funds for resistance—then we will suffer a decline of our world position which will make a major crisis somewhere absolutely inevitable.

Interview, Washington/
U.S. News & World Report, 3-15:26.

4

[On U.S. critics of negotiations with Panama for a new Panama Canal treaty]: These negotiations were not started by this [Ford] Administration. They have been going on for 12 years, under three Administrations of two different parties, making it clear that three successive presidents, of as different personalities as Johnson, Nixon and Ford, have come to the conclusion that it is in the national interest to negotiate a better arrangement for the Panama Canal. They have come to this conclusion not because a local ruler has made certain demands but because of their conviction that our relations with all the countries of Latin America would be impaired if we did not make at least a good-faith effort to negotiate an arrangement.

Interview, Washington/
Los Angeles Herald-Examiner, 5-14:(A)7.

5

Let us face facts. Respect for the dignity of man is declining in too many countries of the [Western] Hemisphere. There are several states where fundamental standards of human behavior are not observed. There are standards below which no government can fall without offending fundamental values—such as genocide, officially tolerated torture, mass imprisonment or murder, or comprehensive denials of basic rights to racial, religious, political or ethnic groups. Any government engaging in such practices must face adverse international judgment.

Before Organization of American States
General Assembly, Santiago, Chile, June 8/
The Washington Post, 6-9:(A)6.

WHAT THEY SAID IN 1976

Paul D. Laxalt
United States Senator, R—Nevada
1

[Saying the U.S. has sovereignty over the Panama Canal]: The fact is that we took over that Canal at the time the French were not able to complete it. We negotiated with Colombia, insofar as the rights to the ground were concerned. We bought out the private landowners on a fee-simple basis. We went ahead and developed the Canal. We have had ruling after ruling on every official level indicating that we have sovereignty in the Canal. The Supreme Court of the United States ruled that we had sovereignty in the Canal. So what we are talking of basically in Panama, we are talking about possibly being coerced out of our own property by the Panamanian people and particularly by the dictator there. So I view this to be a very, very strong issue, and certainly the American people do . . . Colonialism implies, to me at least, exploitation, and if there is a country that hasn't been exploited at all in this situation, it is Panama. We have done tremendous things for the Panamanian economy ever since we built that Canal, and I don't know of anybody who has profited more from the situation than the Panamanians themselves.

TV-radio interview, Washington/
"Meet the Press,"
National Broadcasting Company, 5-16.

Rene Levesque
Premier-elect of Quebec, Canada
2

[Saying his new provincial government will at some time set up a referendum to determine if Quebecers want independence from Canada]: If it is no, we have a four-year mandate and that will be it until the end of the mandate. If it is yes, then we will have the necessary pressure for final negotiations because I don't see Canada—I have too much respect for Canadian democracy—holding by force a very-well-identified population saying, "We want out" . . . You can't be half in and half out, and the problem is that what we used to call "special status" is unfeasible in an old-fashioned federal structure . . . I do not see the Canadian version of federalism loosening up enough in any way to give a

decent and respectable framework for what we seek as our national affirmation.

Interview, Montreal/
The New York Times, 11-22:(A)2.

3

Four-fifths of French-speaking Quebec children never went beyond grammar school until 1960. Now that French Canadians have been educated to get the decent jobs, jobs are still going to the English-speaking segment of Quebec society. We're still the natives. We're getting the short end of the stick. The language, the economics—that's what this [possible Quebec secession from Canada] is all about. The French Canadians will never get a fair shake until Quebec is independent.

Interview/ Los Angeles Times, 12-1:(6)2.

Jose Lopez Portillo
Candidate for the Presidency
of Mexico
4

For me, it is important to look into the eyes of the people . . . The reality of the eyes of the spectators and the reality of the places that I visit [during the election campaign] bring the problems alive to me and fill me with responsibility. I have learned patience in this campaign, patience to listen, to find out, to receive people, to work for 14, 16 and 18 hours a day without losing curiosity and interest, patience to make these hearings an act of service.

Interview, Mexico City/
The Dallas Times Herald, 2-8:(A)21.

Jose Lopez Portillo
President-elect of Mexico
5

[On whether he is politically right or left]: I strongly oppose falling into the trap of revolutionary geometry . . . as a means of classifying the social sciences. The right wing says that Mexico is going left, while the left wing says that Mexico is going right. That must mean that our country has its own way and we are following it. That is the way of justice, of our social democracy.

Los Angeles Herald-Examiner, 7-18:(A)10.

Jose Lopez Portillo
President of Mexico

1

Let us strive to put an end to hate, rancor, fear and impatience. Our first task is to get hold of ourselves and put an end to panic-stricken and frantic activity. Mexico needs to reassert its values, its strength and its confidence that its destiny does not depend on monetary fluctuations or some magic figure that establishes the parity of the peso with the foreign currencies . . . If I could make a call to the dispossessed and marginalized groups, it would be for forgiveness for not having lifted them out of their misery. But I also say to these people that the entire country is aware and ashamed of our backwardness in this respect.
Inauguration address, Mexico City, Dec. 1/
San Francisco Examiner & Chronicle,
12-12:(This World)18.

Allan J. MacEachen
Secretary of State for
External Affairs of Canada

2

From its beginnings, Canada has had to adapt to or contend with the profound influence of the United States. Nevertheless, in ways both apparent and subtle, Canada remains in many respects a nation quite different from the United States, and will continue to evolve nationally along distinct lines. For Canadians, their distinct national identity remains a fundamental concern. I have stated many times that a basic objective of Canadian foreign policy is to reduce our existing vulnerability while at the same time continuing to develop a dynamic, creative and mutually beneficial relationship with our southern neighbor . . . The relationship is not one of equals, and the fact that a lesser power and the world's strongest power can successfully share a continent is high tribute to the conception and the conduct of our bilateral relations. Our relations can never survive inattention, however, and the general sound state of Canada-United States relations is not the result of accident or a preconditioned conformity of views. On the contrary, the successful interaction of two democratic and Federal states, each with its own national interests and domestic constraints, is highly complex because of the open system that each country has for reconciling various domestic interests.
Before Royal Society of Canada and American
Academy of Arts and Sciences, Quebec/
The National Observer, 7-17:11.

Bryce S. Mackasey
Former Postmaster General of Canada

3

[On the English-French language dispute in Canada]: Terrible hatred seems to be spreading across this nation. The French language is suddenly hated for no reason, [and] French Canadians aren't welcome. We're blessed [with a heritage of a united Canada], and we're throwing it away.
The New York Times, 10-26:3.

Michael Manley
Prime Minister of Jamaica

4

There is absolutely no danger whatsoever, there is absolutely no possibility whatsoever of Jamaica becoming a Communist country. It's just not a part of the stream of our history.
The New York Times, 12-16:8.

Claude Morin
Minister of Intergovernmental Affairs
of Quebec, Canada

5

[On the election victory in Quebec of the Parti Quebecois which calls for independence for the province]: Quebec has taken a landmark step toward becoming the master of its own affairs . . . We want to state clearly, without beating around the bush, that in our view the present Federal system should be replaced by a new political order. What we shall propose to the rest of Canada when the time has come is a new type of association which shall take into account requirements of economic interdependence as well as the historical and natural aspirations of Quebecers to be the masters of their own national destiny.
Before Canadian finance ministers, Ottawa,
Dec. 6/The New York Times, 12-7:8.

WHAT THEY SAID IN 1976

Alejandro Orfila
Secretary General,
Organization of American States   *1*

. . . there seems little reason for the United States and Latin America to continue on a collision course. Yet the signs are that this will remain the situation unless the United States develops a clearer understanding of the nature of hemispheric development interests today. The understandings of yesterday no longer hold. Actions, not words, must govern the future of hemispheric relations, and only as both the United States and Latin America demonstrate in practice that they are genuinely committed to their mutlilateral partnership for hemispheric development will the traumas of the present be diminished.

Before Palm Beach (Fla.) Roundtable, Feb. 29/
Vital Speeches, 4-15:406.

2

Latin America is no longer, if it ever was, isolated from the mainstream of world history and politics. It has rather assumed control over its own destiny and is a leading actor in the world political and economic arena. Its nations now rank in the middle range of the developing countries. And Latin America has grown more during the past 25 years than during the previous 200 years of its history, having a population today of 300 million and a gross national product of $225-billion. Yet the Latin American countries are on the verge of an even more profound transformation of their societies. Twenty-five years from now the population will double to 600 million. The central question ahead is will the Hemispheric nations find the vision, the resources and the capabilities required to establish whole new cities, feed, house and educate millions of new citizens, guarantee the protection of human rights and freedom, and both achieve greater social justice and broaden equality of opportunities? I have no doubt that the nations and peoples of the Americas are fully capable of responding to their overriding development challenges—provided they firmly establish regional priorities and that both Latin America and the United States join together in newer and more dynamic ways to assist regional and national development efforts. Cooperation between our nations must become a model for helping to build a world bridge over the greatest chasm of our times—the profound division separating the North and South of our planet.

Nov. 19/ The Washington Post, 11-28:(B)6.

Jacques Parizeau
Finance Minister-designate
of Quebec, Canada   *3*

French Canadians have always been nationalistic. Our language, history, culture and customs are all foreign to the rest of English-speaking Canada . . . English-speaking Canadians have always considered their French-speaking countrymen incompetent and nitwits. "You guys aren't up to it. Let the Anglo-Saxons run the show," is what we've always been told. We've been put down for years by the English-speaking Canadians. But what is happening now [the growing controversy over whether the province should secede from Canada] isn't a struggle between the French- and English-speaking Canadians. It is a fight among French Canadians—those who think the time has come for independence and those who think we're not yet ready. We French Canadians are a pain in the neck to the rest of Canada. We're always yapping like a nagging wife, never satisfied, always wanting more. If I lived in one of the other nine provinces I would react the same way most English-speaking Canadians do to us. I'd think, "Good riddance. Let the Quebecers go. We won't have to worry about them any more."

Interview/ Los Angeles Times, 12-1:(6)1.

P. J. Patterson
Minister of Industry, Tourism and
Foreign Trade of Jamaica   *4*

We reject the system of capitalism because of its history of social inequality and economic exploitation. Likewise, and with equal firmness, we abhor the doctrine of Communism because of its monolithic nature and the imminent danger which it can impose on human freedom.

Los Angeles Times, 3-28:(1)5.

Carlos Andres Perez
President of Venezuela
1

I agree with [U.S. Secretary of State Henry] Kissinger when he says the United States can't tolerate having conditions imposed upon it. [In Latin America,] we're smaller and more humble countries but we can't accept it either. There is a broader receptivity to this now, yes. It's been created because we now have in our own hands part of that decision-making which was only in your [developed countries'] hands before. We're not blaming the great nations for everything that's happened to us. We blame ourselves, too, for our lack of discipline, our individualistic feelings . . . But we're trying to break this vicious circle. We're creating a new world and we hope the developed nations will join us.

Interview, Caracas/
The Washington Post, 1-2:(A)11.

2

. . . within a scant 12 days, an event of exceptional importance for the Hemisphere will take place—the Bicentennial of the independence of the United States of America. That great country was the first to free itself of the yoke of colonialism and to build a powerful, sovereign state. To its people and its government we send our words of solidarity. July 4 will be a day of jubilation for all Venezuelans who will share their joy with the Americans who live among us in our own land. To be coherent and faithful to the frankness with which we speak to our own people and the world, we must say here that the great day of independence for the 200-year-old America will only be marred by a fact which is dissonant with the best traditions of the United States. I am referring to the colonial enclave of the Panama Canal Zone. Pana-

ma . . . is divided; it's sovereignty is removed. And it is in a cordial spirit that we raise our voice in the name of Venezuela, and are sure that it is the voice of all the peoples of Latin America, to say to the great nation of the north that the best homage to Washington and to the thousands of anonymous heroes of the U.S. independence, would be to proclaim to an admiring world that the United States is restoring to Latin America, that they are returning to their legitimate owners, that portion of Panamanian territory.

At National Pantheon, Caracas, June 22/
The New York Times, 7-14:15.

Ronald Reagan
Candidate for the 1976 Republican U.S. Presidential nomination;
Former Governor of California (R)
3

[Saying the U.S. should not give up sovereignty over the Panama Canal]: State Department actions for several years now have suggested that they are intimidated by the propoganda of Panama's military dictator, [Cuban Premier] Fidel Castro's good friend, General Omar Torrijos. Our State Department apparently believes the hints regularly dispensed by the leftist Torrijos regime that the Canal will be sabotaged if we don't hand it over. Our government has maintained a mouselike silence as criticisms of the give-away have increased. I don't understand how the State Department can suggest we pay blackmail to this dictator, for blackmail is what it is. When it comes to the Canal, we bought it, we paid for it, it's ours, and we should tell Torrijos and company that we are going to keep it!

Campaign address, Winter Haven, Fla., Feb. 28/
The New York Times, 2-29:(1)42.

4

[On U.S.-Panama negotiations for a revision of the Panama Canal treaty]: The only reason that has been given so far by the [Ford] Administration for the almost secret negotiations they've been conducting for two years to give that Canal away and then present the

WHAT THEY SAID IN 1976

(RONALD REAGAN)

American people with a fait accompli is that we have been threatened with violence by the dictator of Panama. I think for the United States to set such a precedent to tear up a treaty that has been in existence for almost three-quarters of a century, a treaty which they [Panama] have observed to their own benefit and ours, in which we guarantee their independence in perpetuity, which guarantees that is sovereign United States territory—I do not believe that we should be negotiating that way, and certainly not under the conditions of a threat of violence.

Interview/ The Christian Science Monitor, 6-3:17.

John J. Rhodes
United States Representative,
R—Arizona

1

[On the controversy over whether the U.S. has sovereignty over the Panama Canal]: ... the name of the game is to keep the Panama Canal open. I think it is absolutely of no profit to talk about who owns it. Personally, I doubt very much that we do own it, but we have the right to defend it and we have the right to operate it. I am satisfied that no [U.S.] Administration, and certainly not this [Ford] one, is going to give up that right.

TV-radio interview, Washington/
"Meet the Press,"
National Broadcasting Company, 5-9.

Mikhail A. Suslov
Secretary, Central Committee,
Communist Party of the Soviet Union

2

The Cuban revolution has not only radically changed the face of the country, but also has made an indelible imprint on the whole liberation struggle of Latin America. And if today the possibility of a "second liberation" of the continent is becoming a more and more realistic prospect, this is to a considerable degree the result of the influence of the Cuban example ... The process of

great social changes now going on in Latin America is an integral part of the revolutionary liberation and democratic movement which ... is advancing on a world-wide scale. As a Latin-American state, the Republic of Cuba ... actively participates in the national-liberation movement of the continent.

At Cuban Communist Party Congress/
The Christian Science Monitor, 1-7:30.

Omar Torrijos (Herrera)
Head of Government of Panama

3

[Saying his country will rid itself of U.S. influence and U.S. control of the Panama Canal]: [In the early days of my rule,] the leaders of the Cuban revolution told me to avoid provocations ... I then began to act in a more reasonable way, with the conviction that we will free ourselves but with the knowledge that a struggle of liberation is not carried out in one year. They [the U.S.] are trying to buy us with money. But we idealists have no price.

Santiago, Cuba/
The Christian Science Monitor, 3-17:18.

4

[On his country's efforts to gain control of the Panama Canal from the U.S.]: Patience has limits. We are now following the peaceful route of Gandhi. We are also prepared to follow the Ho Chi Minh route, if necessary. That means terrorism, guerrilla operations and sabotage in a national-liberation war to regain our territory.

U.S. News & World Report, 4-26:24.

5

[On the controversy in the U.S. over his country's desire to gain sovereignty over the Panama Canal]: We don't want our most vital issue to become a political football in the U.S. election campaign. It's too important to us. We are willing to wait, to keep our people calm, providing the U.S. shows good faith in negotiating efforts. [But] if there were an uprising [of students], if there were terrorism, I, as commander of the National Guard, would have two options: to crush them or lead them. And I can't crush them.

The New York Times Magazine, 5-16:26.

Pierre Elliott Trudeau
Prime Minister of Canada   1

Some economists say all you've got to do is get back to the free-market system and make this market system work. It won't, you know. We can't destroy the big unions, and we can't destroy the multinationals; but who can control them? The government. That means the government is going to take a larger role in running institutions, as we're doing now with our anti-inflation controls. [Controls of some sort must continue even after the anti-inflation program ends, because] we don't want to go back to the same kind of society with high unemployment and high inflation. [The solution is] big government—not less authority, but perhaps more.

*Television interview/
The New York Times, 1-11:(1)8.*

2

[The Federal government] has a duty to intervene when necessary to stimulate employment, to redistribute income, to control inflation and pollution, to protect the consumer, to promote conservation, productivity and an adequate supply of the things we need. [But] there is no desire on the part of the government or the people of Canada to impose more regulation on the truly competitive sectors of the economy—the small-business sector, for example. The preservation and strengthening of the free-market sector of our economy is absolutely central to the Liberal view of the Canada of the future. That is why we reject socialism, which seeks ever-greater government ownership and control.

*Before Canadian Club, Ottawa, Jan. 19/
The New York Times, 1-20:8.*

3

Some extreme free-enterprisers have suggested that our best hope for the future lies in the creation of a true free-market economy, a market system designed according to economists' models of perfect competition. I believe they are wrong. Such a system would involve, for example, the breaking up of some of our giant corporations and unions. Do we really want to do that, even if we could? Before you say yes, ask yourself how Canada could be largely self-sufficient in steel, for example, if we didn't have some very large steel companies capable of amassing the enormous amount of capital needed for the job, the sophisticated technology, the managerial experience, and skilled labor force. We need some large corporations because of their efficiency, because of their unique ability to do the jobs that need to be done, because of their ability to sustain and increase our export trade. The problem is not the existence of monopolies or quasi-monopolies in certain sectors of our economy. The problem is how to ensure that their power is used in the public interest and is directed toward the achievement of national goals. In that context, the issue before us is to what extent we will be controlled by government regulation and to what extent we will be controlled by our own sense of responsibility. I think we all favor as little of the former and as much of the latter as is humanly possible.

*Before Canadian Clubs of Ottawa/
The National Observer, 2-28:15.*

4

. . . I think we have to worry, as Liberals, about our future as a national party. It remains for us to keep the national interest in mind, and to preach it . . . in the area of bilingualism, and in the area of the economy and [economic] controls; and this will or will not be the salvation of the Liberal Party— and if I can say so without too much pretention, perhaps also that of Canada. We are the government, [and] if the country breaks up or if certain centrifugal tendencies fulfill

WHAT THEY SAID IN 1976

(PIERRE ELLIOTT TRUDEAU)

themselves . . . we will have permitted this country either to break up or become so divided, for economic, linguistic or regional reasons, that its ability and will to act as one nation will have been destroyed in our time. And we were the government.

At policy session of Liberal Party's Ontario caucus, Toronto/ Los Angeles Times, 10-4:(1)22.

1

[On his current economic program which calls for wage/price controls over a three-year, not 90-day, period]: We wanted people to realize they couldn't look past the control period and figure out how to catch up when the 90 days were over. We wanted them to realize there had to be some change in behavior and in institutions. We wanted them to see that the expectations of continually increasing wealth no longer applied . . . The problem of industrial society today is to accept some kind of restraint, some kind of discipline. We're trying to get Canadians to ask, "How will discipline and restraint be maintained when controls are gone?"

Interview, Ottawa/ Los Angeles Times, 10-21:(2)7.

2

[On the recent election victory in Quebec of the Parti Quebecois which favors independence for the province]: History created this country from the meeting of two realities, the French and the English. This coming together, though at times difficult to accept and hard to practice, has become the fabric of our life as a nation, the source of our individuality, the very cornerstone of our identity as a people . . . The issue [in the Quebec election] was not separation of the province, but sound administration of that province. Quebecers have chosen a new government, not a new country. [Quebec Premier-elect Rene] Levesque has no mandate to bring in separation . . . Can Francophones of Quebec consider Canada as their country,

or must they feel at home only in Quebec? And you know as well as I know that a new sharing of power between Ottawa and the provinces will never give the answer to that particular question, will never make a Francophone feel more at home in Toronto or in Vancouver than he does in Quebec. Quebecers, like citizens of the other provinces, seek personal fulfillment in a free and independent way. The central question, therefore, is whether this growth of freedom and independence is best assured by Canada, or by Quebec alone . . . Canada must not survive by force. [The present Canadian Confederation, founded in 1867,] provides the world with an example in fraternity. This extraordinary undertaking is so advanced on the road to liberty, so advanced in the way of social justice and of prosperity, that to abandon it now would be to sin against the spirit, to sin against humanity.

Broadcast address, Ottawa, Nov. 24/ The New York Times, 11-25:1,12.

3

[Rejecting independence for Quebec]: Our task is to build a more enriching Federalism to guarantee even more firmly the liberty, self-realization and well-being of the people and communities of Canada. When I speak of Canada I do not have in mind an identity that competes with that which a French Canadian and Quebecer, conscious of his or her specific history and roots, holds dear. [I think] rather of a political society, the ideals of which are liberty, equality and, yes, fraternity. I think of a society which, by securing the cooperation of our people, by pooling the resources of our different regions, by making possible the free development of the different cultures of our communities, makes our individual liberty, capacity for self-realization and well-being more secure and better guaranteed than they would be if each community were to attempt to achieve this alone.

At conference of provincial Premiers and Federal officials, Ottawa, Dec. 13/ The New York Times, 12-14:2.

Jorge Rafael Videla
President of Argentina

1

For us, respect for human rights is based not on legal mandates or international declarations, but is a result of our profound Christian convictions on the pre-eminent dignity of man as a fundamental value . . . We will show the same firmness in defending your rights as we now show in demanding your effort . . . The government offers no easy or miraculous solutions. On the contrary, it asks, and will realize, sacrifices, effort and austerity.

Nationally broadcast inaugural address,
Buenos Aires, March 30/
The New York Times, 4-1:2.

Jack H. Warren
Canadian Ambassador to the
United States

2

Our [Canada's] nationalism reflects the awakened aspirations of Canadian society. In that respect it is not different from the spirit of national pride which animates and has animated other societies both old and new, including your own country [the U.S.]. It is not, and should not be regarded as, anti-American. It represents our effort to be ourselves: North Americans with a difference.

Before Los Angeles World Affairs Council, Jan. 6/
Los Angeles Times, 1-7:(3)13.

3

In the post-war years, Canada was often strongly influenced, if not guided, in its actions by reference to the U.S. positions . . . This so-called "special relationship" was not the result of any particular decision; it was a way of life in which the habit of accommo-dating each other in most areas had become enshrined. Indeed, when our government released its major review of Canadian foreign policy in 1970, there was no specific section on the United States. But the mood had changed as a result of a decade of self-examination, and there was recognition in the foreign-policy papers of an important challenge and problem for Canada in "living distinct from but in harmony with the world's most powerful and dynamic nation, the United States." [Then-U.S.] President Nixon's economic measures of August 15, 1971, made us increasingly aware of the problem, and the Canadian government moved thereafter to examine the question more closely. What resulted was a new approach which we call the "Third Option." Having examined the only other two options considered realistic—continuing as before the *laissez-faire* course or actively seeking closer integration with the United States—the government adopted the last of the three options put forward, calling for "a comprehensive long-term strategy to develop and strengthen the Canadian economy and other aspects of our national life and, in the process, to reduce the present Canadian vulnerability" . . . While obviously not a remedy or detailed blueprint for the solution of every problem, the "Third Option" seems to have given expression to the aspirations of Canadians for a greater sense of identity vis-a-vis the United States and may well have proven self-fulfillment in encouraging them to achieve it . . . So let us accept that the evolution of our foreign policy is a natural one which does not detract from the central importance of our relationship with the United States—a relationship so pervasive that it affects all major aspects of Canadian life.

Before Economic Club of Chicago,
April 29/Vital Speeches, 7-15:590.

Asia and the Pacific

Zulfikar Ali Bhutto
Prime Minister of Pakistan

1

[Lamenting the increasing curbs on freedom in India]: The reasons that kept India together—and I'm not against Indian unity; I'm just giving an analysis—is the fact that India had a democracy. India was making it. India was exploding atom bombs; India was making progress in science; India was making general progress; the food problem was being tackled on a grand scale . . . Indians started feeling proud of their nationalism—that "I am an Indian" . . . [Now if] there is suppression and there is inward-looking to the point of forgetting the external . . . of being an Indian, then they're going to start saying, "What's this? What's the point? Isn't it better I am a Maharashtran, I am a Sikh or I am a Rajput?" So the question is this, [that] that kind of a crisis takes place in a polyglot like India—that is a factor which you cannot ignore.

Interview, Larkana, Pakistan/
The Washington Post, 1-24:(A)12.

2

[On his authoritarian rule]: I had a vision of Pakistan, of what we would do, what we would achieve, and I think we have made a big stride. In another year or two, we will have completed a process of the country's historical evolution . . . The qualitative change in their [Pakistanis'] economic and social development and standards will reflect in their political outlook. They will not be then going berserk, tearing each other apart, saying, "I have nothing to lose; I have no stakes" . . . In the villages, if you sit with the lice-ridden people with beards and hair going up to here and there, on the floor with them,

and talk to them, they'll understand. By and large, the people understand. They know that I believe passionately in them and that if I am given the opportunity and the time, I will make this country viable and strong.

Interview/The New York Times, 1-29:3.

Mrs. Nguyen Thi Binh
Foreign Minister of South Vietnam

3

We wish to emphasize the responsibility of the United States to contribute to the reconstruction of Vietnam after the war because in South Vietnam now, in spite of the fact that the war has stopped, that there is no more American presence, that there are no more U.S. bombs, the sequels of the war are felt daily, hourly, and they are weighing heavily on our country. And the situation will last for a long time.

Interview, Moscow, March 5/
The New York Times, 3-7:15.

Leonid I. Brezhnev
General Secretary, Communist Party
of the Soviet Union

4

Peking's frantic attempts to torpedo detente, to obstruct disarmament, to breed suspicion and hostility between states, its efforts to provoke a world war and reap whatever advantages may accrue, present a great danger for all peace-loving peoples . . . We are prepared to normalize relations with China in line with the principles of peaceful coexistence. What is more, we can say with assurance that if Peking reverts to a policy truly based on Marxism-Leninism, if it abandons its hostile policy toward the socialist countries and takes the road to cooperation and solidarity with the socialist world, there will be an appropriate response from our side and opportunities will open for developing good relations between the U.S.S.R. and the People's Republic of China.

At Soviet Communist Party Congress, Moscow, Feb. 24/ The New York Times, 2-25:14.

Zbigniew Brzezinski
Special Assistant-designate to the President of the United States for National Security Affairs
1

We could do more to upgrade the U.S.-[Communist] Chinese relationship to minimize the possibility of a swing in China toward greater normalization with the Soviet Union. [But] I don't think the U.S. can simply abandon the security treaty with Taiwan . . . The U.S. cannot be a viable guarantor of anyone's existence if we welsh on a commitment to maintain the survival of a particular party.

Interview/ Time, 12-27:14.

Jimmy Carter
Candidate for the 1976 Democratic U.S. Presidential nomination; Former Governor of Georgia (D)
2

I do not favor blanket amnesty [for U.S. Vietnam-war draft evaders]. I do favor a blanket pardon. There is a difference. Amnesty means what you did was right; pardon means what you did is forgiven. I cannot equate the actions of those who went to Vietnam thinking it was wrong—many of whom lost their lives—with those who thought it was wrong and defected. But exile for this long period of time is adequate punishment.

Interview, New Hampshire/ Newsweek, 2-2:18.

3

I cannot see any circumstances imaginable under which we need or would use atomic weapons in the Korean area . . . I see no reason to keep them there. What concerns me about that area is that the Japanese, unfortunately, because of their growing distrust of this country, and their belief that

we've not gotten an adequate consultative relationship with them, equate our concern with them to our concern with maintenance of strength in Korea. And I don't think that ought to be a part of the Japanese consciousness. My commitment to Japan would be total. I think this is something that has been ratified by our Congress and the President, and, I think, the people believe that we ought to maintain our forces in Japan. There are only about 25,000, plus about 35,000 in Korea and Okinawa. But I would not be rash about the withdrawal of troops from South Korea. I'd be very careful about that. I'd make sure the Japanese knew what we were doing. I would make sure they understood that our commitment to them is total. I would make sure that they understood my motivations in withdrawing atomic weapons. Then I would make sure that in the four or five years when we get our troops in Korea substantially removed, that [South] Korea would still be able to defend itself against North Korea.

Interview, March 16/ The Washington Post, 3-21:(B)5.

Jimmy Carter
1976 Democratic U.S. Presidential nominee
4

[On U.S. recognition of Communist China]: That is an ultimate goal, but the time is undefined. I would like assurances that the people of Taiwan—the Republic of China or whatever it might be called—be free of military persuasion or domination from mainland China. That may not be a possibility; if it is not, then I would be reluctant to give up our relationship with the Republic of China.

Interview, New York/ Time, 8-2:15.

M. C. Chagla
Former Indian Ambassador to the United States
5

[On the curtailment of freedom in his country]: [The future of India] looks very dark. Frankly, I don't see light at the end of the tunnel. Not today. But there is an important section of the country who are dis-

(M. C. CHAGLA)

senters. I would like to see freedom restored in my lifetime but I doubt that I will. Freedom is indivisible. India is a vast country representing a vast area of freedom. If that is lost, it is a big blow against democracy and freedom elsewhere.

Interview/Los Angeles Times, 8-27:(1)25.

K. M. Chrysler
Chief Canadian correspondent, and former Tokyo bureau chief, "U.S. News & World Report" 1

The Japanese are feared because they work so hard, so cooperatively, so effectively. Their secret weapon is an ability to subordinate corporate as well as individual interests to those of the state. This means that Japanese businessmen have no hesitation in forming a united front, if necessary, to beat out foreign competition for a big, lush order. It's part of their so-called Japan-Incorporated image, and what critics call the "incestuous relationship" between businessmen, bureaucrats and politicians. Additionally, the Japanese are accused of a variety of more-conventional sins, including an under-valued currency and barbed-wire barriers to imports of foreign goods and capital. But what may upset trading partners most is their aggressive salesmanship and what a former U.S. Ambassador to Japan once called an "unfair labor practice"— their willingness to work and to work hard.

Interview/U.S. News & World Report, 11-15:73.

Pete V. Dominici
United States Senator, R—New Mexico 2

At this particular point in history, I know of no conditions under which I would support [U.S.] aid [to Vietnam]. Believe me, I have as much concern about the effects of that war as anyone. I think a lot of mistakes were made, but I also know that 50,000 Americans died there, and that we spent in excess of $300-billion of our resources. It's just not right to think of making retribution to them

for us having been involved in what we thought was right, even though it turned out to be a rather mixed bag. If we are going to have a foreign-aid program, there are many countries more deserving of our help. We have taken many friendly nations for granted, especially in Central and South America. I think our limited resources should go there, and at home, first. It's possible there could be a balance-of-power situation that might cause us to change our minds about Vietnam. We didn't think we wanted to be friends of [Communist] China's, either. But it's a question of China vis-a-vis the Soviet Union, and we choose to be friends of China. I don't see that kind of situation—Russia versus Vietnam or Vietnam versus China, however.

Interview/U.S. News & World Report, 10-25:50.

Pham Van Dong
Premier of Vietnam 3

[The U.S. should] honor its commitment under the Paris [peace] agreement [of 1973] regarding U.S. contributions to healing the wounds of war and post-war reconstruction in Vietnam. For the United States, with whom we are prepared to normalize relations, this is a question of conscience, responsibility and honor, which it can by no means elude.

At conference of non-aligned nations, Colombo, Sri Lanka/U.S. News & World Report, 8-30:67.

Gerald R. Ford
President of the United States 4

[On the death of Chinese Communist Party Chairman Mao Tse-tung]: Chairman Mao was a giant figure in modern Chinese history. He was a leader whose actions profoundly affected the development of his country. His influence on history will extend far beyond the borders of China. Americans will remember that it was under Chairman Mao that China moved, together with the United States, to end a generation of hostility between our two countries. I am confident that the trend of improved relations between the

P.R.C. and the United States, which Chairman Mao helped create, will contribute to world peace and stability.

To newsmen, Washington, Sept. 9/
The New York Times, 9-10:(A)16.

1

I have personally told [South Korean] President Park that the United States does not condone the kind of repressive measures that he has taken in that country. But I think, in all fairness and equity, we have to recognize the problem that South Korea has. On the north, they have North Korea with 50,000 well-trained, well-equipped troops. They are supported by the People's Republic of [Communist] China. They are supported by the Soviet Union. South Korea faces a very delicate situation.

Debate with Democratic Presidential nominee
Jimmy Carter, San Francisco, Oct. 7/
The New York Times, 10-8:(A)19.

Donald M. Fraser
United States Representative,
D—Minnesota
2

I don't think North Korea will launch another war as long as U.S. troops are in the South. And that's why I find [South Korean President] Park's arguments that they've got to impose tight controls on the South because of the threat from the North to be incredible. If our [U.S.] troops were gone, that would be a different matter. But, frankly, my impression is that Park is doing what he's doing just because he wants to stay in power. It's my feeling that we ought to exert maximum pressure on the South Korean government to change course [allow more freedom] while the troops are there because . . . that would leave the Korean government persuaded to reverse course without having to worry about the threat from the North. U.S. forces would serve as

a shield behind which you could have a more open political system.

Interview, Washington/
The Christian Science Monitor, 11-24:4.

Malcolm Fraser
Prime Minister of Australia
3

There had been a view—which was never an Australian view—that because of the United States' strength, countries in [Asia] could sit back and relax and not do what they ought to do for themselves. We would certainly support the statements made by Americans that the United States cannot be expected to do for other countries what they ought to do for themselves . . . Australians certainly don't want a free ride at anyone else's expense. This is one of the reasons why, in a time of fairly strict financial stringency at home, our defense effort and forward five-year defense programming is being very significantly extended. There are things that we feel we must do on our own account. But there are many other things that only the United States can do because only the United States has the material strength and the material power. She is the world's leading free power. There are many things that, if they are not accomplished by the United States, will remain undone.

Interview, Washington/
U.S. News & World Report, 8-9:32.

4

The [Communist] Chinese don't want to have any formal alliances or arrangements with anyone. What we are seeking to do generally in relations with China is to learn, to explore, to communicate . . . when you come to Australia and China, the history, tradition, language, culture and standard of life are all vastly different. Until fairly recently, we had no real communication with China. And I believe very strongly that no matter what the internal ideology of a country may be, it's important in international relations to seek to communicate, to understand. We

WHAT THEY SAID IN 1976

(MALCOLM FRASER)

[Australia] have very close dialogue on many matters with many countries—with Canada, the United States, Japan, with all the Asian countries and, of course, with New Zealand. As far as we're concerned, our communications are quite incomplete unless we also have good, full communication with China.

Interview, Washington/
U.S. News & World Report, 8-9:33.

Indira Gandhi
Prime Minister of India
1

[On her emergency powers and the suspension of certain freedoms in her country]: You can go anywhere and see that there is no police-state atmosphere. In fact, throughout the emergency we have not had to use the police at all and the people are relaxed. If by "openness" or "giving up openness" you mean that we have given up democracy, this also is wholly incorrect. The emergency is intended to deal with grave internal disturbance, which was no less than the breakdown of the country. That dire possibility has been prevented, but the forces which worked for it have not disowned their intentions. In every country, the peacetime rights of citizens are definitely abridged in wartime. The threat to defy laws and bring about a countryside paralysis of government [in India] produced an almost warlike situation. The emergency was a kind of shock treatment intended to tell the country that the nation cannot survive or the future be built if there is widespread lack of discipline, if factories, railways, universities are not allowed to work. Today there is no basic change in our philosophy. We only wish to plug the loopholes and improve the functioning, [especially] of the legal system, so that major social and economic programs can go ahead.

Interview, New Delhi/
San Francisco Examiner & Chronicle, 4-18:(A)23.

Hirohito
Emperor of Japan
2

Today, as I look back over the past 50 years, I recall many joys and sorrows. Above all things, I am deeply impressed that the people, after having overcome national crises and ordeals, have become what we are today. However, when I think of the many victims and their families of the last war and as I still see the scars of that conflict, my heart is filled with great sorrow. I believe that we should not be blinded by the prosperity of the moment. The world changes second by second and our country will have to deal with many problems in the future.

At ceremony marking the 50th anniversary
of his reign, Tokyo, Nov. 10/
The New York Times, 11-11:1.

Hua Kuo-feng
Acting Premier of the People's Republic
of (Communist) China
3

A revolutionary mass debate is going on [in China] in such circles as education, science and technology. It is a continuation and deepening of the Great Proletarian Cultural Revolution. It fully demonstrates the extensive democracy practiced in our country under the system of socialism. We are confident that, through this debate, Chairman Mao's proletarian revolutionary line will find its way deeper into the hearts of the people, and our socialist motherland will be further consolidated.

At banquet honoring former U.S. President
Richard Nixon, Peking, Feb. 22/
Los Angeles Herald-Examiner, 2-23:(A)2.

Hua Kuo-feng
Chairman,
Communist Party of China
4

[Saying his country will purge Party and government officials who gained their positions through connections with the late Mao Tse-tung's wife, Chiang Ching, and other repudiated Politburo members]: The Central Committee is going to launch a movement of consolidation and rectification throughout the Party at an opportune time next year . . . This evil bourgeois trend [of Chiang Ching and her associates] was highly corro-

318

sive to our Party's organism and corruptive of the minds of our Party members. Ganging up for private interest is not allowed. Party workers are servants of the people and must never ask the Party and the people for high posts or for power.

At Chinese national farm conference/
The New York Times, 12-29:1,3.

Alfred le S. Jenkins
Former Director for the People's Republic of China, Mongolia, Hong Kong and Macau, Department of State of the United States
1

The Russians and [Communist] Chinese have different chemistries ... while the chemistry between the Americans and the Chinese is better. All through history the Chinese have tended to look at everyone else as barbarians. Americans are lovable, naive barbarians, but the Russians, they think, are peculiarly adept at being barbarians. The Chinese also think of the Russians as heretics in the secular religion of Communism, and a heretic is harder to deal with than a mere non-believer ... The United States has finally learned that we can't simply overwhelm countries with our power as we once did. We now must use history, psychology and diplomacy and a lot of other things. And China, I think, has learned that it's better to talk, even if it is ineffective, than it is to fight.

Before Dallas Women's Club, Nov. 10/
The Dallas Times Herald, 11-11:(E)2.

Kim Il Sung
President of North Korea
2

In trying to keep South Korea in their grip, the U.S. imperialists aim primarily at tightening their control of Japan. They think that only when they have control over Japan can they treat other countries of Asia as colonies. The U.S. imperialists want to keep South Korea under their thumb partly because they want to make South Korea their permanent raw-material base. It is a fact that they lust for the raw materials in South Korea. Some time ago, I found an article in a certain country's magazine which predicted that

Korea had huge oil deposits, which might possibly touch off troubles in Korea. It looks like the U.S. imperialists are craving for the oil resources found in the continental shelves near the Korean peninsula. To the U.S. imperialists it is also essential to have control over South Korea as a military base. They want to seize the whole of Korea and, further, realize their world domination by using South Korea as their military, strategic base. They want South Korea as a military base to deter the Soviet Union and [Communist] China and tighten their control of Japan.

Interview/ The Washington Post, 11-12:(A)8.

Kim Seong Jin.
Minister of Culture and Information of South Korea
3

I don't think there will be any role for foreign influence in our culture in the future. What I expect of foreigners is that they understand and appreciate our culture as it is. That is all ... Well, technology, if you consider that to be part of culture—I think we can learn from foreign countries about that. But other than that, I don't see any role for foreign culture here in the future.

Interview/ Los Angeles Times, 7-20:(I)1.

Kim Young Sam
Leader, New Democratic Party of South Korea
4

[Criticizing repression in his country]: Freedom and civil rights should go hand in hand with national security. Those two things should not and cannot be separated from each other. The government must give the people a cause to enable them to defend freedom at the cost of their lives. If the present situation continues, perhaps the people may find no reason to fight for their country.

The New York Times, 3-21:(4)3.

Toshio Kimura
Former Foreign Minister of Japan
5

People sometimes say that Japan should spend about the same amount on [foreign]

economic aid that it spends on defense. I do not agree with this approach. If economic aid to the developing nations is to be justified at all, it must be done so on its own terms. If it is not justifiable, we should not be spending a penny on it, even if we were allocating much less of our budget on defense. On the other hand, if aid is justifiable—and I believe it is—we should continue it and expand it even if defense were to take up a much larger share of our budget.

Interview, Tokyo/
The Christian Science Monitor, 4-30:12.

Henry A. Kissinger
Secretary of State
of the United States

1

There are some naive ideas around that if we appeal properly to the [Communist] Chinese that they will somehow take care of our Soviet problems for us; that we can use the Chinese by some undescribed means to bring additional pressure on the Soviet Union. The fact is: No offer of cooperation has ever been made to us by the Chinese that we have refused or that we would not have followed up if it was in our own interest. The worst mistake we could possibly make is to give the Chinese the impression that we are using them for our purposes, and that we are asking them to take additional risks in order to help *us* out. The Chinese have been in business as a major country for 4,000 years. They did not survive that long by letting themselves be used by foreigners. The Chinese need us for security reasons and because they have an interest in world equilibrium. We have, for our own reasons, our own interest in preventing any country from upsetting the balance of power. Therefore, if we both understand our interests properly, we can pursue certain parallel policies without fawning and without giving the impression that there is some gimmick which is going to solve our basic security problem for us.

Interview, Washington/
U.S. News & World Report, 3-15:27.

What is there [for me] to have pangs of conscience . . . about with Vietnam? We found 500,000 American troops in Vietnam and we ended the war without betraying those who in reliance on us had fought the Communists . . . No one could foresee that [the Watergate scandal in the U.S.] would so weaken the Executive authority that we could not maintain the settlement that in itself was maintainable [in Vietnam]. And if you look at what our opposition was saying during that time, their proposals were usually only about six months ahead of where we were going anyway. Some said we should end the war by the end of '72. After all, it took [the late French President Charles] de Gaulle five years to end the Algerian war. And it was a very difficult process.

Interview, London, June 25/
The Washington Post, 7-1:(A)17.

3

[On U.S. relations with Communist China]: It is important to recognize that China's perception of the United States as a strong and resolute force in international events is an important factor in shaping our relations. We will keep Chinese views in mind in framing our approach to important international questions. But equally, if so subtle and complex a relationship is to prosper, the People's Republic of China must take our concerns and problems into account as well. We must deal with each other on the basis of equality and mutual benefit—and a continuing recognition that our evolving relationship is important for global stability and progress. The new relationship between the United States and the People's Republic of China is now an enduring and important feature of the international scene.

Before Seattle Chamber of Commerce and
Downtown Rotary Club, July 22/
Vital Speeches, 8-15:654.

4

Three times in the past 35 years, many thousands of American lives have been lost on the Asian continent. We have learned the hard way that our own safety and well-being depend upon peace in the Pacific, and that peace cannot be maintained unless we play an active part. Soviet activity in Asia is growing. North and South Korea remain locked in bitter confrontation, [and] Hanoi [Vietnam] represents a new center of power and its attitude toward its neighbors remains ambiguous and potentially threatening.

Before Seattle Chamber of Commerce and Downtown Rotary Club, July 22/ The Washington Post, 7-23:(A)8.

1

[On the death of Chinese Communist Party Chairman Mao Tse-tung, and its possible effects on the world scene]: We consider our opening to the People's Republic of China one of the most important foreign-policy actions of the recent period and we don't really expect any change on the Chinese side; but the methods and the nuances are certainly going to change. I don't think even the Chinese know what the impact of the death of such a tremendous figure will be for them. And I don't think any of us know what the new Chinese leaders will do. I would think that, interests having brought us together, common interests will keep us on a parallel course.

To newsmen, Washington, Sept. 9/ The New York Times, 10-10:(A)1.

Kukrit Pramoj
Prime Minister of Thailand
2

Democracy is the only reply from this country to the encroachment of Communism all around us. We cannot fight Communism by another kind of dictatorship. This would only play into the Communists' own hands. We must base our weapon on equal challenges and equal opportunity, the right to have individual choices and individual views. If we put away these things, we are lost.

Interview, Bangkok/ Time, 3-15:36.

Nguyen Cao Ky
Exiled former Premier and former Vice President of South Vietnam
3

America created [South] Vietnam, supported it, chose its leaders and abandoned it. After the Paris agreement, Hanoi and the U.S. got something, but we lost. The country's *raison d'etre* ceased.

Interview, New York/ Los Angeles Herald-Examiner, 5-1:(A)4.

4

[Saying former South Vietnamese President Nguyen Van Thieu was not an effective leader during the war with North Vietnam]: That's the whole thing. Leadership. We know that when you speak about ideology, of course freedom is better than Communist dictatorship. But on the other side they kept their people united and strong because of strong leadership . . . After many years of bombing and all kinds of destruction, they stood on their own feet and continued to accept the suffering. It's not because of ideology but purely of leadership.

Interview/ The National Observer, 5-8:4.

5

When I came out of Vietnam, I had just a tennis bag with me. Your [U.S.] Customs people checked everything. Now [people] are spreading rumors about me that, when I left, I smuggled heroin out with me. With [former South Vietnamese President] Thieu, it's gold. With me, it's heroin. People don't understand. When I was in Vietnam, there was no Constitution. I could kill you if I like. I could take millions of dollars legally if I like. But I'm born honest. That's all. People don't understand that.

Interview/ "W": a Fairchild publication, 6-11:2.

Le Duan
Secretary General, Communist Party of Vietnam
6

The first [Vietnamese Communist] Party Congress [in 1935] brought about the unity

WHAT THEY SAID IN 1976

of members and power of the Party. The second Congress brought about a victory over the French. The third Congress gave directives for building a socialist society in North Vietnam and fighting for the liberation of South Vietnam. The fourth Congress will lead us to defeat poverty, smash all obstacles and achieve our socialist goals, providing happiness for all.

At Vietnamese Communist Party Congress,
Hanoi, Dec. 20/
The New York Times, 12-21:3.

Lee Kuan Yew
Prime Minister of Singapore
1

[When the Association of Southeast Asian Nations was formed,] most people assumed that America and the West had a vital interest in, and would help insure, a non-Communist Southeast Asia. Half a million American troops then in South Vietnam were proof. [But today America and the West have shown that they are] prepared to live with the new [Communist] governments of Vietnam, Cambodia and Laos. As never before, the future of non-Communist Southeast Asia rests in the hands of the leaders and people of non-Communist Southeast Asia.

At ASEAN conference, Bali, Feb. 23/
The Washington Post, 2-24:(A)12.

Lon Nol
Exiled former President of Cambodia
2

[On last year's U.S. withdrawal from the war in Indochina]: The American Army has never been vanquished. But why this time after so much combat in Vietnam, didn't the United States win? . . . What saved Europe [in World War II]? It was determination. But in Southeast Asia, now it's necessary that men submit to dictatorship.

Interview, Honolulu/
Los Angeles Times, 5-26:(1-A)3.

Do Vang Ly
Exiled former South Vietnamese
Ambassador to the United States
3

The war in Vietnam has stopped, but the game is not over . . . American and other Western aid is pouring into [Communist] Vietnam. This aid is helping them rebuild so they can expand in the future. The U.S. should not help Vietnamese expansionism . . . Hanoi has not changed its foreign policy. Americans must realize that Hanoi's friendly attitude to Southeast Asian states and the U.S. is only a temporary short-range tactic. The future role of the U.S. in Asia is linked with the real intentions of Vietnam . . . You cannot ignore Vietnam—it's the key to Southeast Asia. Americans should not be ostriches and put their heads in the sand.

Before Town Hall, Los Angeles, Sept. 13/
Los Angeles Herald-Examiner, 9-14:(A)4.

Mike Mansfield
United States Senator, D—Montana
4

The foremost task for U.S. policy remains to recognize the realities in Indochina. The [Ford] Administration's policy of opposition to trade and commercial relations with Vietnam and Cambodia, and the failure to send an ambassador to Laos, has something in it of the ostrich complex. Although the shooting war is over, economic warfare continues as a cornerstone of U.S. policy. There is no way that a unilateral U.S. trade embargo against Vietnam or Cambodia can be effective in a competitive world. Containment is not a policy. It is only a petulant reaction.

Before the Senate, Washington, April 13/
Los Angeles Times, 4-14:(3)15.

5

[Saying the U.S. should establish formal diplomatic relations with Communist China even if it means breaking relations with Taiwan]: Equivocation over the Taiwan problem has continued far too long. Ambivalence has created a dangerous situation, and further delay could bring about serious long-term consequences for American policy in the Pacific area. [Further delay on the Taiwan problem] may well strengthen the hand of the elements in the [mainland] Chinese leadership seeking to restore greater comity with the Soviet Union even at the expense of the U.S. relationship. The failure to face up to the Taiwan issue will only make the inevitable decision more difficult, controversial and divisive.

Before Senate Foreign Relations Committee,
Washington, Nov. 21/
Los Angeles Times, 11-22:(1)1.

1

We [the U.S.] should pay increasing attention to the Far East, taking into account that ours is not an Asian policy but a Pacific policy. One of the basic objectives should be to get U.S. troops out of Korea. And we should pay constant attention to Japan.

To reporters, Washington/
The Christian Science Monitor, 12-8:42.

Ferdinand E. Marcos
President of the Philippines
2

[On his imposition three years ago of martial law and his assumption of absolute power]: I am one of those who felt guilty about the old system. But I realized I was a captive of it and so did a lot of other people. The [earlier] Presidents seemed to me as if they were just front-men for the oligarchs behind them and, well, I wasn't going to be a front-man for anyone. I wanted to reform and bring about a new society.

Interview, Manila/Time, 1-12:21.

3

I personally believe that [Communist] China and Indochina will be busy trying to consolidate internally in the next five to 10 years, and that it will be to their advantage to develop and engage in normal intercourse with us. Asian nations, including the Philippines, will always be facing the danger of subversion. The principal threat, however,

is internal and not external. Our security will depend on the state of our national health. If our economy should deteriorate, if we are weak and disunited, then the subversives will try to topple the government. Let me say this: Thailand and Malaysia and the other mainland states are in a difficult position. The Philippines and Indonesia are fortunate to be separated from the mainland by water. The leadership in Thailand and Malaysia will have to exercise the highest form of statesmanship in bringing peace to their territories.

Interview, Manila/
U.S. News & World Report, 11-22:65.

Marquita Maytag
United States Ambassador-designate
to Nepal
4

[On Nepal]: When I was up there in the midst of all the Himalayas—I don't think there are words to describe it to anyone. It's overpowering; it equalizes things. It's the wildness, the beauty and simplicity of their way of life. I think they have something very special in their souls and in their spirits that we, as Americans, could benefit from. It's a very sensitive, very deep thing for me. Depth of feeling and caring and consideration and understanding in our Western civilization has almost vanished in pursuit of materialism. That doesn't mean we have to give up everything. But when we see people as content as they are with as little as they have—there's something deeper we need to discover.

Interview, Washington/
San Francisco Examiner & Chronicle, 3-14:
(Sunday Scene)2.

Daniel P. Moynihan
1976 New York Democratic U.S.
Senatorial nominee; Former
U.S. Ambassador to India
5

[On what he learned while Ambassador to India]: Well, they used to have a saying: "What is the good of living in an empire on which the sun never sets if you live in an alley

WHAT THEY SAID IN 1976

(DANIEL P. MOYNIHAN)

where the sun never shines?" I think the lesson I got was that the lesson the colonials taught India was a disaster. The whole British thing—which was basically a decent thing—was concentrated on redistributing the wealth. The trouble is you cannot redistribute wealth where there is no wealth. I mean, you can redistribute the Aga Khan's wealth in a day—but there'll be no difference in the lives of 600 million people. If only they had emphasized production instead of redistribution.

Interview, New York/
San Francisco Examiner & Chronicle, 9-19:
(This World)29.

Jayaprakash Narayan
Indian political leader
1

We have in the country today a complete dictatorship. It is true [the] outward forms of democracy are there. Nevertheless, I hold that there is a dictatorship because . . . power is concentrated in the hands of a single person, [Prime Minister Indira] Gandhi . . . The activities of the opposition parties seem to be totally ineffective. But anyhow, I am not pessimistic. I have faith in the people of this country, and I think there will be a protest generally . . . There seems to [be] economic improvement in the condition of the people to some extent on account of falling prices and greater availability of essential commodities. But, on the other hand, how long this will continue one does not know. So if the economic situation worsens and the political situation remains as it is—or worsens—I don't think the people will accept it for long.

Before Indian political parties,
Bombay, March 20/
The Christian Science Monitor, 5-12:18.

Ronald Reagan
Candidate for the 1976 Republican
U.S. Presidential nomination; Former
Governor of California (R)
2

Our relationship with mainland [Communist] China has been a deterrent and a help,

not only to them because of their sharing of the border with the Soviet Union and the fear that exists between the two countries of each other, but I think that it serves our purpose. I don't believe, however, that in pursuing that relationship we should be persuaded to drop any of our long-time friends or allies, like Taiwan. I think we should say to the mainland Chinese that they accept us and our friendship with the knowledge and understanding that we will not, in return for that, throw any allies aside or break any of our commitments to our allies.

Interview/
The Christian Science Monitor, 6-3:17.

Donald M. Rumsfeld
Secretary of Defense of the
United States
3

Stability in northeast Asia is very important not only to South Korea but Japan, to the economic well-being in the United States and Western Europe . . . There's no question that the government of South Korea is contributing to the stability in northeast Asia, and that's valuable to the United States.

TV-radio interview/
"Face the Nation,"
Columbia Broadcasting System, 11-28.

William B. Saxbe
United States Ambassador to India
4

[On his experiences as Ambassador]: When we first came here [last year], you never heard anything good about the United States or anything bad about Russia. Now you still hear nothing bad about Russia, but you begin to hear something good about the United States occasionally. I think that they [Indians] are beginning to get the idea that we are not infiltrating their government, that we are not interfering in their affairs, or that we're not going to encourage someone to attack them if we don't like their form of government.

Interview, New Delhi, Nov. 17/
The New York Times, 11-18:13.

James R. Schlesinger
Chairman, Washington Study Group on
National Policy; Former Secretary of
Defense of the United States
1

[Saying Communist China depends on the U.S. to curb Soviet expansionism]: [The Chinese] are not motivated primarily by their love of American society or of our social system, which they continuously decry in their internal propaganda. They simply feel that if areas not under Soviet domination in the Eurasian continent were to succumb to Soviet overlordship, then their future would not be one of independence . . . [China's attitude is that of] turning to the barbarian close at hand. That is not altogether flattering for our self-image, but it does underscore that the Chinese respect the potential strength of the United States, and the willingness to use it. [For that reason,] whether there is a period of turmoil or not, it is in our interest that China remain capable of deterring the Soviet Union. We should regard it with great concern if the Soviets were permitted to move against China.
Before Foreign Policy Association, New York/
The Christian Science Monitor, 11-2:12.

Seni Pramoj
Prime Minister-elect of Thailand
2

The total withdrawal of the American forces [from Thailand] will be the right thing, a good thing for the peace in Southeast Asia. It seems to suit the trend of the times and I don't expect other powers to fill in the power vacuum created by this withdrawal.
Interview, Bangkok, April 18/
Los Angeles Herald-Examiner, 4-19:(A)7.

Karan Singh
Minister for Health and
Family Planning of India
3

We [in India] are facing a population explosion of crisis dimensions which has largely diluted the fruits of the remarkable economic progress that we have made. The time factor is so pressing, and the population

growth so formidable, that we have to get out of the vicious circle through a direct assault upon this problem, as a national commitment.
New Delhi, April 16/
The New York Times, 4-17:4.

William C. Westmoreland
General (Ret.) and former Chief of Staff,
United States Army; Former Allied
Commander in Vietnam
4

[On his new book, *A Soldier Reports*, about the Vietnam war]: I wrote it because the military's side never has been told. A soldier has an obligation to report. We shouldn't sweep Vietnam under the rug like a chapter in history that we can't be proud of. We must look at it to learn our errors. After all, five [U.S.] Presidents and the Congress were involved in this. I'm not advocating a witchhunt, but objective analysis . . . I am convinced that history will reflect more favorably upon the performance of the military than upon politicians and policy-makers.
Interview, Washington/
The Washington Post, 1-17:(B)1.

5

Our erstwhile honorable country betrayed and deserted the Republic of [South] Vietnam after [we] had enticed it to our bosom. The handling of the Vietnam affair was a shameful national blunder. The military should not acquiesce to unsound military decisions.
San Francisco Examiner & Chronicle, 11-28:
(This World)2.

H. K. Yang
Vice Foreign Minister of the
Republic of (Nationalist) China
6

Our relationship with the United States is vital to our national existence. We are against the "two-China" policy, the "one-China, one-Taiwan" formula, and the "one-China, two-governments" formula. To think of any other formula [besides the existing

WHAT THEY SAID IN 1976

(H. K. YANG)

one] would indicate a lack of confidence in the United States and ourselves. To negotiate with the Communists [on mainland China] is to sow the seeds of self-destruction for any country. The United States is a big country and can afford to make some mistakes; but we are a small country and can't afford to make mistakes.

Interview, Taipei/
The Christian Science Monitor, 8-9:4.

Giovanni Agnelli
Chairman, FIAT Company (Italy)
1

The Italian Communist Party has really been the only opposition party to the Christian Democrats since the Second World War. This is why we have had the Christian Democrats in power for 30 years—because of the impossibility of the alternative. At the same time, that role in opposition has made the Italian Communists milder, different, trying to prove that they could be an acceptable alternative in Western society, which is a situation different from that of any other Communist party in the world. I'm not saying they are acceptable, but they are surely trying to become so. When a party has one-third of the voters in a country, it represents a vast spectrum of the electorate, not necessarily just the working class. This different category of voters—intellectuals, middle class and others—also makes the Italian Communist Party different from the American popular impression of Communism.

Interview/Time, 5-3:22.

Andrei A. Amalrik
Soviet historian
2

[On his about-to-begin exile from his country]: The movement for human rights and democracy in the Soviet Union has three lines of defense. On the first are those . . . in jails, camps and mental hospitals who take the sharpest blows. Their burden is hardest. The second line are those who live and struggle in the Soviet Union . . . And finally, there are those beyond the boundaries of the Soviet Union in the safest conditions but who still have to continue the struggle. Once I was on the first line, then on the second and now I will be on the third line. There is no difference in principle between the three, only a difference in degree of risk.

Interview, Moscow/
The Washington Post, 6-27:(A)18.

Andrei A. Amalrik
Exiled Soviet historian
3

Russians have always had respect for a strong Army, tough talk and strong personalities. [Karl] Marx said violence was the midwife of history. So if you want to talk seriously to the Russians, you have to talk tough—from a position of strength. They despise you, they consider you an idiot, they do exactly what they want if you talk to them with courtesy and tact.

Before Anglo-American Press Association, Paris/
U.S. News & World Report, 10-25:55.

Giulio Andreotti
Premier of Italy
4

[On how the Italian Communist Party would run the country]: We have to look at various things to determine what their final attitude will be. I don't believe that there is any pretense in the political line that [Communist leader Enrico] Berlinguer has begun. I don't think that the present leaders are insincere when they want to build something different. The problem of independence from Moscow is not the most worrisome to me. It is the problem of whether they really carry out an evolution toward a different Communism, a Communism different from that in the Soviet Union. The Albanian Communists don't depend on Moscow, but they give no sign of wanting to create a different type of political system.

Interview, Rome/
The New York Times, 12-6:16.

WHAT THEY SAID IN 1976

Carlos Arias (Navarro)
Premier of Spain

1

To legalize the Communists [in Spain] is not a criterion for freedom . . . [Exiled Communist leader Santiago] Carrillo has repeatedly placed himself inside an international ideology that would make him a tool of subversion. He symbolizes a group that is not trying to heal old wounds but reopen them. So Carrillo has lost all right to Spanish citizenship and protection . . . The civil war woke me up about Communism and its monstrosities . . . There isn't a single example in the whole world of a Communist Party that has proved with deeds its respect for the rules of the democratic game once it reached power.

Interview/ Newsweek, 1-12:43.

Anne Armstrong
*United States Ambassador
to the United Kingdom*

2

[Defining the dominant theme of Anglo-American history]: Not hostility, but the compromise of differences; not war, but peaceful cooperation around the world; not jealous competition, but the harmonizing of national efforts to achieve a common purpose.

*At U.S. Bicentennial museum exhibition,
Greenwich, England/
The Christian Science Monitor, 6-9:18.*

3

[On U.S.-British relations]: It's so deep, so pervasive, that even if tomorrow someone decided there'll be no more special relationship, it would be impossible. [The British influence] is in our legal system, in our Constitution, in our language and arts; it's the bedrock of our way of government. It's paradoxical that our very British heritage is what led to our revolution, our demand for self-government.

*Interview, London/
Los Angeles Herald-Examiner, 7-11:(A)10.*

Guido Artom
*President, Italian Federation of
Textile and Apparel Industries*

4

Europe, and especially the EEC countries, are troubled by so many internal problems that the push toward unity has slowed down . . . In this regard, Italy finds herself an advanced and vital country split off from her own frozen political structure. My hope is that 1976 will bring the necessary clarification between the "official" and "unofficial" country, giving the masses the responsible answers they have been asking for.

*Interview/
"W": a Fairchild publication, 1-9:17.*

Mark Evans Austad
United States Ambassador to Finland

5

No other country has 800 miles common frontier with a neighbor [the Soviet Union] so different in its political system. This is a fact we have to recognize about Finland. But I have found that while their heads are turned East, their hearts are with us in the West.

*Interview, Helsinki/
The Christian Science Monitor, 4-8:14.*

George W. Ball
*Former Under Secretary of State
of the United States*

6

By our [the U.S.'] incessant attention to the mood and actions of the Kremlin, we have led some of our European friends to suspect that Washington and Moscow were threatening to gang up on them. At the same time, we have given the Western Communists a false respectability. If the [U.S.] President and the Secretary of State can hobnob with [Soviet leader Leonid] Brezhnev and his cronies on the television screens of the world, what is wrong with Italians sharing governmental power with their own Communist Party?

*Before Democratic Party platform committee,
Washington, May 19/
The Washington Post, 5-20:(A)7.*

Max Beloff
Principal, University College, Buckingham, England; Former professor of government and public administration, Oxford University, England   1

What we have now in Britain is government that claims to be acting in the name of the sovereignty of Parliament opposed by groups, like the trade unions, which can defy government because they possess coercive power. In between is the great mass of citizens who are represented in neither way and become hopeless victims of these competing pressures with very little say over their own destinies. The result is increasing discontent, disillusion, apathy—call it what you will—as people find themselves confronted with a reality they've never been asked if they want . . . what's been occurring in Britain for a century or more does correspond to a movement in public opinion which increasingly looks to the state as the ultimate universal provider. As soon as you get any public which regards the state like this, it finds it very difficult to think out any alternative scheme in which the benefits of a state underpinning of society are linked with the benefits of freedom. Until people grasp the simple notion that when they talk about the state benefiting them they really mean the state taking their money and spending it for them, there won't be much change.

Interview, London/
U.S. News & World Report, 3-8:53.

W. Tapley Bennett
United States Ambassador/ Deputy Permanent Representative to the United Nations   2

If life in the Soviet Union is so beautiful, if it really is [a] paradise . . . why is it that so many people want to emigrate? Famous names such as [ballet stars Mikhail] Baryshnikov and [Rudolf] Nureyev and [author Alexander] Solzhenitsyn—no, pardon me, Mr. Solzhenitsyn did not emigrate; he was exiled; they expelled him. But it is not just these famous names; there are countless thousands whose names we will never know who have desired to emigrate . . . We need only to recall the following words of Lenin—mind you, it is not customary for an American delegate to be quoting Lenin—but it seems appropriate here today in these circumstances. Here is what Lenin said: "The people have no need for liberty . . . In a state worthy of the name there is no liberty. The people want to exercise power, but what on earth would they do if it were given to them?" That says it all, doesn't it, as to what the Leninist state thinks about human rights.

Before UN General Assembly's human rights committee, New York, Nov. 26/ Los Angeles Times, 11-27:(1)28.

Enrico Berlinguer
Leader, Communist Party of Italy   3

Our relationship with all other Communist parties is based on friendship, but we are not tied by the policies of Communist countries. We do not see the Soviet Union as a guide; no Communist Party, not even the Soviet Party, has a position of guiding influence.

The New York Times, 1-18:20.

4

The grave crisis that our country is going through will find a democratic solution and one of social renewal only if the Communist Party is called on to participate at a level of equality with popular and democratic forces of different political and ideological orientations in the direction of national political life . . . We are fighting for a socialist society that would be the culmination of the development of all democratic conquests and would guarantee respect for all individual and collective liberties—liberties of religion and culture, arts and sciences. We think that in Italy one can and must not only advance toward socialism, but also build socialist society with the contribution of different political forces, organizations and parties, and that the working class can and must affirm its historical function in a pluralistic and democratic system.

At Soviet Communist Party Congress, Moscow, Feb. 27/ The New York Times, 2-28:12.

WHAT THEY SAID IN 1976

(ENRICO BERLINGUER)

1

[On whether Italy would remain in NATO should his party assume controlling powers in the government]: We are ready to accept the obligations attached to membership until such a time when military blocs are replaced by other security systems. We will honor the duties assumed in the alliance by preceding governments—if we become a member of the government. But we are against interference by other allies in our affairs—especially the United States—using NATO as an excuse.

Interview, Rome/
The New York Times, 3-21:(4)17.

2

As our [Italian Communists'] independence is complete, so is our allegiance to democracy and its rules. We have made it clear that the accession of the working classes to political power can and must be achieved in Italy in a manner fully consistent with democratic institutions, the principles of freedom and the procedures for a change embodied in our constitution. We consider various forms of economic management necessary, allowing wide scope for private enterprise within a national, public program that is democratically prepared and democratically carried out.

Interview, Rome/
San Francisco Examiner & Chronicle, 5-16:(A)20.

3

[On the forthcoming Italian national elections]: The question is not whether the Communists should come to power, but whether the domination of the Christian Democrats and their suffocating power system, which has wrought so much damage and brought Italy to such disorder and poor government, is any longer tolerable.

At rally, Cosenza, Italy/ Time, 6-14:20.

Willy Brandt
Chairman, Social Democratic Party of West Germany; Former Chancellor of West Germany

4

The Communists are large parties in France and Italy, and they won't disappear just because we think their strong appeal to the voters is a bad thing. It would be wrong if by our conduct we contributed to halting the developments that have led to a break-up of the former monolithic bloc of Communism.

Interview, Jan. 23/
The New York Times, 2-5:3.

5

[On the strength of European Communist parties]: The situation in southern Europe is not as critical as some observers have thought. In Portugal only a year ago, many people thought it would be lost to the Communists. Well, the Communists are a strong party—15 per cent in last month's elections—but it is the Socialists that have taken the leadership, and there are two other non-Communist parties . . . In Spain, with many difficulties still to be faced, it is nevertheless clear that if and when there are elections, the Communists will not be a leading party. Two years after the colonels' regime in Greece, there is a conservative government there and a moderate Social Democrat opposition. And in France, what I see is that the Socialists have become the strongest party, whereas only a few years ago people felt only the Gaullists and the Communists were the alternatives.

Interview, Bonn/
The Washington Post, 5-9:(A)18.

Leonid I. Brezhnev
General Secretary,
Communist Party of the Soviet Union

6

[Some circles in the U.S.] portray the policy of the Soviet Union in a false light and refer to an imaginary "Soviet threat" to urge a new intensification of the arms race in the U.S.A. and in NATO . . . In fact, of course, there is no Soviet menace either in the West or in the East. It is all a monstrous lie from beginning to end. The Soviet Union has not the slightest intention of attacking anyone. The Soviet Union has not the need [for] war. The Soviet Union does not increase its military budget, and far from reducing, is steadily augmenting allocations for improving the people's well-being.

At Soviet Communist Party Congress, Moscow,
Feb. 24/ The New York Times, 2-25:14.

1

We have created a new society, a society the likes of which mankind has never known. It is a society with a crisis-free, steadily growing economy, mature socialist relations and genuine freedom. It is a society governed by the scientific materialist world outlook. It is a society of firm confidence in the future, of radiant Communist prospects. Before it lie boundless horizons of continued all-around progress.

At Soviet Communist Party Congress, Moscow,
Feb. 24/ The New York Times, 2-27:3.

2

The Soviet Union's attitude to the complicated processes within the developing countries is clear and definite. The Soviet Union does not interfere in the internal affairs of other countries and peoples. It is a constant principle of our Leninist foreign policy to respect the sacred right of every people, every country, to choose its own way of development. But we do not conceal our views. In the developing countries, as everywhere else, we are on the side of the forces of progress, democracy and national independence, and regard them as friends and comrades in struggle. Our Party supports and will continue to support peoples fighting for their freedom. In so doing, the Soviet Union does not look for advantages, does not hunt for concessions, does not seek political domination, or exact military bases. We act as we are bid by our revolutionary conscience, our Communist convictions.

At Soviet Communist Party Congress, Moscow,
Feb. 24/ Vital Speeches, 4-1:361.

3

The very idea of using nuclear weapons in Europe sounds monstrous to Soviet people.

The European house has become extremely crowded and flammable. There neither is, nor will there be, a fire brigade that could put out the fire if it really were to break out. For Europe and Europeans, peace [has] indeed become vitally necessary . . . Today, more than ever before, it is important to blaze the road to military detente to halt the arms race.

At European Communist party conference,
East Berlin, June 29/
The Washington Post, 6-30:(A)26.

4

The vigorous activity of the Communists in the countries of Western Europe, their perseverance in the struggle for the masses, for uniting the working class and all the forces capable of struggle against the power of the monopolies, for the establishment of truly democratic regimes, for creating prerequisites for the transition to socialism, are bearing fruit. It is thanks to the consistent and tireless struggle for the vital interests of the broad popular masses that the Communist parties of Italy and France, Finland and Portugal, and also of Denmark, the FRG and other capitalist countries have turned into important political forces. Some of the convincing testimonies of this was the outstanding success of the Italian Communist Party in the recent parliamentary elections, a success in which we all rejoice and on which we congratulate our Italian comrades. It is of special importance that, when uniting in the struggle against reactionary imperialist circles with broad democratic streams, including social democrats and christians, the Communists remain revolutionaries, convinced champions of replacing the capitalist system by a socialist one. It is to the solution of this historical task that they subordinate all their activities.

At European Communist party conference,
East Berlin, June 29/ Vital Speeches, 8-1:615.

5

[On reports that his country may be planning to forcibly take control of Yugoslavia]:

WHAT THEY SAID IN 1976

(LEONID I. BREZHNEV)

Authors of such fairy tales try to present Yugoslavia as a helpless Little Red Ridinghood, whom the terrible and bloodthirsty wolf—the aggressive Soviet Union—is preparing to devour. [It is difficult to determine if the root of such statements is] a complete misunderstanding of the principles on which socialist countries build their relations or the cynical belief that the public will swallow any lie if it is repeated frequently enough.

At dinner in his honor, Belgrade, Nov. 15/
The New York Times, 11-16:3.

George S. Brown
General, United States Air Force;
Chairman, Joint Chiefs of Staff

1

Great Britain—it's pathetic now. It just makes you want to cry. They're no longer a world power. All they've got are Generals and Admirals and bands. They do things in great style, grand style. God, they do it well. On the protocol side. But it makes you sick to see their forces.

Interview/ U.S. News & World Report, 11-1:63.

Ihsan S. Caglayangil
Foreign Minister of Turkey

2

NATO remains a necessity for Turkey. The conditions giving birth to NATO are still in existence. True, times are changing, but the basic conditions remain unaltered. Let me state definitely that friendship with the U.S.S.R. does not mean a negation of friendship with the U.S.A.

The New York Times, 2-12:2.

James Callaghan
Prime Minister of the United Kingdom

3

. . . we [in Britain] are still not earning the standard of living we are enjoying. We are only keeping up our standards by borrowing, and this cannot go on indefinitely . . . There can be no lasting improvement in your living standards until we can achieve it without going deeper and deeper into debt as a nation.

Broadcast address to the nation upon
becoming Prime Minister, London, April 5/
Newsweek, 4-19:46.

4

What we [in Britain] need is not so much a change in economic policy as changes in attitudes. This country has felt too long that it has been on the losing side. Well, I think that a country which can be self-supporting in energy—as we shall be in 1980—a country which has skilled scientific manpower and a technological base, a country that has a self-disciplined population—don't tell me that this country can't succeed. Of course it can. We've got to give our people confidence that there is something on the other side of the hill and stop the loser mentality.

Interview/ Time, 5-24:29.

5

[Defending government expenditures]: I was brought up in a family where after my father died we never had more than two furnished rooms. That was denial of freedom. I was unable to go to a university because we could not afford to pay for it. That was a denial of freedom. There was an occasion when I should have had hospital treatment, but I could not because we could not afford it. That was a denial of freedom. The new generation has those freedoms, and that is what public expenditure is about.

Before Parliament, London/
The Christian Science Monitor, 6-11:7.

6

What is the cause of high unemployment [in Britain]? Quite simply and unequivocally, it is caused by paying ourselves more than the value of what we produce. We used to think that you could just spend your way out of a recession and increase employment by cutting taxes and boosting government spending. I tell you in all candor that that option no longer exists . . . You know that we have not been creating sufficient new wealth as fast as we have been distributing it. You know that over the last three years our domestic product has risen by two per cent and the increase in our public expenditures has been 18 per cent. The only long-term cure for unemployment is to create a healthy manufacturing industry that can hold its own overseas and then certainly be able to retain its grip on the domestic market.

Before Labor Party,
Blackpool, England, Sept. 28/
The Christian Science Monitor, 9-29:10.

1

If we [British] are pushed [by our foreign creditors] into a position where we would have to make a choice whether to carry on these [European defense] responsibilities or say, "Sorry, our economic situation demands that we put our own position first," this would be a very serious matter for Europe. I don't want to have to make that choice. I think West Germany, the United States and perhaps Japan have some responsibility here. [The 55,000 British troops in West Germany have] something to do with the stability of Central Europe, something to do with the whole politics of the Western world.

Television statement, London, Oct. 25/
The Washington Post, 10-27:(A)14.

Constantine Caramanlis
Premier of Greece

2

[On his country's dispute with Turkey over Cyprus]: I would make two proposals to Turkey—that the two countries should agree to put an end to the arms race which is detrimental to the welfare of their people, and to conclude a non-aggression pact and seek a peaceful solution of their disputes . . . This is not difficult if good faith prevails, because it is irrational both to preach peaceful coexistence and to undermine it with words and deeds.

Before Parliament, Athens, April 17/
The New York Times, 4-18:(1)10.

Prince Carlos Hugo
Pretender to the Spanish throne

3

Democracy and self-managing socialism are the only answers for Spain. In northern

Europe, monarchy has been a guarantee for change. In Spain, a democratic monarchy would show that you can have change without fear of it getting out of control . . . What we have in Spain [now] is not a monarchy but a hereditary dictatorship. It has neither democratic nor historic roots. Its only roots are in totalitarianism . . . In Spain, the tensions are so enormous and the need for democratic change so radical that the monarchy can have another meaning. [The current] regime wants the people to think that the choice is between them and chaos. But a monarch chosen and elected by the people and committed to democratic change [would prevent a backlash against reform].

Interview, Paris/
The Washington Post, 5-10:(A)1,11.

Santiago Carrillo
Secretary general,
Communist Party of Spain

4

In former years, Moscow, where our dreams began to take on reality, was our [Communists'] Rome. We talked of the great socialist October Revolution as the day of our birth. Those were the times of our childhood. Today we have become adults . . . We have lost the traits characteristic of a church . . . today we have no center that gives us directives . . .

The Washington Post, 7-2:(A)14.

5

Americans should realize that the [Communist] parties in the West don't want to change the strategic balance. It is an element of peace. We don't want Europe under the influence of the Warsaw Pact; we want an autonomous Europe. What we do want is to affect our countries' internal politics without interference. We want a type of socialism with universal suffrage, alternation of government—not control of power for the Communists, but an alliance of forces that in no way would allow a Communist monopoly.

East Berlin/
The New York Times, 7-7:2.

Jimmy Carter
Candidate for the 1976 Democratic
U.S. Presidential nomination;
Former Governor of Georgia (D)
                                                    1

. . . in recent years our Western European
allies have been deeply concerned, and justly
so, by our unilateral dealing with the Soviet
Union. To the maximum extent possible, our
dealings with the Communist powers should
reflect the combined views of the democracies, and thereby avoid suspicions by our
allies that we may be disregarding their interests.

> *Before Foreign Policy Association,*
> *New York, June 23/*
> *The Washington Post, 6-24:(A)6.*

Jimmy Carter
1976 Democratic U.S.
Presidential nominee
                                                    2

[On the advances of some Western European Communist parties]: I think in many
cases they are due to the weakness or the ineptitude of democratic forces to govern suit-
ably. In certain cases, corruption [on the
part of non-Communists] has been a factor
for Communist successes while in others
there has been a certain incompetence or
inability to keep close links between those
who govern. I don't think it is good to intervene directly or indirectly in [foreign
elections] . . . I hope that the countries of
the Atlantic community will make the Italians
and the French understand that Communists
have dual loyalties which most often will tip
in favor of the U.S.S.R. and the Eastern
European nations. This is a threat to their
security and to peace.

> *Interview, Plains, Ga., Aug. 22/*
> *Los Angeles Times, 8-23:(1)7.*

                                                    3

We [the U.S.] should have been much
more aggressive when we attended the Helsinki [European Security] Conference [last
year]—or should have been absent in the
first place. We now have in Eastern Europe

at least a tentative endorsement by our country of the domination of that region by the
Soviet Union. They didn't have that before
the Helsinki accords. It was a very great
diplomatic achievement for the Soviets to
have our promise not to interfere in their
control over Eastern Europe. In response to
our yielding on that point, there was an agreement on the Soviet Union's part that they
would liberalize their policies toward human
rights. They have not fulfilled those commitments.

> *Interview/ U.S. News & World Report, 9-13:22.*

                                                    4

[Criticizing President Ford's statement
that Eastern European countries are not
under Soviet domination]: The Poles, the
Czechs, the Hungarians and the East Germans have been under the domination of the
Soviet Union for a long time. The Soviet
Union has tank divisions and hundreds of
thousands of troops in those countries to
keep them under Soviet domination . . . If
they tore down the Berlin Wall, which way
would the people move? They would move
toward freedom because they don't have
freedom now. And for the President of the
United States to claim that those people in
Eastern Europe are completely free of domination is absolutely ridiculous.

> *Campaigning, Oct. 7/*
> *Los Angeles Times, 10-8:(1)1.*

Jimmy Carter
President-elect of the United States
                                                    5

I have made my position on Yugoslavia
clear; that if the Soviet Union should invade
Yugoslavia, that this would be an extremely
serious breach of peace. It would be a threat to
the entire world, as far as a peaceful world is
concerned. It would make it almost impossible
for us to continue under the broad generic
sense of detente. And whether or not we actually committed troops to Yugoslavia . . . the
conjecture of my opinion is that that would be
unlikely—but I would have to make a decision on a final basis at that point. I might
add that my information from Yugoslavia

has been that the nation is strong militarily, very highly united, very deeply committed to independence, and that the chance for a Soviet invasion would be extremely unlikely.

*News conference, Plains, Ga., Nov. 4/
The New York Times, 11-5:(A)14.*

1

I think the Turkish [military] bases are important to us. I think the presence in a continuing way of our Navy in the eastern Mediterranean is crucial. I think because of a series of mistakes and possible unwarranted intrusion into the Cyprus question that we have alienated to some degree both the Greek and Turkish governments . . . I would hope that we might go ahead and try to ratify an agreement with both Greece and Turkey to continue an adequate military presence in those countries.

*Before Senate Foreign Relations Committee,
Washington, Nov. 23/
Los Angeles Herald-Examiner, 12-2:(A)24.*

Chiao Kuan-hua
*Foreign Minister of the People's
Republic of (Communist) China*
2

There is now a strange phenomenon in the world. Some people are terrified at the mention of the Soviet Union, thinking that it cannot be touched. This is superstition. Soviet social imperialism is nothing to be afraid of. It is outwardly strong but inwardly weak. Alienated from the people, it is essentially feeble. It faces economic difficulties and ever-sharpening class contradictions and contradictions among its nationalities.

*At United Nations, New York, Oct. 5/
Los Angeles Herald-Examiner, 10-6:(A)4.*

Jacques Chirac
Premier of France
3

France is not and will never be hostile to the U.S. Sometimes we have different ideas from those of your country. But I think it is much more important for a nation like the United States to be sure that, in case of a real crisis, France will be the first to be beside them.

*Interview, Paris/
Los Angeles Herald-Examiner, 6-4:(A)8.*

Jacques Chirac
Former Premier of France
4

[Fascism] is absolutely incompatible with Gaullism. This is what differentiates us fundamentally from all forms of Fascism, totalitarianism and collectivism: We never exert an authority which is not legitimate—that is, ratified by the people. The day [President Charles] de Gaulle lost his majority, he resigned within three hours.

Interview, Paris/Newsweek, 12-20:39.

5

It is true that in 1958 the Algerian crisis found its solution in the appeal [in France] to [President Charles] de Gaulle. And in 1968, it was the appeal to [President] Georges Pompidou. Today, it seems again that France is asking herself questions, that she is wondering what her destiny, her future will be. She is hurt by the economic crisis that threatens the economic growth she has become accustomed to. She wonders today if those who lead her are the real embodiments of her hopes.

Interview, Paris/Newsweek, 12-20:39.

Chou Kua-min
*Deputy Minister of Foreign Trade
of the People's Republic of
(Communist) China*
6

On the one hand, [the Soviet Union] uses such political swindles as "relaxation of tension" and "disarmament" to divert the direction of the struggle of the Third World against imperialism. On the other hand, it peddles its old wares such as "international division of labor" in a vain attempt to establish a social-imperialist system, with itself as the sole overlord.

*At United Nations Conference on
Trade and Development, Nairobi, Kenya, May 11/
The New York Times, 5-12:7.*

335

Winston S. Churchill II
Member of British Parliament

1

I think that if there is no coordinated resistance to Soviet expansionism and imperialism in Africa we could see this thing moving nearer home with a Soviet take-over of Yugoslavia following [President] Tito's death or incapacitation. And that, of course, would see the Soviets straddling the northern shores of the Mediterranean which they already dominate with a fleet four times greater than that of the United States. In that context I think one could see the possibility not of nuclear war but of such a large-scale build-up of military power so close to the frontiers of Western democracies that they would just succumb from a combination of external pressures and large-scale fifth-column activity supported from outside.

Interview, London/
Los Angeles Times, 3-21:(1)9.

Dick Clark
United States Senator, D—Iowa

2

It would be the saddest irony if our government, by rushing pell-mell to solidify its relations with post-Franco Spain, were to alienate those very democratic forces whose future success is so fundamentally necessary for the full realization of Spanish-American friendship.

March 3/The Washington Post, 3-4:(A)20.

Liam Cosgrave
Prime Minister of Ireland

3

There are in this country [the U.S.] some people who contribute in the most direct way possible to the violence [in Northern Ireland] —by sending actual guns and explosives. A larger number have contributed, thoughtlessly or otherwise, to organizations nominally engaged in "relief" work, but which have used the money to buy guns and explosives. What they are doing with every penny, dime or dollar they give is helping to kill or maim men and women of every religious persuasion. And they are not helping—whatever they may

think—to bring an end to what they call the British presence in Ireland.

Before joint session of Congress,
Washington, March 17/
Los Angeles Herald-Examiner, 3-24:(A)7.

4

[On IRA terrorism]: Those who kill and maim should know by now the futility of their course. Seven years have brought the toll of unnecessary deaths to some 1,500 and of injured to 18,000. These are not numbers or ciphers in some coding game. They are ordinary men, women and children, like many of you listening to me here today. What cause do those who bomb and shoot on this scale think they serve? Is it a brighter future or friendship with the family and neighbors of the dead?

At political party conference/
The Christian Science Monitor, 5-17:4.

Massimo de Carolis
Member of Italian Parliament

5

[On Communist election gains at the expense of his party, the Christian Democrats]: Until now, the Christian Democrats knew the votes were there and mainly used their power to conserve their influence within the Party. Today, the votes are no longer automatic and the Party must concern itself with winning popular support . . . I do not consider myself right-wing. Unfortunately, in Italy today anyone who is opposed to the Communists is automatically considered a Fascist.

The Washington Post, 12-5:(A)9.

Suleyman Demirel
Premier of Turkey

6

[Criticizing the U.S. for instituting an arms embargo against Turkey last year because of that country's military intervention in Cyprus]: We did not have any dispute with the United States—but the U.S. Congress took the embargo decision. Embargo means hostility . . . I think we share the same way of life and philosophy and that we had commonly decided to defend it. A strong Turkey would be more helpful to defend the common cause. A weak Turkey would be a burden. With the embargo decision, the U.S. Congress has undermined Turkey's defense strength, which means creating a weak friend. We have allowed that there be some U.S. missile bases and other things which mean increasing the risk to Turkey in case of [East-West] confrontation. In case of confrontation, Turkey would be the Number 1 country to be eliminated.

Interview, Ankara, Dec.1/
Los Angeles Herald-Examiner, 12-2:(A)4.

Milovan Djilas
Author; Former Vice President
of Yugoslavia 1

The Italian and Spanish Communists are all right because they have democratic ideals. But the French are Stalinists. The Italian Communists say "our democracy" when they talk to the people. And this is a necessary, positive approach to the existing Constitution. The French Communists—they talk about, "We shall create a popular democracy of the masses," which is Stalinist dogma. The Italian Communist Party is part of the Establishment now. It is unimaginable that the Italian Party would retrogress to the Soviet line if it achieves total power ... Communism is worth trying in Italy but not in France. In France, it would mean civil war.

Interview, Belgrade/
Los Angeles Times, 11-14:(4)6.

Antonio Ramalho Eanes
President-elect of Portugal 2

[On his recent election victory]: [It was] a mandate for democracy, for a state of law in Portuguese society ... the minority must respect the will of the majority. No type of insurrectional activity will be tolerated. Freedom and liberty are possible only when security allows them to be.

News conference, Lisbon, June 28/
Los Angeles Times, 6-29:(1)15.

Gerald R. Ford
President of the United States 3

This Administration would be very dis-

turbed by Communist participation in the government of Italy. For one reason, it would have a very, I think, unfortunate impact on NATO which is, of course, a very vital part of our international defense arrangement. The United States does have apprehension on a broader basis for Communist participation in the Italian government.

San Francisco Examiner & Chronicle, 7-25:
(This World)2.

4

... there is no Soviet domination of Eastern Europe and there never will be under a Ford Administration ... I don't believe ... that the Yugoslavians consider themselves dominated by the Soviet Union. I don't believe that the Romanians consider themselves dominated by the Soviet Union. I don't believe that the Poles consider themselves dominated by the Soviet Union. Each of those countries is independent, autonomous, it has its own territorial integrity, and the United States does not concede that those countries are under the domination of the Soviet Union. As a matter of fact, I visited Poland, Yugoslavia and Romania to make certain that the people of those countries understood that the President of the United States and the people of the United States are dedicated to their independence, their autonomy and their freedom.

Debate with Democratic Presidential nominee
Jimmy Carter, San Francisco, Oct. 7/
The New York Times, 10-8:(A)18.

5

[On his statement during a recent debate that Eastern European countries, such as Poland, are not dominated by the Soviet Union]: Let me explain what I really meant ... They [the Poles] don't believe they are going to be forever dominated—if they are—by the Soviet. They believe in the independence of that great country, and so do I. We're going to make certain, to the best of our ability, that any allegation of dominance is not a fact.

Before San Fernando Valley Business and
Professional Association, Los Angeles, Oct. 8/
The New York Times, 10-9:1.

WHAT THEY SAID IN 1976

Manuel Fraga (Iribarne)
Minister of Internal Affairs of Spain

1

[Saying there are three points of view on the status of the Communist Party in his country]: One: Spain, unlike Portugal, had a bloody, relatively recent civil war. Even leftists remember this acutely. Many people still believe the Communists will try to promote chaos in Spain; that therefore it is foolish to give them any legal status because they are well-organized, disciplined, have ample funds and an international base. The British and Americans, who had their civil wars in the 17th and 19th centuries, find it difficult to appreciate Spanish feelings on this. Two: Others argue the Communists now are recognized and exist everywhere and you can limit but not destroy their well-organized infrastructure; that one must accept and face this situation. They also believe it is less dangerous to expose Communists legally than to leave them to conspire underground. Finally, they insist other leftist parties won't join in the new Spanish democracy if the Communists are excluded. Three: The government's views embrace both opinions. For the present, we consider it wise to accept point one. But after the second phase of our reform program is punctuated by a new, freely elected legislature—probably in June, 1977—it will be time to accept point two. By then, Spanish society will be sufficiently rejuvenated and strong enough to face any problems created.
Interview, Leon, Spain/
The New York Times, 6-19:21.

2

Our government is moving forward toward its democratic objectives while resisting pressures from both right and left extremes. During the first six months of our existence we have amended the succession law and legalized a multi-party system. The second period—in which we find ourselves—will end with our national referendum. This third half-year phase will finish with free Parliamentary elections. This is a steady, pragmatic program, not just words. It is a step-by-step affair with a fixed goal in mind. In method

it may be compared to the kind of technique used diplomatically by [U.S. Secretary of State Henry] Kissinger. I meet one day with liberal leaders, another with Socialists, another with conservatives—even with those officially sent by the Communists. Our policy is set—and the calendar of our timing for each step forward.
Interview, Leon, Spain/
The New York Times, 6-19:21.

David Frost
British television interviewer;
Producer

3

I always cling to the view that Britain will survive its economic crisis—not so much from a blanket "pollyanna" point of view but because I think the British character has the qualities of the ostrich and the lion. Like the ostrich, we probably add to our problems by not facing up to them. But when another 1939 dawns, the British will have the qualities of the lion—provided they are convinced that it is 1939.
Interview/
"W": a Fairchild publication, 1-9:17.

Valery Giscard d'Estaing
President of France

4

[On the possibility of Communist governments in Italy and France]: To implement the program of the left would bring economic disorders. Logic does exist in politics, and logic is stronger than statements. Communists in power will conform to their doctrine, which obviously does not endorse free enterprise, participation in NATO or the construction of a united Europe. Even if the Communists' language seems more moderate today, their basic principles remain the same.
Interview/Time, 5-17:41.

5

People were skeptical of my determination to carry out major changes in French society. They are now convinced that I meant what I said. Major reforms include the lowering of the voting age to 18, the liberalization of divorce, contraception and abortion laws, the liberalization of TV and the setting up of a capital-gains tax. I can't think of a major reform that I have failed to get through. I'm a strange case—both a traditionalist and a reformer, but not a conservative. What concerns me is that France adapt itself to the modern world . . . I'm not in favor of change for change's sake, but because change is essential to adapt France to changing conditions.

Interview/Newsweek, 5-17:48.

1

Nothing which has happened in the world and in Europe during the past few years suggests the prospect of the withdrawal of American troops from Europe. Such a withdrawal would be detrimental to the security of the United States and, obviously, it would be detrimental to the security of Europe. As to the prospect of an autonomous European defense: This is not likely in the immediate future. At present, there are a number of unresolved problems concerning the organization of Europe. Only when these are resolved will it be realistic to raise the problem of a European organization of defense.

Interview, Paris/
U.S. News & World Report, 5-17:51.

2

To understand France, you have to remember that it has one of the oldest political histories in the world. We have been an organized nation for 1,000 years—the only nation in Europe to have a centralized structure for so long. This historical aspect is fundamental to what we are and how we act. It means that France is highly aware of its own personality and is very attached to its independence. France wants to control its own destiny. Besides this, France was a world power of a special type: much more an intellectual and moral power than a material

one. Britain has been a gigantic colonial empire. France, on the contrary, tried to exert political and moral influence rather than try to dominate. It exported its influence and ideas at the time of the French Revolution in 1789 and at the time of Napoleon. I think the best-known statesman to the present generation is still Napoleon. At present, the world faces certain problems in terms of influence. In the North-South dialogue [between rich and poor nations], for instance, the value of proposed solutions counts far more than does the power of the countries which propose the solutions. This is how France has been able to contribute to this dialogue.

Interview, Paris/
U.S. News & World Report, 5-17:51.

3.

[On U.S.-French relations]: The real secret of our understanding springs from the principles that have inspired it. Both countries have shown, without a break and sometimes in dramatic circumstances, an identical passion for independence and liberty.

Washington, May 17/
The New York Times, 5-18:2.

4

Let America view Europe's achievements without misgivings and without apprehension. You [the U.S.] do not fear freedom for yourself; do not, then, fear it for your friends and your allies. An independent, organized and prosperous European community is the best partner for the United States and a guarantee of stability, development and peace.

Before joint session of U.S. Congress,
Washington, May 18/
Los Angeles Herald-Examiner, 5-18:(A)1.

5

[On U.S.-French relations and the U.S. Bicentennial]: In the course of these two centuries, our two countries have remained friends. This example is perhaps unique in

WHAT THEY SAID IN 1976

history. We are fully aware of the role you played in defending our liberty. The French people have not forgotten; they thank you for it. The real secret of our understanding springs from the principle which inspired it. Both countries have [shown] without a break, and sometimes in dramatic circumstances, an identical passion for independence and liberty. Today, two centuries later, this same principle remains at the center of the world's problems: the independence of peoples and the liberty of men. Liberty sometimes seems to us as natural as the air we breathe, but we know very well we must constantly defend it against the forces of intimidation and falsehood to maintain it. My country is ready to make the effort and sacrifices such defense entails. In saying this, I am probably only restating what the greatest of my predecessors have already said before me in the name of France. However, this is not a meaningless repetition. Through me, it expresses the intellectual and emotional endorsement by new generations of French men and women of the positions taken by the preceding generation vis-a-vis the United States.

At the White House, Washington/
U.S. News & World Report, 7-5:Special Section.

1

Europeans are people who have fought among themselves for 2,000 years with remarkable relentlessness, who have different languages, different cultures, different religions, and very strong personalities. Their organization of a confederation is, in my opinion, a task more difficult and at least as creative as the building of the Federal structure in the United States. Realizing this confederation must be our first objective.

Interview/
The Christian Science Monitor, 11-10:22.

Robert A. Haeger
London bureau chief, and former
Bonn bureau chief,
"U.S. News & World Report"   2

Economically, West Berlin is a phony—the most subsidized spot on earth. In the mid-1960s, West German taxpayers were shelling out $1-billion a year to keep the city afloat. Now the bill runs close to 2.5 billion annually. The total so far is in the neighborhood of $40-billion—more than $20,000 per head of West Berlin population—and still climbing. Up to now, there has been a minimum of grumbling about this enormous drain on the Bonn treasury. But how long will younger West Germans—those who don't remember the Soviet blockade, the Allied airlift and the other spectacular clashes of the cold war in Berlin—keep digging into their pockets willingly? And if West German support—financial, political, moral—ever flags, there would be a real possibility of a negotiated deal in which the Communist East Germans would take over. That's the sort of thing those Germans who don't fear war, but who do fear Communist domination, think and talk about.

Interview/
U.S. News & World Report, 11-15:74.

Alexander M. Haig, Jr.
General, United States Army;
Supreme Allied Commander/Europe   3

I believe that the threat of Soviet power is greater today. What we have been witnessing, at a relentless pace, is the propulsion of Soviet geopolitical power to superpower status. This has been . . . primarily an outgrowth of sheer military power. We see this more clearly every day—Angola being the latest manifestation. In this new strategic environment . . . the debate over detente may be far less relevant than a clear recognition that growing Soviet power is with us and will not be controlled by atmospherics or rhetoric. There can be only one answer: Soviet power must be managed by the maintenance of equivalent Western power.

Interview, Brussels/Newsweek, 2-9:35.

4

We know [West Berlin] is not defensible, but it is there, and it stands today as a bastion of the will and unity of the free world. It does not stand there because it is defensible but because it represents a tangible manifestation of our collective will.

Interview, Casteau, Belgium/
U.S. News & World Report, 3-1:38.

1

. . . if you look at the Mediterranean, we have had an evolution in Portugal. It is far from out of the woods and very difficult still. But there have been recent elections and manifestations of a moderate pluralistic outcome. There is an evolution in Spain from which we have some reason to draw encouragement that it will be greater in the direction of moderation, greater integration in European affairs—economic and security. We have the exception of Italy, which is perhaps at the peak of its crisis. In Greece and Turkey we have been wrestling with these insoluble problems, but which I believe were aggravated by American policies, but which now provide some hope of normalization of the alliance relationships. Now, all this is highly dynamic and dangerous, but nonetheless you look at that northern tier of the Mediterranean and it's not a question of being all black—not by a long shot. In recent months, there has also been a growing awareness in the Scandinavian countries —Denmark and Norway—of the need to maintain their guard. Britain is a special problem because of their severe economic bind, but there you still see evenhandedness in austerity not all falling on defense, so that is encouraging. In the U.S., you see the emergence of the highest defense budget in history . . . The simple facts are that if you look at the Atlantic Alliance, plus Japan, you have twice the industrial base and one-and-a-half times the manpower as the Soviet bloc. We are therefore groping with a problem of will and establishing priorities, and this is a do-able task.

Interview, Mons, Belgium/
The Washington Post, 5-17:(A)14.

Peter Hall
Director, National Theatre, London

2

[This is] the miserable '70s, when Britain doesn't believe it can do anything and doesn't want to believe. We're a defeated and neurotic nation whose only joy in life is failure.

Newsweek, 3-22:74.

Roy Hattersley
Minister of State
of the United Kingdom

3

Nineteen-seventy-six is not a year when Britain longs to return to its imperial past. This is not a moment at which we mourn the passing of the empire beyond the sea. It is the beginning of an epoch in which we understand our new role and gladly accept the position in the world which our size, our history, our situation and our character makes our present destiny. We know that the empire will no longer provide an artificially receptive market for our goods. We understand that we can no longer live on the inflated returns of capital invested in the colonies. We realize that we are a medium-sized industrial power operating on the European stage.

At City Club, Cleveland, Ohio, May 24/
Vital Speeches, 7-1:557.

Denis Healey
Chancellor of the Exchequer
of the United Kingdom

4

I think there has been a quantum change in the public's attitude toward inflation. When the last government [of Edward Heath] was in power and unemployment was rising, the [labor] unions applied very heavy pressure for a massive reflation, and the government surrendered to that pressure. It lost its nerve and produced the seizure in the economy in 1973 whose consequences I am still wrestling with. The reaction of the trade unions was to move to the extreme. This time it has been exactly the opposite. Moderate people have been winning union elections all over the country. Union leaders themselves have not only acquiesced in the

(DENIS HEALEY)

suggestions I have put to them, they have volunteered suggestions of their own . . . There is evidence that the basic lesson now accepted throughout the country is that inflation is the major problem, and we shall not get employment moving up until we have inflation under control.

Interview/ Business Week, 3-29:90.

1

We suffer in Britain from a sort of statistical masochism. We always tend to present our problems in the worst possible light in comparison with others . . . Newspapers tend to paint Britain as a sort of Roman orgy of fiscal profligacy, throwing out social benefits on a scale unparalleled in the world.

Dec. 7/
The Christian Science Monitor, 12-9:3.

Edward Heath
Former Prime Minister
of the United Kingdom
2

The rest of the world does not believe that we [British] have shown the will or wisdom as a nation to deal with our problems to give them the confidence which will enable them to go on holding our currency . . . Britain has now come to the end of the present road. The rest of the world knows it. The rest of the world is very sorry. The rest of the world regrets it is unable to oblige any longer.

At Conservative Party conference,
Brighton, England, Oct. 6/
The New York Times, 10-7:2.

Joerg Henschel
Deputy Speaker,
West Berlin Senate
3

The impression in the Western countries is that with the signing [of the four-power Berlin agreement of 1971-72], West Berlin is now a normal place. It is not, and the people [of the city] have the impression that they are a little bit forgotten. [Now] we must find a

new function for West Berlin and a new self-understanding. But that is a psychological and sociological problem for Berliners who lived under certain political circumstances and pressures for 25 years. It is difficult to bring them back to say, "Okay, Berlin is now almost a normal city with certain advantages." That is difficult. They are conservative people who for 25 years knew what they were. Now they are not sure what their special function is.

The Washington Post, 3-8:(A)14.

Peter Hill-Norton
Admiral of the Fleet, British Navy;
Chairman, Military Committee,
North Atlantic Treaty Organization
4

Every piece of information received on Warsaw Pact weapons and activities fits into a clear pattern of relentless determination to achieve superiority, and emphasizes potential and widening military options. This applies in the strategic and theatre nuclear fields, and in all ground, air and maritime forces. It also applies to the Soviet's continuing ability to project its power in distant areas. The evidence is formidable, and gives dramatic emphasis to the need to improve NATO forces.

At NATO ministers meeting, Brussels/
Los Angeles Times, 12-8:(1)16.

Enver Hoxha
First Secretary, Labor
(Communist) Party of Albania
5

Yugoslav revisionism remains a favorite weapon in the hands of the international imperialist bourgeoisie in the struggle against socialism and the liberation movements. The first to come out in support of world capitalism and apply itself with unrestrained zeal to the fight against the revolution and Marxist-Leninism was Yugoslav revisionism, the so-called self-managing socialism. Yugoslav revisionism carries on sabotage and undermining activities among the progressive forces of the developing countries, striving to set their sincere aspirations on a wrong course. Titoite self-management has proven to be an eclectic bourgeois doctrine that has led to permanent political and ideological confusion.

At Labor Party congress, Tirana, Nov. 2/
The New York Times, 11-5:(A)7.

Hua Kuo-feng
Premier of the
People's Republic of (Communist) China 1

[Criticizing the Soviet Union]: The superpower that is most vociferous for "detente" in its quest for world hegemony is deliberately squeezing into every opening and making trouble and carrying out expansion everywhere. It has become the main source of a new world war. However, though wildly ambitious, it is essentially flabby.

At banquet honoring Australian Prime Minister
Malcolm Fraser, Peking, June 20/
The Christian Science Monitor, 6-22:6.

Jacob K. Javits
United States Senator, R—New York 2

Western Europe is approaching a real watershed. If we do not assume the role of partnership with it, it may drift into an economic disaster that will pull us down with it. We could have a depression without any question. There is real danger that Western Europe might become adrift. She could go anywhere. She might become anarchic or attach herself in some way to the Soviet Union. This is a Marshall Plan moment. It doesn't, as the Marshall Plan did, require money from the United States—cash on the barrel. It doesn't require Four Point technical assistance. And it doesn't require military aid, as Greece and Turkey did in the postwar period. It does, however, require the same *attitude* on the part of the United States, with different means. It requires that we act as a partner with Western Europe, not as a superpower that thinks nobody really belongs in negotiations with us except the Soviet Union and the People's Republic of [Communist] China. If we deal with Western Europe as a partner, and establish that kind of relationship with the Western European community, I am convinced we can avert an economic catastrophe over there.

Interview, Washington/
Los Angeles Herald-Examiner, 12-26:(A)5.

Anker Joergensen
Prime Minister of Denmark
3

I think we do need a slowing down of social-welfare programs. Personally, I don't think we are going too fast on these programs, but obviously some people do. My party doesn't have a majority in Parliament so we have to move more slowly. And the economic situation dictates that we move slowly, too.

Interview, Copenhagen/
The New York Times, 2-12:16.

Juan Carlos I
King of Spain
4

It is essential for a true monarchy that the power of the King should never be arbitrary . . . The monarchy should be a supreme power . . . above conflicts and tensions . . . [an arbiter] and defender of the constitutional system and promoter of justice.

Before Advisory Council of the Realm, Madrid,
March 2/The Christian Science Monitor, 3-5:8.

5

The Spanish monarchy has committed itself from the first day to be an open institution, one in which every citizen has full scope for political participation without discrimination of any kind . . . At the same time, the monarchy will ensure the orderly access to power of distinct political alternatives, in accordance with the freely expressed will of the people.

Before Congress, Washington, June 2/
The Dallas Times Herald, 6-3:(A)11.

343

Henry A. Kissinger
*Secretary of State
of the United States*

1

Soviet strength is uneven, the weaknesses and frustrations of the Soviet system are glaring and have been clearly documented. Despite the inevitable increase in its power, the Soviet Union remains far behind us and our allies in any over-all assessment of military, economic and technological strength. It would be reckless in the extreme for the Soviet Union to challenge the industrial democracies. And Soviet society is no longer insulated from the influences and attractions of the outside world, or impervious to the need for external contacts.
*Before Boston World Affairs Council, March 11/
The New York Times, 3-12:4.*

2

. . . we must be concerned about the possibility of Communist parties coming to power —or sharing in power—in governments in NATO countries. Ultimately, the decision must, of course, be made by the voters of the countries concerned. But no one should expect that this question is not of concern to this [U.S.] government. Whether some of the Communist parties in Western Europe are in fact independent of Moscow cannot be determined when their electoral self-interest so overwhelmingly coincides with their claims. Their internal procedures—their Leninist principles and dogmas—remain the antithesis of democratic parties. And were they to gain power they would do so after having advocated for decades programs and values detrimental to our traditional ties. By that record, they would inevitably give low priority to security and Western defense efforts, which are essential not only to Europe's freedom but to maintaining the world's balance of power. They would be tempted to orient their economies to a much greater extent toward the East. We would have to expect that Western European governments in which Communists play a dominant role would, at best, steer their countries' policies toward the positions of the non-aligned.

The political solidarity and collective defense of the West, and thus NATO, would be inevitably weakened, if not undermined. And in this country, the commitment of the American people to maintain the balance of power in Europe, justified though it might be on pragmatic, geopolitical grounds, would lack the moral base on which it has stood for 30 years.
*Before Boston World Affairs Council, March 11/
The New York Times, 3-12:4.*

3

What is the problem with respect to Communism in Western Europe? As Secretary of State, I have an obligation to make clear what I believe the consequences of certain events are, even if we cannot necessarily influence them. I believe that the advent of Communism in major European countries is likely to produce a sequence of events in which other European countries will also be tempted to move in the same direction. This, in turn, is going to produce governments with which the degree of cooperation that has become characteristic of Atlantic relations will become increasingly difficult—in which their own internal priorities are going to be away from the concern with defense—which will create new opportunities for outside pressures and toward a more neutralistic conception of foreign policy. I, therefore, believe that the United States must not create the impression that it could be indifferent to such developments. In many respects, we cannot affect it. And if any government, if any people, votes in a way that will produce a Communist government or admits a major participation of Communists in that government, we will have to deal with that reality. But we should not delude ourselves that it would not mark a historic change that would have long-term and very serious consequences.
*Before American Society of Newspaper Editors,
Washington, April 13/
The Washington Post, 4-17:(A)11.*

4

It is not healthy for the United States to be the only center of initiative and leadership in the democratic world. It is not healthy for Europe to be only a passive participant, however close the friendship and however intimate the consultation . . . Of course, we do not want Europe to find its identity in opposition to the United States. But neither does any sensible European . . .

At International Institute for Strategic Studies,
London, June 25/
The Washington Post, 6-26:(A)9.

1

I believe that the Atlantic Alliance has been greatly strengthened in recent years. I believe that the system of consultations that now exists within NATO, and between the countries of NATO outside the NATO Alliance, is intimate and substantial and reflects the realization of all of the countries that we are united not only for security but as repositories of freedom in the world today.

News conference, Brussels, Dec. 10/
The New York Times, 12-11:8.

Robin Knight
Moscow bureau chief, and former
chief London correspondent,
"U.S. News & World Report"

2

. . . Britain's decline over the last 20 years makes her a much less useful partner than she used to be. Her horizons have shrunk dramatically. This means that whenever an international crisis occurs outside Europe, Washington no longer can count on Britain's active help in the way it did in Korea in the early 1950s and in the Persian Gulf until very recently. Today there are distinct limits to Britain's value as an ally. Much of the blame must lie with the shaky British economy. But it's not entirely a matter of economic weakness. Britain's desire to play an important international role has sharply diminished also.

Interview/
U.S. News & World Report, 11-15:70.

Bruno Kreisky
Chancellor of Austria

3

The Communists play a major role in only two Western European countries, Italy and France. Elsewhere they have a non-value, politically. Therefore, Socialists refuse to collaborate with them, as in Portugal. In France, the Socialists have become stronger than the Communists, so they can work in coalition with them and still dominate. But it is the reverse in Italy. There the Socialists are too weak to count . . . What will happen [in the forthcoming Italian elections in which the Communists may gain power]? I don't know. But I may modestly propose no foreign country should interfere with any suggestions. That would only injure Italian national pride and prove to be counter-productive. There have even been hints that if the Communists are admitted to government, no other solution would remain than to keep them out with a dictatorship, military or otherwise. Yet any threat implying support for dictatorship in the name of law and order would be disastrous. I hope there will never be such a possibility in Italy. It would be disastrous for all Europe. I cannot imagine any democratic government supporting such an idea.

Interview, Vienna/
The New York Times, 6-6:(4)17.

Harold Macmillan
Former Prime Minister
of the United Kingdom

4

The real distinction in Britain is not between Liberals, Conservatives and Labor, but between people who want to make a mixed economy run properly and those who want to destroy the system. If you are a Communist, or even want a pure socialist state, which I suppose [is] what Communism is supposed to be, of course you want to destroy it.

Television interview, London, Oct. 20/
Los Angeles Herald-Examiner, 10-21:(A)4.

Mike Mansfield
United States Senator, D—Montana

5

The idea of maintaining 235,000 military personnel in Western Europe 31 years after

345

WHAT THEY SAID IN 1976

(MIKE MANSFIELD)

the end of World War II makes no sense. This is costing us in the neighborhood of $5-billion a year. When we beefed up our divisions in Europe in 1951, we were assured this was on a temporary basis until the Europeans got back on their feet and could shoulder their share of the defense effort.

Interview, Washington/
Nation's Business, November:36.

Georges Marchais
Secretary general,
Communist Party of France
1

[Criticizing repressive measures taken against dissidents in the Soviet Union]: We cannot agree to the Communist ideal being stained by unjust and unjustifiable acts. Such acts are in no way a necessary consequence of socialism. Our road to socialism is an original road . . . a French road. France today is neither Russia in 1917 nor Czechoslovakia in 1948. [Thus] no [foreign] party or group of parties can legislate for us.

At French Communist Party Congress,
St. Ouen, France, Feb. 4/
Time, 2-16:25.

2

The socialism for which we [in France] are fighting will be profoundly democratic because it will be based on the ownership of the means of production and exchange by society itself as well as on the political power of the masses of the working people in which the working class will play a decisive role. It will [be] profoundly democratic not only because it will create the essential conditions for freedom by ending exploitation, but also because it will guarantee, develop and broaden all the freedoms which the people have won. This refers to the freedom of thought and expression, of creation and publication, the freedom to demonstrate, to hold meetings and to assemble, the freedom of movement within the country and abroad, the freedom of religion and the right to strike. It is also a question of the recognition of the results of general elections—which includes the possibility of a democratic alternation [of government]—recognition of the right of political parties to exist and carry out their activities, of the independence of the system of justice and the rejection of any official philosophy . . . This is the socialism we want for our country, one which cannot be separated from freedom.

At conference of European Communist parties,
East Berlin/
The New York Times, 7-1:12.

Golda Meir
Former Prime Minister of Israel
3

[Criticizing the Soviet Union for anti-Jewish policies]: What do you gain, Soviet Union, from this miserable policy? Where is your decency? Would it be a disgrace for you to give up this battle? We can't accept that teaching Hebrew is counter-revolutionary. We can't accept that three million Jews have no right to have a theatre, have no newspaper. The second greatest power in the world —what are you gaining from this policy?

At World Conference on Soviet Jewry,
Brussels, Feb. 19/
The New York Times, 2-20:5.

Vito Miceli
Former Director,
Italian Defense Intelligence Service
4

I was head of Italian intelligence for four years. I can tell you that the Communist party in every country is directed by a central committee in touch with Moscow. It is not important whether these parties are run by moderate or other factions—that's a romantic notion. They all have internal discipline.

Interview, Rome/
Los Angeles Herald-Examiner, 6-15:(A)8.

Dom Mintoff
Prime Minister of Malta
5

We want to [be] friends with everyone. There are different degrees of friendship.

The goal is for Malta to become a bridge of peace between Europe and the Arab world. We want to stop being a fortress, to stop playing handmaiden to the powerful . . . We want to stay between the superpowers. The Mediterranean should not be divided between them.

To foreign correspondents, Valletta, Malta/
The New York Times, 9-18:2.

Walter F. Mondale
United States Senator, D—Minnesota;
1976 Democratic Vice-Presidential
nominee 1

[On U.S. President Ford's statement, during a political debate, that the East European countries are not dominated by the Soviet Union]: [It was] the most incredible and unbelievable statement ever made by a President of the United States. The President can hire all the experts and the shills he wants in Washington, but he made the statement and he's going to live with it. I have been in many Eastern European countries. Ford's statement will come as a great surprise to them. It will come as a surprise to millions of Americans of Polish, Czech, Hungarian, Romanian, Bulgarian and German descent. The tracks of Soviet tanks are still visible in Prague, where they stomped the Czechoslovakian move for independence. These countries are also under the Soviet's thumb economically. President Ford's statement dramatically underscores why he should get his advice from more than one man. If he had talked with [exiled Soviet author Alexander] Solzhenitsyn, he would have learned some of the truths about Soviet oppression of freedom and liberty in Russia as well as in Eastern Europe.

News conference, Houston, Oct. 7/
The Dallas Times Herald, 10-8:(A)19.

Robert Moss
Editor, "The London Economist
Foreign Report" 2

. . . I'm not altogether certain that in the not-too-distant future we won't see a situation emerge where there will be a new phase in the economic crisis in Britain where our long-patient foreign friends will get fed up with us and stop lending us money unless we set our economic house in order. And I'm not certain that at some point we won't have to face a fairly shattering kind of decision, a decision as to whether we go on further into the kind of socialism our trade-union bosses want, further toward total state regulation of our economy, nationalization of our banks, which is another thing the TUC is calling for, and so on—a communist kind of economy with high import controls, fixed exchange rates, and all the rest of it—or whether we go in a radically different direction by trying to restore sanity, by trying to cut excessive public spending, by trying to provide new incentives for people to make their own business decisions, and the rest of it. But I do know one thing: We will have to face that decision. And I know another thing: Any government that faces that decision will not be allowed to make up its mind without a fairly devastating confrontation with our trade-union movement, if it wants to go back toward curbing abusive union power, toward devolving economic power back to the private sector, and toward cutting excessive public spending.

At National Right to Work Committee awards
banquet, Washington, May 14/
Vital Speeches, 7-1:561.

Daniel P. Moynihan
United States Ambassador/Permanent
Representative to the United Nations 3

The Russians are expansionists . . . No one should get into the habit of thinking that the Russians don't know how to be imperialists. Theirs is the only 19th-century empire to have survived the 20th century—not only to have survived it but to have expanded. They got back parts they had lost. They had lost Lithuania and Estonia and Latvia. They got them back; they got chunks of Poland back. They have a genuine, bona fide 19th-century imperialist condition.

Interview/Newsweek, 1-19:29.

WHAT THEY SAID IN 1976

Daniel P. Moynihan

*Professor of government, Harvard
University; Former United States
Ambassador/ Permanent Representative
to the United Nations*

1

[On what the U.S. should do if the Soviet
Union invades Yugoslavia after President
Tito's death]: Should we defend one Marxist
autocracy against an incursion by another?
Certainly, we should seek to prevent such an
incursion, but do you start the Third World
War over it? No. You don't start the Third
World War to save a bunch of Communist
sons of bitches who do anything they can do
to cause us trouble anywhere else in the world
except along the Danube. Sorry, I have dealt
with the Yugoslavians in the United Nations.
Find me one time Yugoslavians have sought
anything but our disadvantage. Well, to hell
with them in the large. In the particular, we
should like to see them not conquered by
the Soviets. But if the Soviets insist on conquering them, then I'm damned if we should
feed the Soviets a year from now. I think we
should say to the Soviets that any such action on their part is an act of intransigent
hostility which suggests to us no alternative but to prepare for the very worst encounter between them and us. On the other hand, I'm damned if I would fight for
Belgrade. And with that ambiguity, you will
learn with what use you invite the opinion
of professors.

*At Woodrow Wilson International
Center for Scholars,
Washington,
Los Angeles Times, 5-18:(2)7.*

Malcolm Muggeridge

*Author; Former editor,
"Punch" magazine*

2

[Saying Americans have difficulty believing that Britain could become Commun-
ist]: People said that about Czechoslovakia;
they said it about Hungary; they said it about
China . . . The truth is that if and when they
do take over England, it will just be as when
they took over other countries . . . not in any
gentlemanly Etonian way . . .

*Television interview/
"The Second Battle of Britain,"
Columbia Broadcasting System, 3-17.*

Gunnar Myrdal

Swedish economist

3

The difference between America and us
[in Sweden] is that well-planned social reforms are seen here as productive. As we've
accelerated social reforms, our productivity
has gone up. In America, you look on social
reforms as a big government activity, expensive, difficult. Here we come to look on social
reforms as an investment that works . . . We
have not had a war since Napoleon's time.
We have no religious differences, no racial
problems. We have plenty of raw materials.
We have iron ore, we have wood, and when
we were hit by the oil crisis there was a raw-
material boom. My opinion about the Swedes
is that with our history and our raw materials
we should be doing even better.

*Interview, Stockholm/
The New York Times, 10-3:(1)6.*

Peter Oppenheimer

*Economist,
Oxford University, England*

4

British economic policy still tends to lurch
from one half-baked expedient to another. It
lacks the judiciousness and assurance that
come from a clear appreciation of what government can achieve and what must be left
to the economy at large to do.

Los Angeles Times, 3-21:(1-A)5.

Marcelino Oreja (Aguirre)

Foreign Minister of Spain

5

The government has stated that sovereignty lies in the hands of the people and
that they will decide Spain's future course.
There are new laws for the recognition of
political parties and we expect these laws
will be obeyed in recognizing these parties.
[The law] will not include the Communist

Party. The law excludes those who adopt violence and separatism, particularly those parties controlled from abroad. Finally, the judiciary will define which parties contravene the laws of Spain. We do not see any recognition of the legality of the Communist Party. But first we must establish the rules—the judges will decide.

Interview, San Sebastian, Spain/
Los Angeles Times, 9-12:(1)22.

Olof Palme
Prime Minister of Sweden
1

[On the defeat of his party, the Social Democrats, in the recent election]: We've been lucky—44 years is a long time. Sooner or later you lose an election, but then you come back. Conservatives all over will make use of this. They say in Sweden, of all places, people have rejected socialism. I'm sure in Chile they're extremely happy. But it's absolutely wrong to say that people have rejected socialism—they haven't. The bourgeois parties promised more than the Social Democrats. What turned the election was the nuclear-power issue. It may not have been the central issue, but without the campaign being concentrated on it in the past two weeks, we would have won.

Interview, Stockholm, Sept. 23/
The New York Times, 9-24:(A)13.

Paul VI
Pope
2

[Saying Catholics should not vote for Communist Party candidates in the forthcoming Italian national election]: It is not permissible to evade our duty in this election when a profession of fidelity to irreconcilable values and principles is involved ... It is even less tolerable for [a Catholic] to give his support, especially public support, to a political expression which is, for ideological reasons and in historical experience, radically opposed to our religious ideas of life.

At Italian Conference of Bishops, May 21/
Los Angeles Times, 5-22:(1)1.

Robert Pontillon
National secretary,
Socialist Party of France
3

There is a new situation in Southern Europe. There is a dynamism on the left, but we can't reach power without an alliance with the Communists. Unless the U.S. wants to deal only with the likes of [the late Spanish dictator Francisco] Franco and the Greek colonels, [U.S. Secretary of State Henry] Kissinger must admit the reality of Southern Europe, including large Communist parties.

Time, 2-9:40.

Ronald Reagan
Candidate for the 1976 Republican
U.S. Presidential nomination;
Former Governor of California (R)
4

I believe the Soviet Union, in its great upsurge of military spending—its increased truculence—operates from a standpoint that the reason we're [the U.S.] falling behind is that the American people no longer have the will to make the effort. The Russians feel they are more virile—that they are the stronger power. They're ready to sacrifice and do this. And we are the Carthage of our time, in a way ... My belief is that the Soviet Union right now is surging ahead because it sees no intent on the part of our people to do this. The Russians know they can't match us industrially or technologically. But the Soviet Union today apparently is the only country in the world that believes that there could be another war and that there could be a winner of that war.

Interview/
U.S. News & World Report, 5-31:20.

Merlyn Rees
British Secretary of State for
Northern Ireland
5

[Arguing against withdrawal of British troops from Northern Ireland]: It would solve nothing. I have no doubt that withdrawal, abandonment of our responsibilities

WHAT THEY SAID IN 1976

(MERLYN REES)

to citizens in the United Kingdom, would precipitate violence on an even greater scale [than] we have seen so far. And we must not assume that violence would be confined to Northern Ireland. It would spread to Great Britain and also to the Republic of Ireland. Withdrawal would be a shortsighted policy, but above all it would be an irresponsible policy . . . The existence of Northern Ireland, created as it was in the 1920s, and the fears of a divided community, split between the [Protestant] majority and the [Catholic] minority, mean that there would be a very real chance of violence from the very moment that a declaration of intent to withdraw was made. There are parliamentary forces on both sides. Some of them behave with savagery, and react to savagery. They are not taking part in some theoretical discussion in a drawing room, or a weekly editorial conference.

Before House of Commons, London, Jan.12/
The New York Times, 1-13:5.

1

[Announcing the dissolving of the Northern Ireland Convention, whose purpose was to work out a political arrangement between Catholics and Protestants, and a continuation of British rule indefinitely]: It is clearly not possible to make progress toward a devolved system of government for Northern Ireland. My strongly held view is that there is no instant solution to the problems of Northern Ireland. It would be a grave mistake to pretend that there was one, let alone to rush forward with some new devices . . . The Convention was born out of a belief that the people of Northern Ireland themselves ought to have the chance to play a constructive part in seeking a solution to their constitutional problems, in the knowledge that final decisions were for Parliament at Westminster. The Convention did not, however, agree on the central issue—that is, how, in a divided community, a system of government could be devised which would have sufficient support in both parts of that community to pro-

vide stable and effective government.

Before House of Commons, London, March 5/
The New York Times, 3-6:1.

2

All decent people in Northern Ireland must be grateful to [U.S.] President Ford for his forthright condemnation of those [in the U.S.] who support organizations involved directly or indirectly in campaigns of violence in Northern Ireland. To those who do still believe that they are helping the situation or that their money is some kind of charity for destitute families, I say only that they should visit the hospitals of Northern Ireland and see the victims of terrorism for themselves. They then would know where their efforts were being directed.

Before American correspondents, London,
April 7/The New York Times, 4-8:9.

Guy de Rothschild
Senior member, French branch,
House of Rothschild

3

It is rather amusing to note in Europe and in European discussions about European unity, the largest, most important single factor is America.

Before business leaders, Pittsburgh, Pa./
The Wall Street Journal, 8-2:10.

Helmut Schmidt
Chancellor of West Germany

4

The elementary prerequisite for the continued existence of [Germany, East and West] remains its citizens' consciousness of belonging together. This consciousness is a formidable reality that is left to the divided German nation in spite of all. The people here and in the GDR know, spontaneously and unquestioningly, that they are Germans. This is how they see themselves and this is how they are seen by the non-German world in East and West. That consciousness of being one has grown through history. And it is therefore subject to the influences of time and circumstance. It would be careless to overlook this. In political terms, this means that a nation has a right to self-determination as long as it wants to be a nation.

Before Bundestag, Bonn, Jan. 29/
Vital Speeches, 3-15:328.

1

I wouldn't like to see the Communist Party in the government in Paris, or in Rome, or in other places. On the other hand, I do not believe that this must of necessity mean a catastrophe. We have seen Communists as ministers, and even in higher office, in Lisbon, and we have seen them in Reykjavik. Europe has not collapsed, nor has the Atlantic Alliance. I would not like us to predict disaster, if it's possible that such predictions might in the end prove to be self-fulfilling prophecies.

Interview, Bonn/
Time, 5-10:39.

2

There is a certain weakness in our [Germany's] national character tending toward perfectionism. We even make our mistakes in a perfect manner—big mistakes, even crimes. This perfectionist weakness is not something that will evaporate this year or this decade. It's one of those characteristics that have a long period of life in the development of a nation. People also attribute to Germans a certain amount of discipline. This, I hope, will not quickly vanish.

Interview, Bonn/Time, 5-10:40.

William W. Scranton
United States Ambassador/Permanent Representative to the United Nations *3*

The Soviet Union's efforts to manipulate the developing world are very destructive. Using the guise of neo-colonialism to discredit the ideas and forms of freedom, they hope to strengthen the ideas and forms of totalitarianism.

At United Nations, New York, Nov. 24/
The New York Times, 11-25:10.

Brian Sedgemore
Member of British Parliament *4*

[British managers] complain about lazy workers, when any foreign businessman seeking to buy British goods will tell you that if you try to contact many managers outside the hours of 10 a.m. to noon, they are unobtainable. Apparently outside these hours they preside over Britain's decline and fall like Roman generals of old, in their pubs, clubs and sauna baths.

At symposium at London School of Economics/
Los Angeles Times, 3-21:(1-A)5.

Mehmet Shehu
Premier of Albania *5*

[On Soviet leader Leonid Brezhnev's suggestion that his country's relations with Albania be improved]: These renegades [in Moscow] think our Party shifts according to the direction of the wind. They will be bitterly disappointed once again. There is not and never will be any wind or storm that can change the course of our ship, which is always oriented by the infallible breeze of Marxist-Leninism.

The Dallas Times Herald, 12-2:(A)25.

Augusto Souto Silva Cruz
Admiral and Chief of Staff,
Portuguese Navy *6*

[In Portugal] the rich get richer and the poor get poorer. For example, a big multinational company comes here and opens a huge factory, two or three thousand workers. It makes two or three components for something. All the materials are imported, and all the products are exported. It does nothing for Portugal, brings no technology, doesn't help to develop the country at all. It just takes advantage of cheap labor, which is understandable for the businessmen, but what about our people? They look and say, if that is what the capitalist system means, then we should try something else. The other system is Communism. That is why we have to find some new ways, some changed version of capitalism for countries like ours, so it can

(AUGUSTO SOUTO SILVA CRUZ)

work better to solve the problems while we are developing.

Interview, Lisbon, April 27/
The New York Times, 4-28:3.

Mario Soares
Leader, Socialist Party of Portugal   *1*

After the revolution [deposing the Portuguese dictatorship in 1974], the Communists infiltrated the military, the media, the unions, the government. It seemed they would dominate. But [Communist Party leader Alvaro] Cunhal had spent many years in prison and exile and did not know the Portuguese people. For 20 months the Communists intrigued. We Socialists tried to gain the trust of the people. We had only 2,000 Socialists underground when I returned from exile. Now we have 80,000 active members. We won the elections [for a Constitution-making assembly, last year]. The Communists then attempted to discredit the elections. We went to the streets and beat them everywhere. Then [last November] they tried a military coup. They failed. They have now lost most of their key positions in the military and the media.

The Washington Post, 1-30:(A)23.

Sidney Sober
Deputy Assistant Secretary for
Near Eastern and South Asian Affairs,
Department of State
of the United States   *2*

No power in history has shown a more ravenous appetite for foreign territory than the Soviet Union. Ask anyone of numerous countries, from the far north of Europe to the far east of Asia. For instance, the United States has withdrawn from various Pacific islands which it occupied as a result of World War II operations. Can the Soviet Union say the same? In the European area, as merely an example, let it not be forgotten that in 1940 the Soviet Union took over by military force the Baltic states, its independent neighbors Latvia, Estonia and Lithuania. The Soviet Union still holds those formerly free nations in its grip and denies them basic human rights. Lack of religious freedom is only one that might be emphasized. My delegation would like to ask a simple question: Does the Soviet Union intend to hold these formerly independent countries forevermore? Or will the long finger of history, which presides over human affairs with considerable impartiality, call the Soviet Union to account?

At United Nations, New York, Dec. 2/
The Washington Post, 12-17:(A)20.

Alexander I. Solzhenitsyn
Exiled Soviet author   *3*

The West deceives itself by thinking that this dictatorship [in the Soviet Union] stems from Russia's own past and that therefore the West is immune to the disease because its own heritage is different . . . I don't believe the statements of the French or Italian Communist Parties concerning their intentions. One must not forget that Lenin himself always used golden words before coming to power. But once he came to power he showed that he had a well-organized dictatorship run by an iron fist.

Interview/ The New York Times, 8-18:35.

Walter J. Stoessel, Jr.
United States Ambassador
to the Soviet Union   *4*

[The Soviet Union is] a very big, very powerful country with a very formidable military force and a system of government which can control the actions of the population, and so on, and can operate in a certain amount of secrecy. The Russians have an ideology which is fundamentally hostile and which impels them, I think. It gives them a natural inclination to sort of push out and oppose us.

Interview, Moscow/
The New York Times, 9-12:(1)2.

Adolfo Suarez (Gonzalez)
Premier of Spain
1

If political reform has been started as an urgent task, we shall accelerate it with the realism that our time demands. The ultimate goal is very concrete—that future governments should result from the free will of the majority of Spaniards; and for this I ask the collaboration of all social forces.

Broadcast address to the nation, Madrid, July 6/
Los Angeles Times, 7-7:(1)5.

Mario Tanassi
Secretary general,
Social Democratic Party of Italy
2

The [Italian] Communist Party is still closely linked to the Soviet Union. They must be kept out of the government because our democracy would be put into question. There would be a threat to the Atlantic Alliance. Part of our economic crisis stems from the Communist advance. If they won, who knows to what low levels our money would fall.

Salerno, Italy/
The New York Times, 5-27:9.

A. J. P. Taylor
British historian
3

We [British] are, whatever people say, more loosely attached to Europe than, say, Germany or France. Europe has always been for us, in a sense, a nuisance; somewhere we get dragged into wars that are of no concern to us because of the mistakes that Europeans have made. We liberate them over and over again, and then they aren't grateful.

Interview, London/
The New York Times, 6-16:2.

Margaret Thatcher
Member of British Parliament;
Leader, British Conservative Party
4

[Warning of Soviet arms domination]: The Russians put guns before butter. We [Britain]
put just about everything before guns.

At Conservative rally, London, Jan. 19/
The Christian Science Monitor, 1-21:1.

5

[Criticizing the current British Labor government]: It takes a socialist government to boast that the pound is now rising to $1.76 and that the annual rate of inflation is now down to 18.9 per cent. Such is the state we have arrived at under socialism.

Before Parliament, London/
The Christian Science Monitor, 6-11:7.

Paul Vanden Boeynants
Minister of Defense of Belgium
6

Europe can no longer satisfy itself by trusting the Americans [for defense security]. Today we are eating out of the Americans' hand. What will become of us if the United States' nuclear umbrella were to disappear tomorrow? We'd be in real trouble. Europe must unite not only politically but also militarily. It is a necessity for our security. People say that if something goes wrong, the Americans will help us. But let us be cautious. Although it is clear that America's interests, not America's duty, prevent Europe from falling under Soviet domination, it is also clear that the Americans will leave us to our fate if they realize that the Europeans are not prepared to defend themselves or contribute to the necessary effort. The farmer in Nevada does not care about far-away Europe.

Before Christian business executives, Jan. 28/
Los Angeles Herald-Examiner, 1-30:(A)4.

James N. Wallace
Tokyo bureau chief, and former
Moscow bureau chief,
"U.S. News & World Report"
7

The Soviets are firm believers in "peace through strength," despite all their criticism of American leaders for saying essentially the

(JAMES N. WALLACE)

same things. No outsider can hope to understand fully the thought processes that go on inside the Politburo of the Communist Party. But they do seem to have a genuine underlying fear that the West, meaning the U.S., would attack them if it had a clear strategic superiority. So the present Soviet leadership is not going to risk military weakness in relation to the U.S., no matter how much they have to sacrifice to maintain it. Some other things are involved, too. Soviet leaders must recognize—there has been plenty of evidence —that their whole Eastern European empire would break away, or at least greatly change its relations with Moscow, except for the physical presence of Soviet military power. And the Russians are genuinely worried about [Communist] China.

Interview/ U.S. News & World Report, 12-6:46.

Harold Wilson
Former Prime Minister
of the United Kingdom
1

[On the role of the British monarchy]: All I can say is that I would have found the job of Prime Minister a lot harder if there hadn't been a total separation between the head of government and the head of state. The fact that the Queen is above politics is one of the intangible advantages. The other thing is the continuity of the Crown and, in our particular case, the Queen's sheer hard work and deep grasp of every kind of national and international problem. You have an audience every week, lasting about an hour. She sometimes floors you—did floor me very early in my Premiership by referring to a Cabinet committee paper that she had read overnight and that I was saving for the weekend; I felt like some boy who had failed his examination. In Queen Elizabeth's case, she is not critical or quizzical but very active, and you are explaining why you did something to someone who is above the battle. It is very therapeutic and makes you think very hard.

Interview, London/ Time, 10-25:40.

Yevgeny Yevtushenko
Soviet poet
2

[On foreign criticism of repression and lack of freedom in his country]: There will be demonstrations outside the hall when I read [in foreign countries]; there always are. We do not treat foreign writers this way in Russia. We listen to them. We do not accuse them of representing their governments, or all that is worst about their countries. Wherever I go, the questions are all the same—dissidents, dissidents. What do you all know of Russia? Only what your correspondents tell you, and they live in a small group, being informed only by English speakers and dissidents. Western publishers are not interested in any writer who is not in trouble [in the Soviet Union]. We publish more English and American writers than you [in the West] publish Russian. You talk of freedom!

Interview, Stratford-upon-Avon, England/
San Francisco Examiner & Chronicle, 10-10:
(This World)30.

Adnan Abu Odeh
Information Minister of Jordan
1

It is not fair to say the PLO cannot represent Palestinian interests, because we have never really given it a chance to do so. We must simply admit in public that the PLO is an essential factor, among other factors, in the peacemaking equation. This will not necessarily anger Israel. The Israelis also recognize the Palestinians as an essential factor. If the United States, acting as a benevolent third party, does not bring the Palestinians into the peacemaking process, the losers in the long run may be not only the Palestinians, but all moderate Arabs.

Interview, Amman/
The Christian Science Monitor, 11-5:20.

Spiro T. Agnew
Former Vice President
of the United States
2

I do feel that the Zionist influences in the United States are dragging the U.S. into a rather disorganized approach to the Middle East problem. I feel, for example, that we don't have an even-handed policy in the Middle East. There's no doubt that there has been a certain amount of Israeli imperialism taking place in the world. There has been an invasion of the West Bank. The Israeli Parliament is talking about settling on the Golan Heights, on the Gaza Strip . . . and I feel that, because of the Zionist influences in the United States, these matters of aggression are routinely considered to be permissible. The media are sympathetic to the Zionist cause [and the] nation-wide impact media . . . have a tendency not to separate the Arabs into what you might call militant Communist-oriented Arabs and the Arabs that support free-enterprise systems.

Television interview/"Today" show,
National Broadcasting Company, 5-11.

3

[On criticism of his anti-Israel statements]: I resent the fact that an American citizen is not allowed to have an opinion about his country's relations with another country without his motivation being taken into account and questioned. The American Zionists make it very uncomfortable for a person to criticize Israel. They do not accept criticism of Israel as a foreign nation, and they accuse the person making the criticism of racial or religious bigotry . . . The pro-Israel thesis is driven home every day [in the news media]. There is a vacuum of pro-Arab material and criticism of Israel is suppressed. Freedom of the press in America is fiction.

Interview, Amman, Jordan/
The New York Times, 11-11:9.

Yigal Allon
Foreign Minister of Israel
4

The PLO hardly controls 10 per cent of the Palestinian Arab community. It is the representative only of an international terrorist organization. Why should we give them semi-recognition that will frighten to death all the moderate Arabs in the West Bank? Once [the moderate Arabs] realize there is even the theoretical possibility of handing over power to the PLO, they will go to the PLO right away, instead of remaining a moderate, constructive element, as most of them are today.

Interview, Washington/Time, 1-19:34.

WHAT THEY SAID IN 1976

(YIGAL ALLON)

1

If they [the Arabs] knew beforehand that the American and European governments are not going to tolerate any oil embargo and are not going to yield to blackmail but will take economic counter-measures, they will never try to impose any oil embargo. The richest oil-producing Arab country cannot survive one month without supplies from the West. They need food, they need grain, they need machinery. How can they expect the West to supply them with whatever they need without supplying the West with oil, particularly when there are no alternative markets for the oil?

Interview, New York, Oct. 12/
Los Angeles Herald-Examiner, 10-12:(A)12.

2

Whatever things Israel can compromise on, she will do so in free negotiation and without pressure. And what she cannot compromise on, she will not compromise on under even the heaviest pressure.

Tel Aviv, Dec. 30/
Los Angeles Herald-Examiner, 12-31:(A)4.

Yasir Arafat
Leader,
Palestine Liberation Organization
3

The [Lebanese civil] war did keep us [the PLO] preoccupied for a long time. But, instead of being weakened, we gained valuable military experience. Politically, you can see that we are stronger by noting the recent United Nations vote calling for the establishment of a Palestinian state. Ninety nations voted for it. Remember, those states don't cast their votes out of mere sympathy. We also showed our strength at recent Arab summits, whose resolutions not only reaffirmed that the PLO was the legitimate representative of the Palestinian people, but developed that idea by emphasizing the right of the

Palestinian people to establish an independent state in their homeland. These are major victories.

Interview, Beirut/ Time, 12-13:60.

Hafez al-Assad
President of Syria
4

[On Syria's armed intervention in Lebanon to quell that country's civil war]: Syria does not constitute a foreign presence in Lebanon. Lebanon cannot be considered a foreign presence in Syria, Jordan or Saudi Arabia. The Arabs are one nation, and Israel is a foreign body in the Arab world. This is *a priori* and does not need any proof.

The New York Times, 11-16:35.

Abdel Rahman al-Atiqi
Minister of Finance and Oil of Kuwait
5

The talk about high [Arab] oil prices and the 1973 embargo [against the U.S. and other supporters of Israel] should not be used as a black mark against us. When you are in a state of defense you use all your weapons, as you [the U.S.] used the atom bomb against Japan when you found no alternative. Don't forget that the U.S. has cut off food—grain to the Chinese, the Russians and the Communist states of East Europe—in the past. When we had no jurisdiction over our own oil, the big Western oil companies very rigidly prevented us from sending a single barrel of oil to East Europe, in keeping with orders received from the U.S. and British governments. So East Europe became 100 per cent dependent on the U.S.S.R. and Romania. Then, toward the middle of the 1960s, major companies were given orders to relax the restrictions on East Europe somewhat. No, we [Arabs] did not start the policy of boycott and were not the first to think of it. But you have to use all the weapons at your disposal.

Interview, Kuwait/
The Christian Science Monitor, 5-14:(B)10.

Uri Ben-Ari
Israeli Consul General in New York 1

. . . we [Israelis] will decide the proper policies for us. No one else. Even if we end up all alone. It will be very hard to be all alone, very hard. Our people may have to live like we did in 1948. We'll have to cut our standards to one-third of what they are today. Many people may leave the country and become taxi drivers in New York. But you know something about us. You know that even though we are sometimes very divided internally, just as we are now, we will be united if we have a war. And even though I don't look forward to another war, I know we will survive, just as we have survived other wars.

Interview, New York/
Los Angeles Times, 1-18:(4)3.

Leonid I. Brezhnev
General Secretary,
Communist Party of the Soviet Union 2

There is no war in the Middle East at present. But neither is there peace, let alone tranquility. And who would venture to guarantee that hostilities do not erupt anew? This danger will persist as long as Israeli armies remain in the occupied [Arab] territories. It will persist as long as the hundreds of thousands of Palestinians driven from their land are deprived of their legitimate rights and live in appalling conditions, and as long as the Arab people of Palestine are denied the possibility to create its national state. For Middle East peace to be lasting, the security of all the states of the region, their right to independent existence and development, must also be guaranteed. It is not clear how serious a responsibility is assumed by those who, in pursuance of egoistic aims, are making a Mid-East settlement the object of political maneuver and use separate partial agreements to delay, or even entirely place in question, genuine solutions.

At Soviet Communist Party Congress, Moscow,
Feb. 24/Vital Speeches, 4-1:362.

Of late, certain forces are making persistent attempts to undermine Soviet-Egyptian relations. As concerns the U.S.S.R., we remain faithful to the fundamental line of strengthening them. We are prepared to participate in international guarantees of the security and inviolability of the frontiers of all Middle East countries, either in the UN framework or on some other basis. Since we are on the subject, it is our opinion that Britain and France, too, could participate in such guarantees along with the U.S.S.R. and the U.S.A. This could only benefit matters.

At Soviet Communist Party Congress,
Moscow, Feb. 24/The New York Times, 2-25:14.

George S. Brown
General, United States Air Force;
Chairman, Joint Chiefs of Staff 4

. . . I think [Israel has] just got to be considered a burden [to the U.S.]. I had this same conversation with [U.S. Senator Jacob] Javits . . . He said to me: "Can't you see the great strategic value of Israel to the United States?" And I said: "Frankly, no" . . . But my concern there is that they're a burden. Now, if the trends were reversed, then I could see in the long term where it might be a tremendous asset, where they would gain power and could bring about stability in the area. But you see, the problem today is, today there's stability because Israel is strong. She could whip Syria and Egypt handily, and there's nobody else that could check them in that area, unless the Russians took a direct hand . . . [But] the long-term outlook is that the Arab states are going to overcome the deficiency that they've had, which is leadership and technology and educated people . . . It's going to take a complete change in outlook on Israel's part. Up to this point, at least, she's maintained her position, and I must say, if I were in her shoes . . . I'd be in a terrible dilemma because she's surrounded by people who'd just as soon see her pushed into the sea.

Interview/
U.S. News & World Report, 11-1:63.

357

WHAT THEY SAID IN 1976

Jimmy Carter
Candidate for the 1976
Democratic U.S. Presidential nomination;
Former Governor of Georgia (D) 1

I have never advocated withdrawal of Israel to her pre-1967 borders. I think this would not be consonant with the 1967 resolution that the borders have to be defensible. If I were Premier of Israel, I would never yield control of the Golan Heights. I've been there, been in the valley below, visited the kibbutzim overlooking the Sea of Galilee. I would not yield, if I were the Premier of Israel, the promontory to the Syrians. I would not yield, either, control of the Jewish or the Christian holy places [in Jerusalem] if I were the Premier of Israel.

Before Jewish leaders, Beverly Hills, Calif.,
May 20/ Los Angeles Times, 5-24:(1)3.

2

... I think the finest humanitarian act ever performed by the community of nations was the establishment of the state of Israel. I recognize that the only major dependable ally Israel has is our nation. I think a basic cornerstone of our foreign policy should be preservation of the nation of Israel, its right to exist, and its right to exist in a state of peace. And, yes, I think it was a fulfillment of Bible prophecy to have Israel established as a nation. Now, that doesn't mean that I would mistreat the Arabs. I would continue to encourage trade, friendship and better understanding between ourselves and the Arab countries. But I would let this commitment to the right of Israel to exist, and to exist in peace, be well-known and not have it be an indeterminate and shaky thing. It would be an unequivocal commitment of our country, well understood by the rest of the world.

Interview, June/ Liberty, Sept.-Oct.:10.

3

I have never yet had an Israeli leader respond to my direct question that they would favor using American troops under any conceivable circumstance. If there was a mutual agreement between Israel and all her neighbors, and the only basis on which they could declare non-belligerency and recognize the existence of Israel permanently and resolve the Palestinian question and leave Israel in a defendable posture and carve out a permanent peace [was] through the temporary presence of American forces in certain areas within the territory, I might consider it. But I would prefer that those forces be United Nations forces—or multinational forces—and not American forces.

Interview, June 24/
The New York Times, 7-7:12.

Jimmy Carter
1976 Democratic Presidential nominee 4

The legitimate interest of Palestinians is probably the most important aspect of the Middle East settlement. They ought to be recognized. There ought to be territories ceded for the use of the Palestinians. I think they should be a part of Jordan and be administered by Jordan. I think half the people in Jordan are Palestinians themselves. And that would be my own preference.

Interview/
Los Angeles Herald-Examiner, 7-26:(A)6.

5

I believe that the boycott of American businessmen by the Arab countries, because those businesses trade with Israel or because they have American Jews who are owners or directors in the company, is an absolute disgrace. This is the first time that I remember in the history of our country when we've let a foreign country circumvent or change our Bill of Rights. I'll do everything I can as President to stop the boycott of American businesses by the Arab countries. It's not a matter of diplomacy or trade with me. It's a matter of morality.

Debate with President Ford, San Francisco,
Oct. 7/ The New York Times, 10-8:(A)19.

Moshe Dayan
Former Minister of Defense of Israel 6

There must be a way of coming down the hill, of de-escalating [the Middle East arms race]. The only solution is . . . not to give us more arms for our security, but to give us more security so we can have less arms. If I could go to America and make a suggestion, I would say: Cut the billions [of dollars in aid] and provide us with an end-of-war commitment from Egypt. [But Israel] must have a nuclear option . . . With three million people, you can't have 10,000 tanks. We have to have the means to threaten them [the Arabs] and deter them.

Interview, Tel Aviv, Aug. 25/
Los Angeles Herald-Examiner, 8-26:(A)10.

Abba Eban
Former Foreign Minister of Israel
1

[Crediting Egyptian President Anwar Sadat with a relaxation of tensions]: Sadat has given a new face to the Middle East. He had inherited a diplomatic-military conflict with Israel. He turned it into a fight on the economic-social front at home.

Interview/
The Christian Science Monitor, 3-17:2.

2

I still believe that you cannot go back to the 1967 borders as they were. But for peace I could make do with a few limited changes. They might be small in quantitative terms but very important in their quality. For example, a difference between being on top of the Golan Heights and down below might be very small, but it's very important. The difference between a united and divided Jerusalem is nothing in terms of kilometrage, but everything in terms of having a unified capital.

Interview, Herzliyah, Israel/
The New York Times, 4-19:2.

Arie Lova Eliav
Member, Israel Knesset (Parliament);
Former Secretary general,
Israeli Labor Party
3

If America just dropped Israel, saying, "Okay, we've had enough of you—no more

money, no more military equipment," Israel would go all hawkish. Israel would act like a wounded and cornered animal, and a cornered animal does not act dovish. The real Israel hawks would cry: "All the world is against us. All the *goyim* is against us. So we'll go it alone." I call this the Sampson complex. "They have blinded us. They have shorn our hair. Now they laugh at us. So let's grab the pillars and bring down the whole palace." This is a very real possibility. A wise American policy would say to Israel: "We don't want you to disappear; we want you to be strong, But at the same time this is what America wants: For peace, you must give up the conquered Arab land and go back to the 1967 frontiers. This can be done in stages, and the United States will help you. We understand your Holocaust trauma." Many Israelis know this, but they see it through a mesh of suspicions and misunderstandings. They know what the basic American policy is, that it continues, and that they can't change it. Now the time is ripe for the American government to say all this publicly.

Interview, Washington/
The National Observer, 4-10:7.

Emil L. Fackenheim
Professor of philosophy,
University of Toronto
4

You cannot make people forget about the Holocaust, but you can neutralize it. [According to the Soviets and the Arabs,] the Israelis are the new Nazis; the Palestinian Arabs are the new Jews; the Palestine Liberation Organization is the French Freedom Fighters; and Zionism is racism. That means the slate is wiped clean.

At conference sponsored by
American Zionist Federation, New York, Feb. 10/
The New York Times, 2-11:9.

Gerald R. Ford
President of the United States
5

[The U.S. will remain] the ultimate guarantor of Israel's freedom. If we falter, there

WHAT THEY SAID IN 1976

(GERALD R. FORD)

is none to pick up the torch. If we withdraw into ourselves, those who rely on us, those who gain their strength from us are lost. But we will not falter; but we will not withdraw. We will remain steadfast in our dedication to peace and to the survival of Israel.

Before American Jewish Committee, Washington,
May 13/ Los Angeles Times, 5-14:(1)1.

1

Israel is asked to relinquish [occupied Arab] territory—a concrete and essentially irreversible step—in return for basically intangible political measures. But it is only in willingness to dare the exchange of the tangible for the intangible that hostility can be ended and peace attained.

Before American Jewish Committee, Washington,
May 13/ Los Angeles Times, 5-14:(1)20.

Suleiman Franjieh
President of Lebanon

2

[On the civil war in his country between Moslems and Christians]: The abundant blood that was shed in Lebanon will not have been shed in vain if a new Lebanon emerges—for which it was destined to be born in pain, tears and in hope for happiness and prosperity.

Broadcast address to the nation, Beirut, Feb. 14/
The New York Times, 2-15:(1)1.

Pierre Gemayel
Leader,
Christian Phalangist Party of Lebanon

3

[On the Christian-Moslem civil war in his country]: The land we built stone by stone is dying before our eyes while the world forgets us. Our people and our army are dispersed. Our industries are disintegrating. Our land is occupied. There is no legislature, no executive, no judiciary, no security, no sovereignty, no freedom.

March 25/ Los Angeles Times, 3-26:(1)1.

Ashraf A. Ghorbal
Egyptian Ambassador to the
United States

4

[Egyptian] President Sadat has said that the U.S. holds 99 per cent of the cards to make peace in the Middle East. We are moving continuously into amicable relations with the United States and the West in general. We are opening our economy. I think we have proven that we are the masters of our own destiny and of our own house. Within that context we want excellent relations with the United States, but we don't want to cut off our relations with the Soviet Union either . . . We have changed in significant ways. We have invited American business to come to Egypt and invest. We came to you to get the Suez Canal opened. We set out to find a peaceful political settlement with you for the Middle East. All of this for a very simple reason: You have the investment capital, the technology to do things like opening the Canal—the power required to get things done in the Middle East. All these things indicate how close we are moving for a common aim: peace.

Interview, Washington/
U.S. News & World Report, 4-19:57.

5

The signals we get from Israel now are confused. They say they need an end to the state of war in exchange for withdrawal [from occupied Arab territory], but they are building a port on Egyptian land near El Arish, more settlements in Syria's Golan Heights, in Arab Gaza and in the Arab West Bank. Do we believe the withdrawal—or the settlements?

Interview, Washington/
U.S. News & World Report, 4-19:58.

Edouard Ghorra
Lebanese Ambassador/
Permanent Representative
to the United Nations

6

[Blaming the Palestinian guerrilla movement for the civil war in his country]: The world has been baffled by the intensity of the fighting, the passions it has aroused, the large number of casualties and the extent of destruction . . . It is deplorable that those who have been the victim of a gross injustice [the Palestinians, who lost their lands to Israel] are inflicting an injustice of such inhuman proportion on Lebanon and its people. All this could not be justified by any objective of the Palestinian revolution, nor by any principle of morality and brotherhood . . . It is indeed sad for a Lebanese diplomat to stand before this [UN General] Assembly and denounce the actions of the Palestinians in Lebanon . . . [But] they acted as if they were a state or states within the state of Lebanon, and flagrantly defied the laws of the land and the hospitality of its people.

At United Nations, New York, Oct. 14/
The New York Times, 10-15:(A)3.

Valery Giscard d'Estaing
President of France

1

[U.S. Secretary of State Henry Kissinger's step-by-step strategy in the Middle East] was not without merit. If it had not taken place, the risk of a new conflict would have been extremely grave and the fact to have won a delay for peace is in itself a positive result. Secondly, it allowed a certain opening of minds. Discussion of the problem is more open and more complete than it was a year ago. But I have always said that it would not lead to peace in the Middle East because there has to be an over-all agreement for peace and, by its nature, an over-all agreement cannot be negotiated bilaterally. It presumes the involvement of countries that are not presently participating in the bilateral talks, and a participation by European states. Present circumstances, especially the American Presidential campaign, are not favorable to a new initiative. But a new initiative could be taken at the beginning of next year. For me, 1977 should be the year of an over-all settlement in the Middle East.

Interview, Washington/
The Washington Post, 5-16:(A)16.

Nahum Goldmann
President, World Jewish Congress

2

Without Russia [Mideast peace] cannot be done, because the Russians are not strong enough to impose peace, but they are strong enough to sabotage peace.

Interview, Jerusalem/
The Christian Science Monitor, 5-7:7.

George Habash
Leader, Popular Front for the
Liberation of Palestine

3

We believe that a united, democratic state in Palestine, where both Arabs and Jews will live, is the real solution. UN Security Council Resolution 242 is based on acceptance of Israel within its pre-1967 borders; within those borders, Israel occupies 80 per cent of Palestine. What will Palestinians say to us if we accept a settlement that liberates only 20 per cent of Palestine and does not let them return to their homes? Suppose they offered us 50 per cent of Palestine. Would we accept? No! We object to the Israeli state. Nobody can convince me that Zionism is not racist. No Arabs can accept a racist state in Palestine that regards Arabs as second-class citizens.

Interview/Time, 2-9:32.

Chaim Herzog
Israeli Ambassador/
Permanent Representative
to the United Nations

4

[On his country's sovereignty over Jerusalem]: In the past 2,000 years, the city of Jerusalem has not known a more enlightened administration than today, dedicated to the principles of human tolerance and peaceful coexistence. I offer no excuse for our presence in Jerusalem. I owe no apology. We are there as of right.

Before Security Council, United Nations,
New York, March 22/
Los Angeles Herald-Examiner, 3-23:(A)2.

WHAT THEY SAID IN 1976

Amir Abbas Hoveyda
Prime Minister of Iran
1

[On the construction of an Iranian naval base at Chabahar, 60 miles from the Pakistan border]: Iran is not a nation of the Persian Gulf alone; we are a nation of the Indian Ocean. And certainly we have interests in the Indian Ocean. The Persian Gulf is a door to the Indian Ocean. And, therefore, as a power of the Indian Ocean we have to have a base ... We are in a region, in a part of the world, which has not been known for its stability ... Defense is for us insurance for our survival ... We can't have a defense which is third-party insurance. Our defense has to be comprehensive insurance. And it is ... To be in pacts, in military pacts, with other nations, that doesn't harm. But when it comes to the moment when you need your friends, well, usually you get nice words.

Interview, Teheran/
The Washington Post, 2-28:(A)10.

Hussein I
King of Jordan
2

[On the Lebanese civil war]: The Palestine Liberation Organization has weakened, perhaps irreparably, its argument that Jews, Muslims and Christians could live in harmony side by side in a future greater Palestine. It can now be seen that Arabs themselves, citizens of the same country, not only cannot coexist but collide day and night.

Interview/Newsweek, 7-19:47.

Jacob K. Javits
United States Senator, R—New York
3

In Israel, a country where the search for peace has been its principal goal since the day of its creation, there is ... a new psychological climate. Sadly, that climate is a function of a growing sense of political isolation and a staggering economic burden that grows directly from Israel's requirements for arms and military security. There is a growing realization that this economic burden cannot continue indefinitely within the framework of a viable democratic society. Israel, as a genuinely democratic nation, is now caught in the trauma of making difficult decisions that simply cannot be accepted happily by all segments of her population. Israel must solve the problem of a new approach to the peace table in the context of a government able to persuade its people that peace [with the Arabs] will come of sacrifice; that some new steps must be taken in the nation's larger interests.

May 12/The Washington Post, 5-19:(A)10.

Rashid Karami
Premier of Lebanon
4

[On the Christian-Moslem civil war in his country]: I am sure that at least 95 per cent of the Lebanese people reject what has happened. All Lebanese want to live as one family. Once the weapons are taken away, you are going to see Lebanese—Moslems and Christians—kissing each other on the streets. It is better to forget. There is no other way. I think that, after this painful experience, the people are convinced that nothing can be achieved by force, that there must be dialogue. All have agreed to a new reform program for a new Lebanon. For all sides are equal in force, equal in territory, equal in rights. This cease-fire came about because everyone was convinced that it was time to stop the deterioration, to stop the killing. What we want is a peaceful Lebanon, a Lebanon that can satisfy all Lebanese. There is no reason for this cease-fire to break down because all parties have agreed to return to normal, to live together and to save the country.

Interview, Beirut/Time, 2-2:24.

Edward M. Kennedy
United States Senator,
D—Massachusetts
5

The influx of arms into the Persian Gulf is out of control. U.S. sales alone have increased dramatically from a few hundred million dollars five or six years ago to almost seven billion this year. There is no real arms balance, no understanding of the risks of war by accident, and generally poor command

and control over weapons. There is also little evidence of American leadership to avoid instability. On the contrary, our arms policy contributes to instability in this area of traditional rivalries and potential hostility.

Interview/
U.S. News & World Report, 3-18:43.

Khalid (ibn Abdel Aziz)
King of Saudi Arabia

1

Saudi Arabia . . . has never attacked anyone and it is not our policy to do so. Our objective in arming ourselves is first and foremost self-defense. The kingdom is a vast country suffering from a relative manpower shortage in relation to its size . . . We have to compensate for it as much as possible by using sophisticated equipment and military technology. We are certain that friendly governments producing arms, including the U.S., will appreciate [our] motivations and objectives in this regard.

Interview, Riyadh/ Newsweek, 11-22:54.

2

[On the Arab boycott against U.S. firms doing business with Israel]: The boycott is a retaliatory economic measure that the Arabs use to guarantee their own security and to lessen Israel's ability to declare war on the Arab people and occupy their land. Therefore, the boycott is not directed against any other country and it is not based on either racial or religious discrimination. And the Arabs are not the first, nor the only, nation that applies the boycott. The U.S. calls for boycott when its interests are threatened. Didn't it apply the boycott against [Communist] China and Cuba, and doesn't it still do so?

Interview, Riyadh/
U.S. News & World Report, 11-22:89.

Henry A. Kissinger
Secretary of State
of the United States

3

[On the pending sale by the U.S. to Egypt

of six C-130 cargo planes]: We do not seek to replace the Soviet Union and become the major arms supplier of Egypt. [On the other hand,] Egypt has courageously committed itself to pursuing peace and to ending its long-time close dependence on the Soviet Union, while moving toward closer relations with the West and emphasizing economic reconstruction and development. It is clearly in the American national interest to demonstrate that countries which choose the road of peace and moderation will find support and understanding in the United States.

Before Senate Foreign Relations subcommittee,
Washington, March 26/
Los Angeles Times, 3-27:(1)8.

4

The survival and security of Israel are unequivocal and permanent moral commitments of the United States . . . We will never abandon Israel—either by failing to provide crucial assistance, or by misconceived or separate negotiations, or by irresolution when challenged to meet our own responsibility to maintain the global balance of power.

Before American Jewish Congress,
Washington, April 4/
Los Angeles Times, 4-5:(1)1.

5

We understand the complexity of Israel's position. Any negotiation [with the Arabs] will require Israel to exchange territory in return for political and therefore much less concrete concessions. Even Israel's ultimate goals—a peace treaty and recognition from its neighbors—are inherently intangible. But they would be the greatest step toward security since the creation of the state. We do not underestimate the dilemmas and risks that Israel faces in a negotiation. But they are dwarfed by a continuation of the status quo. And we recognize our obligation as the principal support for Israel's security to be understanding of Israel's special circumstances in the process of negotiations. There will be no imposed solutions; there should be negotia-

WHAT THEY SAID IN 1976

(HENRY A. KISSINGER)

tions between the parties that will eventually have to live in peace.

At synagogue, Baltimore, May 9/
The New York Times, 5-10:5.

1

. . . the objective conditions that make for peace in the Middle East are better than they have been in perhaps decades. I believe that all of the parties have come to the conclusion that there is no military solution to their conflict. And some negotiated peace must be sought. Endless conflict will have profound consequences for the peoples involved and profound global consequences, and therefore I believe the parties are now more ready and conditions more ripe for a significant effort for peace than has been the case for a long time.

News conference, Brussels, Dec. 10/
The New York Times, 12-11:8.

Esmat Abdel Meguid
Egyptian Ambassador/Permanent
Representative to the United Nations

2

Israel's intransigence and desire of expansion were—and still are—the only obstacles on the path of achieving a just and lasting peace. If Israel's claim for security is to have any validity, it must be viewed within the broader framework of Arab security.

At United Nations, New York, Jan. 13/
The Washington Post, 1-14:(A)13.

Daniel P. Moynihan
United States Ambassador/Permanent
Representative to the United Nations

3

[Criticizing last year's UN vote condemning Zionism as racist]: If there was some emotion in my speech [during the debate] about the Zionist issue, there was some validity to it. Not since Nuremberg have you seen [and] heard such things as were being said during that debate. That place was reeking with hate and violence. And much of the civilized world

was sitting silent, not taking a position, not having a view. Israel was just a far-away little country of which we knew little . . . But the idea was that it was not just Israel. They were saying, "You're next." They were talking about us.

Interview, New York/
The Dallas Times Herald, 2-8:(A)14.

Muhammed Nashashibi
Secretary, executive committee,
Palestine Liberation Organization

4

Any ultimate solution [to the Arab-Israeli conflict] including the existence of Israel is not only out of the question as far as we are concerned but is beyond comprehension of all Arab states, even if they won't say so now.

U.S. News & World Report, 1-26:34.

Mohammad Reza Pahlavi
Shah of Iran

5

Could the United States afford to see Iran lost? Could the whole world afford it? You can't just live in your dreamland—your "fortress America"—and let all the countries of the world eventually disappear. A false sense of security will destroy you—like nothing. If you pursue that policy, Iran is one country that, if it goes, you are going to feel it badly. If we disappear, don't think that the rest of the region will stay as it is. If we go, the inexorable fate of the region will be that the present source of energy to Europe and Japan, and to some degree to the U.S., will not only be in jeopardy but will probably be cut off . . . If you [the U.S.] remain our friends, obviously you will enjoy all the power and prestige of my country. But if you try to take an unfriendly attitude toward my country, we can hurt you as badly, if not more so, than you can hurt us. Not just through oil—we can create trouble for you in the region. If you force us to change our friendly attitude, the repercussions will be immeasurable.

Interview, Teheran/
U.S. News & World Report, 3-22:57.

1

. . . the Israeli Prime Minister [Yitzhak Rabin] is saying that he expects a war [with the Arabs] in May. I have always expressed the opinion that [UN Security Council] resolutions 242 and 338 [calling for cease-fires, troop withdrawals, peace negotiations] must be implemented. We can't just accept *fait accompli*—the acquisition of land [by Israel] by force—because if you accept it in one place, why should you oppose it someplace else? Israel and the UN must seek real guarantees and formulas within secure boundaries for the future. You can't just risk war every time. The PLO should be at Geneva in some form, because you cannot ignore the existence of so many Palestinians. We have got to accept this. Just as we accept the existence of Israel, we have to accept the existence of the Palestinians, too. It is a reality.

Interview, Teheran/
U.S. News & World Report, 3-22:58.

2

The Palestinians obviously have the sympathy of many people . . . stateless people looking for a home . . . exactly like the sympathy that the Jews had when they were searching for a home. But our good Palestinian friends must know that there is a limit to where they can go and bully the world by terrorism and blackmail . . . They should really open their eyes, reassess their situation and start a new policy, because the actual one is going to lead them nowhere.

Television interview/
"60 Minutes,"
Columbia Broadcasting System, 10-24.

Thomas L. Phillips
Chairman, Raytheon Corporation
3

[On U.S. companies, such as Raytheon, supplying military equipment to foreign countries]: I think every nation has a right to provide for its own common defense. I make no apologies for that. But I do view with some misgivings the wide proliferation of all kinds of arms in the Middle East. When I heard that the United States was willing

to supply Jordan with a defense system, I really couldn't believe it. But looking at the total strategic picture, if we don't supply them, Russian influence is going to get in there.

Interview, Lexington, Mass./
The New York Times, 8-8:(3)5.

Muammar el-Qaddafi
Chief of State of Libya
4

If the Palestinian people who have been expelled from their territory in 1948, if their struggle is "terrorism," then we accept this accusation and it is an honor to us because we support oppressed and colonized people for the restoration of their land and independence and sovereignty . . . The Third World must not be misled with regard to the meaning of terrorism in order to make us give up our struggle against imperialism and colonialism. Zionists are terrorists. It is they who attack schools in the Middle East. They attack properties. This is terrorism, the terrorists over the city of Cairo in their planes when they killed people and workers in factories. This is terrorism.

At non-aligned nations conference,
Colombo, Sri Lanka, Aug. 18/
Los Angeles Times, 8-19:(1)4.

Yitzhak Rabin
Prime Minister of Israel
5

Certainly [the Palestinian issue] has to be solved in the context of a final [Arab-Israeli] peace. But to assert that this is the key to peace, the formula for peace, or the breakthrough to peace, is to misread the realities. It is to put the cart before the horse . . . There are the truths that lie at the heart and the core of the Arab-Israeli conflict [such as the Palestinian goal of Israel's destruction]; and since, to date, the Arab version of peace does not depart from these truths, no honest being can blame us for refusing to cooperate in our own national suicide.

Before joint session of U.S. Congress,
Washington, Jan. 28/
The New York Times, 1-29:13.

WHAT THEY SAID IN 1976

(YITZHAK RABIN)

1

In 1947, when the partition plan of former Palestine to a Jewish state and an Arab state was proposed, we accepted it. The other side rejected, went to war against the plan, against the very existence of the Jewish state, and now they claim that they have suffered from the war that they initiated. Had they accepted the partition plan, there would have been a Jewish state and a Palestinian state, and no one Palestinian would have been in the status of a refugee.

TV-radio interview, New York/
"Meet the Press,"
National Broadcasting Company, 2-1.

2

[On his country's raid on Entebbe Airport in Uganda to free Jewish hostages from Arab terrorists]: In a bold, resourceful and sophisticated effort, the Israeli defense forces have succeeded in carrying out the decision of the government of Israel to save and liberate from captivity the passengers of the Air France plane, who were hijacked by Palestinian terrorists and kept prisoner in Uganda, with their lives in danger ... Anti-Israel terrorism has become a phenomenon of international import, and we do not exempt any government from the duty of fighting for the eradication of terrorism. But above all, we shall persist in this struggle, even though we be alone.

Before the Knesset (Parliament),
Jerusalem, July 4/
The New York Times, 7-5:2.

3

[On the Christian-Moslem civil war in Lebanon]: What is going on in Lebanon is a tragedy. The losers are the Lebanese people, whose country is now half-destroyed. The main blame should be put on the extremist Palestinians. They haven't lost because the Arab world still needs them; it has been using them as a political football for 40 years and

won't stop now. Don't forget that the Palestinians in Lebanon constitute only 10 per cent of all Palestinians. The bulk of the Palestinians are secure because they are either Israeli citizens, live under Israeli administration, or are Jordanians. With the majority, [PLO leader] Yasir Arafat has no influence at all. Because of the special circumstances in Lebanon, I don't see a settlement unless the 300,000 Palestinians there either integrate or move somewhere else in the Arab world.

Interview, Jerusalem/
U.S. News & World Report, 9-6:35.

4

[Egyptian] President [Anwar] Sadat, if you are serious about this word "peace," let us negotiate. You have explained your willingness to make peace to American Senators, Congressmen and television people. However, they are not the parties to peace. A Middle East peace can only be negotiated by us who live here. I have heard what you have said to others. What have you to say to me?

Nov. 21/ The Christian Science Monitor, 11-23:8.

5

[On Israeli-Egyptian relations]: I wish I could say I have a good relationship. Unfortunately, there are no political relationships whatsoever, because Egypt refuses to have them. Once there were an agreement between us, Egypt and Israel could play a major role in changing the destiny of this area. Egypt [is] the biggest Arab country and it is also the leading Arab country. Israel represents the country which is most advanced and progressive in technology and social concepts. The combination of the efforts of these two countries could again bring the Middle East to what it once was— the cradle of Western civilization.

Interview/ Time, 12-6:35.

6

I believe that before you define the question of exact borders [for Israel] you must reach an understanding on what you mean by the term "peace." For me, peace means reconciliation of the Arab countries with the existence of Israel as a Jewish state. This means an agreement to end the state of war and to open the borders to movement of people and goods and to the meeting of minds. When we do talk about defensible boundaries, the yardstick is not Israel's desire for real estate, but lines which will enable Israel to defend itself. Even if we talk in the context of [a full-fledged peace agreement], I cannot accept the principle of total withdrawal [to the 1967 boundaries]. We cannot come down from the Golan Heights, though this does not mean that we have to stick to the present line. In the Sinai, we have to keep presence and control in Sharm el Sheikh as well as a land connection with it— and by land connection I don't just mean a road. When it comes to Jordan, I have to adhere to the policy of my government, which is that we can negotiate a settlement. But if it involves territorial concessions on the West Bank, we have to seek a popular mandate [for such a change] in new elections.

Interview/Newsweek, 12-20:47.

Anwar el-Sadat
President of Egypt

1

The Soviets are refusing to give me arms. They are refusing to reschedule Egyptian debts. What is worse, they are demanding that I pay interest on the military debts . . . [Recent letters] show clearly the Soviet Union is playing a cat-and-mouse game with me. In one year and 1½ years at most, all the arms I have will turn into scrap iron because they are withholding spare parts for arms and the means to overhaul plane engines . . . The Russians are putting economic pressure and military pressure on me unless I go to them begging on my knees. I kneel only to God!

Before National Assembly, Cairo, March 14/
San Francisco Examiner & Chronicle, 3-21:
(This World)14.

2

[Defending the improved Egyptian-American relations]: After the [1973 Arab-Israeli] war, America came to us. Should I have turned it back? Would any real patriot fail to seize an opportunity to prevent the complete American bias for Israel which was Israel's most potent weapon for 25 years before the 1973 war? I still say that 99 per cent of the cards in the game are in America's hands whether the Soviet Union likes it or not, whether the Soviet Union gets angry or not.

Before National Assembly, Cairo, March 14/
Los Angeles Times, 3-15:(1)1.

3

We could have achieved something [toward peace in the Middle East] this year but unfortunately it is the Arab position which is hindering us, not one of the superpowers . . . In spite of any difference between us and the Soviet Union, they agree with us that the proper place for the peace is Geneva, and the same thing with the United States . . . [But] it appears that they [Syria] are not ready, because one day they say they are ready and the next day they say we shan't go. It is always two-faced policies.

Interview/The New York Times, 6-4:(A)3.

4

I don't know whether [the U.S.] Congress will agree if I ask the United States for arms. But I think it's an obligation now. We are friends, and you know my policy. I have proved myself to you. I would like you to convey to [U.S. President-elect Jimmy] Carter this: Let us put a global solution for the whole [Arab-Israeli] problem in 1977. It's time and we are ready for this and I hope Israel is ready, too . . . [Egypt is ready for a peace agreement providing] Israel withdraws from the lands it occupied in the 1967 war . . . and agrees to the establishment of a Palestinian state on the Jordan West Bank and the Gaza sector.

Before U.S. Senators, Cairo, Nov. 13/
The Dallas Times Herald, 11-14:(A)4.

WHAT THEY SAID IN 1976

(ANWAR el-SADAT)

1

When [Israeli] Prime Minister [Yitzhak] Rabin says he would like to sit down with me, this is a pretext for not wanting peace. He is wrong in assuming this approach would lead anywhere, because I would mistrust everything he says and he would mistrust everything I say.

Los Angeles Times, 11-29:(1)11.

2

[On U.S. Secretary of State Henry Kissinger, who is leaving his post next month]: The absence of one man will not do major harm. But I will say for Henry, he is the first Secretary of State with whom I dealt—and I've dealt with four—who changed the image of America for the better. He was not fond of the big stick, like Dulles, weak, like Rusk and naive, like Rogers. He came here during a turning point, when the Arabs had won their first victory over Israel, and he proved to be a man of his word. Israel and the Arabs needed someone in whom both could have confidence. Henry was this man.

Interview/Time, 11-29:28.

3

The Palestinian question is the whole core, the crux of the problem. If we are not going to solve it, we are not going to have the peace that we are after now. The Palestinians must have their state. So Egypt's position will be: the creation of a Palestinian state on the West Bank and the Gaza Strip with a corridor between them, and some sort of agreement upon the relation between this state and Jordan according to what the two parties—the Palestinians and the Jordanians—agree upon . . . I am true in my feeling and true in my vision of permanent peace in this area. Without peace, we can't build our country and achieve the reconstruction that we have already started. Without peace, we can't fulfill the hopes of our people for prosperity. When we say we want peace, we mean it.

Really. And I think I have proved this to the whole world. I always mean what I say. Unless the peace process proves to be a failure before the whole world, I am not putting any effort into preparing for a fifth war.

Interview/Newsweek, 12-13:44.

Elias Sarkis
President of Lebanon

4

[Addressing the nation on the civil war in his country]: I turn to you, realizing that some are still under arms and that the blood of the martyrs and victims has not yet dried. To those I say: We have had enough bloodshed, destruction, waste of effort and loss of opportunity . . . Once more I repeat: enough bloodshed and ruin.

Broadcast address, Beirut, Nov. 7/
The New York Times, 11-8:10.

Saud Faisal
Foreign Minister of Saudi Arabia

5

[On the Arab boycott of foreign firms doing business with Israel]: The boycott is an economic tool used by member states of the Arab League to defend themselves and their people from the territorial conquests and ambitions of Israel. The boycott involves no religious or racial discrimination. It applies equally to Muslims, Christians, Jews and anyone else who would strengthen Israel's ability to wage war on Arab countries and peoples. It is therefore an economic device for assuring the security of the Arab state.

Houston, Tex./Los Angeles Times, 10-17:(1)23.

Alexander M. Schindler
President, Union of American Hebrew Congregations; Chairman, Conference of Presidents of Major American Jewish Organizations

6

[On the U.S. sale of military transport aircraft to Egypt]: I realize that these six planes won't make a bit of difference in terms of the balance of power. But the sale . . . signifies that the United States may go beyond providing just the six planes; it could become a major supplier of arms to Egypt . . . I would hate to make these six planes an issue. But if Egypt really is interested in peace [with Israel], why must the country continue buying arms? I can understand the thrust of American foreign policy, which seeks to draw Egypt into the orbit of U.S. influence. But Egypt needs tractors, bread and technological expertise rather than weapons. Hungry people will do anything, but when a nation has something to lose it is less willing to get involved in armed conflict.

Before Jewish Federation Council, Los Angeles/
Los Angeles Herald-Examiner, 3-20:(A)3.

William W. Scranton
United States Ambassador/
Permanent Representative to
the United Nations 1

I feel strongly that it's important that the Israelis recognize that every time they push forward with more settlements [of Israeli population] in more directions outside of their former perimeters it makes it difficult, very difficult, to allay the suspicions of the Arabs as to their expansionist moves. And that makes it very much harder to achieve a peace. I have never thought that we could get a peace and military and economic security for Israel by making enemies of everybody on the Arab side. That's an absurdity.

At United Nations, New York, March 23/
Los Angeles Herald-Examiner, 5-10:(A)8.

2

[Defending Israel's rescue of its hostage-citizens from Arab terrorists in the recent raid at Entebbe airport, Uganda]: The government of Israel invoked one of the most remarkable rescue missions in history, a combination of guts and brains that has seldom if ever been surpassed. It electrified millions everywhere, and I confess I was one of them . . . [Israel's action] necessarily involved

a temporary breach of the territorial integrity of Uganda. However, there is a well-established right to use limited force for the protection of one's own nationals from an imminent threat of injury or death in a situation where the state in whose territory they are located is unwilling or unable to protect them.

At United Nations, New York, July 12/
Los Angeles Times, 7-13:(1)1;
The Washington Post, 7-13:(A)8.

Ariel Sharon
General, Israeli Army (Ret.) 3

This [Israeli] government is more subservient to Washington than any state in the U.S. Our ministers talk to [U.S. Secretary of State] Henry Kissinger four times a day; they have no plans, no initiative . . . Israel is being over-pressured and there will come a point when Israel will decide that it cannot give in any further. Then there will be a war in which everybody will lose.

Interview/Newsweek, 5-24:38.

Adlai E. Stevenson
United States Senator, D—Illinois 4

The Israeli image is not improving. Two months ago, Israeli officials spoke to me with pride of the trusting relationship between Jew and Arab in Israel and the tranquil Arab acceptance of the military occupation of the West Bank . . . Why has peace been put at risk by the continued establishment of Israeli settlements in the West Bank in violation of the Fourth Geneva Convention which states that "the occupying power shall not deport or transfer parts of its own civilian population into the territory it occupies"? Why provide agitators with a tailor-made issue with which to incite riots in the streets of Nazareth by confiscating Arab-owned land? Why permit the secret purchase of land from West Bank Arabs, in contravention of the Jordanian law which applies to them? Why an ostentatious holiday march through the West Bank by thousands representing a mili-

369

WHAT THEY SAID IN 1976

(ADLAI E. STEVENSON)

tant Israeli minority? The predictable response was more rioting—and at a time when the Lebanese crisis has already heightened the possibility of another Middle Eastern war . . . I am grieved by an Israel isolated; an Israel protected on more than one occasion by only the slender margin of an American veto from censure by the United Nations Security Council, an Israel, which a scant few years ago counted almost every black African country a friend, welcoming to Jerusalem the leading apostle of apartheid . . . Let there be no misunderstanding. America's commitment to Israel is unequivocal. The day America abandons Israel will be its last day as a great power. But America's will is not now tested; Israel's is tested.

May 6/ The Washington Post, 5-12:(A)22.

Robert Taft, Jr.
United States Senator, R—Ohio

1

[Favoring U.S. arms sales to Saudi Arabia]: I don't consider that Saudi Arabia has an enormous military potential. It has contracted to purchase from the United States two to three billions in arms. It is attempting to build up a naval and air-force capability that it hasn't really had. It has a small population. It's a very sparsely populated area even though it's large. It has very large oil resources which must be very tempting to aggressive neighbors—particularly in view of its small population and large but very sparsely inhabited area. I think there's every reason to feel that it's in the interest of stability in the area to have the Saudi Arabians build up their armed services. Also, we should welcome especially the build-up of their naval forces as providing further insurance that the supply lines will be kept open from the Middle East oil fields to Europe and Japan. So, as far as Saudi Arabia is concerned, I think we are pursuing a perfectly sound program of arms sales. Furthermore, I don't feel that the build-up of arms in Saudi Arabia, to the extent that it is presently

planned, constitutes any major threat to the Israelis.

Interview/ U.S. News & World Report, 3-8:44.

Maxwell D. Taylor
General, United States Army (Ret.);
Former Chairman,
Joint Chiefs of Staff

2

We can't wage war effectively in the Middle East at the present time . . . because we do not have the logistic support, the bases which are necessary for us to do so . . . We could intervene, but not effectively for long. We could not sustain combat in that area by ourselves because we would be very greatly exposed in the Eastern Mediterranean to the Soviet fleet. We are without many of the bases we used to count on . . . If we're smart, we won't go to war in that part of the world.

Interview/ Book Digest, November:17.

Malcolm Toon
United States Ambassador to Israel

3

There is a change taking place in the American attitude—not necessarily toward Israel but toward the whole business of foreign aid. This is in part, I think, a heritage of our Vietnam misfortune. It would be unwise for Israel to rely on a level of aid comparable to the one this year or last year . . . I think you can rely on the fact that we will always behave in such a way that Israel's security will not be jeopardized. [But] this, of course, depends on one's interpretations, one's attitude, and it may be that we may have differences of view . . . as to what really constitutes your [Israel's] security, your requirements, and what really meets them.

Interview, Tel Aviv/
Los Angeles Herald-Examiner, 4-11:(A)4.

4

Unless Israel's professed willingness to return occupied [Arab] territory is seen as more than mere rhetoric, the vicious circle of mutual mistrust cannot be broken. [Israel] must find a way to ease suspicions among the Arabs about its intentions in the occupied territories . . . I must point out here that the continued establishment by Israel of settlements in the occupied areas makes it difficult for us to persuade the Arabs that the Israelis are genuinely determined to live up to the commitments they have undertaken in the United Nations.

Before B'nai B'rith Anti-Defamation League,
Jerusalem, Nov. 19/
Los Angeles Times, 11-20:(1)15.

Cyrus R. Vance
Former Secretary of the Army, and
former Deputy Secretary of Defense,
of the United States 1

We [the U.S.] are committed to the survival of Israel. There isn't any question about this . . . If Israel were about to be driven into the sea, my answer would be yes [the U.S. should go to war]—if they [Israel] were to be extinguished as a country.

Television interview, New York, May/
The Dallas Times Herald, 12-11:(A)11.

Aharon Yariv
Director-designate, Institute of
Strategic Studies, Tel Aviv University 2

At the present, the Russian role [in the Middle East] has been lessened. Why? Because the U.S. has great advantages over the Soviets, and the Arabs have an interest in using this advantage. The Soviets can give weapons to the Arabs. They can give economic aid, even though the Arabs don't much care for it. But it is not the Soviets who can deliver to the Arabs territory held by the Israelis. The only nation with that capability is the U.S.

Interview, New York/
U.S. News & World Report, 11-29:23.

Ardeshir Zahedi
Iranian Ambassador to the
United States 3

. . . in the Arab-Israeli war in 1967 and again in 1973, Iran—which is not Arab—was the only country in the Mideast that did not embargo shipment of oil to Europe and the United States. But we have also said that oil in today's world is like bread and water: You cannot deprive people of its use. Iran, as a major supplier of oil, does not believe in using this commodity as a political weapon. As soon as our oil is pumped into tankers, where it goes is no longer our concern. We are simply interested in the economics of oil—and not its politics.

Interview, Washington/
U.S. News & World Report, 1-12:52.

The United Nations • War and Peace

David Brinkley
News commentator,
National Broadcasting Company

1

I don't share the Pentagon's nightmares about the Russians. I don't think they are sweet people or kindly disposed toward us [Americans], but neither do I think they have any idea of starting a war. The [Communist] Chinese? They don't have a history of being warlike people. I don't know any way they could attack us . . . and why should they? The Middle East? It is still unsettled and unstable, but from what I hear when I talk to [U.S. Secretary of State Henry] Kissinger and [Israeli Prime Minister Yitzhak] Rabin, it seems to me that changes are at work. It will drag on and there will be crises . . . but that's all.

Interview, Washington/
The Christian Science Monitor, 8-18:22.

Harrison Scott Brown
Professor of science and government,
California Institute of Technology

2

I happen to think that the UN is a terribly important body. It's all we've got from the point of view of true international organization. But the present state of the UN is most deplorable. The rich-country/poor-country confrontation is threatening to render the whole system impotent. When you superimpose upon that the continuing East-West confrontation, it becomes a hopeless mess. I think the UN has got to be transformed into a body where the main efforts are less along the lines of confrontation and much more along the lines of our working together to create a peaceful and stable world.

Interview, Pasadena, Calif./
Los Angeles Herald-Examiner, 12-26:
(California Living)7.

Jimmy Carter
1976 Democratic
U.S. Presidential nominee

3

. . . peace is not the mere absence of war. Peace is action to stamp out international terrorism. Peace is the unceasing effort to preserve human rights. And peace is a combined demonstration of strength and goodwill. We will pray for peace and we will work for peace, until we have removed from all nations for all time the threat of nuclear destruction.

Accepting the Democratic Presidential
nomination, at Democratic National Convention,
New York, July 15/
U.S. News & World Report, 7-26:79.

4

Contrasting the present function of the United Nations with its original concept in 1946, it has not measured up to expectations. I don't think anybody anticipated that in the 30 years following the establishment of the UN we would have 100 new nations formed. I think we had about 50 in the beginning, and now we have 150, almost all of which are in the UN. It has deteriorated into a debating society. The nations realize that their decisions will not be carried out and have become irresponsible. The Security

Council is almost entirely a negative entity where vetoes prevent decisions from being consummated. [But] I have a strong belief that the United Nations should be continued, that we should give it our support, that if it were not there it would be advisable to create a similar organization from scratch . . . I would make a major effort as President to elevate the importance of the United Nations, still retaining, of course, a veto power within the Security Council to make sure they didn't carry out any actions that were contrary to the best interests of our country.

Interview/
Los Angeles Herald-Examiner, 7-25:(A)6.

Lord Chalfont
Former Minister of State for Disarmament
of the United Kingdom
                                        1

I am deeply sorry if I tread on anyone's dreams, but I feel bound to draw attention to the fact that the nuclear balance, always a fragile and uncertain edifice, is being demolished before our very eyes. The nuclear balance ceases to exist at the moment when one side believes that it has acquired the capacity to deliver an effective nuclear attack upon the other and survive the ensuing retaliation. My proposition is that the Soviet Union is resolved to acquire that capacity in the very near future.

U.S. News & World Report, 9-6:16.

Bob Dole
United States Senator, R—Kansas;
1976 Republican
Vice-Presidential nominee
                                        2

Four times in this country we have gone to war. Each time the harsh light of history reveals that war rarely began for reasons that were self-justifying—but rather because of weakness, wishful thinking and bad leadership.

Campaigning, Presque Isle, Maine, Oct. 25/
The Washington Post, 10-26:(A)4.

Gerald R. Ford
President of the United States
                                        3

The United States is a peace-loving nation, and our foreign policy is designed to lessen the threat of war and of aggression. In recent years, we have made substantial progress toward that goal—in the Middle East, in Europe, in Asia and elsewhere around the world. Yet we also recognize that the best way to secure the peace is to be fully prepared to defend our interests. I believe in peace through strength.

News conference, Washington, Feb. 17/
The New York Times, 2-18:20.

                                        4

Peace today has a special significance—because war today has a special terror. A thermonuclear war today would mean death and destruction on a scale so vast that we can hardly comprehend it . . . Where there is conflict, let us try conciliation. Let us attempt to work out our differences on the negotiating table, rather than in a desperate duel that would leave the world in ashes.

At War Memorial, El Paso, Tex., April 10/
The Washington Post, 4-11:(A)13.

Richard Garwin
Visiting professor of physics,
Harvard University; Former member,
Federal Science Advisory Committee
                                        5

There are many possible causes of nuclear war other than the often-mentioned escalation from conventional fighting or a disarming first strike. One could have accidental war, in which one superpower could inadvertently launch one of a whole stockpile of weapons against some other power . . . Catalytic war is a second possibility. A power possessing a small number of nuclear weapons and a great hate for the two largest powers could, in its own interest, provoke war between them . . . There are tens of thousands of nuclear weapons in the world instead of just a few, and many of these have an explosive power of 20 megatons instead of 20 kilo-

WHAT THEY SAID IN 1976

(RICHARD GARWIN)

tons—capable of destroying an area 100 times larger than the original nuclear weapons . . . Furthermore, we have far less control over most of these weapons than we had over the first few, although we do, at least, have some technical controls for our own. As usual, however, we have been over-concentrating on a few dangers and ignoring the many others that will be the ones to bite us simultaneously. How, for example, would the United States respond to nuclear violence? We have never really practiced the channels of decision. The President, being a busy man, is far more familiar with other things than with the procedures for releasing nuclear weapons or the likely effects of such actions.

At Cambridge Forum panel discussion/
The Washington Post, 1-4:(F)1.

Fred C. Ikle
Director, Arms Control and
Disarmament Agency of the
United States 1

I think it's nonsense to suggest that we automatically would be drawn into a nuclear war if a nuclear bomb were somewhere exploded in anger. There's no reason why that should follow. But we would be affected in the sense that the world would not be the same the morning after the nuclear bomb was first used again since 1945. The impact around the world would be shattering.

Interview/
U.S. News & World Report, 11-8:70.

George F. Kennan
American diplomat 2

I know of nothing in the present undertakings or aspirations of either our government or the Soviet government that could justify the present overwhelming concentration on the purely military aspects of our relationship. Such competition is placing not only the people of these two countries, but

the people of many other countries as well. in terrrible jeopardy which no consideration of political advantage can possibly justify. There is no reason of national interest why this country should not agree at once to the total banning of the testing of nuclear weapons, if others will do the same. There is no reason why this country should not clarify its position on the first use of nuclear weapons—make it plain to ourselves and to everybody else that we will not use these weapons of mass destruction unless they are used against us.

At "Pacem in Terris" convocation,
Washington, December ('75)/
The Center Magazine, March-April:15.

Edward M. Kennedy
United States Senator,
D—Massachusetts 3

In their preoccupation with third- and fourth-generation nuclear weapons, in their fascination with a calculus of numbers that has little real meaning, the superpowers are fast foreclosing the chance to prevent the spread of nuclear weapons around the globe. It does not take 700,000 Hiroshima-type bombs to have a nuclear war; in the wrong hands, it takes just one.

At "Pacem in Terris" convocation,
Washington, December ('75)/
The Center Report, February:9.

Henry A. Kissinger
Secretary of State
of the United States 4

We know from history that great powers will not long accept a diminution of their security or inroads into their interests and that sooner or later they will seek—and find—compensation in some other place or manner. It is precisely this chain of action and reaction that has led to catastrophe in the past and which must be broken if the disasters of history are not to be repeated.

At luncheon, Moscow, Jan. 21/
Los Angeles Herald-Examiner, 1-21:(A)2.

1

Historically, a conflict of ideology and geopolitical interests such as that which characterizes the current international scene has almost invariably led to conflict. But in the age of thermonuclear weapons and strategic equality, humanity could not survive such a repetition of history. No amount of tough rhetoric can change these realities. The future of our nation and of mankind depends on how well we avoid confrontation without giving up vital interests and how well we establish a more hopeful and stable relationship without surrender of principle.

Before Boston World Affairs Council,
March 11/ The New York Times, 3-12:4.

2

The United Nations was born of the conviction that peace is both indivisible and more than merely stability; that for peace to be lasting it must fulfill mankind's aspirations for justice, freedom, economic well-being, the rule of law and the promotion of human rights. But the history of this organization has been in considerable measure the gradual awareness that humanity would not inevitably share a single approach to these goals. The United Nations has survived—and helped to manage—30 years of vast change in the international system. It has come through the bitterness of the cold war. It has played a vital role in the dismantling of the colonial empires. It has helped moderate conflicts and is manning truce lines in critical parts of the world. It has carried out unprecedented efforts in such areas as public health, development assistance and technical cooperation. But the most important challenge of this organization lies still ahead: to vindicate mankind's positive and nobler goals and help nations achieve a new understanding of community.

At United Nations, New York, Sept. 30/
Vital Speeches, 11-1:42.

George B. Kistiakowsky
Professor of chemistry,
Harvard University

3

There are no cases in history of absolutely

insane arms races ending peacefully by simply laying down arms. Arms races usually end up in wars. As the military acquires more and more weapons, it will acquire more and more power, and the military tends to resolve conflict by military means. Here, I am not talking of nuclear weapons alone. Let us bear in mind that in the last year the United States has sold or given away nearly $10-billion worth of non-nuclear arms to Third World countries. The figure for the Soviet Union is not very far below. If the armament race continues, what will be the outcome? I think that a major nuclear war, in which the loss of life would be at least comparable to that of World War II, is not unlikely.

At Cambridge Forum panel discussion/
The Washington Post, 1-4:(F)4.

Gene R. LaRocque
Rear Admiral, United States Navy (Ret.);
Director, Center for Defense
Information

4

Let me emphasize: There is no defense against a nuclear attack. There is no way to shoot down incoming nuclear weapons. There is no way to neutralize nuclear weapons that are in flight. There is no effective way to provide shelter for our civilians, and no certain way to stop a nuclear exchange after it has started. In a war with Russia, fighting could well start with conventional weapons, but when one side begins to lose, the fighting is almost certain to escalate to tactical nuclear weapons, and the inevitable next stop will be a general strategic nuclear war. Now, since there is no way to defend against a nuclear attack, and since a nuclear war will probably be catastrophic for civilization, the only rational course is to avoid nuclear war.

At "Pacem in Terris" convocation,
Washington, December ('75)/
The Center Magazine, March-April:49.

David E. Lilienthal
Chairman, Development and Resources
Corporation; Former Chairman,
Atomic Energy Commission
of the United States

5

If a great number of countries come to

WHAT THEY SAID IN 1976

(DAVID E. LILIENTHAL)

have an arsenal of nuclear weapons, then I'm glad I'm not a young man and I'm sorry for my grandchildren . . . The tragic fact is that the atomic arms race is today proceeding at a more furious and more insane pace than ever. Proliferation of capabilities to produce nuclear weapons of mass destruction is reaching terrifying proportions. We have to decide now what we can do, now, within our own capabilities, to prevent a very bad situation from becoming a disastrous and inevitable one. I therefore propose as a private citizen that this Committee, with its great prestige, call upon the Congress and the President to order a complete embargo to the export of all nuclear devices and all nuclear material, that it be done now, and done unilaterally. Further, unilaterally, the United States should without delay proceed by lawful means to revoke existing American licenses and put an end to the future of pending licensing to foreign firms and governments of American know-how and facilities paid for and created by American taxpayers' funds and American brains.

Before Senate Government Operations Committee, Washington, Jan. 19/ The New York Times, 1-20:2.

Richard M. Nixon
Former President of the United States   1

There are . . . some who believe that the mere act of signing a statement of principles or a diplomatic conference will bring instant and lasting peace. This is naive. There cannot and will not be lasting and secure peace until every nation in the world respects the security and independence of every other nation, large or small.

At banquet in his honor, Peking, Feb. 22/ Los Angeles Times, 2-26:(1)8.

Wolfgang K. H. Panofsky
Director, Stanford Linear Accelerator Center   2

No civil-defense program—large or small

—and no shift in strategic doctrine can change the basic dilemma of our age, that the peoples of both the United States and the U.S.S.R. are in jeopardy in any kind of nuclear conflict. Only bold steps limiting and reducing the dispersion of nuclear arms among nations, both by negotiation and intelligent self-restraint, can offer hope that nuclear catastrophe can be avoided.

Before Congressional Joint Committee on Production, Washington, April 28/ The Christian Science Monitor, 5-26:12.

William W. Scranton
United States Ambassador/ Permanent Representative to the United Nations   3

[On being UN Ambassador]: It's terrible, the problems are impossible, the hours are much too long—and I love it.

To U.S. President Ford/ San Francisco Examiner & Chronicle, 6-6: (Scene)2.

                                                    4

It doesn't surprise me that this is a confrontation period [in the UN] that has been going on the last few years, and at least to some degree I would expect it to continue for some time. After all, there have been tremendous changes, political and otherwise, in the world with the establishment of so many new nations. To avoid war and have peace . . . is practically impossible without change. To have peaceful change is certainly one of the functions of an international organization . . . That there is relative peace in the world today is a great tribute to the United Nations.

Interview, United Nations, New York/ Los Angeles Herald-Examiner, 9-5:(A)13.

Yosef Tekoah
Former Israeli Ambassador/ Permanent Representative to the United Nations   5

One of the reasons I decided to leave the UN was great disappointment . . . I served a total of eight years in the UN, and more than 100 of the 135 member states don't know what democracy is.

Interview/
"W": a Fairchild publication, 6-25:8.

Kurt Waldheim
Secretary General of the United Nations

1

. . . disillusionment [with the UN] persists and on occasion rises almost to fever pitch. We are, in fact, going through such a period in the United States at the present time. [But] for all the criticism which is directed at the world organization, there seems, in the minds of governments at least, to be no alternative in times of trouble to its admittedly imperfect procedures . . . [A] new generation of global problems—the gap between rich and poor nations, food, environment, population, raw materials and the future of the oceans—are too large and complex to be dealt with [by] any one nation or group of nations alone. [The UN] is an imperfect institution with manifest shortcomings. Its public face represents the turmoil and uncertainty of our world and the frustrations and difficulties which governments have in finding their way in the world . . . At such a time, it is essential that governments should come together to discuss their problems and to work out concerted plans for the future . . . We can certainly expect more stormy weather in the year ahead. To my mind, this accentuates the necessity of the institution [of the UN], for the tensions and conflicts exist in any case and cannot be ignored.

Before University of Denver Social Science
Foundation, Jan. 25/
The New York Times, 1-26:10.

2

[On the UN's machinery for peace]: This machinery has little value if it is not used by governments. One of the key dilemmas of the future is whether this unique international resource is going to be properly utilized, or whether nations are going to relapse into those former practices that have brought so much tragedy to mankind, and particularly to Asia. The long, drawn-out agony of Indochina should serve as a lesson in this regard.

At University of the Philippines, Feb. 12/
Los Angeles Times, 2-13:(1)12.

3

[On his job as Secretary General]: There is no family life any more. I have to be here from early in the morning until late in the evening . . . But it's part of the job. I used to say, when my wife was complaining about no family life, I said, "You can't have the cake and eat it. You must accept the challenge." And I always accepted the challenge. Otherwise I wouldn't have accepted this job. And this job is a job which only somebody can really do who is ready to accept the challenge, because it's sometimes a most frustrating job—most frustrating. You want to do so much more . . . But what I want to say is that there are moments when you have satisfaction, if you liberate—if you're able to achieve the liberation of a few human beings who are captured, put in prison, and you are able to get them out; if you are able to settle a border conflict . . . if you are able to contribute to the beginning of a negotiating process somewhere in the world instead of having a new war there—this is a satisfaction, whether it's recognized or not.

Interview, United Nations, New York/
Los Angeles Times, 11-14:(1)2.

4

The post of Secretary General is at the same time one of the most fascinating and one of the most frustrating jobs in the world, encompassing, as it does, the height of human aspiration and the depth of human frailty.

Accepting a new term as Secretary General,
United Nations, New York, Dec. 8/
The New York Times, 12-9:12.

Herbert F. York
Professor of physics,
University of California, San Diego

5

. . . despite 30 years of trying, there has been little accomplishment in arms control and ab-

WHAT THEY SAID IN 1976

solutely nothing in nuclear disarmament. The danger is not that we may accomplish too much, or that we will damage our vital interests by pursuing both arms control and disarmament. The real danger is that we will continue, in the future as in the past, to do exactly nothing until the whole world blows up in our faces.

At "Pacem in Terris" convocation,
Washington, December ('75)/
The Center Magazine, March-April:51.

Charles W. Yost
Former United States Ambassador/
Permanent Representative to the
United Nations
1

In economic matters the United Nations is not going to do the whole job of managing economic interdependence in the world. We would not expect it to. But the United Nations is the organization where everybody is present; that is one advantage. Another is that it already has a very extensive family of agencies working in this vineyard—the World Bank, the International Monetary Fund, the Food and Agriculture Organization, the World Health Organization, and all the rest of them. So much should continue to be done there. These are the operationally important executive parts of the United Nations, the agencies that can get those things done that are necessary to the preservation of mankind over the next few decades. What happens in the General Assembly is quite another matter.

At "Pacem in Terris" convocation,
Washington, December ('75)/
The Center Magazine, March-April:58.

PART THREE

General

Berenice Abbott
Photographer   *1*

If anything represents the present, it is photography. It's nature is *now*. You can't photograph the past or future, so you have to deal with it in its own time, and that takes on a sense of timelessness.

Interview, Washington/
The Washington Post, 4-3:(E)3.

Leon Barzin
Conductor,
National Orchestral Association   *2*

The cultural explosion of the past three decades is over, and today cultural organizations are struggling to keep their status quo. What is needed is more education in the arts if they are not to take second place to time-passing activities when people arrive at a 30-hour work week in the near future. Otherwise, people will become drooling morons in front of TV sets.

Interview/
The New York Times, 4-5:46.

Salvador Dali
Artist   *3*

Drawing is the honesty of the art. There is no possibility of cheating. It is either good or bad.

Cadaques, Spain/ People, 9-27:49.

Agnes de Mille
Choreographer   *4*

Most of the money [given to the arts by the National Endowment for the Arts] is being thrown away. It's being used for political purposes. They're spreading it around geographically, like Kiwanis, because every state has its Senators and Congressmen. What do they care in Alaska if Martha Graham continues creating? Or what do they care in Oklahoma if Ballet Theatre continues? Our intent in the beginning was to help the highest, the *best*. The whole world tendency today is to help the unknowns and the unproven, but all that does is encourage mediocrity. And a mediocre ballet company is worse than no ballet company. The people don't like it, and they're right. If I saw dancing out there without seeing any of the great works, I would hate it, too.

Interview, New York/
The New York Times, 7-4:(2)6.

John Denver
Singer, Songwriter   *5*

Art can be a song, a poem, a movie. Art for me is to create a space for people to realize themselves. I write a song. The song works. The medium of words, music, works. I have said what I wanted to. It's art if someone listens and something happens, something pops up, little pictures, an image. When that picture comes up and you think, "That's right! That's true!"—that's art. It's realizing who you are.

Interview, Aspen, Colo./
San Francisco Examiner & Chronicle, 8-29:
(Datebook)18.

James Dickey
Author, Poet   *6*

Painters such as Jackson Pollock and Willem de Kooning have made America the

WHAT THEY SAID IN 1976

(JAMES DICKEY)

most influential country in the visual arts in the 20th century . . . Our writers, Faulkner and Hemingway and T. S. Eliot . . . are Nobel Prize winners. There's no way that we [in the U.S.] could or should feel any kind of an inferiority complex, because we are the dominant force in the artistic world. I love the European tradition. I love French literature, painting and music; Italian opera and German music—but they are not the force at the present time that the Americans are. The Europeans know it, and the English know it—and they can't forgive us for it.

Interview/
U.S. News & World Report, 3-15:55.

Helen Hayes
Actress
1

It is wrong to think of the arts as frivolity . . . They are as necessary as school and food. They are the food of our spirit.

Before Massachusetts arts commission/
The National Observer, 12-18:6.

Charlton Heston
Actor
2

If I remember this correctly, someone once said that art is not quite the truth. But that art is the lie which helps us understand the truth.

Interview, Dallas/
The Dallas Times Herald, 4-26:(D)7.

Thomas P. F. Hoving
Director, Metropolitan Museum of Art, New York
3

Far from being less pertinent, the fine arts and the art museum will become more important . . . If the art museum does harness the contemporary tools, techniques and aesthetics of the very best aspects of communications, it can go beyond art education, art appreciation and art history, and can become the broadest and most powerful communi-

cator in visual history. This will most assuredly be the next great epoch of the art museum.

At world art conference,
New School for Social Research, New York/
The Christian Science Monitor, 11-11:16.

4

The current period—the Now—of the American art museum is simply a consolidation era finishing off the entire stage of the late 19th-, early 20th-century period. It is a period of tidying-up the last loose threads of the first stage. Encyclopedic collections are being rounded out. Buildings are being finished forever except for their mutable interiors. A rich diversity of art museums and institutions is being achieved. Let me generally characterize it by a personal observation. A few years ago someone asked me: was I trying to bring the Metropolitan into the 20th or even the 21st century? No, I said, I'm not doing anything new. I haven't made any single metamorphosis—and that was deliberate, I hasten to say. I'm just trying to wrap up the 19th-century phase. Innovation will come a little later.

At world art conference,
New School for Social Research, New York/
The Christian Science Monitor, 11-12:26.

Ada Louise Huxtable
Architectural critic,
"The New York Times"
5

Art is always with us, whether we know it or not. We cannot escape art. It is as unavoidable as breathing . . . Art affects everything—from the drive-in to the park benches to the idea of a good life. Art is not the kind of cultural spinach you consume because it is good for you. It is a way of life.

Dallas/ The Dallas Times Herald, 11-14:(F)1.

Raymond Loewy
Industrial designer
6

. . . the world is burdened with archaic objects—noisy autos, garishly unappetizing restaurants, ugly dwellings that look like buildings to break out of rather than places burglars would enter surreptitiously, just to name a few. Wherever I turn, I become aware of unexplored regions of our civilization just waiting for designers to apply imagination. The challenges are out there for all of us.

Interview, Palm Springs, Calif./
Los Angeles Times, 6-27:(Home)29.

George London
Opera singer;
Director, National Opera Institute   *1*

One of the most encouraging things happening in America is the growing public support of the arts. There has been steadily increasing attendance and more money provided by Congress through the National Endowment for the Arts. It's but a fraction of what a great country requires, but the trend is upward. I've always felt that the state of the arts is a reflection of the health of a society. A symbol of an ascendant society is the flourishing of its arts.

Interview/U.S. News & World Report, 12-6:62.

Robert Motherwell
Painter   *2*

For me, painting is like farming or gardening. You can't force it; you must cultivate it at its own speed. That's not to say there aren't magic moments—but I'm sure there are in farming, too.

Interview, Greenwich, Conn./
The New York Times, 2-3:33.

Iris Murdoch
Author   *3*

The most important thing about art is that it tells you what nature is really like, as opposed to what people in their fantasy-ridden way vaguely imagine it's like. Art holds a mirror to nature, and I think it's a very difficult thing to do.

Interview/Publishers Weekly, 12-13:17.

Louise Nevelson
Sculptor   *4*

When I came to New York 55 years ago, to pursue art, the American government didn't feel that art was important. No young country is really in favor of creativity. Art is a luxury when people need bread . . . But that has changed. Now I go to the coast of California, to Florida and Maine, always with my work and for my work. I never traveled in America for that reason, until recently. I find that all over America the seeds have been planted. Like Johnny Appleseed —art seeds have been planted. And they're flourishing and flourishing. Today, artists have academic training—they're professionals in that sense. There must be more than 500 new museums. Art and art history are taught in every school. Art in this country now is like eating. It's a must.

Interview/Newsweek, 7-4:53.

Gregor Piatigorsky
Cellist   *5*

. . . climbing the high mountain which an artist does in his youth is hard, but it is even more difficult to come down the mountain. When you go up, there is acclaim. When you come down, no one. I saw a tennis match yesterday—one man won, the other lost. Some of the strokes of the loser were absolutely immortal, but he was considered a loser. That's not right. When an artist comes down wisely, bravely and safely, we should applaud and shout "bravo!"

Interview, Los Angeles/
Los Angeles Times, 4-4:(5)12.

   6

You know, music, art—these are not just little decorations to make life prettier. They're very deep necessities, which people cannot live without. And every musician, every artist, has a heavy responsibility. Though not all of them realize this, to be true to art they must really forget themselves and devote their lives to something larger in which they believe.

Interview/The Wall Street Journal, 11-29:18.

WHAT THEY SAID IN 1976

John Portman
Architect
1

A building is not for a particular class of people. It sits out in the public, and it should serve everybody. Now, that is a pretty big order. So we have tried to isolate things the human being has within him that produce innate reactions to environmental conditions. If it is innate, since we are all creatures of nature, then nature plays a big part in it. Consequently, I use water in lake form, in fountain form, in brook form. I use water in all kinds of ways, because the human being has a natural affinity for it. The common denominator to all buildings is people. We try to invoke a pleasant response in people.

Interview, Atlanta/
Nation's Business, August:48.

S. Dillon Ripley
Secretary,
Smithsonian Institution, Washington
2

I do not believe museums have anything to gain in the long run without allying themselves somehow with the destinies of education in this country . . . Museums are sylvan sacred groves in which the fruits of the human condition are seen at their finest and preserved for future generations, waiting to teach the past and expose presentiments for the future.

Before American Association of Museums,
Washington, May 31/
The Washington Post, 6-1:(B)3.

Robert W. Sarnoff
Former chairman, RCA Corporation
3

The late President Kennedy once wrote that . . . the arts, "far from being an interruption, a distraction, in the life of a nation, is very close to the center of the nation's civilization." I would hope that even—indeed, especially—in these troubled times, we can allow that purpose and quality to shine forth. The restorative powers of music and drama, of dance and the visual arts, can contribute mightily to helping us all meet our problems with confidence and spirit.

The Dallas Times Herald, 3-22:(B)4.

Maximilian Schell
Actor, Director
4

Sometimes I would rather hear a seven-year-old child playing [Beethoven's] *Fur Elyse* on a piano, with all the mistakes, than to hear it played by a master on a record. As close as you can get to the inventive moment of art—even the child trying to draw for the first time—the better it is, the fresher you see the world.

Interview, New York/
The Christian Science Monitor, 6-3:26.

Beverly Sills
Opera singer
5

There was a time when, if you wanted to hear Mozart, everybody said you had to go to Vienna. If you wanted to see real ballet, it had to be a Russian name; if it was not a Russian name, how could it dance? If you wanted to hear a great symphony orchestra, of course, it was in Europe—it couldn't possibly be here [in the U.S.]. And opera stars—my God, 20 years ago, if the name was unpronounceable it was automatically a great singer. That's all changed today. Our [U.S.] symphony orchestras are among the top five in the world. You can't put ours on the side. As far as opera companies go, let's face it—sure there's La Scala, Vienna and Covent Garden, but there is only one Metropolitan Opera. And American opera stars with perfectly pronounceable names are doing very well. You can't dismiss Price and Horne and Verrett and Arroyo and Milnes, and I may immodestly include myself. We're holding our own extremely well. We have arrived. The day of European supremacy, for my taste, is over. We're one of the great art forces—instead of armed forces—of the world.

Interview/Newsweek, 7-4:74.

John Simon
Film critic, "New York" magazine
                                        1

[On why he writes reviews noted for their harshness]: Because we live in a world full of phonies, full of bad art posturing as art. Cultural and intellectual values are in a steady decline. Education is becoming more and more laughable. Literacy is in danger of disappearing the way the tail fell off the human ape. Students no longer know how to express themselves either in speech or in writing. Newspapers and books are edited so badly that it is clear that neither writers nor the editors know such things as grammar any more. I don't mean to rehearse this whole tragic history, but given this kind of world in which values are going out the window every second, it seems that the least one could do if one has certain standards and notions of excellence, is to defend them as determinately and as dedicatedly as one knows how.
Interview/The Wall Street Journal, 8-5:8.

Benjamin Thompson
Architect
                                        2

[On architects]: I strongly believe that to be professional today means answering a higher level of responsibility for the public good. Our real constituency has changed from private to corporate to public. Our power to affect the lives and environments of people is awesome. The men we work for—boards, committees, agencies—largely will not take those responsibilities. Like lawyers and accountants, we are finally responsible for the impact of our work, for ugliness, destruction, overscale, monotony, chaos, and for crimes against nature, for devitalization of the inner city or—for the reverse.
At New England regional meeting of
American Institute of Architects/
Los Angeles Times, 12-13:(4)9,14.

Wesley C. Uhlman
Mayor of Seattle
                                        3

The arts themselves are one of the basic reasons that cities and towns and metropolitan counties exist in this country. And as we are forced to lower our expectations about the quantity of material wealth which this or any other nation can sustain, the arts give us the chance to raise our expectations about the quality of our lives.
At Associated Councils of the Arts conference,
Seattle/Los Angeles Times, 8-6:(4)16.

Fashion

Marc Bohan
Fashion designer
1

A woman does not have to be embroidered from head to toe to look sophisticated. Style should not be forced, aggressive. There is more freedom today. Life is more casual. People dress up less. Social life is less spectacular, more intimate. One is taken in less by appearance, less by grandiose things.

Interview, New York/
"W": a Fairchild publication, 10-29:13.

Pierre Cardin
Fashion designer
2

There should be only one fashion collection a year, just as there is one big *salon d'auto* a year. That is the only way to give a real surprise to fashion, the only way to really change anything. With as many collections as we have now, nothing is really different.

Interview/"W": a Fairchild publication, 1-23:5.

Andre Courreges
Fashion designer
3

If eventually, in fact very soon, people do not understand what I am doing, I will close down my couture house. In the past I was understood by Americans. The French never understood. Blacks understood better than whites. Now the Americans don't understand, either . . . I cannot show to people who do not understand. That is the hardship of singing when no one listens.

Interview, Paris/
The Washington Post, 3-7:(K)1.

James Galanos
Fashion designer
4

Today anything goes. Evening gowns with boots, funny hats with evening attire. No rhyme or reason for what is done. It shows a lack of interest in refinement and niceties, even for people with money.

The Washington Post, 11-28:(G)4.

Mike Geist
Fashion designer
5

The unisex clothes of the '60s are no longer needed because the tension over women's rights has all but ended. Women have established their equality and they can now dress to suit their identities as women. We now recognize the cult of the individual.

Los Angeles/
Los Angeles Times, 8-12:(4)16.

Rudi Gernreich
Fashion designer
6

The fashion industry is made up of a small court of people who decide things. And today they are more fascistic than ever before. They have so little respect for reality and the problems of reality that they are again projecting elitist fantasy uniforms for themselves. I'm a pro. I work. I create symbols. What are *they* doing?

Interview, Los Angeles/
Los Angeles Times, 10-1:(4)9.

7

Clothes in themselves are not masculine or feminine; it's the people wearing them. I am currently working on the costumes for a very modern ballet and, in one number, all the dancers, male and female, wear the same costume. It's amazing—when a man wears it he looks extremely masculine, a woman terribly feminine. Men and women cannot look alike because they do not look alike.

Dallas, Dec. 5/
The Dallas Times Herald, 12-6:(E)8.

Halston
Fashion designer

1

Eight years ago I went into business for myself against the most terrible odds. The whole tide was against someone who did made-to-order designs. I proved there was a client for high fashion both here and abroad. I'm the impossible designer dream. You know, I live in an ivory tower on 68th Street in New York. I've made a few million dollars. I'm talked about. Everyone thought that kind of style was over. Really, isn't this what America is all about? I went against the grain. Everyone in my trade was going out of business. I had stick-to-it-iveness. I proved that anyone can do it.

Interview, Los Angeles/
Los Angeles Times, 10-24:(5)18.

Norman Hartnell
Dress designer to
Queen Elizabeth II of England

2

Social conditions have altered so. To wear a beautiful dress is all rather corny now. I find the strangled dedication that the modern young girl has to the ugly is rather inexplicable. If fashion reflects the times, the times at the moment must be awfully tatty.

San Francisco Examiner & Chronicle, 7-11:
(This World)2.

Edith Head
Motion-picture fashion designer

3

I've always been a big supporter of home sewing. I mean, wouldn't it be great if every man and woman learned how to sew? For one thing, they'd save a lot of money. And for another, it would help to put some individuality back into American fashion.

Los Angeles Times, 5-6:(4)4.

Carol Horn
Fashion designer

4

People are so brainwashed. They see the way clothes are put together on a mannequin or in a magazine, and they think it has to be that way. I try to get through to them that they have the same options in clothes as they do in, say, cooking. You don't always make the same recipe the same way. You improvise. Your moods change. Your style should change, too . . . Clothes can be liberating, a means of expression. Sometimes I see a girl of 15 who understands this, sometimes a woman of 50. If I have a mission, it's to encourage women to cultivate their own style and taste. I try to make it easier by providing the materials. But, really, it's up to the woman to make dressing herself an adventure.

Interview/
The New York Times Magazine, 2-29:(2)36.

Bill Kaiserman
Fashion designer

5

Where does my creativity come from? It comes from me. You experience things, you travel to different places, see, feel, and somewhere, in some way, that filters into your mind and it gets a buzz. That's when I sit down and do my next collection.

Interview, Beverly Hills, Calif./
Los Angeles Herald-Examiner, 12-5:
(California Living)15.

Jean Sebastien Szwarc
Director general,
House of Saint Laurent, Paris

6

The *haute couture* is like an old grandmother with a heart condition. Everyone expects her to die any moment, but she goes on to bury her children and grandchildren

WHAT THEY SAID IN 1976

(JEAN SEBASTIEN SZWARC)

and her great-grandchildren. The *haute couture* is sick, but she is an invalid who hangs on pretty well.

"W": a Fairchild publication, 8-6:16.

Emanuel Ungaro
Fashion designer

1

[On the "mannish" look of new clothing for women]: There is masculinity and femininity in each person. Some have more of one quality than the other. It makes little difference that there is such a similarity in the clothing of men and women. It is the individual, only, that makes a difference, not his or her clothes.

The Washington Post, 4-25:(H)9.

Gloria Vanderbilt
Fashion designer

2

I don't believe there's any such thing as good taste or bad taste. It's what you like and what you relate to. And if you change —if the fashions you liked 10 years ago or even one year ago no longer appeal to you— it doesn't mean what you liked then wasn't good taste. It's just that you've gone on to another point of view. You should plunge in with great authority and say what you like even if others don't like it. You must believe in yourself. You must have what I call creative will—which is really stubbornness.

Los Angeles/
Los Angeles Times, 8-18:(4)6.

Spiro T. Agnew
Former Vice President
of the United States 1

Too many [in the news media] have gone to advocacy journalism. They write what they feel and build the facts around that . . . they treat everyone badly, and sometimes I think it's getting worse. The commercialization of attacking public people may cost us talent in public life. The attitude of destroying everyone in public life is damaging us overseas. And they do it under the guise of freedom of speech . . .
Interview, Beverly Hills, Calif./
Los Angeles Times, 5-1:(1)20.

Harold W. Andersen
Chairman, American Newspaper
Publishers Association 2

Too many people, including more than a few in positions of influence, believe either that the news media have too much power or that we are not using our power wisely and fairly. If we aren't trusted, we don't have much left. The First Amendment would prove too thin a garment if we ever had to try to wrap ourselves in it to withstand the cold wind of majority opinion convinced that the news media cannot be fair as well as free.
At ANPA convention, New York, May 3/
The New York Times, 5-4:14.

Erik Barnouw
Professor emeritus of dramatic arts,
Columbia University;
Former TV writer, producer 3

[On TV news]: People say that they're going to watch "the news." They don't say

they're going to watch *some* news. They're going to watch "the news." [News commentator] Walter Cronkite says: "That's the way it is," and the viewers feel that they know what's happening. There's nobody more reassuring than Cronkite in making you feel that you are getting it straight, and complete . . . What you see on television news is mainly events that happened where they had camera crews. That means a limited number of cities in the United States and a limited number of places abroad. Television-news people depend largely on the pseudo-events. They decide before anything happens what's going to be important. The only exceptions are fires and floods and other catastrophies that last long enough to get the cameras there. Everything else is an arranged event: press conferences, dedication of buildings, beauty contests, demonstrations. This puts an awful lot of power into the hands of people who are in a position to arrange things of that sort . . . Things that don't happen on the tube don't seem to have really happened. People may read about it in the newspaper, but it doesn't have the reality of something shown on television. What happens on TV sticks in the mind. It's brighter. It's in living color that is more living than anything in your own life. It has fantastic authority.
Interview, Washington/
U.S. News & World Report, 3-1:28.

Daniel Bell
Professor of sociology,
Harvard University 4

It's no accident, though I think it's exaggerated in the terms of its magnitude, that journalism became the hotshot place of the '70s. Being the adversary—uncovering, in-

WHAT THEY SAID IN 1976

vestigating, exposing character—was the real payoff as against the hard work, study and assembling of technical knowledge that was the road of the '60s. In the end, the journalism of the '70s will defeat itself because it will have lacked some of the technical knowledge which would have been gained if there'd been a larger interplay with hard study.

Interview/
U.S. News & World Report, 7-5:Special Section.

Daniel J. Boorstin
Librarian of Congress
of the United States; Historian
1

The question is whether TV has abolished the role of the printing press. This is another example of a new technology forcing the old into new roles. In the case of TV, it has obviously pushed newspapers into new roles. The development of investigative reporting can be explained in part by the new role of TV. TV can give the spot news quicker than newspapers, which have to be printed and distributed. So the newsprint media seek new roles and find new roles. It takes as much inventiveness in finding new roles as in inventing new media.

Interview, Washington/
Los Angeles Times, 11-9:(2)5.

David Brinkley
News commentator,
National Broadcasting Company
2

If it is news in a newspaper, is it not also news on radio and television? No, it isn't. [The test] is whether it's worth knowing. Does anyone care? And how many care? ... Newspapers can print items most of their readers don't give a damn about. We [in broadcast news] can't. We have to do things our own way to suit the medium that we work with.

Before Radio-Television
News Directors Association, Miami Beach/
Los Angeles Times, 12-15:(1)2.

No one who has not been an [TV news] anchorman can understand what a grinding, confining, repetitive job it is. In almost any other kind of work you can arrange your schedule to give you some flexibility. The newscast is fixed and everything else has to be arranged around it. In any other business, if you do something reasonably well you can get promoted. Here, if you do this reasonably well, you stay at it until you die.

Interview/TV Guide, 12-18:8.

Jimmy Carter
Candidate for the 1976
Democratic U.S. Presidential nomination;
Former Governor of Georgia (D)
4

My preference is that the press be open. I personally feel that the Pentagon Papers should have been revealed by *The New York Times,* and I would do everything I could to protect the right of the press to conceal its sources of information and let the responsibility of the press be its major check on how it acted as it deals with sensitive material or with matters that might affect our own country.

TV-radio interview, New York/
"Meet the Press,"
National Broadcasting Company, 7-11.

Jimmy Carter
1976 Democratic
U.S. Presidential nominee
5

[On press coverage of his campaign]: Issues? The local media are interested, all right, but the national news media have absolutely no interest in issues *at all*. Sometimes we freeze out the national media so we can open up press conferences to local people. At least we get questions from them—on timber management, on health care, on education. But the traveling press have zero interest in any issue unless it's a matter of making a mistake. What they're looking for is a 47-second argument between me and another candidate, or something like that. There's [no newsman] in the back of this plane who would ask an issue question unless he thought he could trick me into some crazy statement.

Interview/ Playboy, November:66.

John Chancellor
News commentator,
National Broadcasting Company   1

[On his nightly news telecast]: Your loyalty is not to masses of people who can be manipulated or informed, but to the concept of a very small group. Maybe two. I never think we're in 10½ million homes every night. I don't know what that is—I can't get a mental picture of it. I tend to see a living-room or a kitchen, and a couple of people who are watching the news. And if you can talk to them effectively, then that satisfies the desire to tell somebody what you've done in a report of the day's news.

Interview/
San Francisco Examiner & Chronicle, 1-18:
(Datebook)35.

2

[On the three networks' evening TV news broadcasts]: Competition is healthy. I would not like to see any program get too far out in front. The leading program would become lazy and the one far behind in third place would then try gimmicks simply for the sake of ratings. The viewer is best served, it seems to me, if NBC and CBS—and I wish ABC were up there too—were all within about a rating point of each other.

Interview, New York/
San Francisco Examiner & Chronicle, 7-4:
(Datebook)37.

Charles Collingwood
News commentator,
Columbia Broadcasting System   3

I grew up in radio. I feel very much at home with it. There is a shade more freedom on radio [than on TV] because the technology is less sophisticated and therefore less overpowering. There's me, a typewriter,

a microphone and a guy at the control panel. On TV, you've got cameramen, soundmen, producers, directors—an entourage of people all contributing to your 45-second report. And, of course, there's time. On TV, we usually just provide a headline service—you tell the average story very superficially. Radio gives you a bit more time—and any broadcast journalist will tell you that even an extra minute of air time may be the difference between a good story and a great story.

Los Angeles Herald-Examiner, 9-18:(A)16.

Walter Cronkite
News commentator,
Columbia Broadcasting System   4

I wonder if those [TV] stations that hire the young and beautiful but inexperienced and callous to front their news broadcasts are not getting ripped off . . . [Some people say that all it takes to be a news anchorman today] is to be under 25, fair of face and figure, dulcet of tone and well-coiffed. And that is just for the men! That and to be able to fit into a blazer with the patch on the pocket. This doesn't make a journalist, and I think the public may be more aware of that than the stations . . . Just as it is no good to put out a superior product if you can't sell it, it is far worse to peddle an inferior product solely through the razzle-dazzle of a promotion campaign. And aren't we guilty of that when we put the emphasis in our news broadcasts on performance and performers rather than content? Isn't that really what we are looking for when we examine ourselves to see whether we are indulging in show business rather than journalism?

Before CBS-TV affiliates, Los Angeles, May 5/
Daily Variety, 5-6:8.

5

[On broadcast journalist Barbara Walters' $1-million-a-year contract with ABC]: The Barbara Walters news did shake me up at first, as it did us all, I suppose. There was a first wave of nausea, the sickening sensation

WHAT THEY SAID IN 1976

(WALTER CRONKITE)

that perhaps we were all going under, that all of our efforts to hold network television news aloof from show business had failed . . .[But TV reporters] have been getting show-business salaries . . . since the beginning. It is not very productive, either, to talk about whether she is worth $1-million. Compared to what? Compared to the school teacher? Certainly not. Compared to a rock 'n' roll singer? I'd say certainly yes. It is a marketplace situation. If she can get a million dollars from ABC, presumably ABC feels she is worth a million. If not, heads will roll, I assume.

Before CBS-TV affiliates, Los Angeles, May 5/
The Washington Post, 5-7:(B)12.

1

We [in television] news fall far short of presenting all, or even a goodly part, of the news each day that a citizen would need to intelligently exercise his franchise in this democracy. So as he depends more and more on us, presumably the depth of knowledge of the average man diminishes. This clearly can lead to disaster in a democracy.

Before Radio and Television News Directors Association, Bal Harbour, Fla., Dec. 13/
The Washington Post, 12-14:(B)10.

John De Mott
Department of journalism,
Temple University

2

In order to foster more journalistic objectivity, we need to broaden the range of backgrounds from which the members of our profession are recruited, enlarge the scope of their education, toughen the self-examination and self-criticism aspects of their training, teach them the investigative skills they will need to ferret out the numerous "angles" in any news event, require them to "walk all the way around" each occurrence, challenge their conclusions constantly, encourage them to exploit as thoroughly as possible every re-source possessed by a news-gathering and reporting organization for increasing the variety of viewpoints available in any given situation, and direct them in action designed to stimulate them to think more objectively. Most important of all, perhaps, we must instill in our ranks a sharper skepticism, especially toward those who say there are no objective standards for determining empirical fact, and a deeper commitment to each person's personal quest for objectivity. We need to promote the development of objectivity as a more demanding ideology within our profession; to nourish the social roots of our concepts commanding the effort at objectivity . . . The highest possible degree of objectivity, in journalism, depends upon superior intelligence, creativity, imagination, learning—and humility, great humility.

At Defense Information School,
Fort Benjamin Harrison, Indianapolis, Aug. 12/
Vital Speeches, 10-1:748.

Tom Dillon
Chairman, Batten, Barton,
Durstine & Osborn, advertising

3

It's really not necessary to guess what would happen if there were no advertising, because there are countries in the world in which advertising does not play the part in the economy that it does in the United States. What happens in their internal communications systems? Some countries, like Great Britain and Canada, have advertising operations very much like our own [in the U.S.]; but there are other countries where advertising expenditures per capita are very low. There you will find that freedom of the press tends to be a fiction. To begin with, radio and television must be supported by the state, and they become the official propaganda organs of the party in power. Indeed, the last thing that these parties want to see is commercial television, for commercial television is free-speech television. And what happens to newspapers? They are, to begin with, small, miserable, badly written and badly edited sheets. In the majority of cases, because circulation revenue can't possibly support them, these newspapers are the official organs of various political parties and get their revenues from party funds. The fact of the matter is that, in the absence of advertising revenue, the concept of freedom of the press is a joke.

Before BBD&O executives, New York, July 1/
Vital Speeches, 9-1:679.

Oriana Fallaci
Journalist 1

In the democratic countries, we [journalists] are the only tool of communication between the people and the power. What other bridge does society have but the bridge offered by the journalists? As bad as they accuse us of being—superficial, without culture—we are still the only ones who guarantee to the people the right and the duty to know what happens, to understand it and to intervene somehow. It is far more important and far more moral to be a journalist than a politician.

Interview, Florence, Italy/
"W": a Fairchild publication, 4-30:26.

Fred W. Friendly
Professor of journalism, Columbia
University; Former president,
Columbia Broadcasting System News 2

[The Fairness Doctrine] does not really stimulate radio and TV stations to devote "a reasonable amount of time" to controversial issues. Many stations fear interference by the Federal government, so they avoid trouble altogether by doing as few documentaries as possible. It [the Doctrine] is a rationale for timidity, an excuse for cowardice.

Interview/ People, 8-2:44.

George Gallup
Public-opinion analyst 3

[In international broadcasting,] we're [the U.S.] trying, supposedly, to reflect the truth. Now, I would argue vigorously that

when you listen to a broadcast from the United States—and I would say this applies to all the services—you get a picture of the United States as a sort of crime-ridden country. You get a picture of a lot of chaos in the labor-management world. You get a picture of confrontation, political confrontation. You get a picture that is not a very good one and, I believe, would do far more harm than good. In fact, I've often thought, wouldn't people have a better opinion of the United States if they never listened one minute?

Before U.S. Advisory Commission on
Information, February/
The Washington Post, 11-16:(A)3.

Brendan Gill
Drama critic, "The New Yorker"
magazine 4

Why do people stay at *The New Yorker?* It's certainly not the money. The salaries and pension plan are contemptible! A "Talk-of-the-Town" reporter might average $20,000. A profile writer may earn $5,000 for a piece but he may only do three a year. But *The New Yorker* is a citadel of 19th-century paternalism, like a mill owner. None of the people on the magazine ever wanted to go anywhere else. No one ever left except in death or defeat.

Interview, Beverly Hills, Calif./
Los Angeles Herald-Examiner, 3-10:(B)1.

Barry M. Goldwater
United States Senator, R—Arizona 5

[On broadcast journalism's coverage of politics]: After my [1964 Presidential] campaign, I asked men I knew, like [newsmen] Harry Reasoner, Walter Cronkite and others, and they made a very good answer. They said, "Look, no matter how we may feel about you, whether we like you or don't like you, we can't hide that fact from our eyes or our tone of voice." In that effect, I think they do show discrimination; but I think it's natural. I think they try to do the best job. If I have any criticism of average coverage, it's that

WHAT THEY SAID IN 1976

(BARRY M. GOLDWATER)

there are not enough men who've ever been in the political game, who know what they're talking about.

Interview/ TV Guide, 6-12:10.

Julian Goodman
Chairman,
National Broadcasting Company

1

In television news we do not enjoy all of the freedom guaranteed to the press by the First Amendment of the Constitution. Instead, we operate under an FCC-administered Fairness Doctrine whose declared intent is to prevent one-sided presentation of views on controversial issues. [This means government regulators who are] forbidden by law to intrude on the printed press can stand at a broadcaster's shoulder and make him justify his journalistic judgments.

Before International Franchise Association,
Palm Springs, Calif./
Daily Variety, 2-11:10.

Katharine Graham
Publisher, "The Washington Post"

2

In Washington there is growing pressure, from the intelligence community and elsewhere, for some kind of Official Secrets Act to prevent the press from publishing secrets if the government objects—or for a law imposing heavy penalties on those who leak sensitive material to the press. In my view, these approaches have many defects and few benefits at all. For one thing, no law would stop those who act irresponsibly now; it could instead turn mischief-makers into martyrs, at least in some people's eyes. That is hardly desirable. Second, the controls being discussed would hobble the responsible press by inhibiting our efforts to give context and perspective to the news we print. Third, any such law is bound to be applied selectively and arbitrarily, because of two unavoidable areas of discretion: first, who decides what is secret, and second, who decides whether

to prosecute when something has been leaked . . . It virtually insures that most of the conflicts between secrecy and openness will be resolved one way: in favor of greater official control over the content and even the topics of public debate. And it could make the press more like a bulletin board for official pronouncements, rather than an energetic, independent force.

Before Economic Club of Chicago, Feb. 10/
Vital Speeches, 4-15:398.

3

Many people, especially in government and business, assume the press is hostile, uninformed and likely to distort or sensationalize everything. Many reporters and editors, on the other hand, assume that everything secret is scandalous, and every claim of confidentiality is a cover-up . . . I think the press can do a great deal to reduce the suspicion that persists if we approach the areas of conflict with maturity and sense and make more effort to explain our policies and listen to complaints.

Before Inland Daily Press Association,
Williamsburg, Va., Feb. 24/
The Washington Post, 2-26:(C)4.

Robert Haiman
Executive editor,
"St. Petersburg (Fla.) Times"

4

Today's generation sees the world in living color—in television, movies, billboards. Look at our [newspapers'] drab, dull, gray product. We need something that can jump off the doorstep in the morning and say, "Wow! I'm exciting! Read me!"

Los Angeles Times, 11-26:(1)31.

Paul Harvey
News commentator,
American Broadcasting Company

5

I'm not proud of my profession. Unless it is bleak, black or bloody, you won't see it on page one.

Before Arkansas Baptists, July 3/
The Dallas Times Herald, 7-4:(A)2.

Bobby Knight
Basketball coach, Indiana University
1

I'll tell you the only thing that irritates me about the press. They write some things they don't know a damned thing about. I don't mind a guy interviewing me and then disagreeing with me the next day in the paper. What I don't like is to read things that are totally untrue. One day I called up a writer and asked him where he got the stuff he was writing about. He told me that he couldn't get a hold of me but said that he had some "reliable" information.

Interview, Philadelphia, March 28/
Los Angeles Times, 3-29:(3)1.

Charles Kuralt
News correspondent,
Columbia Broadcasting System
2

We all know there are a lot of Ted Baxters [prima donna newscasters] around. Television abounds with them. And not all of today's anchormen with beautiful hair are bad. But there are an awful lot of anchormen and women in the business today who wouldn't know a news story if it jumped up and mussed their coiffure.

Interview, Boston/
The Christian Science Monitor, 11-30:21.

Bill Leonard
Vice president (Washington)
Columbia Broadcasting System News
3

In large areas of this globe there are no airplane accidents, no riots, no disagreements, no attempts on the lives of leaders. Broadcasting and journalism in most of this world is considered far too important to leave to journalists. I don't believe you really want to face this kind of cure [for the excesses of news reporting].

TV panel discussion/
"Talking Back to CBS,"
Columbia Broadcasting System, 2-15.

Philip Lesly
Public-relations counsel
4

While all responsible media have a policy of being accurate and fair, and will often cor-

rect—in an inconspicuous way—proved errors, there is little recourse from the medium's judgment or treatment. Also, in the growing pressure on the media to capture and hold audiences, there is a tendency toward dramatizing and sensationalizing what comes into their purview. As much as the outsider may question the effect of such dramatizations and selectiveness in uses of material, the judgment of the medium is virtually sacrosanct. All of us who must deal with the media have to recognize that they have this sovereignty and that no one can argue with a printing press or a broadcast tower. Though this presents problems, it's part of the pattern of a free press, and America has the freest press in the world. The media must have as much independence as possible from all sources of pressure, and inevitably they sometimes convert independence into what in other areas would be considered arrogance.

At Federal Bureau of Investigation National
Executive Institute, Quantico, Va., May 9/
Vital Speeches, 6-15:527.

William Loeb
Publisher,
"Manchester (N.H.) Union Leader"
5

[On newspapers endorsing political candidates]: We back people who we think are honorable individuals and deserve our support, regardless [of party, etc.]. For instance, we supported Taft against Eisenhower, and we knew darned well that Taft was [not] going to win. The answer about power is that I have never made any claim to power. This matter of power has come from a national press looking for stories. I have no idea whether I have power or not. Sometimes you might be able to make the difference in a close race, but if you support a man you believe in and the voters are going in the other direction, you could do all the editorials in the world and they would just go right on the way they wanted to go.

TV-radio interview, Washington/
"Meet the Press,"
National Broadcasting Company, 2-15.

WHAT THEY SAID IN 1976

Donald S. MacNaughton
Chairman, Prudential Insurance
Company of America
1

With freedom comes responsibility, and, in the opinion of many, that sense of responsibility has been lacking [in the news media]. Most of us are fed up with glib, shallow, inaccurate reporting and editing—tired of journalistic tastes which prefer sensationalism above the fundamentals—which allow a thespian to pose as a newsman . . . The news media have been surprised in recent years, I think, to find a growing group of critics taking issue with their accuracy and objectivity . . . [The media] should assume the responsibility for establishing sound minimum performance standards for all of the practitioners of [their] profession. For example, it shouldn't be possible, as it is today, for anyone to enter the reportorial or editorial fields without first having acquired the necessary credentials by way of a sound training program. Nor, for another example, should the press discourse on any subject, particularly the complex ones, except through members with an expertise in the subject. Much has been done along these lines. There has been real progress, but much more needs to be done. We also urge that in establishing standards, the news media set goals for the profession as a whole, goals which will change from time to time, but which will always reflect the high degree of quality it should seek.

At annual meeting of
American Life Insurance Association and
Institute of Life Insurance/
The New York Times, 3-7:(3)14.

Darious Mbela
Information Secretary of Kenya
2

. . . what we find in most developing countries is a press that is either the mouthpiece of big-power influence normally alien to us, or a government organ. In the former, the reader is molded to aspire for foreign— and most times decadent—interests, and, in the latter, the reader is blinkered to getting only the information that the government feels is safe to release.

At United Nations Educational, Scientific
and Cultural Organization conference,
Nairobi, Kenya/ Los Angeles Times, 11-6:(1)14.

George S. McGovern
United States Senator,
D—South Dakota
3

I've seen more bias and personal vendettas from syndicated columnists, who supposedly have a chance to think these things over, than I have from television commentators. I think the television commentators are under the restraint of knowing that they are supposed to be objective. The syndicated columnists somehow think they have a license to say anything they damn please. Once they have it in for you, even though you may not understand the bias of it, they can make life miserable for you. I've had two or three of them whom I would gladly dump over the nearest cliff if I had the power to do it.

Interview/ TV Guide, 6-12:10.

German Ornes
Chairman, committee on freedom of the press
and information, Inter-American
Press Association;
Publisher, "El Caribe," Santo Domingo
4

In those American nations controlled by dictatorships, which at the present time are in the majority, the press cannot faithfully reflect the truth of political, economic and cultural developments; they are stopped short by rigid censorship or by a degrading self-censorship . . . More difficult to understand, and equally painful to report, is that even constitutionally elected democratic governments reveal a marked hostility toward the independent press. That obvious hostility is shown mainly in the sustained effort by governments—frequently bordering on intolerance—to stop the free flow of news or to keep newspapermen from access to legitimate sources of news.

Before IAPA executive committee, Sarasota, Fla.,
Jan. 26/ The New York Times, 2-1:(1)4.

William S. Paley
Chairman, CBS, Inc.
1

In the United States, the battle for a truly free press has never been conclusively won. Print journalism has always been defending the most basic rights of the press to report and the people to know against one assault after another. Broadcast journalism never *has* enjoyed the full protection of the First Amendment. Simply because stations are licensed to avoid technical chaos on the air-waves, such crippling restrictions are impos-ed as the so-called Fairness Doctrine, the right-to-reply and the equal-time require-ments in election campaigns. This may sound reasonable on the surface, but they consti-tute unwarranted obstructions that work to the detriment of the public. And, in recent years, both print and broadcast journalism have been the subject of a growing, if irra-tional, suspicion—sometimes expressed in high places—that the press is somehow to blame for unhappy events and trends, merely because it performs its duty reporting them.
Before Anti-Defamation League of B'nai B'rith/
The New York Times, 12-19:(4)17.

Jody Powell
Press Secretary to President-elect of the United States Jimmy Carter
2

I really don't hold [journalistic] grudges. I have felt free to express my disagreement with writers on the campaign. I've had some heated, informative discussions with a writer; but I always considered the discussion over when we walked away from each other. If I ever intimidated anyone by talking to them, it was not apparent in anything they later wrote. People who have reached the stage of their careers where they are reporting politics in Washington are secure enough not to be intimidated—especially by someone like me.
To reporters, Washington, Nov. 23/
The Washington Post, 11-24:(A)7.

Gene Roberts
Executive editor, "Philadelphia Enquirer"
3

Everyone's looking for the patent medi-cine, the gimmick, the one little thing [in] your bag of tricks—two columns of local news or a new consumer column—to solve the problems of metropolitan [news] papers. The problem is much broader and more fun-damental than that; it involves everything from superficial news coverage to generally dull writing. We've gotten so stock and so routinized in our presentation that we're just uninviting for most readers. There are prob-ably 50 or 60 or 70 things we ought to re-examine—page by page, section by section, subject by subject.
Los Angeles Times, 11-26:(1)32.

A. M. Rosenthal
Managing editor,
"The New York Times"
4

[On whether newspaper editors should formulate industry-wide policies on printing statements by terrorists who may be holding hostages or threatening violence]: The last thing in the world I want is guidelines. I don't want guidelines from the government and I don't want any from professional organiza-tions or anyone else. The strength of the press is its diversity. As soon as you start imposing guidelines, they become peer-group pressures and then quasi-legal restrictions. I'm viscer-ally against it. Besides, you have to judge each situation individually, on a case-by-case basis. You have to weigh the human dangers and the journalistic values of each case as it comes up. No policy could possibly cover every case.
Los Angeles Times, 9-15:(1)14.

Richard S. Salant
President,
Columbia Broadcasting System News
5

[Calling for an extra half hour of network evening news]: A good deal of this [time-constraint] problem will be ameliorated, if not solved, if someday we can have an hour of evening news . . . compression inadvert-ently is going to cause some distortion, be-cause you can't get the nuances and the qual-ifications in . . . We all pray for [the addi-

WHAT THEY SAID IN 1976

(RICHARD S. SALANT)

tional time]. We go to bed every night saying: Please, somebody give us the extra half hour.

TV panel discussion/
"Talking Back to CBS,"
Columbia Broadcasting System, 2-15.

1

I submit that the mere stamp of secrecy does not, standing alone, mean that it is outside the scope of valid and proper reporting in a democracy. To take a contrary position is to enact, by our own action or default, an extreme official secrets act—a clear prior restraint imposed by the government, or some officer or unit of the government. And that would be antithetical to everything that a free and independent press stands for. I would emphasize as strongly as I can that I do not mean that it is proper for reporters or news organizations to ignore governmental decrees of secrecy in all circumstances. Reporters and news organizations have an awesome responsibility here—they must weigh such decrees and the consequence of publication most carefully. There must be the most conscientious and expert consideration on our part of whether national security is really involved and whether there are real dangers. The right to know is, indeed, not absolute. But we know all too well, from the proliferation of the secrecy stamp and the suppression of that which is embarrassing and unfavorable rather than what is dangerous, that it is not in the public interest to accept such stamps blindly.

Before CBS-TV affiliates, Los Angeles, May 5/
Daily Variety, 5-6:8.

2

[On ABC's hiring of Barbara Walters as news commentator at a salary of $1-million a year for five years]: A million dollars is a grotesque amount of money. I'm really depressed as hell. If Barbara Walters is a five-million-dollar woman, then [CBS News commentator] Walter Cronkite is a sixteen-mil-

lion-dollar man. This isn't journalism—this is a minstrel show. Is Barbara a journalist or is she Cher? . . . If this kind of circus atmosphere continues, and I have to join in it, I'll quit first . . . It's some damn fool kind of show business, sports business, movie-star business. I hate it. This isn't what we are supposed to do.

The Center Magazine, Nov.-Dec.:23.

John A. Scali
News correspondent,
American Broadcasting Company

3

The pendulum has swung too far in the journalistic zeal to rout out evil. There is almost a tendency not to treat the government as an adversary but as the enemy . . . We are living in the golden age of journalism, and investigative reporting is king. The news organization that doesn't have one, or indeed a team of investigative reporters, is like a cathedral without an organ . . . Of course, we must be vigilant and expose wrongdoing; but we must be on guard that in so doing we do not destroy or damage the structure or the fabric of our society . . . Almost every responsible news organization and responsible individual agree[s] that the government must undertake some covert operations at a time when there is still deep and exceeding danger in the Republic, and when nuclear weapons can incinerate a hemisphere. Yet, somehow, secrets have come out, and as one who has worked with pride as a newsman for 30 years, who believes that the first line of democratic defense is a free press, may I say that as we re-examine government, we also re-examine the press and its role in the crisis situation.

Before ABC Radio Network affiliates, Chicago/
The New York Times, 3-29:53.

Herbert S. Schlosser
President,
National Broadcasting Company

4

. . . the equal-time rule is as out of place in American politics as a live dinosaur in

Central Park. It limits coverage of the major candidates, and its silly results include time for Lar Daly to show off his Uncle Sam suit, a suspension of television work for comedian Pat Paulsen and the cancellation of old Ronald Reagan movies from the late, late show. The inhibiting effects of the equal-time law are well documented. When it was suspended in 1960, we not only had the landmark Kennedy-Nixon debates. In addition, we had a free hand to present the major candidates in a variety of formats. The result was the most extensive campaign coverage television has ever been able to provide. There was a tremendous turnout at the polls. The proportion of eligible voters who actually vote for President has declined progressively ever since. So far as free time is concerned, NBC long ago committed to make available four half-hours of prime television time to the major parties for appearances of their Presidential and Vice-Presidential candidates . . . But . . . we cannot make the time available unless the equal-time rule is repealed or suspended. Otherwise, we would be faced with legally enforceable demands for equal free time from the dozen or so fringe candidates in whom the public has shown only limited interest.

Before NBC affiliates, New York, June 21/
Vital Speeches, 8-15:668.

Daniel Schorr
News correspondent,
Columbia Broadcasting System   *1*

[On his refusal to reveal the source of classified government material he leaked for publication]: . . . we all build our lives around certain principles, without which our careers lose their meaning. For some of us—doctors, lawyers, clergymen and journalists—it is an article of faith that we must keep confidential those matters entrusted to us only because of the assurance that they would remain confidential. For a journalist, the most crucial kind of confidence is the identity of a source of information. To betray a confidential source would mean to dry up many future sources for many future reporters. The reporter and the news organization would be the immediate loser. I would submit to you that the ultimate losers would be the American people and their free institutions. But beyond all that, to betray a source would be to betray myself, my career and my life. I cannot do it. To say I refuse to do it is not saying it right. I *cannot* do it.

Before House Standards of Conduct Committee,
Washington, Sept. 15/
The New York Times, 9-16:69.

Eric Sevareid
News commentator,
Columbia Broadcasting System   *2*

Elections make the press drunk. On the eve of the Presidential primary campaigns, many people in the press . . . take the vow. The heady wine of prediction and prophecy [of who will win and by what margin] will not touch their lips this time. They tell themselves, why try to predict what's going to happen before it happens? That's what elections are for—to tell us the answer. But the temptation is too great; we fall off the wagon every time, frequently on our faces.

May/ The New York Times Magazine, 8-29:57.

3

. . . we are not the worst people in the land, we who work as journalists. Our product in print or over the air is a lot better, more educated, more responsible than it was when I began some 45 years ago as a cub reporter. This has been the best generation of all in which to have lived as a journalist in this country. We are no longer starvelings and we sit above the salt. We have affected our times . . . We have done the job better, I think, than our predecessors, and our successors will do it better than we. I see remarkable young talents all around. That's the way it should be. I will watch them come on, maybe with a little envy, but with few regrets for the past. For myself, I wouldn't have spent my working life differently, had I been able to.

At Washington Journalism Center, June 3/
Vital Speeches, 7-1:567.

WHAT THEY SAID IN 1976

(ERIC SEVAREID)

1

[An] idea I have would get no takers—it's too way-out. News every other day. News broadcasts, newspapers only on Mondays, Wednesdays and Fridays. We could do a better job and let everybody's nerves rest a little while. There is a kind of news pollution. I never thought that news programs would become a staple of TV with such huge audiences. I suppose it is for the same reason that fiction hasn't done very well. Reality has outrun imagination.

Interview/
The Christian Science Monitor, 8-19:27.

Milton J. Shapp
Governor of Pennsylvania (D);
Candidate for the 1976
Democratic Presidential nomination

2

The public depends on the press—radio, TV and newspapers—for all information that is official. Whereas an alderman in a small borough must respond directly to his constituents, who are also his neighbors, when you move up the political ladder to become a Congressman or a Governor and certainly a President, the average voter will form his opinion most often from what he reads in a newspaper, or hears on radio or TV. Not only will a politician's personal record and conduct be judged, but his stand on various issues and his handling of his office is also subject to interpretation by the news media, and this interpretation can and often is quite varied. Reporters, editors and publishers in our American democracy are the guardians of the public's trust; unlike some other governments where they are purveyors of a party line, here they're responsive only to the public and not the propaganda needs of the holders of power. The American press calls attention to the deeds and misdeeds of public officials and, for a good part, they have done an admirable job. But while public officials have a responsibility to the public, the press has an equal responsibility to the same citizens. And

the question occurs: "Who will watch the watchers?" As Jefferson noted so eloquently, we must preserve freedom of the press to report the truth. But the members of the press must themselves show restraint and responsibility in reporting events, for they carry a dangerous power to undermine the basic confidence in government which our people must have if we are to preserve our system of government—and I might say preserving our system of government also includes the preservation of that precious freedom of the press.

Before National Newspaper Publishers
Association, Philadelphia, June 10/
Vital Speeches, 8-1:617.

William Sheehan
President,
American Broadcasting Company News

3

Our [broadcast news] success is dependent upon the size of our audience, but the pursuit of that audience does have bounds. We must not distort, caricature or hype the reality of the news we present because we are, in this area, dealing with the real world. It is not the world of make-believe, and if we gain temporary success by expedient means, we will lose our credibility and the whole process will turn to mush . . .

Before Associated Press Broadcasters,
Minneapolis, June 4/
Daily Variety, 6-8:9.

Red Smith
Sports columnist

4

Writing a column is easy. All you do every day is sit down to a typewriter, open a vein and bleed.

To a journalism class/
Los Angeles Times, 7-16:(3)2.

William F. Thomas
Executive vice president and editor,
"Los Angeles Times"

5

[On whether newspapers should print comments by public officials that were made in

400

private or off-the-record]: The point is you draw the line when the conversation becomes important enough to expose. You report it if it's germaine to his performance, if it's something you think the public ought to know about this guy. I think all this [the resignation of Agriculture Secretary Earl Butz because of a racial remark made in private but reported to and printed by the press] is going to make public officials think several times before they loosen up. I suppose some in the press abuse privacy, and this kind of gossip reporting is bound to have an effect on the interrelationship between members of the press and public figures.

The New York Times, 10-7:18.

Richard C. Wald
President,
National Broadcasting Company News 1

Everybody talks about the possibility of should there be a one-hour nightly [TV network] news. Within five years, I guess there will be a one-hour news . . . Now we live in a world that's two-thirds literate and one-half urban. These people think. They have power. They want more information. They are able to see what you might call the shop-window revolution. They can see something they don't have, and they want to know why they don't have it, and that starts a train of thought, and that starts expectation; and expectation is the mother of change. Really. So that people will want more. It will be expensive not to give it to them. We will give it to them. It's very simple. And there will be . . . somewhere in these United States an all-news television station, probably more than one.

Before National Association of Broadcasters,
Chicago, March 22/
The Washington Post, 4-18:(K)2.

2

We [in broadcast journalism] are poor in abstract explanation. Television finds it very hard, partly because it exists in a time frame—you can't go back and look at something again—to do some kinds of analyses that print finds itself peculiarly suited for . . . I would not want to rely on television to explain the gold crisis to me.

U.S. News & World Report, 8-2:22.

Barbara Walters
Co-host, "Today" show,
National Broadcasting Company Television
3

[On criticism of the million-dollar-per-year salary to be paid her when she joins ABC News as a commentator this fall]: If you're comparing a million-dollar salary to a Congressman who earns $42,000 a year, then nobody's worth [a million], if you talk about it that way. But how about [TV talk-show host] Johnny Carson and his $3-million a year . . . or [actress] Mary Tyler Moore or [comedian] Redd Foxx or the sports figures and their salaries? The whole thing gets very hypocritical. However, if you approach it from the aspect that I work hard, I'm good at my job, I know my business—then it takes on another meaning.

Before ABC affiliates, Los Angeles, May 25/
Los Angeles Times, 5-27:(4)24.

Barbara Walters
News commentator,
American Broadcasting Company
4

The worst failing is that television can lie. TV producers can make it lie. Also, it can be very superficial. For example, a 30-second political commercial often distorts. You can see this being done with superb editing and repetition. I hope that audiences are so sophisticated that we don't fool them too much. And I think they are . . . I don't think that any commentator now can make or break a candidate. If you are selective and listen enough, you'll get a fairly complete picture. Now I'll give you the positive side [of TV]. When someone is on television, even if it's edited, you hear what he has to

WHAT THEY SAID IN 1976

say. Nobody says, as you might read in a magazine: "He smiled coyly; he smiled charmingly; he smiled meanly; he growled." You see and hear exactly what he said and how he said it. When he smiles, you decide whether the smile was coy or sly or mean. What you see is what you get. I'd rather be interviewed on television than by a newspaper. I'd rather live by exactly what I said and be quoted by that and be judged by that.
Interview/ U.S. News & World Report, 10-11:43.

Walter B. Wriston
Chairman, Citicorp
(Citibank, New York)
                                                    1

Power without accountability is an invitation to trouble. History teaches that when any sector of our society grows too powerful it is only a matter of time before that power is curbed. Usually the sector affected, be it business or labor or the police or the press, fails to appreciate why society is reacting as it is to what they perceive to be right and just. The news business which makes its money criticizing others reacts to criticism the same way you and I do. [Former] Senator [J. William] Fulbright recently wrote that not all people who suggest the news business could be improved are Fascists, even though editors go "into transports of outraged excitement, bleeding like hemophiliacs" from the pin pricks of their critics. Like other sectors of our society whose power has become very great, some in the news business seem to believe that the end justifies the means. The "truth" must be revealed, no matter how obtained or how irrelevant, or how, in the judgment of legal authority, adverse to the public interest. A dedication to the truth is a noble objective. However, some truths are more significant than others; some have no significance. Some, for the protection of privacy, some for reasons of state, should not be told at all. If we are to preserve the First Amendment—a guarantee of freedom not only almost unique in political history, but also precious to our democracy—the media should reflect that the effective functioning of a democracy requires the most difficult of all disciplines, self-discipline. The freedom of us all rides with the freedom of the press; but its continued freedom and ours will depend in the end upon the media not exploiting to the fullest their unlimited power. It can and must criticize the government, but it cannot replace Constitutional authority by saying no secrets are valid.
Before the Management Conference,
University of Chicago, March 11/
Vital Speeches, 5-1:424.

Michael J. Arlen
Author

1

What makes [author] Norman Mailer interesting is those very sensible demons that propel him out of the house, because without going out of the house, what can you do really? You commit yourself to a lack of experience. There ought to be a Federal law to prevent most writers, and certainly novelists, from being full-time novelists. You've got to get out of the house.

Interview/"W": a Fairchild publication 6-11:2.

2

It's important [for a writer] to be spontaneous. It's no good trying to turn the past into a series of tableaux that you can hold and turn around so as to present them in the best light. You have to proceed by impulse, to become deeply involved yourself—and if there isn't that sort of involvement, why write at all? Why simply join the hubbub? If what I'm writing doesn't matter, deeply, to me, why should it matter to a reader?

Interview/Publishers Weekly, 8-30:248.

Richard Armour
Author; Professor emeritus of English, Scripps College

3

There are problems with writing humor at an advanced age. The quick play with words involves a more youthful zest than serious writing. Sharpness wanes with age.

Interview/Los Angeles Times, 7-18:
(Book Review)3.

Isaac Asimov
Author

4

Science fiction is the hardest writing there is. On top of the usual problems of character and action, you've got to create a whole new society and make it believable. I can spend 300 hours on a science-fiction novel. A mystery novel takes 200 hours. But I can write a normal-length non-fiction book in 70 hours. I write from memory, then check my facts. I do all my own typing, all my own research, make all my own deals—no agent. Some critics say I'd write better if I wrote slower. That's like telling a sprinter he'd run better if he ran slower. If I try to write slowly I can't write at all. What the hell, I'm not trying to be Shakespeare, I'm trying to be clear!

Interview/People, 11-22:110.

Saul Bellow
Author

5

New York is not a center for literature and the arts. New York is a place where all the stuff gets packaged and where auxiliary or associated careers are made in publishing, in editing, among agents, among literary journalists, and for hustlers. But as for literature, it doesn't thrive in promotional centers like New York.

Interview/Publishers Weekly, 11-1:22.

6

So many current critics . . . remind me of nothing so much as the figure of the man who steps to center stage with his thumbs looped in his suspenders, giving off an air of tremendous confidence, as if to say, "I've got the poop." Well, as I see it, he doesn't have the poop, just the suspenders.

Interview, Chicago/
The New York Times Book Review, 12-5:92.

WHAT THEY SAID IN 1976

(SAUL BELLOW)

1

... a writer should reach as many people as possible—not with a message but with a point of view arising from his freedom as a writer, the non-partisanship of his heart, and the happy responsibilities of the imagination. When it is going well, a novel affords the highest kind of truth; a writer can lay claim to a disinterestedness that is as great as that of a pure scientist—when he is going well. In its complicated, possibly even mysterious, way, the novel is an instrument for delving into human truths.

Interview, Chicago/
The New York Times Book Review, 12-5:92.

2

[On his winning this year's Nobel Prize for literature]: I have no very distinct sense of personal achievement. I loved books and I wrote some. For some reason they were taken seriously. I am glad of that, of course. No one can bear to be ignored. I would, however, have been satisfied with a smaller measure of attention and praise. For when I am praised on all sides I worry a bit. I remember the scriptural warning, "Woe unto you when all men shall speak well of you." Universal agreement seems to open the door to dismissal. We know how often our contemporaries are mistaken. They are not invariably wrong, but it is not at all a bad idea to remember that they can't confer immortality on you. Immortality—a chilling thought. I feel that I have scarcely begun to master my trade. But I need not worry too much that all men will speak well of me. The civilized community agrees that there is no higher distinction than the Nobel Prize, but it agrees on little else, so I need not fear that the doom of universal approval is hanging over me. When I publish a book I am often soundly walloped by reviewers—a disagreeable but necessary corrective to self-inflation.

At Nobel Prize banquet, Stockholm, Dec. 10/
The New York Times, 12-11:3.

3

Writers are greatly respected. The intelligent public is wonderfully patient with them, continues to read them and endures disappointment after disappointment, waiting to hear from art what it does not hear from theology, philosophy, social theory, and what it cannot hear from pure science. Out of the struggle at the center has come an immense, painful longing for a broader, more flexible, fuller, more coherent, more comprehensive account of what we human beings are. At the center, humankind struggles with collective powers for its freedom, the individual struggles with dehumanization for the possession of his soul. If writers do not come again into the center it will not be because the center is pre-empted. It is not. They are free to enter if they so wish.

Nobel lecture, Stockholm, Dec. 12/
The Washington Post, 12-13:(C)2.

Peter Benchley
Author

4

I look upon my novels as entertaining stories that within them say something about the people they involve. There are those who don't agree. There are those who agree more than I think they should. [Cuban Premier] Fidel Castro thought that *Jaws* was a marvelous metaphor about the corruption of capitalism. Somebody else wrote me that *Jaws* was a political allegory—the shark was [former President] Nixon, etc. The Italians regard it as a hugely profound study of the human condition. And so on. People ask me if I have thought of writing a "serious" novel. I assume that means that rather than have a story be the primary thing it should be an exploration of terribly important themes—man's relation to the cosmos, or something like that. I'm not ready to do that yet. When I get to feeling I'm ready to tell that story, then I'll do that—and I'll be accused of writing a terrible rip-off of something else.

Interview, New York/
The Christian Science Monitor, 7-8:25.

Bernard A. Bergman
Book editor,
"Philadelphia Sunday Bulletin"
1

[On book awards]: I constantly rail against them, and how meaningless they are. How can those battle-scarred judges, honest enough but with hidden axes to grind, really choose the best books? So the politicking is awesome, particularly in the Pulitzers. And why can't the National Book Awards be promoted so that more people will know about the winners and buy the books? Publishers run their authors ragged touring the country to plug their books on radio and TV and in interviews, yet who has thought of one idea that would dramatize the Awards ceremony with a dramatic TV show?

Interview/Publishers Weekly, 5-31:111.

Daniel J. Boorstin
Librarian of Congress of
the United States; Historian
2

Reading enlarges awareness in a way that TV can't. TV has a limited number of channels. Books have an infinite number of channels. They are there all the time. They are not subject to government control or supervision. There is no requirement for a certain amount of religion or uplift. A book does not have to be uplifting at all. It can be as heterodox, as disrespectful, as unbalanced as the author wishes. The last refuge of the free and the brave is the book, while TV becomes increasingly government-controlled and supervised. One of the great things about books is they can be read secretly and privately. That is one reason why books have such explosive force in the world. You can hide a book under the mattress, but you can't do the same with a TV set. Books can seep into the interstices, and can play all kinds of roles which TV can't. In more and more parts of the world where freedom retreats and where government uses force to prevent people from learning and won't change its TV programs, books seep in. So the book remains the hope of freedom, really. It is necessary when more and more countries

shut down freedom of the press and all the rest.

Interview, Washington/
Los Angeles Times, 11-9:(2)5.

Jorge Luis Borges
Author
3

Behind writing there should be emotion. Writing has to have feeling, emotion—sadness. I don't think happiness makes for literature. Wistfulness does. It makes for poetry, no? Feeling sorrow over things.

Interview/"W": a Fairchild publication, 7-23:16.

Lillian Bradshaw
Director, Dallas Public Library
4

People today are all specialists. People are personalized. Each has his own specific needs and specific information needs. People don't come to the public library just for a good book to read any more. The public library is a place to come for something special in the way of information. He wants it quickly, too. There are businesses out there that can rise and fall on the answers and information we give them . . . Librarians of old were like censors, telling people what they ought to read. But no more. The new approach is more positive. It's "what do you need and how can I, the librarian, help you find it." We no longer sit in judgment of others and try to bend them to our ways . . .

The Dallas Times Herald, 11-7:(D)6.

Barbara Cartland
Author
5

People can't write what hasn't happened. That's why my books are so good. I've done it all.

Interview, Los Angeles/
Los Angeles Times, 7-4:(10)7.

6

Why do my books sell? Because all my heroines are virgins, and they stay virgins

WHAT THEY SAID IN 1976

(BARBARA CARTLAND)

until they get married. That's what people want . . . What publishers have failed to realize is that one cannot have pornography and expect that to be enough. There must be something spiritual behind it; and if publishers had a lick of sense they would recognize that fact.

Interview/ The Dallas Times Herald, 10-31:(G)1.

James Dickey
Author, Poet
1

Crowds turn out at a poetry reading for even a poet that nobody has heard of or who has a very slender reputation. Auditoriums of colleges fill up as long as the poets speak. When a poet of national or international reputation—such as Robert Lowell or Archibald MacLeish—comes, you cannot buy your way in. The reason for that is that people are fed up with the rhetoric of politics and journalism. They instinctively turn—whether they would say so in so many words or not—to the poet as the last repository of the true, authentic human voice of one person speaking truly and imaginatively to another person. The poet is not trying to sell anything, not trying to get anybody to fight wars, not trying to get anybody to vote for a political candidate, but just telling this other person how he feels about his life and about existence in general.

Interview/ U.S. News & World Report, 3-15:56.

E. L. Doctorow
Author
2

. . . I see curious likenesses between politicians and writers. In the first place, both normally address themselves to populations rather than individuals. Writers and politicians are one person speaking to many. Of course, a difference is that we writers take office and then we create our constituencies. That is to be a shade more arrogant than the politicians. But we have a saving grace: The power we assume is of no prac-

tical use to ourselves. If we are lucky, we have our greatest influence when we are dead.

Before Authors Guild/
The New York Times, 4-11:(4)17.

Roger Donald
Editor-in-chief,
Little, Brown and Company, publishers
3

. . . right now everybody's publishing books about how to change your personality — how-not-to-feel-guilty-about-saying-no books, meditation books, pop psyche and pop psychology. I don't understand it. Doesn't anybody like themselves any more?

Interview/"W": a Fairchild publication, 3-19:8.

William Gaddis
Author; Winner, 1976
National Book Award for fiction
4

I feel like part of the vanishing breed that thinks a writer should be read and not heard, let alone seen. I think this is because there seems so often today to be a tendency to put the person in the place of his or her work, to turn the creative artist into a performing one, to find what a writer says about writing somehow more valid, or more real, than the writing itself.

Accepting the National Book Award, New York/
Los Angeles Times, 5-2:(Book Review)3.

Alex Haley
Author
5

[On writing]: There's nothing I'd rather do, except perhaps be a surgeon. In many ways it's similar delicate, careful work, and I *act* like a surgeon. When I'm writing I take six showers a day, and wash my hands maybe 20 times. And it's a physical thing with me. When it's going well, I find myself tapping my foot in rhythm with the keys, as if there's a cadence going. I like to do first drafts at night, when I'm tired, and then do the surgical work in the morning when I'm sharp. And I love writing on a ship at sea. In fact, if

I had my druthers, I'd spend half the year at sea.

Interview/ Publishers Weekly, 9-6:12.

Andrew Heiskell
Chairman, Time, Inc.
1

Reading and writing, next to talking and eating, is man's most common activity. Despite the electronic age and its concomitant marvels, we still give, and get, the message often by the sight of type on the printed page. For the most part, we take for granted the power of print—maybe because it has been always with us. But every now and then someone puts pen to paper, reminding us of that exciting mental pursuit called reading —and the subsequent effect of written words on a person's perceptions, decisions or actions. Think for a moment of the unimaginable frustration of not being able to read or to write. What a joyless condition that would be. Think also of the enormous responsibility we who use professionally the written word must bear. Certainly no less than those who communicate through wire or ether, by satellite or microwave.

At Public Relations World Congress, Boston/
The National Observer, 9-18:13.

Frederic Hills
Editor-in-chief,
McGraw-Hill Book Company, publishers 2

When you ask yourself what happens to the few writers who can be called "genius" in America, why their powers seem to wane as they get older, you have to look at what the media does to authors. There are many known cases of the media chewing them up and spitting them out. Hemingway and John Steinbeck come to mind. I think Nabokov gives the supreme example of a literary career that has been totally oblivious to the response of the media. He's as invulnerable to praise as he is to criticism.

Interview, New York/
"W": a Fairchild publication, 3-19:8.

Harry Hookway
Chief executive, British Library, London 3

[Saying that, due to production cost increases, publishers may soon be unable to afford to issue hard-cover books]: Already some publishers of scientific works are printing books in facsimile from the author's typed manuscripts, and I think this will spread to other scholarly works. Librarians in charge of great collections like ours are having to relate their plans for storage space and new buildings to what is likely to happen in communications. Frankly, we don't know what is going to happen . . . We could build the biggest library in the world and then find hardly anyone is reading, but using television and other audio-visual methods instead . . . The pattern and use of reading is changing. Books nowadays are packed with illustrations. You see adults reading books of picture strips which 20 years ago were printed only for children. Imagine a situation where the act of opening a book, and finding what you want in it and reading it becomes unimaginable. Librarians and architects planning libraries that will stand into the next century have got to think of these things. Already, to retrieve some data, one has to consult a computer and command an image on to a screen. Does anyone know where we shall be in 30 years? I am still convinced the book has a future. There is nothing like a book. You can put it in your pocket, read it, browse about in it. You can't do that with microfilm.

Interview, London/
The Christian Science Monitor, 1-23:18.

Irving Howe
Author, Editor
4

Jewish writers don't write about their children; they write about their childhood. I think it was Graham Greene who said that an unhappy childhood is a writer's goldmine.

Interview, New York, Feb. 9/
The New York Times, 2-16:26.

Christopher Isherwood
Author
5

All that I'm trying to do as a writer is tell

WHAT THEY SAID IN 1976

(CHRISTOPHER ISHERWOOD)

my reader how I feel. I believe that by being absolutely frank about oneself, one builds the most surprising bridges with other people. If you ever make the kinkiest confession, reveal the secret of secrets, expose something that no one else could have experienced—sure as hell you're going to get a letter from a stranger saying, "That's exactly how I feel—how did you know?"

*Interview/Los Angeles Times, 12-5:
(Book Review)16.*

Rona Jaffe
Author
1

I spend a year thinking about what I'll write. I'm in that germination stage right now. People never understand—and it's impossible to explain—why I get glassy-eyed in the middle of a conversation or pass them by on the street. I'm working. When I sit down at the typewriter, I don't want to stare at an empty sheet of paper. I want to know exactly what I'm going to say, to feel as if I can hardly wait to begin.

*Interview/Los Angeles Times, 10-3:
(Book Review)2.*

Clara Stanton Jones
*Director, Detroit Public Library system;
President, American Library Association*
2

Libraries have been very deeply established in the ethic of America. They go right along with the flag. For a period of time they played a role in the Americanizing of millions who came over here from Europe, who learned English by reading books in English. At that time, libraries were a community center. People had that, the church, a political party, and not much else . . . It's becoming clearer and clearer to me that libraries must become more visible, and just as we have had to introduce modern business methods in book ordering and charging out, librarians more and more are managers, people who take their place in the community in an

active way. But how can you tell people to appreciate reading a book when reading is an undeveloped skill? Libraries are in danger today, not because Americans don't appreciate them, but because our educational system is in the state it is. If you give up this basic freedom of reading—and we talk about the right to read, not the privilege to read—the other freedoms go along with it.

*Interview, Chicago/
The Dallas Times Herald, 8-2:(B)1,5.*

Herman Kogan
Book editor, "Chicago Sun-Times"
3

Sometimes the people who make the best-seller list do it as a result of heightened promotion, very skillful public-relations campaigns; but often it's a reflection of what they're thinking out there. The how-to books are the big things that go now—everything from how to revamp your entire life by breathing deeply, and all that sort of jazz, to how to determine your cat's astrological sign. There's a book called *Cat Astrology*, and I'm sure it'll go because the publishers are interested in making a big buck. Primarily, publishers are interested, I think, in making a buck. I don't deplore the fact that it's no longer a gentleman's profession. I don't think it ever *was* that.

Interview, Chicago/ Publishers Weekly, 6-21:18.

Jerzy Kosinski
Author
4

On television, the commercials stress the gleaming exterior, the sleek design, the air conditioner. They do not show the spare tire, which implies a blowout—disaster. I focus on the spare tire in my novels. Life is not only about the four wheels; it is about the spare tire and the time when you need it. The artist—the writer, the painter, the journalist—he focuses on the unpleasant. He should not expect to be welcome.

*Interview, Dallas/
The Dallas Times Herald, 11-17:(E)1.*

1

[On why he is reluctant to have his books made into motion pictures]: They're [filmmakers] not after making movies. They're after making deals. Whenever a man calls, I listen to him and wait for him to call my book a "property." Any man who calls my book a property is not going to make a movie, not from *my* novel. "Property?" I say, "You want a real-estate man," and I hang up. Films are basically about plot and action, and to transfer my novels into a film would strip them of the very specific power they have and that is to trigger in the reader his own psychological set-up, his own projecting. Film has the very opposite effect. It doesn't trigger anything from within. It sets things from without and you, the viewer, are there to be an observer, not a participant ... When I write a novel, I'm entirely on my own. It is entirely my project, my responsibility from beginning to end. I even have control over my covers. I'm very, very possessive about it. But in a film you have to begin to question, who is the author? Is it the one who wrote the script? Is it the director? What about the studio? What about the editing room? The point I'm making is that a film is a collective effort, the exact opposite of a book. And in a film, where would I, the *author*, be?

Interview/The New York Times, 11-21:(2)14.

John V. Lindsay
Former Mayor of New York

2

A lot of my friends and colleagues were very surprised I chose to do a novel. I've found that when people in government read books, it's generally economics or history. They *never* read novels—they're just not interested. And there's this love of pigeonholing people: once a politician, always a politician. But I believe in a bit of role reversal once in a while. If Norman Mailer can run for Mayor, why can't I write a novel?

Interview, New York/
Publishers Weekly, 2-2:20.

Larry McMurty
Author

3

There are certain writers who ... squeak out 300 words a day at the expense of sitting seven or eight hours in front of a typewriter. Well, I can tell you frankly I wouldn't be a writer if I had to suffer like that to do it ... I have always thought the agony of writing has been overstated, and that it needn't be an agony at all.

Interview, Washington/
The Christian Science Monitor, 2-6:16.

Scott Meredith
Literary agent

4

I'm part salesman, part lawyer, part literary critic, part father confessor. I get calls from clients who are broke and can't pay their bills, from clients who are drunk or who have been arrested for beating their wives. One writer called from a neighbor's to tell me his house was on fire and all his manuscripts were burning. Why did he call me? Because he wanted to talk to someone who would be sympathetic ... and I was.

Interview, New York/Newsweek, 3-1:76B.

Henry Miller
Author

5

I don't like the New York type [of writer] at all—ultrasophisticated, analytical, critical of everything. I hate the intellectual, and I hope I'm not put down as one. I want to be an intelligent man, but not an intellectual. I would say that a writer should try to write only from the instinctive urge that we all get. We're all creative; we all have the urge to sing, to dance, to paint, to write—but most of us have squelched it.

Interview, Pacific Palisades, Calif./
Los Angeles Times, 4-4:(Calendar)3.

Iris Murdock
Author

6

What a novelist should be trying to do is produce a work of art. How she does that

(IRIS MURDOCK)

she has got to decide; but I don't think a novel should be a committed statement of political and social criticism. Novelists do enlighten people, they are great sources of education, but that's just incidental. They should *aim* at being beautiful.

Interview/ Publishers Weekly, 12-13:17.

Harold Robbins
Author
1

When I wrote my first book, I knew almost nothing about the business of writing. But I was self-confident because I'd led a wild life and known a lot of wild characters. I dipped into my experience and began to feel my way gradually. I discovered, for example, that one person or one life probably doesn't have enough ingredients to make a novel. Nor does a day-to-day journal of living make very interesting reading. A novelist takes liberties. He combines a number of interesting characters into one. He takes the exciting highlights of a number of careers and boils all of it down into a tight little group of adventures involving one or two central characters. The objective is to get rid of the boring stuff and to encapsulate only excitement into a time-frame and action-frame that holds the readers' interest.

Interview, Beverly Hills, Calif./
Los Angeles Times, 2-22:(Home)25.

2

There's a difference between novelists and *writers.* [Norman] Mailer is a writer. Mailer is afraid of the novel. He writes good ideas. But he doesn't write novels. Philip Roth? *Portnoy's Complaint* was a one-line joke. [Saul] Bellow bores me. [Ernest] Hemingway was a jerk. My favorite novelist is John Steinbeck. He wrote about people out of his lust and passion. I also like to read the old swashbucklers—Dumas, Dickens—too. Those were people who wrote about the times and people in them. Those are the things that I want to write about.

Interview/ People, 7-19:44.

Irwin Shaw
Author
3

Each morning I wake up with fear and trembling, knowing the typewriter is waiting for me. I'm afraid that maybe I don't have it any more, or maybe I never had it. Then, I just force myself to start writing . . . I found that endurance is a prime virtue for a writer. There are too many literary flashes in the pan. Everything in a writer's life should prepare him for the future. As writers, you must cling to the belief—however ill-founded—that you have talent. You should turn a deaf ear to criticism. And do not despise money; poverty will not make you a glorious stylist.

At Santa Barbara (Calif.) Writers Conference/
Los Angeles Times, 7-4:(Calendar)66.

Sidney Sheldon
Author, Screenwriter
4

I can't understand writers like Lillian Hellman who say they agonize over every word. Slow calculation may be their way, but to me a writer writes, loves writing and does it easily because that's simply what he was born to do.

Interview, Beverly Hills, Calif./
Los Angeles Herald-Examiner, 9-22:(B)1.

Tom Tryon
Author; Former actor
5

[Saying he prefers writing to acting]: In Middle America, an aura still hangs over you from the silver screen and people want to talk about Hollywood. I'll do it, if they want, but I find it all very boring. Nowadays, if someone comes up to me on the street and says, "Say, aren't you a movie star?" I say, "No, I'm not." But if someone says, "Hey, I read your new book," my eyes light up like a Christmas tree and I'll stop and talk gladly.

Interview, New York/ Publishers Weekly, 7-5:15.

Leon Uris
Author
6

One thing that even my worst critics admit is that I'm a hell of a good storyteller.

For some reason or other, my mind seems able to organize all that material. Possibly other things suffer in the writing, but by now you might say that I've outlived most of my critics. And although I don't look forward to breaking in a whole new generation of them, I am up to the task.

Interview/ Parade, 5-9:24.

1

You have to know what you're getting into [as a writer]. You can't have any illusions. Apply the seat of the pants to the seat of the chair. If you have excellence and the power to persevere, you can eventually break the door down. All you can do is hope you've got talent. If I had known in the beginning what I know now . . . well, you always ask yourself could I do this again? You see, then I was driven. Now I'm committed.

Interview/
Los Angeles Herald-Examiner, 7-30:(B)3.

Kurt Vonnegut, Jr.
Author

2

There is a shortage of readers. We're publishing more books than we can pay attention to. It's like an infantry charge—thousands of people go over the top, but few make it. We [the U.S.] send more writers over the top than all the rest of the world. It's wasteful, but there it is.

The New York Times Book Review, 8-29:6.

Irving Wallace
Author

3

[Publisher] Alfred Knopf sent me a contract that had beautiful embroidered ribbons but virtually no money. Alfred thought that writers degrade themselves by working for money but that publishers can do it.

Interview/"W": a Fairchild publication, 4-16:2.

Robert Wedgeworth
Executive director,
American Library Association

4

We are a society that is overwhelmed by the media—not just radio and television, but films, recordings and print. People are reading more, not less. And they aren't reading just books. They're reading digests, magazines, film clips. Reading is essential to the use of all the other media. Many people thought libraries would become obsolete because of the new media developments. But instead, libraries have become even more important.

Interview, Chicago/
The Christian Science Monitor, 10-6:4.

Jessamyn West
Author

5

I'm no Gore Vidal. I know evil exists, but I sort of soft-pedal it in my books. I might start out brimming with fiery anger, but by the time I'm finished, I've turned soft. For example, a neighbor of ours had a public-address system, and he kept it blaring noisily over the neighborhood. He was a hideous fellow and I started to write a story about him. But when I stepped inside the character, I began to understand him. He'd lived under the thumb of his parents, under the domination of his wife, and the loudspeaker was the first time he'd really found a chance to be heard, to let his voice carry. I've had similar experiences many times—anger at first, then I grow soft. The outcome inevitably is sympathetic writing because I like myself, and I always identify with the people I write about. Once I become the character in a story, there's no alternative. I have to be nice to myself.

Interview, Napa Valley, Calif./
Los Angeles Times, 10-10:(Home)43.

Morris West
Author

6

There is still only one test of a storyteller: Can he hold the reader? All the rest is dispensable.

Interview/ People, 12-6:115.

411

WHAT THEY SAID IN 1976

Alan D. Williams
Editor-in-chief,
The Viking Press, publishers   *1*

The industry is more competitive now than it has ever been. The literary agent who once might have been looked on with suspicion is the main beneficiary of the competition. Publishing houses know they need an author the agent represents, and now the whole feeding and caring of agents have changed.

Interview, New York/
"W": a Fairchild publication,
3-19:8.

Peter B. Bensinger
Administrator, Drug Enforcement
Administration of the United States
1

Heroin is the Number 1 priority because it is the most dangerous to the person using it, and as a result of that use the social consequences, the public-safety consequences, tend to be the greatest . . . The recidivist—the person who gets rearrested the most—is a heroin addict. An additional problem is that it's the kind of drug that is required every four or five hours. It's disruptive to a person's personal life. People on heroin aren't able to stay at work regularly. It's psychologically, as well as physiologically, very damaging . . . I think the direction of the Federal government in focusing on heroin is appropriate, because the results of the activities of these addicts have generally been the most disruptive, not only to themselves but to their communities.

Interview, Washington/
The National Observer, 5-1:16.

Joseph L. Bernardin
Roman Catholic Archbishop of Cincinnati;
President, National Conference of
Catholic Bishops
2

The 1973 [U.S.] Supreme Court abortion decisions have made abortion-on-demand a fact throughout the United States, with the result that our country now faces a startling and terrifying reality: With the approval of the law, one million human lives are destroyed each year by abortion. Considerations of health or economic distress cannot account for all of this. The plain fact is that many of these human lives are destroyed simply because others find it convenient to destroy

them. I think it is important to underscore the fact that the Supreme Court did not legalize abortion in just a few exceptional cases. In effect, it legalized abortion-on-demand. The 200-year-old tradition of the American people and the Judeo-Christian principles on which this nation was established are clearly opposed to abortion-on-demand, and a large segment of the American people today are opposed to abortion on demand.

Interview/ U.S. News & World Report, 9-27:27.

Bertram S. Brown
Director, National Institute of
Mental Health
3

Despite heroic efforts during the past quarter century to reduce the stigma attached to mental illness, public perception of the mentally ill continues to be significantly clouded as well with shame, suspicion and hostility. American towns continue to pass ordinances designed to exclude those who have been treated in a mental hospital; middle-class neighbors fear their property values will erode if a halfway house or boarding home for former patients were to be opened down the block; and people will talk openly about a heart attack or surgery for cancer, but still keep secret their depression or that of a family member. The image of mental-health research—its respectability and worth—undoubtedly suffers also because the very beneficiaries of its efforts are themselves suspect. Troubled people, many believe—including many in positions of influence and power—need most to develop self-control and discipline, even to be punished, but certainly not helped. Mental-health problems are, for many, a fiction, a conven-

(BERTRAM S. BROWN)

ient rationalization for those who would pamper the "morally decayed" or the "ethnically flawed" among us. If the goal of mental health is devalued or rejected, so, too, is the mental-health research community and the Federal institution that serves its purpose.

The Washington Post, 6-17:(A)28.

Edmund G. Brown, Jr.
Governor of California (D)
1

[On why he signed his state's right-to-die bill]: There's a very ancient moral doctrine that there's moral obligation to sustain life through artificial and extraordinary means. Machines should serve humans rather than the reverse. It ill-serves a human being to be hooked up to one of those technological machines and be treated as though the person was subhuman.

News conference, Sacramento, Oct. 1/
The Dallas Times Herald, 10-2:(A)6.

John Bunker
Professor of anesthesiology,
Stanford University
2

Not more than 20 per cent of surgery is done to prevent death or prolong life. The rest is done to improve the quality of life, and we have no systematic data on the value of the results.

Interview/The New York Times, 1-27:24.

Robert N. Butler
Director,
National Institute on Aging
3

Two-thirds of every dollar that the Federal government expended in health [in the U.S. last year] was spent on the population over 65 years of age. Yet, we do not have a medical school in the United States where medical students are required on a routine, regular basis to have training in a nursing home. This is true even though at the moment we now have more patients in nursing homes than we do in American hospitals . . . In the field of mental health, we also have many

grave problems. It is often striking for people to learn for the first time that, for a variety of reasons, 25 per cent of all of the suicides which are committed in the United States are accomplished by people over 65 years of age. And among the reasons for this is the absence of an adequate, effective network of mental-health services with people to sit and listen, to be attentive to and to help other people resolve their many difficulties, fears and concerns.

The Washington Post, 6-10:(A)18.

Earl L. Butz
Secretary of Agriculture of
the United States
4

If our diets are not far, far better today in this country than in the past, when people ate larger quantities of so-called natural foods and home-processed foods, how come each generation of children turns out to be taller than their parents, with broader shoulders and better coordination? Why do our young athletes of today so consistently outperform those who came before? Why do so many past records of human achievement, both physical and mental, crumble in the dust of the marks set by the youngsters of today?— youngsters raised on commercially processed foods, youngsters raised on manufactured foods, on industrially processed foods, on foods the health faddists say are poisonous. About the most-manufactured thing about our food supply today is the artificial worry about food quality . . . The biggest problem we have with our food in this country today is eating too much of it. If our current food supply is not nutritious and delicious, how come we see so many people overweight from eating it?

Before Institute of Food Technologists,
Anaheim, Calif./
The National Observer, 6-26:11.

Hugh L. Carey
Governor of New York (D)
5

Tuition and costs in medical education are rising steeply. There is a real danger that medicine will become the private privilege of those who are already rich enough to take on these increasing costs. I believe that whatever the fiscal constraints under which government must operate, it has a responsibility to see to it that this does not happen.

*At New York University
School of Medicine Alumni Day, April 10/
The New York Times, 4-11:(1)44.*

Jimmy Carter
*Candidate for the 1976
Democratic U.S. Presidential nomination;
Former Governor of Georgia (D)*　　1

[Calling for a mandatory and universal national health-insurance program]: I would want to give our people the most rapid improvement in individual health care the nation can afford, accommodating first those who need it most, with the understanding that it will be a comprehensive program in the end . . . We have built a haphazard, unsound, undirected, inefficient, non-system which has left us unhealthy and unwealthy at the same time.

*Before Student National Medical Association,
Washington, April 15/
Los Angeles Herald-Examiner, 4-16:(A)3.*

2

I favor a nation-wide, comprehensive, mandatory health-insurance program. It ought to be financed partially from Federal funds. Also, employees and employers ought to contribute to the cost of the health program. Patients should retain the right to choose their doctor and place of treatment; I want to keep the personal relationship between doctors and patients. The plan should be designed to minimize unnecessary medical costs. We now have a wide disparity of length of stay in hospitals, a wide disparity of charges for the same services, a wide difference also in the chance of one's undergoing an operation; it depends on what

geographical area in which the hospital might be located.

Interview/ U.S. News & World Report, 5-24:23.

Jimmy Carter
*1976 Democratic
U.S. Presidential nominee*　　3

I'm opposed to abortion; I think abortion is wrong . . . I don't think government ought to do anything to encourage abortions, and I think we ought to have a nation-wide effort through my own persuasion as President, if I'm elected—through sex education and access to contraceptives, for those who believe in their use, family-planning programs, better adoptive procedures—[to] do everything we can to minimize the need for abortions. I see abortions as evidence of a failure to prevent unwanted pregnancies. And this has been my position all the time. I'm not in favor of a Constitutional amendment that would totally prohibit abortion, or that would give states local option. I think that's the wrong approach to it.

*Interview, Los Angeles, Aug. 23/
Los Angeles Times, 8-24:(1)16.*

4

We now have an almost uncontrollable inclination to build health care facilities that are not needed. We've got too many beds, for instance, in some areas of our country and [are] still building them. [There is] very little correlation between meeting a community's need between the private and the public installations. We've got too much emphasis on in-patient care—sometimes almost forced on the patient—by the unwillingness of the insurance companies to pay unless a patient is an in-patient. I think we need to have more emphasis on out-patient care. I think we've gotten too much advanced technology going into medicine when sometimes the return on the investment is very slight. We've got too much emphasis on the treatment of disease once it's become serious, and inadequate routine preventive care. We've got too little monitoring of the in-

(JIMMY CARTER)

clination of doctors and insurance companies to kind of orient the patients into accepting health care beyond their own needs.

Interview, Los Angeles, Aug. 23/
Los Angeles Times, 8-24:(1)16.

Morris E. Chafetz .
President, Health Education Foundation;
Former Director, National Institute on
Alcohol Abuse and Alcoholism   1

When [alcohol] is used safely it helps us answer our very human need to be in communication with others, the need to break out a bit, let go and soar. And there is a safe way to drink . . . Most people don't realize that alcohol is an anesthetic, not a stimulant. In moderate amounts, it appears to stimulate because it inhibits the "new" part of the brain —the part that records new learning, judgment and social controls—as well as the brain centers that make us aware of exhaustion and discomfort. A little alcohol makes us feel physically able and emotionally freer. With increasing doses, however, alcohol puts these brain centers to sleep. Then the "older" part of the brain—the center for our primitive, less-socialized impulses—begins to take over. Sufficient dosage can put us to sleep for keeps, by anesthetizing the centers that control breathing and heartbeat.

Los Angeles Times, 11-28:(2)6.

Robert B. Choate
Chairman, Council on Children,
Media and Merchandising   2

There are 14,000 [TV] ads for edible products, and most of the products are nutritionally worthless. Or the advertising is nutritionally worthless. I think kids recognize that what goes into their mouths is important, but out of the content of television messages, they pick up no nutrition wisdom. Instead, they are urged to eat something because it is star-shaped or purple or sugared. Very seldom is there anything to indicate, for example, that something has calcium— or what it does to you. We've got 14,000

ads pretending to tell them about food— which sure as hell don't tell them about nutrition.

Interview/Los Angeles Times, 4-2:(4)8.

James Coleman
Assistant professor of social science,
California State Polytechnic University,
San Luis Obispo   3

People who advocate the medical approach [to aiding drug addicts], based on the notion of addiction as something completely involuntary, are pursuing the right goal—more humane treatment for addicts— but by the wrong means. There is no question that addicts, by and large, are predatory and antisocial. In that regard, I cannot say that I have a great deal of sympathy for them. But it is just as true that they have been treated very harshly and unjustly by our society. I think we must change our legal system, not by having the courts declare addictive behavior involuntary, but by having the legislatures adopt more humane and realistic programs. Until the states stop trying to terrorize people into doing what they think best for them, the opiate problem will not be solved. The idea of addiction as completely involuntary behavior should be disposed of as quickly as possible, for it only aggravates the problem. But at the same time we must move in the direction of more humane and less oppressive treatment of the addict.

The Center Magazine, Nov.-Dec.:51.

Rene Dubos
Professor emeritus of microbiology,
Rockefeller University   4

You can have all the systems of healing invented in the world; they function only to the extent they help you to put into use those resources that you are born with that help you fight disease. There exists in the structure of each and every one of us a phenomenal resiliency that allows us to face up to all kinds of physical and mental disorders.

At "Ways of Healing—Ancient & Modern"
symposium, San Francisco/
The National Observer, 3-13:10.

Renato Dulbecco
Winner,
1975 Nobel Prize in cancer research   *1*

[On smoking]: The fact that it [lung cancer] has not been prevented, and that 60,000 Americans are killed by it every year, must be squarely attributed to lack of adequate action by the government, and its failure to heed the many calls made by responsible scientists over the last two decades. As a cancer researcher and as a medical man I am shocked by this lack of action [against smoking], and I question the credibility of the government as a promoter of health.

At Senate hearing, Washington, Feb. 19/
The Washington Post, 2-20:(C)5.

William Dunn
Chief pyschologist, Philip Morris
research and development center   *2*

The most important reason people smoke is to obtain the effect of smoke in the body. We've done considerable research on just what is the nature of that effect. It would appear somehow or other—and we don't know how—smoke acts as an agent to assist in regulating the arousal of emotion. We live in a complex civilization. The more complex, the more we must control our emotion. We are not allowed to fight and to run. We must stand there and cope. We are constantly being aroused emotionally, but we have to control these feelings. And the degree to which we control these emotions, the better off we are in this complex society. Cigarettes, in my opinion, help control these emotions.

Richmond, Va./
The Washington Post, 5-16:(F)2.

Robert L. DuPont
Director,
National Institute on Drug Abuse   *3*

There is no question that alcohol and tobacco are causing us far more health problems than marijuana does ... There are health risks associated with all the drugs [alcohol,

tobacco and marijuana]. If a young person does use [one of them], I would encourage them to use less of it ... Personally, my view is that we do not have to threaten young people with imprisonment to discourage use of marijuana.

News conference, Feb. 12/
The Washington Post, 2-13:(A)7.

Nanette Fabray
Actress   *4*

Helen Keller has said that, given her choice between deafness and blindness, she would have chosen blindness. That's because a blind person is still able to interact with other people socially. He can sit in a room with others and talk, listen to music, enjoy the radio, or even television, with them. But a deaf person is extremely lonely, and often very afraid. After all, it is communication with others that sets us apart from a tree, or a flower ... or the animals.

Interview, Chicago/
The Dallas Times Herald, 10-24:(I)9.

John H. Filer
Chairman,
Aetna Life & Casualty Company   *5*

... why do you suppose it is that in most states with a no-fault [automobile] liability system that has a low threshold—in other words, a fairly modest amount of medical expense and wage loss beyond which an injured person may sue and recover for pain and suffering, etc.—why is it that the medical expenses seem to turn out to be consistently higher than in places where the law does *not* have that characteristic? We can't prove it statistically, but the evidence satisfies us that collusion between lawyer, doctor and accident victim adds millions of dollars to the public's cost of auto insurance. Why is it that we see evidence from time to time of one fee schedule for a non-insured medical or dental procedure and another for the insured individual? And what is it about the more impersonal practice of medicine that has con-

(JOHN H. FILER)

tributed to the dramatic change in medical malpractice litigation and awards in recent years? Could it be that in the minds of the public the doctors have turned into businessmen rather than professionals, with their focus on their own income, security and convenience rather than the well-being of the patient? . . . What the system and its woefully inadequate self-policing or regulatory mechanisms seem to be doing includes these things: a) reducing sharply the confidence of people in the medical profession; b) increasing the cost of medical care directly and indirectly through insurance costs; and c) hastening the day of government intervention either directly or through a regulatory process. But yet what the profession started out to do was heal the sick.

Before Connecticut Society of Certified Public Accountants, New Haven, Oct. 5/ Vital Speeches, 12-1:118.

Gerald R. Ford
President of the United States
1

Hospital and medical services in America are among the world's best, but the cost of a serious and extended illness can quickly wipe out a family's lifetime savings. Increasing health costs are of deep concern to all and a powerful force pushing up the cost of living. The burden of a catastrophic illness can be borne by very few in our society. We must eliminate this fear from every family. I propose catastrophic health insurance for everybody covered by Medicare. To finance this added protection, fees for short-term care will go up somewhat, but nobody after reaching age 65 will have to pay more than $500 a year for covered hospital or nursing-home care nor more than $250 for one year's doctor's bills. We cannot realistically afford Federally dictated national health insurance providing full coverage for all 215 million Americans. The experience of other countries raises questions about the quality as well as the cost of such plans. But I do envision the day when we may use the private health-insurance system to offer more middle-income families high-quality health services at prices they can afford, and shield them also from catastrophic illnesses.

State of the Union address, Washington, Jan. 19/ The New York Times, 1-20:18.

2

I disagree with the decision of the Supreme Court: their initial decision to limit states' rights to ban abortion, and their more recent decision—the one which says the husband doesn't have to give consent, and that a minor child doesn't have to get consent from the parents, for an abortion. I think those decisions are wrong. On the other hand, I do not believe that a national prohibition against abortion by a Constitutional amendment is a practical solution. I have supported—because I think it might be a practical and moral solution—an amendment which would permit each state, or the voters in each state, to make the decision on that state's abortion policy.

U.S. News & World Report, 9-20:17.

Park S. Gerald
Harvard University Medical School
3

Cancer is a thousand problems for which we have a common name. Each disease will have its own environment and genetic aspects and its own treatment. What it means is, don't expect a cure for cancer because there is no single cancer. It's our emotions that lump them together, not their biology. There will be a thousand cures for a thousand cancers. We're pecking away at the genetics, but we're still just nibbling at the edges.

The National Observer, 8-21:1.

William Harvey
Member, National Advisory Council on Drug Abuse
4

For years we have been content to study the drug user, but many of us have been concerned about the feelings and motivations of the substantial number of people who don't take drugs or alcohol of any kind. [A recent St. Louis survey of these non-users] seems to be saying that we should strengthen those institutions [religion, the home, etc.] and family ties so that teen-agers who want to carve out their own identity can do so without the exhilaration they think they might get from taking drugs. If they can get the exhilaration they need from other sources— it may be religion, a hobby, or just feeling good about themselves—it is a way of allowing them to seek and find their own identity, which appears to be one of the big reasons kids turn to drugs.

The Christian Science Monitor, 11-16:1.

Richard G. Hatcher
Mayor of Gary, Indiana
1

We should examine, research and explore the concept of [heroin] decriminalization and we should conduct a small number of tightly controlled heroin-maintenance experiments. There are more than 500,000 addicts in this country, and the number is increasing every day . . . it is important that the subject be brought out into the open. The social cost of illegal drug trafficking is sucking the life from American cities.

At 1976 Congress of Cities, Denver/
Los Angeles Herald-Examiner, 12-2:(A)16.

William D. Hathaway
United States Senator, D—Maine
2

[Criticizing alcohol advertising]: Many millions of American youth are bombarded every day with many thousands of messages about drinking from many hundreds of glamorous, friendly, healthy, adventurous, sexy—and in some cases venomous—people telling them of the joys and benefits of drinking.

At Senate subcommittee hearing, Washington,
March 8/The Christian Science Monitor, 3-9:1.

Raymond T. Holden
Chairman,
American Medical Association
3

A physician who does good work and who satisfies his patients has never needed advertising. The only ones who would try to benefit [from the lifting of restrictions on doctor advertising] would be the less-skilled, less-ethical physician.

U.S. News & World Report, 1-26:62.

Jacob K. Javits
United States Senator, R—New York
4

The medical profession, acting from understandable desire to help sick people, has often accepted innovations in practice, only to have them later prove to be of limited value or dangerous. It is too late to assess an innovation when it is ready for general medical use. We must begin to anticipate problems and plan their solution.

At science policy meeting, Warrenton, Va./
The New York Times, 4-5:23.

Yousuf Karsh
Photographer
5

[On the medical profession, which he once hoped to enter]: Arrogance is never part of the great physician. One is likely to find vanity. But that is necessary. Vanity is self-enoblement striving for perfection. It makes a person want to do things his way—but correctly.

People, 1-12:71.

Gerald L. Klerman
Professor of psychiatry,
Harvard University
6

The health-care system is increasingly called upon to deal with the quality of life rather than its prolongation . . . My own prediction is that as our society becomes more urban, more industrial, more mobile, more individualistic, medication will be even more central as a means of coping with distress

(GERALD L. KLERMAN)

and improving the quality of life. The future belongs to illness . . . Every adult would like to be relieved of tension, guilt, insomnia. We would all like the health-care system to make us more sexually potent, more beautiful, more intelligent, live longer and happier. Every child could use help with furthering his personal, physical, psychological, cognitive and emotional development. The future probably will produce drugs which will do many of these things. The question then will be not what is morally right, but is it effective, at what cost, is it safe?

*Before American Association for the
Advancement of Science, Boston/
Los Angeles Herald-Examiner, 2-29:(E)3.*

Alfred G. Knudson, Jr.
*University of Texas Health Science
Center, Houston*   1

We can reduce cancer, but we can never get it to go away. We'll never eliminate cancer, because to do so you would have to eliminate spontaneous mutations. In a sense, cancer is the price we have to pay to evolve.

The National Observer, 8-21:1.

Halfdan Mahler
*Director general,
World Health Organization*   2

Long life without improvement in the quality of life is one of the tragic sequels to technological development in many countries. It is therefore clear that, in virtually every society, a redefinition of health goals is required.

*At World Health Organization
annual conference, Geneva, May 4/
The Washington Post, 5-5:(A)11.*

Jean Mayer
*Authority on nutrition;
President-designate, Tufts University*   3

The United States is the only country I know of which has male foods and female

foods. You go to the local Ramada Inn and you'll find all the ladies of the auxiliary of the hospital eating chicken croquettes or sole, and you find all the men of the sales force eating those big slabs of bleeding meat —even though, from the cardiovascular viewpoint, one can wish that they would reverse their tastes. But I think the more men sit at their desks all day, the more they want to be reassured about their maleness in eating those large slabs of bleeding meat which are sort of the last symbol of *machismo*— the motorcycle of the middle-aged.

*Lecture sponsored by College of Physicians of
Philadelphia and SmithKline Corporation/
The National Observer, 7-10:13.*

Walter J. McNerney
*President,
National Blue Cross Association*   4

Administration of Medicaid has been too casual so far. The day when a guy with a license and a patient with an illness met in a never-never land is over. There is too much money available. You need strong and sound management in the administration of this kind of program.

U.S. News & World Report, 9-13:55.

Frank E. Moss
United States Senator, D—Utah   5

[On doctors who pad Medicare bills, falsify claims, participate in kickback schemes, etc.]: There comes a certain point when physicians, like other lawbreakers, must be put in jail. To do otherwise, as we have been, is to make a mockery of the laws we have enacted and to ridicule the great majority of honest physicians who observe them . . . The long and short of it is that the message that we have given physicians is, "Go ahead and steal. The worst thing that can happen to you is that you will be asked to pay back some money. The odds are you will never be caught. And if, by some accident, you are caught, you have had the use of all this money for several years."

Before Senate Finance Committee,
Washington, July 28/
Los Angeles Herald-Examiner,
7-29:(A)6.

1

[On his experience masquerading as a Medicaid patient in New York]: When you get to see a practitioner, your visit will be brief, usually from three to five minutes, and the examining-room will be tiny. You will be given a general examination no matter how specific your complaint. If blood pressure is taken or a stethoscope is used, the odds are it will be done through your clothing. It is likely that you will not be touched; Medicaid doctors don't like touching their patients . . . [The inside of the clinics] will be dirty. Cleanliness is not prized in Medicaid mills; it costs too much money. The floors look like they haven't been swept in a month and the restrooms are abominable . . . At some point, the doctor will take blood. The taking of blood confirms that treatment has been rendered to the patient, but, perhaps just as important, samples presented to clinical laboratories will generate a return of $15 each from the laboratory. In addition, you are going to be asked for a urine sample; you will be given a number of X-rays and perhaps a shot or two. You can count on receiving several prescriptions, and in most cases you will be directed to a particular pharmacy. If you're not sick, you won't be told you're not sick. If you are sick, the odds are you won't be helped.

Before Senate Special Committee on Aging,
Washington, Aug. 30/
The New York Times, 8-31:1,46.

Daniel P. Moynihan
Professor of government, Harvard
University; Former United States
Ambassador/Permanent Representative
to the United Nations   2

[On abortion]: I believe in the usual am-biguous position. I'm not against abortion. I mean, I wouldn't prevent anyone who wanted to from getting an abortion; but I'm damned if I think that the Supreme Court should be saying that no legislature can forbid it. I think it's entirely within a legislature's power to forbid it . . . At the very least, you'd like to have a country where if someone didn't like abortion they could go to a state where they don't allow it. I think the framers of the Constitution would have been very much surprised by that Supreme Court decision. I know what we're going to do. We're going to have more and more, and there will be a Constitutional stand. And that's only the half of it. Don't kid yourself. You have something that's gone out of the culture when you commence to think of these things as matters of convenience . . . But it's no longer a sacred culture anyway. We know that. And if you don't have a sacred culture, pretty soon life is not sacred.

Interview, New York/
Los Angeles Times,
4-22:(1)7.

Max H. Parrott
President,
American Medical Association   3

I firmly believe that private fee-for-service practice can serve . . . the country in an ever more positive manner. In saying "ever more positive," I mean that fee-for-service practice is just as capable of new modalities as any other form of practice. These modalities increasingly include multi-specialty and single-specialty group practices. Almost a fourth of all non-Federal physicians engaged in patient care, excluding interns and residents, are in group practice . . . and only 8.4 per cent of the groups are prepaid. More and more fee-for-service groups are settling around hospital campuses . . . so that in addition to relating to a campus, they can relate physically—though not functionally—to each other. Thus, within a convenient radius, the patient can be referred to the appropriate

(MAX H. PARROTT)

physician . . . and have a latitude of choice . . . in contrast with the limitations of an HMO closed panel. The general point to be made is that the fee-for-service system has flexibility . . . which includes giving the patient the time he needs. Its very hallmark is the doctor-patient relationship . . . which increasingly includes seeing the patient as "a whole man" . . . with physical, emotional and mental characteristics that are medically interrelated . . . rather than seeing him as a mere slice of disease and then hurrying him on his way. All of these attributes of the fee-for-service system are important to the quality of care.

At Oregon State University, April 19/
Vital Speeches, 6-15:535.

Max H. Parrott
Former president,
American Medical Association 1

While the health professions—particularly physicians—traditionally have emphasized the *quality* of care . . . the government places unusually heavy emphasis on cost containment . . . all pretensions to quality assurance notwithstanding. This is all well and good—up to a point. And that point is where cost containment begins to erode quality assurance. Because high-quality care—like any high-quality service—cannot be provided at less than its basic cost. And when this critical juncture is reached, the only other way to further reduce costs is to limit *access* to care. Without safeguards, both quality and access can be limited . . . especially under governmentalized systems where medical expenditures must compete with other budgetary priorities. For example, it's no secret that under Britain's National Health Service, more than 500,000 patients are now awaiting access to elective care . . . and some of them will have to wait up to two years. Furthermore, Sir Keith Joseph, a former Health Services Secretary, described himself—when in office—as Britain's biggest slum landlord. He meant that many of Brit-

ain's hospitals were built in the 19th century . . . that their sub-standard quality can actually endanger patients . . . and that only 40-odd new hospitals have been built since World War II. In short, while the public sector should be a partner with the private sector in assuring patients of care . . . it should never become the overseer.

At University of California, Santa Cruz,
Sept. 25/Vital Speeches, 10-15:14.

Mary Pendery
Assistant clinical professor of psychiatry,
University of California, San Diego;
Chief, alcoholism treatment program,
Veterans Administration Hospital,
San Diego 2

It is interesting that many people who are not working closely with alcoholics in the various stages of their problems, or recovery, are afraid that the "disease concept" [of alcoholism] is dehumanizing. I hear this from many of my own colleagues, my fellow psychologists. But in the group therapies and other settings where alcoholics are in treatment, probably the single most helpful concept to them in their own recovery is this disease concept. The disease concept gives them an explanation which to them is humanizing after the terribly dehumanizing experiences they have been through.

Group discussion, Center for the Study of
Democratic Institutions, Santa Barbara, Calif./
The Center Magazine, July-Aug.:38.

William Rader
Medical director of alcoholism recovery
services, San Pedro and Peninsula Hospital,
California 3

[On why so many young people drink]: It's a fad, like long hair and LSD in the '60s, or bisexuality in the '70s. Alcohol is the drug —and it *is* a drug—of their choice, and parents are comfortable with it because it's something they themselves use. The parents are making the illness worse because they say, "At least they're not smoking marijuana."

And it's easier to get this drug than others because it's right in the house. Alcohol is the Number 1 drug-abuse problem among teenagers today.

Interview/People, 8-23:46.

Frank J. Rauscher, Jr.
Director, National Cancer Institute   *1*

We see a predictable increase in cancer today. But we're going to see even much more, for a variety of reasons, unless current trends are turned around.This is because of contamination of our environment and because of continuing use of tobacco and other known carcinogens. There's another very interesting trend: As this country approaches a zero-population-growth rate in births, and as our health care improves, we're going to have an older population. Most cancers are essentially diseases of older people. So, as we live longer, we're going to see an increase in cancer due to that factor as well.

Interview, Washington/
U.S. News & World Report, 2-9:61.

    2

Much of the science is done. We know how to prevent many of the cancer cases. We just have to apply what we know . . . We now know that up to 90 per cent of the cancers are not genetically produced. Something from outside has caused these cancers. This is a godsend. Knowing this, we ought to be able to do a better job of finding carcinogens and getting rid of them . . . [But there will be] no overnight miracles [in the fight against cancer]. This is going to be a slow eroding of the 100 diseases that we call cancer.

Before National Newspaper Publishers
Association, Washington, March 19/
Los Angeles Herald-Examiner, 3-20:(A)5.

Ronald Reagan
Candidate for the 1976
Republican U.S. Presidential nomination;
Former Governor of California (R)   *3*

I think any comparison of our pluralistic [medical] system in America, compared

to those countries such as England, Sweden, that have put in national health insurance reveals that government medicine is more expensive, government medicine is less efficient. And we [in the U.S.] have, I believe, the finest health care to be found any place in the world, and we should think twice before we throw that system away.

Interview/The Christian Science Monitor, 6-3:16.

E. Kash Rose
President-elect, Hospital
Financial Management Association   *4*

The patient today is king. He can choose what doctor he wants, and that doctor is answerable to him for delivering quality medical care. But a physician working for a hospital no longer functions only for his patient. The physician's employer's interests would have to be reckoned with in decisions that should take into consideration only the patient's best interest—and out the door goes that fundamental, personal relationship between patient and physician . . . What it all comes down to is this: A hospital is bricks and CAT scanners, beds and bedpans. By putting physicians on a hospital salary, that physician becomes another part of the hospital. He does not function in it for the benefit of the patients only, but becomes part of the hospital itself, another building block, another financially controllable consideration, a part of the profit motive. A hospital and a doctor must remain economically separate. This freedom ensures that the patient remains the primary consideration in the delivery of health care in America today.

Before Hospital Financial Management
Association, Monterey, Calif., Sept. 23/
Vital Speeches, 11-15:70,71.

C. H. William Ruhe
Senior vice president for scientific affairs,
American Medical Association   *5*

The [routine] physical examination is not going to protect a person from anything. It's not a treatment, although it assumes that

WHAT THEY SAID IN 1976

(C. H. WILLIAM RUHE)

kind of proportion in some people's minds: "I've been through this battery of tests and I'm all right. It's okay for me now to go out and over-eat and stay up late." A physical is a reasonable assessment of the present state of the body. The individual should use judgment in his own estimate as to what is meant by the physical examination. The physical should not become some kind of fetish or ritual that must be observed. It doesn't guarantee anything for the future.

Interview/ The National Observer, 9-11:10.

Charles Sanders
General director,
Massachusetts General Hospital
                                                            1

[On the increasing costs of hospital care]: Whatever we do . . . inflation is bound to send costs higher, and so will our strong commitment to providing the best medical technology. Americans want and expect high-quality care. I think it has to be recognized that absolute containment of costs is incompatible with comprehensive quality health care. Costs are important to consider, but so is the need for good care.

Interview, Boston/
The National Observer, 6-19:10.

Alexander M. Schmidt
Commissioner, Food and Drug
Administration of the United States
                                                            2

I am growing increasingly concerned about the safety of some of the so-called organic foods, and think there should be more local regulation of health-food stores. After all, one of the reasons that there are food additives is so that food can be shipped safely without need for careful refrigeration. Some health-food stores look like the stores of my childhood—food hanging from the ceiling, and so on. Our authority extends only to products sold in these stores that have been shipped in interstate commerce; the stores themselves come under state health depart-

ments. The danger is that many people think that organic food is very nutritious and safer than other foods; but that is not always the truth. If you don't preserve food well, you can get sick from it. If you don't handle it and store it properly, you can get sick. And some organic food contains more naturally occurring toxins than do processed foods.

Interview/
U.S. News & World Report, 2-23:54.

3

The [pharmaceutical] industry is schizophrenic [in that it is] a public-service industry that is also dedicated to maximizing profits. [That is] the best argument [for a regulatory agency such as the FDA].

Interview, Rockville, Md./
The Washington Post, 11-15:(A)3.

Samuel K. Skinner
United States Attorney for the
Northern District of Illinois
                                                            4

The 1970s have witnessed the greatest rip-off in history, as literally millions of dollars in hard-earned and sorely needed tax dollars have been mismanaged, squandered, wasted and stolen from Federally funded health programs [such as Medicaid]. As a result, Federal health-care programs have become a mockery and simply do not provide the quantity and quality of medical services which the poor, the sick, the disabled and the old both need and deserve, and which Congress intended to provide.

Before Senate Special Committee on Aging,
Washington, Nov. 17/
Los Angeles Times, 11-18:(1)17.

Leo H. Sternbach
Medicinal chemist;
Inventor of Valium (tranquilizer)
                                                            5

Through the development of Valium, I achieved a goal which was of value not only to the company for which I was working but, in addition, to humanity. As a chemist, I

424

could have developed some horrible poison gas for warfare or something like that, and of such achievement I would not be particularly proud. But Valium is something of real value to people. It's not something which everybody should take, because it's generally recognized that a certain amount of anxiety is needed to stimulate enthusiasm. If you don't care about anything, you won't do anything. So one needs a certain amount of anxiety. But anxiety can become so strong that it incapacitates some people, and that's where Valium helps.

Interview, Montclair, N.J./
Parade, 6-27:10.

Richard S. Sternberger
Rabbi; Chairperson, Religious Coalition
for Abortion Rights   *1*

[Opposing a Constitutional amendment to outlaw or further restrict abortion]: We believe very strongly in a woman's right to make her own choice [regarding abortion]. We're a pro-choice organization, not a pro-abortion organization. We believe that this is a matter of individual conscience—that a woman has to make this choice in consonance with her conscience and with her religious beliefs—and that is not a legal matter. Secondly, we believe very strongly in the separation of church and state, and we are very, very concerned about the imposition by law of any theological stance, whatever it be, on the citizens of this country.

Interview/
U.S. News & World Report, 9-27:27.

Jokichi Takamine
Chairman, committee on alcoholism,
American Medical Association   *2*

The three constant factors in alcoholism are the agent—alcohol; the host—the drinker; and the environment. No matter what may pyramid on top of this or proliferate from it, those three things are constant. And obviously this is true for other diseases; that is one of the reasons why the disease concept was applied to alcoholism. Since then, I think

too many people think of alcoholism solely as a medical disease. In our haste to clarify what alcoholism is, I am reminded of something said long ago by H. L. Mencken, that for every problem there is a solution which is short, simple and wrong. That is a pitfall into which many of us in alcoholism may have fallen.

Group discussion, Center for the Study of
Democratic Institutions, Santa Barbara, Calif./
The Center Magazine, July-Aug.:31.

Lewis Thomas
President, Memorial Sloan-Kettering
Cancer Center, New York   *3*

My feeling about cancer is not just the optimism of one with a commitment to—or, as some might say, a vested interest in—research. There are enough clues around to make me realistically optimistic. For instance, there are those cancer patients whose tumors mysteriously undergo spontaneous remission, and disappear. We have combinations of drugs now that can cure some cancers, especially rapidly growing cancers in children that were fatal 10 years ago. And there is the long history of cases that suggest that cancer may be a failure of the immune system and thus hint that a natural mechanism for the elimination of malignancy is lying behind the scenes waiting to be uncovered.

Interview, New York/
The New York Times Magazine, 7-4:109.

4

Doctors are needed, of course, to cope with a number of specific problems for which medicine has something to offer. But I think the doctor's role in disease is essentially to guide us to the balance of nature, to the fact that so much of human illness tends to be self-limiting and spontaneously reversible.

Interview, New York/
The New York Times Magazine, 7-4:109.

Joel Warren
Director, Leo Goodwin Institute for
Cancer Research, Fort Lauderdale, Fla.   *5*

[Saying there will never be a "cure" for cancer]: What has happened in technologi-

WHAT THEY SAID IN 1976

(JOEL WARREN)

cally advanced countries, and particularly in America, is the rise of the notion that, given enough time and given enough money, we can bring these things under control and stamp them out. We have gotten to the idea that cancer is something that's going to be conquered. Because of this, we view any hazard as something that is technologically avoidable. But cancer is not a technological disease . . . There's no question that many of our tumors are environmentally caused. Smoking, asbestos, radiation levels—these things have got to be controlled. But I disagree that the environment causes most cancers. There are probably thousands of causes of cancer . . . every species that we know of has a basic rate of cancer. You could take a hundred people and put them in a lead-lined cave in Colorado. You could keep them away from all of the things believed to cause cancer—don't let them smoke, for instance. Of those people, 25 to 30 per cent would get cancer if they lived beyond the age of 60.

Interview, Fort Lauderdale, Fla./
The Dallas Times Herald, 12-26:(A)34.

The Performing Arts

MOTION PICTURES

George Abbott
Stage producer-director-writer

1

Motion-picture acting can't be equated with real acting. It's bits-and-pieces stuff. A director can make Gary Cooper look like an actor. He can make 20 shots of an actor saying, "I do," and pick the one really good "I do."

Interview, New York/
The New York Times, 4-28:34.

Alan Alda
Actor

2

I'm aware there's a stereotyped picture of actors, though many don't fall into it. What keeps some true to it is that the actor's life is so passive. He has to wait for an agent to call and tell him that maybe he can work. He auditions and waits again. Then, if he gets a job, the agent takes over, like a parent, and negotiates his contract for him. So he has very little control over his life. It isn't a healthy experience. It's not what normal men and women do. Plus, it's natural to be attracted to the business out of a need for approval and applause. Just putting those factors together you can see that it might be difficult for an actor to grow up.

Interview/McCall's, January:16.

Robert Aldrich
Producer, Director

3

[On film criticism]: There's no winning the critical game. If you're half smart, you abandon that elusive hope. You make the picture that you find attractive or interesting, and you make it as well as you can. If the critics like it, great. If they don't, forget them. There's no way to placate them, or to know what next year's in-vogue, trendy critical acceptance level is going to be.

Interview, Los Angeles/
The Christian Science Monitor, 4-9:20.

4

The demise of the star system is tragic. The industry is getting more and more hooked on having to make bigger and bigger pictures with fewer and fewer people who are growing older and older. As for replacements, there's nobody on the bench. Nobody knows who will be the Steve McQueen of 10 years from now; and the sad thing is, they don't care.

Interview, Los Angeles/
The Christian Science Monitor, 4-9:20.

Irwin Allen
Producer, Director

5

[On "disaster" films]: It gives members of an audience a great sense of self-satisfaction to vicariously live through a crisis in heroic style. If your film makes the whole thing so real to them that they become totally immersed in the adventure to the extent that they forget they're merely onlookers, you have accomplished what I believe to be the greatest draw for bringing people to the motion-picture box-office.

Interview/Daily Variety, 7-28:5.

Eric Ambler
Author

6

[Saying writing for films is an "occupational hazard"]: It's a hazard because very little screenwriting is writing. It's drawing blueprints for someone else to make a movie.

WHAT THEY SAID IN 1976

(ERIC AMBLER)

The hazard is it earns large sums of money which tend to raise the living standard. Therefore, the writer gets to a point where he is reluctant to reduce. He wants to go on making movies—not because he enjoys it, but because he wants to make the same kind of money. That is where the hazard lies.

Interview, Clarens, Switzerland/
Los Angeles Times, 2-15:(Calendar)33.

Lindsay Anderson
British director
1

The biggest catastrophe in show business in the United States is the rise of the agent. Actors were better off when they were run by the studios. Now they have the power to be stupid.

Interview, New York/
San Francisco Examiner & Chronicle, 7-11:
(Datebook)23.

Samuel Z. Arkoff
Chairman and president,
American International Pictures
2

What the studios are doing now are super versions of the same formulas. That's necessary because there is tremendous entertainment on television today. Television can't present anything too big; you rarely see long-shots on TV shows; nor is there much action, outside of fistfights and car chases. Movies have to give the public something more.

Los Angeles/
Los Angeles Herald-Examiner, 5-23:(B)2.

James Baldwin
Author
3

In the same way that the [blaxploitation] film craze may have inadvertently cleared the way for more-valid works, the spate of pornographic films—which I haven't seen— may prepare the way for more-valid work in the area of love and sex. In any case, only a puritan can produce a pornographic film.

Interview, Washington/
The Washington Post, 5-2:(G)8.

Ralph Bellamy
Actor
4

[Hollywood] isn't fun any more. In the 1930s everyone had fun, and that photographed. You could see it in the attitude of the performers. Today, as a result of TV and bigger budgets, there is a severe time limit. Everything must be done punctually, under intense pressure. That's communicated to the screen. Now everybody is breathing down your neck to get the job done. Today it's all lawyers and accountants. What we need are more showmen, the kind of tough guys who ran the studios. They were son[s]-of-bitches and they were czars but they shaped a grander industry. The aura that used to surround the business is gone— destroyed forever by the men with their ledgers and Ivy League suits.

Interview, San Francisco/
San Francisco Examiner & Chronicle, 12-5:
(Datebook)29.

Ingmar Bergman
Director
5

When I was a child I played with my own little projector, and I guess I'm still playing. When I walk into the studio with all the actors and cameras and lighting and settings, I feel that it's so strange, that I'm playing a game. But they take me seriously; they pay me for it. I still have the feeling of a child, going into a room and taking out my toys and playing a game with them.

Interview, Munich/
The New York Times, 10-17:(2)15.

Bernardo Bertolucci
Director
6

. . . I've never merely been interested in illustrating literary works. I told Moravia, when I was to make a film from his novel,

The Conformist, that I would have to be unfaithful to the text to be faithful to the spirit of the book. My films are not illustrations of film scripts, either. I write the scripts as well as I can and then work from the memory of them—I don't open the script when I'm to shoot. I'm inspired by the set and the actors I have before me.

Interview, Rome/
Los Angeles Times, 4-20:(4)11.

1

Only politicians can get the Fascist codes on censorship off the books. The fight must be for total freedom of expression and this includes the freedom to produce pornography.

The New York Times, 10-10:(2)20.

Maurice Bessy
Delegate general (director),
Cannes Film Festival

2

All the countries—big and small—want to make pictures, but it is very difficult to find *auteurs* and directors making great films. I attribute this to the pace at which they must work in today's world. With only one or two exceptions, they are almost compelled to turn out at least one picture a year —and for the creative person this is the worst thing in the world. In France, we had a great writer called Racine. In his lifetime he wrote only 13 plays, and of those, only three have become classics, which have withstood the passage of time. In today's world the film-maker needs money to live and so necessity forces him to produce more than that which he is capable of doing really well. An *auteur* cannot make more than five or six great pictures during his lifetime. But today's creators are under what I think is an unreasonable pressure from which the old masters did not suffer. In my opinion, one of the greatest American creators is Orson Welles. How many pic-

tures has he made? Maybe 12 or 13 in all his years in films.

Interview, Los Angeles, Calif./
The Hollywood Reporter, 3-8:14.

Marlon Brando
Actor

3

. . . that's all films are—just an extension of childhood, where everybody wants to be freer, everybody wants to be powerful, everybody wants to be so overwhelmingly attractive that there's just no doing anything about it. Or everybody wants to have comradeship and to be understood. They become lullabies. They're tell-me-again-daddy stories. That's all television is: Tell me again, daddy, about the good guy and the bad guy and the strong guy and Kung Fu and Flash Gordon. People love to hear the stories; they love to hear the lullabies.

Interview, Montana/
Los Angeles Herald-Examiner, 5-23:(D)7.

4

Acting is an empty and useless profession. I do it for the money because for me there is no pleasure . . . I'm convinced that the larger the gross, the worse the picture. [Directors Ingmar] Bergman and [Luis] Bunuel are visionaries, wonderful artists and craftsmen. How many people in the world have ever seen one of their films or ever heard of them? How can you take movies seriously? You go on the set with the script in your back pocket. You take it out and read: "Let's see . . . in this one Brando plays an Indian who attacks the stage coach." Okay, let's roll 'em. Commercialized glop, not worth thinking about.

Interview, Tetiaroa (South Pacific)/ Time, 5-24:74.

Genevieve Bujold
Actress

5

[On why she dislikes promoting her films]: If [a film] is a flop, it's because the public doesn't want to see it. I can't do anything

(GENEVIEVE BUJOLD)

about that. If you try to talk people into seeing something they don't want to see by peddling yourself, then you become a saleswoman and a prostitute, and I am neither.

Interview, Beverly Hills, Calif./
San Francisco Examiner & Chronicle, 8-29:
(Datebook)13.

George Burns
Entertainer
1

[On his winning this year's "Oscar" for best supporting actor]: I've been in show business all my life and getting this award proves one thing: If you stay in this business long enough, and if you get to be old enough, you get to be new again.

San Francisco Examiner & Chronicle, 4-4:
(This World)2.

Richard Burton
Actor
2

I think all actors, perhaps all artists, go through a period when they run out of intellectual energy or stamina. You become average for five years or so; then, suddenly, you wake up, and it's coming back. It's a cycle, circular. You're at the top, and you go to the bottom; there's a dreadful time at the bottom, and then you climb up again. Then there's the question of luck, and I think you make your own luck.

Interview, New York/
Los Angeles Times, 4-25:(Calendar)35.

Michael Caine
Actor
3

Somebody once told me that if you want to be a leading man you must always be the leading man. Better to be a leading man in a bad film than have a minor part in a good film. It was the worst single piece of advice I ever got. It is better to be the camera

operator on something good than to be the director on a piece of rubbish.

At American Film Institute seminar,
Beverly Hills, Calif./
Los Angeles Times, 1-23:(4)1.

Dyan Cannon
Actress
4

I'm so tired of all the violence [in films], the chicanery. I want more love stories, stories of men and women having fun together, without coyness, without futility. I had to leave *Taxi Driver* before it was over. Who needs it? I don't read newspapers for the same reason. It's always the same old stories, with nothing changed but the names. They never tell you what new flowers are growing.

Interview, Los Angeles/
The New York Times, 9-3:(C)6.

John Carradine
Actor
5

Today's directors could never be as good as the ones working 30 years ago. They have no background . . . The master craftsman was John Ford, probably the greatest director I've worked with and I think I've worked with them all . . . Frank Capra was probably the greatest director for women . . . I can't say who was the worst director, but Henry Hathaway and Otto Preminger were definitely the most unpleasant. They believed they could make an actor out of fear and trembling. But I don't scare that easily. I wouldn't take it. I've worked with some holy terrors. If they don't like my work, I tell them to get another boy. No one screams at John Carradine.

Interview/"W": a Fairchild publication, 7-9:6.

John Cassavetes
Actor, Director, Writer
6

Most of my movies have not done well at the box-office. *Minnie and Moskowitz* was a delightful picture, a nice picture, but you couldn't pull people into the theatre. *Shadows* played in one theatre in the United States and I couldn't even get my best friends to see it, although for some crazy reason it is a legend on college campuses and in Europe. *Faces*, which I love, did not play in Europe, although that didn't bother me because I knew it was an American film. I really never know if a film is artistic or commercial. For instance, I thought [*A*] *Woman* [*Under the Influence*] was artistic so I took it to the New York Film Festival. They rejected it because it had no ending. I made the film and I know that, if anything, it was a series of endings. In fact, I never wanted to let go. It's not my ego, but I wanted to choke them . . . Film-making is a craft that I want to keep learning. I'm in love with it and I would make films for nothing, and do, and pay for them myself or with the help of my friends. I don't feel I have a responsibility to anyone if I'm going to take my own losses. I've lived my whole life that way and I'm really not afraid.

Interview, Los Angeles/
Los Angeles Times, 3-7:(Calender)33.

Francis Ford Coppola
Director

1

[On high salaries asked by many actors]: The problem is not really actors . . . being outrageous or greedy. It is that the studios are crippling the industry by not developing talent. Actors today are like salmon swimming upstream. If they make it, they are worth a fortune and who can blame them for asking what they can get? . . . We should go back to the old studio system of developing talent. Each studio should put up $500,000 a year into a fund to provide actors with opportunities to work in experimental theatre or workshops. But the studios are shortsighted. They want to know what they are going to get *this* year.

Los Angeles Times, 2-9:(4)10.

George Cukor
Director

2

I think style is terribly important. You do *The Women* differently than you do *Camille*; the text dictates the style. It's not a conscious thing; you don't think, well, I will do it this way or that to make the style a certain way. It just happens; it's an interpretation—the style of acting and style of presentation. You're the same person, you don't have another brain, but you adapt. I do a melodrama one way, a comedy another. That shows how wonderfully versatile I am.

Interview, Los Angeles/
The New York Times, 12-24:(C)13.

3

I wish the pictures today weren't so hopeless. I wish you could respect them more. I wish they could get you more involved emotionally. You see some pictures where you don't really care if anybody lives or dies. People must have some emotional thing to get them to attend to the picture. And I don't like all this vulgarity; these pictures may have shock value, but I don't think they're comforting.

Interview, Los Angeles/
The New York Times, 12-24:(C)13.

Bette Davis
Actress

4

. . . though they called my time the Golden Era of Hollywood, it was no more golden than it is today. It was just harder. I don't know how I did it, making all those pictures every year. For almost all my 18 years at Warners, we worked 40 weeks a year and often Saturdays. One time I was making two movies at once—one in the day and one by night. My first year at Warners I had 25 parts. But that's how I learned my profession. Back then we were more disciplined, more trained. We all came up through the theatre and somehow we loved the profession more.

Interview, Weston, Conn./
"W": a Fairchild publication, 10-15:47.

431

WHAT THEY SAID IN 1976

Dino De Laurentiis
Producer

1

This is an industry for one man. In the '30s there was Zanuck, Zukor, Goldwyn and Mayer. Now it isn't so bad and that's the trouble. It's now a conglomerate. Conglomerate? Conglomerates can't make movies.

Interview/ Los Angeles Times, 11-28:(Calendar)1.

2

I try always to make a picture for an audience. If you think a picture is for the reviewers or the [Motion Picture] Academy, you might as well quit. Critics don't mean anything at the box-office. The audience doesn't read reviews except for just a very few movies. You release a picture by Fellini or Bergman, then the critic is imporant. Only then.

Interview/ Los Angeles Times, 11-28:
(Calendar)60.

Brian De Palma
Director

3

The older [film] critics always think in terms of the Establishment—and they're always 30 years behind. They'll continue to rave about the directors they grew up loving: Visconti, Fellini, Antonioni, maybe Hitchcock, Hawks or Ford. Of course, they're all great directors. But when a young director makes a film, he's considered a tawdry imitation. All the while, the "master" is in his dotage, making half a dozen films that are pretty bad. Anyone who says that Hitchcock's last film [*Family Plot*] was a masterpiece is a fool. The man has clearly lost his sense of timing, of cinema. He's 75! You can't be a genius forever. The fact is, the big-grossing directors are the younger ones.

Interview, New York/
Los Angeles Times, 9-19:
(Calendar)31.

Kirk Douglas
Actor

4

[John] Barrymore's pathetic ending seems

to me to sum up the price one pays when he is in the public eye and doesn't know what it is he wants. Who knows what lurks inside any star—[Steve] McQueen, [Paul] Newman, [Marlon] Brando? It is a very strange life. A star lives in a world of make-believe that has to be played against the world of reality . . . It was while looking at my work that I realized that the theme to my career could be found in the very first picture that I made. I said to Barbara Stanwyck in *The Strange Love of Martha Ivers* that "it is not her fault or my fault. It is just the way things are. No one gets what one wants in life." And that is the way it is. A struggling actor looks at a star and thinks the star has it made. But the star is looking for something else.

Interview, Los Angeles/
The Dallas Times Herald, 2-8:(F)1.

Blake Edwards
Producer, Director

5

This town [Hollywood] is brutal about even one failure. They nailed [director] Stanley Donen to the cross about *Lucky Lady* . . . completely forgetting his list of hits, among them *On the Town, Funny Face, Singin' in the Rain,* and dozens of others. The same goes for [director] Peter Bogdanovich, after *At Long Last Love,* whose plusses were merely such box-office blockbusters as *Last Picture Show, What's Up, Doc?* and *Paper Moon.* It's miserably unfair. In other businesses, including sports, a man's overall record is considered. If a baseball player hits .300, he's a big man. One bad game does not unmake a quarterback. Only in this [the film] business does one failure have them barking at your heels.

Interview, Los Angeles/
Los Angeles Herald-Examiner, 9-23:(B)5.

Robert Evans
Producer

6

The producer is not a dying breed but a greedy breed today—with some exceptions. You can't just go by dollars and cents when you produce a film. It takes a lot of heart. But too many producers today are dealers, promoters and entrepreneurs. They don't live through the picture.

At San Francisco Film Festival, Oct. 17/
Daily Variety, 10-19:6.

Douglas Fairbanks, Jr.
Actor
1

[Recalling the early, "big studio" days in Hollywood]: I found life here dreary, frustrating, dull, boring and only occasionally fun, as it can be fun on some special day even in a Siberian prison. It was not a fairy-land or Baghdad or Xanadu . . . News was fed out by well-organized publicity departments and the movie magazines that lived by the trash of the studios. And the public received it all . . . The talk of Hollywood as having been a Babylon—none of that was true. Wild parties? Well, they have them in Dubuque, Iowa, too. This wasn't the place for a Babylon. You didn't have the people for it and you didn't have the time.

Interview, Los Angeles/
Los Angeles Herald-Examiner, 3-24:(C)14.

Peter Falk
Actor
2

[On director Ingmar Bergman]: Guys like that are the real thing. They don't get up every morning to find out the latest best-seller. They have their own demons, and they make movies about them.

People, 8-9:22.

Federico Fellini
Director
3

To be a director gives you a sense of power, of fantasy, even if you have doubts. The possibility to create is in itself regenerating. I don't think God was unhappy when he was creating all the things he is said to have done. I am not talking about the result

but the operation. You are invaded by something else. I think I am lucky to be in movies.

Interview, Rome/
Los Angeles Times, 4-18:(Calendar)30.

James Ferman
Secretary,
British Board of Film Censors
4

I am not a guardian of public morals, but I am strongly against sadism and sex-ploitation in the movies. I can conceive of no society that would not place some limits on what is permissible on the screen . . . These terrible little [sexploitation] films have a place on the periphery; they can be a safety valve for the many people with sexual hang-ups. But I think they are now threatening to take over completely . . . I believe our society is not as permissive as we are led to believe. Most people in this country still value family life and the old morality. I think someone has the duty to say, "This far and no further." We have come very far, very fast. A pause for thought now would do no harm.

Interview, London/
Los Angeles Times, 1-2:(4)15.

Peter Finch
Actor
5

I simply won't play in an overtly violent film, because it makes me personally sick . . . And the excuse isn't good enough when producers and directors say they put it in movies because it exists. I personally don't want to go to the abattoirs for an afternoon's entertainment . . . Explicit sex I'm not asked to do, but I don't think I would . . . The ultimate pornography is violence, though . . . And there are racist pictures which pretend not to be . . . I stand quite firm on not contributing to this sort of thing. I've been lucky enough to be able to say no, because I have enough bread for my children. And even if I didn't, there are other things to do—radio or something . . . Nearly all artists worthy

(PETER FINCH)

of the name feel like this. Some say, oh, they can't stem the tide alone; but these are the same who failed to stem the tide of Hitler.

Interview, New York/
The Christian Science Monitor, 12-10:35.

Jane Fonda
Actress

1

[On the dearth of good women's roles in films today]: It's not just rhetoric. It's true. The only explanation is that the women's movement has made such a tremendous impact that it has become more difficult to use certain female stereotypes. The male ones persist—the cowboy, the cop—but the glamour girl or the kind of characters I played before wouldn't hold up. The old female roles have been done away with, but the financiers of movies—those men who run the multinational corporations—can't figure out which new female stereotypes are bankable. The realities that confront most women haven't been proven [to appeal] at the box-office, whether it's two female friends, or a woman out looking for a job.

Interview, London/
The New York Times, 10-31:(2)17.

Joan Fontaine
Actress

2

I stand fast. That's why I haven't done movies and TV for so long. I have standards and I refuse to tear them down and be seen on the screen any other way. I am offered parts as a dipsomaniac, nymphomaniac, you name the maniac and it has been offered to me. I won't do them; I don't have to prove myself to anybody or prove to myself that I can act those parts. I think audiences are being cheated. There are so few straight people writing scenarios today that all the women seem to come out as hideous creatures. The romantic male-female thing is gone. Love and devotion are gone . . . It's not that I want to see merely a return of

gracious living. I'm more concerned about a return to ethics.

Los Angeles Herald-Examiner, 6-22:(B)1.

Betty Ford
Wife of President
of the United States Gerald R. Ford

3

When I was a girl in high school I never dreamed about growing up and being married to a President. In fact, in those days, like most school girls, my hopes were of going to Hollywood and perhaps having the opportunity to glide across a highly glossed floor with Fred Astaire . . . And, because of the magic of movies, I've danced and laughed and cried my way through several lifetimes . . . Like millions of people, the President and I love the movies. Movies light candles of the imagination; they enrich our dreams and expand our understanding. May we always be a land that loves make-believe and story-tellers . . .

At American Film Institute
salute to William Wyler, Los Angeles, March 9/
Los Angeles Herald-Examiner, 3-11:(B)1.

Milos Forman
Czech director

4

The American cinema doesn't work in waves. It has a steady lack of massive masterpieces, but every year something great comes out that is exciting to see. With exceptions, most other countries are flooded with cheap products and flirting with pornography for the bourgeoisie. If any country is at the top of interesting film-making today, it is the U.S.

Interview, New York/
The Christian Science Monitor, 4-1:26.

James Franciscus
Actor

5

An actor can talk about the joy of being a link in the chain of communication, the pleasure of being involved in the creative process. But it's basically a selfish experience. An actor is given a chance to live out all his fantasies. Beneath the makeup of every serious actor there's a little boy running around playing cowboys and Indians, getting paid for what is essentially fun and games. There's still another irony. The audience applauds the actor, but it should be the other way around. The audience has tolerated him while he works out his fantasies . . . and afterward the actor should applaud the audience, by way of saying thanks.

Interview/ Los Angeles Times, 2-1:(Home)25.

William Friedkin
Director
1

. . . I don't find many movies that give me the feeling I used to have when I was 12, of being carried away by the events on the screen . . . The simple premise of D. W. Griffith was that you introduce a character or a group of characters to the audience, make them sympathetic and identifiable and then get them into trouble. The people in my films respond to life with basic solutions, not subtle or high-blown solutions . . . I'd never make a nihilist film. I'd never make a film saying life is rotten. Mysterious, strange, touched with corruption, maybe, but ultimately worth living and experiencing on even the most dangerous levels . . . It's still a three-act world. Life may not have third acts, but drama better.

Interview/ Los Angeles Times, 4-2:(4)1.

Giancarlo Giannini
Actor
2

I consider myself the type of guy who is much less interesting than the characters I portray. That's why the characters are so different from one another. That's why I play such fanciful characters. I know there are many actors who try to portray themselves. But I feel it's much more fun to be able to portray others than to know oneself intimately. It would be almost im-

possible to portray myself in front of a camera.

Interview, New York/
The Christian Science Monitor, 5-24:30.

Lew Grade
Producer
3

I'm a great believer in stars. If I want them, I don't care what I pay for them. If you think about actors who've become stars, they're there because of past performances. So what you're paying for are expert performances. I wouldn't pay for cameos . . . I don't see the sense in that. But I'll always pay for star performances. I'm a visualizer, remember; not a creator. People bring me an idea. I say yes or no. Then, when I read the script, I straightaway visualize someone in the role. After that, it's just a question of going out and getting him.

Interview, London/
Los Angeles Times, 7-18:(Calendar)34.

Joel Grey
Actor, Entertainer
4

[Comparing performing on the stage and in films]: In the theatre, one has the individual moments and nights which stick to your bones and that's it. In films, however, there is a record, a permanent record, and you better be good.

Interview, Beverly Hills, Calif./
Los Angeles Times, 7-12:(4)11.

Dave Grusin
Composer, Conductor
5

[On music for motion pictures]: Music as an art form has nothing to do with film as an art form. When they work together, it's an accident. Music has to be, and should be, sublimated for the benefit of the film. I find, more and more, there's too much music in American films. The tendency is for American film-makers to let music try to save certain areas, especially problem

435

(DAVE GRUSIN)

areas, of a film. With records, music is primary; with film, it's secondary.

Interview, New York/
Variety, 4-28:61.

Joan Hackett
Actress
1

To be an actor and a film actor are two totally different things. I heard someone say, "If you can get her, great; but God protect me because she'll kill me on the screen." That means, if you're pretty, maybe you shouldn't act too good in films, for the guys who are hiring their leading ladies. It means better to walk with a limp.

Interview, Los Angeles/
Los Angeles Times, 7-11:(Calendar)35.

Anthony Harvey
Director
2

Films [today] have a preoccupation with the agonies of life, and one often comes out feeling desperate from films. It's harder to make films about hope instead of despair.

Interview, Los Angeles/Daily Variety, 9-1:3.

Goldie Hawn
Actress
3

There are different kinds of films—message films and films for fun. I did [*The*] *Duchess* [*and the Dirtwater Fox*] because it was pure comedy, entertainment, laughs. It was important for me to do something like this, for my career. But it's also important for people to feel that this kind of movie is still alive. There are terribly depressing films around now. We're in a terribly depressed situation, and it's important that the people who have the gift to make people feel good should *do* that. There are only a handful of us.

Interview, New York/
The Christian Science Monitor, 7-21:22.

Edith Head
Motion-picture fashion designer
4

Secretly I envy conventional dress designers, because they bring out a new line of clothes once a year or so, and it seems like a leisurely pace to me. You see, every time I receive a new script, it's a new season. Many years I've worked on 20 or 30 films. That's an incredible number of seasons to pack into a 12-month span. But my envy is just fleeting fancy. I have no serious complaint. I really wouldn't trade my career for anybody's. The wonderful part of my work *is* the constant need for creativity. There's no routine about it. I never do the same project twice. Every script, every actor, every director presents a new challenge, a different language to learn, perhaps a baffling problem to solve. I go into battle each time, asking myself: Is this going to be a good one or not? I'm inclined to be optimistic about the outcome, but the total experience is like watching a film by my good friend Alfred Hitchcock. The dominant emotion for me, all the way through, is one of suspense.

Interview, Los Angeles/
Los Angeles Times, 7-18:(Home)17.

Sherman Hemsley
Actor
5

Acting is using all those feelings you've had in life and channeling them into the characters you play. Anger, sympathy, hate, love, inferiority, superiority—it's all there inside you, and you have to pluck out what you need and project it to an audience.

Interview, Los Angeles/
San Francisco Examiner & Chronicle, 7-11:
(Datebook)34.

Katharine Hepburn
Actress
6

. . . don't you think acting is something either you can do, or not do? It's sort of a knack. It's a quirk. [At first] I didn't know what the hell I was doing. I'm not sure I do now. I enjoy it, but I don't take myself as seriously as I would if I were a really good painter or writer. I think it's a charming talent, but it's not like a singer. What you can do, you take for granted. It's all involved in selling yourself. "Here I am. Look at me. I'm fascinating." I think that's embarrassing. I know exactly how fascinating I am and how fascinating I *amn't*. It's exhausting being fascinating.

Interview, New York/
The New York Times, 1-16:27.

1

G-rated? I don't know what that means. If it means that this picture [that she is making now] can be seen by the entire family, that is true. It's about time that someone made pictures that can be. One is in danger of becoming an old crab, of being accused of belonging to a past generation. But I must express my utter distaste for the kind of films that are being made today. Couples rolling around in the dirt, simulating sex; buildings burning; fake sharks gobbling up people. This is considered "fun fare." "Ain't it a scream!" they say. Well, it's not a scream. It's boring, simply boring. Abnormal freaks are a bore to me.

Interview/
The Dallas Times Herald, 9-16:(C)1.

2

I thought *Jaws* was asinine. It could have been so much better. I call movies like *Jaws* and *The Exorcist* the "Boo Series"—someone jumps around the corner and yells "Boo!" I'm amazed grown-up people love the Boo Series so much, but they do. That's why these remakes of *King Kong* will be enormous successes. Dear, dear, *dear*. Is this all we have to write about? *God!*

Interview, New York/ People, 10-11:64.

Charlton Heston
Actor

3

I've worked for women directors on stage, but never in a film. I think it would be much harder for a woman to direct a movie. A mov-

ie director has to be a captain. That is not a woman's role.

Interview, Dallas/
The Dallas Times Herald, 4-26:(D)7.

Alfred Hitchcock
Director

4

Suspense is the key. I would never make a who-done-it. That doesn't interest me. It is seeing exactly what happens, and then anticipating what will happen next, which intrigues an audience.

Interview, Los Angeles/
Los Angeles Herald-Examiner, 3-21:(B)1.

5

I made it a point over the years to put the film on paper in advance. I certainly don't improvise with all those electricians and workers waiting there. I prefer improvising in my office. Architects put a building on paper and don't improvise at the site; composers don't go out in front of an orchestra with a half-finished musical score, asking for a flute player to sound an interesting note they'd like to play with and write down. They all write it out in advance. Why can't this be done with a film?

Interview, Los Angeles/
The Dallas Times Herald, 3-25:(C)8.

6

My appearances in my films are as brief as possible because I can't stand the indignity of being an actor any longer than I can help it.

Interview/"The Merv Griffin Show,"
Metromedia Television, 4-8.

Dustin Hoffman
Actor

7

I'd rather have a critic dump me than praise me. When a critic says a movie is great, he's just building up the importance of his job. Critics do to movies what plant lovers do to plants. They water them until they die. It's called assassination by adoration. Why we take these people seriously I can't imagine. If you were looking for a baby to adopt, would you adopt the child of [critics] Paulene Kael and John Simon?

People, 5-3:56.

WHAT THEY SAID IN 1976

William Holden
Actor

1

I care about the movies. But you have to look at movies two ways. It's an art business and a business art. The art business is making film and accomplishing something by it, creating. The other is that it helps you to realize necessities. You get involved in artistic endeavors you don't like because the money from them makes [other] artistic endeavors possible.

Interview, Los Angeles/
Los Angeles Herald-Examiner, 11-3:(B)1.

2

For me, acting is not an all-consuming thing, except for the moment when I am actually doing it. There is a point beyond acting, a point where *living* becomes important. When you're making a movie, you get up in the morning and put on a cloak; you create emotions within yourself, send gastric juices rushing up against the lining of your stomach. It has to be manufactured.

Interview, New York/
The New York Times, 11-12:(C)6.

Anthony Hopkins
British actor

3

There's a tendency in England to walk on stage and make beautiful sounds. English actors trained in the [Royal] Academy are dependent on external technique. They study speech, voice, movement and fencing. Americans are more internally oriented. They're more dependent on heart, less on voice and speech. I prefer the texture of this country [the U.S.]. You don't get that "My Lord, off to the Tower with her." You get the realistic type of acting here. It's marvelous.

Interview/
Los Angeles Herald-Examiner, 2-22:
(TV Weekly)5.

Tab Hunter
Actor

4

Hollywood has a tendency to drain and discard people, like TV. It uses up people. Luck

plays a very important part in everything out there. I think if you like people, you like people. You don't put them in categories. Out there everything reminds me of the Tennessee Williams play I was in on Broadway, *The Milk Train Doesn't Stop Here Any More,* where they hung bells around the necks of lepers to tell them apart from the rest. In California they categorize you immediately. It's so plastic. They just care if you're groovy or "with it" . . . When you've been a product of Hollywood and been subjected to as much crap as I have, it's not conducive to your own development . . . It's see-through plastic of the worst kind.

Interview, Middleburg, Va./
The Washington Post, 5-27:(C)1.

John Huston
Director

5

When I cast a picture, I do most of my directing right there in finding the right person. I use actors with strong personalities, ones who are like the characters they play. Take Laurence Olivier—he's probably the greatest of all, and he can assume any role and take on any shape. It's a marvel, really, but that's a kind of virtuosity that does not serve my purposes, much as I admire its art. I'd rather get the real article.

Interview,
Puerto Vallarta, Mexico/
The New York Times, 2-15:(2)15.

Glenda Jackson
Actress

6

We have a lot of good writers today, but not one of them can write about women. They can't seem to realize that they themselves are not God's gift to the world, that women are capable of energizing anything, except maybe putting a spoke in the man's wheel. Either we are the sex object or the sex goddess, the mother or the whore.

Interview/
Los Angeles Herald-Examiner, 11-11:(B)1.

1

. . . eventually I discovered that not depending on the external look of me was a plus; it freed me to get on with my work. You see, having to always protect a face rather excludes you from life, doesn't it? It really must have been a terrific strain when acting was all looks-oriented for women. Yet, there is still that hangover in our business that says women are what they look, not what they are.

Interview, New York/
"W": a Fairchild publication, 11-26:12.

2

[On "Oscars" and other awards]: I don't think you can elevate art by awarding, and you certainly can't elevate acting . . . It's not like a race where you know who's fastest because he's the first one past the finish line . . . Awards are nice pats on the back, that's all.

Interview, New York/
The Christian Science Monitor, 11-29:35.

Dean Jones
Actor

3

I'm often asked why I'm willing to settle for so little as an actor, meaning the Disney films, I guess. Well, I've never felt that way. I don't think anyone should ever underestimate the importance of making people laugh —no matter what the medium. The more seriously an actor can play a comic movie situation the funnier it becomes. It takes concentration and timing—also facial expressions that often have to convey a feeling that words can't. But when this is done properly it can light up an audience and make it laugh . . . I won't do anything violent or play any part that I think is degrading to the human race. I feel too many actors excuse too many objectionable movie scenes on the basis that it was the director's fault and that they were only following orders. I still think a man is morally responsible for his actions—on and off the screen.

Interview, Tarzana, Calif./
The Christian Science Monitor, 4-2:19.

Pauline Kael
Film critic, "The New Yorker" magazine

4

The Supreme Court ruling on pornogra-

phy, throwing things back to the communities, really wrecked the possibility for Americans to continue in the direction Bernardo Bertolucci opened up in *Last Tango in Paris.* Because of the decision, the big studios won't finance anything now that deals with eroticism on any serious level. Whereas the porno film-makers aren't scared of anything. If they close in one town, they move to the next or chop out a few scenes and change the name of the movie. Artists are hamstrung. Cities are flooded with porno movies, but there is no serious treatment of the relationship between the sexes on screen and it is something we all want. The only people who don't want it are the people who don't go to the movies.

At Los Angeles Film Exposition, April 3/
Los Angeles Times, 4-5:(4)12.

Fay Kanin
Screenwriter

5

. . . it's not so much the films that are made, it's the ones that *aren't* made. My disappointment today is that our parameters are narrowing and that we're making films within such certain limits, films that have "hype" in them, that are melodramatic, or violent. Well, that is an aspect of life here, abroad, everywhere. But there's more; there has to be room for more. I hate that we have all become bonanza-makers.

Panel discussion/
Holiday Inn Companion, Jan.-Feb.:16.

George Kennedy
Actor

6

. . . I have very little patience with performers who keep questioning the director, asking, "What's my motivation here? How was my life influenced and shaped up to the moment the audience first sees me on the screen? Is each of my actions explainable by something that happened before?" Acting should not be that complicated. Spencer Tracy said it better than anyone: "Just learn the lines and don't bump into the furniture." That's what acting is all about. I would add one brief note to it:

439

WHAT THEY SAID IN 1976

(GEORGE KENNEDY)

Actors should not confuse their on-screen roles with their off-screen lives.

Interview, Los Angeles/
Los Angeles Times, 4-25:(Home)70.

Irvin Kershner
Director
1

Film is and always has been poor propaganda. Individual films don't do a thing to change people's minds about anything. I did documentaries for years. But films work best when they're emotional, when they move your emotions. I don't think you can teach much with films, but you can get people to see things they haven't seen, to see in a different perspective, and make them feel things—or feel about things—that they have never felt about.

Interview, Mexico City/
The Christian Science Monitor, 8-19:17.

Cloris Leachman
Actress
2

So often actors are compared to children. It is because they both react to freedom. The child needs his freedom to play and the actor needs that freedom to explore. That is the lone valid comparison of actor to child.

Interview, Houston/
The Dallas Times Herald, 6-6:(E)5.

Jack Lemmon
Actor
3

[Directing a film] will make you a better actor because it makes you concentrate more on the whole, rather than just your own part in it . . . As an actor grows, he begins to think more and more like a director . . . The really fine performances are simple . . . and you can be terribly distracted when performers don't do that because they've got a "great moment" going . . . It may be fine acting but wrong acting.

Interview/
The Christian Science Monitor, 3-4:26.

4

We have a lot of crazy people in this business. You have to be a little nuts to be an actor. By nuts, I mean you have to have experienced trauma in your life, tragedy, if you're going to be able to step into a role and portray tragic emotions. Some people think that *all* actors are crazy, and I know that some are—emotionally and psychologically screwed up. But the majority are not that total. We're all kind of crazy—but think of how crazy we'd be if we weren't actors. Crazy, maybe—but not dumb. No good actor is dumb. You've got to interpret emotions. No good actor can be told by a director what to do, and then merely turn it on. It has to come from inside, from a life which has let the actor know trauma.

Interview, Columbia, Calif./
San Francisco Examiner & Chronicle, 8-22:
(Datebook)13.

5

Comedy is more difficult [than drama], I think, because there is no gray area. An audience knows when something is supposed to be funny, and if it doesn't work it lies there like an omelet. In drama, you have to hold interest; in comedy, if you don't get the laugh, it's right out the window. Believe it or not, comedy is deadly serious. The minute you play comedy without being serious—forget it.

Interview, Los Angeles/
The Hollywood Reporter, 10-27:15.

Sergio Leone
Italian director
6

The Western, in my opinion, is an extraordinary vehicle for a message. Because of the enormous audience it reaches it belongs not just to America but to the entire world. You can put into a Western anything you want because it's a formidable vehicle . . . The Western has been stripped of national boundaries. When I made *A Fistful of Dollars* I was reminded of the Italian *comedia dell 'arte.* The great themes are classical. For me, Homer was the best writer of Westerns ever.

Interview, Rome/
San Francisco Examiner & Chronicle, 2-29:
(Datebook)21.

1

I think a director must be very flexible with actors. With the Americans, for example, there are no problems because they're extremely competent and they understand what the director wants. Nevertheless, you can't give any actor a chance to argue. When I direct, I'm a real despot. I have my ideas, and the actors must be content with me.

Interview, Rome/
San Francisco Examiner & Chronicle, 2-29:
(Datebook)21.

Mervyn LeRoy
Director
2

[Today] we have a few good directors, a few good writers, but not enough. You know, there's nothing easier than writing a filthy story; but try to come up with a *Waterloo Bridge*, a *Best Years of Our Lives*. Pornos make money, but I'd be ashamed to take it. Also, there's a small group of artsy-craftsy New York critics that seem to equate bafflement with art . . . We need pictures with warmth, "heart," if you will. The audience is there, but they want something to root for.

Interview/
Los Angeles Herald-Examiner, 3-27:(A)15.

Joseph E. Levine
Producer
3

Any commodity has to be sold. And films are no exception. Get the picture into as many theatres as possible in as short a time as possible and spend as much money as possible advertising it. That's my method . . . This is a circus business and I never forget it. You've got to let the public know. At one of those exhibitors luncheons I gave some years ago, I showed them 1,000 $1,000 bills. A million bucks. We used 24 bank guards to deliver them. "Next time you see this money," I told the people there, "it'll be in newspapers, on television and on the hoardings." That's the way to sell a film.

Interview, Deventer, Netherlands/
Los Angeles Times, 9-19:(Calendar)35.

Shirley MacLaine
Actress
4

[On finding good women's roles in films today]: It's practically impossible. Robert Redford and Paul Newman. Michael Caine and Sean Connery. Warren Beatty and Jack Nicholson. I think they'd rather play with each other than play with us . . . The only women that the movie-makers in Hollywood know are housewives and hookers. Out of my 37 roles, 14 were hookers. Hollywood must realize that portraying *real* women would be a commercial success.

Interview/People, 5-10:27.

5

Films are tied up with the moral tone set by a government; and when you have a government as corrupt as our last one [in the U.S.], the artist must assume the responsibility for telling the truth. Films can help eliminate the double vision the American public has of our country, our values, our future; they can contribute a clarified vision, a moral perception of our social problems.

The New York Times, 9-3:(C)6.

Louis Malle
Director
6

My role is that of a troublemaker. I want to wake people up, to make them worry, to rethink their values. So many people are sleeping a lot these days. They have been so completely brainwashed by television, by advertising and by their daily routine. For me, the ideal spectator is a prolongation of myself. He, too, must draw his own conclusions. I want him to do some homework. My films are not TV dinners.

Interview, New York/
The New York Times, 11-19:(C)6.

Being a director is like being a thief. You steal bits and pieces of the lives around you, and you put them into a movie.

Interview, New York/
The New York Times, 11-19:(C)6.

Rouben Mamoulian
Director
1

A lot of films that are obsessed by sex in its most mechanical and coarse manifestations, and violence at its worst, have been made while the world has been making incredible strides scientifically. We are walking on the moon, sending a vehicle to Mars. But spiritually and morally we have retrograded atavistically to the time when we used to live in the trees. After millions of years, homo sapiens have discovered sex and murder, blood and violence. It's a sad, bad situation, this appeal to sensationalism. The hopeful sign is that we have lost a great deal of our audience. Now, coming from me, the remark about losing audience being hopeful sounds strange. It's hopeful because 10 or 12 years ago, in this country alone, 90 million people saw films every week. Today the audience is only 17 million. That's an enormous loss. The film industry, because of its complexity and costliness, is subject to the law of supply and demand. When people stop buying tickets to the cheap, sensational films that are made just to make money, such films will no longer pollute our culture.

Interview/
Los Angeles Herald-Examiner, 8-30:(B)3.

Marcello Mastroianni
Actor
2

It is difficult to measure up to images. That's why it is easier for an actor to have a relationship with an actress than [with] a non-actress. Actresses understand the problem. You don't have to perform for an audience. An actress knows that, beneath the image, actors are no different than others. With an actress, you don't have to play a role. Remember, too, that actresses are usually beautiful. And beauty is a miracle. It is exciting to discover that an actress is not really like her publicity, to find the real person there—gentle, intelligent, fragile. This can be an exciting discovery. And nobody knows, just you. Her real personality is a big secret, except to you.

Rome/ Los Angeles Times, 5-30:(Calendar)38.

Paul Mazursky
Producer, Director, Writer
3

You can't complain about a system that gives you absolutely complete creative freedom to make a film with no stars and with actors the studio didn't even see [such as his latest film, *Next Stop, Greenwich Village*]. Somebody backed *Dog Day Afternoon*, which was not a sure-thing property with or without [Al] Pacino. And somebody backed *Nashville*, a film with two dozen people in it instead of a star, and with an unconventional structure. Still, I'm concerned about the system, because the risks keep getting greater all the time, and so does the tendency in the studios to work with what seem to be very commercial ingredients. They're afraid of the word "sensitive." The greatest problem is what do you do about violence, because violence makes money almost every time. The executives may hate violence, but they're stuck with it, at least until something else makes money.

Interview/ Los Angeles Times, 2-27:(4)1.

Darren McGavin
Actor
4

Being an actor doesn't require a hell of a lot of brains. Acting doesn't require intelligence. Talent and intelligence aren't necessarily equated. Intelligence can get in the way of talent. If you have intelligence, it's hard to bear some of the terrible things you're in as an actor. You'd like to go out and shoot yourself. You'd like to walk off the set. You'd like to go ape. Besides, nobody wants an intelligent actor. Say the words, hit the mark and get in front of the camera—that's what they want [from an actor].

Interview/
Los Angeles Herald-Examiner, 4-28:(B)4.

Ray Milland
Actor

1

There are no more [movie] tycoons. A tycoon in the old days was more like the Czar of all the Russias. When Louis B. Mayer walked into a room, the place would hush. [Today, Sam] Spiegel walks in and people shout, "Hi ya, Sam, how 'ya doin'?" A tycoon was a man with a private train, and they don't even have trains any more.

Interview, Los Angeles/
"W": a Fairchild publication, 1-23:9.

Jeanne Moreau
Actress

2

. . . the movie industry is as important to the U.S. as building cars. It's really the American art, the dream machine. Life goes to cinema and cinema goes to life—the preoccupation and the reality.

Interview, Los Angeles/
"W": a Fairchild publication, 1-23:9.

3

I've never tried to pretend. Most people feel acting is pretending, but for me it is not that. It is to feel to the core of your body and mind so you can express yourself, open yourself up and be truer than life. Nobody's going to spend a lot of time watching someone who's untrue.

Interview, Washington/
The Washington Post, 6-25:(B)3.

Michael Moriarty
Actor

4

For an actor . . . what is so important is getting involved with good people for whom you feel some affinity. It's so important to feel this . . . chemistry, so that you are willing to take greater risks with the material and with yourself. In film, especially, it's so important to have a director you trust because you're so much in his hands. An actor and a director can have a deeply creative relationship—if the trust is there, if the

chemistry is right. That's just it, you see; there are a lot of wonderful people I'd like to work with but never will just because I don't feel this. When you come together to do a production, it's a marriage—a brief marriage, but a marriage nevertheless.

Interview, Washington/
The National Observer, 2-14:18.

Paul Newman
Actor

5

To make the perfect movie I would get together with [director] Robert Altman and work out an idea about communication. We would hire the people we would want— with no thought given to their box-office potential. We would sit down with the script writer, rehearse and get the crew together. The day before we were to start shooting we would shut down the project and go our separate ways, since it wouldn't be necessary to photograph the movie. The artistic satisfaction would be in the creating of it. Everything else is unnecessary and repetitious. If creating is the true artistic experience, then the audience's reaction is only the redundancy.

Interview, New York/
The Dallas Times Herald, 6-27:(D)4.

Jack Nicholson
Actor

6

[On spontaneity]: When you're working, you don't want to "act" if you don't have to. It can be interpreted a million ways by the people that see it, but ultimately the camera photographs exactly what's there. That goes for a vase or an emotion . . . The more integrated this is, the more depth you have in the character, the more levels of reality that he's functioning on at once, the more lifelike it is. It's as simple as this: If you're playing a scene that involves escaping from a fire . . . you must find ways of surprising yourself into momentarily believing that there is something like a fire there . . . You tap whatever feelings you actually have about fire, that you share in common with

(JACK NICHOLSON)

most people. The character's expression is then shaped through his particular characteristics, which also have to be created . . . You should work in the interrogative mood all the time. You should be asking questions of the character, not making statements as the character. These are things which, experience seems to have shown us, dredged the subconscious.

Interview, New York/
Los Angeles Herald-Examiner, 4-12:(B)4.

David Niven
Actor
1

[On the great studio moguls in the early days of motion pictures]: They came mostly from the ghettoes of central Europe, from the most horrendous backgrounds. They came to this country and were given sanctuary; and my theory is that—when they built their dream factory—they made movies about a country that they saw through rose-colored lenses. They were not all that lovable, and their blacklists and that sort of thing were despicable. But they were great showmen, and millions of people per week bought tickets to their movies. They saw only the great good things, and their movies mirrored that. When the Depression came, they pressed on, making nonsensical things that had nothing to do with reality—but they were great, in a way, because they took people's minds off the awful horror that was going on. And I think that's happening again now. That's why the movies are booming again. When there are unattractive disasters going on in the world, depressions and things, people go to the movies . . . It's strange.

Interview, New York/
The Christian Science Monitor, 6-10:27.

Kathleen Nolan
Actress; President, Screen Actors Guild
2

Congressmen and the public in general think of actors in terms of one night of the

year—the Academy Awards, when we all appear in our rented tuxedos and rented evening gowns, arriving in our rented limousines. The fact is that less than 1 per cent of our members earn more than $100,000 a year. The guild has 85 per cent unemployment, and the earnings of 77.7 per cent are below the poverty level.

Interview, Los Angeles/
The Dallas Times Herald, 2-15:(F)4.

Al Pacino
Actor
3

The type of film I like to make is more energetic, socio-political. I like to play character roles. I try as much as I can to be different. You don't have time to build a character in a film, so I try to find a metaphor; even if I can have this illusion, it propels me . . . Theatre is so much more creative for me. Movie life is too fragmented, too mechanical. The result is that it's very difficult to find a momentum.

Interview, Leukerbad, Switzerland/
"W": a Fairchild publication, 8-6:14.

Jack Palance
Actor
4

Frankly, I'm tired of acting. I think a lot of actors are. Why? Well, I think some of us would just like to go out and wander through the hills for a while. Acting is not what most people think it is. It's been romanticized.

Interview/The Dallas Times Herald, 2-13:(E)9.

Gregory Peck
Actor
5

The audience . . . looks for recognizable personalities. The best acting is when the audience recognizes the [actor]. But it is very dangerous. The actor must be honest and interesting. The audience wants to see how this fellow they know will go about facing life and death. It is much easier for an actor to put on a Scottish accent and a putty nose than it is to play himself.

Interview, Dallas, June 14/
The Dallas Times Herald, 6-15:(C)1.

444

Arthur Penn
Director
1

[Films are] financially rather healthy, but they've nearly lost whatever boldness and individuality they had a few years back, and I think that's a grave loss . . . There's a degree of caution in the air that's unproductive. Caution is not the way art gets made.

Interview/ The Christian Science Monitor, 5-27:26.

David V. Picker
Vice chairman, and president of the feature-film division, Paramount Pictures Corporation
2

[The film business is] not as much fun any more because people don't trust each other any more. [Some years ago at United Artists,] we used to have a picture in release before anything was signed. Today I won't believe anybody until I get it in writing. It's terribly sad. We've lost sight of the fact that we have a goal. We spend 95 per cent of our time without seeing that goal. When I got to Paramount in January, the first thing I did was settle six lawsuits, all brought because nobody trusted each other. That's not what the movie business is about. We all sit back and try to stop the other guy from doing something or to keep from getting screwed by somebody. We're an industry bonded together by mistrust and held together by greed.

At entertainment-law symposium, University of California, Los Angeles, Nov. 6/ Daily Variety, 11-8:11.

Roman Polanski
Director
3

This is the most important thing in film-making: When you set your story somewhere, it has to happen *there*—very French if it happens in France, very Polish in Poland. If you set it in Transylvania you must be sure it's very Transylvanian. You *must* establish where it happened. If the setting is a land of fantasy, you have to know every-

thing about that land. You have to know the life of the imaginary place and then conform to the rules. The more lies you tell, the more you have to pretend they are true. That's where a lot of movies fail: You feel all the details are wrong; you just aren't convinced.

Interview, Paris/ The New York Times, 2-22:(2)15.

4

. . . I think great literature is unfilmable because it's real value lies in the way it's written and not what it's about. Faulkner, for example, is a great writer, but there has never been a good film made out of any of his novels. That doesn't mean it can't be done, just that it's impossible to render the real value of literature through a camera. Assuming you have no inhibitions about the masterpiece, how do you render in images what has been achieved by words? You are forced to be pictorially literal, or to use parts of the book as a commentary or as internal dialogue. But that's not the way. The most perfect writing is poetry, but how can you translate a poem by Baudelaire into film? All you can do is show the story of the poem, and that's not it at all.

Interview, Paris/ The New York Times, 2-22:(2)15.

5

To me, cinema, and any form of art, is entertainment first. Of course you express ideas, but first you entertain. Or else you should be writing philosophical tracts. Everyone seems so convinced now that, when you create something artistic, you must pledge part of your soul to every film you make. I think the best you can do now is to give people entertainment and a few hours of joy. In this moment, when everyone is so convinced of his rightness, the best thing is just to give them some relief.

Interview/ The Washington Post, 6-11:(B)13.

WHAT THEY SAID IN 1976

(ROMAN POLANSKI)

1

. . . I don't read reviews. There is little I can learn from them, and I find that the critics are becoming more and more insulting. That is something new and disturbing. Reviewers have become personal in their comments, and they seem more interested in puns, alliteration and jokes than in informing their readers about a film's merits.

Los Angeles Herald-Examiner, 7-7:(B)7.

Sydney Pollack
Director

2

The new Hollywood will be less flamboyant, perhaps less spectacular than in the past, but more real. But so much has changed during the last 10 years, especially the taste of the public. In the past, people went to the movies to see something diametrically opposed to their everyday existence. Now they want the exact replica of reality. And the difference is entirely in this opposition. It is not because romance has been buried. Far from it. There will always be love stories, but the 1976 movie-goer is much more of a realist.

Interview, Brussels/
The Hollywood Reporter, 2-5:16.

Robert Radnitz
Producer

3

Movies are not only an entertainment medium, they're an educational medium. And these don't have to be divergent qualities. I don't mean I'm setting out to crusade in every movie. But at the end of every film, people will hopefully see that—although the characters may be different than they are—there's a common thread of humanity that runs through all of us. I feel that about everything I've done.

Interview, New York/
The Christian Science Monitor, 5-14:26.

Oliver Reed
Actor

4

I don't like intellectual films too much . . . Political things don't interest me much because they're always on TV and in the newspapers and magazines, and it's constantly affecting our lives . . . I much prefer to see the sorts of films that I make—pure entertainment. It used to be *a la mode* to watch movies about wives with their hair in curlers ironing knickers, and the husband coming home and beating her up and screaming about the children, and the children running away. But I think there's too much of that in our own lives . . . Movies are becoming more and more an escapist medium.

Interview, Oakland, Calif./
The Christian Science Monitor, 10-13:35.

Alain Resnais
Director

5

I don't like doing adaptations. I prefer working from original scripts, specifically written for the cinema. But it's very difficult to find an author who will write a script without being sure that the film will be made. When I ask someone if he wants to make a film with me, the answer is usually yes. But at that moment he is doing something else and can only work on the script on weekends or a couple of days a week. So to get a film ready takes about a year or more. Several times, I've tried to start off three scriptwriters on different scripts at the same time, but I could only use them when they were free. So it takes a lot of time. By the time the scripts can be shown to a producer, the budget has become too inflated and the film is not made. So one can easily finish up with two projects, each taking a year of work, and each of which comes to nothing because no one can raise the money. In short, it is not a matter of choice. On the contrary, I find it very difficult to make a living with so few films. It's one of the problems of my life.

Interview, Paris/
The New York Times, 10-10:(2)17.

1

When I make a film, I always feel I am a bit like an archeologist who finds a block of stone and earth in the desert and in this block there is a statue. So with great care he tries to clear away the earth in order to make the statue appear. But he doesn't really know in advance what is going to be there. The whole thing is to know precisely when to stop chipping away, so that you don't end up by breaking a leg, or a nose, or the statue itself.

Interview, Paris/
The New York Times, 10-10:(2)18.

Burt Reynolds
Actor

2

[On his becoming a director]: . . . my ego doesn't need stretching any more. I could walk away from the adulation I get as an actor and never miss it. I'd much rather be a chess player than a chess pawn. Besides, there are a lot of good actors coming along to take my place on the top 10. What we need are good directors. Most of the young directors I've met only want to sit around and discuss, "Do you work from the inside out, or from the outside in?" Which is intellectual bull. They don't know even know where to put the camera.

The New York Times, 8-27:(C)6.

Cliff Robertson
Actor

3

These newfangled superstars with their studied careless look are faking it. They're so worried about protecting their manhood they don't have the guts to do something important once in a while, a movie that might shake up an audience for real. Where are the big stars with the courage to play a s.o.b. and not hide behind a protective gloss? Sure, we've got some younger actors who are willing to go all the way with a part, guys who don't care that audiences may find the character they play truly objectionable. We've got Dustin Hoffman, Robert DeNiro, Al Pacino, a couple more maybe. But where the hell do these other guys get off? The ones who sit at home in Malibu refusing to read a script

until there's a guaranteed $2-million offer to do the movie. How dare they be so arrogant! Most actors overreact to their own publicity. Acting isn't deal-making; it isn't a contest. A real actor reads every script he can get his hands on to look for a part he can sink himself into completely, that mythical perfect role he was born to play. To hell with the image, the brown Mercedes, the Gucci loafers and the $200 jeans.

Interview, Los Angeles, Sept. 30/
Los Angeles Herald-Examiner, 10-1:(B)1.

Ginger Rogers
Actress, Entertainer

4

[On why the films made with Fred Astaire in the 1930s and '40s were so popular]: Our movies were entertaining, full of hope and joy and happiness, with good sounds and good viewing. When you came out of the theatre, you went dancing down the street. Our movies didn't leave you with any problems. You didn't come out saying, "Why did I pay that money to hear those foul words and see that sex scene that is anti everything I believe in?"

Interview, New York/Esquire, August:130.

Mickey Rooney
Actor

5

You never hear the stories about how actors and actresses feel when their marriages to someone outside the business break up. When it's happened to me, it's always, "Oh, the poor woman." I've been brokenhearted a lot, but no one prints that . . . I think that people in the motion-picture business are the most stable people you'll find anywhere. They just have the tendency of marrying unstable people.

People, 5-24:92.

Maximilian Schell
Actor, Director

6

Some directors in Hollywood go home at the end of the day when the actors do; then

(MAXIMILIAN SCHELL)

the film is turned over to an editor. But I see my films all the way through to the end. Acting takes 10 weeks, and the job is over. Directing takes two years out of your life, especially when you write, scout locations, film, edit, and help with the distribution and promotion, as I do. It's more fulfilling than acting, but it's also more wounding to get bad reviews as a director than as an actor.

Interview, New York/
San Francisco Examiner & Chronicle, 5-30:
(Datebook)16.

John Schlesinger
Director
1

. . . since every director's career is going to be a checkered one, and we can't have hits all the time, we have to take chances. We no longer live in a golden era in which directors went under contract to a studio that guaranteed a certain amount of work each year. In the '40s, a director never had to worry about where the next film was coming from. You just made films, one after the other, some good, some bad. That's how all the great reputations were made. Now it's a big gamble, and every time you make a film your whole future is at stake. That's why I'm always anxious to get the next one prepared while the old one is being released.

Interview/
San Francisco Examiner & Chronicle, 11-7:
(Datebook)14.

Robert Shaw
Actor
2

[On his performing in "commercial" films after training in the classical form]: I wake up in the middle of the night, frequently, with pain and humiliation and a great deal of shame at some of the work I've done in films. And I would do a good movie any day, regardless of the money. Unfortunately, there aren't many. And, ironically, if you are not successful now and again [success meaning

box-office], nobody asks you to be in any movies at all. For years the studios would say, "Shaw's pictures make no money; he's not an international star."

Interview, Pamplona, Spain/
The Washington Post, 2-3:(D)2.

Richard Shepherd
Producer
3

The quality of films recently has not merited lines queuing up . . . Very often a film gets made because "so & so" is committed. That generates the film financing. Forget "so & so" —how good is the raw material? Too many films are motivated for the wrong reason.

Interview, Los Angeles/
Daily Variety, 3-1:3

John Simon
Film critic, "New York" magazine
4

[On women's roles in films]: Hollywood, as always, is lagging behind, afraid of treating an actress as a sex symbol, as she used to be treated, or as the sort of tough bitch that Barbara Stanwyck and Joan Crawford used to play. They're afraid that any kind of treatment will offend either the *avant garde* or the rear guard of women. So, out of this uncertainty, they make women's roles very insignificant. As a result, no real actresses show up, or, if they do, there is nothing significant for them to do.

The New York Times, 2-8:(2)19.

Neil Simon
Playwright, Screenwriter
5

Every time I write anything, I never think it will get on. I'm always prepared that when I show it to somebody for the first time they'll say, "This is dreadful; what have you been doing all this time?" But what tends to happen is I put down a couple of lines at the typewriter and I think it's funny, and then I add a few more, and pretty soon I'm getting calls from the studio and soon they're making deals and talking contracts. I don't even *want* them to like everything I do. I want them to like only the ones *I* like, only the things *I* think are good.

Interview, Burbank, Calif./
Los Angeles magazine, February:65.

1

[On why he prefers writing for the stage to writing for films]: I saw a rough cut of [his new film] *Murder* [*by Death*] the other day, and a great line change occurred to me. But what could I do about it? When a film is finished, the only change possible is a cut. But I am by nature a rewriter. I love rewriting. It's perhaps the best thing I do. I'm never happier than when I spot a line or a bit that needs fixing and I go back to that hotel room and rewrite ... But on a movie you have at best two weeks of rehearsal, and most of that time is spent blocking positions and moves. The actors don't really get into it until they're on camera, and then it's too late. So you have to be 100 per cent sure of the script going in, and a rewriter like me is never 100 per cent sure. I work from feelings, from what's inside me. I can't analyze it; it's the strangest thing—a gift, I guess.

Interview, Los Angeles/
The New York Times, 6-6:(2)5.

Sam Spiegel
Producer

2

The star system as I knew it doesn't exist any more. Today's stars are puny in comparison. In the old days I used to give lavish New Year's Eve parties and the actresses would sweep into the room in magnificent gowns; they were larger than life. Now the stars are undersized. The men have acting ability but they lack style. That is one of the results of the counter-culture in this country: It has eliminated the value of style.

Interview, Los Angeles/
The Dallas Times Herald, 3-19:(B)10.

Rod Steiger
Actor

3

[On acting]: I find it fulfilling, disturbing,

aggravating, paralyzing, terrorizing, panicking, sufficient, insufficient, boring, dull, but above all, necessary—to me. I'm over-sentimental about it. I consider it an art. I refuse to consider it anything else. I consider people who can do it special.

Interview, New York/
The Christian Science Monitor, 4-26:22.

James Stewart
Actor

4

What we had in the '30s and '40s were some dedicated men. They had the God-given talent to know good stories, what the public wanted to see, who should play the parts, and they wanted to do everything in good taste. They weren't part of oil companies or making pictures by committee, the way it's done today.

U.S. News & World Report, 3-15:40.

5

I never sat down and tried to analyze my style, but you know, I've always been fascinated by one thing in particular, by the vulnerability of a character, vulnerability not to great catastrophes and so on, but just to the things of everyday life. And so, even in the Westerns, you had riding and gun battles and everything like that; but you also try to bring into this the vulnerability of the character you're playing. That's what always interested me.

Interview, Washington/
The Washington Post, 10-4:(D)1.

6

It's sad that the big studios are mostly gone now, and with them the moguls—such as Samuel Goldwyn—who built Hollywood. They created the glamour and the magic by having a tremendous love for the motion-picture business. Now there are books that say the men were cold, vicious, terrible people who ran factories and turned out sentimental, gushy stuff—but that is nonsense. These men knew their jobs, and were geniuses in their own right. Their years were the golden years of Hollywood.

Interview/U.S. News & World Report, 11-15:86.

WHAT THEY SAID IN 1976

Lee Strasberg
Artistic director, Actors Studio
                                    1

There is very little stimulus to actors today. They get to the top and begin to loaf. We really haven't seen what talent can do in this country. An actor is like a violinist who has played only little gypsy pieces, and said, "What else is there?"

Interview/
The New York Times, 11-26:(C)2.

Peter Strauss
Actor
                                    2

Some actors think about the Porsche and the pool and, "Finally I can get rid of the wife because I can afford the alimony." Not me. I just don't want to fall into what I call "the trap." The chocolate-brown Mercedes, the jacuzzi, one good piece of turquoise, the best table at the Palm, handball at the health club, and the Star of David around your neck because suddenly you're proud to be a Jew. A wise Russian named Michael Schepkin once said that an actor is forever carving a statue of snow. I guess what I'm really desperate about, aside from ending up in the "Whatever Happened to" books, is success in a mediocre world.

Interview/
Los Angeles Times, 9-26:(Calendar)31.

Richard Thomas
Actor
                                    3

. . . in his work an actor is vulnerable all the time, offering himself to an audience for approval, never knowing whether or not he's going to end up with egg on his face. But in real life the vulnerability holds greater terror. Equipped with lines provided by writers, an actor can be bright, witty, charming, intelligent and extremely well-informed. But turn an actor loose in the outside world without a script, and he might prove to be a babbling idiot. That's scary enough to make a coward out of the bravest among us.

Interview, Los Angeles/
Los Angeles Times, 5-30:(Home)20.

Francois Truffaut
Director
                                    4

[On directing children]: When I make a film with them, they change, physically and emotionally, during the shooting. By the time the film ends, they are different. The story of a child is much richer than that of an adult. There is always a double level of meaning. There is the child himself, and then all humanity is represented, too. And even though the spectator's biography has not been the same as the child's, the film turns him back to his own childhood. Sometimes it is very difficult to direct children. You try something over and over and then have to let it go. But when it works, it's 10 times better than with an adult.

Interview, Paris/
The New York Times, 9-26:(2)15.

                                    5

I am afraid of abusive cinema. Cinema can create a very strong emotion simply by showing a person slap someone. I feel very strong emotion in a Hitchcock film where someone merely says something cruel. That's why I get angry when I see a picture where a person kicks someone in the stomach. People who film things that are too violent are people who don't know how to film . . . whereas a Hitchcock works with very few elements— he really feels things. It's the same in conversation. When people are very violent in defending a thesis, this violence is aimed at convincing *themselves*. Someone who is genuinely convinced speaks softly.

Interview, New York/
The Christian Science Monitor, 12-1:30.

Roger Vadim
Director
                                    6

I'm not attracted to see violent movies; but I think they serve a social purpose, because people with tendencies toward violence can transfer this potential just by going to a violent movie. The violence on the screen becomes a kind of necessary therapy. It keeps violence off the street. It's like saying you should never give a child a toy gun. If you deprive them of this kind of toy, the child becomes bizarre. They have frustration and they explode. Unless somebody invents a pill to eliminate all violence, movies are a good substitute.

At San Francisco Film Festival/
Daily Variety, 10-27:10.

Jack Valenti
President, Motion Picture
Association of America   *1*

Movies are attracting big audiences again. The fact is that people badly need some light in their lives—and good stories about fascinating characters provide that . . . People are looking for giants—heroes who can be emulated—and the movies happen to be full of actors who at least play that role well.

U.S. News & World Report, 3-15:40.

Gore Vidal
Author   *2*

There is no such thing as a pornographic movie. There are only pornographic audiences.

Interview/
"W": a Fairchild publication, 4-2:5.

    3

Particularly during the classic period in Hollywood, they used to say the director is the brother-in-law. The producer was all-important. He picked the writer, or writers, and he got the script. Once he had the script, then he would pick the cast; then, as an afterthought, he'd assign a director to it, the way you would a lighting man. Nobody wanted to be a director because you had to get up early and deal with actors all day long. The big people were the producers, the creative people were the writers and, in between, the. sort of nothings were the directors.

Interview, Beverly Hills, Calif./
Los Angeles Times, 4-18:(Calendar)27.

Hal B. Wallis
Producer   *4*

I get the feeling of working for different audiences these days, and I can't say I like it. Whether the people are really satisfied with the material they're getting on the screen these days I don't know. But the fact that old movies are so popular on TV, and in the theatres for that matter, tells me something. You can only bust a car up so many ways or only go to bed so many ways, and after that you've got to think of something better to do in movies. I'm waiting for the day, and looking forward to it confidently, when you can make movies that give you joy and satisfaction.

Interview, Los Angeles/
Los Angeles Times, 10-4:(4)1.

John Wayne
Actor   *5*

[Westerns are] the best vehicle to tell a story in our medium. The cowboy is American folklore, and every country understands every other country's folklore. And a man on a horse has always been the top hero. Look at the monuments—they're always a man on horseback.

Interview, Carson City, Nev./
The New York Times, 1-27:33.

    6

[On those who say he plays himself on the screen]: It is quite obvious it can't be done. If you are yourself, you'll be the dullest son of a bitch in the world on screen. You have to act yourself, you have to project something—a personality. Perhaps I have projected something closer to my personality than other actors have. I have very few tricks. Oh, I'll stop in the middle of a sentence so they'll keep looking at me, and I don't stop at the end, so they don't look away, but that's about the only trick I have.

Interview, Los Angeles/ Daily Variety, 1-29:10.

Lina Wertmuller
Director
1

[On making commercially successful films]: The law of the world is economic. Besides, financial success means a big audience. Look, I could make a very refined and intelligent movie for a very educated audience, but that would make me a traitor to the function of cinema. Cinema has to be a great social service. It is the art of our times, and we are trying to build great mass civilizations.

Interview, New York/
The National Observer, 2-21:22.

Nicol Williamson
Actor
2

Acting is all I know. But it's a painful, difficult profession. Actors are very insecure, vulnerable people, and we all need a little mercy in our lives. An actor is a guy who has to put a big bold face on, no matter how flimsy he feels.

Interview/The New York Times, 10-29:(C)6.

Robert Wise
Producer, Director
3

. . . film-making itself is probably the greatest of all international fraternities. There's a camaraderie that develops immediately. You may have a language barrier, and we've all worked in foreign countries where we have had them, but somehow or other you immediately get down to that common denominator of what it is you're doing at that particular moment, and you're doing it together. And it's just a marvelous, marvelous feeling.

Panel discussion/
Holiday Inn Companion, Jan.-Feb.:17.

Irene Worth
Actress
4

You know what a salmon does when it wants to go upstream? It feels about for the point of maximum energy in the water, the point where the water whirls round and round and generates a terrific centrifugal force. It looks for that point, and it finds it, and the water quadruples the salmon's own natural strength, and then it can jump. That's what an actor has to do with the text. The point of maximum energy is always there, but it takes finding.

Interview, New York/
The New York Times, 2-5:26.

William Wyler
Director
5

It takes more than one person to make a good film. I've never been able to make a good picture without a good story, good actors, good cameramen—good everybody. In my case, it was never a one-man job like some directors—Bergman, Fellini . . . I could never claim to be an *auteur* when making films from scripts by Lillian Hellman, Robert Sherwood, Sidney Howard, or Preston Sturges—even though I'm one of the few directors in Hollywood who can pronouce *auteur* correctly.

Interview, Beverly Hills, Calif./
The Hollywood Reporter, 2-20:12.

6

I don't believe in imposing myself on an audience. I try to tell the story with my medium, with my camera, the best way I know how. I'm not a writing director. I always needed a good story, a good script, good actors, a good cameraman. I never thought of doing something where people say, "Oh, that's Wyler" . . . Some of the directors don't seem to care or give a damn about anybody except their own feelings. They use the camera as a toy. They say, "to hell with the audience, that's the way I want it." You know, there's a very fine line between self-confidence and arrogance.

Interview, Beverly Hills, Calif./
The Washington Post, 3-7:(F)6.

Frank Yablans
Producer
1

[Lamenting the poor acting roles today]: Just look at who the big stars were last year—an ape, a shark and a lobotomy victim. When you see that, you know we've got problems.
Interview, New York/
"W": a Fairchild publication, 11-26:10.

Franco Zeffirelli
Italian director
2

The Italian cinema is lost, almost without hope. [Italian films] are dominated by politics and pornography, and no interesting young directors are in sight.
Interview, Carthage, Tunisia/
Los Angeles Herald-Examiner, 6-13:(B)4.

Howard Zieff
Director
3

The making of movies is not as wonderful as you'd like it to be. It's not an ideal laboratory that isolates you and the actors to make this wonderful thing. You have to deal with all the humanity of the executives, and the budgets, and everything . . . There are times when you're joking on the set, and it's fun. But most of the time . . . it's anguish . . . You look forward to the satisfaction of when it's completed—when you can sit at the Moviola without having to deal with personalities, and the editor, and you can put it together. It's like preparing a meal for hours, and finally sitting down and enjoying it.
Interview, Los Angeles/
The Christian Science Monitor, 1-14:23.

MUSIC

Claudio Arrau
Pianist
1

In Europe, when you hear a great new operatic talent, it generally is an American. I think that their general education is much better than that of the Europeans, and they know their parts much better. Part of this is due to the influence of Maria Callas. Giulini [the conductor] told me that she knew a score as well as he did. After Callas, you can't get away with lack of preparation or sloppiness.

Interview/The Dallas Times Herald, 1-14:(E)6.

Janet Baker
Art-song singer
2

Voice is a start. With some people it is the finish, too, and that is really wrong. It is a method of communication—not a means of self-glorification. It is only a means to an end, and that end is trying to make other people feel what the creative genius is saying. If you can make somebody feel that, then it doesn't matter what your voice is like.

Interview, Washington/
The Christian Science Monitor, 3-15:19.

Daniel Barenboim
Pianist, Conductor
3

[On Mozart piano concertos]: There is so much characterization and individuality in each concerto that you can't ever absorb them completely. No matter how often I play them, they don't get any easier. The music is so expressive yet so naked, at least for me. The dynamic range is not large, but within its restrictions the wealth of color is enormous, posing problems of balance and articulation and phrasing. It becomes a proofstone of a performer.

Interview/The New York Times, 5-7:(C)20.

Tony Bennett
Singer
4

I had rough times, knocking around as a youngster, trying to make it as a singer. Once I shared a room in New York with five other guys. We had two beds in the room and about 30 cents apiece for food. I mean, it was spaghetti at every meal, and we were glad to get it. But I'm not complaining about rough times. Everything I've done, every little experience, has helped me interpret lyrics. The difference between a singer just starting out, and a singer who makes an audience believe a song, is a difference learned by doing plenty of walking on life's many highways.

Interview, Beverly Hills, Calif./
Los Angeles Times, 8-22:(Home)22.

Alan Bergman
Lyricist
5

Lyrics aren't poetry. The primary function of a lyric is to sing. The combination of word and note makes a lyric. A lyric belongs in a time frame. Poetry can be read at any time, and it stands by itself. A lyric has to be changed if it doesn't sing. Let me give you an example in an Irving Berlin song. "They say that falling in love is wonderful." That line by itself is nothing. But put it to Berlin's music, and it sings. It becomes something because it combines with the melody.

Interview, Los Angeles/
Los Angeles Herald-Examiner, 4-1:(B)6.

Leonard Bernstein
Composer, Conductor
6

It's a remarkably lucky thing, being able to storm your way through a Beethoven symphony. Think of the amount of rage you can get out. If you exhibited that kind of rage on the street or in an interpersonal relationship, you'd be thrown in jail. Instead, you're applauded for it.

Interview, Washington/
The Washington Post, 1-7:(B)3.

Victor Borge
Entertainer, Musician
1

. . . too many musicians approach music like it's auto mechanics or something. One guy sitting there all starched and stiff, playing the flute as if it was all part of some serious religious ceremony. Musicians should realize that they can't get off on a piece every time they play the damned thing. That's impossible. It's like in ballet, where you can jump until you have jumped your highest. And after you have jumped your highest all you can do is repeat that jump. Everything is limited, even the universe, if you believe what Einstein told you. It is still repetition. All you can do is put it in a different order or in a different combination. No matter how great you are you are still bound to repeat yourself. The real excitement with music is the environmental effect it creates.

Interview, Los Angeles/
Los Angeles Herald-Examiner, 3-21:(B)5.

Antonia Brico
Conductor
2

When I go to the universities, so many students say, "I want to be a conductor." They think that is so easy. I have worked very hard, and I don't know if every girl would be willing to sacrifice and go through what I did—deprivation—things one holds dear—marriage, children. So many people say, "Well, if I hadn't married, I would be a great artist." But they *did* marry. The point is that they *did* make that choice. You have to sacrifice. To me, it was the thing I wanted most in all the world. And I was very consistent about that.

Interview, New York/
The Christian Science Monitor, 1-7:16.

Eugene Conley
Artist in residence,
North Texas State University;
Former singer,
Metropolitan Opera, New York
3

Here [in the U.S.] you have only one operatic name which carries any weight and that's the Metropolitan. And they are aware of it. Managements want their singers to have that handle, too, because it makes the product a little more salable. So they've really got things under control. People don't look at Chicago the same way. And San Francisco—they're on the go all the time, but people will not accept being a member of the San Francisco Opera as having the same value namewise as being a member of the Metropolitan. There should be four or five major opera companies—and I see no reason why there shouldn't be in this country, as big as it is—that would be comparable to one another and that the general public would recognize as such.

Interview, Denton, Tex./
The Dallas Times Herald, 4-22:(E)10.

Franco Corelli
Opera singer
4

I have always been afraid. In the beginning, I didn't have the B or C, and I was afraid I wasn't born to be a singer. Then I did have the B and C, and I was afraid to lose it. Sometimes I get up in the morning and the voice doesn't answer. If I'm on holiday and not singing I worry if it's still there. I tape every performance. After the performance I spend three hours listening. I am exhausted, I need rest, but I can't sleep. If the performance was good I can't sleep for joy. If the performance was not good I don't sleep for despair. What is this life? It's the life of a prisoner, in a hotel room, in front of the television or playing solitaire. You know, I was born free. I was born just 50 meters from the sea in Ancona [Italy]. Caruso said it best: "We tenors know our beginning but not our end."

Newsweek, 3-15:58.

WHAT THEY SAID IN 1976

Mac Davis
Singer
1

I love playing the small-town fairs. Here's where I meet the grass-roots people—honest, hard-working, sincere folks. They stood in the rain in Springfield, Missouri—20,000 of them. And at the Ohio State Fair, when about 25,000 showed up, it started to rain while I was singing *I Believe in Music.* I went inside for cover, but I could hear this beautiful sound of all those people out there continuing to sing *I Believe in Music* like a rondelay. It was one of the high points of my life.

Interview/ Los Angeles Herald-Examiner, 1-11:
(California Living)5.

Sammy Davis, Jr.
Singer, Entertainer
2

There used to be a sense of urgency when we walked into a recording studio, a commitment that you felt when you looked around and saw some of the great heavyweight musicians in the band; their presence inspired you and it was healthy. But today you go in, and the studio is almost empty, and some guy will say, "We're just doing the piano and rhythm track today. We'll add the strings later; and if we don't like 'em, we'll have some other cat write some more strings." So you wind up just singing to a tape. It's like artificial insemination! Jesus, if I'm going to have a baby, I don't want a guy shooting a needle in my wife's arm, or wherever . . . How can I do my best in a recording situation when I don't have cats like Buddy Collette or the Candoli Brothers or George Rhodes' orchestra sitting around and digging what I'm doing and encouraging me with a smile? This takes all the joy out of it! It's the same thing when I do the *Tonight Show* [on TV]. I can really cook when I'm on that show, when I hear the cats in the band saying, "Yeah, Sam!" That's still the name of the game. You take away that personal element and it all becomes sterile. You're into Orwell's *1984.*

Interview, Burbank, Calif./
Los Angeles Times, 6-27:(Calendar)37.

John Denver
Singer, Songwriter
3

I think people see themselves in me. The music is of a kind that touches people of all different ages, from all different backgrounds. People are finding value in it that's more than just entertainment, more than just pretty. For a long time now it hasn't been okay to acknowledge certain things about yourself. For example, that you love your old lady; that it feels good to be out in the sunshine; that every once in a while on a rainy day you feel sad; that life is good. As I have been able to communicate those things for myself and to reach a large audience, that gives them support in feeling those things . . . Nobody else is singing these songs. Everybody else is talking about how hard life is, and here I am singing about how good it is to be alive!

Interview, Denver, Colo./
The New York Times, 3-28:(2)18.

4

It's important for me to write songs, as it is for most musicians today. It came, I think, out of the '60s, with all the young people involved in music. It came from the need to express oneself, and out of the absence of opportunities for people to do that. Kids who couldn't communicate with their parents, and with each other, could write it down in a song.

Interview, Aspen, Colo./
San Francisco Examiner & Chronicle, 8-29:
(Datebook)18.

James DePreist
Music director, Quebec Symphony Orchestra;
Principal guest conductor,
National Symphony Orchestra, Washington
5

[Saying black composers should be recognized for their contributions to music forms other than just classical]: We shouldn't fall into a trap of relegating jazz and certain aspects of pop music to a lower level than classical music. It's true that our concern today is with classical music. But our concerns should be broader. It's a mistake not to include spirituals and jazz. This is a vital aspect of our [blacks'] tradition. It could be the most vital aspect.

At symposium of black classical composers, Washington, Dec. 2/ The Washington Post, 12-3:(B)17.

Neil Diamond
Singer, Songwriter

1

I really assimilate everything I've heard in music. I've drawn upon all of the choral music and black music and country music and rock 'n' roll and Broadway... I'm like the Will Rogers of pop: There isn't a musical form that I've heard that I haven't liked.

Interview, Sacramento, Calif./ Los Angeles Times, 2-15:(Calendar)70.

2

I have a great feeling for the stage. I think if I hadn't been a songwriter, I might have easily gone on and been a stage performer, an actor. The satisfaction you get from being on stage is more instantaneous than the satisfaction you get from writing. But when it's over, it's over. Whereas a piece of music that you write can go on for a long time and still be satisfying.

Interview, Los Angeles/ Los Angeles Herald-Examiner, 8-3:(B)1.

Bob Dylan
Singer, Songwriter

3

Almost anything else is easy except writing songs. The hardest part is when the inspiration dies along the way. Then you spend all your time trying to recapture it. I don't write every day. I'd like to but I can't. You're talking to a total misfit. Gershwin, Bacharach —those people—they've got songwriting down. I don't really care if I write. I can say that now, but, as soon as the light changes, it'll be the thing I care about most.

Interview, Malibu, Calif./ TV Guide, 9-11:8.

Arthur Fiedler
Conductor, Boston Pops Orchestra

4

I never play to the audience. I never play to the gallery. I come out and I do my business and I try to play a Strauss waltz or Sousa march or Beethoven symphony as well as I know how. To me, music is something that must be performed with love and kisses.

Interview/ Lately (the Sheraton hotel magazine), Vol. 1, No.2.

5

I'm a middle-of-the-road guy. People like the things they know, and I play the music they like. I'd have trained seals here if people wanted them... You plan a musical program the way a master chef plans a menu. You have a tempting appetizer, a fresh salad with a piquant dressing, a robust main course, a carefully chosen dessert.

The Wall Street Journal, 7-29:25.

6

If you take the five best orchestras in the country and compare them—it's impossible. It's like comparing five beautiful women: One has lovely eyes, another has a beautiful disposition.

Upon being presented with the Sword of Loyola Award of Loyola University Stritch School of Medicine, Chicago/ The Dallas Times Herald, 12-12:(F)9.

Ernest Fleischmann
Executive director, Los Angeles Philharmonic Orchestra

7

...there are only 1,500 musicians of world class on this planet, and they must be handled with care and respect. You're dealing with very special people. Musicians are such a nervous lot. So tense! Von Karajan, you know, loves to fool around with gadgets and experiments, and he once wired his players to measure their heartbeats and pulse rates— that sort of thing. The test showed *tremendous*

457

WHAT THEY SAID IN 1976

elevations just prior to and during performance. Terrible stress! And not only are musicians constantly on display, they must subjugate their own considerable egos to the conductor's, which causes predictable problems. Then, when it comes time to negotiate a contract, management traditionally looks upon these special animals as auto workers! Or teamsters! That's the problem right there. American orchestras have become militant in recent years—and we see strikes—because management negotiates on a *them vs. us* basis.

Interview, Santa Monica, Calif./
The New York Times Magazine, 4-11:37.

Eugene Fodor
Violinist
1

Music is a living art and a certain amount of dramatics enters into my work. Paganini, who had the most successful career in music history, was known for his theatrical approach. But I don't subscribe to acting onstage other than how the music affects me. It would be false and it would be deceiving the audience. I mean, doing things like having a string break while you are playing.

Interview, Dallas/
The Dallas Times Herald, 9-17:(B)4.

David Gockley
General manager, Houston Grand Opera
2

[On why opera is booming in Houston]: I am extremely concerned with what others call opera and what I call "musical theatre" becoming more American—something Americans can look at as their own rather than something Italians liked in 1880. This can only be done by making the experience more total in a visual and musical sense, by casting singers as much for their acting as their vocal abilities. But we had to begin by breaking down the barriers that kept people from accepting opera—the price of the tickets, the language of the performance,

the theatricality or lack of it, the idea that opera was a kind of a closed club for elite types.

Interview, Houston/
The New York Times, 2-29:(2)19.

Jerry Goldsmith
Composer
3

A painter begins with identifiable colors, a palette, a brush, perhaps a model. A writer begins with a large vocabulary and some real-life characters, perhaps disguised but nevertheless real. A composer, however, has almost nothing to start with. There are 12 different tones, and that's all he brings to the game. Each assignment becomes an agonizing experience. Where shall I begin? What notes shall I play? What combination of sounds will be at once so melodic and original and attention-grabbing that the audience will be hooked? To me, 95 per cent of the agony is finding a departure point, a place to begin . . . I've heard some say the music just writes itself, but I'm skeptical. My guess is creative people are reluctant to admit they suffer in the process of creation. But I see suffering as an inescapable part of the experience. I agonized for over a month, looking for an approach to [the scoring of the film] *Logan's Run.* Once I found it, the music took off like a racehorse.

Interview, Los Angeles/
Los Angeles Times, 9-19:(Home)74.

Eydie Gorme
Singer
4

When I was a little girl, the classics were Puccini and Verdi. The composers were around 200 years old. Today, music is much more simple, more basic and, to me, a lot more dull. Elton John and Alice Cooper are freak shows. And I don't say that with malice. I know Alice. He's a doll. But his music . . . Like most things great, songs need time to mature, to become great. But in this era a tune is a hit today and forgotten tomorrow. Composers are given an assignment Wednesday and told they must have the material finished Thurs-

Interview, Beverly Hills, Calif./
San Francisco Examiner & Chronicle, 10-10:
(Datebook)28.

Donald Gramm
Opera singer
1

No matter how professional you are, the lack of response from an audience makes you think: "What am I doing wrong?" And an enthusiastic response encourages you. But I have yet to see it fail—when you are up for a performance and thinking, "this is going very well," someone from the audience will invariably come up to you afterward and say, "Oh, tonight was good—but last Tuesday you performed so beautifully!"

Interview, Santa Fe, N.M./
The Dallas Times Herald, 9-2:(C)6.

John Green
Composer-conductor
2

It's been the age of the amateur. We've been through a terrible period of do-it-yourself and me-too-ism. "If he can do it, I can do it, too" —that's one of the destructive lies of recent times. Not everybody is an Irving Berlin or a Benny Goodman or a Leonard Bernstein. The professional stage and screen is for professionals. When the upcoming generation recognizes this—that there is a vast difference between a moderately talented amateur and an importantly talented professional—we'll see new talents emerging again.

Interview/
The Dallas Times Herald, 7-11:(D)6.

Bernard Haitink
Permanent conductor, Concertgebouw Orchestra, Amsterdam; Artistic director, London Philharmonic Orchestra
3

[On orchestra touring]: Once I'm on my way I start to enjoy it, but I don't see much

THE PERFORMING ARTS—MUSIC

reason for it. Too many orchestras are traveling now without a real purpose. It's like the Olympic Games, and I don't like that . . . An orchestra should tour only when it has a face of its own. When the Chicago Symphony comes to Amsterdam, that's okay. But touring just to stay alive—that's bad.

Interview/ The New York Times, 11-21:(2)35.

Vladimir Horowitz
Pianist
4

I'm absolutely against competitions [for music students]. In competitions winners are chosen by elimination, not by excellence, and sometimes, when the winner goes out on his own, there is not enough excellence. Also, sometimes, it's political; it does not smell good.

Interview, July 24/
The New York Times, 7-26:30.

Jose Iturbi
Pianist
5

Conducting? No, it's not a precise science. I love to watch these types who make a big gesture for a little *pizzicato*. They're funny. Still, the audience loves them. Yes, there were great conductors—Toscanini, Kleiber, Monteux, Walter. But, somehow, they didn't have to do so much dancing around.

Interview, Beverly Hills, Calif./
Los Angeles Herald-Examiner, 11-16:(B)1.

6

. . . there are three types of artists, in my view: many *before* the concert; many *after* the concert; but far fewer *during* the concert.

Interview, Beverly Hills, Calif./
Los Angeles Herald-Examiner, 11-16:(B)1.

7

[Saying he still gets butterflies]: Before, during and a little bit after a performance. Why? Well, if you start to think of all the possibilities of what can go wrong—you cannot come back and correct it. Technically, theoretically, we should have impeccability

(JOSE ITURBI)

in a performance. But not in one performance have I gone out on stage and returned and said, "Ah, it was good." Never.

Interview, Philadelphia/
The Washington Post, 11-27:(C)6.

Burl Ives
Singer

1

When I sing, I lose my sense of self. All my energy and imagination is condensed into a character telling a story. Through me, like a current, emotion and words and stories flow. Between the audience and me, I build a bridge of poetry and music. It joins us together, binding our lives and, in a true spiritual sense, making us richer for the experience.

Interview/
Los Angeles Times, 12-5:(Home)35.

Herbert von Karajan
Music director and conductor,
Berlin Philharmonic Orchestra

2

Many conductors travel all over to conduct. I am never away from my orchestra for more than 16 days at a time. I always want to get it to the point where if something goes wrong, it's my fault.

Interview, Washington/
The Washington Post, 11-8:(C)3.

3

Baton technique is what the people see, but it is all nonsense. The hands do their job because they have learned what to do. In the performance, I forget about them. The molding comes when the orchestra and conductor come together in a sort of union. Things happen that are too delicate for words. It is the music that takes you away. It is mystical: You are so concentrated you forget everything else.

Interview, New York/Time, 11-29:81.

Walter Kerr
Drama critic, "The New York Times"

4

Music can be profound using no words at

all. It's the nearest thing to ESP. You can make immediate contact with the thing itself without intervention of words or pictures. If you were making a hierarchy of the arts, music would be the most profound.

The Dallas Times Herald, 3-22:(B)4.

Dorothy Kirsten
Opera singer

5

I was auditioned by the Met five years before I joined the company and was offered a contract. I refused it then . . . I felt I was not ready, that I did not have enough experience. I wish more young singers would think that way today. If young singers asked my advice, I'd tell them to pace their careers, not to sing too many roles too early. Your voice must be mature to sing some roles. You've got [to] learn to say "No," or you'll burn yourself out. There is a lot of pressure now to learn a lot of roles and to move about quickly to fill as many engagements as possible.

Interview, New York/
Los Angeles Times, 1-3:(2)11.

Lili Kraus
Pianist

6

The style of a composer, or of a writer or a dancer, is how they "speak." Each has his own language. To understand them, we who are performers, readers or audience must learn to speak their language. Only a fool would not know that Mozart—the man with the deepest soul, which he expressed with the fewest words—has his own way of speaking to us, and that you do not speak his words as you would those of Beethoven or Wagner. These are other languages. As musicians, we have to be multilingual in order to perform. We must also know how to read between the lines of these languages, so to speak, and to be aware of undercurrents, of the meaning of the most abstract symbols. Too much accent, for example, or too much agogic freedom would destroy the crystal-clear ocean that Mozart is. Beethoven is something else. He speaks in interruptions, *crescendi* which end in a *subito piano* and vice versa. Brahms is again something else. His language is that of big, wonderful round harmonies and melodies. They are never very, very deep, but hover with mastery on the edge of sentiment. With them, as with Mozart, it is the job of we, the performers, to glean from the music its essence, and then to fuse this with our essence in order to consummate the union. In this way, a piece is born anew, quite unlike any other union which another may form with the same piece.

At Texas Christian University/
The New York Times, 8-1:(2)15.

Peggy Lee
Singer
1

When that kind of music [rock] took over, I was destroyed emotionally. I didn't understand it; I couldn't find my place in it. I told myself if that's where music is going, I don't want to go along, so I'd better find something else to do. But after a while, I made a conscious effort to study and understand what the younger musicians were doing. Gradually I came over; I realized there were some new, wonderful things evolving. Some of the soft rock is very interesting, and the Latin songs are something I can understand. More good songs are coming along all the time. There is a dearth of beautiful ballads, but I can always go back to the great songs of Cole Porter, George Gershwin, Otto Harbach and Jerome Kern, Rodgers and Hart, Rodgers and Hammerstein.

Interview/
Los Angeles Herald-Examiner, 9-5:(E)2.

James Levine
Music director and principal conductor,
Metropolitan Opera, New York
2

In opera, a production must exploit the emotional effect of music. What happens on stage cannot confine your imagination. *Papier mache* icons are fake and you know it. A production fails when it has a suppressing effect on the music. I've sat through operas where what

is happening on stage has nothing to do with the music, and the musical experience is destroyed.

Interview, New York/
The New York Times, 2-1:(2)17.

3

For myself, I have two goals. I want to work with other musicians, straining every fiber of our guts, conviction, knowledge and skill to lay out a performance about which the composer would say, "That's my piece!" I have no certain way of knowing I am doing that, but everything I do is geared to what my instincts, skills, knowledge, experience and research lead me to believe that it is. That assessment will vary from performance to performance. The composer gave us a piece and it has infinite aspects; those aspects need to be brought into a just proportion in any given performance. The challenge lies in the variables. There is no objective end—the goal changes with every performance. Second, I would like to affect the general system of our musical life in a way that will make it more possible for that kind of thing to happen more consistently. It would be very easy to crawl into the guest-conductor cocoon, traveling around with my own hand-picked associates, performing under ideal rehearsal conditions. There are those who do that. But you've got to work with one chorus and corps of singers and orchestra and audience, and under a variety of conditions, for the art form to progress—all the significant musical and theatrical work that's ever been accomplished has been done that way. And that is what I and all of us want to do.

Interview/
The New York Times, 10-10:(2)21.

Richard Lewis
Opera singer
4

I would like to be looked upon as an actor-singer or a singer-actor rather than just a singer. Because one has to act with the voice, act with the words, act with the facial expressions, not just gestures alone. What comes

WHAT THEY SAID IN 1976

(RICHARD LEWIS)

from the heart and the mind through the voice is really what tells and what the audience is moved by. I would prefer to be moved by a person who is using the voice, and knowing that they are singing with the mind and their heart, and using that sound that they make in the throat as a medium for this.

Interview, Boston/
The Christian Science Monitor, 4-1:27.

Rolf Liebermann
General director, Paris Opera
1

If you are dependent on a government [for support], you can never be sure about the future. Right now I am on my fifth Minister of Culture.

Time, 9-13:59.

Guy Lombardo
Orchestra leader
2

Our music is the popular music as it's written—popular music as the composer wanted it played, so you'll know what we're playing without all the embellishments that take away from the beauty. I mean that every song that is a song is a beautiful thing, in my opinion, and I don't believe in people butchering it up.

Interview, Fort Lauderdale, Fla./
Los Angeles Times, 2-19:(1)1.

Lorin Maazel
Musical director, Cleveland Orchestra
3

Too many concerts are given by too many orchestras. You get the professionalism of mediocrity, and it grinds on like some kind of dreadful machine that never stops. I'd like to see the day when there is much more music made, but on a much less pretentious level. I think it's better when a lot of young people get together in city-block orchestras, or duets, or trios. But getting together 50 rather poor musicians, calling them the Someplace Philharmonic, with a women's committee, a junior committee, a fund-raising program and a

Ford Foundation grant—that consecrates them forever. They all join the union so nobody can be fired, and for 45 years the oboe tries to play what he cannot. That's the in-between world I would like to see us do away with by withholding our patronage.

Before college students/ People, 1-12:28.

Henry Mancini
Composer
4

The music world has changed irreversibly. For example, when I wrote the title song for [the film] *Moment to Moment* with Johnny Mercer in 1965, the first record we had on it was by [Frank] Sinatra. Those are the kinds of thrills you used to be able to have as a songwriter; somebody coming along like Frank, or Andy Williams, selling millions of records. Nowadays, part of the rock syndrome is that most artists write their own material and even a movie song is very difficult to get off the ground . . . Even if Sinatra did a song of mine now, it would be very hard to get airplay. They don't care who you are; it's just a matter of fitting a format, using up radio time to get top ratings.

Interview/
Los Angeles Times, 6-20:(Calendar)92.

Barry Manilow
Singer
5

I've played big arenas—10,000 people, old people, young people, all that stuff. I think I could have a decent conversation with any of the people who come to hear me. I mean, I don't get dope addicts. But I do offend some people. I think maybe it's because I'm not controversial. I mean, I don't wear funny hats or funny glasses. I even hang around with people who don't know anything about music. There's more to life than the music industry, and I always figure that someday they'll take the music away from me.

Interview, New York/
The New York Times, 12-3:(C)2.

Zubin Mehta
Musical director, Los Angeles
Philharmonic Orchestra
1

If an orchestra likes a conductor, they play music with much more love, that's for sure. Musicians are not machines. They cannot be coaxed. You cannot order a musician to play with heart. If the musician doesn't like the conductor and doesn't feel inspired either by his personality or knowledge, he *cannot* open up to him, I know . . . when my orchestra and I have a little bit of tension, they play correctly and give a more exciting performance, but there's no love in it.

Interview, Los Angeles/
The New York Times, 9-5:(2)24.

Robert Merrill
Opera singer
2

[On New York's Metropolitan Opera]: There was a time when I did 25 or 30 operas each season at the Met. Ah, it was a magnificent place then, with a glamorous history, marvelous traditions and great musicians. But today the Met needs money. So the managers are economizing. Oh, there are still some great stars left, but we no longer have the glamor, the excitement or the quality. For the most part, the Met is like a factory, with busy directors moving the cast about. And that's not opera. Audiences are thrilled by the singing, not costumes, sets and action. Those are just dessert. They are making a very great mistake.

Interview, Chicago/
The Washington Post, 6-22:(B)3.

Bette Midler
Singer
3

The nature of this business eats you up . . . The very nature of the business breeds fear. Everywhere there is bitterness and jealousy. The worst part of having success is to try finding someone who is happy for you. You don't really find that, not in this business.

News conference, Philadelphia/
Los Angeles Times, 3-3:(1)2.

Mitch Miller
Musician; Former record producer
4

Artists are expendable in today's [music] industry. In the years right after World War II and into the early 1960s, we had absolute freedom. If we made mistakes, it was no big deal, as long as there were not too many. I was regarded as a sort of genius in the industry because I could come up with innovations. We devised a million little strategems and shortcuts. You had to go in when things were red hot and forge them. Today's music isn't made, it's manufactured.

Interview, Chicago/
The Dallas Times Herald, 7-5:(D)6.

Eugene Ormandy
Musical director,
Philadelphia Orchestra
5

People say to members of my orchestra, "How do you keep up such a demanding schedule?" and my players—my beloved players—reply, "If the old man can do it, we can do it." That's my philosophy. If the conductor gives, the orchestra gives. If the conductor rests, why should the players try? It's no secret. We work like slaves. Today I am studying Brahms *First*. I never stop studying it. There is always more to learn.

Interview, Los Angeles/
Los Angeles Times, 7-13:(4)8.

Ray Price
Singer
6

My music is based strictly on grass-roots country music, but I haven't decided what country music is. I've always wondered if it's a "Madison Avenue" word. Jimmy Rodgers was once called a hillbilly; then his music became known as country, and later it was country-and-western. But there's only 32 bars of music, no matter how you play it. To me, music is either good, bad or indifferent. You either like it or you don't . . . Country music is something everybody can relate to. Maybe it's a lesson to people, showing the pitfalls of life. It's the contemporary music of today,

WHAT THEY SAID IN 1976

and 10 years from now it'll still be the story of what is happening to human beings.

Interview, Nashville, Tenn./
Los Angeles Herald-Examiner, 2-18:(B)5.

Ruggiero Ricci
Violinist

1

The old Russian school [of violin-playing] did whatever sounded attractive—a lot of *glissandi*, beautifully done, with elegance and polish. You hear it in Heifetz. The Russians developed a set of very effective cliches. They were the originators of the most imitated style of string playing, and they made an enormous impact that left its influence on all of us. The new Russian school is schmaltzy—much more romanticized. They use slower *tempi*, exaggerated *rubati*, an excess of vibrato—the long notes have too much vibrato and the passing notes are white. Still, it's a successful formula. People love sugar and sentimentality. We [in the U.S.] sell corn to the Russians and they sell it back to us.

Interview, New York/
The New York Times, 1-18:(2)15.

Richard Rodgers
Composer

2

Music popularity tends to run in cycles. Young people are now demanding more professionalism in their music, although many of their favorites were much more trained musicians than they let on. One of these days, rock and roll will be left behind, at least for a while, and the young people will move on to something else. Straight melody, I hope.

Interview, New York/
The Christian Science Monitor, 12-8:28.

Leonard Rosenman
Composer

3

I discovered, when I began working in

films and TV, it meant a sharp blow to my status among serious musicians. They refused to regard me as a real composer, a man worth listening to in a concert hall. Turning it around, to the extent I earned a reputation as a serious composer, it became difficult to find jobs in movies and TV. Producers who'd heard I was working in concert halls considered me a long-haired dreamer, not commercial enough for show business . . . It isn't fair to exclude long-hair music from the world of entertainment. It's just as unfair to put a label of good, bad or indifferent on music written for TV or films. I'd rather find a way of interweaving the music we hear in concert halls with the music we hear in theatres and on TV.

Interview/
Los Angeles Times, 6-6:(Home)43.

Mstislav Rostropovich
Exiled Soviet cellist;
Musical director-designate, National
Symphony Orchestra, Washington

4

Music and art are a whole spiritual world in Russia. In Russia, when people go to a concert, they don't go to it as an attraction, as an entertainment, but to feel life. I have seen photographs of concert audiences in the Soviet Union . . . the faces are all so intense, so drawn, faces of people searching for the meaning of existence. I cannot permit myself not to think about the faces of those people. The intensity is part of the hardships they have endured.

Interview/
The New York Times Magazine, 4-18:15.

5

[Prokofiev] was my greatest teacher of music. He opened my eyes for certain colors in music. He always wore bright, multicolored jackets. That's normal now. In those days in Russia, people wore only black and gray. He saw music sometimes in terms of color—low oboes, he used to tell me, were dark brown. Very often he treated musical instruments as if they were living beings.

For example, slow, low notes on the tuba made him think a beetle was sitting in the note. With great pleasure he would listen to the beetle climbing from one note to another.

Interview/"W": a Fairchild publication, 10-1:2.

Julius Rudel
General director and conductor,
New York City Opera

1

The City Opera has had more influence outside New York than any other company. The kind of opera we espoused has been accepted—the kind of opera that emphasizes theatre, music, drama; the kind of opera that doesn't put all its money on a couple of cards, a couple of big European stars. We don't mind seeing our whole approach to opera being taken up elsewhere.

Interview, New York/
The New York Times, 9-3:(C)2.

2

One could, if one wished, put an opera company together in two weeks: the time it would take to borrow scenery, hire singers, rehearse a professional chorus and orchestra and get a conductor and stage director to inject a modicum of order into the chaos. This is done rather regularly in some cities, and I used to be one of the lion tamers tossed into the pit. Such Instant Opera can occasionally result in some very exciting performances, even if the stately columns wave in the breeze and the stage director is a retired traffic cop . . . But most of the time it is artistic disaster, and attracts an audience which clings to old memories and the occasional high notes omitted by some "name" singer.

Interview/
Los Angeles Times, 11-14:(Calendar)1.

Roger Sessions
Composer

3

I am not discouraged in regard to the state of music today . . . That which prompts my

lack of discouragement is my conviction that gifted young people are as anxious as they ever were to create music, and that those whom I consider gifted are neither, in my judgment, discernibly less gifted nor fewer in number, or less serious in their aims, than those I have known in previous generations.

The Washington Post, 3-28:(K)4.

Bobby Short
Singer, Pianist

4

[On performing in intimate cabarets]: Intimacy breeds conversation, noise and ultimate destruction. I loathe the woman who comes to the piano just so she can bask in the spotlight and show off her unblemished shoulders. And I abhor having my severest critic wave his cigar an inch from my nose. The very nature of being a saloon singer is contradictory to being a good singer. That's why I prefer a concert hall where people come to listen.

Interview/
Los Angeles Herald-Examiner, 2-8:(D)2.

Beverly Sills
Opera singer

5

How did I get to be a singer? It was Galli-Curci recordings. Before my mother put on the coffee in the morning, she was cranking up this little $10 Victrola and putting on her records. I was raised with the noise of perking coffee and the cranking, cranking, so that Galli-Curci could do her bit in the morning.

Interview/Newsweek, 7-4:74.

6

There haven't been as many productions of American operas as there should be because it's so expensive to mount a new production. It costs at least $150,000, and often much more. So good American operas are not performed enough, while some of the old war horses go on and on. But that's beginning to change, because there is a new generation

WHAT THEY SAID IN 1976

of directors and stages that are ready to take chances.

Interview/ U.S. News & World Report, 10-25:65.

Georg Solti
Musical director,
Chicago Symphony Opera   *1*

An orchestra needs iron discipline. Whether it's a benign or not benign dictatorship, you must take orders from somebody. Once you don't, the borderline between anarchy and liberty very soon arrives.

Interview, New York/
The New York Times, 5-9:(2)17.

Stephen Sondheim
Composer-lyricist   *2*

Music is always easier for me to write [than lyrics] because it has to do with emotional atmosphere. I *love* music with a passion, and always have. As for lyric-writing, well, to tell you the truth, I find it emotionally frustrating. And bloody hard work. Hard work the way running round the block is hard—just pushing and pushing until finally you think you're going to drop dead from exhaustion, until you let the lyric stand because you can't get it any better. Sometimes, of course, you do get it better. But more often you don't. And occasionally you talk to another lyric-writer two years later, after the show has closed, and he'll give you the solution. "Why didn't you think of using the word *chair*?" he'll ask. And you'll say, "My God, I just didn't *think* of it."

Interview, New York/
The New York Times, 1-4:(2)5.

Paul Sperry
Lieder singer   *3*

There's no question that singing at the Met or at La Scala would make me much more saleable around the country. But I'd much rather sing songs. Songs are what I love best.

I've got to feel passionately about a song, and the way I get to feel passionate is to dissect it from top to bottom. The first thing is to understand the poem that's been set to music. Always, I go to the original published form of the poem, and read it as a poem on the printed page—in its own rhythm and aura. Then, I read it as the composer set it, following the reflections, the rising and falling line, so that if there is a particular high note which I know is going to be very expressive, I'll put that into the reading. Then, I try to think *why* the composer made that choice. If I understand everything about why a composer set a poem the way he did, then the music will take care of itself.

Interview/ The New York Times, 2-8:(2)24.

Isaac Stern
Violinist   *4*

Believe it or not, a great soloist is, above all, a concept, a powerful idea. Even when an audience can't define that idea precisely, they respond to it. By the same token, I can think of certain violinists who can play all the notes in the world. But they will not make it as great soloists because the audience senses they are too narrow, too stupid.

Interview/
The New York Times Magazine, 2-22:40.

Michael Tilson Thomas
Music director,
Buffalo Philharmonic Orchestra   *5*

Concert societies are still governed, by and large, by people who want music on the old European model. They like the ceremony of music and get a lot of security out of going to concerts, hearing nice old melodies which evoke a kind of lost "nobility." They like conductors who are smooth, elegant and foreign; who do well at cocktail parties with older and wealthy people. It's a handicap for many artists to be American and committed to shaping their music as it demands now to be heard. I know a number of important American artists who don't have the right opportunities because glamorous but often predictable or even second-rate foreign-style artists are preferred by the influential.

Interview/ U.S. News & World Report, 12-27:65.

Tatiana Troyanos
Opera singer   1

There isn't enough time to prepare operas today. Everybody is so booked up, you're lucky if you have a few days of rehearsals. You're forced to go all over the place or you don't have a career and you're not in demand. I resent it. It's crazy.

Interview/Newsweek, 3-22:78.

Barry Tuckwell
French-horn player   2

[On French-horn player Gottfried von Freiburg]: He tried for everything—and no matter if he cracked a few notes. His was a full-bodied sound that projected throughout the hall without being a loud sound. It inspired me more than anything I had ever heard. Good music-making requires risks. This applies to every instrument, but the risks are greater on the horn. You may be able to get by playing for total safety, but it won't be worth tuppence musically.

The New York Times, 2-15:(2)20.

Bobby Vinton
Singer   3

I'm simply not a star in the sense of having a sensational voice. As a singer, I'd have to be classed as not much more than ordinary. If I just sat by indifferently, hoping people would notice me, I'd never amount to anything . . . Unless a singer's voice is pure gold, there's no point in waiting for something to happen. You have to make it happen . . . I'm convinced I have to keep in touch, or they'll forget about me, because there are always new boys coming along, new faces, new personalities eager to take my place. Another reason I have to keep plugging away

at promotion is that I'm not really "in." I'm not contemporary. I don't write much of my own material. I sing old-fashioned songs. That can be a problem even for a truly great voice; and for an ordinary singer like me, it's a major challenge.

Interview, Los Angeles/
Los Angeles Times, 5-9:(Home)24.

Frederica von Stade
Opera singer   4

The whole power of music is so incredible, really . . . Music has a whole physical reaction. It can make you cry, laugh—or it can just touch you. It is bigger than humanity. Performing artists are both protected by music and responsible to it. It's like a shell of aspiration and protection. That's what music has been to me, and I've been very happy and very lucky. And I've loved it. Even the downers have been worth it. In ten years I may be selling apples, but there will still be the experiences I have had of meeting people like Janet Baker and Jackie [Marilyn Horne], the great conductors, and great artists. It is something that you love so much, you are afraid you are going to lose it—until you realize the experiences you've already had you can't lose.

Interview, New York/
The Christian Science Monitor, 1-7:17.

5

[I want] to become as greedy as possible about artistic standards. I just don't think it's worth doing "instant opera," dashing in and out for some enormous fee. I've been lucky enough so far to work with some of the most inspiring directors around—Strehler, Abbado, Solti, Peter Hall, Frank Corsaro. Opera is a bit like tennis in this respect—you perform better and learn more when you're surrounded by the best. When you're around people of such dynamism, interest and energy, you feel as if your motor has been turned on for the first time.

Interview, Washington/
The Washington Post, 9-14:(B)6.

WHAT THEY SAID IN 1976

Porter Wagoner
Country-music singer

1

In the last few years country music has come the furthest distance it ever has . . . the sounds themselves have gotten better. People used to look at country music as backwoods music, because they had only heard about it. Now it's better presented in every way . . . and it has better quality in every way— instrumentally, and in the use of better recording facilities. It *sounds* better. So people are listening, and it'll keep growing . . . Country music is not so sophisticated that you have to sit trying to figure it out. The world has gotten people so busy figuring out the complications of computers, and just *living* in a place like New York City . . . But country music is so basic that you don't have to be a genius. It connects with the way people were brought up and want to live.

Interview, Nashville, Tenn./
The Christian Science Monitor, 11-5:30.

Christine Walevska
Cellist

2

An artist lives more or less in a cocoon. You practice by yourself, then you go and rehearse with the orchestra. Nobody thinks of saying, "Would you like to have lunch or can I show you the town" or something like that. So I go back and have lunch with myself, and I see something of the place, take a nap before the concert, get dressed, iron the concert gown—ha!—take a cab to the concert hall. I play, they all say, "Oh, mar-velous . . . great . . . fantastic . . . please come again soon, bye-bye!"

Interview, New York/
The Christian Science Monitor, 11-1:23.

Lawrence Welk
Musician; Orchestra leader

3

My whole life, you might say, is based on longevity. Music changes, but I don't. Most of the people who star with me—my musical family—find they can't get away from me. I'm the father; they're my children. I think we produce a better product that way . . . When you keep people together for a long time, the work becomes just a little finer.

Interview, Los Angeles/
TV Guide, 7-17:26.

Alec Wilder
Composer

4

[On old pop songs]: I thought there were songs that I loved that I didn't need to hear any more. But I *do* need to hear them. It's like trains. I can't get over the sound and smell of a steam locomotive, hearing the whistle in the night. Songs are part of my emotional being. And I'm not ashamed of it at all. I've written half a ton of concert music. It's an entirely different point of view. And yet I go back to songs like I go back to an old friend, to a garden, to a fireplace, to a cat that's come back after being away.

Interview, New York/
The New York Times, 10-1:(C)25.

THE STAGE

George Abbott
Producer, Director, Writer
1

A hell of a lot of directors think you get fun by being funny. If it's a good show, you get fun by being real. I saw a horrendous production of *Room Service*. It was all mugging. Mugging is for kids. Mugging is pins—like in the circus. It's strange about the English. They're so good in serious acting. But they have no standards, as we [in the U.S.] do, when it comes to comedy. They just love cheap comedy—pie-in-the-face. I despise that kind of thing. It's the lowest form of humor. Cruelty is also supposed to be very funny. I dislike all things that have to do with hurting people for fun.
Interview, New York/
The New York Times, 4-28:34.

2

I think the level of performance today is very high. You don't have the stars you used to, but that's because they don't try to build up stars. And that's not a bad thing. Stars were made at the expense of other people. An actress like Ethel Barrymore never looked at anybody else on the stage. There are still some musical-comedy stars who only look at the other actors on opening night. After that, they do what they want.
Interview/"W": a Fairchild publication, 4-30:6.

Edward Albee
Playwright, Director
3

. . . I think not every playwright should direct his own work. But if you can stay sober, if you're reasonably articulate, know how to work with actors, and if you can re-member what you intended when you wrote the play, and if you're willing to put up with the tedium—as well as the excitement—of directing, you can probably, if you're somewhat objective, end up with a fair representation of what you intended.
Interview, New York/
The New York Times, 3-28:(2)5.

Brooks Atkinson
Former drama critic,
"The New York Times"
4

In 1976, the American theatre is not magnificent or powerful, but it is alive . . . It will be less and less a part of show business and more a form of community art and ideas. Subsidies are becoming more and more common . . . Theatre will continue, no matter what happens. It is, among many other things, an obsession.
Before American Theatre Association,
Los Angeles, Aug. 8/
Los Angeles Times, 8-10:(4)10.

George Balanchine
Director, New York City Ballet
5

The principle of classic ballet is woman. The woman is queen. Maybe women come to watch men dance, but I'm a man. I know. The man is prince consort. It's like Elizabeth and What's His Name, or the Dutch one. If the women were less important, it would not be ballet. The woman's body is more flexible; there is more technique. Why? Why is Venus the goddess of love, not a man? That's the way it is. Woman is like that. They don't have to fight, go to war. Men can be Generals if they want, or doctors, or what-

WHAT THEY SAID IN 1976

(GEORGE BALANCHINE)

ever. But the woman's function is to fascinate men, to make them work. Men write poetry to dedicate it to woman. Otherwise, there would be no poetry, because who would it be dedicated to?

Interview, Paris/
The New York Times, 10-6:37.

Mikhail Baryshnikov
Ballet dancer

1

Dance is big. Complex. Dancing is about everything—emotional control, physical control and spirit. It's happiness. It's sadness. I mean, [it's] feeling, pure feeling. It's your attitude to the steps, to the music, to what you're doing with all of it. It is your life.

Interview, New York/
Los Angeles Times, 8-25:(1)27.

David Birney
Actor

2

The stage is where I began; it's what I wanted to be; and a lot of promises I made to myself have to do with that work. But, you know, this is America. Television and films are obviously significant. I guess what I find sad about it, if you think back over the careers of some of our best actors, very few of them go back [to the stage] . . . It's no accident that some of our best actors, best minds, best writers, best people are out here [in Hollywood] working in this [films-TV] business— one, because they can contact large numbers of people; and second, because the problems are great, great in New York. A Canadian actress that I worked with doing a couple of plays said that being a stage actor in this country is like being a tinsmith. It's like a past art that nobody is terribly interested in any more. The action, and the money, to be fair, is here [in Hollywood].

Interview, Los Angeles/
The New York Times, 11-17:(C)28.

George Burns
Entertainer

3

Vaudeville died when the talkies came in. For a dollar and a half you got a comfortable seat, and a picture, and then you had the Rockettes and 70 musicians; you couldn't compete with that, you know—and on the way out they'd make out your income tax. They gave you a better show—what's the use of kidding? And vaudeville got so set in its routines. You always knew a wire act would open the show; then there'd be a two-man dancing act; then there'd be a sketch; then there'd be one of the headliners; then there'd be Powers' elephants . . . all great acts, but you saw them year in and year out, and always in the same spots.

Interview, New York/
The National Observer, 1-24:18.

4

Who knows what "timing" is? Timing is having good ears. An audience laughs. When they stop laughing, you speak. That's timing. And if you talk over a laugh, you're an idiot. Anybody can be a straight-man—just wait for the people to stop laughing and then start talking. They laugh . . . you stop . . . you smoke . . . you tell your next joke . . . and they laugh again. And if the laughs are big, you blow your smoke out easy. If the laughs are not too big, you just take a little puff. So, that's timing.

Interview/
Los Angeles Herald-Examiner, 9-6:(B)1.

Richard Burton
Actor

5

I sweat and shake in the wings. But once I'm on I don't think I show my nerves. When I played my first performance [of his current *Equus*] I was terrified I'd lost the ability to command. But the minute I walked out on the stage in front of the audience I knew I still had the authority, the presence, whatever, and I breathed a secret sigh. That's another intangible of acting—the ability to "take stage."

Certain actors have it, others simply don't. I don't know whether it's sex or power or fame or a mixture of all those things. Actually, it can't be fame, because when I first discovered I had stage presence I was 25 and nobody knew my name.

Interview, New York/
The New York Times, 4-4:(2)10.

Joseph Chaikin
Actor, Director
1

[Saying he prefers the stage to films and television]: [In movies and TV] the audience is, in fact, not present—that is, not while the acting is taking place. The kind of acting in which the actor pretends he is actually living these experiences has its place, definitely. Sure, I like to imagine Elizabeth Taylor is Cleopatra or something of that sort. But that isn't acting that acknowledges the actor-audience contact. When I am on stage I feel that I am the audience in action—that is, I am acting for the audience in its basic emotions.

Interview, New York/
The New York Times, 3-7:(2)5.

Hans Conried
Actor
2

There aren't that many plays being written today. [Playwright Neil] Simon is of course marvelous and he sells tickets. But if I had to give a weakness of today's American playwrights, it would be that most live in New York and write for New York audiences. That is very limited.

Interview, Dallas/
The Dallas Times Herald, 8-25:(E)9.

Agnes de Mille
Choreographer
3

I'm really like a playwright. That is my real value as a choreographer. I tell a story, and I tell it well. My big strength is not in the lyrical development of movement, but in the telling dramatic gesture—and the funny one.

That's what comes easily for me, and I hit it like a bull's-eye.

Interview, New York/
The New York Times, 7-4:(2)1.

Colleen Dewhurst
Actress
4

I'd love to work on Broadway every year, but it would mean I would have to limit myself to only one medium, and I can't come out every September with a new Broadway show. I love the theatre, but every time a show closed on me, I'd be out on the street again. It's hard to make a living that way.

Interview/"W": a Fairchild publication, 9-17:24.

Martin Esslin
Professor of drama, Stanford University;
Former director, radio drama department,
British Broadcasting Corporation
5

[On the difference between British and American actors]: The difference in quality is often attributed to the role of the professional theatre schools in England against the role of university drama departments in America. To my way of thinking, the universities provide a fine liberal-arts education, but they are not especially geared for training professional actors. Lacking that background, American actors tend to be talented but with limited range . . . The English actor from the beginning of his or her training will constantly be moving from Shakespeare to the moderns and back again . . . Where Americans excel is in the musical theatre—the English simply can't sing and dance and tap as well as the musical actors here [in the U.S.]—and these people *do* come out of a craft-type training that the straight-drama people don't. It's just the reverse in England, with our highly trained legitimate-theatre actors, but with our poorly skilled musical-theatre people.

Interview, Stanford University/
San Francisco Examiner & Chronicle, 12-12:
(Datebook)42.

Cy Feuer
Producer
1

The essential thing in musical theatre is to involve an audience. That has to be done in terms of how people are feeling today, not how they were feeling yesterday. It's the subscriber of 30 we have to concentrate on now, not the one of 70.

Interview/
Los Angeles Times, 4-25:(Calendar)48.

Margot Fonteyn
Ballerina
2

I think the dancer cannot be separated from the person. It's the whole picture that counts on stage as it does in life—everything together, gradually building like coral.

Interview, Los Angeles/
Los Angeles Herald-Examiner, 6-2:(B)1.

John Gielgud
Actor
3

When I see theatres like the new mausoleum in Washington, the Kennedy Center, I get depressed. Theatre has a sort of squalor that's necessary to give it a kind of pungency.

Interview/Newsweek, 11-29:76.

Brendan Gill
Drama critic,
"The New Yorker" magazine
4

I don't consider myself a critic. I'm a reviewer . . . A critic addresses himself to the author, the creator. A reviewer addresses himself to his audience. So, in reviewing plays, I try to write what it's like to be watching a particular play.

Interview/
The Washington Post, 2-29:(F)4.

David Gockley
General manager, Houston Grand Opera
5

You don't have big Broadway shows any more. You've just got gimmick shows like

[A] *Chorus Line*, with only 16 or 17 people. *Camelot* could never be produced today. The effect has been to ruin the creativity and experimentation that used to take place. Shows on Broadway are shows that have succeeded someplace else, like *Chorus Line*, or they're formula shows whose elements—stars and composers—have succeeded before.

Interview/"W": a Fairchild publication, 11-26:2.

Billy Goldenberg
Composer
6

Too many plays and musicals are concerned with looking backward. I don't mean history should be neglected, but there's a tremendous amount of fascinating activity in current life. Not nearly enough is written about it. I'm astonished when producers go wild about an incident in the life of Queen Victoria, or a love story taking place during the War of 1812. What excites me is finding out what makes people tick right now. I'd love to write a musical about paranoia. If the present is too close, let's try the future.

Interview/
Los Angeles Times, 10-17:(Home)34.

Martha Graham
Dancer, Choreographer
7

[Saying that dance had an uphill struggle for acceptance in the U.S.]: It was because we were once a new country and dance was not an intrinsic part of our inheritance. It had been imported from Europe. But today, there are more wonderful dancers in this country and in the world than there have ever been. There is a terrific interest in the dance. It is even a dedication, more than an interest.

Upon receipt of Medal of Freedom award,
Washington, Oct. 14/
The New York Times, 10-15:(A)12.

Peter Hall
Director, National Theatre, London
8

[On criticism that the high cost of the new National Theatre complex will financially hurt regional theatre in Britain]: If the National Theatre's costs, already pared to the bone, become any kind of threat to the health of the very profession that theatre exists to nourish, then it would be a negation of what we stand for. The new National Theatre is intended to serve the theatre at large: to increase audiences; to provide a focus; to give more work to actors and directors and more opportunities to playwrights; to loan its stages to regional and fringe theatres when and if it wants them.

The New York Times, 3-10:24.

1

The function of this place [the National Theatre] is to aid the debate of society with itself. Theatre is one of the few forums left where living people gather to confront problems and go out in some respects changed.

Newsweek, 3-22:74.

Joseph Hardy
Director
2

[On opening nights]: I'm depressed and lonely, because when a play opens the director's work is all done and nobody wants him any more.

Interview/The New York Times, 12-24:(C)2.

Rosemary Harris
Actress
3

I think it's marvelous that so many revivals are being done. I think new generations of audiences are growing up and want to see [them]. I think that the classics are being done more today. About 20 years ago, to do a classic was courting disaster. Now there's *The Glass Menagerie,* with Maureen Stapelton, and Vanessa Redgrave is coming to do *The Lady From the Sea.* This gives a boost to theatre. I think that in the past there was a sense of hangdog if you were in a revival. Now you can glory in it. Producers are always looking for new scripts to make them a fortune, but here are these plays right under their noses.

Interview, New York/
The New York Times, 2-11:46.

Helen Hayes
Actress
4

I have no idea why playwrights are rejecting the theatre, shrinking away from it, except that there's an awful lot of time and energy and mental vitality that goes into writing a play. When my husband [the late playwright Charles MacArthur] got in a jam while writing a script, he would reluctantly use some beautiful lines he was saving for something else, some future masterpiece— and he acted like he was spending his last dime. Playwrights are often like that, spending their thoughts reluctantly. It's a hard way of life, and I don't think that playwrights in America get as much back from it as they should.

Interview/
U.S. News & World Report, 9-13:61.

Katharine Hepburn
Actress
5

The terrible thing about acting in the theatre is that you have to do it at night. If I could only perform in the morning, I'd be the happiest actor in the world. I could just take over the matinees and let someone else play in the evening. I love the matinee audiences. They're happy and I'm happy because . . . I'm wide awake!

Interview, New York/
The New York Times, 1-16:27.

Rock Hudson
Actor
6

I've spent 25 years being Charlie Movie Star. Now I want the confidence of theatre acting, where there's no director saying, "Cut. Let's do it again." On the stage, you're on your own. It's terribly exciting. You really feel a sense of responsibility.

Interview, Beverly Hills, Calif./
San Francisco Examiner & Chronicle, 5-2:
(Scene)16.

WHAT THEY SAID IN 1976

Eugene Ionesco
Playwright

1

They say I do theatre of non-communication, but that's totally false. Only the critics say that. My theatre is not absurd, not at all. In the early days of the '50s, "theatre of the absurd" was a new name to distinguish the new theatre from the old, because there was a rupture between the two and there was a lot of talk about absurdity from people like [Jean-Paul] Sartre. But in fact there is a lot that is absurd in life. I often meet people who ask me to write "theatre of the absurd." I ask them, "How do you know it is absurd?" And they reply, "Because the critics say so."

Interview, Washington/
The Washington Post, 11-24:(B)3.

Robert Joffrey
Director, Joffrey Ballet, New York

2

[On criticism that his company does pop, disposable ballets of little lasting merit]: What people say is their business, but I really don't care. I'm grateful that audiences like us. A very important part of the Joffrey Ballet is that it relates to audiences. A company must both preserve its heritage and create contemporary things for the dancers. Not every ballet we have will last forever. The ballets created at the moment are important because the dancers have to dance about their times, to use music and ideas and people that are of their times.

Interview, New York/
The New York Times, 3-7:(2)10.

Michael Kahn
Artistic director,
American Shakespeare Theatre,
Stratford, Connecticut

3

. . . at the heart of Shakespeare is language —rhythm, stress, meaning. I've been concerned with American actors and audiences getting involved with that language—making it their own, without denying the fact that it is still in verse, still "Shakespearean." When I started, there were two ways of doing

Shakespeare in America—first, butchering the text, which comes from the Method, where "talkin' well is phony," and second, the watered-down Gielgud style practiced by American actors who went to RADA or LAMDA and came back with English technique. My idea of American Shakespeare is to try to bring the same kind of life and reality to it that you would to a modern play, but doing it *through* the text.

Interview/The New York Times, 8-22:(2)5.

Gene Kelly
Actor, Dancer

4

· [On the dancing he used to do in musicals]: We considered what we did an art form, even though it was popular. I never wanted to dance to Brahms or Tchaikovsky; I wanted to dance to George Gershwin and Jerome Kern. The dancing that is being bought and paid for, and is being subsidized, today is classic ballet. Classic ballet has finally come to the conclusion that it can incorporate some popular dancing in it. I used to get up on a soapbox and say, "We steal from you, why don't you steal from us?" Now they're starting to.

Interview, Beverly Hills, Calif./
The New York Times, 5-10:32.

Pauline Koner
Dancer, Choreographer

5

[On her forming a new dance company]: People said to me, "You're insane to start a company now. This is the time you should enjoy life." Twenty-five years ago, I began a course called "Elements of Performing," to drag out of kids the tools you need to have an impact on stage. I want to transfer this knowledge, and I owe it to this generation. I say especially this generation because I saw the art of performing disappear and the art of acrobats take its place. Technique has become an end in itself. It's "How high can I get my leg?" At the inception of modern dance, the point was to get it from the guts. Today's emphasis on technique has externalized modern dance.

Interview/The New York Times, 10-15:(C)14.

Eva Le Gallienne
Actress
1

Live theatre will never die. It fills a need. Nothing can replace that sense of an experience shared—that communion between actor and audience. Actors today are spoiled. They don't have a hard enough time. The great actors all started very young. Mrs. Fiske was eight, Maude Adams was four, Mme. Duse was four. They didn't go to college and waste all those years. You learn acting by having to, by playing before a paying audience. Too many young actors today—and there are too many—think acting is easy. I don't think they realize that it's a very great art—can be—and that it takes all your life and that you never get to the end of it.

Interview, Los Angeles/
Los Angeles Times, 12-19:(Calendar)84.

Alan Jay Lerner
Playwright, Lyricist
2

I think we're beginning to see a neoclassic, neoromantic—well, neoprofessional theatre. I always thought it was rather depressing during the '60s and early '70s when people kept saying, "We've got to bring the young into the theatre." I'm all for bringing everyone into the theatre, but to tailor something for the young is the rankest kind of commercialism. I mean, who are you then? You're just somebody trying to dish up something for somebody. The point is, theatre has never been for the young or the old or the middle-aged. It's for people, that's all, and that's all it should be. It is not a popular medium. Heavens, more people see a soap opera during the week than ever saw *Gone With the Wind* or *My Fair Lady* on the stage. In some ways I think we alienated our audience by trying to cater to the immature. Imagine if someone had said to Shakespeare, or Gershwin, or Mozart, "Write something for 16-year-olds." That's no way to get lasting theatre. The audience was alienated, but I think they're coming back now.

Interview, Washington/
The Washington Post, 2-29:(F)3.

Sam Levene
Actor
3

The glamour of the theatre? That's a lot of bunk. It's not glamour; it's hard work, getting a part, getting yourself "up" for the performance night after night, keeping your concentration—and, when it's over, they forget you.

Interview, Los Angeles/
Los Angeles Herald-Examiner, 12-19:(D)7.

Herman Levin
Producer
4

[On his revival of *My Fair Lady*]: This is the classical musical show of the American theatre. I think a classical musical has every right to be done over, just as a classical play is done. Basically two kinds of people will come: those who saw it before, and those who didn't see it before.

Interview, New York/
The New York Times, 3-22:21.

Jerry Lewis
Comedian, Entertainer
5

A good performer doesn't think about the audience first. He starts with himself. He's looking to satisfy his needs through giving other people pleasure. That kind of selfish, selfish act I have no qualms about. I'll be that selfish.

Interview, New York/
The Dallas Times Herald, 12-7:(C)7.

Joshua Logan
Director, Playwright
6

There is nothing audiences like better than an accident on stage. That, I think, is an exaggeration of the secret of the theatre: Each performance is unique, it's slightly different, it's live, it's happening now. It's its own "accident." Nothing stays exactly the same, the way it does in the movies. Audiences cough, laugh, listen, applaud. They know that sometimes an extra bit of applause will make the actors do a little more. There's a sense of

475

WHAT THEY SAID IN 1976

(JOSHUA LOGAN)

spontaneity, of excitement—a festive thing that happens when you go to see a play—that you can't get anywhere else.

Interview, Los Angeles/
Los Angeles Times, 5-26:(4)16.

Shirley MacLaine
Actress, Entertainer

1

I feel terror, sheer, pure, unadulterated terror from top to bottom when I'm on stage. These [performers] who get a laugh and then relax—that's not me. Being a dancer, I'm a masochist and so I must love fright. Frank [Sinatra], Liza [Minnelli] and Sammy [Davis, Jr.] say I'll never get over it, and that I shouldn't. They say that when they forget to be afraid, then they're not as good.

Interview, New York/
The New York Times, 6-25:(C)2.

2

[On her musical cabaret act]: You really find out about your personality when you're performing live, on stage. There's nothing more exposing. You're not a character, you're yourself—singing, dancing, telling jokes. If you make an ass out of yourself, you know it right away. Even your philosophy is exposed, because you've got to get up every night to feel happy. If you're not in good physical or psychological health, it shows. If your sense of humor is default, it shows . . . Audiences are used to technological product—films or TV—but when they see you live, it's all hanging out in front of them. It's an honest form of communication.

Interview/
Los Angeles Times, 10-3:(Calendar)33.

Ted Mann
Artistic director,
Circle in the Square theatre, New York

3

I always said that where it was at were plays that dealt with people, with families, with their interactions. I'm glad to see that the pendulum is swinging back in that direction, to plays that people can relate to. As

long as there are people, there will be theatre; and if you do good plays with good actors, they will come to see you.

Interview, New York/
The New York Times, 3-8:33.

Armina Marshall
Playwright, Producer, Director

4

The problem in the theatre today is getting proper plays and proper playwrights . . . Plays today are not really plays—only mood pieces. I want plays that have a beginning, a middle and an end. A play must be about something and by a playwright who knows structurally how to do it. Too many plays are without any real design.

Interview/The New York Times, 1-1:12.

Mary Martin
Actress

5

Movies were not fun for me, and I don't see any point in doing anything you don't have joy in. Making movies was so static and it bored me to death. I think now, because of television when things have to be shot so quickly, there must be some difference. But it was so sterile, and you just sat. Boresville. I like something that has some dynamics. I'm a ham. I like to play it and hear it and have the rapport of the audience. When we'd go on the road [with a play], I adored it. It kept me alive in a part to open every week somewhere else; but, again, it required total devotion. I'd go for years without going out to lunch, without talking to friends, without going shopping. It was the only way I could do it. There was no compromise.

Interview/Los Angeles Times, 4-20:(4)6.

Tony Martin
Singer

6

We're a toy. Entertainers are not a necessary commodity. We're not food or shelter or clothing. As long as you stay good enough, you're fine. But you can be an unknown overnight. Only politics is rougher that way. An entertainer can overcome a bad review but he can never overcome empty seats. Getting those behinds in the seats is the name of the game.

Interview, Chicago/
The Dallas Times Herald, 12-6:(E)5.

Burgess Meredith
Actor
1

It's theatre, not movies, that stores memory patterns [for an actor]. In a play, you have a longer interest and sometimes traumatic rehearsals. You sculpt a play as an actor. You have a stronger sense of the moment . . . [Films] just don't bring the actor the kind of happiness that theatre does. I remember every day of *Little Foxes* in Westwood last summer, but not one afternoon of *The Hindenburg.*

Interview, Los Angeles/
Los Angeles Herald-Examiner, 1-11:(E)6.

David Merrick
Producer
2

The problem with both stage and screen right now is that they are constantly being upstaged by the news, so the writers drop back to nostalgia, to revivals. Well, I don't *like* revivals . . . The theatre has lost all its writers to Hollywood. The stage seems to have lost the glamour it had once upon a time. But I'm still stagestruck, and I'll be back.

Interview/ The New York Times, 10-15:(C)6.

Yoko Morishita
Ballerina
3

When I'm on stage, I'm thinking all the time. This is my strength. What I'm always thinking about is the role, not the technique. I want to impress the audience not with how long I stand on pointe, or how high I leap, but with the feeling of the role—the deeper, inner meaning. This is what I am studying all the time. When I was dancing Aurora, I was thinking about her character—a mixture of the dignity of a princess with the naivete of

a young girl. This is what I was always trying to communicate to the audience.

Interview, New York/
The New York Times, 7-11:(2)1.

Robert Morse
Actor
4

I loved having done *How to Succeed* [*in Business Without Really Trying*], but that was 15 years ago. There should have been a few others [hit shows] between then and now. You don't go to Robert Redford and say, "I loved you in *Barefoot in the Park.*" If I had the equivalent of *How to Succeed* in the dress business I would have 50 stores by now and be able to retire. But the show closes—and all shows close—and, when it does, you are back at the beginning.

Interview, Dallas/
The Dallas Times Herald, 9-12:(E)1.

Ivan Nagy
Ballet dancer
5

I don't think we [dancers] are really that creative. If I look at a composer, a choreographer, a painter, a sculptor—they are creating. A pianist, a singer, a dancer . . . we are just instruments. I'm a dancer. I'm an instrument for a choreographer who creates the whole thing. I have to participate . . . Even if two or three or five or 100 people have to do the same thing, I will be different, because it is my individuality which makes it different from other people. But I think the choreographer is the creative artist. We are just like puppets, like marionettes.

Interview, New York/
The Christian Science Monitor, 1-26:23.

Anthony Newley
Actor, Singer, Composer
6

I swear to you every creative person is unhappy. I will brook no interference on that. You have to put show business in the proper perspective. It's a search for approval. As I've grown older, I realize how stupid that is.

WHAT THEY SAID IN 1976

(ANTHONY NEWLEY)

I can't enjoy it too much having to get the approval of my audience. But it has become my meal ticket.

Interview, Los Angeles/
Los Angeles Herald-Examiner, 12-15:(B)1.

Wayne Newton
Singer

1

I just have this basic philosophy of entertaining: Listen, people come into a showroom, they've been hassled getting reservations, the wife has a new hairdo and probably hit the old man for a dress, they had to tip the maitre d' for a good table and maybe they're still not sitting where they want. When a performer comes out on stage, the audience doesn't need its religion or political beliefs threatened. They want to be entertained. I'm not trying to teach anything. I don't allow political humor. If I go to see a guy sing, that's what I want to see him do. And you have to act the right way. People don't want to think you're doing them a favor by showing up.

Interview, Las Vegas, Nev./
Los Angeles Times, 2-29:(Calendar)48.

Mike Nichols
Director

2

I have a theory why comics are often irascible and self-concerned and tend to stay up all night with a coterie: There's no period of time between the work and the reward. For a comic, the laugh *is* the reward. The rest of us work at something, and after some time there is a reward. The actor has to wait until the end of the performance, but the comic gets a response after every line.

Interview/The New York Times, 11-26:(C)4.

Laurence Olivier
British actor

3

. . . when you're talking about comedy, you're talking about the highest achievement in the theatre. I don't subscribe to the view that tragedy is harder than comedy. Comedy is harder, and it's more important than

tragedy. I've been impatient when I felt I should do tragedy out of service to the medium. I don't get pleasure out of it; it's a stern duty.

Interview, Los Angeles/
The Washington Post, 1-28:(C)4.

4

Americans seem to think that the English theatre is infinitely superior in some mysterious and miraculous way. Let me say that your [U.S.] theatre, from an actor's point of view, is equally mysterious—and, at its best, equally miraculous . . . I have known and been an avid fan of the American theatre for the best part of 50 years. Looking back, it comes as a great surprise to me that my personal ventures on Broadway number only ten.

Interview, New York/
The Dallas Times Herald,12-12:(F)5.

Joseph Papp
Producer

5

In today's theatre, subscription plans are essential. An audience absolutely has to be guaranteed. People talk about these culture ventures happily, but, unless people go to them, it's empty, dangerous talk. Ideal theatre can be serious, is serious, but in an interesting way. You have to leave theatre feeling and knowing more about yourself than when you went in. Theatre maintains an enormous spirit and zest, but the spirit of the audience is vital to it. It is a mutual understanding, theatre people and audiences.

At civic luncheon, Baltimore, April 20/
The Washington Post, 4-25:(G)13.

6

My interest lies in a single artistic idea—either in a play or in a particular performance. The fact that I operate on a large scale is not basic to my notions at all. If something becomes successful and reaches a thousand people, that's great, but it's not necessary. I'm interested in the smallest thing: creation

478

itself . . . It's the history of all my work. People get confused. They see only scope and entrepreneurship. But I work on a very small scale, which is looking a writer in the eye and talking about the play. The fact that the Shakespeare Festival has a $10-million budget and 300 to 400 people on payroll is merely the administrative result of an essential feeling about art—in particular the theatre, which is my outlet. Its effect on society is interesting to me, but it's not central to my life. Whether I reach 40 people or 5,000 doesn't matter to me.

Interview, Los Angeles/
Los Angeles Times, 7-25:(Calendar)48.

Arthur Penn
Director

1

The theatre was supposedly on its way out until fairly recently. It was responding to a kind of convulsion that took place in society in the '60s. The play of ideas, or the play as such, seemed inappropriate . . . Now there's a more contemplative response, and people are returning to the theatre to encounter emotion and idea . . . This is back "in"—and it's not *Hair* or strip-to-the-buff and play rock and blow them out of the theatre. It begins to be a place where we talk about experiences we know. There is a constant and genuine hunger for the theatre that never goes away.

Interview/
The Christian Science Monitor, 5-27:26.

2

In film, whether you ascribe to the auteur theory or not, a certain authorship does devolve upon the director, who's running the entire army that makes the film. In theatre, I've always thought the best director is the most inconspicuous. The play should never seem manipulated by one hand.

Interview, New York/
The New York Times, 12-12:(2)4.

Harold Pinter
Playwright

3

I've never been able to sit down and say,

"Now I'm going to write a play." I just have no alternative but to wait for the thing to be released within me. The way I go about things is to write the whole thing off very quickly—pouring a drink, having a cigarette, getting up and stumbling around. Something is taking place and my task is just to allow that thing to take place and follow it. So that one series of facts determines another and one image breeds another.

Interview/Newsweek, 11-29:77.

Christopher Plummer
Actor

4

Please don't make me look like I'm this classical actor. I think of myself as a contemporary one, too. The thing about the classics, however, is that you always need to go back to them. They call on the peak of your talents. It's like the Olympics of theatre.

Interview, Beverly Hills, Calif./
Los Angeles Times, 8-27:(4)23.

Eleanor Prosser
Acting chairman, department of drama,
Stanford University

5

For me, perhaps the most important ingredients of theatre are absolute honesty, which necessarily entails humility, and an eagerness to share every insight, every emotion and every fleeting moment with the audience. If the audience is dismissed—as it often is when a director and cast revel in the private ecstacies of their own creativity—theatre does not exist.

Interview/
The Christian Science Monitor, 11-8:(B)5.

Lynn Redgrave
Actress

6

Reviews can be terribly destructive. That's why I don't read them any more. If you get bad reviews, and people still buy tickets and seem to like you when they see your performance—well, that's not so bad. But when a

WHAT THEY SAID IN 1976

(LYNN REDGRAVE)

bad review keeps people away, that can be terrible. And sometimes you just don't get it out of your mind. Even a good review can be bad. I remember when I was playing the mute daughter in *Mother Courage* at the National Theatre. One very respected reviewer, in a very serious paper, spent two whole paragraphs talking about a particular piece of business I had done, and how wonderful he thought it was. I dare say he meant to be kind, but for the rest of the run—and that play ran a very long time—I never again could do that piece of business without having it flash across my mind what the reviewer had said about it. And, of course, I never again got it completely right.

Interview, New York/
The Dallas Times Herald, 3-22:(D)5.

Ginger Rogers
Actress, Entertainer   1

[On her nightclub act]: Why am I doing what I'm doing? Because entertainment is not with us any more. Entertainment seems to be a nasty word. Instead of entertainment, we are seeing people disemboweled. Everything is ugly, everything is violent, everything is obscene, everything is permissive. They call all of this ugliness entertainment. That's not entertainment. What I am doing is entertainment. It's dancing, humor and fun. It's nice people in a happy atmosphere. There's not a four-letter word in the whole show. *That's* entertainment.

News conference, Dallas, May 13/
The Dallas Times Herald, 5-14:(F)10.

Gene Saks
Director   2

I'm in a business where anyone can be an "authority"—absolutely anyone. The theatre is full of "authorities," but if I didn't know more than most of them, I'd kill myself. I'd have to. Otherwise, what would be the

point of even being in the theatre?

Interview, New York/
The New York Times, 6-18:(C)2.

Alan Schneider
Director; Director-designate, drama
division, Juilliard School   3

Where once shows traveled from New York to the regions, now they come from the regions to New York. At this point, I think *all* theatre is regional—New York is just one of the regions. The growth of theatre outside of New York is not only inevitable, it is necessary, because it is making theatre part of our national consciousness.

Interview, New York/
The New York Times, 9-19:(2)5.

Dan Seltzer
Professor of English,
Princeton University; Actor   4

[On his experience acting in a Broadway play]: I've been exposed to the gritty realities of play production in New York City. And although a good bit of the acting itself was rewarding, the over-all experience was unspeakably depressing. The two words which rule most decision-making on Broadway are greed and stupidity.

People, 8-23:50.

Neil Simon
Playwright   5

You have to be crazy to think of your plays as works of art. That would be like writing under the title, "An important new play by Neil Simon." That's pretentious. A work of art is qualitative . . . I haven't the slightest idea if what I'm writing is going to be a hit or a flop, or good or bad. It just feels good as I'm writing it.

Interview, New York/
Los Angeles Herald-Examiner, 2-29:
(California Living)28.

1

[On his moving from New York to Los Angeles]: I am now referred to as "a New York influence." Whatever the hell that is. This geography business! As if where you live has anything to do with how well you write. I've had people ask me seriously, "But how can you *think* out there [in L.A.]?" Ridiculous! I could have written *Plaza Suite* here or *California Suite* in New York. I wrote *Heartbreak Kid*, which I feel is my best screenplay, in Majorca, not in Manhattan. A writer takes his world with him. There's no geography to audiences either. People say to me, "Yeah, terrific line for L.A.—but will it get a laugh in New York?" Of course it will. If it's funny here it'll be funny in New York, or New Haven or Wilmington or Minneapolis or in the movie version in some small town in Oregon. People are people. Theatre is theatre.

Interview, Los Angeles/
The New York Times, 6-6:(2)5.

Red Skelton
Comedian

2

So many comedians today are a long way from comedy. I'm not condemning them, but I am saying that very few comedians were ever clowns or mimes, and that is the basis of comedy.

Interview/
Los Angeles Herald-Examiner, 12-30:(B)1.

Stephen Sondheim
Composer-lyricist

3

[On recent musicals he has admired]: Actually, "admire" is an odd word, because there is very little I admire. For me, the word means something I'd like to sign my name to, and I see very little I'd like to sign my name to that I haven't already signed my name to, if you know what I mean. My favorite musical on Broadway at the moment, by far, is *The Wiz*, because it captures the most elusive quality there is—joy. I really admire that because I personally don't know how to do it. If I con-

sciously sat down and said I wanted to write something that would send people out of the theatre *really* happy, I wouldn't know how to go about it.

Interview, New York/
The New York Times, 1-4:(2)5.

Lee Strasberg
Artistic director, Actors Studio

4

The movies have siphoned off a good deal of the pure entertainment that previously only the theatre supplied. If people could see Paul Newman, Marlon Brando and Al Pacino in good plays, then the theatre would be what it should be today. The problem for the theatre is to create an environment that will be stimulating to the best actors. Talented actors will not come back to the theatre for money—the theatre cannot possibly give them as much as they get in movies. The only thing the theatre can give them is excitement and artistic satisfaction. We have more and greater theatrical talent [in the U.S.] than anywhere in the world. What we need is to create a theatre of national standing and international reputation. When there is a home, people find their way there.

Interview, New York/People, 12-13:105.

Glen Tetley
Former artistic director,
Stuttgart Ballet

5

[On his resignation from the Stuttgart Ballet]: I don't know if anyone can really say exactly what went wrong or even what really happened, but I certainly learned that being the director of a huge company like Stuttgart takes 100 per cent of your time—the catch is that being a choreographer also takes 100 per cent of your time.

The New York Times, 3-21:(2)2.

Sada Thompson
Actress

6

If you've been exclusively in film, the stage seems artificial. For me, it's natural to be on

WHAT THEY SAID IN 1976

a stage. It's a perfectly natural way to tell a story. Everybody is there on the stage. You don't have to consider film technique where you're doing somebody else's closeup but you yourself are out of the picture. I think it's much more natural to see both people if the two are reacting to each other. They tend to overdo closeups. The similarities are there, also. In film or on stage, it's not only the words spoken. An interior monologue goes on in you all the time.

Interview/
Los Angeles Herald-Examiner, 3-17:(A)11.

Jack Weston
Actor
1

I have always been a great admirer of Bert Lahr. He was my idol—a physical comic who could communicate so much through his face, his eyes, the curl of his lip, the way he used his hands. Zero Mostel, too, and James Coco and the great Bobby Clark were all influences. They were all part of a marvelous school of physical comedy that's dying—or dead. The material is no longer being written. We have cerebral comedy now—Woody Allen and Mel Brooks. It's "ha-ha" instead of "ha-ha-ha!" I'm not knocking that kind of comedy. But if you only knew the laughter you get with comedy from the older tradition. You hear laughs that sound like thunderclaps! I get goosebumps in the middle of a scene—a couple of times I've almost wept with joy, right on stage [in the new play, *California Suite*]. To

look out there and see people doubled over, unable to straighten up in their seats . . . The polite laughter you hear with verbal comedy is fine, but maybe people are getting a little tired of it. With the physical comedy in those two sketches in *California Suite*, people in the audience my age, middle-aged, say, "My God, here it is again!" And the youngsters say, "My God, I've never seen anything like it!"

Interview, New York/
The New York Times, 7-25:(2)5.

Peter Wood
Director
2

The only reason directors generally don't like stars is that stars are such a pain in the ass. But that's what you're paid all that money for—to deal with pains in the ass.

Interview/
"W": a Fairchild publication, 2-6:2.

Irene Worth
Actress
3

The audience has the right to expect what a child expects when it goes to the theatre for the first time. What is that? To name it is to lessen it. But it's what a little boy I know said to his godmother when she took him to see *Peter Pan*. When the play ended, he said, "Oh, curtain, curtain, please don't come down." That's what I want for the theatre.

Interview, New York/
The New York Times, 2-5:26.

TELEVISION AND RADIO

Danny Arnold
Producer
1

The [TV] network depends on its share of audience. It doesn't want to offend anybody [with its programming]—which is pretty difficult to do. I wouldn't like to start out with that kind of job—you know, to say, "I'm going to do something that everybody is going to like." If you do something that everybody likes, of necessity you abdicate all points of view, you eliminate all controversy, and what you wind up with is a kind of innocuous pablum.

TV program/
"You Should See What You're Missing,"
Public Broadcasting Service, 11-26.

Erik Barnouw
Professor emeritus of dramatic arts,
Columbia University;
Former TV writer, producer
2

. . . there are enormous pressures from among better-educated people for more news, more documentaries, more cultural programs [on TV]. And some of the network news departments themselves would desperately like to do more things of this sort—some of which have gotten a lot of attention. There are people in Hollywood who feel that they can expand the subjects of drama—that audiences are ready now to handle more-complex themes. But the fact remains that those who run television networks still measure success in terms of selling advertising. So it looks to me as if television will continue pretty much along its present path—no quantum leap in any direction for the moment.

Interview, Washington/
U.S. News & World Report, 3-1:27.

Terrel H. Bell
Commissioner of Education of
the United States
3

TV has created a great interest in sports. If only we could get some of that interest into the works of Shakespeare. TV has the potential to tell people, "Hey, you can take a much higher road than you're taking, and out of it you'll get a lot more fulfillment and gratification." Our human misery and sadness and murder—most of it—is caused by the greatest malady of all, universal ignorance. And what is the most powerful means of getting at that? Education is one way, and the educational system ought to be a lot better than it is. But television, too, could help. It could do much more to help us keep on learning how to learn.

Interview/ TV Guide, 5-15:13.

Jean-Paul Belmondo
Actor
4

[Saying film stars should not appear on television]: People have got to pay if they want to see a major star. Stars like Lee Marvin do both cinema and telly. But he's a has-been. It's all right to appear in serials if you're over the hill.

The Hollywood Reporter, 3-11:3.

Carol Burnett
Entertainer
5

I've done three [feature] pictures and I've found there's a snobbism among movie people concerning actors in television. They have a way of dismissing them as being good only for the little screen. I did [the feature film *Pete 'n'*] *Tillie* with Walter Matthau. He likes to goad

483

(CAROL BURNETT)

people. Once he asked me, "Why do you do all that TV garbage week after week?" I asked him, "How many movies do you do a year?" He said, "It averages about two and a half." "How long does it take you to make them?" I asked. "Oh," he said, "about eight, 10, 12 weeks." I said, "It takes you 10 weeks to make a piece of garbage. It only takes me four days."

Interview, Los Angeles/
Los Angeles Herald-Examiner, 11-19(B)1.

Johnny Carson
TV talk-show host 1

[On how he handles his *Tonight* TV program]: I'm a comedian. I'm not out there to lead everybody out of Armageddon. All the guys who have tried it—from Les Crane to David Frost—have gone off . . . basically, it's an entertainment show. If you start taking yourself too seriously and try to make great social change, you might as well hang it up. The ratings will go right down the toilet. It's different with an actor like Paul Newman. He can go on screen and be somebody else. But I'm out there every night. I'm "Johnny Carson."

Interview, Los Angeles/
The Washington Post, 8-8:(F)3.

Jimmy Carter
1976 Democratic U.S. Presidential nominee 2

I know there's a very narrow dividing line between censorship on the one hand and a minimization of violence and sex on television . . . [As President,] I think the best thing that I could do is perhaps to express my concern to those who comprise or form those presentations and hope for voluntary —maybe stricter—self-policing in that respect. I would not hesitate, as President, to express my concern about it, and I think that the President's voice would have a beneficial impact, perhaps. But I would be cautious

about how to do that because I'm really strongly opposed to any sort of censorship. I think that if parents and purchasers of goods, who comprise the viewing audience, say, [of] television, if they knew that the President was also concerned, that they might very well let their own displeasure be felt in a more vivid and effective way.

Interview, Los Angeles, Aug. 23/
Los Angeles Times, 8-24:(1)19.

Peggy Charren
President,
Action for Children's Television 3

It seems to us that TV, when it's well done, actually stimulates reading rather than blocking it out. Ask any librarian: If a show is in any way based on a book, kids will storm the library for it. This has happened recently with the books of Laura Ingalls Wilder, which are the basis of [TV's] *Little House on the Prairie.*

TV Guide, 9-4:10.

Paddy Chayefsky
Playwright, Screenwriter 4

Most of the people I know in television are sensible, devoted people. My fear is that they're not going to stay that way. It's an industry built on hysteria—you drop your rating share, and a minute later hysteria sweeps through the network. The basic philosophy in television in dealing with new ideas is to say, "No." After all, 99 per cent of the time you will be proved right. My feeling is that people watch things that are familiar. If you put something unfamiliar on and leave it on long enough it will become familiar. But that's not the way it works. There used to be two seasons a year. Now if you don't make it the first week of the new season, you're out.

Interview/
"W": a Fairchild publication, 11-12:47.

5

Television coarsens all the complexities of human relationships, brutalizes them, makes them insensitive. The point about violence is not so much that it breeds violence—though that is probably true—but that it totally desensitizes viciousness, brutality, murder, death so that we no longer actively feel the pains of the victim or suffer for the mourners or feel their grief. When the *Hindenburg* blew up, the reporter broke down on the radio. I can't imagine anything like that happening today. I imagine a detached, calm description of the ship going up in flames: "I do believe there will be no survivors." We have become desensitized to things that are usually part of the human condition. This is the basic problem of television. We've lost our sense of shock, our sense of humanity.

Interview/ Time, 12-13:79.

James Coco
Actor

1

[On his recent, short-lived TV series]: I don't regret [having done] it. That's the difference between New York actors and Hollywood actors. The Hollywood actor in a flop sits around his pool in Beverly Hills getting a depressed ulcer. The New York actor goes home and says, "Okay, I'm ready to do a play." I've been in 800 flops that closed in New Haven. So 13 weeks in a TV series is a long run, baby!

*Interview, New York/
San Francisco Examiner & Chronicle, 8-8:
(Datebook)13.*

Robert Coles
*Research psychiatrist,
Harvard University Health Services*

2

Television is a great transforming element in the lives of children, as radio was in the '20s and '30s. If you observe these children, you find they do get brainwashed to a degree—mesmerized by the "tube"—to the point where they even parrot commercials. But there comes a point when that begins to stop. After *Batman* and *Superman* and, yes, *The Electric Company*, the natural process of growing up takes over. There is just so much

the children can take. They become bored, they don't listen, they go outside and play and fight, just like kids have always done. It is childhood asserting itself over a technological instrument . . . One has to be careful [about violence on TV], but I think some common sense should prevail. Children who are already troubled and who see violent things can be hurt by it, just as some normal children who see constant violence on TV can find a sanction for violent acts of their own. But I part company with people who underestimate the capacity of children to maintain a perspective. In general, I think children can play with toy guns, they can see violence on television, and still grow up to be normal children—and, indeed, not really be all that affected by what they have seen.

*Interview, Washington/
U.S. News & World Report, 9-6:60.*

William Conrad
Actor

3

Most of television is crap. *Cannon* [his former series] was crap. I was delighted to see it cancelled . . . I don't mean to demean *Cannon* by calling it crap. It's as good as anything else on television. It's what the audience wants. If they wanted something better, they wouldn't be watching it. It's just that I don't watch much television. I prefer to do other things with my time.

*Interview, Chicago/
Los Angeles Times, 9-16:(4)26.*

John Denver
Singer, Songwriter

4

Television is an incredible, mind-blowing, possibly devastating, sometimes uplifting medium and it reaches a whole lot of people with its worst and its best. I hope to make my contribution on the "best" end.

*Interview, Denver/
The New York Times, 3-28:(2)18.*

485

WHAT THEY SAID IN 1976

Thomas Elmendorf
Former president,
California Medical Association 1

One of the lessons of television is that violence works. If you have a problem with someone, the school of TV says to slap him in the face, stab him in the back. By aggressive acts, the bad guy, for example, may gain control of grazing land, gold mines, nightclubs, and perhaps the whole town. Not until the very end is he usually punished. And, as in the case of *The Godfather* . . . punishment may never really occur. Because most of the program has shown how well violence has paid off, punishment at the end tends not to have much of an inhibitory effect . . . studies have shown that viewing violence blunts a child's sensitivity to it. They become jaded to violence on the screen. They condition themselves to avoid being upset by the gougings, smashings and stompings they see on TV. If they did get involved, their emotions could be shattered . . . What happens when these children grow up and no longer are under parental control, when they are conditioned into thinking that violence works, and when they have a diminished sensitivity to violence? What happens to these children when they grow up and *do* have access to weapons? What happens when they grow up in a world apathetic to violence?

Before House Subcommittee on
Communications, Los Angeles, Aug. 17/
Vital Speeches, 10-1:765,766.

Peter Falk
Actor 2

Television can be a terrific medium, but the economics prevents it. There's no proper balance of the people in charge to give the audience what it wants and the other responsibility to set a standard and see if the audience would respond to something else if given the chance. I spend an afternoon with people and I find people funny. They're really funny. I look at TV and I don't find the so-called jokes funny, the one-liners that are supposed to be funny. If the audience finds that funny, maybe it's because the audience

has been conditioned. They're cued in. When they don't think it's funny, they wonder, "Is there something wrong with me?"

Interview, Los Angeles/
Los Angeles Herald-Examiner, 2-20:(B)3.

Barbara Feldon
Actress 3

There is a certain amount of snobbery involved in discriminating between TV and movie stars. In England, performers seem to divide their time between film and television and stage appearances without any barriers going up. I don't know if it's justified, but there is a feeling in our business [in the U.S.] that you can't cross over, that being available on TV makes you less desirable for the movies. Perhaps there's something to it. I haven't been in enough movies to know. But Dick Benjamin, for one, has told me that you can notice a distinct difference between TV and movie celebrities. Movie fans are more inclined to be awe-struck, to treat you as something special. TV has a familiar tone. The people on movie screens seem to become vessels of fantasy, and getting too close may spoil the fantasy.

Interview, Washington/
The Dallas Times Herald, 2-29:(D)5.

Seymour Feshbach
Professor of psychology,
University of California, Los Angeles 4

I don't feel the evidence supports the idea that televised violence begets imitation to any important degree. Depiction of a violent event on TV is not necessarily an instruction on how to do it, nor a message saying you *should* do it . . . People suspend disbelief while reading or watching fiction, but they know the difference between fantasy and real life.

TV Guide, 11-13:37.

Peter Finch
Actor 5

As for entertainment TV, it caters to the lowest common denominator. It asks the public what it thinks is best, and the public hates change and innovation . . . Even in Shakespeare's day the groundlings cried for more farce. You can corrupt any art form.

Interview, New York/
The Christian Science Monitor, 12-10:35.

Fred W. Friendly
Professor of journalism, Columbia
University; Former president,
Columbia Broadcasting System News 1

The [TV] networks are running out of situation comedies, cop shows and Chers. They're drying up and they're desperate. That's why I predict we will see news shows dominate prime time in the next few years. There's no shortage of material. Look at it this way—the only thing that replenishes itself every day is the news.

Interview/ People, 8-2:47.

David Gerber
Executive vice president
in charge of production,
Columbia Pictures Television 2

[Saying the battle for ratings and profits by the TV networks has worked against quality programming]: It makes the networks play safe with the kind of shows they will buy. They won't take any chances on new types of programming. The pressure to be Number 1, to maintain high ratings, has affected the quality of shows. There is an apathy setting in [among viewers]. People might start thinking—"hey, maybe we don't have to stay home. Maybe we're not missing anything." When they figure they are not missing anything, when they go out and do something else or go into another room, then television is in trouble. And that's what might be happening right about now.

Interview/ TV Guide, 2-14:7.

George Gerbner
Dean,
Annenberg School of Communications,
University of Pennsylvania 3

[On TV violence]: . . . violence is among the cheapest and easiest-to-use of all dramatic devices. Almost any story must show people changing in some way: winning or losing, learning, getting rewarded or punished. If you want to show all this in terms of complex human psychology, you need a highly talented playwright and talented actors. That costs money. It is much easier and cheaper to resolve the story just by having the good guy shoot the bad guy. Violence is the quick way of showing who wins, who has power.

TV Guide, 11-6:9.

Lillian Gish
Actress 4

I'm afraid television is making the same mistakes the movies did. The movies started playing down to people. The people who made pictures thought, "They're so dumb out there, you've got to spell it out." The movies killed a lot of interest that way. Television should be more intelligent. They've lost a lot of intelligent people in the audience. There's nothing that causes me to switch programs quicker than the lack of intelligence. And look, we had to go to the BBC to tell us our history. Alistair Cooke and the BBC, in *America*, had to do what we should have done ourselves.

Interview, Los Angeles/
Los Angeles Herald-Examiner, 2-25:(B)5.

Julian Goodman
Chairman,
National Broadcasting Company 5

We [in TV] are highly visible and our policies and practices are laid on the line every day in millions of homes. Success and failure of any venture comes swiftly, and broadcasting has become extraordinarily sensitive to changes in public sentiment.

Before International Franchise Association,
Palm Springs, Calif., Feb. 10/
Daily Variety, 2-11:10.

Lew Grade
British producer 6

If there is a substantial audience for a [TV]

(LEW GRADE)

show, don't pull it off the air just because it hasn't captured the biggest ratings. If a sizable number of people like a show, they should be able to see it. We [in Britain] don't take a show we believe in off the air because it hasn't reached as vast a public as we would like. We keep it on. We have the courage of our convictions. You have to be concerned with the taste of the minority of the public, as well as the majority; and I think American broadcasters would do well to concentrate more on prestigious programs.

Interview, London/
San Francisco Examiner & Chronicle, 2-1:
(Datebook)6-TV.

Merv Griffin
TV talk-show host 1

It's easy to put it down but, my God, television affords so many things: instant news, sports, the documentaries that take you all over the world. Look what it's doing during this particular economy. If you figure out what it costs to go out to dinner, hire a babysitter, go to a movie, park your car, buy the gasoline—the wear and tear, getting dressed and everything—and compare it to sitting at home and, now with cable, seeing some of the finest performances in the Movies of the Week, it can't be that bad.

Interview/Holiday Inn Companion, July:12.

Arnold Grisman
Executive vice president,
J. Walter Thompson Company, advertising
2

My major fear is that things [on TV] will continue getting worse. The media, competing for audiences, keep pushing each other to think up sexier sex and ghastlier violence . . . This process of steady escalation leaves the audience jaded. What shocked us a few years ago doesn't shock us any more . . . [It] makes us more tolerant of violence perpetrated against other people. If we hear of a

real-life shooting today, we only shrug. We've all seen thousands of shootings on TV.

TV Guide, 11-13:40.

Lawrence K. Grossman
President,
Public Broadcasting Service
3

I always looked upon the word "network" as the television term for program distribution. Unfortunately, the word "network" has become the code word for centralized control. The fact is that public television's network system is vastly and inherently different from the CBS, NBC or ABC version of networking. In commercial television, after all, the money goes from the networks out to the stations. The ultimate power, therefore, lies with the networks. In public television, the money goes from the member stations to PBS. Control and power, therefore, reside in the stations. PBS' job, indeed its only reason for being, is to satisfy the needs and to serve the requirements of its member stations. So if we call PBS a network, it's a very different kind of network from what the commercial networks are all about.

At PBS membership meeting, Los Angeles,
Feb. 10/Daily Variety, 2-11:1.

4

[Public TV is] not simply another market for an unsold commercial project. We have to be certain that what we broadcast is something quite special. But public TV is where the real opportunity lies for creative television. Commercial TV has only one source of revenue—advertising. They must program what advertisers will buy. Our revenue sources are much wider—public funds, subscription funds, corporate grants, foundations. Consequently, the spectrum of our programs can be so much wider. But we also have responsibilities. Our membership is largely white upper-middle-class. If we were commercial TV, that's the audience we'd program for. As public TV, we must program for audiences we never hear from—the disenfranchised, the minorities.

Los Angeles/Los Angeles Times, 2-16:(4)16.

Hartford N. Gunn, Jr.
Vice chairman,
Public Broadcasting Service 1

As far as I have been concerned, there really have been only two fundamental objectives over the past six years since the founding of Public Broadcasting Service. First is to develop a public television system to provide all Americans, regardless of backgrounds, social or economic status or geographical location, with free access to the best cultural, informational and educational resources that the world has to offer. The second objective was to insure the independence and freedom of the system from those who would try to abuse it and use it for their own narrow and sometimes even dangerous personal purposes.

At PBS membership meeting,
Los Angeles, Feb. 10/
Daily Variety, 2-11:13.

Vance Hartke
United States Senator, D—Indiana 2

The First Amendment is your [TV's] defense and should always be such. But you cannot hide behind the First Amendment as a defense for unlimited profits at any social cost . . . The First Amendment assures the access of multiple voices to the marketplace of ideas. It does not assure protection of the status quo. It protects your right to select the content of your programs, but it protects your rights to profits only when you are fulfilling your public trust . . . Is it really necessary that human violence be exploited for acquiring and holding mass television audiences? "Family viewing time" seems to have compacted the nightly violence into a very short time period when the viewer often has no other choice but a police drama or action-oriented show . . . The trend in the future for your industry must be greater sensitivity to the viewers' rights, to minimizing the social costs which an economist would say you "externalize" rather than absorb internally through increased production costs. For example,

violence may be cheap for you, but very expensive for the children who watch it.

Before National Association of Broadcasters,
Chicago, March 22/ Daily Variety, 3-23:1.

John Houseman
Actor, Producer, Director 3

[In early television,] the opportunity to do good work wasn't because the shows were done live. That it was live was a necessity we had to deal with. The important factor was that television was young and experimental. It was ready to try things. There's no question that television was better then. Not all the shows were great shows. But television was new and had a lot of vitality, a lot of energy and a lot of talent.

Interview/
Los Angeles Herald-Examiner, 4-4:(TV Weekly)5.

Kim Hunter
Actress 4

Television eats up performers, but it's even more destructive to writers. There's no way, without becoming virtually a hack, that you can turn it out week after week after week . . . Television writers are being eaten by their own livelihood. The theatre has become the only place a writer can write his own material.

Interview/"W": a Fairchild publication, 8-20:2.

Ross Hunter
Producer 5

Movies made for television have to skip innuendos and nuances because there is no time to concentrate on these things. The producer of films for TV is a manufacturer while the producer working for the large screen hopes to be a creator.

Interview, Dallas/
The Dallas Times Herald, 11-28:(G)3.

Robert M. Hutchins
President, Center for the Study of
Democratic Institutions 6

If you accept my major premise that tele-

WHAT THEY SAID IN 1976

(ROBERT M. HUTCHINS)

vision is making us what we are, then television is making the culture we are going to have. You have to ask yourself what kind of thing on television would give us the kind of civilization that you would like to see. The key word is civilization . . . if what you are trying to do is to attract 40 million watchers so that you can run up your rates or get bigger advertising contracts, I don't think the ultimate result is in doubt; it's going to be lousy. And, as a result, if you accept my major premise, American culture is going to become lousier.

Television interview/ Center Report, February:23.

Daniel K. Inouye
United States Senator, D—Hawaii

1

TV has the power to do good or evil, to make or break a politician, the power to elect or defeat the President of the U.S., if you [broadcasters] wanted to. You are the most powerful segment in the country. The people who really run the country are broadcasters. They are the opinion-molders.

Before National Association of Broadcasters,
Portland, Ore./
Los Angeles Herald-Examiner, 10-28:(A)7.

Jesse L. Jackson
Civil-rights leader;
President, Operation PUSH
(People United to Save Humanity)

2

[Criticizing pay cable TV]: Ultimately we know that no TV is free, but present network TV is at least available to a larger audience of people, as compared to pay cable TV . . . Pay cable runs the danger of becoming class TV. Our opposition to pay cable grows out of the fact that a larger listening audience, including millions of poor familes, would be cut off from good TV programming by this system of taxation, since they could not afford to pay.

Before House Communications Subcommittee,
Washington/
The Christian Science Monitor, 7-30:5.

Nicholas Johnson
Chairman, National Citizens Committee
for Broadcasting; Former Commissioner,
Federal Communications Commission

3

[Television] is destroying the mental health of our people by constantly preaching, "you are nothing as a person; your meaning in life comes from the products you consume, your car and your hair spray" . . . Virtually every component of the rising rate of heart disease can be countered by avoiding things which television constantly promotes—obesity, cholesterol, nicotine, alcohol, a lack of exercise. What does television tell us? "Eat more, drink more, smoke more, and—for heaven's sake—don't touch that dial!"

San Francisco Examiner & Chronicle, 4-4:(A)13.

4

. . . in Britain, television is used more like a typewriter. Television for them is simply electronic equipment; it is content-neutral. It is something used by everybody in the society. It is not an industry with a bunch of specialists in it. So that the very best writers in Britain write for television just as much as they write for the theatre, or write novels. And the very best actors and actresses who appear in London theatres and British films, appear also in television. Professors and other people who have something to say in Britain are accustomed to go on television and say it. There are opportunities for them to do so. That is an accepted thing. If you are commissioned to give a public lecture, you often go on television and give it. Of course, that is not true in our country [the U.S.]. Here, television has been taken over by three enormous corporations who run it for their own profit-making purposes. These corporations have television program-manufacturing facilities in Los Angeles that look like aerospace plants. And they keep turning out the programs.

Interview/ The Center Magazine, July-August:53.

5

We advocate neither the abolition of all violence from American television nor censorship of any kind . . . We do not believe that television should be limited to a Pollyanna view of the world—even for children. Violence may be necessary to an occasional television program of significant artistic value; it may be essential to an understanding of the day's news events. What we do believe is that there can no longer be any doubt that there is more violence in American television than there needs to be, for either artistic or commercial purposes. There is no longer doubt that it is doing us grave injury as a people. Information about its location, extent and sponsorship can be a constructive service to all who care about this national tragedy.

The Christian Science Monitor, 8-2:13.

Don Johnston
President, J. Walter Thompson Company, advertising
1

[Criticizing violence in TV programs]: We're not attacking television. That would be foolish because we depend on it . . . [But] it seems clear to us that we have a responsibility—and that we should do something about it. We will continue to speak out against television programming that promiscuously exploits violence. We are counseling our clients to evaluate the potential negatives of placing commercials in programming perceived as violent. Our motivation is primarily social, but there are certain business considerations that confirm our recommendations.

Before American Advertising Federation, Washington, June 8/ The New York Times, 6-9:53.

Shirley Knight
Actress
2

The public is so lulled into sub-existence by pap and porno and soap. If you want to see the whole collapse of society in miniature, get up at 6 a.m. and watch TV until it goes off—the game shows, the humiliation of those people for money, the afternoon pap, the violence at night.

Interview, Los Angeles/ Los Angeles Herald-Examiner, 4-21:(B)1.

Norman Lear
Writer, Producer
3

You will find very few members of the creative community—few actors, writers, directors or producers—who will not agree that gratuitous sex and violence is to be condemned at any hour. The simple fact is that if networks had not wished gratuitous violence on the air waves they control, it would not have been there. We read today of the giant advertising agencies who now condemn TV violence. They are the same agencies which paid millions and millions of dollars for years and years of television violence before it became popular to condemn it.

Before House Communications Subcommittee, Los Angeles, Aug. 18/ The Washington Post, 8-19:(B)9.

4

[The networks] have to listen to the public, communicate with the creative community, be more aware that they must program in the public interest, not just in the advertising interest. You do that by being more aware of what the public interest really is, and you learn that by listening to the public, not only to each other. When the public is upset about violence, you become upset about violence. And then you do something about eliminating it. But you don't sit behind closed doors with a government agency and come up with a piece of cosmetic nonsense [the "family hour" concept] that cloaks the real issue. Violence was simply pushed to nine o'clock—available to all the same children anyway. Violence was not diminished by five seconds or one gunshot.

Interview/ The Christian Science Monitor, 11-10:24.

Jack Lemmon
Actor
5

There are great limitations to TV. You can't move around very much . . . I wouldn't want to do a series or an anthology. You get too locked in. I'd go crazy on TV. All the things I might want to do, good or bad, you

(JACK LEMMON)

couldn't do. Because TV must appeal to the least common denominator.

Interview/The Christian Science Monitor, 3-4:26.

Warren G. Magnuson
United States Senator, D—Washington
1

Today there is a growing consensus that gratuitous violence on TV is no longer an acceptable norm. The use of this kind of violence for the sole purpose of attracting and maintaining audience attention is a common programming practice. Violence portrayed without showing the human consequences is cheap and it degrades the viewer and the industry . . . The child viewer trying to get in touch with reality is a victim when subjected to this type of programming. To suggest that television, the most persuasive tool available to advertisers for sophisticated and mature human beings, is not affecting children who do not have the experience to distinguish the truth from falsehood or exaggeration from understatement, is ludricrous. Reinforcement of the child's inner fears, doubts and confusions, mixed with simplistic solutions to complex human problems, is the devastating effect of gratuitous violence on television . . . Decision-makers involved in television programming must recognize that their programs do have an effect on their viewing audiences. They cannot wash their hands of responsibility for their decisions.

*Before the Senate, Washington, Oct. 1/**

Karl Malden
Actor
2

[On the mental states through which a series lead actor progresses]: The first year, you've just accepted the show and the challenge is there. You resolve that you're going to turn it into a hit. When it's picked up for the second year, there's the excitement of having made it a hit. The third season, you're sure that you have a hit. You wonder, "How long is it going to run?" The excitement isn't

quite there the way it was. By the time the fourth season begins, you are really concerned about repeating the same character and you think, "My God! I signed a five-year deal!"

*Interview/
Los Angeles Herald Examiner, 2-18:(C)14.*

Jean Marsh
Actress
3

Television is an entirely unpredictable medium. It's like creating a super recipe. You must have precisely the right ingredients in precisely the correct amount. Only then will it come out good and proper.

*Interview/
San Francisco Examiner & Chronicle, 1-18:
(Datebook)27.*

Donald H. McGannon
*Chairman and president,
Westinghouse Broadcasting Company*
4

It's hard to justify a prime-time [TV] schedule that does not have any regularly scheduled news or public-affairs programming. It is difficult to accept a schedule that is more than 50 per cent crime, violence and "adult content" in the face of rising youth crime, venereal disease and alcoholism. We must face the hard reality that commercial television is not held in universal high regard.

*Before NBC affiliates, New York, June 21/
The New York Times, 6-23:67.*

Newton N. Minow
*Former Chairman,
Federal Communications Commission*
5

[On how TV has changed since 1961 when he called it a "vast wasteland"]: I think the medium still tends to waste its potential in many respects. However, there has been enormous improvement, particularly in the area of news and information. In 1961, the nightly national-news broadcast was 15 minutes long and didn't have the impact that it does now. You didn't have programs like *60 Minutes.*

There weren't many informational specials, like the half-hour Presidential-primary reports. As far as entertainment is concerned, there's been a basic fallacy in the minds of the programmers. They *consistently* underestimate the intelligence and sophistication of their audience. They don't realize that *television itself* has elevated that level. I would say that the most important educational institution in this country is not Harvard or Yale or the University of California, but television. Broadcasters are caught in a dilemma. They want to reach the majority *all the time*, which is an impossible task. When newspapers take readership surveys, they usually find that the most popular feature is the comics. But that doesn't mean you turn the whole paper into comics; you try to present a balance, with news and editorial pages. The same has got to be true with television.

Interview, Chicago/TV Guide, 10-16:6.

1

[On TV's "family hour" concept]: The concept of saying there are certain periods when anybody can watch and know there's not going to be blood and gore is a good one, but it's hard in practice to make sharp definitions. I do think the argument that it cuts the "meat" out of the programs is exaggerated. I realize [FCC Chairman] Dick Wiley . . . has been criticized for trying to do something with the family-viewing hour, but that's his job. There ought to be a constant running battle between the FCC and broadcasters. If there isn't, the country's in trouble, because it means one side has put the other to sleep.

Interview, Chicago/TV Guide, 10-16:8.

John H. Mitchell
President,
Columbia Pictures Television

2

[On poor-quality commercial TV]: The roster of executives in the three networks shows that no one has ever produced or written anything—the two keys to creativity.

Newsweek, 2-16:72.

Mary Tyler Moore
Actress

3

[On her winning a number of "Emmy" awards over the years]: The unusual thing about winning is that the more "Emmys" I have, the more important they become. You might think I would become careless, but that's not true. I keep thinking I've done it all, and then suddenly there's another "Emmy." Then I think I've got to do better and set my sights higher. It's a circle that makes you work harder instead of less.

Los Angeles Herald-Examiner, 5-19:(B)1.

Jack Palance
Actor

4

There was some excitement then [in the late '40s]. There were better plays and better people writing, directing and acting. There seemed a reason for it. Then deterioration set in. I think what finally did it to me was television. After *Requiem for a Heavyweight,* good television disappeared. When, against my better judgment, I agreed to do that circus series [*The Greatest Show on Earth*], I just didn't realize how much work was required to produce—a nothing. It wrecks your day. It wrecks your week. If you don't watch out, it wrecks your life.

Interview/TV Guide, 3-27:19.

Andre Previn
Musical director,
London Symphony Orchestra

5

I cannot believe the fears that everybody watching television in America is too stupid to enjoy a performance of a Beethoven symphony. The BBC is really spectacular that way. If they deem something to be of interest, it is broadcast in absolutely prime time. They look at our scheduled repertoire before the start of the season searching for the unusual. When we did Messiaen's *Turangalila* Symphony, they said: "That hasn't been on before. Well, let's put it on." For an hour and a half on Sunday evening!

Interview, New York/
The New York Times, 3-14:(2)15.

WHAT THEY SAID IN 1976

Tony Randall
Actor
1

When something really good is being done [on TV], it should be on all three networks at the same time, just like a Presidential address. Then it would have great ratings, and everyone would see the things he *ought* to see . . . It takes a bit of highhandedness, takes someone to say, "Now you're going to see what's good for you, just tonight, not every night of the year." It could be done, it could be commercial then, if it were on all three networks. It would pay its way handsomely, we'd all feel better for it, and we'd *be* better for it.

Interview/TV Guide, 12-4:32.

Johnnie Ray
Singer
2

People come up to me in the supermarket and they say, "Aren't you still singing?" They don't mean to be rude, but if you are not on television every 20 minutes or have a hit record every time they turn on the radio or have a film out, they think you've retired. Americans are the most over-entertained people in the world. They have more spare time, more money to spend than anybody. And TV. TV just gobbles up entertainers.

Interview, Los Angeles/
Los Angeles Times, 11-1:(4)4.

Hal Roach
Former motion-picture producer
3

. . . TV is an intimate form of entertainment and should have its own type of production. What I'm talking about is this: Let's take *All in the Family* which is supposed to be one of the tops. The minute they start to do anything, hundreds of people laugh. They say it's done before a live audience. Why is it done before a live audience? Laurel and Hardy—who've been as funny on TV as any show before or since—had no laugh track. If they're funny, you laugh; if you don't think they're funny, you don't laugh. Now, if you were in an apartment and it had a well and

across the well was a couple having an argument and you could see and hear them—it could be very entertaining as long as they didn't know you were looking at them. But as soon as they know that you are looking and listening—I mean, the whole thing stops. If *All in the Family* wants to be an intimate form of entertainment—well, as soon as 100 or 200 people laugh, it's no longer intimate.

Interview, Los Angeles/
Los Angeles Times, 7-4:(Calendar)34.

Elton H. Rule
President,
American Broadcasting Companies
4

Whether a child watches five hours of television a week, or 25, his viewing is an important part of his life. Knowing that imposes an awesome responsibility on all of us in the television industry, and we have committed ourselves in the strongest possible terms to live up to that responsibility. But the quality of our efforts can only be as good as the use to which they are put in the home. For parents who pay little or no attention to their children's television viewing, television is no more than an electronic baby sitter, an informative and entertaining gadget whose value will vary from child to child in unpredictable—and sometimes undesirable—fashion. This we must try to avoid. On the other hand, for parents who grasp firmly their share of the responsibility, who actively involve themselves in their children's viewing experience, television can be—and will be—a significant and constructive contributor to the growth of the generation of young people that will take over where we, their parents, leave off. That is the goal all of us should work toward.

Before Rotary Club of Los Angeles, Sept. 3/
Vital Speeches, 10-15:26.

Eric Sevareid
News commentator,
Columbia Broadcasting System
5

Every new development of communications in the direction of the mass of people has been opposed by intellectuals of a certain stripe. I am sure that Gutenberg was denounced by the elite of his times; his device would spread dangerous ideas among the God-fearing obedient masses. The typewriter was denounced by intellectuals of the more elfin variety; its clacking would drive away the muses who apparently were accustomed to the scratching of the quill pen. The first motion pictures were denounced; they would destroy the legitimate theatre. Then the sound motion picture was denounced; it would destroy the true art of the film, which was pantomime. To such critics, of course, television is destroying everything. It is destroying conversation, they tell us. Nonsense. Non-conversing families were always that way. It has, in fact, stimulated billions of conversations that otherwise would not have occurred. It is destroying the habit of reading, they say. This is nonsense. Book sales in this country during the lifetime of general television have greatly increased and well beyond the increase in the population . . . TV is debasing the use of the English language, they tell us. My friend [journalist] Alistair Cooke, for one. Nonsense. Until radio and then TV, tens of millions of people living in sharecropper cabins, in small villages on the plains and in the mountains, in the great city slums, had never heard good English diction in their lives. If anything, this medium has improved the general level of diction. Intellectuals of the type I am objecting to have always hated anything that the generality of people liked. They must, to preserve their distinctiveness, their eliteness, even those who claim they love humanity.

At Washington Journalism Center, June 3/
Vital Speeches, 7-1:563.

Robert Stack
Actor
                                                    1

[On television]: You have to remember the frame of reference within which you function. You've got to have an audience, a big audience. The ratings must hold up. The show must work in that sense. That has to be the first consideration. The actor wants moments to fulfill himself. Richard Boone put it the right way: "An actor in a television series

has to try to make a moment out of drinking a cup of coffee." The point is, the opportunities for fulfillment aren't many. You have to study how you can use what's available.

Interview/
Los Angeles Herald-Examiner, 7-7:(B)8.

Peter Strauss
Actor
                                                    2

I don't have the traitor instincts that most actors have about TV. They work in theatre, then go on to television, and the minute they hit some degree of success, they end up in a film and never look back at television again. I personally like TV. I like the pace; I like where it's going and what it's doing. All of a sudden, television is starting to find itself with a great richness of material, stories that might have been put aside at the film studios and never done. As an actor, I find that intriguing.

Interview/"W": a Fairchild publication, 10-1:2.

Tom Swafford
Vice president, program practices,
Columbia Broadcasting System Television
                                                    3

[On the controversial "family hour" concept]: One of our disappointments has been that we feel not many producers have tried to comply with it; they haven't even asked about "family hour" . . . There's been a cop-out by producers. A couple of producers have told us "we'll do everything we can to destroy the 'family hour.'" A lot of people thought "family hour" would be *Gentle Ben* and *Father Knows Best* [which was never the intent of the networks' "family hour" concept]. I can't understand the opposition to it. That's one reason some of us are gratified it is being tested in the courts.

Los Angeles, May 5/ Daily Variety, 5-6:10.

Dick Van Dyke
Entertainer
                                                    4

Networks believe they have to put in something for everyone [in a TV show]. That's

495

WHAT THEY SAID IN 1976

(DICK VAN DYKE)

what they call demographics. Maybe the network will scream, but I don't agree with that philosophy. I know, when I sit down to look at television, I want to see what I want to see. That's why I scream at *Wide World of Sports* when I want to see a track meet and I have to sit through a "demolition derby" before they finally get around to the track. And then, it's only part of a track meet . . . [And] you can't necessarily have the guests you'd prefer. I've been working over a compilation of guests for the season. NBC will look it over, cross out certain names and substitute others. Then, you have to write sketches around guests who've been picked instead of picking guests because they fit sketches that you've already written. Obviously, if you suit the sketch to the actor instead of the actor to the sketch, you immediately inhibit the comedy imagination from taking off. You start off handicapping it; confining it, if you will.

Interview, Los Angeles/
The Dallas Times Herald, 7-14:(E)3.

Richard Widmark
Actor

1

I know I've made kind of a half-assed career out of violence, but I abhor violence . . . Everywhere you look on films and on television you see violence. You can't tell me that doesn't have some effect on young minds. We now have a whole generation that has been brought up on television. These kids have been subjected to violence all their lives. That kind of exposure has got to desensitize them . . . TV producers seek the lowest common denominator, and that means violent action. Of course, everyone is interested in violence. Evil is always interesting.

Interview, Valencia, Calif.
The Washington Post, 12-28:(C)2.

Robert D. Wood
President, Columbia
Broadcasting System Television

2

You don't start out to make a bad show. But safer and on the air is preferable to different and off the air.

Newsweek, 2-16:72.

Muhammad Ali
Heavyweight boxing champion
of the world   *1*

[On the movie being made about him]: Can you imagine, in just 34 years I lived enough for a serious movie company to make a major motion picture about my life. You know they're serious—look at all those trucks and wires they got outside. And my life ain't even *started* yet.

Interview, Miami/
The New York Times, 11-7:(2)1.

Irving Berlin
Composer-lyricist   *2*

[On his health at 88 years of age]: It's like a Broadway show still out-of-town. Not bad enough to close, but it needs a lot of work.

Los Angeles Herald-Examiner, 5-20:(B)2.

Leonard Bernstein
Composer, Conductor   *3*

I'm a public person when I conduct and a private person when I compose. I take on a whole other personality. When I'm composing I'm much more introspective, inward-turning. I tend to brood more. When I'm that way I watch myself conducting on television and think, "What is he doing standing on that box carrying on like a nut?"

Interview, Washington/
The Washington Post, 1-7:(B)3.

4

As one gets older one gets more jealous of one's time. It's running out. Suddenly, with a shock, you think maybe you have 15 or 20 years left, especially if you've gone through life being young . . . I don't mind that I've aged, that my hair is white, that there are lines in my face. What I mind is this terrible sense that there isn't much time. So much has to be done before it's too late. That kind of pressure makes it harder. It makes you a neurotic, and that saps your energy.

Interview, Washington/
The Washington Post, 1-7:(B)1.

David Bowie
Rock musician   *5*

I have never considered myself a rock freak. In fact, hitting the rock scene was just a way of becoming enough of a force to say what I wanted to say. I always felt I would make a quick flash, like a comet, flare, shine very bright, then fade away and never be seen again. Otherwise, it becomes a career, and who wants a career in rock and roll? I'm not a rock musician. It was only a grand means to an end. I've always wanted to be a film director.

Interview, New Mexico/
San Francisco Examiner & Chronicle, 6-27:
(Datebook)18.

Edmund G. Brown, Jr.
Governor of California (D)   *6*

I've never been a big spender. Certainly not in my personal life—as my friends will attest—and not in the public offices I have held. I am not a fiscal conservative. I'm just cheap.

Interview/ Playboy, April:69.

WHAT THEY SAID IN 1976

(EDMUND G. BROWN, JR.)

1

Some people have a very large sense of their own ego. I don't particularly have that sense, that idea of the typical personality that comes out of wanting to be Number 1, to be the top, to be the best, the whole achievement trip. I don't know—you have to judge other people's egos yourself. Yes, I have an ego. But people who think the world revolves around them—I don't think that's accurate about me. Ego is a driving energy. I tend to think that doesn't apply to me, but obviously there are some forces working here.

Interview/The Washington Post, 5-9:(H)8.

Genevieve Bujold
Actress

2

I have no plans. I am like a woman who is always in labor. Every day I have a new contraction, and my whole life changes. That's [one] reason why I do not give interviews. Whatever I tell you now will be obsolete by next week. I know where my child is at this moment, but I don't know where life will take us tomorrow. I live each day at a time and make every minute work for me until the minute is over. Then I go on to something else. I am totally alone in this world.

Interview, Beverly Hills, Calif./
San Francisco Examiner & Chronicle, 8-29:
(Datebook)13.

Richard Burton
Actor

3

I rather like my reputation, actually, that of a spoiled genius from the Welsh gutter; a drunk, a womanizer. It's a rather attractive image . . . It's actually difficult to make me unhappy. I think it was Shaw who said life is a tragedy for those who feel, and a comedy for those who think; and I think I belong to the latter category. It's always very amusing. Even when others think it's my drama, I see the funny side. Periodically, when I'm on stage, in full flow, I think: What are you doing here? I'm suddenly watching myself, and I can't help smiling, because it's all so absurd.

Interview, New York/
Los Angeles Times, 4-25:(Calendar)39.

Glen Campbell
Singer

4

Now I really feel the need to go back home [to Arkansas], float down the Missouri River and fish for bass and crappies. It's real peaceful, and remote from things like telephones. I'm a take-me-as-I-am person, and all the rest is water under the bridge. You can't change yesterday any more than you can predict what's going to happen tomorrow. What I try to do is live with myself and please me. If I can't do that, I can't please anybody else or live with anybody else.

Interview/People, 3-29:46.

Truman Capote
Author

5

I'm the greatest genius of all time.
Interview/"W": a Fairchild publication, 4-30:6.

Jimmy Carter
1976 Democratic
U.S. Presidential nominee

6

I'm impatient with inattention to duty or lack of a deep commitment to a cause. I'm very demanding, I think, on my fellow political workers, and maybe I'm not as inclined as I ought to be to compliment or congratulate people who do a good job. I believe that I am stubborn, which may be a weakness or a defect. Tenacious is another word. Once I set my mind to do something, I find it very hard to deter from it. I make a lot of mistakes. Sometimes I've elected to admit them; sometimes maybe I admit them freely because I know they are going to be revealed anyhow.

Interview, Plains, Ga./Parade, 10-31:6.

Prince Charles
Prince of Wales

7

At the moment [at age 27], I don't feel like becoming domestic—so I personally feel a good age for a man to get married is around

30. After one has seen a great deal of life, met a large number of girls, fallen in love every now and then, one knows what it's all about. I do have to consider marriage a bit more carefully, particularly because whoever it is that I marry, I hope I shall be married to for the rest of my life. In my position, the last thing I could possibly consider is getting divorced.

Interview, London/
Los Angeles Times, 4-17:(1)3.

Hans Conried
Actor
                                                    1

I had to become a character actor. In Hollywood 35 years ago, you had to be beautiful to become a star, and I didn't look like anyone or anything.

Interview, Dallas/
The Dallas Times Herald, 8-25:(E)9.

John Denver
Singer, Songwriter
                                                    2

The mountains open me up. I don't like the city. The city is very fast and hectic. I get a tired feeling when I have concrete under my feet. In the mountains, it's quiet. I'm more in touch with the life around me and with myself. When you lose sight of the earth, the leaves, the bugs, the trees and the stars, you lose sight of yourself . . . Because of the success I've attained in show biz, all the TV and the record people now are so nice to me. They want to know what they can do for me—would I like this and would I like that? But in the mountains I know who I am. I'm not important there. Something there keeps me straight. The mountains have been a real blessing to me. My life is so completely full.

Interview, Beverly Hills, Calif./
Los Angeles Herald-Examiner, 11-9:(B)1.

Bob Dylan
Singer, Songwriter
                                                    3

My being a Gemini explains a lot, I think. It forces me to extremes. I'm never really balanced in the middle. I go from one side to the other without staying in either place very long. I'm happy, sad, up, down, in, out, up in the sky and down in the depths of the earth. I can't tell you how Bob Dylan has lived his life. And it's far from over.

Interview, Malibu, Calif./
TV Guide, 9-11:3.

Chris Evert
Tennis player
                                                    4

I can't see doing this [tennis] for more than three or four more years—I mean, what do you do after you've won everything there is to win? All my life, tennis has been my main interest. I've missed a lot. I don't know much about the theatre; I don't read many good books because it takes too much mental energy, and I need all I have for tennis. I used to run back to the hotel room after every match so I could rest up for the next one. I'm not doing that this year. I want to see the cities where I play. I want to meet new people and open myself up more.

People, 2-16:12.

Jose Ferrer
Actor
                                                    5

I'd never play another role if I could afford not to. I'm no Laurence Olivier. I never believed I was born to act. I could give it up in a minute.

Los Angeles Herald-Examiner, 5-18:(B)3.

Gerald R. Ford
President of the United States
                                                    6

I am the first to admit that I am no great orator or no person that got where I have gotten by any William Jennings Bryan technique.

Time, 2-2:11.

George Foreman
Former heavyweight boxing
champion of the world
                                                    7

There was a time when I felt I didn't need boxing any more. But I was only fooling my-

(GEORGE FOREMAN)

self, like a man who tries living without food. I need the punching and the sweat and the sacrifice. It's what makes me what I am, what makes me different. I'd be nothing without boxing.

Interview, Livermore, Calif./
Newsweek, 1-26:38.

Joe Frazier
Former heavyweight boxing
champion of the world
                                                    1

A lot of people told me maybe I should retire after that fight in Manila [with heavyweight champion Muhammad Ali]. I came out of that fight with respect. I could have quit. The people who told me to quit were my friends, people who loved me and didn't want me to get hurt. But what am I going to do—sit around thinking about it all the time, watch old films and wait for a heart attack? I got to be myself; I got to go to the gym, work out, run. I got to be with my boys. I love my wife, my four beautiful daughters and little son, but I got to be doing my thing. My wife wakes me in the morning when it's time for roadwork. She don't really want me to go, and sometimes I don't really want to go. But I got to. It's my life.

New York/Los Angeles Times, 3-21:(3)12.

J. Paul Getty
Industrialist
                                                    2

I suffer no guilt complexes or conscience pangs about my wealth. The Lord may have been disproportionate, but that is how He—or nature, if you like—operates.

Time, 5-24:41.

Buddy Hackett
Entertainer
                                                    3

Today I'm better [professionally] than I was yesterday, and tomorrow I'll be better than I am today. The difference will be infinitesimal, but it will be. Living and being

and doing will make it that much better. At some point there'll be a decline, and when I'm 62 I'll walk onstage—and nothing will come out. Then I'll go home, sit by the fire, and pat my dead dog.

Interview, Las Vegas, Nev./
Los Angeles Herald-Examiner, 8-12:(B)1.

Audrey Hepburn
Actress
                                                    4

I don't care any more if I don't go around the world, if I don't see more than I've seen. I feel very saturated—in the good sense, not in boredom. I haven't enough time to think about everything I've done and seen. Living is like tearing through a museum. Not until later do you really start absorbing what you saw, thinking about it, looking it up in a book and remembering—because you can't take it all in at once.

Interview/McCall's, January:128.

                                                    5

[On her not having made a film for eight years]: You're going to think I'm so corny, but my wish is not to be lonely. And to have my garden . . . Don't get me wrong. I've enjoyed the klieg lights, the soundstages, the camera and the hard work making films. But if you ask me what I want from life, it's not glamour or money. I don't know what I would've done in the movies during the past eight years, anyway. It's all sex and violence. I don't like guns, and I can't strip because I don't have the body for it; I'm too scrawny. So I don't know what the future holds . . . But whatever happens, the most important thing is growing old gracefully. And you can't do that on the cover of a fan magazine.

Interview, New York/
San Francisco Examiner & Chronicle, 4-4:
(Datebook)15.

Katharine Hepburn
Actress
                                                    6

I never read anything about myself. It might be lies, and that would annoy me more.

So I live in my own dream world. First of all, you must please yourself.

Interview/The Dallas Times Herald, 9-16:(C)1.

1

Acting is not a great talent. I've got a nice little talent and I was born at the right time and I had the right kind of looks and I was kind of classy and I sounded better than some people and I've done pretty well with what I have—whatever it is.

Interview, New York/
Los Angeles Times, 10-10:(Calendar)46.

2

I don't think I'm the least bit peculiar, but people tell me I am. My greatest strength is, and always has been, common sense. I'm really a standard brand—like Campbell's tomato soup or Baker's chocolate.

Interview, New York/People, 10-11:64.

Charlton Heston
Actor

3

I want to win, and I always have, since those days back in high school. I want to succeed, to get into as many things as I can, and accomplish them all. To be Number 1—in films, in any sport I attempt, in social work, in my activity for the government promoting this country, in the American Film Institute, as president of the Screen Actors Guild, or on any of the other numerous committees of which I'm a member. I bite off more than I can chew; I over-extend; I take on more projects than I can possibly accomplish. Who knows why?

Interview, Los Angeles/
San Francisco Examiner & Chronicle, 11-7:
(Datebook)19.

John Huston
Motion-picture director

4

I'm not rich. I've spent it as I've gone along. That's the secret of my longevity—I *have* to work. But I've had a hell of a good time, a

better time than a lot of the Hollywood fat cats.

Interview, Puerto Vallarta, Mexico/
The New York Times, 2-15:(2)15.

Elsa Lanchester
Actress

5

In one respect I'm glad I'm no sexpot or clotheshorse. Since I usually look frumpy on screen, I can hardly help but look better in person. When people meet me—and as long as I'm clean and don't smell—they think I'm terrific.

Interview, Los Angeles/
Los Angeles Herald-Examiner, 7-14:(B)1.

Sophia Loren
Actress

6

I adore good music and good books. I am an outstanding cook and I will tell you a secret. The aroma of string beans moves me to tears. This alone is happiness.

San Francisco Examiner & Chronicle, 10-24:
(Datebook)24.

Shirley MacLaine
Actress

7

I have always tried to pursue my own identity, to do the things that I think are important. I knew I would probably never become a great actress, because what goes on beyond the camera is so much more interesting to me than what goes on in front of it. I have never tried to live according to someone else's rule book. But I think I have always been hardworking, honest, seeking. Someone who tried to find out the truth.

Interview, Las Vegas, Nev./
McCall's, August:52.

Stanley Marcus
Chairman,
Neiman-Marcus stores

8

I'd like to live another 100 years so I could really accomplish everything I want. The

(STANLEY MARCUS)

world is so interesting, there are so many exciting facets and exciting people, one life isn't enough. I'd like to have two or three different careers. I'd like to go into archaeology and I've always wanted to be a newspaper publisher. There are still so many areas that I really don't know anything about.

Interview, Dallas/
The Dallas Times Herald, 12-12:(D)1.

Billy Martin
Baseball manager, New York "Yankees"
1

Having a temper isn't a bad thing. Jesus had a temper and took up the whip. Temper is my greatest asset.

Interview/"W": a Fairchild publication, 7-23:16.

Walter Matthau
Actor
2

I've heard about all the research Al Pacino and Robert De Niro do for their roles, and I think they're both excellent actors. I have a hunch, though, that most of those guys are just trying to convince the critics that they're serious, hard-working actors. But I don't have to throw myself into a role that way, because I've *lived* everything. I've been a waiter, a gambler, a pimp, a murderer. I'm from the ghetto, and the only time I do any research is when I play aristocracy.

Interview, Los Angeles/
The New York Times, 8-13:(C)6.

Paul McCartney
Singer, Musician
3

[Comparing his married life now with when he was with the Beatles rock group]: Now I'm more mature. I'm not happier than I was as a single man with the Beatles. But *as* happy, in a different way. I used to wake up to chicks and old drinks, but that horror has been removed from my life. Now it's a whole other thing. I have my own kids in the morning when I wake up.

Interview/ People, 6-7:38.

Margaret Mead
Anthropologist
4

I tend to be "bread" to people—something you want to eat every day—to people who are "wine" to me. There is nobody who is bread to me—not in the sense that I have to have them around every minute—and never has been; it's not anything I want. See, I don't want people to be dependent on me. Bread is a point of dependency.

Interview, New York/
Los Angeles Times, 12-3:(6)8.

George Moscone
Mayor of San Francisco
5

My greatest strength is a proper evaluation of my talents and weaknesses, which are almost one and the same. I know just how smart I am; I know just how dumb I am; I know just how far I can go. And I've been able to settle for it.

San Francisco Examiner & Chronicle, 1-18:
(This World)2.

David Niven
Actor
6

I'm not a terribly ambitious actor. I've always stayed within the type-casting frame. Anybody in movies does. I've done my best, and followed the advice of [Clark] Gable and Spencer Tracy—"Get there on time, know the jokes, take the money, and go home at six o'clock."

Interview, New York/
The Christian Science Monitor, 6-10:27.

George Peppard
Actor
7

[On what he would be doing if he had all the money possessed by the wealthy character he played in the TV series *Banacek*]: What I do now. What is there to do? You can only wear one suit of clothes at a time. My passion is music; I can afford symphony tickets and lots of records. Reading and fishing don't cost much. I have a nice camera, and I love good works of art. I really don't care about the trappings. And you know something? Banacek didn't, either.

Interview, Beverly Hills, Calif./
The Dallas Times Herald, 4-23:(E)7.

Donald Pleasance
Actor   1

I just *have* to work. I can't be choosy. I get neurotic if I don't work. I can't bear the thought of being left with all those great blanks on the calendar, of doing nothing . . . Even if only three days pass between my finishing one role and being asked to do another, I'm sure I'm finished. I think: That's it; they've found me out; nobody's ever going to ask me to work again.

Interview, London/
San Francisco Examiner & Chronicle, 6-13:
(Datebook)20.

Tony Randall
Actor   2

The truth is I am a phony . . . I am not a learned man, despite the fact that I appear on opera shows and people think I am brilliant. What I am is a fan, and fans are not meant to be taken seriously as authorities . . . I am self-educated, an autodidact—in other words, a phony. I don't have a true education. I don't have a college degree. I went for a year and a half to Northwestern and took several courses at Columbia extension. But a well-educated man in the world of our grandfathers was expected to know history, mathematics, Greek, Latin and Hebrew, logic and philosophy. I don't have any of these subjects. I have developed a passionate interest in two things—music and painting. I've made myself a Number 1 fan of the opera. But I can't read music, play an instrument, or even understand any of the languages opera is sung in. That's not real knowledge. I spend hundreds of hours studying paintings in the great museums around the world. I have a passion for cubism and, if I had un-

limited funds, I would have nothing but Braques and Picassos in my house. But people presume because of these hobbies and my big words that I have a wonderful education, and I do little to disabuse them. So, that makes me a phony.

Interview, New York/
The Christian Science Monitor, 11-11:30.

Don Rickles
Comedian   3

[On his acerbic humor vs. his real personality]: People who know me love me. They know I'm human. I've got a wife, children, two dogs and a mother, and I don't go around dressed as Adolph Hitler. I started out to be an actor, but when people laugh at things you say, it's difficult to get the role of the King of England.

Interview/
Los Angeles Herald-Examiner, 6-22:(B)1.

Ginger Rogers
Actress, Entertainer   4

. . . in my entire career I've only had two years when I did zero. And even then, I knew it was only a hiatus. I got tired of sitting on a leaf. I've got to be in the traffic, with the horns tooting. When I was a kid, I played hard. Then I grew up and worked hard . . . Even when I'm not working, I paint. I've got 30 canvasses ready now for a show. I play eight sets of tennis a day. If I wasn't performing, I'd be painting, sculpting or using a potter's wheel. I'm not the rocking-chair type.

Interview/The Washington Post, 4-19:(C)7.

Irwin Shaw
Author   5

I don't want to be remembered—I want to be read.

Interview/People, 2-16:56.

Beverly Sills
Opera singer

1

When I go on the [TV] talk shows, I'm not speaking as the stereotyped prima donna with horns coming out of her head. I wasn't raised in a very well-to-do family where I was sent off to become the opera star. Nor was I raised in a ghetto where I had to struggle to exist. When I go on the talk shows, I project what I am—an intelligent and well-educated girl from Brooklyn.

Interview, New York/
The New York Times, 10-10:(2)39.

Stephen Sondheim
Composer-lyricist

2

You could say that my life-style is very ordinary, very simple and unglamorous. I'm neither a party-goer nor a hermit. As the years go by, I find that I want to spend more and more time with fewer and fewer friends . . . the people I like are the people who are in touch with themselves and who are not smug: people who are troubled and do something about their trouble—not wallow in it.

Interview/People, 4-5:70.

Rod Steiger
Actor

3

I have been called "difficult," but I found out that was a misinterpretation, meaning that you attempt to preserve your independence and your perspective on living. If that is "difficult," then I am "difficult." If it is "difficult" to fight for logic, to belong to no one but have the respect of most, then I am "difficult." And I pray I will be continued to be called "difficult."

Interview, New York/
The Christian Science Monitor, 4-26:22.

Virgil Thomson
Composer

4

[On being 80 years old]: I like talking to young people. I like being among them. Not too young—teens are not my realm—but

anything over 25. Max Jacob used to say that, after 30, everybody's the same age.

Interview, New York/
The New York Times, 11-25:38.

John Wayne
Actor

5

. . . my movie image actually is of a fellow who—regardless of the color of his hat—has white shining through its brim. I like to think of myself as the patriarch and baron of all the domain I survey and the champion of the underdog. Somewhere in between is the character that I am. A man's character and personality are made up by the incidents in his life. Mine has been made up of one thing in *reel* life, and of probably every dramatic experience that a human being could have in *real* life. Somewhere in between there lies John Wayne, or stands John Wayne. I seldom lie.

Interview, Newport Beach, Calif./
The Saturday Evening Post, March:57.

Mae West
Actress

6

I don't drink. I don't smoke, and my mental attitude is right. You have to keep your thinking in the right direction. I'm always positive about everything—myself and the world. It's just my way of thinking. I'm never depressed . . . I don't recognize any such thing as a calamity . . . and that way, if there is a calamity, it just passes.

Interview, Los Angeles/
The Christian Science Monitor, 4-2:18.

Shelley Winters
Actress

7

With luck and good health you get along, right? I am not going to fight for youth. My dream is to weight 140 pounds—around 20 to go. I have had a long career in the movies; I started in 1944 when I was 11. There's been a lot of chaff in the wheat, but there's a lot of wheat in the chaff.

Interview, New York/
The New York Times, 6-18:(C)8.

Philosophy

Muhammad Ali
*Heavyweight boxing champion
of the world* 1

A lot of women rule their men. Or their "boys." No real man could let himself be ruled by a woman. They nag and they try to push him around. But if he lets her, then he's not the man. She's the man. All this power women have over men—it's love. If I don't love you I'll slap you around and say, "Get out of my life." If I love you a lot I'll slap you around and tell you to get out. But then I won't sleep and I'll think about you all night and I'll call you. That's the only power women have over men. It's nature to run from something that runs after you. And it's nature to chase something that runs away from you. As soon as a person finds out how much you love them, then they got power.
*Interview, Landover, Md./
Los Angeles Times, 4-30:(3)6.*

Herb Alpert
Musician 2

To me, a musician is comparable to an athlete who goes through certain calesthenics in order to perform a particular function, whether it's football, baseball, boxing or playing the trumpet. A basic rule of these calesthenics is not to worry about perfection but just to synchronize body motion and timing, keeping the muscles alive and in balance. It's like riding a bicycle, and on a larger landscape it's like traveling through life. It's pointless to tilt one way or the other, buffeted around by excessive tensions or anxieties. The only way to go is to keep in mind the key word—balance—then proceed.
*Interview, Los Angeles/
Los Angeles Times, 11-7:(Home)65.*

Saul Bellow
Author 3

I think of Sidney Smith, a much-admired 19th-century English clergyman, and his advice: "Short views, for God's sake, short views." Nobody can make an impression by speaking at great length nowadays. Falsehoods are all around us, and it is better to break through with short truths.
*San Francisco Examiner & Chronicle, 11-21:
(This World)2.*

4

What is at the center now? At the moment, neither art nor science, but mankind is determining, in confusion and obscurity, whether it will endure or not. The whole species—everybody—has gotten into the act. At such a time it is essential to enlighten ourselves, to dump encumbrances, including the encumbrances of education and all organized platitudes, to make judgments of our own, to perform acts of our own. [Joseph] Conrad was right to appeal to that part of our being which is a gift. We must hunt for that under the wreckage of many systems. The failure of those systems may bring a blessed and necessary release from formulations, from an over-defined and misleading consciousness. With increasing frequency, I dismiss as merely respectable opinions I have long held—or thought I held—and try to discern what I have really lived by, and what others live by. The struggle that convulses us makes us want to simplify, to reconsider, to eliminate the tragic weakness which prevented writers—and readers—from being at once simple and true.
*Nobel Lecture, Stockholm, Dec. 12/
Los Angeles Times, 12-13:(1)1.*

505

WHAT THEY SAID IN 1976

George C. S. Benson
Former Assistant-Secretary of the Army of the United States; Founder, Claremont (Calif.) Men's College
1

It's hard for Americans to understand, but both China and Russia teach ethics in their state-run schools. Citizens of these Communist nations are taught respect for the individual. And there is no organized vice in either Russia or China. Corruption, if discovered, could cost officials involved their heads. It's a sad commentary on U.S. society when we must rely on policemen or prison guards to teach or enforce ethics, including the right to personal property. Corruption begets corruption. When some trade union or segment of our society is corrupt, the unit of government which ignores it is equally guilty of corruption.

Los Angeles Herald-Examiner, 4-18:(A)12.

Irving Berlin
Composer-lyricist
2

The worst part of getting old is that all your best friends are gone.

Los Angeles Herald-Examiner, 5-20:(B)2.

Kingman Brewster, Jr.
President, Yale University
3

Power and wealth can both be achieved by sheer acquisitive manipulation. But success, even to the powerful and to the wealthy, is measured by the extent to which they feel that, by what they have done, they have added something to the fulfillment of others.

At Yale University baccalaureate ceremonies/ The New York Times, 5-16:(4)19.

Leonid I. Brezhnev
General Secretary, Communist Party of the Soviet Union
4

Every Communist party is born of the working-class movement of the country in which it is active. And it is responsible for its actions first of all before the working people

ple of its own country, whose interests it expresses and defends. But it is precisely this that provides the basis for the Communists' international solidarity. For, in distinction from the ineradicable strife, as Lenin put it, between the interests of the exploiters, who fight over profits, markets and spheres of influence, working people of all countries have no such contractions. Their interests and aspirations are the same. On the other hand, it is apparent that the more influential a Communist party is in its own country, the weightier can be its contribution to the struggle for the Communists' common goals on the international scene.

At conference of European Communist parties, East Berlin/ The New York Times, 6-30:10.

Edmund G. Brown, Jr.
Governor of California (D)
5

Even a superficial reading of history indicates there has rarely been a period of self-indulgence on such a mass scale as there is in America in 1976—the idea that the sum total of life is the accumulation of more and more creature comforts and status symbols that are expensive to maintain. Some of it is normal and good, but it certainly has limits; and I don't support the materialism you find in so many magazines and other media today.

Interview/ Playboy, April:72.

6

If one-man, one-vote works in Los Angeles, it ought to work in Rhodesia. If honesty is important in Washington, it's also important in Italy, Chile and Japan . . . If the cities sink, so do the suburbs right afterward. If the blacks can't make it, then the whites won't be long to follow. We are living on a small planet; we are interdependent.

San Francisco Examiner & Chronicle, 5-16: (This World)2.

Warren E. Burger
Chief Justice of the United States
7

In the disorders that began in the 1960s, I suspect that my reactions were much like most others of my generation. I resented that young people who were given what seemed unparalleled opportunities for education, without the barriers of birth or class that exist in other societies, saw fit to tear down, to occupy, to burn rather than learn. Occasionally I went into rowdy crowds not to talk but to listen. On the streets in Washington, in Georgetown, and occasionally in Alexandria, I observed objectionable conduct. But I also saw peaceful protests, including the quiet demonstrations of young men and women with saffron robes and shaved heads, singing and praying in public. I watched others with long hair, simple clothes, knapsacks and bedrolls—most of them orderly and clean, and only a few otherwise . . . The perception of a true revolution in the making rested on the burning and bombing of college buildings and other public buildings, but I overlooked the positive side—the protest against materialism, against the misuse of natural resources, against pollution of the quality of life, and against a war that could not be satisfactorily explained. It was like the age-old yearning of Thoreau for Walden Pond, and, even if unrealistic and unattainable, perhaps it has helped all of us to a renewed awareness of values of the spirit.

At University of Pennsylvania
commencement, May 28/
Parade, 7-18:14.

Michael Caine
Actor
1

In England we have football pools, where people win a quarter of a million dollars and they're instantly rich. But their lives fall apart. They buy the wrong furniture, the wrong wine, the wrong house in the wrong place. Others say, "I won't let it change my life. I'll just live like I always did." Which is fine, but it's not being rich. It's just being what you always were—with a lot of money. To me, being rich is using money as a toy, a tool and a weapon.

Interview, Beverly Hills, Calif./
San Francisco Examiner & Chronicle, 4-11:
(Datebook)13.

Paul D. Cameron
Associate professor of human development, St. Mary's College of Maryland
2

As we are entering an era of childlessness, our [study] results suggest that America may rapidly become a much more dangerous place to live. Children are associated with greater altruism on the part of their parents. Besides being cute, little humans may well be enriching the well-being of the race beyond their weight . . . While it always hurts psychologists to endorse "ancient aphorisms," it does appear that childlessness is associated with selfishness. As our society is starting to choose childlessness more frequently, perhaps it is time to pause and weigh the possible negative effects of such a choice against the apparent advantages.

Before Eastern Psychological Association,
New York, April 22/
Los Angeles Herald-Examiner, 4-23:(A)17.

Jimmy Carter
Candidate for the 1976 Democratic U.S. Presidential nomination; Former Governor of Georgia (D)
3

There are those who believe it is not worthwhile to try, that human nature never changes, that the human condition is fixed forever and that all struggle for human betterment is futile. I do not believe that. I believe that the essence of a worthwhile life is in the striving. I do not fear failure, but I do fear the resigned acceptance of what is mean or mediocre or wrong.

Before California State Senate,
Sacramento, May 20/
The Washington Post, 5-21:(A)3.

Jimmy Carter
1976 Democratic U.S. Presidential nominee
4

I try not to commit a deliberate sin. I recognize that I'm going to do it anyhow, because I'm human and I'm tempted. And Christ set some almost impossible standards for us. Christ said, "I tell you that anyone who looks

WHAT THEY SAID IN 1976

(JIMMY CARTER)

on a woman with lust has in his heart already committed adultery." I've looked on a lot of women with lust. I've committed adultery in my heart many times. This is something that God recognizes I will do—and I have done it—and God forgives me for it. But that doesn't mean that I condemn someone who not only looks on a woman with lust but who leaves his wife and shacks up with somebody out of wedlock. Christ said, Don't consider yourself better than someone else because one guy screws a whole bunch of women while the other guy is loyal to his wife. The guy who is loyal to his wife ought not to be condescending or proud because of the relative degree of sinfulness.

Interview, Plains, Ga./ Playboy, November:86.

Edward M. Davis
Chief of Police of Los Angeles   *1*

Ten years ago, one-third of all marriages ended in divorce. Today, 50 per cent end in divorce. This cycle of destruction for the American family is going to continue because of the new morality which permits people to do what they want, when they want, without acquiring some sense of responsibility.

San Francisco Examiner & Chronicle, 12-19:
(This World)2.

E. L. Doctorow
Author   *2*

. . . politicians are born knowing exactly what writers know about language: that it can change reality. They know that history does not exist except as it is composed; that good and evil are construed; that there is no outrage, no monstrousness that cannot be made reasonable and logical and virtuous; and no shining act that cannot be turned into a disgrace.

Before Authors Guild/
The New York Times, 4-11:(4)17.

Elizabeth Douvan
Professor of psychology,
University of Michigan   *3*

One interesting development over the last 10 to 15 years has been the remarkable turn of the young toward the very old. Beginning with the hippies, but continuing on, the youth culture has developed a significant respect for really old people. Old men who, for years, had wandered on our campus with complete anonymity are now approached and engaged in conversation. Young students in graduate school decided that their real interest in socialization and development lay in the upper reaches of age distribution, not in early childhood. Jessamyn West's story, *Sixteen*—about a young woman's growth in response to her grandfather's imminent death—became a favorite. Gutman theorized that contemporary youth were in many respects psychologically like the very old. *Harold and Maude* became an underground film classic. What I make of this affinity is another sign of the muddy and ambiguous picture we have of adulthood. The young look to the very old as perhaps the right consultants about adulthood. After all, the old have successfully navigated this period. Perhaps the young are looking for a definition of adulthood with which they can identify.

At conference on youth sponsored by Center for
the Study of Democratic Institutions and
Illinois Humanities Council, Chicago/
The Center Magazine, May-June:15.

Rene Dubos
Professor emeritus of microbiology,
Rockefeller University   *4*

In my opinion, the difficulties of our time, or of any time, for that matter, are not reasons for discouragement. History shows that crisis usually fosters renewal and heralds new phases of creativeness, always different from the past. The most interesting characteristic of human beings is that they can transcend social as well as biological determinism. Animals are almost completely prisoners of biological revolution. But human beings are blessed with the freedom and with the inventiveness of social evolution. They can retrace their steps and start on a new course whenever they see danger ahead. They can integrate the raw materials of the earth with the knowledge derived from past experience and from new learning in a continuous evolutionary process of creation.

Before College of Physicians of Philadelphia/
The National Observer, 2-28:15.

Richard Eberhart
Poet
1

What do you have to count on in life? Nothing. When you're young, you think you do. But you don't. Fate always intervenes. Look at me. I don't know anything more about the truth now that I didn't when I was 16. And I know nothing about death. But it doesn't worry me. I know where I am. Hopefully, you learn at least that in the end.

Interview, Cape Rosier, Maine/
The Washington Post, 7-18:(E)1.

Oriana Fallaci
Journalist
2

Success is when you achieve something in general, not for yourself only. To earn a little more, to sell many books, to be interviewed, to be known—this is not success. In one field, I did have success—demonstrating that women can do what men do, and even better.

Interview, Florence, Italy/
"W": a Fairchild publication, 4-30:27.

Arthur Fiedler
Conductor, Boston Pops Orchestra
3

No one should ever finish being interested and curious. I'd like to live to be 1000—for the sake of doing things.

San Francisco Examiner & Chronicle, 8-1:
(This World)2.

Gerald R. Ford
President of the United States
4

History and experience tell us that moral progress comes not in comfortable and complacent times, but out of trial and confusion. Tom Paine aroused the troubled Americans of 1776 to stand up to the times that try men's souls, because the harder the conflict the more glorious the triumph.

State of the Union address, Washington, Jan. 19/
The New York Times, 1-20:18.

5

There are no adequate substitutes for father, mother and children bound together in a loving commitment to nurture and protect. No government, no matter how well-intentioned, can ever take the place of the family in the scheme of things.

At International Eucharistic Conference,
Philadelphia/
Los Angeles Herald-Examiner, 8-13:(A)9.

Erich Fromm
Psychoanalyst
6

[Albert] Schweitzer said at the end of his life that it was not necessary to believe in God. He was a pessimistic humanist, and I suppose I am, too. In the end, the only important thing is our human activity, in which we can express love. Life has no meaning beyond that.

Interview/ Publishers Weekly, 9-13:42.

Willard Gaylin
President, Institute of Society, Ethics and Life Sciences, and clinical professor of psychiatry, Columbia University
7

[Saying he disagrees with the image of man as an aggressive animal]: I think it's distorted. I don't deny there may be a case for the existence of aggressive impulses in human beings, but I think an even stronger case can be made for man's also being a caring, loving animal. There's a tremendous volume of literature to support that. Secondly, I believe that to live with an exclusively aggressive image of ourselves is dangerous and destructive . . . The truth of the old cliche—that psychological self-definitions tend to become self-fulfilling —still stands: What we feel we are in large part determines what we will be. The way we view ourselves and our institutions is the way we and our institutions are going to become. If we see ourselves as essentially destructive by nature, contained only by the instruments of fear and by the power of society, we can indeed become just that.

Interview, Croton-on-Hudson, N.Y./
The Christian Science Monitor, 9-30:15.

Valery Giscard d'Estaing
President of France
1

All the great things in human history attest to the fact that freedom is synonymous with invention, creative energy and indefinite power to renew and improve. It is proof that, far from hampering progress, freedom is its very soul. And it is up to us to prove this by making changes that are needed for implementing reforms required by the course of development. Indeed, nothing is more essential to the world today, nothing is more worthy of the aspiration of a statesman, than to illustrate, through actions, that a free society is also the best of progressive societies.

Before joint session of U.S. Congress,
Washington, May 18/
Los Angeles Herald-Examiner, 5-18:(A)2.

Arthur J. Goldberg
Lawyer; Former Associate Justice,
Supreme Court of the United States
2

Part of liberty is to respect the right of dissent. You can't have liberty if everyone thinks the same.

At California State University-Los Angeles,
commencement, June 11/
Los Angeles Herald-Examiner, 6-12:(A)5.

Samuel Gorovitz
Chairman, department of philosophy,
University of Maryland
3

Moral philosophy alone cannot provide solutions to moral problems any more than law alone can eliminate legal problems or economics alone can eliminate economic problems. We must always reach beyond philosophy in addressing problems in the world. But we should be wary of reaching without it.

The Washington Post, 11-7:(B)2.

Paul Harvey
News commentator,
American Broadcasting Company
4

[On how he explains his success]: I sometimes answer that question facetiously when it's asked. I just say, "I get up earlier than most." I've been blessed with good health and so I can get up with enthusiasm at four o'clock in the morning. Then, too, as a student of biographies, I've learned that the one common denominator in the lives of men who become successful is that they get up when they fall down. They get up and dust themselves off—and prevail.

Interview/The New York Times, 6-6:(2)21.

S. I. Hayakawa
Candidate for the 1976 California Republican
U.S. Senatorial nomination
5

We all believe in the equality of opportunity. That's fine. But liberals have gone beyond that, saying we must have equality of reward. That means that if we all try out with the San Francisco *Giants,* we all get a job with the San Francisco *Giants.*

Before Republican women/
Los Angeles Times, 5-15:(2)12.

Helen Hayes
Actress
6

People don't talk much about life's grandeur. Excess and ugliness seem to be the thing in much of the film world and the theatre, too. The publishing world seems seized by the same graffitic mentality. This is the show-and-tell age: show and tell everything, especially if it is seamy or depraved. [There is] a developing moral numbness to vulgarity, violence and the assault of the simplest human decencies . . . Decency and honesty, honor and dependability, unselfishness, compassion and, yes, good manners and good taste are still basic to the good life for the individual and the community. Civilization exists by virtue of self-restraint and consideration for others. But a vast effort will be required if we are to slough off the rather slovenly clothing of the past few years.

At Marymount College commencement,
Tarrytown, N.Y./
The Wall Street Journal, 5-27:14.

1

I think fame is a burden to anybody. It's what we all want and what we wish we could get rid of the minute we get it. I don't think it's much of a pleasure, because it makes you self-conscious. Self-consciousness is not a happy state of being.

Interview, Sarasota, Fla./
The Dallas Times Herald, 11-17:(E)1.

Katharine Hepburn
Actress
2

We live in a distressing time when upper-class children steal things out of stores. Why? Because they are bored. Their lives offer no challenge. If they don't like their school courses, they drop out, slop out. They're not made to do anything. If they don't like their teachers, they quit. It was not my business to like my teachers. I was in school because I had to be.

Interview/
The Dallas Times Herald, 9-16:(C)1.

3

Success! Our terrible concentration on money and success has made life intolerable for people who feel they haven't achieved them. Your sense of values gets cockeyed. I don't think success matters a bloody bit. What matters is you do with what you've got to offer. The full development of your faculties as God gave them to you—that's success.

Interview, New York/
Los Angeles Times, 10-10:(Calendar)46.

Matina S. Horner
President, Radcliffe College
4

[On success]: People have real trouble with the word. I don't define it the way society has traditionally. To me, a highly successful life integrates personal and professional objectives in a way consistent with one's talents, aspirations and energies—unconstrained by external stereotypes and irrelevant assumptions . . . The hardest struggle is to achieve a balance.

Interview/ People, 6-21:61.

Tab Hunter
Actor
5

In society, people are concerned with who you are when *what* you are is so much more important. People are all trying to "make it," and all that. Success—success is only personal happiness. If you're happy, then you're a successful person.

Interview, Middleburg, Va./
Los Angeles Times, 7-11:(Calendar)40.

Juliana
Queen of the Netherlands
6

Nineteen seventy-six appears to have been gloom. We see lasting discord, even wars in the world, little reconciliation, little progress and too many people failing. And with all of this there is the frightening lack of respect for each other's life and well-being, of all life on earth, that is visible again and again in dozens of terrifying shapes. However, all of this is no cause for surprise in a world inhabited by four billion egoists, all of them inclined to fancy themselves to be the focus point of the world.

Christmas broadcast to the nation, Dec. 25/
The New York Times, 12-26:(1)3.

WHAT THEY SAID IN 1976

Herman Kahn
Director, Hudson Institute
1

[Saying that man, in the future, will not be faced with the kinds of pressures and dangers and problems as in the past, and that this freedom may present its own problems]: Freud once said that, for most people, their touch with reality is the long arm of the job—the needs of work. You take that away from them and most people can, and will, lead delusive lives. They won't be in touch with reality. That's probably the biggest problem coming up. It's a little bit like a family which has always been relatively poor and comes into more money than it ever dreamed of, and goes on a splurge and goes bankrupt again.

Interview, Croton-on-Hudson, N.Y./
The Dallas Times Herald, 2-22:(B)3.

2

There's a well-known Chinese-Italian curse: may you live in interesting times. And a well-known proverb happy is a country whose annals are few, happy is a country without any history. Dullness is happiness. There are people who can't stand happiness. The French can't—it's one of their single biggest weaknesses. But security, growth, dynamism, creativity—all these things come under boredom.

Interview/Newsweek, 7-4:30.

Henry A. Kissinger
Sceretary of State
of the United States
3

Tension is unavoidable between moral values, which are invariably cast in absolute terms, and efforts to achieve them, which of necessity involve compromise.

Before American Jewish Congress, Washington,
April 4/Los Angeles Times, 4-5:(1)1.

4

Our democratic systems have disproved the doctrine that only repression and authoritarianism could advance human well-being. On the contrary, the industrial democracies . . . have demonstrated conclusively that it is in freedom that men achieve the economic advance of which ages have dreamed.

At ministers meeting of Organization for
Economic Cooperation and Development,
Paris, June 21/The New York Times, 6-22:10.

Sophia Loren
Actress
5

When I was little I used to dream of having a wooden pencil holder like my companions at school. I dreamed of simple accessible things, and—even if no one believes me—I'm still like that today. Inner peace is a gift nobody can buy. The world changes, while the family is the only true thing.

Interview/People, 2-2:12.

Clare Boothe Luce
Former American diplomat
and playwright
6

There is a decline of Western Christian civilization and many of the signs of collapse are present, among which is a general failure of will in this country [the U.S.]—a feeling "I want to get mine while the getting is good," a general lack in the country of a sense of duty or obligation and a tremendous desire for what's been called "entitlements"—what the state owes me as an individual, or owes my family . . . If you really want to be cheerful, you can look on the fall and decline of Rome as the beginning of a great new period in European history. So it's quite likely that if the West declines and falls—which it gives every sign of doing—that this may mean the beginning of a great new period in civilization, perhaps a renaissance in the Orient, with the Chinese the great nation of the future.

Interview, Washington/
"W": a Fairchild publication, 4-16:9.

512

1

[On the sexual revolution]: The ordinary thing would be for a girl today to shop around before she gets married. Virginity is lost very early and considered no big deal. I don't know —it may be just because I'm of a different generation, but it seems to me there was more mystery, romance and charm about the old ways than there is now. I think sex has become very public. I know that I don't want to see those movies and read porn books. It's very hard to speak of morals and mores in an age where they do not exist, isn't it? I don't know anything that shocks anyone any more.

Interview, Washington/
"W": a Fairchild publication, 4-16:9.

Richard W. Lyman
President, Stanford University
2

If the only leadership we as a people will dignify with our trust is a leadership of saints and saviours . . . we are in for some tough times indeed. We are in danger of coming to believe that no one can be trusted to speak of moral issues or enlist moral energies unless he or she owns nothing, carries no organizational responsibilities, possesses no authority or office or status—in short, is untrained and inexperienced at coping with problems in public life.

At "Time" magazine conference on leadership, Washington/The Wall Street Journal, 11-12:10.

Ferdinand E. Marcos
President of the Philippines
3

I feel that the younger generation is a profound lot. You cannot just foist decisions on them. You have to explain. Every generation is an experimenting generation. But our generation is not just an experimenting generation. It is a thinking generation.

San Francisco Examiner & Chronicle, 10-24:
(This World)2.

William J. McGill
President, Columbia University
4

The 20th century was to have been an era characterized by an uninterrupted growth of civilization made possible by the elimina-

tion of hunger and disease. It was to have been guided by rapid expansion of education which would free the mass of the world's people from their historic bondage in ignorance and poverty. We have managed to take a number of important steps toward these humane objectives. Man has conquered disease. He has learned how to bring water to the deserts and to enrich the soil so that it produces food in abundance. Man has walked on the moon. But we have also discovered that improved education in the 20th century has not diminished our contentiousness nor has it armed us effectively against simplistic dogma. We are ruled today more by passion and paranoia and less by the sophisticated skepticism of the rational mind than were our 19th-century antecedents. We have not managed to eliminate racial antagonisms in the world and we have not succeeded in eradicating hunger and poverty. Instead, we have succeeded in concentrating industrial growth and material consumption among a few nations which have been willing to share their resources only to the extent of bargaining for political advantage among the starving people of the earth. It is not a very distinguished record—whether we consider it as a failure in the fulfillment of a potential clearly evident at the end of the last century, or whether we think of that failure in terms of the performance of the political and educational leaders of our own times.

At National Conference on the Causes of Popular Dissatisfaction with the Administration of Justice, St. Paul, Minn., April 8/Vital Speeches, 5-15:467.

Margaret Mead
Anthropologist
5

Prophets and scholars alike agree that the world needs ways in which human beings can be made whole again. We have become fragmented by bureaucracies, mass production, impersonal decision-making on a scale so large that decisions have become increasingly dehumanized, in which one stroke of a distant pen can condemn millions to starvation, or bring water to a million drought-ridden people . . . The statistics of population growth, car manufacture, grain sales, costs of trans-

WHAT THEY SAID IN 1976

(MARGARET MEAD)

Atlantic transport, barrels of oil or tons of cement boggle the minds of both planners and consumers, and any sense of the costs and benefits to living human beings vanishes . . . If we are to make this planet safe for our children and their children . . . there is no other way [than] to . . . teach them to think in terms of the whole. We will cripple the next generation if we condemn them to live in a town where there are no old people or no children, no unfortunates in need of help and no handicapped in need of care, no people of a different skin color, no one who speaks a different language, where everyone is rich or everyone is poor, where everyone works at the same kind of job, or where all are consumers for whom all the necessities of life come from far away . . . Human settlements are not "consumer items"; they are not "frills" nor can they be separated from the whole problem of development or energy use, or productivity, any more than they can be separated from human dignity.
At Habitat Forum, Vancouver, B.C., June 7/
The Washington Post, 6-20:(C)6.

1

[To assume that] if you give people equal opportunity they can all do the same thing with it is a sham, a hypocrisy of the worst sort that has been destroying an awful lot of people. What I want to emphasize very heavily is [that] the only way you give people equal opportunity is to recognize their differences, one from another.
Before Justice Department
equal-opportunity project, Washington/
Los Angeles Times, 9-15:(1)2.

Henry Miller
Author

2

. . . I don't have too much regard for intelligence. I don't have great regard at all for great thinkers, because I don't think it's thinking that's ruling the world. It's action. And feeling most of all, feeling beyond everything.
Publishers Weekly, 3-8:10.

Charles A. Mosher
United States Representative, R—Ohio

3

Perfection is not the human destiny. In a way, it's the imperfections that are the dynamic qualities in the human condition.
Interview/ The Washington Post, 12-20:(A)8.

Joe Namath
Football player, New York "Jets"

4

You've got to take care of yourself first. That can sound mighty cold—okay, buddy, first of all, look after yourself—but you have to take care of yourself. If you're not home in your head and your heart from the git-go, you can't be on the level with anybody else. But if you are at home now, if you get along with people, if you are sincere and try to be right, then you can be honest with the rest of the people. You have to experience all this to understand.
Interview, Palm Springs, Calif./
The Dallas Times Herald, 2-22:(C)5.

Linus Pauling
Chemist

5

I am forced, as I think about what has happened in the world during my lifetime and as I observe governments in their processes of making decisions, to conclude that the coming century is probably going to be one in which the amount of suffering reaches its maximum. Unless we are wiser than we have shown ourselves to be in the past, we chemists and we citizens, we advisers of the government and we government officials, there will be a catastrophe during the coming century, perhaps a series of catastrophes. The human race might survive. By 2076, we shall, I hope, have solved these problems, and from then on we may have a world in which every person who is born will have the opportunity to lead a good life.
Before American Chemical Society, New York/
The National Observer, 5-8:13.

Harold Pinter
Playwright

6

However boldly or vigorously one acts or

makes any connection with a thing or a person, nevertheless these things are really taking place in a mist. To arrive at a lucid appreciation of what is taking place is impossible. Perhaps it can only be achieved through art. In life I don't think it can be achieved.

Interview/Newsweek, 11-29:77.

Donald Pleasance
Actor
1

Why do I play so many sinister parts? I'll tell you. The fact is that I don't view the human race very benevolently, and I understand villians more. I just don't identify with the guy who always lives straight and upright, and wins in the end. I haven't found life like that. Handsome men are not always successful. They don't always get the girl. The old myth of the boring prince and Cinderella has gone out of the window. . . I don't take life too seriously any more. I've discovered the whole thing is covered with a very thin layer of chocolate, and that it's really all rather hard underneath.

Interview, London/
San Francisco Examiner & Chronicle, 6-13:
(Datebook)20.

Roman Polanski
Motion-picture director
2

If I am nostalgic, it is for friends and situations more than for the place. But I don't think you can ever have them back again, even if you try. Going back somewhere doesn't necessarily bring back what you have loved or admired. Quite the contrary, it's usually a disappointment. Certain things have happened, and they will never come back again.

Interview, Paris/
The New York Times, 2-22:(2)15.

John Portman
Architect
3

To be successful, you must show great perseverance in what you are doing. And, most important, you must enjoy what you are doing. You can work hard, but if you don't enjoy it, you ought not to do it.

Interview, Atlanta/Nation's Business, August:47.

Ronald Reagan
Candidate for the 1976 Republican U.S. Presidential nomination; Former Governor of California (R)
4

We have to recognize that the moral standards that have grown up down through 6,000 years of civilization should not be cast aside simply because they are old. They have been tested by time. And it begins with every individual watching his own particular efforts. It isn't any good for the fellow to sneer at politicians if at the same time he is running a fast deal in his own existence.

Interview/The Christian Science Monitor, 6-3:17.

J. Edgar Rhoads
Chairman emeritus,
J. E. Rhoads & Sons, Inc.
5

In America, we have too much interest in making money and not enough in the things that make for real happiness—public service, unselfishness, friendliness, willingness to help others. We forget: Power creates the desire for more power, and, when you get more power, you often overlook others' rights. I hope our country will become a happier place and measure profits more in human relationships and less in dollars. I hope we will sincerely follow, every day of the week, what we know to be the right course. Our problems as a nation may increase. Greater wisdom, understanding and spiritual guidance are needed throughout the country to combat them. I feel that character, as well as ability and capital, is vital for human institutions to endure for long.

Interview, Wilmington, Del./
Nation's Business, July:34.

Ginger Rogers
Actress, Entertainer
6

If you're sincere in what you display, that strikes a chord in the heart of the viewer. I can look at a photograph in the newspaper and see the sincerity, or lack of it, in someone's eyes. Sincerity can make someone look beautiful, even if his features aren't.

Interview, New York/
The Christian Science Monitor, 3-17:26.

WHAT THEY SAID IN 1976

(GINGER ROGERS)

1

. . . I do not believe you are what you eat, although I do try to eat well. I believe you are what you think. Your thinking gives you the ability to have joy. Something my mother made me appreciate was the importance of disciplining your thoughts. Discipline is what the world has lost.

Interview, New York/
"W": a Fairchild publication, 3-19:7.

2

Success is three-fourths hard work, and the rest is whatever ingredient you need to complete the requirement.

Interview/The Washington Post, 4-19:(C)7.

Artur Rubinstein
Pianist

3

Contrast makes everything alive. You know sadness only when you have been gay, and you know happiness only if you have been unhappy. Otherwise, things become boring.

Interview, New York/Time, 3-29:53.

4

After reading many philosophers, the one theory I support is life. Life is accessible around us, what we can grasp with our five senses. All the other things, life after death and so on, are guesses. We have to suffer through life. Let's take it as it is. The good side nobody can take away from us: love, ideas, wishes, pleasures, music, poetry, painting. I prove it to myself now at 89. I am a passionate lover of life, unconditionally.

Interview, Paris/
Los Angeles Times, 7-22:(4)13.

Donald H. Rumsfeld
Secretary of Defense of the
United States

5

I'll reflect on a decision I've made that might be wrong, but I've never been much for hand-wringing. I don't sit down and ask myself: "Are you sure you're happy?" I never agonize, because, if you do, you won't be able to cope. What you do is just keep establishing priorities, and, when the work builds up, you stop, take that which is important, delegate the rest and move on.

Interview, Washington/People, 4-19:14.

Helmut Schmidt
Chancellor of West Germany

6

Anyone who thinks that democracy consists of free discussion is mistaken. Democracy is a matter of discussion first, then a matter of decision.

San Francisco Examiner & Chronicle, 10-24:
(This World)19.

Maurice Sendak
Author/illustrator of children's books

7

To be a baby is to be all. The world belongs to babies. They don't know anyone else is in it. It's them and someone who comes to feed them. It's probably the best time of our lives, until we realize we have to share it with a daddy, a brother and a sister and a cat and a dog and a house and a street and a world and America and England. And it keeps stretching out and out and out. That's what growing up is all about—a compromise all the way.

Interview, Ridgefield, Conn./
People, 2-9:49.

R. Sargent Shriver
Candidate for the 1976 Democratic U.S.
Presidential nomination; Former
United States Ambassador to France

8

As society grows more complex, the family becomes more essential—as the one place where a sense of trust, a degree of discipline, a capacity to love can all be nurtured, and often as the only place where people are cherished because of who and what they are.

New Hampshire/
The Washington Post, 2-28:(A)15.

John R. Silber
President, Boston University
1

As a consequence of our success in extending opportunity through education, we have encouraged not merely the true democratic belief that everyone has a right to his own opinion but the counterfeit view that anyone's opinion is as good as that of any other. And we have destroyed the central core of moral instruction, in higher education no less than in primary and secondary education, by accepting as cultural dogma the view that all value judgments are relative and of equal validity. The equal validity of individual judgments on subjects of greatest moral importance is a commonplace doctrine of our educational program. The difference between saying that anyone's opinion is as good as any other's and that everyone has a right to his own opinion is neither obscure nor difficult. Everyone has a right to his own opinion, no matter how wrong, how ignorant, or even how stupid he may be. And he has a right to express that opinion. But there is no justification for the belief that each person is equal in judgment, in discernment, or in knowledge to every other person. "That all men are born to equal rights is true," said John Adams. "Every being has a right to his own as clear, as moral, as sacred as any other being has . . . But to teach that all men are born with equal powers and faculties . . . is as gross a fraud, as glaring an imposition on the credulity of people as ever was practiced by monks, or by Druids, [or] by Brahmins."
Before Society for College and University Planning, Washington/ The National Observer, 10-2:15.

Isaac Bashevis Singer
Author
2

For the Orthodox Jews I am a non-believer. I like to write about sex and love, which is not kosher to the Orthodox people. I believe in God, but I don't believe that God wants man to run away completely from pleasure. If he has created men and women with a great desire to love and be loved, there must be something in it; it cannot be all bad. Love and sex are the things which give life some value, some zest. Miserable as flesh and blood is, it is still the best you can get.
Interview, New York/ The Washington Post, 12-28:(C)3.

B. F. Skinner
Professor of psychology, Harvard University
3

No human being is really creative. Things happen and then you let them stand or wipe them out, depending on whether they please you—whether you're reinforced by them or find them aversive. I certainly believe that I did not direct my life. I didn't design it. I never made decisions. Things always came up and made them for me. That's what life is.
Interview/"W": a Fairchild publication, 5-14:2.

Page Smith
Historian
4

Despite the way they do things, in young people there are the seeds of redemption. It's the living, unquenchable human spirit saying to what is, "That won't do."
Interview, Santa Cruz, Calif./ San Francisco Examiner & Chronicle, 6-27: (Scene)4.

Alexander I. Solzhenitsyn
Exiled Soviet author
5

[On Communism]: All my life and the life of my generation, the life of those who share my views, we all have one standpoint: better to be dead than a scoundrel. In this horrible expression of Bertrand Russell ["better Red than dead"] there is an absence of all moral criteria. Looked at from a short distance, these words allow one to maneuver and to continue to enjoy life. But from a long-term point of view, it will undoubtedly destroy those people who think like that. It is a terrible thought.
Television interview, London/"Panorama," British Broadcasting Corporation, 3-1.

WHAT THEY SAID IN 1976

(ALEXANDER I. SOLZHENITSYN)

1

Genuinely human freedom is inner freedom, given to us by God: freedom to decide upon our own acts, as well as moral responsibility for them ... I think it will not be too much for us to acknowledge that in some renowned countries of the Western world in the 20th century, freedom has been degraded in the name of "development" from its original soaring forms; that in not one country of the world today does there exist that highest form of freedom of spiritualized human beings which consists not in maneuvering between articles of laws, but in voluntary self-restraint and in full consciousness of responsibility, as these freedoms were conceived by our forefathers.

Upon receiving Freedoms Foundation's American Friendship Award, at Hoover Institution/ The Christian Science Monitor, 8-9:27.

Francois Truffaut
Motion-picture director

2

The more people around us show irresponsible behavior, the more responsible I have to be ... I must reproach many artists for pretending they don't care about life, when in fact they care about it enormously ... They pretend because of snobbism and a certain mental confusion. They feel that if they admitted their love of life, it would imply an acceptance of the society in which they live ... I don't mean to cheat or to pretend that life is more beautiful than it is ... But in this great arena of contestation that one has today, there can be a difference between criticisms directed against society and one's feelings toward life ... We must look beyond the end of the century; we must work toward the years 2003 or 2004 ... I would never indicate on screen that I shared the suicidal attitude of many people today. It's a question of responsibility ... and I love life.

Interview, New York/ The Christian Science Monitor, 12-1:30.

Barbara Tuchman
Author, Historian

3

Our standards have shriveled to a point where phoniness is now accepted. From TV to magazines, advertising has created a culture in which nobody expects to say or to listen to or to hear the truth.

The Christian Science Monitor, 4-12:14.

Ernest van den Haag
Adjunct professor of social philosophy, New York University

4

[Criticizing pornography]: [One view] is that society consists of individuals, each independent of each other, and that the task of the government is merely to protect one individual from interference by others. That is not my view. My view is that no society can survive unless there are bonds among its members, unless its members identify with each other, recognize each other as humans and do not think of each other simply as sources of pleasure or unpleasure. For once they do, then they may come to think of people as kinds of insects. If one disturbs you, you kill it. Once you no longer recognize that a person is fully human, like yourself, you can do what the Germans did to the Jews —use the gold in their teeth. Human solidarity is based on our ability to think of each other not purely as means, but as ends in ourselves. Now, the point of all pornography, in my opinion, is that it invites us to regard the other person purely as a subject of exploitation for sexual pleasure.

At debate on pornography, New York/ The New York Times, 11-21:(2)26.

Mike Wallace
News correspondent, Columbia Broadcasting System

5

Surely there's been no time in the country's history—in the world's history—when words have been such an industry as they've become today. On newsstands, at magazine counters, on radio and television, on billboards, the bombardment is never-ending,

518

the din, if not deafening, at least confusing . . . I can't help wondering if we aren't all vastly over-communicated, if words haven't become a kind of Muzak for us, a background hum that fills the silent gaps of time in which, otherwise, we might just sit and think . . . What I'm saying is that perhaps all of us put up with too much word garbage, served up just to fill up newspaper space, magazine pages and broadcast time—just because the space, the pages and the time are there. Perhaps we're too passive about refusing what isn't worth our time. Perhaps we should let the word-merchants *know* when they're selling us shoddy merchandise, by not buying what they're peddling—yes, [by] not listening to what they're saying. By turning off. Perhaps we should opt for more silence. More contemplation. More digesting of those fewer words we find useful, moving, ennobling, stirring, thought-provoking.

CBS Radio commentary/
Los Angeles Times, 3-10:(2)7.

John Hall Wheelock
Poet
1

[On old age]: As life goes on, it becomes more intense, because there are tremendous numbers of associations and so many memories. So many people you loved are gone. It's almost two societies, the living and the dead, and you live with them both.

At gathering honoring him, New York, April 7/
The New York Times, 4-9:26.

Elie Wiesel
Author
2

There is chaos everywhere. We have conquered space, and left the streets to the murderers. We have conquered everything, and we don't know where we are going . . . [Former U.S. President] Nixon is popular in [Communist] China, and [current U.S. President] Ford is popular in Russia . . . Politics

used to be public, and sex private, and now it is the opposite. Could it really be we are witnessing the ultimate decline of mankind? . . . I am afraid of the answer.

At Bicentennial Conference on
Religious Liberty, Philadelphia, April 27/
The Washington Post, 4-30:(D)19.

John H. Williams
Chairman, The Williams Companies
3

The guy who rises to the top is the one who has a little more drive than the others. But, on top of that, he has to be sort of lucky. Most of the time, if you talk to a successful man about his success, he'll say at some point in the conversation that he was just a little bit lucky in being at the right place at the right time. I don't want to belabor that point, however, because while I'm a firm believer in luck as an ingredient in success, I also feel successful people manage to create much of the so-called luck for themselves.

Interview, Tulsa, Okla./
Nation's Business, April:56.

Walter B. Wriston
Chairman, Citicorp
(Citibank, New York)
4

I grew up believing and being taught to believe that every individual in our society could make a contribution. It didn't make any difference what it was that he did. My father was born in a log cabin in a territory of the U.S. His father was a circuit-riding preacher in the Wyoming Territory. And my father wound up as president of a great university. All he had going for him was a very fine mind and driving energy and a firm belief in the opportunity of the U.S. I grew up in a college town without any money in the house. But I believed that if you worked and got educated, you got opportunity. You can't prove by me that it ain't true.

Interview/Newsweek, 7-4:64.

Religion

John C. Bennett
Visiting professor, Claremont (Calif.)
School of Theology; President emeritus,
Union Theological Seminary
                                                          1

One of the main elements in what I call the humanizing of theology of today is the movement away from the belief that most of the human race—because it has not been converted to Christ—is destined to eternal punishment. It is reasonable to believe that those who do not accept a particular religious faith will be deprived of a great good; but to follow up that deprivation with the fires of hell is now for most Christians an incredible way of thinking about God's dealing with people.

At religious conference,
University of Southern California/
Los Angeles Herald-Examiner, 11-20:(A)7.

Peter Berger
Lutheran sociologist,
Rutgers University
                                                          2

An enormous demoralization is going on [in the U.S.], and that is the gist of our crisis. It is not just a crisis in the political arena but reaches down to private life. It goes from the bedroom to the White House. We are uncertain about our values and the meaning of life. Religion used to give us our values, but we now live in an age of secularization.

The Christian Science Monitor, 4-12:14.

Ingmar Bergman
Motion-picture director
                                                          3

God and I separated many years ago. We have nothing to do with each other now. We are on this earth, here; this is the only life, from beginning to end; and, when the end comes, the light is switched off. You exist and you don't exist. That's the whole thing, the remarkable thing. Life is just as cruel and beautiful as it is, and no Gods, nobody except yourself and other human beings on this earth, has anything to do with it.

Interview, Munich/
The New York Times, 10-17:(2)15.

Edmund G. Brown, Jr.
Governor of California (D); Candidate for
the 1976 Democratic U.S. Presidential
nomination
                                                          4

Religion in the world as I understand it involves the relation of God and man. A lot of conventional thinking appears to say that everything is secular. That's never an interpretation that most humans in history have held and not one that most Americans hold today. There are limitations, but human pride sometimes blinds us to them. We must become more humble, more aware of the dependence among man, nature and God.

Interview/The New York Times, 6-4:(A)12.

Jimmy Carter
Candidate for the 1976 Democratic
U.S. Presidential nomination;
Former Governor of Georgia (D)
                                                          5

. . . in 1967 I realized that my own relationship with God, with Christ, was very superficial. And because of some experiences I had·that I won't describe involving personal witnessing in states outside of Georgia among people who were very unfortunate . . . I came to realize that my Christian life, which I had always professed to be pre-eminent, had really been a secondary interest in my life. And I formed a very close, intimate relationship with God, through Christ, that has given me a great deal of peace, equanimity and the ability to accept difficulty without unnecessarily being disturbed, and also an inclination on a continuing basis to ask God's guidance in my life. It was not a profound stroke, a miracle. It wasn't a voice of God from heaven. It was not anything of that kind. It wasn't mysterious. It might have been the same kind of experience as millions of people have who do become Christians in a deeply personal way. I don't think God is going to make me President by any means. But whatever I have as a responsibility for the rest of my life, it will be with that intimate, personal, continuing relationship.

News conference, Raleigh, N.C., March 19/
The Washington Post, 3-21:(A)6.

1

There are good Baptists and bad Baptists. There are good Jews and bad Jews. There are good Catholics and bad Catholics. But the judgment of who's bad is one that is best left to God. I learned from my early years that you should not judge other people because, while you look at the mote in your brother's eye, you should be more concerned about the beam that is in your own eye.

At Jewish Educational Institute,
Elizabeth, N.J., June 6/
The New York Times, 6-7:22.

Jimmy Carter
1976 Democratic U.S.
Presidential nominee

2

One thing [we] Baptists believe in is complete autonomy. I don't accept any domination of my life by the Baptist Church—none. Every Baptist church is individual and autonomous. We don't accept domination of our church from the Southern Baptist Convention. The reason the Baptist Church was formed in this country was because of our belief in absolute and total separation of

church and state. These basic tenets make us almost unique. We don't believe in any hierarchy in church. We don't have bishops. Any officers chosen by the church are defined as servants, not bosses. They're supposed to do the dirty work, make sure the church is clean and painted and that sort of thing. So it's a very good, democratic structure.

Interview, Plains, Ga./
Playboy, November:86.

W. Sterling Cary
Former president,
National Council of Churches

3

If the church is not an instrument of liberation, it is not the church. I hear many people say this is not the time for social action [by the church]. I don't think the church has the right to say it's not a time to be faithful [to its total role embracing] worshiping and bearing testimony. [There are] black churches all over this land that are embarrassed by the poor and the oppressed. It's shocking how few black Christians are fighting for reform of the criminal-justice system that is wiping out our black community . . . It is surprising how few black churches are leading a fight for reformation of our welfare system . . . I don't hear the black church raising hell with the demonic power and principalities, but I do see us going to beautiful sanctuaries which cost a lot of money and occupy them one or two hours and leave them empty the rest of the week.

At Howard University School of Religion
convocation, Nov. 11/
The Washington Post, 11-12:(D)14.

Michel J. Crozier
Founder and director,
Centre de Sociologie des Organisations,
Paris

4

There has been a decline in religious feeling in Western society for the past 100 years without affecting democracy. There now seems to be some kind of religious revival—a search for the sacred, for help in human

521

WHAT THEY SAID IN 1976

(MICHEL J. CROZIER)

uncertainties. Often this search is in a strange sect, but established religions are finding ways to use these new religious feelings to some extent. However, there has been a real disintegration—for good, I believe—of established religion as a political force. I don't mean in the sense of dictating political decisions. But, till recently, the Catholic Church especially was rather efficient in directing people toward decisions and getting obedience. In France, for example, the Catholic Church, although careful not to impinge in politics, had an indirect political impact because people felt it was a stable institution. Because of what the Church represented, churchgoers were pillars of the established authority. All this is true no longer. Religion will develop in the direction of feelings, of mysticism, of giving help to people—but it will not develop as an established authority. This is part of the decay of established authority all through the Western world. Previously, the church helped buttress the social order, just as the educational system and the army did. But now the buttresses have gone. They could be rebuilt, but it would take a long time. They could also be rebuilt with other institutions taking the place of the old ones.

Interview, Paris/
U.S. News & World Report, 3-8:67.

Simcha Dinitz
Israeli Ambassador to the United States 1

When Israel achieved its statehood in 1948, the 650,000 Jews there were not fighting merely for themselves but for the entire Jewish people everywhere—in Israel, in the Soviet Union, and even in the United States. This is the essence of Zionism. This spirit of universality and unity, this combinating of shared history and common purpose, is the essential element in the survival of the Jewish people. If this unity is ever challenged, it is not only Israel that will be in mortal danger but American Jewry and Jews the world over.

Before American Jewish Congress,
Washington, April 2/
The New York Times, 4-4:(1)24.

Gerald R. Ford
President of the United States 2

For millions of men and women, the church has been the hospital for the soul, the school for the mind and the safe depository for moral ideals.

At Eucharistic Congress, Philadelphia, Aug. 8/
Los Angeles Times, 8-9:(1)1.

3

I believe that prayer in public schools should be voluntary. It is difficult for me to see how religious exercises can be a requirement in public schools, given our Constitutional requirement of separation of church and state. I feel that the highly desirable goal of religious education must be principally the responsibility of church and home. I do not believe that public education should show any hostility toward religion, and neither should it inhibit voluntary participation, if it does not interfere with the educational process.

Interview, Washington/
Los Angeles Herald-Examiner, 10-9:(A)8.

Theodore Freedman
Director, program of community service divisions, Anti-Defamation League of B'nai B'rith 4

Most Jews believe that prayers and sectarian observances of religious holidays have no place in public schools and are firmly committed to the principle of separation of church and state as the means of safeguarding the religious freedom of all Americans. [While the Jewish people are] firmly committed to the values of religion and its centrality in Jewish life and believe religious training is an essential aspect of every child's education, such education, in our view, is the prerogative and responsibility of the home, synagogue and the church.

Before B'nai B'rith national executive committee,
Boston, May 29/ The New York Times, 5-30:(1)28.

Joseph Graham
Professor of philosophy,
University of St. Thomas, Houston 5

We are beset on every side of evil unleashed.

Pornography is no further away than the corner drugstore and, increasingly, the television tube. We live in a world in which spiritual values are tolerated to the extent that their presence does not interfere with the unlimited satisfaction of sensual appetite.

At Patrimony of Truth Congress,
Vancouver, B.C./
Los Angeles Herald-Examiner, 5-15:(A)7.

Cary Grant
Actor
1

. . . when England and America were more religious and the church had more attendance, it was a more moralistic behavior. All I know is they had a belief in their government when they were brought up with a religious background. Now it's all part of a large pattern of disintegration. Its progress is not toward happiness, or doesn't seem to be.

Interview, New York/
Los Angeles Times, 1-11:(Calendar)27.

Andrew M. Greeley
Catholic priest; Sociologist
2

[Criticizing the church's ban on artificial birth control]: What the church . . . has to do is develop a positive teaching about sexuality, which will help men and women grow in love. Life together is both intensely rewarding and intensely difficult. Surely the church has more to say than just "Don't use the pills." We are not saying anything more. That is the problem. We are not helping people live together with joy and happiness—just "Don't use the damn pill" . . . Prohibition of birth control was cultural, not just ecclesiastical. It was necessary to keep the human race going. Now we have a whole new situation. I don't think it has been taken into consideration by the church.

Interview, Chicago/
Los Angeles Times, 4-6:(2)5.

Mark O. Hatfield
United States Senator, R—Oregon
3

[On charges that some of the worst crimes in history have been committed in the name of religion]: We have to distinguish between what man does to pervert the truth and what it says in the Old and New Testaments. I don't think we can blame the church as a whole. We have to recognize it is made up of sinners.

At National Town Meeting, Washington, Feb.18/
The Washington Post, 2-20:(C)6.

Irving Howe
Author, Editor
4

[The problem of preserving Jewish identity] troubles those Jews who are not religious, or who are lukewarmly religious, or who join a synagogue or temple for social or sentimental reasons than out of genuine faith; and especially those Jews, perhaps the majority, who do not regard themselves as believers, yet feel an attachment to certain values in Jewish life or to the agonies of modern Jewish experience, so that it becomes a matter of honor to maintain one's identification . . . Perhaps the strongest response to my book [*World of Our Fathers*] is part of that last tremor of historical consciousness that comes over a culture when it is in an advanced stage of disintegration. It is hard to know whether that response signifies a strong desire for a reassertion of Jewish experience or a last hurrah, of sorts, for the vanishing immigrant Jewish culture. [Young Jews can] turn back in simulations of nostalgia—can hold an "East Side festival" with pushcarts, peddlers and other attributes of immigrant life, as one Jewish community did last year—but the experience is fading.

Before American Jewish Congress, Washington/
Los Angeles Times, 5-22:(1)28.

Jesse L. Jackson
Civil-rights leader;
President, Operation PUSH
(People United to Save Humanity)
5

The value of God-consciousness as a part of the cosmic hierarchy has been slowly removed from the experience of this generation of young people. When God is removed, then man, because of a few "godlike" maneuvers, is

(JESSE L. JACKSON)

elevated to the level of God. And man can only *play* God.

At Bicentennial Conference on Religious Liberty,
Philadelphia/ The New York Times, 5-3:9.

Jan Jadot
Archbishop and Vatican apostolic delegate
to the United States   1

[Saying that, for theological, not socio-logical, reasons, women will never be or-dained priests in the Roman Catholic Church]: The Church has been organized accord-ing to the will of Christ; I do not see any positive indication about the ordination of women in the structure of the Church. I see women, especially sisters, so anxious to be ordained. I am afraid they are losing some-thing. They have to discover the place of women in society, in religion ... We are dis-covering now equal rights for everyone ... The feeling is that sexual discrimination is not acceptable. This is bringing into our social life more open possibilities for women. We are feeling this happy situation on the Church lev-el [but not women as priests].

Before National Federation of Priests Councils,
Houston/ Los Angeles Times, 3-27:(1)28.

Hans Kung
Theologian; Director,
Institute for Ecumenical Research,
Tubingen, West Germany   2

Today the Roman Catholic Church suf-fers a kind of leadership vacuum. It is a little the same that is happening in the United States at a political level. Or even in Italy. This is why there is immobility and exceed-ing rivalry. The first necessity is to find again a leadership.

Interview, Rome/
The New York Times, 4-8:16.

Marcel Lefebvre
Roman Catholic Archbishop of
Lille, France   3

The rite of Mass today is a bastard rite. The sacraments today are bastard sacraments. We

want to have prayers like our ancestors. We want to keep the Catholic faith ... If I had done earlier what they teach priests in sem-inaries to do now, I would have been excom-municated. If I had taught then the catechisms they teach now, they would have called me a heretic.

Lille, France/ Time, 9-13:63.

Franklin Littell
Professor of religion, Temple University   4

Religious liberty is a right and truth which is not government's to deny or to grant. Government may only recognize it and pro-tect it, for it stands on higher ground.

At Bicentennial Conference on Religious Liberty,
Philadelphia, April 24/
The New York Times, 5-3:9.

Paul VI
Pope   5

[Christ] places himself in the mainstream of civilization and divides it into two differ-ent and often opposed currents. On one side—his side, that of Jesus Christ—there is the cur-rent of peace and universal brotherhood among those who are his followers. On the other side is the stream of violence, division and conflict, and in the end, that of war. On one side, the current of those who are poor of spirit, of those who are seeking the king-dom of God, of those who believe in eternal life; on the other, the current of those who are selfish and who seek an earthly kingdom, those whose trust is in time alone ... that make force and aggressive and oppressive revolution the blind reason for the destinies of peoples.

At Palm Sunday Mass, Vatican City, April 11/
Los Angeles Times, 4-12:(1)1.

6

[Criticizing Catholics who support the Italian Communist Party]: Sometimes the dearest friends, the most trusted colleagues, the brethren sharing the same table, priests, the religious are precisely those who have turned against us. Christians will find among their brethren in the faith discord, opposition and even treason in these days. Protest is a habit; unfaithfulness has become almost an affirmation of freedom.

> *At weekly audience,*
> *Vatican City, May 12/*
> *Los Angeles Times, 5-13:(1)1.*

Roger L. Shinn
Professor of social ethics,
Union Theological Seminary   *1*

Religious wars tend to be extra furious. When people fight over territory for economic advantage, they reach the point where the battle isn't worth the cost, and so compromise. When the cause is religious, compromise and conciliation seem to be evil.

> *Time, 7-12:33.*

Henry Siegman
Rabbi; Executive vice president,
Synagogue Council of America   *2*

The fervent activism of the 1960s has definitely receded. People are taking a more personal view of religion—especially young people. Many Jews who used to be mounting the political barricades are wearing *yarmulkes* in public, lighting Sabbath candles, keeping dietary laws; and, for the first time in this century, the momentum in membership and enthusiasm seems to be shifting from reform Judaism to the more traditional branches of the faith—conservatism and orthodoxy.

> *U.S. News & World Report, 1-5:52.*

Leon-Joseph Cardinal Suenens
Roman Catholic Archbishop of
Malines-Brussels; Primate of Belgium   *3*

We [Christians] are a people of continuity and tradition, but at the same time we have to be oriented to the future. We need Christians committed to the world to come . . . Youth today are allergic to tradition. We have to face the fact that, with youth of today, it is the future which has credibility.

> *Washington/ The Washington Post, 3-12:(D)14.*

James L. Sullivan
President,
Southern Baptist Convention   *4*

There never was a time when our nation sensed the need for what Baptists can deliver more than now. A world that had thought we were an ignorant, barefooted, one-gallused lot was jarred out of its seat when it found out that . . . our voluntary gifts in a year are approximately $1.5-billion, and that on an average Sunday our churches baptize about three times as many people as were baptized at Pentecost.

> *Newsweek, 10-25:70.*

George C. Wallace
Governor of Alabama (D);
Candidate for the 1976 U.S.
Democratic Presidential nomination   *5*

We must remember that those who do not believe in God have no conscience . . . the real relaxation of tension will come when the leaders of the world realize there is a supreme being, and [He] is, in the long run, really the solution.

> *At religious gathering, Birmingham, Alabama/*
> *Los Angeles Times, 5-30:(1)26.*

Walter S. Wurzburger
Rabbi; President,
Rabbinical Council of America   *6*

We must halt the alienation of our spiritually sensitive youth from our religious institutions. If religion is to emerge as a vibrant and dynamic force in the American scene, we cannot afford to squander the opportunities and spiritual energy provided by the quest for authenticity and spiritual meaning on the part of our young people.

> *Before Rabbinical Council of America,*
> *Fallsburgh, N.Y., May 27/*
> *The New York Times, 5-28:(A)16.*

Space · Science · Technology

Edwin E. Aldrin, Jr.
Former American astronaut
1

[On the aftermath of his having walked on the moon in 1969]: When the trip was over and we returned, I would have preferred to be back in the simulator than have all that attention focused on the event. I felt like a puppet, at the beck and call of everything and everybody. That's what was overwhelming. I had been thrust into a new life. I was uptight. I was speaking in the halls of Congress; I met kings and queens. I went from an astronaut to the Astrodome. I made public appearances . . . A football or a baseball player knows he has to be pleasing to the fans. An entertainer knows he has to have acceptance. The livelihood of the players and the entertainer are dependent on being pleasing. But the livelihood of the astronauts didn't depend on being celebrated people.

Interview/
Los Angeles Herald-Examiner, 4-30:(A)11.

2

We are being forced to go back and ask ourselves why we got involved in the space program. Most people find it hard to accept the fact that we went to the moon because the President of the U.S. wanted to beat the Russians in something. We were embarrassed in Cuba, [and] by *Sputnik*—that's why we got the directive to go to the moon . . . I think the objective of beating the Russians was a good objective. We decided to get something else out of it as well, so we evolved a plan as we made our landings. But one thing I can assure you—we didn't go to the moon to bring back rocks. You have to ask yourself what would the world be like today if we had decided not to go? What would the Russians

be doing if their confidence had not been set back? Would the uncommitted nations of the world have had any choice but to follow?

Interview, New York/
The Christian Science Monitor, 5-13:30.

George Basalla
Science historian,
University of Delaware
3

Scientists cultivate the image of remote, logical and humorless individuals.

Before American Association for the
Advancement of Science, Boston/
The Christian Science Monitor, 2-25:4.

David L. Bazelon
Chief Judge,
United States Court of Appeals for the
District of Columbia Circuit
4

The multitude of new statutes aimed at controlling technology are of particular concern to me because of my position on the U.S. Court of Appeals here in Washington. At present, over two-thirds of our business involves Federal administrative action—far more than any other court in our country—and all signs point to a continuing increase. More and more, these cases are on the frontiers of science and technology: What are the ecological effects of building a pipeline for badly needed oil across the Alaskan tundra? Does the public health require removal of lead additives from gasoline? How can society manage radioactive wastes from nuclear reactors which remain toxic for centuries? Shall we ban the *Concorde* SST or Red Dye #2? . . . Significant or not, decisions involving scientific or technical expertise present peculiar challenges for reviewing courts. The problem is not so much that judges will impose their

own views on the merits. The question is whether they will even know what's going on.
Before American Society for
Public Administration, Washington/
The Wall Street Journal, 12-10:12.

Daniel J. Boorstin
Librarian of Congress of the
United States; Historian   1

People assume that because a new technology comes in, therefore the old must be abandoned. This is a misconception. There is a tendency for a new technology not to displace but to transform the old into a new role. When the telephone came in, it was predicted it would displace the mail. No one would write letters any more. When radio appeared, one of the consequences was thought to be that it would displace the telephone. Why use an instrument that required a wire? We still have bicycles; I gather the market is flourishing not in spite of the automobile but because of the automobile. Television did not abolish radio. There are more radios than ever. But radio plays a different role now. We listen to it in the car and watch television when we get home.
Interview, Washington/
Los Angeles Times, 11-9:(2)5.

Ray Bradbury
Science-fiction writer   2

We go to Mars because the universe terrifies us and we would solve that terror. We go there because death is a mystery and life an even bigger one. We go there because, as Ahab said, this was rehearsed by thee and me a billion years before the oceans rolled.
San Francisco Examiner & Chronicle, 7-18:
(Scene)3.

3

[On the *Viking* mission landing on Mars]: I think the important thing to emphasize is this—that, as of today, we have touched Mars. There is life on Mars, and it is us—ex-

tensions of our eyeballs in all directions, extensions of our sense of touch, extensions of our mind; extensions of our heart and soul have touched Mars today. That's the message to look for there. We are on Mars. We are the Martians.
Television interview/
The National Observer, 7-31:3.

4

Touch a scientist and you touch a child. The best scientist is open to experience and begins with romance—the idea that anything is possible. The dream comes first—then you put the foundation under it.
Los Angeles Times, 8-9:(1)16.

Fletcher L. Byrom
Chairman, Koppers Company   5

Those who attack growth are likely also to attack the technology that makes it possible. I remember a story set down by the late Paul Goodman. "Just the other day," he said, "I listened to a young fellow sing a very passionate song about how technology is killing us, and all that. But before he started, he bent down and plugged his electric guitar into the wall socket." I suppose that soon after man discovered how to make fire, some child burned his fingers. It is just as likely that neighbors of that ancient Prometheus brandished their clubs and called for an end to the evil force that could scorch skin, devastate forests and emit billows of noxious smoke. Fortunately, reason prevailed. Fire became one of man's most useful tools . . . Technology, contrary to what many believe, has not hastened the depletion of our resources. It has made it possible for us to get eight times more energy from a ton of coal than we did in 1900. It has made it possible for the advanced nations to devote less of their gross national product to raw materials and to turn more of their effort toward education and other services that enrich human life. It holds the promise of providing substitutes for those materials that cannot be replaced . . . One scientist has estimated that, without chemi-

WHAT THEY SAID IN 1976

cal fertilizers, insecticides and machinery, only one-fourth of the world's people could be fed; the other three-fourths would be doomed to starvation. In this one area of controversy, I think we have no feasible alternative. It hardly matters whether we view technology as a master that holds us captive or a servant that holds the promise of greater liberation than we have ever known before. On this finite planet, our only hope for salvation lies in the search for new knowledge.

At conference on alternatives to growth,
Texas/ The National Observer, 1-24:11.

Barry Commoner
Director,
Center for the Biology of Natural Systems,
Washington University, St. Louis
1

Science has a well-justified reputation for approaching the truth. Why? Not because we are any more truthful than anyone else, but because we have a tradition of making our mistakes in public—that's called publication. What stands in the way of a scientist faking his results is the certain knowledge that he's going to be checked.

The New York Times Magazine, 11-7:74.

Michael De Bakey
Heart-transplant surgeon
2

We live in an age of fear of the unknown. It is partly the result of the atom bomb. You must not fear the unknown, otherwise we wouldn't have science. The natural history of science is the study of the unknown. If you fear it, then you're not going to study it, and you're not going to make progress.

San Francisco Examiner & Chronicle, 9-12:
(This World)2.

Loren C. Eiseley
Professor of anthropology and the history
of science, University of Pennsylvania
3

Thousands of people in laboratories are working to understand bits of the world. But

when you get down to the final essence—where the Why replaces the How—our knowledge is limited, because we are finite mortal creatures . . .

Interview, Philadelphia/
The Christian Science Monitor, 2-11:19.

Gerald R. Ford
President of the United States
4

[Announcing the re-establishment of a White House Office of Science and Technology Policy]: Now, as we enter our third century, science, engineering and technology are more important than ever in meeting the challenges and opportunities which lie ahead for this nation and the world. This new office will provide an important source of advice on the scientific, engineering and technological aspects that require attention at the highest levels of government.

Washington, May 11/
The Washington Post, 5-12:(A)21.

5

[On the successful landing on Mars of the *Viking I* spacecraft]: It is amazing to think that, in the span of a single lifetime, the exploration of air and space has grown from the dreams of a very, very few individuals to such a massive cooperative reality. We have gone from a flight of a few seconds and a few hundred feet to a year-long journey to Mars, crossing some 440 million miles.

Telephone talk with NASA officials,
Washington, July 20/
Los Angeles Times, 7-21:(1)18.

Philip Handler
President,
National Academy of Sciences
6

Although much is written concerning the scientific method and the ethical code of scientists, these concepts reduce rather simply to the imperative of honesty, dispassionate objectivity, and the obligation to publish descriptions of one's procedures and findings in such [a] way as to permit verification. But establishing truth with respect to technical controversy relevant to matters of public policy, and doing so in full public view, has proved to be a surprisingly difficult challenge to the scientific community. To our simple code must be added one more canon: When describing technological risks to the non-scientific public, the scientist must be as honest, objective and dispassionate as he knows he must be in the more conventional, time-honored, self-policing scientific endeavor. This additional canon has not always been observed. Witness the chaos that has come with challenges to the use of nuclear power in several countries. Witness, in this country [the U.S.], the cacaphony of charge and counter-charge concerning the safety of diverse food additives, pesticides and drugs. We have learned that the scientist-advocate, on either side of such a debate, is likely to be more advocate than scientist, and this has unfavorably altered the public view of both the nature of scientific endeavor and the personal attributes of scientists. In turn, that has given yet a greater sense of urgency to the public demand for assurance that the risks attendant upon the uses of technology be appraised and minimized.

The Washington Post, 11-30:(A)14.

1

How very privileged we are—we who have lived through the last half-century of science, that historic few decades in which the mind of man first came really to understand the nature of the atomic nucleus; first learned the history of our planet and identified the forces that continue to refigure its surface, the habitat of our species; the time when man's mind first engaged the immense sweep and grandeur of the cosmos in what we believe to be its true dimensions; the time when our species commenced upon the physical exploration of the solar system. Ours is the fortunate generation that, for the first time, came to understand the essential aspects of the marvelous phenomenon which is life, a phenomenon describable only in the language of chemistry; came to understand the mech-

anisms that have operated over the eons of biological evolution. In short, ours may well be the first generation that knows what we are and where we are. That knowledge permitted the acquisition of new capabilities whereby we utilize an extraordinary assemblage of synthetic materials, each created for specific purpose, whereby we manipulate our environment, communicate, move about, protect our health, avoid pain and even extend the power of our own intellects ... In a historic sense, the scientific endeavor began only yesterday, yet we have come a wondrous distance from our primeval ignorance in so short a time ...

*Before general assembly of
International Council of Scientific Unions/
The Washington Post, 12-22:(A)18.*

Charles McC. Mathias, Jr.
United States Senator, R—Maryland
2

[On the dangers of abuse of computerized personal-data systems and the use of Social Security numbers as a form of universal identification]: The fact that the police chief or credit bureau or employment office or department-store credit manager in San Francisco could push a button and get all the intimate details of a man or woman who lives in Bangor, Maine, is of course awesome in its efficiency but frightening in its implications. It would really mean that there is no way to go "West" any more to leave your past behind you ... There are many law-abiding citizens who don't necessarily want or deserve to have every detail of their private lives spread upon a semi-public record that makes it impossible for them to earn a living or carry out the ordinary activities of day-to-day life ... The danger of the computer is that its capacity is utilized without some kind of deliberate philosophy of use ... For example, with the use of the criminal data bank system, I've always felt that the Justice Department should be allowed to state very clearly the philosophy of using that system—who is to hold the key to it, under what circumstances the key would be delivered up to anybody who sought information out of the system ...

WHAT THEY SAID IN 1976

(CHARLES McC. MATHIAS, JR.)

Computers can be dangerous. Computers talking to computers lack this kind of judgmental quality. [And without it,] that's how 1984 happens.

The Christian Science Monitor, 4-14:7.

Bruce C. Murray
Director, Jet Propulsion Laboratory,
Pasadena, California
1

By the exploration of the solar system we find out . . . who we are. *Viking* [the Mars landing project] costs about as much as a fortnight of the Vietnam war. I find these comparisons particularly poignant: life versus death, hope versus fear. Space exploration and the highly mechanized destruction of people use similar technology . . . and similar human qualities of organization and daring. Can we not make the transition from automated aerospace killing to automated aerospace exploration of the solar system?

The Christian Science Monitor, 7-19:8.

Alan C. Nixon
Former president,
American Chemical Society
2

I believe the scientist has a responsibility to bring to the attention of the American public any problems in his field of science. Pollution is largely the result of chemistry, but our profession has not been very active in bringing this to the attention of the public. This came much later, usually the result of being caught by a government agency.

Before American Academy for the
Advancement of Science, Boston/
The New York Times, 2-22:(1)34.

Prince Philip
Duke of Edinburgh
3

I suspect that one of the great problems is that people see themselves as either technologists or, for the sake of argument, intellectuals. I think the danger is that one begins to suspect the other. I think the technologists tend to suspect the intellectuals, who are always playing with words and generally criticizing and rationalizing and arguing. The intellectuals look at the technologists as merely spanner-wielding grease monkeys who haven't got a solid bone, who have no cultural aspirations, no social conscience at all. I think this is nonsense, this division. All people have got a social conscience or are capable of having it. All people have the capacity to be intelligent and to enjoy cultural activities. Until we recognize we are all on the same side and that we need the same qualities in people, whether they are technologists or intellectuals, it is only when they begin to work together that we are going to get some kind of rational balance between development, conservation and preservation.

TV-radio interview/"Issues and Answers,"
American Broadcasting Company, 7-4.

Simon Ramo
Vice chairman, TRW, Inc.
4

The problem of wise, full use of science and technology lies not in any lack of availability or promise of science and technology *per se.* It is the *interface* of technological with non-technological factors that is critical and controlling. The whole is a "systems" problem. For instance, in choosing where and how to apply science and technology, it would be helpful to have clearer national goals. For a "systems approach" it is required that we know what we are after before we expect to get very far. We cannot make satisfactory decisions on what to do without an understanding of the trade-offs and options. We need to be in a position to compare the "good" that can come from technological advance against the "bad," and the cost. As to our employment of technological change, we can be likened to a bunch of carpenters, sawing and hammering away, often getting fingers in the saws and hitting our own thumbs and each other's heads as we swing our hammer, who don't know quite what we are trying to build, who sense an unsatisfactory situation, and who meanwhile blame the saws and the hammers.

Before National Bureau of Standards, Washington/ The National Observer, 4-24:17.

Carl Sagan
Director, Laboratory for Planetary Studies, Cornell University
1

I think civilizations are known in the long perspective by what they do—by the historical turning points which they initiate. We now have, because of our technology, a unique opportunity to explore our surroundings in space. The practical advantages are immense, even in the medium-range time frame. The return does not come the year after you go there; it takes a little time. But the opportunity to compare our planet with other planets that have had different histories gives us a perspective on the alternative fates of worlds. We live on a world that is structured in a certain way, and we wish to understand how to make it go in one direction rather than another. You can't experiment on it, because, if you make a mistake, you're in trouble—consider, for example, altering the climate. But nature has kindly provided us with natural experiments on the nearby planets. By examining them, we can gain profound insights into how our planet works and how to make it work better. Human beings have been as successful as they are because of our curiosity and intelligence, and also because of our spirit of exploration and adventure. At this point in human history, the surface of the planet Earth is fully explored. And at just this same moment, other worlds suddenly become accessible to us. I think it is in the deepest human tradition to seize that opportunity.

Interview/ U.S. News & World Report, 8-30:53.

2

. . . I think the money spent on *Viking* [the Mars landing project] is an amazing bargain. The project and planetary exploration in general costs a tiny amount. It is something between 10 and 15 per cent of the NASA budget, which itself is only a few per cent of the Department of Defense budget. It is small

amounts of money compared to what we spend on all sorts of other things. With that money we explore our surroundings in space; we calibrate our planet against neighboring planets. That has all sorts of practical applications for weather, for geology and for biology, as we are now discovering. We have a way to give vent to our heritage of exploration, which we can no longer do because the whole earth is explored. We can continue that marvelous human tradition. And, finally, we approach the deepest questions that mankind has asked—as long as there have been men—on the origin, nature and fate of life and of worlds. I think civilizations are known not only for feeding and housing people, but also for how they add to our view of ourselves and the cosmos.

TV-radio interview, Burbank, Calif./
"Meet the Press,"
National Broadcasting Company, 9-19.

Henry B. Stelling, Jr.
Brigadier General and Director of Space, United States Air Force
3

The United States and Soviet use of and dependence on space is growing. In a decade, space systems will play a major role in deterring warfare, will support virtually all military forces and could strongly influence the outcome of conflicts. It's within this context that the [space] shuttle will arrive.

U.S. News & World Report, 4-26:86.

Wernher Von Braun
President, National Space Institute; Former Deputy Associate Administrator, National Aeronautics and Space Administration of the United States
4

[On the decreasing U.S. interest in space exploration]: When you look at the promises of space in terms of benefits to be made over the next 10 to 20 years, this is one of the best investments that can be made. If we submit to the sorry fact that this is the end, that there is no further growth, this will have such tragic consequences to mankind as a whole that the survival of man as a species will be in danger.

News conference, Washington/
The Christian Science Monitor, 2-17:24.

Sports

Muhammad Ali
*Heavyweight boxing champion
of the world*
1

I want to be the first black heavyweight champion to retire while I'm on top and well-invested. Joe Louis wound up defeated. Joe Walcott, Ezzard Charles, Sugar Ray wound up defeated. Archie Moore, Kid Gavilan, Jack Johnson—all of them. Not one great black fighter in history got out with the money and as champion.

*Interview, Louisville, Ky./
Los Angeles Times, 12-12:(3)1.*

George Allen
*Football coach,
Washington "Redskins"*
2

The worst moments of my life are when I wake up in the middle of the night and can't remember whether we won or lost our last game. If I remember that we won, I get on my knees and give thanks. If, however, I remember that we lost, I am destroyed by the thought of it and regret that I ever woke up at all.

Los Angeles Times, 7-13:(3)3.

Walter Alston
Baseball manager, Los Angeles "Dodgers"
3

[In baseball] you have to be relaxed. You aren't butting heads with anybody in this game. You've got to be patient . . . Running is an example of what we're talking about. The fastest way to run to first base is to run relaxed. You also have to relax to catch a ball, or even pitch it, and I know damn well you can't hit it if you aren't relaxed . . . Stay loose and keep your hands soft. And I think a lot of that is up to the manager. If a

manager is too keyed up, his hitters may try to rip the sawdust out of the ball, and some of his pitchers will try to throw it through the catcher's mitt. That's the hard way to play this game. The best way is low-key, and if the manager is low-key his players will relax, too.

*Interview, Butler County, Ohio/
Los Angeles Times, 2-2:(3)1.*

4

I've never been in favor of long win streaks. I'd rather win two or three, lose one, win two or three more. I'm a great believer in things evening out. If you win a whole bunch in a row, somewhere along the line you're going to lose some, too. Fans tend to get too excited by streaks of either kind. I think the press does, too. There should be a happy medium . . .

*Interview, Philadelphia, May 6/
Los Angeles Times, 5-7:(3)4.*

5

[On managing]: When it comes to knowing when to bunt, when to bring in your infield, and when to lift a staggering pitcher, almost anybody with a basic knowledge of baseball can do it. The big part of managing is in knowing everything you can about your players and then making sure you're getting the most out of them.

*Interview, Los Angeles/
The Christian Science Monitor, 9-24:15.*

Sparky Anderson
Baseball manager, Cincinnati "Reds"
6

There are guys on the bench in this league who better hope nothing happens to the man in front of them. I think there are very few who could be regulars with some other team. A guy who plays a day or two at a time, maybe 70 games a year, might have pretty good figures. Maybe he didn't have to hit against Tom Seaver or Andy Messersmith or Jim Palmer or Catfish Hunter. But playing 70 games in a row is something else, and then he's going to see the Cat or Seaver out there looking at him. There's been a lot of them I could name. Play them two days straight and it's "bench me or trade me." If expansion comes, just wait and see what the new clubs get, because there isn't that much talent around. The man I marvel at is the one that's in there day after day and night after night and still puts the figures on the board. I'm talking about Pete Rose, Stan Musial, the real stars. Believe me, especially the way we travel today, flying all night with a game the next night and then the next afternoon, if you can play 162 games, you're a man.

Interview, Tampa, Fla./
The New York Times, 3-29:41.

1

I'm convinced the DH has no place in baseball. It's not right that you can send up one of your big bombers to bat for the pitcher. The pitcher is part of the game. Part of my thinking is, this thing could make the manager extinct [by depriving him of the opportunity to make defensive moves]. I've shown occasionally that I'm ignorant. This way [with the DH], I don't get a chance to show it.

New York, Oct. 19/
Los Angeles Times, 10-20:(3)1.

2

[On the new right of players to play out their options]: I'm sick about it. Not about players getting all that money—in today's inflated times, that part doesn't bother me. But it gives too much escape for people. A player can get mad and play out his option. I think you have to be able to have disagreements. The next two years in this business are going to be the most critical we've ever seen. If they don't put a stop to this stuff, no

young manager's going to be able to handle it . . . We have a family type thing on our club and I don't know how long it can last if we have guys playing out their options. You've got to work together. Now, a guy playing out his option might play like hell, but you can't tell me there's the same relationship between him and his teammates. There's not the same feeling of togetherness. I hear guys say, "I need security." I say security is the worst word ever invented. If a man doesn't fear what's down the road, what's going to make him work?

Interview, Thousand Oaks, Calif./
Los Angeles Times, 11-2:(3)7.

Mario Andretti
Auto-racing driver   *3*

Taking a car from its newborn stage through life is a thrilling experience. You're dealing with an unknown quantity. How is it going to react? You try to get everything out of it, like the guy with a new girl friend.

Interview, Long Beach, Calif./
Los Angeles Times, 3-26:(3)4.

Roone Arledge
President,
American Broadcasting Company Sports   *4*

The journalism in sports is one of the poorest things television has done. Commentary on sports is an area where TV can certainly show more guts. Television has a tremendous handicap to begin with. It has a desire to please the people who are selling the rights. Newspapers and magazines talk bluntly about an event. The next time, they have no difficulty when they want tickets for press coverage. But the networks are competing with each other and there's a tendency to want to be nice to the people who can give them a chance to beat their rivals.

Interview, Innsbruck, Austria/
Los Angeles Herald-Examiner, 1-12:(B)5.

Arthur Ashe
Tennis player   *5*

You can see the writing on the wall for a lot of tournaments—big money no longer lures

WHAT THEY SAID IN 1976

(ARTHUR ASHE)

the top players when they can make thousands of dollars off endorsements. You have to commit yourself to a nine-month schedule when you go on the WCT tour, and some players . . . just won't do that.

Interview, Dallas/
Los Angeles Herald-Examiner, 5-4:(C)7.

1

What pro tennis needs to insure its continuing success is one person who is in charge of everything—a commissioner, a Pete Rozelle [NFL commissioner]. We still lack a lot of clockwork precision at the business level of the game. And mostly it's because we have too many people sharing decisions where there should really be only one. I think we have to take a hard look at things and answer the question: How many players are we trying to feed each week? Right now we have more players than we have places at the dinner table. Pro tennis should probably be divided into five zones—American, European, South American, Australian, and the Rest of the World. Set it up like pro golf. If a man makes the cut, he plays. If he misses, he doesn't. That way, the strongest people are always going to be playing in the most important tournaments.

Interview/ The Christian Science Monitor, 11-1:18.

Red Auerbach
President and former coach,
Boston "Celtics" basketball team

2

One thing that used to aggravate me a lot was when I'd see coaches with 15 or 20 seconds left to play, and they'd be down by one point, and they'd sit there with pads and pencils drawing out a special play. They've got a month of practice and many, many games behind them. If they don't have a play set to go with 15 seconds or less, what the hell have they been doing all this time? It's ridiculous.

Interview, New York/
TV Guide, 3-13:32.

Bill Bradley
Basketball player,
New York "Knickerbockers"

3

The end of an athlete's career is like an old man dying. There's the nostalgia of the past—reflections of success, the failure, the pain. The difference is, the old man dies. The athlete goes on living.

Interview/ The Dallas Times Herald, 5-13:(C)1.

Hubie Brown
Basketball coach, Atlanta "Hawks"

4

The trouble with athletes today is that they are great at rationalizing. Too many won't stand up and take the blame and admit they didn't produce. When one does, you have a rare man.

The New York Times, 5-16:(5)6.

Jim Brown
Actor; Former football player

5

[Football today is] like show business, a production straight out of Warner Brothers. In my day there was total genuine feeling. We played on another level. There was a lot more honor involved. There's too much acting today. I don't know how to conceive of the guy today who goes across the goal line and busts the ball no matter if his team is 40 points ahead or 40 behind. That makes a circus act of the game. The beauty of sport to me is that it's real. If it's going to be acting, we might as well take 50 reshots of everything to get it perfect.

Los Angeles Times, 8-25:(3)2.

William B. Bryant
Judge, United States District Court
for the District of Columbia

6

[Saying the NFL's annual draft of college players is illegal]: The essence of the draft is straightforward: The owners of the teams have agreed among themselves that the right to negotiate with each top-quality graduating college athlete will be allocated to one team, and that no other team will deal with that person. This outright, undisguised refusal to deal constitutes a group boycott in its classic and most pernicious form, a device which has long been condemned as a *per se* violation of the antitrust laws . . . It leaves no room whatever for competition among the teams for the services of college players, and utterly strips them [the athletes] of any measure of control over the marketing of their talents . . . What is important to note is that the owners are wholly cognizant, and indeed virtually concede, that the current system results in lower salaries for some players than they would receive in a free market . . .

Court opinion, Washington, Sept. 8*/
The Washington Post, 9-9:(A)1,10.

William F. Buckley, Jr.
Political columnist;
Editor, "National Review"
1

[Lamenting the fact that he is too busy to get involved in the sports world]: I've never seen a major-league baseball game. I've never seen a professional football game. And that's not an affectation. I just happen never to have seen one . . . I feel very deprived because of the excitement people get in my own office, for example, over who won the baseball game yesterday. And when I'm listening to the radio news, driving somewhere, and they say who won the games, it means nothing to me and I feel deprived. Because, after all, life is substantially made up of the little spices you get in the course of a dreary existence. Sport is a tremendous spice and I feel sorry for myself, as I feel for other people who don't, for instance, enjoy food.

Interview, Los Angeles/
Los Angeles Times, 12-13:(3)8.

Dick Butler
Supervisor of baseball umpires,
American League
2

There's a tremendous pressure all the time on an umpire. They live in a fish bowl. Everything they do is watched, and their reputa-

tions follow them just like a ballplayer's. Usually it takes a new umpire four or five years to sell himself. The players, the managers, they just don't want to believe in a new ump. In the minors, you can afford to make some mistakes because you're growing up like the ballplayers. Here [in the major leagues] you can't. There's a lot of money indirectly involved in the outcome of every game.

Interview/Los Angeles Times, 4-22:(3)8.

Dick Button
Figure skater
3

That is something about skating that not many people really understand: It is not only athletic. To rush about the ice and flail your arms is not enough. The interesting part is to see whether skaters sail over the chasm or whether you have to put up a ladder and climb over.

Interview,
Colorado Springs, Colo./
Los Angeles Times, 1-31:(3)7.

Clarence S. Campbell
President,
National Hockey League
4

I've said it time and again, and I know that there are many students of human behavior who disagree with me. But, with my considerable experience, I feel that the safest and most satisfactory reaction to being fouled is by retaliating with a punch in the nose.

Los Angeles Herald-Examiner, 4-2:(D)9.

Jim Campbell
General manager,
Detroit "Tigers" baseball club
5

[On the free-agent system of allowing players to play out their options]: I said it a long time ago that baseball never will be the same. Baseball was built on the tradition of developing your own players. Now a team can buy a championship. Is that the way

WHAT THEY SAID IN 1976

(JIM CAMPBELL)

baseball is supposed to be? Another thing players aren't taking into consideration is that these new rules will benefit a very few outstanding players. It will work against the journeyman. The money has to come from somewhere.

The New York Times, 10-24:(5)12.

Joseph Carrico
Chairman,
United States Davis Cup Committee 1

[Criticizing countries which refuse to play other countries because of political differences]: We find it intolerable to mix politics with tennis. People who want to play politics should go play with themselves, and people who want to play tennis should play among themselves. The Davis Cup has been deteriorating in quality year after year because of this continual political interference. We have got to get the governments out of tennis.

San Francisco Examiner & Chronicle, 7-11:
(This World)16.

Jimmy Carter
1976 Democratic U.S. Presidential nominee 2

I believe [sport] does have a real value in life. I was on the varsity basketball team in high school and, when I was in submarines, I was the pitcher on our baseball team. I learned there, obviously, that you have to be mutually dependent to achieve an identifiable goal, and you have to learn how to accept either defeat or victory with some degree of equanimity and look to the next contest with hope and anticipation. I think you have to yield sometimes your own selfish aspirations for the common good and be able to deal with one another in an open, sometimes competitive way, but not a personally antagonistic way. I think those are some of the lessons that you learn from team sports and I hope that I remember them.

Interview, Los Angeles, Aug. 23/
Los Angeles Times, 8-24:(1)18.

A. B. (Happy) Chandler
Former commissioner of baseball 3

Baseball is operating from Justice Holmes' interpretation of baseball . . . as not being a business. But that was in 1922. Baseball is a tremendous business now and is subject to trust and antitrust laws. The reserve clause needs to be amended to fit the 1970s, but it would be against the interests of the owners and players to have the whole thing thrown out.

Interview, Versailles, Ky./
Los Angeles Times, 3-7:(3)4.

Nester Chylak
Baseball umpire, American League 4

[On umpiring]: This must be the only job in America that everybody knows how to do better than the guy who's doing it. Sometimes I have this fantasy: The manager's been popping off all day and his team's just blown a big lead. I call time and walk over to the dugout and say very politely, "Excuse me, sir. Your second-baseman just booted one with the bases loaded."

Interview, Boston/
Los Angeles Times, 4-22:(3)1.

Jonathan Cole
Professor of sociology,
Columbia University 5

[On dishonesty in sports]: There is a high level of cynicism in our society today. The old image of sports as an escape from social realities is dying. People tend to consider bending the rules a general condition of sports today. It's not a matter of evil individuals, for the most part. The programs are corrupted. The structural and social pressures on coaches and programs to be successful, competitive from a business standpoint in order to survive, cause the deviant behavior. Sports institutions, amateur or professional, sometimes feel they must play illegal games in order to survive.

The New York Times, 11-7:(5)10.

SPORTS

Dave Cowens
Basketball player, Boston "Celtics"
1

Pro basketball isn't really [physically] rougher now. It's just different. When you defense a great shooter, you simply use more of your body to get in the way of his body. This is known as "positioning yourself." The shooters are so deadly today that unless the defender positions himself, there is no way he can stop them . . . Basketball is tame compared to the way it used to be. I can remember when Bob Cousy got roughed. The *Celtics* would then send in a guy named Jungle Jim Loscutoff to take care of the offender. Jungle Jim was called an "equalizer." Every club in the league had an equalizer. You don't see that any more.

TV Guide, 4-17:16.

Bill Curry
Assistant football coach,
Georgia Institute of Technology;
Former professional player
2

The real creativity in football is coming from the colleges. I'm not saying all professional coaches are dullards. I am saying that, scouting for the *Packers* last year, I saw, conservatively, 200 football teams, and I can tell you that I was surprised and unbelievably impressed with the quality of coaching in college football.

Los Angeles Times, 7-12:(3)2.

Dave DeBusschere
Commissioner,
American Basketball Association
3

[On the effects of a ban of the reserve system]: . . . I wonder if there would be *that* much player movement in an open system. I think most players are like me . . . if I had my way, I would have stayed in Detroit forever. That's my home. Cazzie [Russell] and Kareem [Abdul-Jabbar] went to Los Angeles, but what has that proved so far? Are the *Lakers* superior? What happened to the *Warriors* when Cazzie and Clyde Lee were taken away? . . . it made room for kids coming up who proved

better for the team. I'm just wondering out loud; I know all the arguments for control because I grew up with them. But only time and, yes, perhaps the failure of some franchises could prove whether, in the long run, open competition might actually lower the general salary scale and increase the continuing search for talent.

Interview/
San Francisco Examiner & Chronicle, 2-1:
(Sunday Punch)8.

Tom Dempsey
Football player, Los Angeles "Rams"
4

[On the pressure of kicking]: . . . you have to be a nut to look forward to the pressure the way we [kickers] do. When I walk out there, every eye in the place is on me, plus the TV cameras, which means I don't know how many million more sets of eyes. No one man wins a game alone, but a team can lose a game if a kicker blows it.

Los Angeles Times, 3-8:(3)2.

Bing Devine
General manager,
St. Louis "Cardinals" baseball club
5

Almost every club [next year] will have people playing out their options. So in one year you'll have this great mass of free agents. And after that, you'll have a whole new game. It's been coming since the war. You had thousands of guys who came home from the war wanting to play baseball, and all those towns wanting to have minor-league teams. Then television came along and the trend got reversed. You soon had fewer minor leagues. Then you had the amateur draft and you no longer could go out and sign anybody you wanted. Finally, there were fewer players at the minor-league level; there were more college men in a hurry; there was more money at the top; basketball and golf and football were flooded with money. All sports became professionalized. In baseball, we should have seen it coming and prepared for the transition. Instead, we had dramatic scenes . . .

New York/The New York Times, 11-7:(5)3.

537

WHAT THEY SAID IN 1976

Conrad Dobler
Football player, St. Louis "Cardinals"   1

[On why he breaks the rules]: Aw, screw the rules. They're just there to provide a little control in a violent game. But tell me how many times defensive linemen head-slap or grab me. Huh? We don't bitch. No, if an individual puts me in a position where it's either cheat or he'll get my quarterback, then you better believe I'm going to cheat.
Interview, Riverside, Calif./
Los Angeles Times, 11-13:(3)1.

Terry Donahue
Football coach,
University of California, Los Angeles   2

Most of the appeal [of coaching football] comes down to what we mean by the idea of a challenge. I can't imagine any challenge that compares with going out and trying to win a big football game. First, you put in a plan and an organization, then you put both into action, and in 60 minutes you get the answer on a wild Saturday afternoon in a great stadium. All teaching is involved with the ego, you know. Your opponent feels the way you do, and there you are in front of thousands of judges, people judging who was the best teacher. There's no thrill like it.
Interview/Los Angeles Times, 8-22:(3)9.

Julius Erving
Basketball player, Philadelphia "76ers"   3

[On having a businesslike attitude toward sports]: I think you have to. You have to combine a business approach with the emotional approach. You have to play with enthusiasm, make sure you're mentally prepared to do the job physically. I think being professional means knowing what you should and shouldn't do, and that it's a job.
Interview, Philadelphia/Money, December:55.

Charles O. Finley
Owner, Oakland "Athletics" baseball club   4

The very wealthy clubs are going to destroy the game of baseball. I just lost six players

who signed with other teams for $9-million, and I can't hack it in baseball any more. We've [the *Athletics*] had five consecutive division championships and three straight World Series championships, and we can't pay our bills . . . I do not blame the athletes at all. If I was one, I'd be out there trying to get the same thing. The blame falls on two things: no leadership, and stupidity on the part of the owners. They are literally destroying themselves; the handwriting is on the wall. There is no way you can pay a football player $900,000 in salary, a basketball player $700,000 or a baseball player $500,000 and still survive. Last year, Sal Bando received $80,000 from the *A's*; he just signed with Milwaukee for $1.4-million for five years. Bert Campaneris got $72,000 last season, and he just signed with Texas for $190,000 a year for the next five. Rollie Fingers made $72,000 with us, and signed with San Diego for $1.5-million for five years. Don Baylor made $32,500 at Oakland, and signed with California for $1.6-million for six years. Gene Tenace received $40,800 from us, and went to San Diego for $1.6-million over six years. And Joe Rudi was paid $67,200 by us, and signed with California for $2-million over five years. You wonder how I lost them? Well, I tried to sell three players last June for $3.5-million. My plan was to position myself so that I could have taken the money and bought free agents at the end of the season. But my plan was delayed by the person who calls himself the Commissioner of Baseball [Bowie Kuhn], who singelhandedly destroyed the Oakland *A's* [by blocking the sale]—I say it was delayed because it comes up next week in court and I am enthusiastic about my chances of winning.
News conference, Los Angeles, Dec. 8/
The New York Times, 12-9:63,67.

Bill Fitch
Basketball coach, Cleveland "Cavaliers"   5

If someone were to drop in from another century and watch a basketball game, can you imagine what he'd think if you explained to him that there's this little hole; if the ball

goes in the hole, your kids eat; if it doesn't, they don't eat.
Los Angeles Times, 4-30:(3)2.

George Foreman
Former heavyweight boxing champion of the world *1*

[On whether he worries before fights, such as his forthcoming bout with Joe Frazier]: Of course. And every day I get a little edgier. What do I worry about? I really don't know. But each day that goes by it gets a little worse until I want to say, "Come on! Get it over with!" Yes, it happens every fight. Almost every. A couple of times I went in and I was scared because I *wasn't* nervous. "Gotta hurry and get some butterflies," I thought.
Interview, Uniondale, N.Y., June 8/
The New York Times, 6-9:37.

Ed Garvey
Executive director, National Football League Players Association *2*

Players are tired of being treated as pieces of property to be bought and sold at the whim of the employer. They are also saying that they will no longer tolerate being told where they must play for their entire career. The player wants freedom and he wants it now.
Los Angeles Herald-Examiner, 3-21:(C)8.

Steve Garvey
Baseball player, Los Angeles "Dodgers" *3*

[On high salaries paid to players]: I am neither stunned by the salaries nor overly concerned by the likelihood that they will continue to go up. There is a variance in the degree of profit throughout baseball, but, by the figures I get, all the clubs *are* making a profit. Baseball is still the best buy for the fan, and by that I mean it's the best buy in show business, the area we belong to. We're entertainers, and it's not out of line for us to be paid as much as a headliner in Las Vegas.
Interview/Los Angeles Times, 12-6:(3)8.

Calvin Griffith
Owner, Minnesota "Twins" baseball club *4*

[On the increasing costs of running a sports club]: I don't know if we can survive any more. I do know our family is the last of its kind in sports and there will never be another one. From now on, owners are going to have to be associated with other businesses so they won't have to depend on sports to feed their kids. Or they're going to have to be men who were born wealthy, who have zillions of dollars, and are just looking for a sports team to buy so they can have something to do with their time.
Los Angeles Herald-Examiner, 3-21:(C)8.

5

[Criticizing the proposed $3-million-plus sale of three Oakland *Athletics* players to the Boston *Red Sox* and New York *Yankees*]: I think it is a terrible thing when two teams, the *Yankees* and *Red Sox*, go out there and start bidding to see who can buy a championship team. I think this just shows what the owners have been saying about the wealthy clubs getting the top players is true. It just shows how necessary a reserve system is if we are going to have fair competition.
The Dallas Times Herald, 6-16:(D)8.

George Halas
Chairman, Chicago "Bears" football team *6*

In addition to talent, you need only three things to play football well: size, speed and desire. Modern athletes are bigger and faster than we were, of course, but they don't have any more desire. The most competitive guys have always been and will always be the hardest to beat.
Interview, Chicago/
Los Angeles Times, 8-13:(3)6.

Roland Hemond
General manager, Chicago "White Sox" baseball team *7*

[On *White Sox* owner Bill Veeck]: Veeck knows everything there is to know about run-

539

(ROLAND HEMOND)

ning a baseball team. He can count a big stack of tickets just by riffling through them with his thumb. He can tell you what kind of grass you ought to have in the outfield. He can tell you what pitch a pitcher is having trouble with. I've never worked as hard in my life trying to keep up with him, and I've never enjoyed myself more.

People, 4-19:53.

Dave Hill
Golfer
1

Winning is fun, but when I say that, I may not make myself clear. The fun of it is just playing the game. It's a trying game, an individual game, one that tests your patience. Winning is always fun, but if you don't win, it's no big deal. If you do win, 20 years from now who knows the difference? Three weeks from now, who's really going to care?

Interview, Miami/
The Dallas Times Herald, 7-5:(C)3.

Lou Holtz
Football coach, New York "Jets"
2

To win football games, you have to be able to run when everybody knows you're going to run and you have to be able to pass when everybody knows you're going to pass. Then you have to be able to do the unexpected in either situation, too.

News conference, New York/
Los Angeles Herald-Examiner, 2-11:(D)10.

Red Holzman
Basketball coach,
New York "Knickerbockers"
3

I won't say that yesterday's players took defeat any harder, but they took it harder for a longer period of time. They would just sit in front of their lockers and never seem to get over it. But, even after a hard defeat, most of today's players are laughing and joking a half hour later and I'm not knocking it. After all,

what good does it do to brood over something that's gone. The best thing is to start getting yourself mentally ready for the next game, and today's player does that a lot better than we did.

Interview/ The Christian Science Monitor, 3-19:35.

Bob Howsam
President and general manager,
Cincinnati "Reds" baseball club
4

The history of long-term [player] contracts isn't very favorable. Once players get that kind of security, they are inclined not to produce on the field. The fans are smart. They are the first to notice when a player is not putting out. I always have felt a great obligation to the fans. They keep us going. They have a right to expect every man to produce to his maximum . . . I think the one-year contract is best for the player as well as the club. It gives the player a chance to profit by his play on the field. He doesn't get complacent. He is always putting out his best.

Interview/
Los Angeles Herald-Examiner, 12-8:(D)9.

James Hunt
Auto-racing driver
5

People say the way to win is to do it as slowly as possible. You do as little as you have to. If you are in a position to win, why win by a lot? That is easier said than done. The temptation when you take an early lead is to get away and build up a cushion so you can relax later. But you can't panic doing it. The fact that you're leading is all that counts. You have to concentrate on doing a steady job and grinding down the opposition. You don't have to beat them into submission, just steadily provoke them into it. This is the mental approach, and I'm still learning. I have a lot of winning to do before I can say I have mastered the art of winning.

Interview/
Los Angeles Times, 3-23:(3)4.

Reggie Jackson
Baseball player, Oakland "Athletics"
1

[On high salaries paid baseball players]: The owners set the precedent by paying astronomical money to certain players. Players talk and are taken aback when they find out what other guys are making. You've got Tom Seaver making $200,000 a year. Pigs get fat and hogs go to market—that's one of [Oakland manager] Charlie Finley's sayings . . . [What should determine salary is] putting fannies in the seats. The amount of money is nebulous. Take Henry Aaron. Every game this year, 2,000-3,000 extra people will come out to see him because it's his last year. Multiply that by 162 games. See what I mean? Richie Allen didn't have a good year, but people still come out to see him. A fella is a commodity. I'm just trying to see it from the owners' point of view . . . I have a hard time believing athletes are over-priced. If an owner is losing money, give it up. It's business. I have trouble figuring out why owners would stay in if they're losing money.
Interview, Rotonda, Fla./
Los Angeles Times, 3-9:(3)1,3.

Reggie Jackson
Baseball player, Baltimore "Orioles"
2

[On what he expects in contract negotiations with a ball club]: I have other alternatives. I have a real-estate business, a Pontiac dealership, a television contract, and obligations to people who work with me. Life has more to offer than hitting a ball over a fence. "Come to me and let's talk," I say. Let the Baltimore *Orioles* and Reggie Jackson hammer out something that's amicable to both sides. They must listen to what I have to say. Treat me like a human being. Treat me like a man. But in such a way that it isn't all business. In such a way that I still have some little boy in me, still some rah-rah in me, so I can play the game.
Time, 4-26:74.

K. C. Jones
Basketball coach, Washington "Bullets"
3

People see what they want to see, and most pro basketball fans have limited vision after they get past the scoring column. They look to see how many points a player gets and that is how they judge him. It makes no sense, but it's true.
Interview/ The Christian Science Monitor, 2-11:10.

Michael Killanin
President,
International Olympic Committee
4

I think in a way that the [Olympic] Games have been too successful, too big. If you look back to the post-war years they began quite modestly but have grown very rapidly. London in 1948 did them reasonably, then came Helsinki which were again small-ish, then Melbourne where the distance limited the size. But when the Games went to Rome, things changed. In Italy there is a vast amount of money available for sport. The Games there were huge, and then came Tokyo and Munich. I think if you look at those last few countries, you can see that the opportunity was taken to show themselves to the world through the Games. And the amount of money being spent has gone up and up.
Interview, Montreal/
The Christian Science Monitor, 7-9:10.

5

[Criticizing Canada's refusal to admit Taiwan to the 1976 Montreal Olympic Games if it uses the name Republic of China]: I admit we've had a very heavy blow from this political interference. I hope we'll never be put in such a damnable position again. I think the world is fed up with politicians getting involved in sport . . . This extremely dangerous precedent, where an individual country has been refused permission to compete, never before has happened in the history of the Olympics. I'm extremely sorry for the Republic of China athletes who can't compete. I anticipated all sorts of problems, but not this one.
News conference, Montreal, July 11/
Los Angeles Times, 7-12:(3)1.

WHAT THEY SAID IN 1976

Billie Jean King
Tennis player

1

. . . the game of tennis is mental. Anybody at the top can serve an ace, rifle a forehand crosscourt, a backhand down the line or smash an overhead into oblivion if they practice enough. All the stars can do it. It's when you walk out on the court, knowing you and your opponent both have all the shots, that something else must determine the edge. More often than not, it's psychology that takes over, a self-awareness that makes you understand the pressure situations and gives you the confidence to produce the right shot at the key points of the match.

The New York Times, 1-14:42.

2

I loved being a pioneer [in women's professional tennis]. There are five or six of us who knocked ourselves out promoting the women's tour those first two years. The women players today have it easy. They play for big prize money, they get tons of coverage and attention, and they are protected, coddled. Some of them don't even realize that it was just a few years ago that we were playing for peanuts, and we had to scrape for every bit of publicity we could get.

Interview, London/
The Washington Post, 6-27:(D)4.

3

When I returned to the United States from England in 1968, after winning Wimbledon for the third time, nobody knew who I was. I don't know what the public thought women's tennis was, but they certainly weren't paying much attention. It was just there. But today there is so much more motivation for women players—so much more chance for a girl to become a star. Money is what keeps the older players in the game now, and money is what is attracting the best new players. Even though it's still a man's world at the pro level in all sports, women are starting to catch up. It may take another ten years, but I think we're going to get there.

Interview, Palm Springs, Calif./
The Christian Science Monitor, 11-8:14.

Bobby Knight
Basketball coach,
Indiana University

4

The whole game of basketball boils down to playing as well as you can no matter who you are playing or where you play. Match-ups, offenses, defenses and all that don't mean anything. My major concern as a coach is to take these ten guys and get them playing what they do best. You've got to motivate them. You've got to get them ready to play every time out. I don't think there is anything to peaks and valleys in a season.

Los Angeles Times, 1-6:(3)2.

Chuck Knox
Football coach, Los Angeles "Rams"

5

. . . losing is what drives football crowds away. People don't like to identify with a loser. Take Buffalo last year. The *Bills* set an NFL record for points scored—and finished with an 8-6 record. And this year their season ticket sale is off 20,000. A lot of points don't entertain your fans if you lose.

Interview/Los Angeles Times, 7-13:(3)6.

6

There's always too much emphasis on the quarterback. Everybody is a quarterback. Every fan identifies with the quarterback. The quarterback gets too much praise for the good things, too much blame for the bad. The quarterback is important, but he's just another part of the team.

News conference, Long Beach, Calif./
Los Angeles Times, 9-8:(3)3.

Philip Krumm
President,
United States Olympic Committee

7

[Criticizing the IOC's decision to go ahead with the 1976 Montreal Olympic Games despite Canada's refusal to admit Taiwan to the Games if it uses the name Republic of China]: This blatant and unwarranted action casts aside all of the Olympic principles and the code under which we are pledged to hold the Games. We have turned the Olympic Games into a competition between nations. Political power determines who can compete, instead of a world competition as demonstrated by the skills of friendly nations.

July 11/ Los Angeles Herald-Examiner, 7-12:(C)2.

Bowie Kuhn
Commissioner of Baseball 1

[Arguing against elimination of the reserve system]: The economic consequences to the clubs could be enormous. The minor leagues—140 clubs which provided entertainment for 12 million last season—if not erased completely, could be seriously curtailed. I think you could expect bankruptcies, sharp retrenchment of franchises and great dissatisfaction among the players themselves as the money gravitates to the top—to the super stars—at the expense of the majority of players.

New York/ The Washington Post, 1-4:(C)2.

2

Today there is a very well-organized, well-led [player] union. The union has made great strides for the players and many of those are very much in order. But there comes a time when the fans want to see tranquility more than they want to see a lot of fighting over more increases, more benefits. The fans, by and large, feel that the athletes are well treated in baseball, and I'm sure at the same time they recognize there are areas for improvements. But they don't want to see it pushed too hard. Maybe the attitude of the union is a little shortsighted as it pushes too hard for change and upsets the equilibrium of the game.

Interview, New York/
The Washington Post, 2-7:(C)1.

3

[Announcing his nullification of a $3-million-plus sale of three Oakland *Athletics* players to the Boston *Red Sox* and New York *Yankees*]: The spectacle of the *Yankees* and *Red Sox* buying contracts of star players in

the prime of their careers for cash sums . . . [is] anything but devastating to baseball's reputation . . . even though I can understand that their motive is a good-faith effort to strengthen their club. If such transactions now and in the future were permitted, the door would be opened wide to the buying of success by the more-affluent clubs, public suspicion would be aroused, traditional and sound methods of player development and acquisition would be undermined and our efforts to preserve competitive balance would be greatly impaired.

New York, June 18/
The Washington Post, 6-19:(C)2.

4

The strong identity of the American League, strong identity of the National League, is what makes the World Series the greatest sports event in the country. The [football] Super Bowl is a nice event. But the World Series, I think, is the champ, and the only reason is the sharp competition between the two leagues.

Interview/ The Washington Post, 11-18:(F)4.

Tom Landry
Football coach, Dallas "Cowboys" 5

People expect too much of the Super Bowl game. They fail to realize that it has to be a defensive battle. In our system today—the three-game playoffs—you can't put together enough winning games without a great defense. Under the old system, when division winners met in a single game for the NFL title, an offensive team could win it once in a while. But the 1960 *Eagles* were the last to do it without a defense. In a series of games, the strongest defensive teams survive.

Interview, Florida/
Los Angeles Times, 1-18:(3)8.

Bill Lee
Baseball pitcher, Boston "Red Sox" 6

. . . winning and losing isn't that important to me. I can walk off the field a happy and contented man as long as I know I've pitched

(BILL LEE)

well. Maybe other guys have to win to feel good, but I don't. In my opinion, people live too much for the moment, when it's actually the over-all picture that's more important.

Interview, Los Angeles/
The Christian Science Monitor, 3-3:7.

Bob Lemon
Pitching coach, New York "Yankees"
baseball club; Former pitcher,
Cleveland "Indians"
1

[On the reserve system]: I still believe in it. I think the owners should have something to protect themselves. It's very sad to see baseball going through what it is now. There's no more loyalty to your ball club. I appreciated the *Indians* putting me through my journeymanship in the minors. To me, it's like growing up, [and] when you're 15 or 16, dumping your parents.

At his election to the Baseball Hall of Fame,
New York, Jan. 22/ The New York Times, 1-23:25.

Johnny Longden
Former jockey
2

You know, people say, "Oh, [horse] racing . . . hoodlums and gamblers" . . . But the image, it's not true. This may be the cleanest sport of all, and the people who run it are continually trying to improve it, to protect it, to work with the people below them. For years, the stewards wouldn't talk to the jockeys. Now they do. After all, everyone is in it together. Racing enabled me to meet the Aga Khan, Churchill, Prince Philip. But I've also met just as many wonderful people on the backstretch. I'd do anything to help racing.

Interview, Arcadia, Calif./
Los Angeles Times, 2-14:(3)6.

Dave Lopes
Baseball player, Los Angeles "Dodgers"
3

My philosophy is to do anything you can to make the other team nervous. A running team puts a lot of pressure on the other side. You pressure the catcher, obviously. But, in addition, you put a lot of heat on the infield.

One of those guys in the middle has to be moving, and that opens up another hole to hit through. And very often, the pitcher eases up a little. All this makes the game more exciting for the fans . . . because there's so much action. The most entertaining ball club is one that's aggressive on the base paths. It's a funny thing: Running brings your team together —and also brings the crowd to its feet.

Interview/ Los Angeles Times, 2-22:(3)8.

Joe Louis
Former heavyweight boxing champion
of the world
4

I would never get nervous before a fight. I only got nervous after we got our instructions in the center of the ring. Just those two or three seconds, between the time we got our instructions and the time the bell sounded to start the first round. As soon as I felt myself land a punch, my nervousness disappeared. I would always try to land a punch right away, just to calm me down. It always made me feel better.

Interview, Las Vegas, Nev./
Los Angeles Times, 1-28:(3)1.

5

Million-dollar purses and guarantees have spoiled the [boxing] game. I never got a guarantee in my life. I fought for a percentage of the gate. If I won, I got the biggest percentage; the challenger got the shorter end. So what happens [today]? Very ordinary fighters like Jerry Quarry and Ken Norton—they get big guarantees, make more money losing than champions in my day made while winning. Fighting for the title used to be an honor. Now it's just another big payday.

Interview, New York, Nov. 30/
Los Angeles Herald-Examiner, 12-1:(D)14.

Dave Maggard
Athletic director,
University of California, Berkeley
6

There are enough countries in the world that think the [Olympic] Games are important; but the Games are dying a slow death for the United States because they no longer mean as much to us. Our emphasis is on professional sports, not Olympic sports.

San Francisco Examiner & Chronicle, 8-15:
(This World)2.

Billy Martin
Baseball manager, New York "Yankees"
                                        1

Baseball is a field of honor. It's not just a game or a living—it's a way of life. It's always been that way with me. You've got to feel that way when you're in love with baseball . . . When you go out to the park, you have a lot of responsibility. You're a manager, a policeman, a brother, a friend—a combination of everything. I've even had players talk to me about their personal life.

Interview, Anaheim, Calif./
Los Angeles Times, 5-17:(3)9.

                                        2

Discipline has got to start in the clubhouse. You can't have a country-club clubhouse. Last year, the game would start and some of the players would come out to [the] bench an inning later. Now the players fine each other if they're not out there for the anthem, and the guys who aren't playing aren't complaining and moaning. That's the way it is with a winning club . . . When I came here, no one wore a shirt and tie on road trips. A couple of guys came on the plane looking like girls. All I ask is that when they go from one town to another they dress like we think representatives of the *Yankees* should dress. After they get to the hotel, they can dress like they want . . . There was no static. There was no objection. I simply said, "If you don't wear a shirt and tie, I'll fine you."

Interview, New York/
The Dallas Times Herald, 8-1:(C)6.

Joe McDonald
General manager, New York "Mets"
baseball club
                                        3

I am really concerned about the future of the game. I think the game is in great jeopardy. The demands that the players are making, and which it appears the owners will have to accept in some form, could really put our sport on touchy ground . . . The owners are being stripped of virtually every bargaining tool. This is certain to result in a spiraling of salaries that will bring many franchises to the verge of bankruptcy.

Interview, St. Petersburg, Fla./
Los Angeles Herald-Examiner, 3-21:(C)8.

George McGinnis
Basketball player, Philadelphia "76ers"
                                        4

[On his high salary]: Am I worth the money? That's a hard question for me to answer. But I really don't think so; you know, deep down inside, I really don't think so. My agent tells me all the time not to say this, but that's really the way I feel. It's hard for me sometimes to comprehend the money I've got. How can I be worth $3-million to play basketball when, if everybody else played for free, I would too. That's how much I enjoy it . . . I really don't know how to evaluate my salary in terms of attendance, or what the club makes. All I know is that it's very hard to comprehend that a guy's making that kind of money. And that guy is me.

Interview, Philadelphia/
Los Angeles Herald-Examiner, 2-1:(B)7.

John McKay
Football coach, Tampa Bay "Buccaneers"
                                        5

The teams that go farthest in this game are those that have three things: good players, good coaching and good morale . . . It takes more than athletes and coaches to win football games. It takes an indefinable something else. On a team with good morale, the players respect what the coach is doing and pull together in a common cause instead of looking for someone to blame. The coaches, for their part, have to sell themselves to the players.

Interview, Tampa, Fla./
Los Angeles Times, 2-11:(3)7.

WHAT THEY SAID IN 1976

Tom McMillen
Basketball player,
New York "Knickerbockers"
1

I suppose in basketball we are in the entertainment industry. The spectators have a vicarious interest—a need to feel the pulse of something physical after being so wrapped up in the mental parts of their lives. To them, sports has something of a role of the stage in Elizabethan times. It has a value. For the athlete, there are very few feelings that match playing good and winning, and feeling the excitement of the crowd. That feeling is very hard to replace. Athletes are willing to accept so many of the downs of losing to feel a few ups.

Interview, New York/
The Washington Post, 12-26:(D)2.

Tom McVie
Hockey coach, Washington "Capitals"
2

Coaching in the NHL without coaching experience seems ignorant to me. Whether you're shoveling snow or coaching hockey, you have to start at the bottom, ride 10,000 miles on a bus, serve your apprenticeship. Five years ago I was no more qualified to come to the NHL than to fly to the moon. But in the last five years, I've been a coach, a general manager, a public-relations man. I've been a trainer when the trainer didn't show up. I've been a player when we've been short of players. I'm organized enough, disciplined enough to do a better job than most coaches. A coach never told me anything that I don't remember it.

Interview/The Washington Post, 1-27:(D)1.

James A. Michener
Author
3

[On the popularity of sports]: I don't really know why ordinarily sane people—men particularly—can get caught up in such nonsense to this degree ... but it's all right. It's healthy. It externalizes a lot of inner tensions. It hooks you onto something a little bigger than you are ... a universal experience. It drives one to such odd extremes. Bennett Cerf, my deceased publisher, always sensed that there

was something about him I didn't like, something that kept us from being good friends. He finally asked me what it was, and I told him I could never be comfortable with anyone who was a *Yankee* fan, which he was. I told him I thought there was something fundamentally sick about being affiliated with the *Yankees*.

Interview, Bucks County, Pa./
Los Angeles Times, 7-25:(Book Review)3.

Johnny Miller
Golfer
4

I could never be as good as [Jack] Nicklaus. I guess I am not sufficiently motivated. I don't lie awake at night worrying about whether I win a lot of major championships. I couldn't care less. I am not a driver—not the way Gary Player is, Lee Trevino, Arnold Palmer, Hale Irwin, and even Nicklaus, who is really dedicated. I am more like Julius Boros or Gene Littler. I like to win, but it's not life or death with me. I think it will help my longevity. Take a guy like Hubert Green. He's so intense; in 10 years he will be talking to the trees.

Dublin, Ohio/Los Angeles Times, 5-28:(3)2.

Marvin Miller
Executive director, Major League
Baseball Players Association
5

I think the reserve clause has been a cover for incompetence among most owners. These hysterical voices about the reserve clause come from a deep-seated inadequacy in dealing with people. They can't deal with people unless they can order them around. That's the real meaning of these hysterical voices [calling for continuation of the clause].

The New York Times, 3-11:49.

6

[Criticizing Baseball Commissioner Bowie Kuhn for nullifying the $3.5-million sale of three Oakland *Athletics* players to other teams]: I consider it sheer insanity. I think the potential in terms of the damage to the best interest of the game is tremendous. At the moment, just guessing, I would say it's done several things: It's raised the potential for litigation which would last for years, and I think it has raised the potential which perhaps other owners do not yet understand. He [Kuhn] is asserting a right to end all club-owners' rights with respect to all transactions. Whenever there's a trade made, he can decide that one team did not get enough value, and he can veto that deal.

June 18/ Los Angeles Times, 6-20:(3)10.

1

Players of 22 or 23 who are at the height of their physical prowess cannot understand their mortality. The average career is four and three-quarters years. But that's one of the refreshing things about representing players: their spirit. They seem to say we're all going to live forever.

Interview, New York/ People, 7-26:17.

2

[On whether professional athletes are paid too much]: If we had a completely rational system, then I think it would be legitimate for people to compare salaries. If the majority agreed to a base system on society's needs, then the top priorities should be for cancer research and the like. If we had such a system, then it would be fair to ask, "What does playing ball mean?" But we don't have that kind of system. Our system is hodgepodge. It's based on all sorts of rational and irrational things. If a particular skill is in short supply or it is vital to society's needs, then there will be high compensation. If a rock star fits the tempo of the times, then people will pay to buy his records. This has nothing to do with whether society needs rock stars. The fallacy of comparing athletes' salaries with other professions is that it makes a stupid assumption. If a ballplayer made less, would a teacher be paid more? Absolutely not. If a ballplayer makes less, then the rich owners will make more.

The Dallas Times Herald, 11-17:(C)1.

3

[On whether players' new free-agent status will sharply increase salaries]: I don't have the hysterical fears of some who think salaries will go through the roof. I believe no such thing. It will stabilize at a point where it is uneconomic to pay more. These are salaried people, and I do not believe that businessmen by and large will pay salaried people more than they are worth. You may make a mistake now and then, but not as a general rule.

Los Angeles Times, 11-23:(3)6.

Joe Morgan
Baseball player, Cincinnati "Reds"

4

The mistake a lot of managers make is "I know all, I know best." That isn't necessarily so. I think a manager's job is to keep 25 guys pointed toward one goal. No manager can expect to keep 25 guys completely happy, but he can keep them pointed toward one goal ... Everything that [*Reds* manager] Sparky [Anderson] talks about is the team. I can go 4-for-4, but if the team plays bad, I'm still part of that bad. Everything is the team winning, not finishing second or third. Sparky thinks they shouldn't give bonus money for finishing second or third. That's what he thinks of winning.

Interview, New York/
Los Angeles Herald-Examiner, 5-9:(D)11.

Manny Mota
Baseball player, Los Angeles "Dodgers"

5

[On being a pinch-hitter]: I don't think about the pressure. This is my job, and I think about the job. I watch every move their [the opponents'] pitchers make—the guy on the mound and the pitcher throwing in the bullpen. I want to know what they're doing different. Maybe they haven't got their best pitch tonight. Maybe it's better than usual. People who concentrate 100 per cent aren't nervous. Haven't you noticed that? How can you be nervous if you're concentrating? Concentration is the only chance I've got. I think about my job.

Interview/
Los Angeles Times, 6-29:(3)1.

WHAT THEY SAID IN 1976

Joe Namath
Football player, New York "Jets"
1

Football is a tremendous challenge. I mean, a quarterback doesn't just get the ball, go back and throw a pass. Before that, he has to choose from 100 plays and call the right one. Or he has to notice what way the guy on defense is pointing his feet and whether he is being set up. The game is sophisticated. Some people laugh at that; they say, "Oh, those sonofabitches go out there and hit each other and all that." But it's not that way. If they only understood. You get 11 guys lined up here, and 11 guys there, and so much goes into it. It is like a chess game, but you have to coordinate the mental with the physical actions. It is no different from playing in the streets back home. We're gonna try to beat them, we're gonna have some fun, and we're gonna come out on top.
Interview, Palm Springs, Calif./
Los Angeles Times, 2-15:(3)8.

Ilie Nastase
Tennis player
2

I think if somebody screams at me from the crowd, I should be able to scream at them too. Yes, I get out of control. Everybody is out of control sometimes. But I pay probably $40,000 in fines in my life, and I am the only one to get fined. People don't understand— everybody has a different temper. Off the court I am like everybody. But not on the court. You're dead if you're shy on the court.
People, 9-27:82.

Martina Navratilova
Tennis player
3

It's much easier to play against someone you really hate. My problem is there aren't too many people I don't like.
Los Angeles Times, 2-27:(3)2.

Byron Nelson
Golfer
4

I don't think today's iron player is any different than it was then [in the 1940s]. You hear a lot of talk about the changes in implements, graphite shafts, investment casting of irons, larger sweet spot, things like that; but mostly they're cosmetic. I don't see today's players hitting the ball any closer to the pins than Hogan or McSpaden or Snead or I did. The last real change that affected play was development of the sand iron and the pitching wedge, and that was back in the early '30s. That eliminated the fear of the bunker or the rough around the green. Other than that, most of the changes have been made to sell clubs, like new designs in automobiles.
Interview, Roanoke, Va./
Los Angeles Times, 1-11:(3)6.

C. M. Newton
Basketball coach,
University of Alabama
5

[On the perils of coaching]: When you're hired you're fired. The date just hasn't been put in.
Los Angeles Times, 5-26:(3)2.

Jack Nicklaus
Golfer
6

People wonder why I continue playing and working so hard after winning 16 major championships. There are two reasons. I still like to play tournament golf; I plan to continue it as long as it remains a challenge for me and as long [as] I feel I can compete without embarrassment. The second reason is that I would like to go down in history as the greatest golfer of all time.
Interview, North Palm Beach, Fla./
Los Angeles Herald-Examiner, 4-4:(C)4.

Chuck Noll
Football coach, Pittsburgh "Steelers"
7

[On the imporance of defense]: Before you can win a game, you have to not lose it.
The Dallas Times Herald, 1-17:(C)1.

Ken Norton
Boxer
1

[On his forthcoming heavyweight title bout with Muhammad Ali]: I look at this fight like the old mechanic and the young mechanic, making the same kind of repairs. The young guy goes down the line, by the book, to do his job well. It may take him longer, but he gets the job done. The older guy, through his experience, knows the short-cuts; he knows how to get around a certain problem and still get the job done. I'm the younger guy. I'm still learning. I expect Ali to come out with something different at the beginning of the fight. But he'll have to revert to what he knows from his experience as the fight progresses.

Interview, Gilman Hot Springs, Calif./
Los Angeles Herald-Examiner, 8-23:(C)8.

Walter F. O'Malley
Chairman,
Los Angeles "Dodgers" baseball club
2

I think the leaders of football, baseball and basketball should get together and form a strong allegiance. They should present Congress with a strong bill that would allow them to function without all the incumbrances that beset them now. What would be in the bill? First, football and basketball would have to be given the same rights under the antitrust laws that baseball now enjoys. Secondly, a modified version of the reserve clause would have to [be] worked out to keep players from jumping around from team to team. Third, we would have to protect against raiding whereby one team goes into another team's territory, as Oakland did to San Francisco. And, finally, a way must be worked out for sports to self-discipline themselves. We have to stop running to the courts every time a dispute comes up. We must work out a system, fair and equitable, that is satisfying to both the players and the owners.

Interview, Los Angeles/
Los Angeles Herald-Examiner, 3-2:(C)9.

Jesse Owens
Former Olympic track champion
3

The Olympics have become the whipping post of a thing called politics. Nationalism has taken precedence over individualism. Some have tried to use the Olympics as the stage to publicize their ideologies. Others have made it a rostrum of hate and prejudice. But the Olympics are kept alive by man, and not nations, and man will prevail . . . There is no way to snuff out the camaraderie of athletes of all nationalities . . . You have to be there to appreciate it.

Los Angeles Times, 7-4:(3)1.

Jim Palmer
Baseball pitcher, Baltimore "Orioles"
4

[On the big salaries being paid to new free-agent players]: I don't blame the players. It's like leaving your son alone in an ice-cream store. He'll eat himself sick. I thought the owners would have restraint. The players say, "If two or three teams go out of business, so what? Baseball will go on." And they're right, unless you play for one of those two or three teams . . . I don't know what real effect the free-agent system will have. I predict, however, the number of free agents may increase ten-fold and that salaries will continue to go up. Rich teams like the *Red Sox* are trying to beat the crush by paying through the nose now. They can afford to sign 18 players to long-term contracts because they know salaries may be even worse later.

Interview/Los Angeles Times, 12-6:(3)8.

Gabe Paul
President,
New York "Yankees" baseball club
5

People are your main revenue source by far, the people you draw into your stadium to watch the team. You even get 20 per cent of the revenue on the road. So it's a judgment situation [player salaries], and a high-risk one: You pay for the players, you win the pennant or come close, and you draw people. Your next big income comes from television, but [Player Association head] Marvin Miller is wrong when he says you get 150 per cent of your payroll from TV before you even take the field. Forgive him, he knoweth not. The percentage of club dollars put into players'

(GABE PAUL)

salaries has doubled in ten years, and might double again in the next two. After that, your only significant income comes from advertising—in your program and on your fence. After that? I guess you pass the hat.

Interview/The New York Times, 12-3:(B)5.

Bob Prince
Baseball announcer,
American Broadcasting Company;
Former baseball announcer,
Pittsburgh "Pirates" 1

Calling a game with cold dispassion is a cinch. You sit on your can, reporting grounders and two-base hits lackadaisically. You've got no responsibilities. But rooting is tough. It requires creativeness. It also fulfills your function, which is to shill. You are an arm of the home club who is there to make the listener happy.

Interview/
Los Angeles Herald-Examiner, 3-10:(D)2.

Tommy Prothro
Football coach, San Diego "Chargers" 2

Coaching is an unnatural way of life. It's natural for me because I'm used to it, but it would be unnatural for most persons. Your victories and losses are too clear-cut. Your emotional peaks are higher, your valleys lower. It's like riding a roller coaster. We're like children who ride a roller coaster all our days.

Los Angeles Times, 7-13:(3)3.

Bob Pulford
Hockey coach, Los Angeles "Kings" 3

There is great satisfaction in seeing a team execute what you are trying to coach. There are peaks and valleys for a coach as there are as a player, but with a coach they are more prominent. You can be extremely disturbed by what happens or doesn't happen in a

game . . . I can feel when I've prepared the team right, done everything I think I can do to get the players ready. Then, if you win, you feel good; if you lose, you don't like it. But when you don't have the feeling you did all you could, that's when a coach really feels bad. That's the tough time.

Interview, Los Angeles Times, 10-1:(3)8.

Jerry Quarry
Former boxer 4

This will surprise some people because I was at it so long, but the truth of the matter is that I hated boxing. It is a cruel, vicious sport—nothing more than two people trying to kill each other—and the more vicious it gets, the more people like it. I'm not an animal. Maybe that's why I didn't become champion.

The New York Times, 1-4:(5)3.

Lance Rentzel
Former football player 5

Football played a great and positive influence on my life. But when it's time to quit, it's time to quit. Then you go on to other things . . . It wasn't difficult for me at all. I never viewed myself as just an athlete and I never thought my life would be over when I left the game. What you have to understand is that it can all end at any time. When it happens, it's a rude awakening for many athletes because they can't adjust. One minute you're on a pedestal and the next minute someone yanks the pedestal right out from under you.

Interview/Los Angeles Times, 2-1:(3)7.

Paul Richards
Baseball manager, Chicago "White Sox" 6

I know baseball can't live with the complete abolition of the reserve clause. There's no relation of baseball to football or basketball's situation becaue they have the college system to develop players. If we [in baseball] have to spend $1-million or more a year developing players, and then a player has a

right to leave, the owners will decide they won't spend this money.
Interview, Waxahachie, Tex./
Los Angeles Times, 2-22:(3)10.

1

Today's athletes run faster and make a lot more plays in the field. But the name of the game is still pitching and it ain't goin' to change. Pitching was 80 per cent of baseball when John McGraw managed and it's still 80 per cent of baseball.
Interview/ The Christian Science Monitor, 6-14:25.

2

I don't think managing has changed. You just take the players and find out what they can do and what they can't do; you have them do what they can and try not to put them in a position where they might be called on to do something they can't. It's the same old story. You try to cheer up the ones who are going bad and leave the ones who are going good alone.
Interview, Chicago/
Los Angeles Times, 7-2:(3)6.

Frank Robinson
Baseball manager, Cleveland "Indians"

3

What I'm trying to build is a team that will make the routine play all the time. I don't care about the spectacular play because it isn't going to help you that much. What kills a manager is when one of his infielders boots an easy double-play ball or one of his hitters can't sacrifice the tying run from first to second base with the team's power coming up. The point is, if you can't get that kind of execution regularly, you can forget about pennants.
Interview/ The Christian Science Monitor, 6-1:30.

John Robinson
Football coach,
University of Southern California

4

Coaching football is a creative thing—and there's no greater feeling than to create some-

thing. You're like a builder, an artist, an orchestra conductor, a playwright or a man who designs bridges. The football coach takes 100 parts, 100 individuals, and creates one part—a team.
Interview/ Los Angeles Times, 8-22:(3)9.

Bob Rosburg
Golfer

5

The tension [in big-time tournament golf] is unbelievable. You are out there on your own—you, a big golf course and a little white ball. The crowd pushes in so close you feel like you're in prison. You can't get away from anybody. You can't get a drink of water without 5,000 people watching every move. I know. I've been through it. I've seen it break strong men. I have seen men panic. I have seen them freeze. I have seen others say, "To hell with it," and go to something else.
Interview, Bethesda, Md./
The Dallas Times Herald, 8-15:(D)2.

Pete Rose
Baseball player, Cincinnati "Reds"

6

I enjoy playing baseball. Call it being a hot dog, call it basal metabolism, call it anything—I play with enthusiasm, and when I lose that it'll be time to get out. I've got about this much ability [hands held two inches apart], this much desire [two feet apart], and this much enthusiasm [arms outstretched]. A guy introduced me at a banquet: "Here's a fellow who can't run, can't throw, can't hit home runs, and he's going to be in the Hall of Fame" . . . I haven't missed a game in two and a half years. I can go to the park sick as a dog and, when I see my uniform hanging there, I get well right now. Then I see some of you guys [the press], and get sick again.
Upon receiving Professional Athlete of
the Year award, New York, Jan. 8/
The New York Times, 1-9:37.

7

I believe in having a reserve clause of some type. I've got a couple of different businesses

WHAT THEY SAID IN 1976

(PETE ROSE)

of my own and I can see the owners' side as well as the players' side. I don't know too much about this whole thing, but I believe an owner who makes the initial investment in a ballplayer should be protected in some way. [I] don't think it's right for some kid to come out of high school, get a big bonus and an opportunity to play in the big leagues, and then, after he becomes a star, tell the owner he's going to play for him one more year and that's it. On the other hand, I think you need a system for the players, too. A guy who comes to mind right off the top of my head is Bill Plummer on our club. He plays behind Johnny Bench, the best catcher in the world. Because he plays behind the best, he sits on the bench and rots. I don't think that's right either.

Interview, New York/
The Dallas Times Herald, 2-26:(E)7.

Darrell Royal
Football coach, University of Texas   *1*

The only way I know how to keep football fun is to win. That's the only answer. There is no laughter in losing.

Los Angeles Times, 7-8:(3)3.

Nolan Ryan
Baseball pitcher, California "Angels"   *2*

Don't get the idea I'm opposed to money. A man has to be paid for what he delivers. But once you get a respectable sum and keep pressing, pressing, pressing for more, you become unhappy, and soon money occupies more of your thoughts than your playing . . . I read about these asking prices of three and four hundred thousand dollars and I kind of laugh, because I haven't seen a ballplayer worth even $250,000. [Willie] Mays and [Roberto] Clemente might have been exceptions, but that's an awful lot of money for playing baseball.

Interview, Palm Springs, Calif./
Los Angeles Herald-Examiner, 3-29:(C)2.

Vin Scully
Sports announcer,
Los Angeles "Dodgers" baseball club and
Columbia Broadcasting System   *3*

Football is to baseball as blackjack is to bridge. One is the quick jolt; the other the deliberate, slow-paced game of skill. But never was a sport more ideally suited to television than baseball. It's all there in front of you. It's theatre, really. The star is the spotlight on the mound, the supporting cast fanned out around him, the mathematical precision of the game moving with the kind of inevitability of Greek tragedy. With the Greek chorus in the bleachers!

Interview, Los Angeles/
Los Angeles Times, 6-20:(TV Times)4.

Tom Seaver
Baseball pitcher, New York "Mets"   *4*

In baseball, my theory is to strive for consistency, not to worry about the "numbers." If you dwell on statistics, you get shortsighted; if you aim for consistency, the numbers will be there at the end. My job isn't to strike guys out; it's to *get* them out, sometimes by striking them out.

Interview/The New York Times, 1-11:(5)5.

Bill Sharman
Basketball coach, Los Angeles "Lakers"   *5*

[Saying basketball is a team game]: It's always great to have the best player, but sometimes one, two or even three outstanding players are not enough to win consistently. Basketball is a game where you don't have time to stop and think about what you're going to do every time you go down court. It's a game where players must react instinctively; and only a great deal of time and experience brings them together.

New York, March 9/
The New York Times, 3-10:37.

Mark Spitz
1972 Olympic swimming champion   *6*

The [1972] Olympic Games were the culmination of my [swimming] career. I swam in everything that I held the world record in, won and got out. I got out because there just wasn't anything for me to do in swimming any more. I have a great amount of satisfaction within me because the gold medals I won meant I accomplished what I set out to do. I don't believe there are too many athletes in the world that go out on top. For some reason, they just keep hanging in there. I think it takes courage to say, "That's it, baby, I quit!"

Interview, Marina del Rey, Calif./
Los Angeles Times, 6-13:(3)3.

Willie Stargell
Baseball player, Pittsburgh "Pirates"
1

[Disagreeing with ball-club owners who say that an end to the reserve clause would result in many players jumping clubs]: A ballplayer doesn't enjoy moving his family from one town to another any more than anybody else does. I don't think there would be any mass jumping. I know, for myself, I wouldn't put an ad in a newspaper saying, "Have bat, will travel."

Los Angeles Times, 2-26:(3)2.

Rusty Staub
Baseball player, Detroit "Tigers"
2

I don't care what club I'm with—the fans love me wherever I've been. Why? Because I bust my back out there. I play well, and I generally have a relationship with the fans that goes beyond merely playing a game. I always try to relate to them. I never consider myself above them. I never look down at them . . . I think the reason I get along so well with so many different types of people is that, despite my so-called progressive attitudes about life in general, I still have that old approach to the game of baseball.

Los Angeles Times, 2-18:(2)3.

Hank Stram
Former football coach, Kansas City "Chiefs"
3

It's only a game when you win. When you lose it's hell.

Los Angeles Times, 7-8:(3)3.

Lynn Swann
Football player, Pittsburgh "Steelers"
4

Everything is political to some extent, but I think football has gone beyond that necessary for it to be a good strong institution, a profitable business, entertainment . . . I'm referring to all of football. Not just decisions on the [player] fines, but the decisions everywhere else—the court cases, and the draft being illegal, people being political about rules because their team's composed of certain talent and can do certain things, so they can [get] a rule change on this or a rule change on that which would help their team. Those kind of politics.

Interview, Pittsburgh/
Los Angeles Times, 10-28:(3)6.

Fran Tarkenton
Football player, Minnesota "Vikings"
5

[On the players' new option rights freeing them from being bound to one team]: Regardless of what people say, the option clause will not be the ruination of sports. Actually, it is very healthy. You're not going to see a mass exodus with people running all over the lot. In fact, there are things other than money that motivates athletes. I think most of them prefer a club and a city where people are positive and there is no abrasive environment.

Interview, New York/
Los Angeles Times, 5-16:(3)4.

Bob Tucker
Football player, New York "Giants"
6

The important [player-vs.-management] issues are things like pension and the individual contract. If I sign for $20,000 for one year, I can be dropped after one week and all I've got is one-fourteenth of that salary, and I'm through. That's not right. That's a one-way street. Pensions are important to men who take the pounding we do, week after week, because when I'm 45 years old I'm not going to be in as good physical shape as those who didn't subject their bodies to what we do. And if I play in a game like the Pro Bowl,

WHAT THEY SAID IN 1976

(BOB TUCKER)

sponsored by the league, and get hurt so badly I can't play next year, my team doesn't have to pay me anything. Things like that are where we require protection. But all the public hears is Rozelle rule, Rozelle rule, and antitrust. Sure, we would like some modification on [that], but that's not where the hangup is.

Interview, Palm Springs, Calif./
The New York Times, 2-1:(5)3.

Ted Turner
Owner, Atlanta. "Braves" baseball club   1

The communication between the players and owners hasn't been good. The players have lawyers and agents and associations to do all the talking. The players themselves should sit down and talk with the owners. I like the players. They're a good bunch of guys. They've worked hard to be champions. They enjoy what they're doing. Everyone wants to be a baseball player, even more than being a newspaperman. They're always being asked for autographs. They're on national television. They fly around the country, first class. The girls recognize them. Everyone wants to be a hero, doesn't he?

Interview/The Dallas Times Herald, 6-6:(C)4.

Thomas Tutko
Psychologist, San Jose, (Calif.)
State University   2

When you try to approach some of the things we do in sport from a logical standpoint, they make no sense at all. Think about it. Here is a sports hero. What does he do? He carries this pig's bladder 100 yards across a white line on the grass, and we all say, "He's a great guy!" Why? Does it make any sense?

San Francisco Examiner & Chronicle, 1-18:
(This World)2.

3

How many million youngsters are we sacrificing along the way so that ten players can entertain us in a pro basketball game? I'm

concerned with how many good athletes have been scarred by injury or burned out psychologically by the time they were 15 because they were unable to meet the insatiable needs of their parents, their coach, their fans or their own personal obsession; or are rejected and made to feel ashamed because of their limited athletic prowess. We'll tolerate almost anything in the name of winning—cruelty, insensitivity, drugs, cheating and lying . . . Is it any wonder the sports field is overrun with neurotic behavior?

Los Angeles Times, 7-9:(3)3.

Bill Veeck
Owner, Chicago "White Sox" baseball club   4

This is an illusionary business. The fan goes away from the ballpark with nothing more to show for it than what's in his mind. When you sell a chair, or a house, or a car, you can develop a contented customer based on the quality of your product. Three years from now he can look at it with a feeling of satisfaction—"Best buy I ever made." But in baseball, all he ever walks away with is an illusion, an ephemeral feeling of having been entertained. You've got to develop and preserve that illusion. You have to give him more vivid pictures to carry away in his head.

Interview/TV Guide, 6-5:15.

Dick Vertlieb
General manager,
Golden State "Warriors" basketball team   5

I don't believe in "dynasties." People grow old and you get unlucky in the draft. A lot of things happen. The only "dynasties" we've had in pro basketball were the old Minneapolis *Lakers* and the Boston *Celtics*. But those days of just one league and eight or nine teams are over. Today you have 18 NBA teams plus the ABA competing for talent. Our primary goal is to continue to be respectable.

Interview, Oakland, Calif./
Los Angeles Herald-Examiner, 3-5:(C)8.

Bill Virdon
Baseball manager, Houston "Astros"
1

[On the designated-hitter rule]: I know some people think it takes away from the strategy aspect of the game, but I think the good things about it outweigh the factor. I like to see a pitcher like Catfish Hunter go all the way instead of being taken out for a pinch hitter in a close game. I like to see a .300 hitter like Cecil Cooper batting instead of a pitcher. And I think the fans like these things too ... It does make it easier for a manager when he doesn't have to worry about whether to pinch hit for the pitcher, but that isn't why I like it. I just think it's better for the fans. In fact, if I had the right to make just one change in the rules, I'd have three designated hitters, not one.

Interview, Cocoa Beach, Fla./
The Christian Science Monitor, 4-1:11.

Kermit Washington
Basketball player, Los Angeles "Lakers"
2

I don't like to be known as a fighter or a bully, because it isn't good for kids to think that's a part of playing ball. It isn't. And violence begets violence. There's always someone stronger or meaner and it only takes one good elbow or cheap shot to end a career. I want to play aggressively, sure, but I never want to hurt anyone. I'll only say that if you let a player intimidate you, you have to go against him the rest of your career, so you have to put a stop to that.

Los Angeles Times, 11-18:(3)5.

Earl Weaver
Baseball manager, Baltimore "Orioles"
3

From what I've observed, owners don't fire managers merely for losing. They fire them if the public is complaining. In some cases, the public will say it wasn't the manager's fault. But when it blames the manager, the owner feels he has to move, and the lovable old skipper gets thrown out on his can ... In most cases, the "public" is the press. If the press writes that the fans feel the manager is doing a bad job, that usually means the *press* feels he's doing a bad job.

Interview/
Los Angeles Herald-Examiner, 4-22:(C)2.

Jerry West
Basketball coach, Los Angeles "Lakers"
4

Even though I love this life and always have, the one thing it doesn't do is satisfy my drive to win. Winning, believe me, is the only thing that's going to make me happy on this level. It's such a great feeling when things go right. That's why if you really are involved, the way I feel I am now, you just can't cast it aside when you lose. It hurts, it really does.

Interview/ Los Angeles Times, 10-29:(3)6.

Maury Wills
Sports commentator,
National Broadcasting Company;
Former baseball player
5

[Saying baseball does not demand as much physical exertion by players as do other sports]: Baseball players run [only] 90 feet at a time. Watch a baseball player along about mid-season, in July and August, when he should be at his peak. Particularly, check one out after he's hit a triple and, I guarantee you, most of them will be huffing and puffing after they get to third. And if it's an inside-the-park home run, with a slide at the plate, well, you can bet that he just hopes his teammates make it a long inning so he can get a breather. Then, too, unlike just about any other sport, baseball players don't have an action assignment throughout the game. In most sports, you're responsible for a one-on-one battle with your counterpart. Whether it's offense or defense, you'd better be moving *someplace*. In baseball, a right-fielder can go out to his position and never have a ball hit to him. And then, when he gets to the plate as a batter, he can go 0-for-4 and literally the extent of his exertion is walking from the dugout to the plate and back again ... and maybe of course a strenuous kick at the water cooler.

Interview, Marina del Rey, Calif./
Lately (the Sheraton Hotel magazine), Vol. 1, No. 2.

WHAT THEY SAID IN 1976

(MAURY WILLS)

1

It's every player's dream—whether he's a major-leaguer or a minor-leaguer—to manage some day in the big leagues. That's the pinnacle, the ultimate in baseball. But look at what can happen to you: There's absolutely no security. Twenty-five players determine how long you stay. You have to be a diplomat. You have to communicate with the press and you have to communicate with management.

Interview/Los Angeles Times, 3-21:(3)6.

Ralph C. Wilson
Owner, Buffalo "Bills" football team

2

[On his paying player O. J. Simpson $400,000]: The idea of paying that kind of money to one athlete is ridiculous. It makes a mockery of everyday endeavor. It upsets the salary structure of your team. And it poses a big risk for ownership because of the injury possibility. In football, the chances of losing a player for the season are far greater than in basketball and baseball. But I see Simpson as a genuine superstar. He is good for our franchise. And he also grew with our club. I would never pay the money he is getting to an outsider, because the rest of the squad would resent it.

TV Guide, 5-29:21.

John Wooden
Former basketball coach,
University of California, Los Angeles

3

Youth needs models more than critics. If a coach is a loud, raving maniac, how can he expect his players to be anything but? I read in some early basketball book that a player who loses his temper is going to be outplayed. I think the same is true for a coach.

Interview/Los Angeles Times, 3-26:(3)9.

Mickey Wright
Golfer

4

[On women golfers competing directly with men]: It's out of the question. There's just no comparison . . . There's talk that the women are better around the green, chipping and putting. That's not true. The men are better. The women are getting better, but they haven't caught up yet. The big difference is coming out of the rough. Women simply don't have the strength to get it out the way men do. And that's part of the game. When I was at my peak, I'd sometimes wish I was an invisible creature for a few weeks and could compete with the men. Just for the competition. I think the competition would have been good for me. But as far as girls competing against the men on a regular basis, there's no way. There just isn't any comparison.

Interview, Pinehurst, N. C./
The Dallas Times Herald, 9-12:(C)7.

Cale Yarborough
Auto-racing driver

5

During a race, it's like I become a machine and the machine becomes a man. I talk to my cars, baby them, shout at them, praise them. I feel them live and breathe in my hands.

Los Angeles Herald-Examiner, 12-31:(C)14.

Elizabeth Athanasakos
Director,
National Commission on the Observance of
International Women's Year 1

We can say there is not going to be any discrimination in our laws, but two years later there's another election and suddenly the types who don't want their wives to operate bulldozers are deciding they've got to pass new laws to "protect" the women—or the girls, as they'd call them. And suddenly you're protected right out of your equal pay and right out of your jobs . . . I wonder whether we aren't missing the boat in not educating the men and working on changing their attitudes and getting them to accept the changes that are going on. We have overlooked sensitizing the men and re-educating them. We complain about it, but we haven't done anything to teach men it is not unmasculine if a wife happens to have a different kind of education and may earn more money.
Interview, Washington/
The Christian Science Monitor, 7-19:14.

Brigitte Bardot
Actress 2

I don't want to be classified as a "liberated" woman. I find that those who are don't give much care toward being a woman. So many of the so-called liberated women are badly dressed, badly made up, sour, ugly, stupid. They do whatever they can to be awful. They're aggressive. They provoke confrontations. But a woman doesn't have to be like this. Every girl can have the air of being lovely. It's not necessary for a woman to be a Venus, but a woman should underline her best sides.
Interview, Paris/
San Francisco Examiner & Chronicle, 6-6:
(Datebook)20.

Marisa Berenson
Actress 3

I agree with some of the points of women's lib—that women should have just as much right to do certain things, that they can be just as talented and intelligent and can earn just as much money. Why not? What I don't like about it is the idea of competing with men to be on the same level in every way. Women should keep their femininity and stay women . . . Nowadays they're becoming men, and it's not attractive . . . or positive.
Interview, New York/
The Christian Science Monitor, 3-19:21.

Urie Bronfenbrenner
Professor of human development and
family studies, Cornell University 4

Women will not achieve liberation if what they aspire for are the values and the behaviors of the men who have been locking them out of the man's world. Not long ago I was at a meeting of a large advertising conference at which a leading woman executive told everybody: "Look, we women can outsell, outmaneuver, outdo men at their own game. We can fool more people than you can fool." That's what I see as a dangerous trend. If women sell out to the male values, to the values of a power-oriented male society—that I think is a snare and a delusion.
Interview/ U.S. News & World Report, 6-7:47.

Yvonne B. Burke
United States Representative,
D—California 5

. . . the experiences that we have as women from the time we are very small children are considerably different [from men]. We are more aware of certain things. And as we grow up, our experiences as wives give us a greater

WHAT THEY SAID IN 1976

(YVONNE B. BURKE)

awareness of, for instance, consumer pricing. That's just a result of a woman's experience. A woman happens to have a great responsibility in the everyday operation of a household, so she has a greater concern with the problems of the consumer. Furthermore, as a result of the role and experiences that women often play, they have a tremendous interest in education. I also believe that women have a great interest in achieving a peaceful society. That is probably because over our lifetimes we're taught to try to compromise, to be peaceful, to seek peaceful solutions rather than aggressive solutions to problems. So I believe that women tend to be more interested in arriving at settlements and compromises of international disputes. We don't have a different viewpoint [from men], but, given different experiences, we often arrive at different conclusions. Any society that excludes any one part of that society from decision-making is not truly representative, and decisions are not made on a representative basis. That's what's happened to the United States. That's what's happened to the United States Congress. Women have been excluded and, as a result, we have not had decisions that represent all the American people.

Interview/ U.S. News & World Report, 4-26:49.

James Caan
Actor
1

I believe that the husband should be the head of the household, that he should be the boss . . . I know it's nonsense to believe that a woman doesn't have the same natural instincts and shouldn't have the same rights as a man, but that's the way I was brought up, and I can't seem to get past it. I really believe that, if she's married, a woman's place is in the home—at least until the kids are grown. Gloria Steinem [feminist] can lead a march to my house with torches, but 70 per cent of the women I know agree with me.

Interview/ Newsweek, 1-26:36.

Taylor Caldwell
Author
2

Women shouldn't have the right to vote. In ancient Rome, women had the right to vote and became active in government. That was the end of Rome. The only good thing Mussolini did was to take away the right of women to vote.

Interview/ People, 3-8:66.

Liz Carpenter
Co-chairman, ERAmerica
3

[On commentator Phyllis Schlafly's campaign against ratification of the ERA]: We don't think she's been *that* successful. How can she be when 34 states have ratified the amendment, and 110 organizations have come together to support it? What she has done is foster a lot of myths, like saying that the amendment will mean more abortions, more busing, the changing of relationships between husbands and wives, and coed bathrooms. It's all lies.

Interview, Washington/ The New York Times, 3-8:20.

Coy G. Eklund
President, Equitable Life Assurance Society
4

Just a few short years ago, most men probably believed that women only want to work until they land a husband; married women only work for "pin money"; it's a shame for a man whose wife has to work; a mother's place is with her children at home; and working women create unemployment. So, even now, some of us are surprised to learn that, without working women, this nation has an inadequate work force. Today about 35 million women work. If you would remove them all from their jobs and endeavor to fill those jobs with unemployed men, that would mean filling 35 million jobs with 4½ million unemployed males! It would leave 30½ million jobs vacant, and the national economy would immediately come to a screeching, grinding halt! This nation cannot maintain its present economy without the very substantial number of women in the work force . . . What we must all come to understand is that women work for the same reasons men do: to support themselves and their families; and also, importantly, for the satisfaction and fulfillment that meaningful work provides for all of us. But what makes it somewhat different—and more difficult— is the biological fact that women exclusively must gestate and birth our offspring. Additionally, society has seen fit to burden them with the homemaking, child-rearing roles to an almost exclusive degree. Therein lies the problem. Women must resolve that dilemma of role duality—on the one hand, marriage, home and family, and, on the other, a professional career—an inherent conflict of interest that no doubt produces a visceral anxiety for many women and which seems to call for decision either to "be a woman" or to "be a success." Women seem confronted with unsatisfying either/or choices. That dilemma must be resolved. Hopefully there is an emerging realization that there can be a new model of a successful woman—a female ambivert—who somehow integrates professional achievement with a personal life wholly fulfilling.

At New York University, April 24/
Vital Speeches, 6-15:539.

Betty Ford
Wife of President of the
United States Gerald R. Ford 1

What's this about the liberated woman being a career woman? A liberated woman is one who feels confident in herself and is happy in what she is doing. A woman who is satisfied with her life at home is just as liberated as a woman with a career outside the home. What is important is that a person has the option to decide the direction of her own life, and that she makes that decision herself, without pressures restricting her choices.

Interview, Washington/
Good Housekeeping, August:24.

Betty Friedan
Founder, National Organization for Women 2

I believe that the Equal Rights Amendment

failed for several reasons. One was that there was this expensive campaign of lies . . . false propaganda that played on women's fears. But what the defeat also showed was the degree to which we have allowed the women's movement to be taken over by extreme groups . . . Things like *Ms.* magazine, for instance, which trivialize the movement and give it an image that is alienating, I think, for the majority of women. Then, too, there's been a divergence of energy in the movement to battles for personal power . . . The group that calls itself the majority caucus, and whose motto is "Out of the mainstream, into revolution," took control of the NOW organization. Now, you're not going to pass something like the Equal Rights Amendment if your energies are devoted to taking your own organization, which should be fighting for the Equal Rights Amendment, out of the mainstream of American society. Some of us are beginning to believe that all this was not a coincidence . . . somewhere all this is being manipulated.

Interview, New York/
The Dallas Times Herald, 3-24:(E)1.

3

The women's movement does not mean the end of marriage. The women's movement does not mean going off and living in an all-female commune. The women's movement does not mean taking the power away from men and reversing the tables on men. On the other hand, women are moving into the mainstream of society. They are now working at better jobs and aspiring to better jobs. They are demanding and getting a decision-making voice. Equality for women with men is what it's all about. It does mean a complex and subtle but real restructuring of every institution.

Interview/Book Digest, October:27.

4

What does woman want? Well, ultimately one would have to answer the question, what do human beings want? And it is a very big and mysterious question. We want to live.

WHAT THEY SAID IN 1976

(BETTY FRIEDAN)

Life is its own answer. In essence, the women's movement is an affirmation of life, that woman should live as fully and freely as possible. And she couldn't do that in the confinement of the role in which she has been locked and in which her own mind had been locked, denying so much of her own personality . . . Real liberation is when we can affirm all that we are, our tenderness and our gentleness and our sensitivities, all those things that have been considered feminine before, which are good things; and also our strength and our courage and our assertiveness. And then we can move freely—from the coziness and the warmth of a home that should be a genuine haven, from love for a man or for children, from new affirmations of each other as women—out to the larger society and have our voice in it and confront its really major problems that we share with men.

Interview, New York/
Los Angeles Times, 12-5:(5)22.

Francoise Giroud
Secretary of State for
Women's Affairs of France
1

I have the impression that American women feel gypped, and this is one reason for their vigorous reaction in women's lib. After all, they colonized and opened up your country, sharing all dangers and hardships with the men—and then this equality vanished. In terms of written law, almost everything necessary has been done to establish equality of women in the U.S.A., France and Sweden. But many things remain in terms of application. In France, women have held a strong position in family and private relationships. They were always important in the arts—for example, painting and writing. But the *Code Napoleon* was strongly biased against women and regarded them as the property of men. This heritage has not yet been erased.

Interview, Paris/
The New York Times, 3-31:37.

Francoise Giroud
Secretary of State for Cultural
Affairs of France; Former French Secretary
of State for Women's Affairs
2

I don't have a taste for power, as such. I would rather do things. Men care about power because, for them, power is linked to sexual performance. Women achieve positions of power out of a need to do something, not because we need reassurance.

Los Angeles Herald-Examiner, 11-7:(A)9.

Barry M. Goldwater
United States Senator, R—Arizona
3

[On the women's movement]: Which movement? I love every little movement a woman has . . . I don't mind what a woman does as long as she's home in time to cook dinner.

The Washington Post, 2-22:(Potomac)5.

Princess Grace
Princess of Monaco
4

I'm very much a feminist at heart. I think women can do whatever they set their minds to do. But I also think that, in a man-woman relationship, the man should be the head of the family and unchallenged by woman. It's a partnership in that two people should keep their own identities . . . not squash the other. But it can't be fifty-fifty and work. If a woman goes into marriage thinking that, she's in for a big shock because she has to give more than fifty per cent to make her marriage successful. Her job is to be the homemaker, the wife and the mother. Even when she goes back to work, she still has these three responsibilities, and it won't fit into a fifty-fifty . . .

Interview, Paris/ McCall's, March:136.

Barry S. Greiff
Psychiatrist,
Harvard University Business School
5

There's no question that the women's liberation movement has helped awaken the consciousness of America to the fact that women have a capacity to deal with a number of complex business, political and economic issues. When men become threatened, however, they talk of "women's lib" in a pejorative way. One reason is that their territory has been invaded. That is a fact. One of the things that is going to occur in this country is "job collision." By that I mean people are going to be colliding for jobs that were exclusively and primarily for the male ... There might be reverse discrimination because of the fact that companies are under social, moral and legal pressure to hire more women. But rather than call it reverse discrimination, it might be better to call it an effort to achieve a fair balance. At the same time—and I really want to make this point— if a woman is going to enter the business world, then she's going to have to do all the things a man does.

Interview/ U.S. News & World Report, 9-27:80.

Barbara Howar
Author
1

Any woman who tells you that she can hold down a career—not a job, but a career—and raise children and keep up with a man and a home and social life and a sex life—and not suffer for it—is lying. It is not possible. Any woman who tells you having your own career or own identity is enough, she no longer needs a man, either knows something I don't know or has taken up with women. I think women's lib is terrific, though. I think that those ladies have done a great deal of good in changing the law and making people aware.

Interview/ People, 5-3:18.

Rona Jaffe
Author
2

I think women are more fascinating now. In fact, I think men are more fascinating now. The women's lib movement has given men the opportunity to be gentle; and women no longer talk about men—they talk about activities.

Interview, Los Angeles/
Los Angeles Herald-Examiner, 9-12:(F)2.

Suzanne Keller
Professor of sociology,
Princeton University
3

Studies have shown that men, while they may pay lip service to such aspects of women's liberation as equal pay for equal work, are more wedded to—hence less willing to change—the traditional domestic and sexual side of male-female relations. This then prevents them from going along with new developments and assuming their share of household and child-care responsibilities on any significant scale, even where their jobs permit it, which most do not. There are some—few exceptions—men who do make a temporary stab at house husbandry—duly reported as the anomalies or curiosities they are ... If men are willing or unable to change themselves, how can the women who associate with them become liberated? It still takes two to tango.

At Colloquium on Changing Life-Styles,
Princeton University/
The National Observer, 6-5:14.

Mary Wells Lawrence
Chairman,
Wells, Rich, Greene, advertising
4

I was a girl at the time when there was no women's-lib movement, and nobody was thinking very much about promoting women. And yet through the years I managed. I never at any time experienced any discrimination whatever because I was a girl. In fact, I'd say people helped me because I *was* a girl. And I've just had a terrific life. That could only happen in America. I'm one of those typical symbols, I think, of what can happen to somebody who didn't have any money and didn't have a spectacular education. If you're willing to really get out and just work your little head off, I don't care if you're green, purple, blue, female or male, you have a very good chance of accomplishing the kind of life and lifestyle you want to accomplish. I worked very hard, and so I made it.

Interview/ Newsweek, 7-4:68.

WHAT THEY SAID IN 1976

Lawrence P. McDonald
United States Representative, D—Georgia 1

Thomas Edison and those who invented time-saving devices for women, like the washing machine, are the true [women's] liberationists. Screwballs who run around screaming women's lib, free love, nickel beer and abortion are kooks and a menace to women.

Interview, Washington/People, 7-5:58.

Madeline H. McWhinney
President,
First Women's Bank, New York 2

My feeling is that there are very good women and very good men. There are all kinds of talents. I don't think talent has anything to do with sex, whether it's management ability or anything else. Now that we're getting women with the proper training and they're being given the opportunities, you're going to see the same proportion of women rising to the top as men . . . There's a lot of resistance. In a lot of fields, there are very few women—and the men who are there are finding every legal way they can to prevent the entrance of more women. But times are changing, and those men are passing off the stage. Because of economic necessity, they're going to have to bring the women in, whether they want to or not.

Interview/U.S. News & World Report, 4-26:53.

Jeanne Moreau
Actress 3

. . . life is so hard for men—the fight for life, the immediate necessity for producing, the little time that is left for day-dreaming, the necessity for a man to be always in a pace that is faster and faster. Men are rivals; they are like roosters. And now that the women have started to speak up, they feel betrayed in a way, I am sure. And they feel more lonely, I am sure, too.

Interview, Washington/
The Christian Science Monitor, 8-9:15.

Louise Nevelson
Sculptor 4

For a long time, for women, a society was like a frame on a picture and you couldn't move out of it. Words are the most dangerous weapons on earth. Women listened to those words, about how they had to wear petticoats, they have to have corsets, garters. Now we wear pants. In my time, women had to get married. No one asked why. That was the way society was. The men were good to the women—that's true. Well, I'm good to my dogs and cats. Women had to cater to men. They couldn't show off their brains. Well, I wouldn't want to be in the horizontal position most of my life. Is that a terrible thing I'm saying? My *work* made me a total woman. Otherwise I'd have been a lackey to some man.

Interview/Newsweek, 7-4:53.

Anais Nin
Author 5

The woman of the future, who is really being born today, will be a woman completely free of guilt for creating and for her self-development. She will be a woman in harmony with her own strength, not necessarily called masculine or eccentric or something unnatural. I imagine she will be very tranquil about her strength and her serenity, a woman who will know how to talk to children and to the men who sometimes fear her . . . The woman of the future will never try to live vicariously through the man, and urge and push him to despair, to fulfill something that she should really be doing herself. So that is my first image—she is not aggressive; she is serene; she is sure; she is confident; she is able to develop her skills; she is able to ask for space for herself.

At Celebration of Women in the Arts/
Los Angeles Times, 3-30:(4)5.

Alejandro Orfila
Secretary General,
Organization of American States 6

The women's movement is ridiculous. Women now have the freedom to move the world. They have the chance to convince the man in the best possible moment when men can be convinced. They can have all the influence and none of the responsibility. The women's movement amuses me but it is ridiculous. They will be losing more than they are gaining if they get the so-called equality. In being different they gain much more than what they have in being equal, for what they have otherwise is more important.

Interview, Washington/
The Washington Post, 1-23:(C)3.

Jacqueline D. St. John
Associate professor of history,
University of Nebraska, Omaha
1

Attitudes and perceptions change slowly, but we must begin to change America's view of feminists and feminism. There are indications that someone is listening to us besides the FBI and the CIA. Thoughtful Americans are beginning to see the necessity for comprehensive, developmental child care; social security for homemakers—perhaps even wages for housework; changes in estate, marriage and family laws; and the recognition of rape as a political act of violence against women. Others are beginning to recognize that sexism is still alive and well in American society—and that women as well as men are sexist in their attitudes. For example, does society condemn a man who says, "I'm proud to be a male chauvinist!"? Would anyone react with laughter and approval if he said, "I'm proud to be a racist!"? How does one react to a woman who states, "I'd never work for a female boss!" or another woman who proclaims proudly, "I don't believe in the feminist movement; I'm happy to be a woman!"? Our media image, individually and collectively as feminists, needs improvement. Media people still refer to feminism as "women's lib" and avoid serious discussions of women's issues while devoting too much media time to sports, especially football— and to the "face on the barroom floor" of the Omaha Press Club.

At Women's Equity Day Conference,
Omaha, Aug. 28/ Vital Speeches, 10-15:6.

Barbra Streisand
Actress, Singer
2

I'm all for women's liberation; do it because you feel it. All women should call their own shots, not in a militant manner but with the conviction that they've got a hell of a lot to offer other than looking pretty and passive.

Interview/ People, 4-26:100.

Lina Wertmuller
Motion-picture director
3

I reject absolutely the distinction between the sexes. The role women have was invented by men for practical reasons. For centuries, men have had in their homes this servant and lover who has been a garbage can to throw things into—his frustrations at work, his vanity, his humiliations, the fact that he wants clean underwear. He has been taught since childhood that he has to be a man, not a human being. Take off his manly crown and then he will become a human being.

Interview, New York/
The National Observer, 2-21:22.

Barbara M. White
President, Mills College
4

I am convinced that liberation of women as full-fledged human beings will prove to be the most significant expansion of human rights in the latter part of the 20th century.

San Francisco Examiner & Chronicle, 9-26:
(This World)2.

Helen B. Wolfe
General director, American Association
of University Women
5

Many unemployed women feel that their identity as women is especially threatened by working women. If full-time homemakers perceive employed women as the ones pushing for ERA, they too can feel that working women deny the validity of their roles as homemakers . . . We must make it clear that

WHAT THEY SAID IN 1976

(HELEN B. WOLFE)

ERA and the women's movement does not envision the interchangeability of men and women. It is not a denial of the uniqueness of women. It is not an effort to destroy workable social models for men and women. One strategy that is important is the recognition of the validity of the role of full-time home-maker, wife and mother. To allow a suggestion that this is not as valid a model as that of the working woman will be counter-productive. However, we must also insist that the role of the working woman is also valid. Neither is a better model than the other, and neither is contemptuous of the other.

At Middle Atlantic Regional Conference,
June/Vital Speeches, 8-15:671.

The Indexes

Index to Speakers

C

I

J

M

Y

Z

Index to Subjects

A

Aaron, Henry, 541:1
Abbado, Claudio, 467:5
Abdul-Jabbar, Kareem, 537:3
Abortion—*see* Medicine
Acheson, Dean, 125:5
Acting/actors, 410:5, 427:1, 429:4, 430:2, 430:3, 432:4,
434:5, 435:2, 435:4, 436:1, 436:5, 436:6, 437:6, 438:2,
438:3, 438:5, 439:2, 439:3, 439:6, 440:2, 440:4, 441:1,
442:4, 442:4, 443:3, 443:4, 443:6, 444:3, 444:4, 444:5,
447:2, 447:5, 447:6, 449:3, 449:5, 450:1, 450:2, 450:3,
451:6, 452:2, 452:4, 453:1, 470:2, 471:1, 471:5, 475:1,
475:5, 475:6, 477:1, 477:4, 478:2, 480:4, 481:4, 483:5,
490:4, 492:2, 495:1, 495:2, 499:5, 501:1, 501:7, 502:2,
502:6
  age: 430:1
  agents, 427:2, 428:1
  external looks, 439:1
  fright/nerves, 470:5, 476:1
  salaries, 431:1, 444:2
  stars, 427:4, 435:3, 442:3, 447:3, 448:2, 449:2, 469:2,
  482:2, 483:4, 499:1
  "talking stage," 470:5
  women's roles—*see* Motion pictures
Acton, Lord, 257:3
Adams, John, 517:1
Adams, Maude, 475:1
Adultery, 507:4
Advertising—*see* Commerce
Africa, pp. 281-299
  Angolan aspect, 290:3
  black majority rule, 127:4, 282:3, 285:2
  change, 297:4
  Chinese (Communist) aspect, 290:5
  Communist/socialist aspect, 284:2, 288:4, 289:3,
  290:5, 291:2, 291:3, 294:1, 294:4, 295:1, 295:3,
  296:1, 296:2, 297:3, 298:3, 299:1
  coups d'etat, 282:2
  Cuban aspect, 290:5, 293:2, 297:3
  environmental aspect, 104:3
  European aspect, 293:3
  Israeli aspect, 292:1, 369:4
  Libyan aspect, 291:4
  Organization of African Unity (OAU), 293:1
  South African aspect, 298:1
  Soviet aspect, 282:5, 285:1, 289:2, 290:5, 293:2, 293:3,
  298:2, 336:1
  United Nations aspect, 293:1
  U.S. aspect, 122:2, 126:4, 130:6, 131:2, 136:1, 138:2,
  282:3, 286:5, 292:2, 293:3, 298:2
  way of looking at things, 286:1
  See also specific countries
Aga Khan, 544:2

Age/youth, 262:1, 403:3, 497:2, 497:4, 504:4, 504:7, 506:2,
508:3, 513:3, 517:4, 519:1, 525:3
Aggressiveness, 509:7
Agnew, Spiro T., 230:2, 247:5
Agriculture/farming:
  food:
    foreign-policy aspect, 124:1, 125:4, 131:2, 145,4,
    149:3
    pesticides, 527:5
    supplies, 43:3
  government involvement in, 46:4, 47:1, 53:3
  incentives, 43:2
Ahab, 527:2
Air Force, U.S.—*see* Defense
Air transportation—*see* Transportation
Alaska, 114:5, 119:3, 120:3, 526:4
Albania, 327:4, 351:5
Alcohol—*see* Medicine
Algeria:
  French aspect, 320:2, 335:5
  population, 100:1
Ali, Muhammad, 12:5, 500:1, 549:1
Allen, Richie, 541:1
Allen, Woody, 482:1
Altman, Robert, 443
Altman, Robert, 443:5
America/U.S.:
  affluence, 14:3
  American Revolution, 20:4, 46:2, 89:3
  "anesthesias," 23:2
  anything-is-possible attitude, 26:6
  "Belle Epoch," 22:2
  Bicentennial, 15:1, 15:2, 15:5, 20:4, 21:2, 24:4, 25:2,
  26:5, 46:2, 132:2, 140:1, 144:3, 178:2, 309:2, 339:5
  change, 25:1, 26:6
  character of people, 17:5
  choices, 13:2
  citizens of world, 26:2
  confidence in, 16:1, 17:2
  criticism/attitude, self-, 12:4, 12:5, 13:3, 14:1, 17:3,
  19:1, 19:3, 21:4, 24:3, 24:4, 26:5, 27:1, 128:4
  decay, 13:6
  Declaration of Independence, 89:3, 166:6, 178:2
  destiny, rendezvous with, 23:4
  dream, American, 12:2, 16:2
  foreign attitude toward, 19:1, 19:4
  "Future Shock," 25:1
  history, making of, 19:5
  ideals, 14:4
  individual, importance of the, 20:3
  ingenuity, 22:1
  innocence, pretentions of, 14:2
  involvement/participation in, 15:4, 19:2

F

K

M

N

S

U